D1559135

Africanisms in Afro-American Language Varieties

# Africanisms in Afro-American Language Varieties

---

*Edited by Salikoko S. Mufwene*

*with the assistance of Nancy Condon*

The University of Georgia Press

Athens and London

Athens, Georgia 30602

Set in 10/13 Times Roman by
Tseng Information Systems, Inc.
Printed and bound by Thomson-Shore, Inc.
The paper in this book meets the guidelines for permanence and durability of the Committee on Production Guidelines for Book Longevity of the Council on Library Resources.

Printed in the United States of America
97 96 95 94 93 C 5 4 3 2 1

Library of Congress Cataloging in Publication Data
Africanisms in Afro-American language varieties / edited by Salikoko S. Mufwene, with the assistance of Nancy Condon.
p. cm.
Includes bibliographical references and indexes.
ISBN 0-8203-1465-X (alk. paper)
1. Afro-Americans—Language. 2. English language—United States—Foreign elements—African. 3. English language—United States—Variation. 4. African languages—Influence on English. 5. Black English. 6. Americanisms. I. Mufwene, Salikoko S. II. Condon, Nancy.
PE3102.N4A35 1993
427'.973'08996—dc20 92-8225
CIP

British Library Cataloging in Publication Data available

# Contents

# Introduction

*Salikoko S. Mufwene*

The papers published in this book are revisions of those presented at the International Round Table on Africanisms in Afro-American Language Varieties, sponsored by the National Science Foundation (Grant BNS-8709868) and hosted by this editor at the University of Georgia during February 25–27, 1988. The term "Afro-American" was borrowed from Alleyne (1980) as a cover term for the creoles and semicreoles[1] that have emerged in the New World since the seventeenth century out of the contact of Africans with speakers of the European languages from which the bulk of their vocabularies has been selected, at least in form. As used here, the term is in no way restricted to North America; it covers as much the American Black English vernacular (BEV) and Gullah as those typologically, if not genetically, related varieties spoken in the Bahamas, the Caribbean, and Central and South America. (For a comprehensive list of the language varieties, see Hancock 1977 and, with more details, Holm 1989.)

The meeting was prompted in part by an increasing realization among creolists that the contribution of the African substrate languages[2] to the structures of creoles and semicreoles of particularly the New World and the Indian Ocean was more likely than had been acknowledged by proponents of either the language bioprogram hypothesis (LBH) or the superstratist hypothesis (SupH). According to the LBH, best formulated by Bickerton (1981, 1984), radical or prototypic creoles are invented by children.[3] As for the SupH, best expressed in relation to BEV recently by scholars such as D'Eloia (1973) and Schneider (1983, 1989), and in relation to French creoles by Chaudenson (1973, 1979, 1988), African-American language varieties (AALVs) and their counterparts of the Indian Ocean owe the greater, and the most central, part of their systems to the nonstandard dialects of the European languages that lexified them. Whatever contribution the African languages have made to the grammars of these language varieties is putatively minimal and/or postformative (i.e., subsequent to their crystallization). The assumption on the extent of African linguistic contribution is explicitly stated by Chaudenson (1979, 1988), echoed by some proponents of the complementary hypothesis[4] (CompH), such as Mühlhäusler

(1986) and Baker and Corne (1982, 1986), and was embraced by Bickerton (1984) for creoles such as Tok Pisin that have had a long stable and expanded pidgin stage.

This editor has, however, assumed that what Baker and Corne (1982, 1986) characterize as postformative stage may well be considered one of the stages of the creolization process qua formation of present-day creoles (Mufwene 1986a). As restated and clarified by Baker (1990; see also Chaudenson 1986, 1989) the original settlement communities in the Indian Ocean and presumably also in the New World (see Singler, this volume) were small homesteads in which the proportion of slaves to masters was either less than 1 or even, hence not significant enough to lead to the new linguistic systems called pidgins or creoles. It was only one or two generations later, after a massive influx of slaves without a concomitant increase in the superstrate population, that drastic restructuring of the lexifiers started. To be sure, creole populations had started earlier, speaking new, slightly restructured colonial varieties of the lexifiers, which served as models for the new generations of slaves (Chaudenson 1979, 1988; Baker 1990). In relation to French, Chaudenson characterizes these new colonial varieties as "français approximatif," that is, approximations of French (also translated below as 'approximate French'). This characterization applies, mutatis mutandis, to other colonial varieties of French that developed under similar conditions.

It is, however, the second stage of restructuring, with the massive influx of slaves disrupting the sociolinguistic status quo, that is assumed to have started the creolization process; that is, the development of a new vernacular whose form is due basically to insufficient exposure to the lexifier in a contact situation typically involving several languages.[5] This is the very stage when (for this editor and apparently for Chaudenson 1979, 1988) substrate influence was possible. Yet Baker and Corne (1986) seem to have had a later stage in mind, when later generations of slaves made the representation of some ethnolinguistic groups (e.g., Eastern Bantu in Mauritius) particularly important and likely to affect part of the creole system. A case in point is the agglutination of the French article to several nouns, on the pattern of Bantu noun class prefixes, in Mauritian Creole (Baker 1984).[6] However, as Singler (this volume) shows, substrate influence from some specific substrate groups was likely from the very beginning of the creolization process, especially when this is not associated or equated with nativization (see also Lefebvre and Robertson, this volume).

This editor wondered whether one of the reasons why claims for African substrate contributions to the New World's creole systems failed to be convincing for superstratists and proponents of the LBH did not lie in the ways the hypotheses had been formulated. Several examples of the shortcomings may be cited here, including: (1) the random selection of substrate languages in, for example, Turner (1949), Allsopp (1977), Alleyne (1980), and, more recently, Holm (1988); (2) the fact that some scholars have capitalized on the lexicon (particularly Allsopp 1977) whereas debates on the genesis of creoles has focused on their morphosyntax (e.g., Bickerton 1981, 1984; Alleyne 1980) and occasionally the phonology (as in Turner 1949; Alleyne 1971, 1980); (3) absence of sociohistorical backing, for example, in Lefebvre's (1986) claim that Haitian Creole is relexified Fon (the shortcoming is overcome in this volume); and (4) the neglect in almost all strong substratist studies of the role that the lexifiers themselves may have played in those cases in which grammatical (phonological, or semantic) influence could as easily be traced to them. It was generally difficult not to notice slackness of heuristic rigor and incompleteness in some of the arguments.

The above comments are not intended to suggest that research was necessarily more rigorous for the LBH and the SupH, although in many cases the SupH was better documented sociohistorically.[7] Until Singler (this volume) such information has been generally lacking in substratist studies. In any case, the tide has generally been against substratists, especially those claiming dominant or significant African contributions in AALVs, and the onus had fallen on them to convince proponents of these other views.[8]

The purpose of the 1988 Round Table on Africanisms in AALVs was to give proponents of various versions of the substrate hypothesis (SubH; Mufwene 1990a) an opportunity either to adduce new evidence or to construct better arguments with old evidence, and, most of all, not to neglect the sociohistorical conditions backing their genetic claims. It was an invitation to substratists to articulate more explicitly the nature and extent of the African linguistic contributions that they advocate and to justify their claims with evidence that answers questions commonly raised by proponents of both the LBH and the SupH. Generally, objections to substratist accounts have had to do with extensive geographical and societal multilingualism in Africa and with historical social and economic facts on the peopling of New World plantations. To make sure that this challenge was present during the Round Table, nonsubstratists were also included in the program, for example, Philip Baker, Francis Byrne, Marta Dijkhoff, Guy Hazaël-Massieux, Thomas Markey, Salikoko Mufwene, Edgar Schneider, Arthur Spears, and Sarah Thomason.[9] The right conditions were set up for new hypotheses and research avenues, some of which are discussed in the Postscript.

The papers in this book reflect more the result of the interaction described above than the original presentations at the Round Table. In the spirit of continuing the dialogue on unresolved issues, both the lead papers and their discussions have been rewritten in a collaborative effort to reflect progress made during the regular sessions and the informal evening workshops on themes such as definition and identification of "Africanism" as well as dimensions of "continuity." The organization of the book is also more consistent with the revised papers than with the meeting program. Since the theme of the Round Table was already highly focused, I doubt that the arrangement can be justified to everybody's satisfaction, especially since some papers may fit as much in one category as in another. The discussants' papers, especially those covering two lead papers, were often a decisive factor because they gave a slant for placement in one or another of the categories. However, in a number of cases, especially in part 3, the lead papers themselves converged well enough (even in constraining the scopes and orientations of the discussants' interventions) to justify their position in the book.

Although all the papers published here are innovative in their own ways, those in parts 1 and 2 deserve special note. They make this book unique in focusing on conceptual problems that are fundamental in discussing African contributions to AALVs. They either address questions that have been unduly ignored in the literature or articulate in more explicit terms working assumptions that may help narrow the gap between different positions on the genesis of AALVs. The following two questions are particularly salient: (1) What in the first place do we mean by "Africanism"? (2) Must there be identity between a rule of language L1 and a rule of L2 before seeking to determine whether, given the circumstances of the development of L2, its rule may have been transferred from L1?

In the remainder of this introduction I will highlight some of the main points of each paper, cross-referencing each with the others and trying to capture their interrelatedness. In general the issues addressed and the questions raised are numerous and diverse, reflecting the complexity of the subject matter investigated by the authors. Since every paper focuses on a significant subset, with its own individual perspective, I thought it more equitable to summarize them separately in order to highlight their individual strengths and, through the cross-references, the areas where they converge. This approach also enables me to sometimes provide the research context in which some of the contributions must be interpreted.

Among several questions, Lawrence Carrington draws attention to the inadequacy of characterizing the notion "Africanism," relative to AALVs, as African peculiarity. According to him, such a characterization suggests, misleadingly, that the very features that are central in the definition of AALVs are peripheral to their systems. That is, Africanisms are suggested by such a characterization to be foreign elements, so to speak, in the systems that they help define. For this editor, the inadequacy is aggravated by the fact that in the New World these language varieties have been associated primarily with people of African descent. Although Carrington does not go so far as to reject the term "Africanism" itself, he proposes that it be interpreted consistently with the fact that AALVs have developed from the contact of Africans and Europeans and have been subject to influences from primarily these parties. This position does not, of course, amount to denying influence from Universal Grammar and, as Huttar, Hazaël-Massieux, and others in this volume note, from other, adstrate groups.

Africanisms must thus be understood as contributions made by Africans to the lexica and structures of AALVs, on a par and in competition with "Europeanisms" and other contributions. Aside from proposing criteria for identifying linguistic features as Africanisms or Europeanisms, Carrington also addresses the question of whether it is justified to consider Africanisms only relative to the formative stages of AALVs. His position is that formative and postformative inputs should count; they contribute at whatever stage to shaping the individual varieties.

George Huttar's paper is a suitable rejoinder to Carrington's, arguing more, however, for caution in the search for Africanisms. The particular nature (idiosyncratic or general) of the features being investigated and the specific sociohistorical conditions of the formation of the relevant AALVs should determine whether such linguistic contributions should be attributed to specific African languages. It is misguided to dwell on some specific language when a feature is areal or shared by most of the African languages that were in contact during the formation of AALVs. Several studies have, in fact, argued that such areal features had a strong chance of being selected in the systems of Atlantic AALVs (see, e.g., Manessy 1985a, 1985b, 1988; Gilman 1986; Koopman 1986; and Faraclas 1987, 1988).

Huttar also argues that "we can do better by investigating those areas of language less likely to be subject to European influence" or the "result of universals," for example, suprasegmentals, onomatopoeias, ideophones, proverbs, greeting formulas, and the structures of conversations and folktales. He is joined in this invitation by Guy Hazaël-Massieux, who suggests that some cognitive domains over which the superstrate group had little control (e.g., religion, sorcery, and dance) seem to reveal more African influence; and by Marcyliena Morgan, who focuses on communicative styles. Though Huttar's paper does not address the question of which factors determine the particular influence that prevails under specific conditions, it serves the field well in showing that a language is more than its morphosyntax and that research on African contributions to AALVs need not be restricted to the latter area, a point echoed by John Rickford. According to Huttar, sound research on Africanisms will progress well by "combining careful linguistic and anthropological fieldwork with the results of the historian's work."

In addition, Huttar addresses two other important questions. The first is that of adstrate influence from American Indian languages, which should not be neglected, especially in the case of creoles such as Ndjuka. He is joined in this view again by Hazaël-Massieux and Ian Hancock. The second question is that of unequal availability of facts about the African languages. Instead of waiting for African scholars, students of Africanisms may well have to investigate, on their own, aspects of African languages which bear on their research. Claire Lefebvre works in this direction.

More and more studies now attempt to relate aspects of creole genesis to second-language acquisition phenomena (see, e.g., several contributions to Andersen 1983) and to outcomes of language contact that are nonetheless different from pidginization and creolization (e.g., Thomason and Kaufman 1988). In the linguistic literature, the terms "substratum" and "superstratum" thus refer variously to languages with not quite the same sociohistorical statuses. Morris Goodman's demonstration that, since Hall (1950, 1966), creolists have used the concepts "substratum" and "superstratum" at variance with the tradition in historical linguistics could not be more opportune.

To be sure, "substratum" as used by Hall (e.g., 1966:107) was not a total shift from the historical linguistics usage. Even though the use already diverged from the tradition, he meant, in the case of the New World, the replacement of the slaves' African languages by the AALVs. However, his characterization of the "superstratum" as "the official European language which is [socio-politically] dominant in the region where a creole is spoken" has led to the sociological interpretation of "substratum" which is now dominant in anglophone creolistics. Those comparing creolization with other contact phenomena should thus pay attention to the different ways the terms are used.

Goodman's next point, that substrate influence need not be absorbed intact by the reference language and is adjusted to the latter's overall system, is quite consonant with the theme of Norbert Boretzky's paper, which comes next. The same point is also made by Thomason. Goodman's other observation, that "African influence has . . . been greatly exaggerated by some ideological reasons during much of the past half century," is as relevant as his own criticism of Bickerton's substratophobia in areas other than the lexicon. In short, linguistic facts combined with sociohistorical information on the genesis of AALVs determine whether a particular feature is an Africanism. Those wishing to pursue the debate in this book should remember this advice, as ideological preconceptions often get in the way of sound investigation.

One of the strongest objections to substratist accounts of the source of AALVs' features has been that their systems do not exactly match those of the relevant African languages (see, e.g., Bickerton 1986a). Norbert Boretzky argues that rule borrowing (or transfer) in creoles operates in the same way as in noncreole languages: the borrowing (or transferring) speakers often select only some aspects of rules that are otherwise complex; thus the transfer is selective and partial.

He also notes that "the substratum languages did not cease to be spoken in the new territories but were being used over several generations." This point, made plausible by the sociohistorical scenario presented by Singler (this volume), increases the likelihood of substrate influence because speakers of the same native languages are likely to influence their new common language with the same interference features and reinforce each other. Several contributors to this book share this assumption, particularly Alleyne, Lefebvre, and Robertson.

A couple of Francis Byrne's observations in his discussion of Boretzky's paper are particularly worth highlighting here. First, linguistic hypotheses are provisional, being subject to further testing and revisions. This is true not only of formal linguistics but also of theorizing in areas such as creole genesis, where facts have been particularly elusive. As most papers in parts 2 and 3 show, the issues arising from, and the factors involved in, creole formation are complex; we are only beginning to identify the relevant ones. Second, a "continuum of possibilities within the creolization process" makes it dangerous to assume that what applies to Creole X necessarily applies to Creole Y, an observation that Alleyne states in slightly different terms. A prerequisite to several of our generalizations thus involves sorting out facts pertinent to individual creoles. Most universalists, substratists, and superstratists should plead guilty on this count. Fortunately, however, the trend is changing, and the papers in this volume mark an important milestone in shaping the direction of future research in creole genesis.

Byrne also draws attention to a problem that I will paraphrase as follows: would the systems of several Atlantic creoles have been predominantly isolating even if the Kwa and Mande languages had not been involved in their formation? What is learned from those creoles in whose formation the Kwa languages either were not involved (e.g., Tok Pisin) or may have played only a minor part (e.g., Palenquero, per Maurer 1987)? As argued by Mufwene (1990a, 1990b), such studies seem to weaken the case for the (original) LBH in favor of other alternatives. It is, however, possible that a more accommodating version of Bickerton's (1988, 1989) lexical learning hypothesis, which should recognize both the possibility of reanalysis in transfer (as Boretzky shows) and a context-based role of markedness in the selection of grammatical features (Mufwene 1989, 1991b), can account for variation in the grammatical structures of creoles.

Focusing on Guadeloupean French Creole, Guy Hazaël-Massieux argues against extreme universalist and substratist accounts of creole genesis. He favors, instead, convergence accounts that explain the conditions under which lexical items and grammatical features of primarily popular French[10] (or its counterparts in the case of other creoles) were selected. Without ruling out a perhaps determinative role of the substrate languages' patterns in the selection process, he highlights the filtering role of universal factors such as semantic transparency (Seuren and Wekker 1986) and perceptual salience (Naro 1981; Mufwene 1991b), which disfavored atonic grammatical markers. He also notes the role of chance similarity with forms of substrate languages. Hazaël-Massieux insists that the French forms or structural features that have been selected by creoles need not have been dominant in the lexifier. They may have been peripheral features that were consistent with the emerging grammatical systems, and their "importance may have been hypertrophied in the particular context of creole colonies. These expressions may thus have served as models and thus have been overgeneralized."

According to Hazaël-Massieux, the selections made by creoles were generally not exclusive of other alternatives nor necessarily regular; the lexifier itself was, or is, not monolithic. However, like Huttar, he recognizes that the likelihood of exclusive African contributions may not be denied in some cognitive domains; for example, in "cooking, ethnomedicine, sorcery, religion, dance, and individual and private activities over which the masters had very little control." But none of this suggests, according to him, an exclusive or dominant African contribution to creole grammar. This position sets him on an interesting collision course with Lefebvre, for instance, regarding serial verb constructions. Such conflicting analyses show once more how difficult it is to account satisfactorily for the development of creole grammatical features. There seems to be no uniform genetic explanation that accounts for every aspect of any creole, which makes more critical the exchanges published in this book.

Philip Baker's endorsement of the Bickertonian LBH (within his CompH model) as the default account of creole grammatical features need not be interpreted as a denial of African substrate influence. Rather, it is an invitation for substratists to articulate the conditions, particularly sociohistorical and demographic (from his point of view), under which grammatical influence from any particular African language or language group was likely and perhaps comparable to the more obvious substrate influence in the lexicon.

Baker also observes that influence affecting the system of a creole may occur at any stage of its development, provided the right conditions are met. This position suggests a gradual rather than an abrupt development of creoles, which is consistent with the three major "events" he identifies in the peopling of the creole territories and the shiftings of proportions of Europeans, Africans, and Creoles. The proportion of Creoles, those born in the colony, to both of the others has a significant bearing on the amount of substrate and superstrate contributions to the new linguistic systems.

Among the many complications that Baker draws to the attention of substratists is the fact that the creole systems are neither static nor homogeneous (especially regionally), which defies any simplistic account of creole genesis in terms of uniform substrate influence. It follows that the genesis of creoles must be accounted for on a case-by-case basis before any cross-systemic generalizations can be attempted. The contributions by, particularly, Alleyne, Singler, Lefebvre, and Robertson go precisely in this direction.

Arthur Spears's discussion of Hazaël-Massieux's and Baker's contributions makes it possible to further examine the positions of these lead papers in light of other discussions in this book and elsewhere. First, he brings back to mind Carrington's position that Africanisms should be treated on a par with Europeanisms (in the case of French creoles, Gallicisms). What matters is coming up with a hypothesis that explains how some of the lexifiers' grammatical patterns were selected into the creole systems and why different creoles with the same lexifier sometimes selected different variants of the lexifiers' patterns. This question applies equally to creole features patterned on African languages, well in line with Baker's CompH.

Spears adds complexity to Baker's position on the genesis of creoles by hypothesizing that the development of Haitian Creole may not have been as homogeneous a process as the literature suggests. Not only must the process have been as gradual as Chaudenson (1979, 1988) and Baker and Corne (1982, 1986) have argued is true for Indian Ocean French creoles, but also today's Haitian Creole may be the result of a merger of different regional and social linguistic varieties of the late seventeenth and eighteenth centuries. The strong African grammatical influence hypothesized by Lefebvre (1986, in this volume, and elsewhere) may be through only one of the varieties under propitious conditions yet to be accounted for. Spears thus draws attention to a more complex, and historically quite likely, view of creole genesis than most creole geneticists have presented. There may have been more French influence in some varieties of Haitian Creole than in others.

In correlating the putative "Africanization" of Haitian Creole with "recreolization," Spears speaks only of changes undergone by *some* of the regional and social French-derived varieties that preceded today's Haitian Creole, not all of them. This, of course, leads to a new picture of today's social and regional linguistic variation in Haiti. Note, however, that Baker's invitation to study older text samples of creoles has a bearing on the above observation.

Mervyn Alleyne argues that child language development, from which universalist hypotheses of creole genesis have derived their apparent strength, is subject to environmental input from the languages spoken in the area. His position is quite in line with the trigger hypothesis, discussed recently by, for example, Lightfoot (1989). This very aspect of language development, Alleyne suggests, must have allowed African linguistic, like cultural, continuities. He also argues against generalizations that ignore the fact that "each region of African America and each segment and layer of the Afro-American population remain different and distinctive" in the New World. African linguistic influence need not have come from a single group, nor from the whole of black Africa. Much was determined by which particular ethnolinguistic group was important "in the early formative period of the slave society," a perspective which has a parallel in the founder principle of population genetics regarding the transmission of genes. In the case of Jamaican Creole, Alleyne argues that the substrate influence is particularly from the Twi-Asante group, who "throughout the post-Columbian history of Jamaica . . . have served as custodians of African culture." He claims they did this through their Maroon communities, which allowed them stability and homogeneity as a group while isolating them from European influence. Much of today's Jamaican Creole is putatively based on this early Maroon system, with perhaps minor contributions by other ethnolinguistic groups.

In his paper Ian Hancock explains how his componential hypothesis of creole genesis, which in the case of the English Atlantic creoles takes into account the African languages, the various dialects of metropolitan English, the West African Creole component, other languages, and the Bickertonian bioprogram, can account for the varying African influence in AALVs. According to Hancock, "each creole-forming social and linguistic matrix [is] an independently developed phenomenon, growing out of the coming together of different proportions of its 'ingredients' or components under different circumstances."

Thus the "ingredients" that favored a particular African influence in one creole are not necessarily replicated, at least not in the same combination, in another. The shared aspects of English Atlantic creoles may be due to their common Guinea Coast English component, to similarities in the varieties of metropolitan or colonial English that lexified them locally, or to the language bioprogram. In a different vein, Hancock also joins Spears in noting that creoles of the same lexifier have sometimes selected different features from the latter. This state of affairs makes aprioristic some attempts to account for such differences in terms of decreolization or, to use Hancock's own term, metropolitanization.[11]

Calling for a principled account of different influences, Hancock also claims that the LBH and the convergence hypothesis complement each other in the selection of creole features. The formation of a creole itself is presented as "an ongoing process, [with] each generation innately negotiating with the linguistic mix available to them for patterns to be retained or rejected in the creole." Arguing that "high mortality rates in the Caribbean ensured that incoming Africans . . . made up the biggest part of the rising population, and that the emerging model was in a state of continually being created by second-language . . . speakers," Hancock makes allowance for African influence of any kind to have occurred at any stage of its formation.

Hancock's position does not seem to be in conflict with the scenario of creole development proposed by Chaudenson (1979, 1989) and Baker and Corne (1982, 1986; see also Baker 1990, this volume), although they emphasize surprisingly different components. (Unlike Baker and Corne, Chaudenson attributes most of the creole features to superstrate influence.)[12] All of them make allowance for substrate influence from the time we can identify a pidgin or creole as developing; namely, the particular stage when the lexifier no longer functions as the sole target (cf. Baker's 1990 "off target") and new constructions that are not attested, or are not so conspicuous, in the lexifier become typical in the emerging language. Chaudenson, of course, insists on the role of the precreole, "français approximatif" input; Baker and Corne favor the bioprogram; and Hancock argues for selection in the complex matrix of the languages available. They are closer to each other than might at first appear to be the case; future studies may help sort things out, especially in the light of the selection principles that Hancock calls for (see also Mufwene 1989, 1991b).

In his discussion of Alleyne's and Hancock's papers, Salikoko Mufwene focuses on questions that must be addressed in order for us to learn the most from their genetic hypotheses, which he does not consider mutually exclusive. He starts by hypothesizing the conditions under which African languages must have continued to be spoken. Despite the often-invoked societal and geographical multilingualism of black Africa, Mufwene notes that individual multilingualism, which has been observed so often about the same part of the world, must have favored the survival of some African languages, especially on account of the plantation economy conditions discussed by Singler (this volume). Some of the languages used by subsets of slaves on different plantations are likely to have left their marks in different creoles of the New World, though the linguistic constraints regulating the possibility of such influence (Mufwene 1989, 1991b) cannot be overlooked. Consistent with Hancock's componential matrix, which varies from one geographical setting to another, Alleyne's thesis is shown to be theoretically conceivable, calling for further research. The likelihood of significant substrate influence in one setting does not entail the same situation in others, which is one of the consequences of Hancock's componential hypothesis.

Mufwene also highlights the relevance of the population genetics notion of the "founder principle" to Hancock's componential matrix, especially since the ethnolinguistic makeup of the plantation community at the formative stage of its creole must have determined a great deal of its system (see also Singler, this volume). He dwells on this to emphasize the closeness of Hancock's, Chaudenson's, and Baker and Corne's positions on the genesis of creoles. Raising some questions on the possibility of recreolization suggested by Hancock, Mufwene joins Spears (this volume) in suggesting the alternative possibility of the development of a nonmonolithic creole community in which different AALVs may have developed either concomitantly or at different times. One could thus note more African substrate influence in one creole variety than in another, since the conditions for such influence either to obtain or to spread may not have been met uniformly in the community.

While sticking to the conclusion that "earlier Black English and BEV are predominantly, though not exclusively, dialectal English in character," (i.e., neither creole nor creole derived by decreolization), Edgar Schneider argues for a more eclectic genetic account that makes allowance for substratist and universalist accounts of some of their features. Cases of African substrate influence seem to include those features of BEV, such as the perfective *done* + verb construction, that are also attested in British or American dialects of English and whose selection and partial reinterpretation seem to have been determined by the existence of morphemes with similar functions in some African languages (see Singler's condition of convergence, this volume). This position is quite akin to Hazaël-Massieux's on French creoles. However, there are putatively fewer such cases in BEV than in their Atlantic creole kin.

Schneider insists rightly on the following aspects of BEV and English creoles, among others, which have too often been poorly highlighted in the literature: (1) "the superstrate was not a standard variety but . . . a mixture of various [nonstandard] dialects . . . from various parts of the British Isles" (see also Hancock, this volume); (2) reference to "somewhat mystical overall varieties such as 'West African languages' or 'English dialects' " does not shed much light on genetic issues, since the West African languages, and likewise the English dialects, differ from each other in several of the features they are collectively invoked to have influenced—several papers in this book are a departure from this weakness; (3) BEV is far from being a uniform variety (see also Spears 1987), and arguments for dominant superstrate or substrate influence must bear this fact in mind; and (4) variable features, especially those with low frequencies, should not be discussed as though they had no noncreolelike alternatives.

Variation in the sizes of the plantations and in the proportion of the African population to the English and other ethnolinguistic groups must account not only for the variable attestations of features typically identified with BEV but also for the possibility that the sources of these features may not be identical. This is especially true where convergence of English and African linguistic features, perhaps combined with some putative universals, may be assumed to be a plausible explanation. Schneider thus echoes both Alleyne's and Hancock's contributions. The reality of AALVs is just too complex for scholars to be content with simplistic uniform explanations.

In his discussion, J. L. Dillard questions particularly the reliability of ex-slaves' narratives as representative of either the earliest stages of BEV (about 250 years ago) or its form in the second half of the nineteenth century. Aside from suggesting that the language reported through the Work Projects Administration and Federal Writers' Project was more representative of the time of the interviews (1930s) than of the 1860s, Dillard draws attention to text editing before publication and raises questions on the selection of interviewees.[13] The basilectal and female populations seem generally to have been underrepresented, and the conduct of interviews by white middle-class males could have affected the form of the language.[14] Dillard believes that "a philological approach [to the narratives] may yield some results which the polemic approach has failed to produce"; hence the texts must be treated as "representative of the literary tradition of black speech," presumably like Gullah as used by writers such as Charles Jones (1888), Ambrose Gonzales (1922, 1924), Albert Stoddard (1949), and now Virginia Geraty (1990).[15] Generally, difficulties in accounting for the genesis of AALVs are thus compounded by the status of historical texts.

John Singler presents sociohistorical information that bears on hypotheses of

African substrate influence on AALVs. To this editor, his contribution seems to constitute a particularly suitable introduction to the third part of this book, which groups together papers defending diverse African influence on these languages. Singler starts by noting that the nativization of AALVs was protracted (see also Lefebvre, this volume); "high mortality and low fertility [among the slaves] were characteristic of all the colonies," which continued to import more and more labor from Africa (see also Hancock, this volume). This state of affairs, combined with "the structure of plantation societies[,] served to encourage retention of African ethnicities and, with them, retention of African languages." Substrate influence was quite likely under any of the following conditions: compatibility of features of some substrate languages with those of the lexifier, presence of unmarked features in some substrate languages, or degree of homogeneity of the substrate languages or an important subset thereof.[16]

Assuming that much of the morphosyntax of creoles is determined in their first formative stage, Singler then adduces demographic facts about different phases of slave importation into Saint Domingue (including Haiti) and French colonies to show that the western Kwa group, especially the Ewe-Fon, was in a position to influence the structure of Haitian Creole in particular. Until 1710, the Ewe-Fon constituted about half the slave population, and they always made up about one-third of the later importation of slaves. Under the condition of protracted nativization noted above, and assuming Singler's condition for the possibility of substrate influence, the incoming Ewe-Fon must thus have been in a position to reinforce the original structural features of Haitian and related Caribbean French creoles.

Singler concludes that his study "does not, and cannot, by itself demonstrate the presence of substratal influence upon Haitian Creole, but it does show where best to look for the substratal input that would have wielded that influence." Nevertheless, it provides long-awaited sociohistorical support to Lefebvre's thesis that Haitian Creole's syntax is essentially (Ewe-)Fon, though the vocabulary is primarily French (1986, this volume).[17]

Claire Lefebvre clarifies her relexification hypothesis, which is akin to Sylvain's (1936) position that Haitian Creole is Ewe-(Fon) with French vocabulary. Invoking essentially the same sociohistorical conditions as Singler does for this dominant substrate influence, she explains that Fon is adduced as representative of a group of Western Kwa languages which are typologically and genetically related.

She also addresses a heuristic problem which any student of the genesis of AALVs must face: whether assumptions about the influence of eighteenth-century African languages can be supported by today's varieties of the same languages. Note that even though today's varieties are being used faute de mieux, many of those features attributed to seventeenth- and eighteenth-century nonstandard varieties of European languages putatively continue to date. This is at least Chaudenson's (1990) position, and it is apparently also assumed by defenders of the superstrate hypothesis regarding BEV. The absence of such features from the lexifiers' standard varieties, where they may have neither existed nor been dominant to begin with, does not ipso facto entail their non-existence in the lexifiers.

In the same way, the African languages that came into contact with the European languages in the New World were regular, everyman's spoken varieties, not the expert varieties used by, for example, storytellers. There are no accounts of major structural changes which have affected African languages over the past three or four centuries comparable to those leading to the split of Niger-Congo languages. Whatever changes have occurred must be minor and do not invalidate the kinds of comparisons undertaken by Lefebvre and other students of the genesis of AALVs, at least not any more than they invalidate comparisons of the same languages with today's nonstandard varieties of European languages.

The rest of Lefebvre's paper is an illustration of some of the similarities between Haitian Creole and Fon. Although she admits that the structural correspondences are not perfect (see also Boretzky, this volume), the data raise the question of whether these partial similarities may be completely ignored by defenders of alternative genetic positions. It is important to remember that there is no simple unilateral account of the genesis of AALVs. In this particular case, it would be surprising if a group that was dominant during the formation of Haitian Creole had not played a determinative role in the selection of its features, even though they are shared by the lexifier. The ways in which determinative influence may have operated are yet to be articulated, though Mufwene (1989, 1991b) addresses some of the relevant questions in regard to markedness which Lefebvre also invokes.

Readers should remember that like Singler and Robertson (below), Lefebvre questions one of Bickerton's (1981, 1984, 1988, 1989) working assumptions: that Haitian Creole, like its other Atlantic kin, was "created" or "invented" by children. I personally do not believe this; it is not necessary to equate creolization with nativization in order to defend the role of the language bioprogram qua Universal Grammar. The absence of any particular formal features which distinguish creoles formed by adults from those putatively formed by children makes the equation unmotivated (Mufwene 1990a, 1991b).

Sarah Thomason's discussion of Singler's and Lefebvre's papers is generally an invitation to investigate contributions of superstrate, substrate, and other influences on creole systems in the broader genetic linguistics contexts of language change and shift due to contact (see also Boretzky, this volume). The paper is also an invitation to compare the superstrate language not only with the dominant language or language group during the formation of a pidgin or creole but with all the languages. As the presence of "marked features" (presumably from the point of view of their attestations worldwide)[18] in some pidgins and creoles has been attributed to the fact that the features are shared by the vast majority of the languages in the contact situation, it is aprioristic to disregard minority languages of the contact situation. In fact, convergence, which has proved in many cases to be a more plausible explanation than, for example, innovation by children, argues against focusing too much on exclusive, or dominant, substrate or superstrate influence.

Thomason also addresses the question of the suitability of today's linguistic varieties in our investigation of creole genesis. Her position is generally that "three hundred years is not a very long time in language history, so most structures present now were also present then." In addition, Thomason observes that contrary to a widely established position in creolistics, grammatical morphemes may be transferred into another, or a new, language (as illustrated, by the way, by Robertson in the next paper). On the other hand, critics are warned against looking for perfect matches; the transferred features must be adjusted to the overall system of the host language, a point also made by Boretzky and Goodman. Overall, there are no simple explanations or other genetic accounts that apply across the board to all creole languages, a position that echoes Alleyne's and is consistent with Hancock's componential hypothesis. Each pidgin and creole must be explained in light of the specific sociohistorical makeup of the setting of its genesis.

After adducing sociohistorical evidence to support the assumption that the Ịjọs were the Africans primarily involved in the formation of Berbice Dutch, Ian Robertson presents linguistic evidence bearing on the assumption that (Eastern) Ịjọ has influenced much of the grammatical system of this AALV, including the form and position of its markers for tense and aspect, nominal plural, negation, and postpositions. The role of the lexifier is acknowledged when facts speak for such influence, and convergence is clearly part of Robertson's genetic hypothesis. His main thesis is that Bickerton's (1984) LBH cannot account for the structure of Berbice Dutch. This AALV could not have been formed by children; they would not have had the knowledge of Ịjọ presupposed by the substrate features that distinguish Berbice Dutch from other Atlantic creoles.[19]

Needless to say, if Berbice Dutch is truly a creole, then it raises questions about one traditional assumption about the social setting of pidgin and creole genesis, namely, extensive societal multilingualism in the contact community and the need to develop a lingua franca within the substrate group. On the other hand, Robertson corroborates Thomason's assumption (this volume) that homogeneity of the substrate group and/or typological kinship with the superstrate group make it possible even for features considered marked (from the point of view of their distribution among the world's languages) to find their way into a creole. There are, however, some unanswered questions, such as why the order of major syntactic constituents in Berbice Dutch is subject-verb-object (SVO) and not subject-object-verb (SOV) (Mufwene 1990b), since both Ịjọ and Dutch have a predominant SOV order. Nevertheless, such questions do not invalidate the hypothesis of significant substrate contributions to Berbice Dutch, which seems to be a clear instance of a mixed system.

John Holm's working assumption in this volume is adequately captured by the following excerpt:

> Since there is evidence that creoles acquire their features from a number of different sources (superstrate, substrate, and adstrate languages, creole-internal innovations, universals of second language acquisition, and combinations of all or some of these), the question often arises as to which of these is the source of a particular feature.

His paper is concerned particularly with establishing the role of African languages in the selection, or retention, of labiovelar stops and palatalized consonants in AALVs of different lexifiers. He argues that African substrate influence is the explanation, especially when, as in the case of labiovelar stops, no model from the superstrate languages may be invoked. Since the sounds "are relatively rare among the world's languages," no bioprogrammatic universals may be invoked to account for them, either. Holm does not rule out convergence in some cases of palatalization; for example, that of velar consonants in English AALVs, for which influence from Irish English must have been significant in some genetic settings.

Hazel Carter characterizes Jamaican Creole as a tonal language, "syllable timed" and "having double rather than phonemically long vowels." She attributes this feature to the fact that most of the African substrate languages that came into contact with English have the same prosodic features. The variation attested in Jamaican Creole, especially regarding vowel length, is attributed to the coexistence of competing systems since its beginning; African languages vary extensively, both inter- and intrasystemically, with regard to this feature. Some languages have neither long vowels nor double vowels, and in some languages vowel length is not phonemic—it is just phonologically conditioned.

Carter argues that if English played any part in the development of this prosodic system, its role must have been that of accommodating the vowel length that may have persisted in some of its varieties to the African double vowel system. According to her, English had generally already shifted since the Great Vowel Shift to a vocalic system without phonemic length, although some nonstandard varieties may have preserved it. Even if these varieties may have introduced phonemic length here and there, the dominant pattern seems to be the double vowel system.

Whether Carter's attribution of a double vowel system to Jamaican Creole is correct (cf. Rickford's discussion), it contributes greatly to research on the genesis of AALVs in noting that both the lexifier and the substrate languages were typologically disparate, and there is no reason to assume that one single monolithic system must have emerged from the inception of the creole. (A similar observation is made in this volume in the papers by Spears and Schneider.) The idea of competing systems as a result of diversified influence from diverse varieties of both the lexifiers and substrate languages deserves attention because it eliminates the need to invoke postformative influence to account for some variation, especially where likeness is perceived with the lexifier. (Cf. also Spears's and Hancock's remarks regarding decreolization in this volume.)

In his discussion of Holm's and Carter's papers, John Rickford argues that "creolistics as a field needs to use more sophisticated means of analyzing and accounting for [inter- and intrasystemic] variation." The coexistence of competing systems within AALVs may be more the rule than the exception; genetic studies ought to highlight those features which are not absolute, just as they should indicate whether the features they discuss are central or marginal within their systems. Marginality, he notes, does not entail late addition to the system, since variation within a language variety may date from its inception. This may be the case with labiovelar stops in Gullah.

Rickford also notes that the genetic issues often do not have clear-cut answers. Further, the possibility of substrate influence does not necessarily exclude the possibility of convergence with other influences, especially in the case of palatalization, where influence from the lexifier seems possible. He also draws attention to Weinreich's (1953) position that while structural correspondences between two systems help determine what may be transferred from one to the other, actual transfers are also determined by nonstructural factors such as the natures of other languages known and the size and relative prestige of the group learning the target language. This point is particularly significant because individual multilingualism has always been typical of most Africans.

Rickford addresses several questions arising from Carter's paper, especially from the fact that long or double vowels are not attested in all AALVs (an observation consistent with Alleyne's and Hancock's papers). He also notes that there are differences between these New World languages and their West African counterparts such as Krio and Nigerian Pidgin English. He observes that his questions may not be answered conclusively until genetic studies are combined with sociohistorical information to reveal which African systems were represented at the different settings of the formation of different AALVs (an important theme in Alleyne's paper). Transterritorial migrations complicate the scenarios further.

Charles DeBose and Nicholas Faraclas's paper is best understood in the context of the traditional question of whether the grammar of the Black English vernacular is creolelike and creole derived (Stewart 1968, 1969; Dillard 1972, 1985) or English-like (Fasold 1972, 1976, 1981; Labov 1972, 1982; D'Eloia 1973; Schneider 1982, 1983, 1989). The latter position may be interpreted in one of two ways. The origin of BEV may lie in nonstandard dialects of British and American white colonial English, with its typological kinship to English creoles due to their having the same or similar lexifiers (D'Eloia 1973; Schneider 1982). On the other hand, BEV may have a creole ancestry, but its grammar has now converged so much with that of white nonstandard English that it may putatively have the same rules as the latter, with only quantitative differences in the application of variable rules (Labov 1972, 1982; Fasold 1981).[20]

The creole origin position may be interpreted to suggest that ultimately the grammar of BEV was determined primarily by the African substrate languages, an interpretation denied by both William Stewart and J. L. Dillard (personal communication, 1983) but endorsed by DeBose and Faraclas, or that BEV has descended by decreolization from an erstwhile, Gullah-like creole. The alternative and viable position that BEV may be akin to other English AALVs only typologically (B. Bailey 1965; Mufwene 1983) and may otherwise represent a case of partial creolization (Mufwene 1987; Holm 1988, 1991; Schneider 1990) is overlooked here. Nevertheless, DeBose and Faraclas's paper is the mirror image of Schneider's contribution: both are generally more conciliatory, acknowledging more input from either the substrate or the superstrate languages.

Focusing on the tense-mood-aspect system and the distribution of the copula, DeBose and Faraclas argue directly that BEV and Nigerian Pidgin English have very similar systems. Since the latter's grammar is allegedly like that of its substrate languages, which are said to be typologically similar, BEV's grammar must reflect dominant influence from the same group of languages. The reader should remember that, based on the authors' introduction, this indirect defense of the substrate hypothesis does not exclude possible superstrate influence, which would entail convergence (the genetic position advocated for some other facts in this volume particularly by Thomason and Rickford, and to some extent by Hazaël-Massieux).

Charles Gilman focuses on an aspect of the genetic debate which Rickford (this volume) finds to be insufficiently studied: the nonstructural factors determining the transfer and, from Gilman's point of view, the retention of substrate or nonmetropolitan features. The general argument is that AALVs have too often been expected, too gratuitously, to develop in the direction of their acrolects. Gilman identifies several sociological factors which must have sometimes prevented assimilation and at other times encouraged dissimilation. The former category includes the linguistic impacts of slave revolts and maroonage, African-based/oriented religions, loyalty to black ethnicity or identity, and political liberation movements. The second category is best illustrated by Rastafarianism, which "combines the factors of low social status, pride in blackness, identity with Africa, religion, and geographical identification with the West Indies." Gilman argues that AALVs' "continued distinctness relies not only on the preservation of older creolisms but also on the continued innovation in directions distinct from the metropolitan varieties." As a group they have experienced both recreolization and decreolization to different extents and in different ways. Gilman suggests the possibility that one aspect of an AALV may be decreolizing while another may be recreolizing, contrary to the tradition of seeing the development only in one direction.

In her short discussion, Marta Dijkhoff raises the question of whether it is justified to treat creoles as exceptional or requiring different kinds of accounts. Her point is prompted by Gilman's claim that the "forces maintaining the distinctness of creoles from the metropolitan forms are the same social constructs which maintain languages or their varieties distinct in noncreole situations." This echoes Thomason's general question of whether the principles invoked to account for creole genesis differ in essence from those generally invoked to account for contact-induced change or shift.

Selase Williams advocates an Afrocentric approach to studies of Africanisms, arguing that Eurocentric approaches have missed a lot of features that look like English only at face value but are otherwise Africanisms. Focusing on the variable regional pronunciations of word-final /θ/ and /ð/ in Afro-American speech, namely, [t, d, f], he argues that their attestations in British varieties of nonstandard English do not account for their regional distribution among African Americans. The distribution is correlated with settlement patterns from Africa in the eighteenth century (during the same critical period identified by Singler, this volume), though the British dialects must have reinforced the trend where there was convergence. He also argues that the selection of substitutes for the English standard pronunciations was determined both by which ethnolinguistic group was dominant in what geographical area during the formative stage and by the variant that was most compatible with the dominant African linguistic system. Williams makes a distinction between "retentions," which are easier to identify, and "continuities," which have normally been adapted to the new system and are harder to identify. This is, of course, reminiscent of Spears's (1982) "camouflaged" features.

Echoing one of Huttar's suggestions, Marcyliena Morgan moves the discussion of linguistic Africanisms to the level of communication styles. She uses the notion of "counterlanguage" for a form of indirection which exploits ambiguity of reference and irony and places the target, originally a person in authority, in a position in which he or she cannot respond verbally. This speech style, which is apparently pervasive in Africa, is shown to be one of the most camouflaged Africanisms at the macrolevel, confirming Spears's (1987) observation that much is yet to be analyzed about AALVs before we can determine whether they are converging with or diverging from varieties of their lexifiers. Morgan's paper shows that discussions of influence in AALVs need not be restricted to their mechanical aspects. More studies of their functional-pragmatic aspects should enrich our understanding of what counts or does not count as Africanism. Perhaps we may ultimately develop not only a more comprehensive picture of Africanisms but also a scale of whether formal or nonformal characteristics are more easily identifiable as Africanisms.

Overall, the papers discussed above show how complex the question of African contributions to systems of AALVs is. Each paper sheds light on different facets of the subject matter. Though they offer no final explanation—no single hypothesis has ever done this—they provide a richer understanding of the problem and raise several productive research questions for the future. They enrich research on African substrate influence especially by the novelty of several questions addressed or raised and by new perspectives given to some old questions. One such question is whether substrate and superstrate influences should be considered exclusive of each other or may be assumed in a number of cases to converge.

This book is also enriched by the two historiographic essays in part 4, which help shape a more informed scholarship on the subject matter of Africanisms in AALVs. Michael Montgomery's paper is intended to develop a fuller picture of the development of studies of Africanisms. According to the author, this research question was already open to debate in the early nineteenth century, as evidenced by the denial of the African origin of some possible Africanisms (e.g., *tote* 'carry') and by citations of terms whose European origin was difficult to identify (e.g., *buckra* 'white man'). Even such a strong defender of the British dialect foundation of Gullah as Bennett (1908, 1909) is shown to have been interested in Africanisms and to have published only observations that matched the attitude of his time toward African contributions to American culture. Montgomery concludes with an invitation for students of Africanisms to use the files of the Linguistic Atlas of the Gulf States (Pederson et al. 1986, 1990), in which several Africanisms qua loan translations are very likely to be determined.

Glenn Gilbert's paper is a report of the factors and people that converted Melville Herskovits from a defender of the European origin of African-American culture and language to a prominent advocate of Africanisms. In Gilbert's own words, "Herskovits 'rediscovered' the creolist hypothesis (paradigm) of the origin of Gullah, and Black English in the Southeast generally, in the United States." Herskovits usually discussed language in connection with aspects of African-American culture, an approach that has influenced some scholars today (e.g., Alleyne 1980, this volume).

To be sure, much of the current research on Africanisms in AALVs owes a lot to Sylvain (1936) and Turner (1949), both of whom are commonly cited not only in this book but also generally in the literature on the genesis of AALVs. I regret not including short essays on them. William Stewart's paper on an aspect of Turner's work unfortunately did not meet our already overextended deadline, and there was no adequate substitute for it. All the lead papers in this volume were volunteered, and none had been proposed for Sylvain. We must thus be content with the impact of their works as reflected by the citations here and there in the literature.

Both the Round Table and this book would not have been possible without the assistance of the meeting's sponsor and several people. I am grateful to the National Science Foundation for funding the Round Table and subsidizing the publication of this book and to Linda Adams for managing the original grant very efficiently. I also thank Cindy Jones, Denise Ferguson, Jennifer Bone, and Jennifer Maxey for transcribing the recordings from the Round Table's discussion sessions and workshops (especially Cindy and Denise) and for typing on computer most of the papers that did not come on disk. Jennifer Eason's help with implementing last-minute corrections and Lioba Moshi's feedback on this Introduction are also much appreciated. I am very much indebted to Nancy Condon for editing the style of virtually every single paper in this book, making sure that the language was as accessible as possible, and for doing much computer work necessary in readying the manuscripts for the publisher. Last but not least, I thank Melinda Conner for the patient and diligent copyediting that has minimized the number of editorial imperfections in this book, as well as the editorial staff of the University of Georgia Press for their assistance through all stages of the book's production. I am solely responsible for all the remaining editorial shortcomings.

## Notes

1. The term "semicreole" is used by Holm (1988) for varieties such as the American Black English vernacular (BEV) and Réunionnais. These share several grammatical features with the creoles to which they are genetically related (Gullah for BEV and Mauritian Creole for Réunionnais), but there is no consensus on whether the similarities are due to decreolization (see, e.g., Stewart 1967, 1968; Labov 1972, 1982; Fasold 1981 for BEV; Cellier 1985) or partial creolization (see Mufwene 1987 for BEV; Chaudenson 1979, 1989; and Baker and Corne 1986 for Réunionnais).

2. In this paper, as in most others in this book as well as in the anglophone creole literature, the term "substrate" is used for languages of the socioeconomically subordinate group during the formative stages of Afro-American language varieties. Compare, however, Morris Goodman (this volume) and Chaudenson (1990) for objections to this usage.

3. The later version, called the lexical learning hypothesis (Bickerton 1989), differs from the earlier one not in the central role that children putatively play in the formation of creoles but in the assumption that the syntax of the new languages is predetermined by properties of the unmarked lexical items selected for the creoles.

4. This term was used for the first time at the Round Table, patterned after Mufwene's (1986a) title "The Universal and Substrate Hypotheses Complement One Another." The position is that neither the LBH nor any version of the substrate hypothesis (SubH) can account fully for the systems of individual creoles. There are, however, differences among proponents of the CompH regarding whether substrate influence becomes effective during or after the crystallization of a creole (Mufwene 1991a).

5. Baker (1990) appropriately uses the term "off target" to say that the slaves at this stage were not attempting to speak the metropolitan variety of the lexifier but rather an already diluted contact variety used by the colonists and their earlier generation of slaves in the homestead system. This corresponds to the variety Chaudenson (1979, 1986, 1989) calls "français approximatif." Note also that by then the term "creole" was already used for colonists and, later, for slaves born in the colony before it was used to describe the language that came to be associated with the slave population.

6. Note that according to Baker and Corne, the Bickertonian bioprogram is primarily responsible for creolization. They exclude the possibility of substrate influence during this phase of creole development because children, who are credited with creolization, did not speak their parents' native languages; hence they could not be influenced by them. The term "generation" is used here following Chaudenson 1979 on the model of generations of, for example, computers, rather than the human generations of approximately twenty-five years suggested by some of the literature.

7. One notices also the same wealth on sociohistorical information in Baker and Corne 1982, 1986 to back their CompH.

8. In retrospect, the onus should have been on superstratists and even more on proponents of the LBH, since the new languages had been created by the substrate groups for communication among themselves (Whinnom 1971; Mufwene 1991b) in the absence of (sufficient) exposure to the lexifier. Assuming the least effort principle, African speech habits should have been considered first when forms and structures of the new languages diverged from those of the lexifier. (One has to assume here that divergence is established after considering the nonstandard varieties of the lexifier which were used in the colonies and not simply by comparing the AALVs with the standard varieties.) Substrate systems may have determined even the selection of forms and structures from among the alternatives available in the lexifiers. Even though other principles related one way or another to Universal Grammar must have been involved (Mufwene 1989, 1990a, 1991b), the fact that some structures are shared by creoles around the world does not necessarily amount to evidence in support of the bioprogram qua Core or Universal Grammar.

9. These individuals are not necessarily opposed to substrate influence. Most acknowledge it as partial or restricted to particular domains, as their contributions to this volume reveal. In fact, some of them now acknowledge a greater African contribution than they did before.

10. French creolists distinguish "le français populaire," the nonstandard varieties brought to the colonies from Europe, from "le français approximatif," the contact variety developed in the colonies. According to Chaudenson's (1979, 1986, 1989) model, which Hazaël-Massieux shares, the features of popular French that were selected by French creoles were mediated by the approximations of French that preceded them.

11. Spears (1987) cautions likewise against hasty attempts to account for features of the American Black English vernacular in terms of either convergence with, or divergence from, white nonstandard English.

12. This difference can be ironed out easily if, as in Mufwene 1991b, the role of the bioprogram qua Universal Grammar in the creolization process is reduced to that of a body of principles and constraints guaranteeing that the emerging system will be a language (as opposed to a nonlanguage). The difference may boil down to

a matter of emphases being placed on different aspects of the process. After all, the lexifier has generally provided most of the morphological building blocks.

13. See G. Bailey et al. 1991, and Rickford 1991 for similar problems regarding the reliability of transcriptions of recordings made by some of the field-workers of the same project.

14. See also Mufwene 1991c for the latter point regarding the Quaterman Gullah sample from the same WPA project.

15. In just the opposite way, Williams (1895) characterizes Gonzales's Gullah as purer than that spoken by the Afro-Americans themselves. Mufwene (1986b) accuses all these writers of maximizing the distribution and concentration of basilectal features in their texts. Mille (1990) observes, for instance, that Ambrose Gonzales's earlier Gullah texts, written in the nineteenth century, are closer to today's Gullah than the later ones written in the twentieth century. In the later texts Gonzales was putatively responding to his readers' interest in the alleged quaintness of Gullah.

16. For the last criterion see also Thomason 1983; Sankoff 1984; Mufwene 1986a; Gilman 1986; Faraclas 1988; and Keesing 1988. For the first criterion, see also Muysken 1983; and Hagège 1985. Compare Mufwene 1989, 1991b for an alternative interpretation of markedness which is situation-relative.

17. See, for example, Lefebvre 1989, 1990; Lefebvre and Massam 1988; and Lefebvre et al. 1989.

18. Mufwene (1989, 1991b) argues that features shared by most of the languages in the contact situation should be considered unmarked relative to the setting, even if they are not commonly attested among the world's languages. Whatever the difference in their interpretations of 'markedness,' Thomason and Mufwene agree that the "creators" of pidgins and creoles actually select from among alternatives available to them, and those that are the most widely shared have a better chance of being adopted by the new language, although there is room for permanent variation.

19. In a way, any successful demonstration of substrate influence in the basic system of a creole disputes (indirectly in some cases) the position that the language must have been formed by children resorting to their bioprogram. The preservation of substrate features generally suggests that they were transferred from the relevant languages by those who could speak them; that is, the adults who came from the relevant parts of Africa in the case of AALVs. Even if children could have selected them from a highly heterogeneous and variable pidgin spoken by their parents, such a selection would presuppose a filtering role of Universal Grammar that is not the same as that assumed of Bickerton's bioprogram (especially 1981, 1984).

20. This second BEV-qua-English-dialect position may be significant only historically. Labov (1985, 1987) has now abandoned the convergence hypothesis in favor of a divergence hypothesis. According to Bailey (1987), who shares that position, the putative divergence started about seventy-five years ago. This hypothesis remains as controversial as any other. For instance, Spears (1987) prefers

that people simply speak of independent development (see also Mufwene 1988), especially since a great deal remains unknown about creoles, BEV, and white nonstandard English.

## References

Alleyne, Mervyn C. 1971. Acculturation and the cultural matrix of creolization. *Pidginization and creolization of languages*, ed. by Dell Hymes, 169–86. Cambridge: Cambridge University Press.

———. 1980. *Comparative Afro-American: An historical-comparative study of English-based Afro-American dialects of the New World*. Ann Arbor: Karoma.

Allsopp, Richard. 1977. Africanisms in the idioms of Caribbean English. *Language and linguistics problems in Africa*, ed. by Paul F. Kotey and Haig Der-Houssikian, 429–41. Columbia, S.C.: Hornbeam Press.

Andersen, Roger, ed. 1983. *Pidginization and creolization as language acquisition*. Rowley, Mass.: Newbury House.

Bailey, Beryl Loftman. 1965. Toward a new perspective in Negro English dialectology. *American Speech* 40.171–77.

Bailey, Guy. 1987. Untitled contribution to *Are black and white vernaculars diverging? Papers from the NWAVE XIV panel discussion*, ed. by Ronald Butters, 32–40. *American Speech* 62.1.

Bailey, Guy, Natalie Maynor, and Patricia Cukor-Avila, eds. 1991. *The emergence of Black English*. Amsterdam: John Benjamins.

Baker, Philip. 1984. Agglutinated French articles in creole French: Their evolutionary significance. *Te Reo* 27.89–129.

———. 1990. Off target? [Column]. *Journal of Pidgin and Creole Languages*. 5.107–19.

Baker, Philip, and Chris Corne. 1982. *Isle de France Creole: Affinities and origins*. Ann Arbor: Karoma.

———. 1986. Universals, substrata and the Indian Ocean creoles. In Muysken and Smith, eds., 163–83.

Bennett, John. 1908. Gullah: A Negro patois. *South Atlantic Quarterly* 7.332–47.

———. 1909. Gullah: A Negro patois, part 2. *South Atlantic Quarterly* 8.39–52.

Bickerton, Derek. 1981. *Roots of language*. Ann Arbor: Karoma.

———. 1984. The language bioprogram hypothesis. *Behavioral and Brain Sciences* 7.173–221.

———. 1986a. Creoles and West African languages: A case of mistaken identity? In Muysken and Smith, eds., 25–40.

———. 1986b. Beyond *Roots*: Progress or regress? *Journal of Pidgin and Creole Languages* 1.135–40.

———. 1986c. Beyond *Roots*: The five-year test. *Journal of Pidgin and Creole Languages* 1.225–32.

———. 1988. Creole languages and the bioprogram. *Linguistics: The Cambridge survey*. Volume 2. *Linguistic theory: Extensions and implications*, ed. by Frederick J. Newmeyer, 268–84. Cambridge: Cambridge University Press.

———. 1989. The lexical learning hypothesis and the pidgin-creole cycle. *Wheels within wheels: Papers of the Duisburg symposium on pidgin and creole languages*, ed. by Martin Pütz and René Dirven, 11–31. Frankfurt am Main: Verlag Peter Lang.

Cellier, Pierre. 1985. *Comparaison syntaxique du créole réunionnais et du français*. Université de la Réunion.

Chaudenson, Robert. 1973. Pour une étude comparée des créoles et parlers français d'outre-mer: survivance et innovation. *Revue de Linguistique Romane* 37.342–71.

———. 1979. *Les créoles français*. Paris: Fernand Nathan.

———. 1986. And they had to speak any way . . . : Acquisition and creolization of French. *The Fergusonian impact*, ed. by Josua A. Fishman et al., 1.69–82. Berlin: Mouton de Gruyter.

———. 1989. *Créoles et enseignement du français*. Paris: L'Harmattan.

———. 1990. Du mauvais usage du comparativisme: le cas des études créoles. *Travaux du Cercle Linguistique d'Aix-en-Provence* 8.123–58.

D'Eloia, Sarah G. 1973. Issues in the analysis of Negro nonstandard English: A review of J. L. Dillard's *Black English: Its history and usage in the United States*. *Journal of English Linguistics* 7.87–106.

Dillard, J. L. 1972. *Black English: Its history and usage in the United States*. New York: Random House, Vintage Books.

———. 1985. *Toward a social history of American English*. New York: Mouton.

Faraclas, Nicholas. 1987. Creolization and the tense-aspect-modality system of Nigerian Pidgin. *Journal of African Languages and Linguistics* 9.45–49.

———. 1988. Nigerian Pidgin and the languages of southern Nigeria. *Journal of Pidgin and Creole Languages* 3.177–97.

Fasold, Ralph W. 1972. *Tense marking in Black English: A linguistic and social analysis*. Arlington, Va.: Center for Applied Linguistics.

———. 1976. One hundred years from syntax to phonology. *Papers from the parasession on diachronic syntax*, ed. by S. Steever, C. Walker, and S. Mufwene, 779–87. Chicago: Chicago Linguistic Society.

———. 1981. The relationship between black and white speech in the South. *American Speech* 56.163–89.

Geraty, Virginia. 1990. *Porgy: A Gullah version*. Charleston: Wyrick and Company.

Gilman, Charles. 1986. African areal characteristics: Sprachbund, not substrate? *Journal of Pidgin and Creole Languages* 1.33–50.

Gonzales, Ambrose E. 1857–1924. *Laguerre: A gascon of the black border*. Columbia, S.C.: The State Printing Company.

———. 1922. *The black border: Gullah stories of the Carolina coast (with a glossary)*. Columbia, S.C.: The State Printing Company.

Hagège, Claude. 1985. *L'homme de paroles*. Paris: Librairie Arthème Fayard.

Hall, Robert A., Jr. 1950. The African substratum in Negro English. *American Speech* 25.51–54.

———. 1966. *Pidgin and creole languages*. Ithaca, N.Y.: Cornell University Press.

Hancock, Ian F. 1977. Appendix: Repertory of pidgin and creole languages. *Pidgin and creole linguistics*, ed. by Albert Valdman, 362–91. Bloomington: Indiana University Press.

Holm, John. 1988. *Pidgins and creoles*. Volume 1. *Theory and structure*. Cambridge: Cambridge University Press.

———. 1989. *Pidgins and creoles*. Volume 2. *Reference survey*. Cambridge: Cambridge University Press.

———. 1991. Atlantic creoles and the language of ex-slave narratives. In G. Bailey et al., eds., 231–48.

Jones, Charles C. 1888. *Negro myths from the Georgia coast, told in the vernacular*. Boston: Houghton Mifflin.

Keesing, Roger M. 1988. *Melanesian Pidgin and the Oceanic substrate*. Stanford: Stanford University Press.

Koopman, Hilda. 1986. The genesis of Haitian: Implications of a comparison of some features of the syntax of Haitian, French and West African languages. In Muysken and Smith, eds., 231–58.

Labov, William. 1972. Is the Black English vernacular a separate system? *Language in the inner city: Studies in Black English vernacular*, by W. Labov, 36–64. Philadelphia: University of Pennsylvania Press.

———. 1982. Objectivity and commitment in linguistic science: The case of the Black English trial in Ann Arbor. *Language in Society* 11.165–201.

———. 1987. Untitled contribution to *Are black and white vernaculars diverging? Papers from the NWAVE XIV panel discussion*, ed. by Ronald Butters, 5–12. *American Speech* 62.1.

Lefebvre, Claire. 1986. Relexification in creole genesis revisited: The case of Haitian Creole. In Muysken and Smith, eds., 279–300.

———. 1989. Instrumental *take*-serial constructions in Haitian and in Fon. *Canadian Journal of Linguistics* 34.319–37.

Lefebvre, Claire, Anne-Marie Brousseau, and Sandra Filipovich. 1989. Haitian Creole morphology: French phonetic matrices in a West African mold. *Canadian Journal of Linguistics* 34.249–72.

Lefebvre, Claire, and Diane Massam. 1988. Haitian Creole syntax: A case for DET as head. *Journal of Pidgin and Creole Languages* 3.2.213–42.

Lightfoot, David W. 1988. Creoles, triggers, and Universal Grammar. *On language: Rhetorica, phonologica, syntactica. A festschrift for Robert P. Stockwell from his friends and colleagues*, ed. by Caroline Duncan-Rose and Theo Vennemann, 97–105. London: Routledge.

Manessy, Gabriel. 1985a. La construction sérielle dans les langues africaines et les langues créoles. *Bulletin de la Société de Linguistique de Paris* 80.1.333–57.

———. 1985b. Remarques sur la pluralisation du nom en créole et dans les langues africaines. *Etudes Créoles* 8.129–43.

———. 1988. L'extraposition du prédicat dans les créoles à base lexicale anglaise et française. *Languages and cultures: Studies in honor of Edgar Polomé*, ed. by Mohammad Ali Jazayery and Werner Winter. Berlin: Mouton de Gruyter.

Maurer, Philippe. 1987. La comparaison des morphèmes temporels du Papiamento et du Palenquero: arguments contre la théorie monogénétique de la genèse des langues créoles. *Varia Creolica*, ed. by Philippe Maurer and Thomas Stolz, 27–70. Bochum, Germany: Brockmeyer.

Mille, Katherine. 1990. *A historical analysis of tense-mood-aspect in Gullah Creole: A case of stable variation*. Ph.D. dissertation, University of South Carolina, Columbia.

Mufwene, Salikoko S. 1983. *Some observations on the verb in Black English vernacular*. Austin: African and Afro-American Studies and Research Center, University of Texas.

———. 1986a. The universalist and substrate hypotheses complement one another. In Muysken and Smith, eds., 129–62.

———. 1986b. Number delimitation in Gullah. *American Speech* 61.33–60.

———. 1987. Review article on *Language variety in the South: Perspectives in black and white*, ed. by Michael Montgomery and Guy Bailey. *Journal of Pidgin and Creole Languages* 2.93–110.

———. 1988. Starting on the wrong foot [Column]. *Journal of Pidgin and Creole Languages* 3.1.109–17.

———. 1989. Some explanations that strike me as incomplete [Column]. *Journal of Pidgin and Creole Languages* 4.117–28.

———. 1990a. Transfer and the substrate hypothesis in creolistics. *Studies in Second Language Acquisition* 12.1–23.

———. 1990b. Creoles and Universal Grammar. *Issues in creole linguistics*, ed. by Pieter Seuren and Salikoko Mufwene, 783–807. *Linguistics* 28.

———. 1991a. La genèse des créoles: quelques questions pour la recherche à venir. *Questions créoles, questions linguistiques*, ed. by Jean Haudry, 21–36. Presses de l'Université Jean Moulin.

———. 1991b. Pidgins, creoles, typology, and markedness. *Development and structures of creole languages: Essays in honor of Derek Bickerton*, ed. by Francis Byrne and Thom Huebner, 123–43. Amsterdam: John Benjamins.

———. 1991c. Is Gullah decreolizing? A comparison of a speech sample of the 1930's with a speech sample of the 1980's. In G. Bailey et al., eds., 213–30.

Mühlhäusler, Peter. 1986. Bonnet blanc and blanc bonnet: Adjective-noun order, substratum and language universals. In Muysken and Smith, eds., 25–40.

Muysken, Pieter. 1983. Review of *Roots of language*, by D. Bickerton. *Language* 59.884–901.

Muysken, Pieter, and Norval Smith, eds. 1986. *Substrata versus universals in creole genesis*. Amsterdam: John Benjamins.

Naro, Anthony J. 1981. The social and structural dimensions of a syntactic change. *Language* 57.63–98.

Pederson, Lee, Susan Leas McDaniel, and Marvin H. Bassett, eds. 1986. *The linguistic atlas of the Gulf states: A concordance of basic materials*. Ann Arbor: University Microfilms.

Pederson, Lee, Susan L. McDaniel, Marvin H. Bassett, Carol Adams, and Michael Montgomery, eds. 1990. *Linguistic atlas of the Gulf states*. Volume 4. *Regional matrix of the linguistic atlas of the Gulf states*. Athens: University of Georgia Press.

Rickford, John R. 1991. Representativeness and reality of the ex-slave materials, with reference to Wallace Quaterman's recording and transcript. In G. Bailey et al., eds., 191–212.

Sankoff, Gillian. 1984. Substrate and universals in the Tok Pisin verb phrase. *Meaning, form, and use in context: Linguistic applications*, ed. by Deborah Schiffrin, 104–19. Washington, D.C.: Georgetown University Press.

Schneider, Edgar Werner. 1982. On the history of Black English in the USA: Some new evidence. *English World-Wide* 3.18–46.

———. 1983. The diachronic development of Black English in the USA: Some new evidence. *Journal of English Linguistics* 16.55–64.

———. 1989. *American earlier Black English*. University: University of Alabama Press. Originally published as *Morphologische und syntaktische Variablen im amerikanischen Early Black English*. Frankfurt am Main: Verlag Peter Lang, 1981.

———. 1990. The cline of creoleness in English-oriented creoles and semi-creoles of the Caribbean. *English World-Wide* 11.79–113.

Seuren, Pieter, and Herman Wekker. 1986. Semantic transparency as a factor in creole genesis. In Muysken and Smith, eds., 57–70.

Spears, Arthur K. 1982. The Black English semi-auxiliary *come*. *Language* 58.850–72.

———. 1987. Untitled contribution to *Are black and white vernaculars diverging? Papers from the NWAVE XIV panel discussion*, ed. by Ronald Butters, 48–55. *American Speech* 62.1.

Stewart, William. 1967. Sociolinguistic factors in the history of American Negro dialects. *Florida Foreign Language Reporter* 5.11, 22, 24, 26.

———. 1968. Continuity and change in American Negro dialects. *Florida Foreign Language Reporter* 6.3–4, 14–16, 18.

———. 1969. Historical and structural bases for the recognition of Negro dialect. *Report of the Twentieth Round Table Meeting on Linguistics and Language Studies*, ed. by James E. Alatis, 239–47. Washington, D.C.: Georgetown University Press.

Stoddard, Albert H. 1949. Animal tales told in the Gullah dialect. Washington, D.C.: Library of Congress. Record albums and mimeo transcriptions.

Sylvain, Suzanne. 1936. *Le créole haïtien: morphologie et syntaxe*. Wetteren, Belgium: Imprimerie De Meester; Port-au-Prince: Chez l'auteur.

Thomason, Sarah G. 1983. Chinook Jargon in areal and historical context. *Language* 59:820–70.

Thomason, Sarah G., and Terrence Kaufman. 1988. *Language contact, creolization, and genetic linguistics*. Berkeley: University of California Press.

Turner, Lorenzo Dow. 1949. *Africanisms in the Gullah dialect*. Chicago: University of Chicago Press.

Weinreich, Uriel. 1953. *Languages in contact*. New York: Linguistic Circle of New York.

Whinnom, Keith. 1971. Linguistic hybridization and the "special case" of pidgins and creoles. *Pidginization and creolization of languages*, ed. by Dell Hymes, 91–115. Cambridge: Cambridge University Press.

Williams, Rev. John G. 1895. A study in Gullah English. *Charleston* (S.C.) *Sunday News*, February 10. Author's manuscript in the University of South Carolina library, Columbia.

# Part One

## *Conceptual Background*

# On the Notion of "Africanism" in Afro-American

*Lawrence D. Carrington*

In this paper I express dissatisfaction with the current usage of the terms "Afro-American" and "Africanism" and propose some criteria for identifying an Afro-American feature as Africanism. The intention of the exercise is to foster consensus on terminology in dealing with those aspects of the study of Afro-American that require reference to substrates or to other historical sources of Afro-American language varieties.

## The Term "Afro-American"

The term "Afro-American" has been used by Alleyne (1980) to refer to the English-based language varieties that have resulted from African-European contact since the fifteenth century A.D. Alleyne does not explicitly define the term. He uses the label initially as an ethnogeographic identifier of New World blacks and later applies it to language varieties particular to that group. Although the specific languages that he treats are English based, he does not exclude historically and culturally similar varieties having other lexical bases. Indeed, his table 1 (1980:11–13) allows comparison of examples from varieties having Iberian, French, and mixed lexical bases. Black Africa and African-America are separate but linked entities, yet their separateness does not lead Alleyne to exclude Krio from the varieties he considers Afro-American. The side of the Atlantic on which the speakers of a variety reside is not a determinant of membership in the category.

The need for a term like "Afro-American" rests on three bases. The first two are matters of academic convenience; the third is a socioemotional concern. First, we must be able to refer collectively to the subset of creoles that are structurally similar and straddle the Atlantic with reference to their structural similarity and regardless of their lexical sources. Second, we must recognize that the contemporary state of some of the varieties of these languages has challenged the accuracy of the label "creole." The third reason is the persistent need to affirm the Africanness of the data set under study.

I suggest that in its widest application the term should refer to those languages in the Americas, the Caribbean, and the Western coast of sub-Saharan Africa which are the historical outcomes of the linguistic contact associated with the transatlantic slave trade, the related plantation systems, and colonization. This definition would embrace varieties now described as Dutch-, English-, French-, Portuguese-, or Spanish-lexicon[1] creoles and their related postcreole varieties. The combination of the geographical and historical criteria would exclude the French-lexicon creoles of the Indian Ocean, despite their structural similarity to the Atlantic French-lexicon creoles, as well as languages such as Afrikaans and the French-influenced versions of Sango.

## X-isms

When applied to a language, the suffix *-ism* suggests peripheralness and peculiarity. Among its definitions of "-ism" the *Concise Oxford Dictionary of Current English* (*CODCE*) includes "(4) of peculiarity in language (Americanism, Gallicism, archaism)" (532). Crystal (1985) does not list any X-isms, but Pei and Gaynor (1969) list several of the kind under discussion here, for example, *Americanism, Gallicism, Hellenism, Hebraism, Hiberinicism, Irishism, Italicism,* and *Negroism*(!). Their definition of "Americanism" is explicit: "A word, expression or grammatical or syntactical form or construction which is peculiar to or characteristic of English spoken in the U.S.A. or which is not in current use outside the U.S.A." The others are less concisely defined, but all are roughly similar: a word, expression, or syntactic construction characteristic or reminiscent of the language or group in question.

An X-ism in language Y is a peculiarity of Y, or in the use of Y, that is attributable to the exposure of Y, or its users, to language X either in the past or in the present. The term usually signals that the source of the X-ism is different from that of the main body of Y and frequently implies that the X-ism is not integral to the functioning of Y.

The application of the X-ism can be at different levels. Let us use the example of a Gallicism in English. A native speaker of British English[2] who uses the expressions *haute couture* or *coup de grace* in a stream of speech can be described as using a Gallicism, that is, a French word or expression introduced by the user for an expressive purpose. The user need not command French nor even be conscious of the foreignness of the expression.

At another level, the legal term *assize* in reference to a court of law is a Gallicism in that it is present in English as a result of its contact with French. The word is of such long standing that it is no longer seen as foreign, but it is nevertheless a Gallicism. The older the Gallicism, the less likely it is to be perceived as such, until eventually only specialists in the history of the languages in question may be aware of its foreign provenience.

It should be noted here that there is an underlying assumption that English exists as an entity apart from French, and that at some time the Gallicism was a loan and was not integrated into the system of the receiving language. In keeping with this idea, it is not reasonable to talk of an Anglicism in English if one is limiting English to the speech of the British Isles.[3] The first application of X-ism, then, is a feature in Y that is or has been imported from X.

Let us take another case. There is a group of people who are described as Italian Americans. A large proportion of them speak American English. Within their speech, one may identify a peculiarity (note the term) that is not present in the speech of other speakers of American English. If it is mainly[4] Italian Americans who manifest the feature, we can legitimately label the feature an Italianism in American English. If the feature in question is paralleled in dialects of Italian or can be shown to be a result of transfer, the label is further justified. However, a feature of the speech of Italian Americans does not need to be manifest in an Italian dialect to be labeled an Italianism. The contact of English and Italian in the United States may have produced in the English spoken by the relevant group features which are not present in the Italian spoken by the subjects or formerly spoken by those from whom they inherit the identifier 'Italian.' Even if a language acquisition expert is able to pinpoint the reason for the feature and to describe it in technical terminology, it does not change the acceptability of the label 'Italianism' as an attribution of source.

But a constraint applies to the case. The term 'Italianism' can only be justified within this example if the language the speaker is using qualifies as English. Under this circumstance, the speaker's control of the medium would be such that the feature to be labeled would be a minor feature of the language although not necessarily of the user's output. This constraint is necessary if we are faced with intermediate varieties which do not represent a consistent, stable, and recognized norm[5] and are produced by persons whose acquisition of the English language is incomplete. The second application of the term "X-ism" would then be a feature in Y that is residual from a time when users of the X-ism spoke language X, or a feature in the contemporary use of Y by the X-influenced group, that is the outcome of the contact of X and Y.

## "Africanism"—An Unsatisfactory Label

The term "Africanism" is unsatisfactory because it is too general in its reference to endure as a primary classificatory term. When linguists wish to refer to the source of an element in a given language or language group, the practice is to label the element by the language, or at least the language group, from which it comes. "Africanism" refers to an entire continent with a multiplicity of language families, let alone languages, as the source or identifier of certain features of Afro-American. When Turner (1949) used the term, it might have been more acceptable because at that time it was important simply to wrest from Europe what was legitimately African.[6] The continued need for its use and for discussion of its scope is an acknowledgment of the paucity of information on the African languages relevant to the case of Afro-American. This paucity bespeaks the absence of descriptions of African languages before the twentieth century, the tentative nature of the African data in studies of Afro-American, and, to some extent, how recently the assumption that the Africans and their descendants were mute participants in the development of their languages was rejected. Ideally, the term should shrink in its usefulness as it is replaced by terms such as "Yorubaism," "Kwaism," or "Fanteism."

"Africanism" has been used to refer to features, devices, elements, or structures in Afro-American which are also present in a language or group of languages indigenous to the continent of Africa. Neither of the two applications of X-ism discussed earlier seems adequate to cover the African legacy to Afro-American.[7] Afro-American is the product of contact between Europe and Africa. The African legacy cannot therefore be described as either peripheral or peculiar. Unless we modify the scope of the first and second applications of X-ism, Africanism will remain too restrictive a term for our purposes. It cannot have the stated connotations because the parties in contact are both intrinsic to the product. By the same token, the terms "Gallicism" in French-lexicon Afro-American and "Anglicism" in English-lexicon Afro-American must be suspect.

The peripheral status implied in the label may be tolerable in respect of lexicon because it is theoretically possible to close temporarily the list of the lexicon, to quantify the proportion of items that are of a particular provenience, and to recognize that the proportion of African items is lower than that of European items. Describing them as Africanisms would then be of similar but not identical value to describing words of English provenance appearing in the repertoire of Yoruba speakers as Anglicisms.[8]

Such a tallying procedure would not be acceptable for grammatical features. Using the label for grammatical features, devices, or structures is less appropriate than applying it to lexical elements because it is more likely that languages will show common structures than that they will have identical lexical items. Simple numerical differences and the laws of chance make this true. Hence, the likelihood is high that a grammatical feature may be characteristic of many more languages than those particular to the Afro-American contact situation.

For purposes of illustration, let us follow Koopman (1986) and assume that predicate clefting in Haitian is a feature that comes through to Haitian from the West African languages that she identifies. It seems inadequate to label such a feature *-ism*. We can argue that the frequency of grammatical features is highly dependent upon the nature of the communication. It would thus be quite unrealistic to quantify the relative frequency of grammatical or semantic features attributable to African as opposed to European sources.[9]

Beyond frequency lies the matter of relative importance of a feature in a language. It is difficult to achieve weightings of the grammatical or semantic features of a language such that one would be rated as more important or more critical than another. Even if this were feasible, its undertaking would be a wasteful exercise simply to rescue the suffix *-ism*.

It is worth recalling that the term "Africanism" was used initially when African contributions to Afro-American were considered to be a list of residual lexical items and a few sporadic peculiarities of phonetics and grammar.[10] The slow rate at which that view has been changing may well be partly due to the labeling of the category. However, if we consciously acknowledge the inadequacy of the term, we should be able to focus on the substantial matter of how to characterize the African legacy.

## Criteria for the Status "Africanism"

The term "Africanism" in relation to Afro-American should be used to describe a feature transmitted from a time when the user of Afro-American or his or her historico-cultural community spoke a language indigenous to the African continent. It should not suggest peripherality or peculiarity, though some Africanisms may be peripheral or peculiar to a given variety of Afro-American; some may be static and others productive.

I now propose criteria for classifying features that are manifest in Afro-American on the basis of whether they are also manifest in (a) languages that are not part of the historical contact setting of Afro-American;[11] (b) languages known to be the result of comparable sociolinguistic contact phenomena; (c) African languages relevant to the development of Afro-American; or (d) European languages relevant to the development of Afro-American.

1. If a feature $F_1$ of a variety of Afro-American is manifest in a relevant African language and a relevant European language, then—independently of its presence or absence in other languages—it is a *shared feature*.
2. If a feature $F_2$ of a variety of Afro-American is manifest in a relevant African language but not in a relevant European language, then—independently of its presence or absence in other languages—it is an *Africanism*.

**Table 1. Feature Identification Matrix**

| | *Other languages* | *Contact languages* | *Relevant African* | *Relevant European* | *Status of Feature* |
|---|---|---|---|---|---|
| Feature $F_1$ | ± | ± | + | + | shared |
| Feature $F_2$ | ± | ± | + | – | Africanism |
| Feature $F_3$ | ± | ± | – | + | Europeanism |
| Feature $F_4$ | ± | + | – | – | contact |
| Feature $F_5$ | ± | – | – | – | Afro-American |

3. If a feature $F_3$ of a variety of Afro-American is manifest in a relevant European language but not in a relevant African language, then—independently of its presence or absence in other languages—it is a *Europeanism*.
4. If a feature $F_4$ of a variety of Afro-American is not manifest in a language relevant to the genesis or development of Afro-American but is manifest in known contact languages, then—independently of its presence or absence in other languages—it is a *contact feature* in Afro-American.
5. If a feature $F_5$ of a variety of Afro-American is not manifest in a relevant African language or in a relevant European language, nor is it manifest in known contact languages or other languages contingent on the Afro-American case, then—independently of its presence or absence in other languages—it is *proper to Afro-American*.[12]

Table 1 summarizes the position.

"Feature" must be interpreted in its broadest sense. It cannot be limited to forms, devices, structures, or strings thereof but must include the functions and meanings with which these elements are associated. The term should subsume lexical items, function morphemes, idioms, word order at phrase and clause level, morphological rules, feature-meaning relationships, feature-function relationships, transformations, and nonsegmental phenomena.

Established linguistic reasoning on how to interpret the occurrence of similar phenomena in different languages can be applied to the case of Africanisms. The critical point is that a feature in Afro-American cannot be related conclusively to a relevant African language unless there is some acceptable supporting conceptual, semantic, formal, distributive, or communicative similarity between the features in the putatively related varieties. Identifying a feature as an Africanism requires a systematic consideration of feature-meaning and feature-function relationships in the variety of Afro-American and in the relevant African language(s). Not all features may be sufficiently supported for conclusive assignment to the category of Africanism; a large number of features will remain suspected Africanisms without much likelihood of confirmation. That circumstance should not invite a relaxation of the criteria for Africanisms. It simply has to be accepted as evidence of the limitations in our historical knowledge and reconstructive methodology.

As for lexical items, the phonetic shape of the Afro-American feature must be related, given the known dynamics of formal change, to a feature in a relevant African language. In addition, its meaning, function, or communicative value must similarly be related to such a language, given the normal dynamics of semantic change and functional shift (e.g., *fufu* in Jamaican Creole [JC], and *e-fúfu, fufúú* in Twi). In the case of function words, evidence must be provided of a similar or the same grammatical function in a relevant African language. If phonetic similarity can also be established between the Afro-American word and its putative African etymon, so much the better (e.g., *se* in JC and *sè* in Twi), but this prerequisite is not necessary.

The case of idioms is somewhat different from that of lexical items but similar to the case of function words. Here, the feature of Afro-American must relate to the relevant African language by showing a similar technique for the representation of reality without any necessary reference to phonetic shape. What are commonly listed as calques would fit into this category, with the requirement that they show similarity of conceptualization of the meanings that they are intended to express (e.g., items such as 'eye-water' in JC and Guyanese Creole [GC] and parallel expressions in several African languages noted in Allsopp 1976).

A feature like word order would require that the sequence of components be similar and have the same or similar grammatical or communicative function as in the relevant African language. (See Robertson, in this volume, for examples of postpositioned locatives in Berbice Dutch [BD] and Ịjọ.)

Morphological and word-formation devices of Afro-American may be assigned to Africanisms when they have parallels in their form, form class, independent meanings, or linkage behavior. (See Robertson, in this volume, for examples of postposed pluralizer *-apu* and nominalizer *-jɛ* in BD and Ịjọ.)

Suprasegmental features such as tone and intonation would have to be identified by their similarity of shape and assigned to Africanism on the basis of their distribution, at least, or their function. One of the reasons for this provision is that the change of lexical set during historical transmission could have affected the maintenance of nonsegmental phenomena so much that we are obliged to consider residual presence rather than active patterning.

The term "relevant language" needs discussion. What is a relevant language? Quite simply, it is any language that is historically identifiable as a language used by linguistically influential participants in the contact that produced Afro-American. This requires careful interpretation. In the case of the European languages, it is obvious that the lexical source language of a given variety of Afro-American is a relevant language. But relevance should not be extended to the linguistic type of the language concerned. For example, in the case of Jamaican, English is a relevant European language but Germanic is not a relevant type of language. As for the African languages, historical data on the sources of the Africans, their languages or ethnic affiliations, and the like will signal relevant languages. In addition, the linguistic type of the languages identified is also relevant. Hence, in the case of Jamaican, Twi is a relevant language, and equally the class Kwa (and more specifically Akan) is relevant.

The reason for this skew in the interpretation of relevance is that it is the Africans who were experiencing language shift, and, as native speakers of their languages, they would have had access to analyses of their speech derived from their native speaker competence. That would place the typological resources of their languages within their personal scope. It is true that the Europeans also had available their analyses as native speakers of their languages, but they were not the parties who underwent the language shift in which we are interested. This view implies rejection of the notion that children, if indeed they are the locus of creolization, had access only or primarily to a pidgin used by their parents.[13]

## Time of Access

The issue of access that would have allowed a feature to be part of the repertoire of an Afro-American user introduces a historical component to our reasoning. One of the views which must be countered at this juncture is the idea that Africanisms are tied in some sense to *early* contact in a "formative" period of Afro-American.

There are two objections to this. First, any insistence that some arbitrary period of formative contact is the only one relevant to the identification of Africanisms denies the evidence that the process of stabilization and growth of the language varieties must have been gradual beyond the elementary pidginization phase. Second, it undervalues the fact that until the end of the slave trade (at different dates for each of the relevant countries) there was a continuing input of new Africans from the west coast of the continent.[14] The continued input of these Africans would have meant that linguistic replenishment would not have ended with the stabilization of Afro-American varieties in the New World but would have continued into the nineteenth century—earlier for some of the colonies, later for others. Whether a feature is of early or late provenience in the history of Afro-American does not diminish the legitimacy of its being considered an Africanism.

Further, the fact that a feature was recorded late does not mean that it was not available prior to its being recorded. Indeed, it can be argued that even where a feature is a late development in a putative source language, its presence may well have been structurally possible from a much earlier period than its notation in the variety under examination. In the lexical domain, for example, new words in a language are rarely formed out of elements that are unacceptable within the morphophonology of the language. The late presence of a lexical element must therefore be viewed as an accident of the lexicon or the need for an item rather than as an indicator of a shift in the language, unless there is some inconsistency in the behavior or shape of the element by reference to established elements. New elements themselves (other than borrowings), then, can still be indices of the nature of the language prior to their appearance. A similar argument, and indeed a stronger one, would apply regarding grammatical features.

Briefly, then, it is the entire period of the trade in slaves which must be regarded as relevant to the identification of Africanisms in Afro-American. Changes in the sources of slave supply after the assumed establishment of Afro-American do not disqualify 'postformation' inputs from eligibility.

## The Question of Universals

The issue of universals must also be addressed. The assignment of a feature of Afro-American to the category "Africanism" by the procedures I have proposed would be irrational unless one had a clear position on the relationship between universal features of language and the features of particular languages.

The discovery of Universal Grammar, and, by extension, other universals governing the nature of languages and the processes that they undergo in response to social change, is being undertaken by three routes:

1. In-depth analysis of individual languages with the rationale that if there are universals, they must be discoverable by thorough deep investigation of *any* language.
2. Comparative study of the structure of a widening set of languages with the intention of accumulating evidence of similarities of principles.

3. Analysis of a subset of languages presumed by their histories to have shallow culture-induced layers over a presumed innate structure.

For our present purposes, I think that there is absolutely no incompatibility between the idea that a feature could be both a putative universal and an Africanism, an Austronesianism, or any other X-ism.[15] The point is that universal status is in addition to specific status, not a substitute for it.

## Notes

I thank my colleagues Ian Robertson and Valerie Youssef for discussions that clarified my thinking on several aspects of this paper. I further acknowledge the comments of Salikoko Mufwene on the original version presented at the Round Table.

1. Or any combination of these lexical types.

2. For reasons which will become apparent below, my illustration must deal with a restricted geographical version of English.

3. One could speak, though, of an Anglicism in the use of American English. It would be interpreted to mean a Britishism.

4. I would prefer to be able to say *only,* but allowances have to be made for non–Italian Americans who may be operating linguistically within the sphere of influence of Italian Americans and might have features of their speech.

5. It is easy to recognize here a possible kink in the argument. Intermediate varieties produced by Italians (let us say elderly or newly arrived) using English would show features which many would argue are parallel to features established in languages called "creole." I suggest that there is an important difference in that the intermediate features in the Italo-American case are transient, on either an individual or a community basis. The comparable features in a "creole" would be established rather than transient.

6. Note, too, that Turner very carefully sought to assign the African elements of Gullah to specific languages. His use of "Africanism" was as a summary rather than primarily categorical.

7. I am using the term "legacy" in a completely nontechnical sense in order to avoid the use of words like "component," "feature," "device," and so on, which carry special connotations within linguistic usage.

8. This should not obscure the obvious fact that Anglicisms in Yoruba would be *loanwords,* whereas the Africanisms of Afro-American cannot be so described.

9. For example, it would be nonsensical to count the frequency of predicate clefting cases in Haitian and compare it with the frequency of the use of *di* as a possessive particle.

10. Allsopp (1976) offers the word "apport" as a neutral term that could encom-

pass the contribution of a specified group to a language born of the type of contact that produced Afro-American. Hence, one might speak of the "African apport" to Afro-American. Regrettably though, I find that "apport" appears in the *CODCE* with a meaning that could well provoke an uproar in our context. It is defined as "production of material objects by supposedly occult means at spiritualist séance; object thus produced." The term is listed as obsolete.

11. It should be noted that Afro-American has been in contact with indigenous American languages whose influence must be accommodated within the definitions and procedures by which source is assigned to a feature of a language. For the time being it is easier to overlook this detail.

12. Note that "proper to" does not mean 'exclusive to.'

13. Avoiding a discussion of this controversial point, I draw attention to my observations on time of access below, specifically to the assertion on the continuity of input from Africa for the duration of the slave trade.

14. It is pointless to argue that Afro-American (or some pidgin or creole) was extant on the west coast of Africa and so new slaves already spoke it. Unless the indigenous languages had been totally exterminated, the transported African would still have been a native speaker of one of them.

15. See also Mufwene 1986.

## References

Alleyne, Mervyn C. 1980. *Comparative Afro-American: An historical-comparative study of English-based Afro-American dialects of the New World*. Ann Arbor: Karoma.

Allsopp, S. Richard. 1976. The case for Afrogenesis. Paper presented at a conference of the Society for Caribbean Linguistics, University of Guyana, August 1976.

Cassidy, Frederic G., and R. B. Le Page. 1980. *Dictionary of Jamaican English*. Second edition. Cambridge: Cambridge University Press.

*Concise Oxford dictionary of current English*. 1982. Seventh edition. Oxford: Oxford University Press.

Crystal, David. 1985. *A dictionary of linguistics and phonetics*. Oxford: Basil Blackwell.

Fyle, C. N., and E. D. Jones. 1980. *A Krio-English dictionary*. Oxford: Oxford University Press.

Koopman, Hilda. 1986. The genesis of Haitian: Implications of a comparison of some features of the syntax of Haitian, French, and West African languages. *Substrata versus universals in creole genesis*, ed. by Peter Muysken and Norval Smith, 231–58. Amsterdam: John Benjamins.

Mufwene, Salikoko S. 1986. The universalist and substrate hypotheses complement one another. *Substrata versus universals in creole genesis*, ed. by Peter Muysken and Norval Smith, 129–62. Amsterdam: John Benjamins.

Pei, Mario A., and Frank Gaynor. 1969. *A dictionary of linguistics*. Totowa, N.J.: Littlefield, Adams and Company.

Turner, Lorenzo D. 1949. *Africanisms in the Gullah dialect*. Chicago: University of Chicago Press.

# Identifying Africanisms in New World Languages: How Specific Can We Get?

*George Huttar*

Studying the history of any language, creole or otherwise, involves asking where a particular item in the language came from and by what path, or through what changes, it got to its present state. Answers may be in terms of internal and/or external history of the language. In the case of New World creole languages, the question usually means asking in the first place whether an item comes from language universals, superstrate languages, or substrate languages. Questions about superstrate languages then subdivide into looking at the various candidate European languages, basically English, Dutch, French, Spanish, and Portuguese. The substrate languages get us looking first of all at Amerindian versus African sources, and the latter lead us to European-based pidgins with which slaves may have been in contact in Africa. Then, within African or Amerindian, we attempt to get more specific, identifying either a specific language family (e.g., Cariban, Bantu) or perhaps even a specific language (e.g., Kalina, Kikongo). In this paper I make some claims about how specific it is appropriate to be in claiming a particular source for a particular linguistic item and propose some research emphases which should allow us to get more specific about some of these sources.

When I first proposed this topic to the organizer of this conference, I had a rather negative impression of the surprising frequency with which claims about origins were made in the literature with much greater specificity than I thought the evidence warranted. But even the little I have managed to do since then in sampling the vast literature dealing with New World creole origins has made me more optimistic. Some recent writers are being more cautious in their claims; better still, some are adducing enough additional evidence to make greater specificity defensible.

Little of what I have to say is new; rather, I am trying to bring together ideas from several sources, many of them too long in my consciousness to allow me to acknowledge where I first picked them up. The sources include anthropologists, historians, and linguists specializing in Spanish, French, Dutch, English, and Portuguese areas of the New World on a subject of concern which has already been a matter of scholarly attention for a century (see references in Delafosse 1925; Castro 1980). While my focus is on creole languages, the study of Africanisms in New World languages cannot be neatly divided into creoles, on the one hand, and noncreole varieties of European languages, on the other. Such an arbitrary division can hinder more than help any pursuit of African origins in either type of language, even assuming we can always agree into which category to put a particular language.

As one more preliminary matter, let me make explicit what I believe to be the position of all of us at this Round Table: we are not pursuing origins as what Carrington (1987:90) calls "a ritual goal," but rather we hope that such historical studies, in making the heritage of today's speakers of creoles more specifically known, may contribute in some way to goals important to such speakers.

I am not directly concerned here with the universalist versus substratist discussion, important as that is; yet my remarks are not unrelated to it. First, if we agree that some linguistic items are less likely to be a product of innate or other universal factors than others, and so are more apt to be language specific, then the more language-specific ones will be by definition more useful in determining specific origins than the more universal ones.

Second, if a particular item can be shown to very likely have African roots, then only with correspondingly less certainty can it be attributed to universals (e.g., bioprogram). I agree, however, with Mühlhäusler's (1986:286) position that being able to relate a particular item in a creole to a particular potential substratal source is not a sufficient demonstration that the item did in fact arise from, or only from, that source and not from, for example, universally operating factors.

In asking about origins behind a particular creole language or group of such languages, we are asking two sorts of questions. One is, Where did creole language X come from? One way to answer this question is in terms of whether a particular language was brought to the New World en masse from Africa, developed completely in the New World, or somewhere in between. The second sort of question is, Where did item Y in creole language X come from? The answers to this question for all Y's in language X constitute another way to answer the first question.

By "linguistic item" I mean any unit, system, or other identifiable feature of a language, whether in some sense "real" or the product of linguists' reification. An item may be a form, a construction, a system of units such as tones or consonants or pronouns, or a way of distributing a set of meanings across a system of forms, such as kin types or color terms.

The growing literature on creole languages of the New World frequently addresses questions of origin. Given the various factors that potentially obscure the issue, the answers given are sometimes surprisingly specific. I believe a number of claims about origins have been too specific, or too incautious in the specificity of their claims, at three different levels: (1) assuming African influence where language universals, the influence of other languages, or both are just as likely (e.g., several "African" items in Delafosse's [1925] description of the creole of the interior of French Guiana are almost certainly of English origin); (2) assuming a particular African language family (e.g., Kwa) when other language families, also likely from an extralinguistic historical point of view, may be involved (see, e.g., Corne's [1987] comments on the possibility of Bantu sources, at least for some Indian Ocean creoles, for the verb fronting commonly assumed to derive from Kwa sources); and (3) assuming a specific language (e.g., Yoruba) when closely related, similar languages are also a possibility. (Although this last still occurred fairly recently, I mention here only Baudet's [1981:106] criticism of a work from half a century ago, Sylvain 1936.)[1] While such errors are understandable because of the factors that make more specific identification of origins difficult, they are not thereby excusable. Let us look at some of these factors, some briefly, some at greater length. None of them is unfamiliar to us—many, for example, have been discussed by de Granda (1978)—yet a recapitulation of them here gives us a basis for proposing methods for overcoming them.

First, although we are not directly concerned here with the question of universals versus substrates or superstrates, the existence of linguistic universals does make the question of origins more difficult to answer. For if some items are very commonly found in languages, then their presence in a particular creole by virtue of their arising independently in many human languages is indistinguishable from their occurring because the creole inherited, borrowed, or appropriated them from some specific substrate or superstrate language. (And even if we have some reason to assume the substrate option in a particular case, the range of possible source languages is very wide.) What this means for research into specific origins is that it pays to focus attention on areas less likely to be a result of universals. That can mean general areas like the phonological shape of most lexemes, which we know to be fairly language specific or at least family specific. Or specific linguistic items that are rarely attested, such as the *m-* or *mi-* inserted after transitive verbs in certain syntactically and phonologically defined environments in several of the creoles of Suriname (Huttar 1986b).

In this connection even onomatopoeic forms, sometimes dismissed as too universal to be of value for origins research, are useful. While they may generally be more iconic than other lexemes, they typically are only partly so and remain partly conventional. That the firing of a gun is represented by *bang* in English but by *gbóou* in Ndjuka, for example, should not only suggest that more than universal principles of onomatopoeia are operating here, but also, with the doubly articulated stop in the Ndjuka form, should encourage us to find out how this same noise is represented by ideophones in a variety of West African languages. More important, the fact that Ndjuka and other creoles of Suriname have many ideophones representing nonauditory characteristics for which English has no ideophones (e.g., Ndjuka *líyéé* for smoothness, *fánn* for whiteness, *tyakatyáka* for disorderliness) indicates a source for the number and use of ideophones in these creoles that is neither universal nor superstratal. Again, careful comparison with West African languages of various families is indicated.

Second, contact with superstrate languages in the various stages up to, through, and after creolization obviously reduces significantly the number of items available for the search for specific African sources. Put more optimistically, easily identifiable items of European origin reduce the job left to be done in identifying substrate sources. But if we are using the latter items as clues to the specific origins of a people, then the greater the European influence on the language in question, the worse off we are. We obviously can get further in languages like those of Suriname, where the intensive contact period with European superstrate languages was comparatively brief, than in most languages of the Caribbean, where the contact with the superstrate has remained important over the centuries. This may occasionally mean that we can use information from the former group of languages to help resolve questions about the latter. But this method is very limited in applicability because the history of the slave trade has been so different for these different territories: their slaves were brought by different nations from different parts of Africa (or from elsewhere in the New World) at different times.

For either group—languages with or without long superstrate contact—we can also do better by looking at those areas of language less likely to be subject to European influence. For example, de Granda (1978) and Alleyne (1980) agree that lexical items are in general more easily replaced under language contact than are phonological or phonetic and morphosyntactic ones, a position with which few would argue. Mühlhäusler (1986:128–29) proposes:

> As a general principle, it can be postulated that the more arbitrary an area of grammar, the more readily can languages borrow from one another. With regard to the formation of developmental continua such as the pidgin-creole continuum, this implies that substratum influence will be most

> pronounced in the areas of lexical semantics, prosodic phonetology, some segmental phonetology, and pragmatics. On the other hand, superstratum influence will be strongest in lexical morphology and segmental phonetology. Syntax, inflectional morphology and derivational morphology are relatively independent of substratum and superstratum influences.

Mühlhäusler's three-way division suggests that "lexical semantics, prosodic phonetology, some segmental phonetology, and pragmatics" are areas that will be most useful in determining specific substratal influences, while lexical morphology, for example, will be least helpful.[2] Yet even within the area of lexical morphology, certain domains of meaning are less likely than others to have been influenced by the European languages because they were kept secret, they were simply irrelevant to the European masters, or for other reasons.[3] In some domains, not only lexicon but a more extensive linguistic system may be available for study, as in Dalby's (1971) and especially Bilby's (1983) work on a religious language surviving in Jamaica. The case of Berbice Dutch (Smith et al. 1987) demonstrates that under certain sociohistorical conditions even everyday domains of vocabulary can be heavily influenced by a substrate. But that is so far an exceptional case, although it does remind us not to be closed to the possibility of other such cases coming to light.

We return to Mühlhäusler's "lexical semantics" below. By "prosodic phonetology" we may understand the form and function of phenomena such as stress, lexical and grammatical tone, intonation, length, and rhythm. Carter (1987) provides a clear example of the approach that should be most fruitful for origins research: looking at the suprasegmentals of a New World creole in detail and as a system and comparing them with similar phenomena, again as systems, in various African languages.

In the "pragmatics" area we may be permitted to include highly ritualized areas of language use, such as proverbs and greeting formulas (see, e.g., Naden 1986 on greeting rules in Mampruli of Ghana), areas which should therefore be fruitful for our purposes. For example, the typical greeting exchange among Ndjukas involves an opening whose form varies with the time of day, and usually with the sex of the addressee and the relative ages of the two interlocutors. The reply consists of an almost exact repetition of the opening, with a specific change made at the end. The first speaker then inquires after the other's general well-being, again in a form dependent on the time of day. The second speaker repeats most of that inquiry in the reply and immediately follows it with an inquiry into the first speaker's well-being. The first speaker replies with a similarly vague but affirmative statement that all is well, whereupon the second speaker may utter a simple affirmative interjection or may elaborate on it.

Such an exchange pattern does sometimes occur among English speakers (viz., "Good morning." "Good morning." "How are you?" "Fine, thank you. How are you?" "Fine, thanks." "Good."), but it is not as standard or unmarked as among the Ndjukas and differs in its literal content. A survey of what is said in analogous situations in various cultures should tell us how likely such structures are to be a result of innate factors alone (not very likely, I suspect) and in what specific parts of the world similar structures occur—in particular, among what peoples, language families, or language areas in West Africa.

More generally, the whole area of specifics of language use referred to as "ethnography of communication" should have escaped the obscuring action of the superstrate more than areas of language knowledge more easily brought from the tacit to the conscious level—which may amount to the same thing as Mühlhäusler's criterion of being less arbitrary. To take another example, Maroon societies in Suriname (e.g., Saramaccans, Ndjukas) employ palavers (Ndjuka *kuútu*) in which parties in a dispute speak to the paramount chief only by directing their comments to a "speak person" or "answer person" (Ndjuka *píki man*). Replies from the chief are likewise passed through this functionary. Here again we seem to be dealing with a feature of this kind of communication event which is more likely substratal than innate. If such a palaver structure is African, we can again seek to be more precise and investigate in what areas in Africa such a way of conducting palavers is found, or was found some centuries ago—or, for that matter, in what areas a distinct communication event classifiable as a palaver is recognized.

Similarly, although perhaps "pragmatics" is not the most appropriate rubric for this area, I would urge the study of creole and African discourse structures,[4] including the structure of extended monologues such as folktales, the sort of utterances not likely heard often from Europeans. Likewise conversational structure: while conversation between European and African was likely too "artificial" to follow the established patterns of either African or European languages, conversation among slaves presumably could have continued in African molds, at least when the discourse structures of the languages of the two interlocutors were similar. In general, I believe the structure of discourse, as opposed to that of words, phrases, and clauses, is an area for which it is hard for native speakers to be made aware of their unconscious knowledge. I further assume that such areas are likely to be particularly resistant to change. Thus more descriptions of discourse structures of New World creoles would clearly be desirable. We do have a few so far (e.g., Grimes and Glock 1970; Park 1980; Broderick 1985; Frank 1986; Glock 1986; and Wilner 1986). Singler (1988) compares discourse functions of utterance-final *o* in basilectal Liberian English and languages of various families of West Africa and refers to forthcoming work in which he argues that Liberian English has adopted "a Kru strategy for narratives and procedural texts . . . [with] consequences for the Liberian English tense-aspect system as well" (138).

Before leaving the area of Africanisms being eliminated by the overlay of the superstrate, I should also mention the less widespread phenomenon of competition from non-African substrate (or "adstrate") languages—that is, Amerindian languages. Valdman (1978:174–75) lists forms from Arawakan, Cariban, and Tupi origin in French creoles of the Antilles. The creoles of Suriname likewise have lexemes from the same three general sources (on Ndjuka lexemes from the Tupi language Oyampi, such as Ndjuka *tamanúa* [cf. Oyampi *tamanúa,* Portuguese *tamanduá*], see Huttar 1989). Many of these lexemes refer to items presumably introduced to the (ex-)slaves by the Indians, such as implements used in the processing of cassava. But others, such as those for some local plants and animals, perhaps would have been named with African lexemes, as so many other such items were, had the Indian sources not been available.

One more variant on the problem of the original African sources being obscured by the replacive action of other languages is that implied by Taylor (1963) and made explicit by de Granda (1978): that a Portuguese (or English—see, e.g., Hancock 1986) pidgin or creole may have begun replacing African items long before influence from European superstrates in the New World continued the process (for yet other possibilities, see Holm 1986:265).

A third factor obscuring the specific African source of a particular item is the great similarity among many languages in areas from which we know slaves were taken (but see Hair 1970:60 on the lack of lexical similarity among, e.g., Kwa languages). Such similarity is found in phonological, grammatical, lexical, and semantic areas. Coarticulated labiovelar stops, for example, are found all the way from the Atlantic across the West African bulge into the Central African Republic (Welmers 1973:47). Serial verb constructions using 'to surpass' to express comparison are found in languages of the Kwa, Mande, and even Chadic families (Huttar 1981; see the more extensive survey in Stassen 1985). Koopman (1986) uses parallel structures in both Kru and Kwa, and to some extent Mande and Gur, languages in comparing Haitian Creole syntax with "West African," on the one hand, and French, on the other. Ndjuka *potopóto* 'soft, weak; muddy' relates equally to Yoruba *potopoto* and Kikongo *potopoto,* both meaning 'mud.'[5] The use of the same lexeme (*gogó*) for 'buttocks' and for the 'base' of, for example, an arrow, as in Ndjuka and Saramaccan, is also found in languages of the Jukunoid, Grasslands Bantu, Cross River, Mande, and West Atlantic families.

To get around this problem, more attention must be given to specific areas of specific African languages. For example, what is the distribution of co-articulated stops in each language? Do they occur only word-initially? Again, the details of comparative constructions with 'surpass' are quite different in Chadic and Kwa languages, as well as from one Kwa language to another. It is encouraging to see the trend in recent years toward more detailed studies of specific structures (e.g., Arends 1986a, 1986b) and toward studies of linguistic systems, not only isolated items (e.g., Boretzky 1983a, 1983b).

Along with this more detailed look at the languages, or in fact as the framework in which such a look must take place, is an examination of linguistic items as they relate to one another, and not only in isolation. For example, there has been a great deal of study of individual lexical items and where they may have come from, but comparatively little of systems of lexical items or of the conceptual habits that such systems may perpetuate or reflect (cf. Huttar 1983)—what Mühlhäusler refers to, I suspect, under "lexical semantics." Yet such habits are probably much less impervious to superstrate influence, and thus all the more useful for getting at African origins. Little has been done in this area by creole scholars (results of one empirical study are presented in Huttar 1975); I suggest that the work of ethnosemanticists like Brent Berlin (e.g., 1976), Paul Kay (e.g., 1971; Berlin and Kay 1969), and Cecil Brown (e.g., 1984; Witkowski and Brown 1985) would provide us with a good methodological starting point, as well as some specific questions to ask about creole and African languages.

Looking more closely at a greater variety of African languages also will help us partly overcome a fourth obstacle to origins research: the fact that some African languages are more thoroughly described than others. An obvious remedy is to continue the more detailed study of a greater number of languages in the pertinent geographical areas. Of course, most of this further study of African languages can be aimed only at the languages as they are spoken now, which brings us to a fifth source of obscurity of origins: the substrate and superstrate languages involved in the formation of New World creoles are the languages of two or three centuries ago; yet, with some notable exceptions, we must deal with records of both as they have been spoken in the last few decades. This is especially true when we are concerned with the syntactic details, discourse structures, esoteric lexical items, and details of phonetics and phonological systems which are apt to be most helpful in pinpointing specific origins. We can in a few cases refer to older records of the languages we are interested in (see Hair 1970 for a catalog of most of the earliest extant works on languages of West Africa), but this method is applicable to only a few items (such as individual lexical items) in only a few languages, and not at all to most New

World creoles. Usually the best we can do is make sure we do not violate some well-established diachronic universal in getting from a putative origin form or structure to its putative modern reflexes.

When we ask where a particular language, or the language of a particular group of people, came from—whether instead of or by means of asking about where specific items in a language came from—we are essentially asking where a particular group of people came from. This has, in fact, been a major concern or motivation of much of the work on creole language origins. From this consideration it is clear that we have the additional resource of looking at any number of nonlinguistic items in the culture concerned, as well as whatever oral traditions about the history of the group may have been preserved. The latter may only be helpful for some groups and may give us no more clues than a couple of personal or place names. But the former, especially in cases in which the European cultural superstratum has not wiped out most traces of African culture, looks more generally promising. For example, what are the details of the rules and terminology for the playing of *waree* or *agi,* including the social conditions in which it is appropriate to play the game? (For example, among the Ndjukas it appears to be played most often with the recently bereaved during their initial mourning period.) Lichtveld's (1931) study of the distribution of Spider and Rabbit as the trickster hero in West Africa exemplifies the use of nonlinguistic cultural materials to get more specific about the origins of creole-speaking peoples, as does the Herskovitses' (1941) work on religions of Suriname and of Dahomey.

But in culture, as in language, we are again often faced with the unknown degree and nature of change between the time of our investigation and the time of the slave trade. Mintz (1975) has made clear that preservation or transmission of Old World cultural traits, especially systems of traits or institutions, can hardly be assumed to be a straightforward matter. But he also points out that some institutions are likely to be more readily preserved or transmitted than others, and that beliefs and attitudes may likewise persevere more clearly than institutions (483–87). The following quotation will make my discussion more specific:

> Purely for purposes of argument, I would suggest that many motor habits, the emphasis on the folktale as a pedagogical device, ceremonial use of the drum, the trickster motif, and certain features of verse-singer and chorus refrain might be parts of a West African cultural substratum; possession by specific gods with specific characterological attributes would be attributable—at least in some measure—to culture-specific African traditions;

> some social-organizational features having to do with descent are conceivably traceable to lineage organizations. . . . The principal point I wish to make . . . is that we cannot view the phenomenon "culture" as homogeneous and undifferentiated, whether we are seeking to trace the origins of particular values or practices, or to understand what happens when a culture changes and reintegrates. (Mintz 1975:486–87)

From this it follows that certain parts of cultures, like certain parts of languages, will be more useful to us than others in getting a clear picture of the origins of a group—that is, a picture less clouded by the effects of superstrate language and culture. Thus we may do well to examine basic beliefs and attitudes of a group rather than look only at the institutions that have grown out of them; or to focus our research efforts on some of the areas Mintz suggests, or similar ones—ones that did not require for their preservation numbers of people or other tangible resources unavailable to the slaves. Hazaël-Massieux (1985:9–10) specifically suggests the areas of cuisine and music as ones likely to still be revealing of substrate origins.

Another such potentially fruitful area of research, one embracing both language and culture, is proverbs. Collections of proverbs have been published, for example, for some Caribbean creoles; but it remains for systematic comparative work to be done to explore the possible sources of specific proverbs, of whole repertoires of proverbs, and of the cultural values that proverbs encode. The partial independence of literal meaning and encoded cultural value can be illustrated by the Ndjuka (and Saramaccan) proverb, *Te i o leiki san i o nyan a Sonde, i mu leiki san i kisi a Sataa* 'When you're going to figure out what you'll eat on Sunday, you must figure out what you catch on Saturday.' The proverb encodes a sentiment about the necessity of preparation that may be reflected in the proverbs of a wide variety of cultures (see Huttar and Huttar 1988) but is expressed, in terms of its literal referents, in a way presumably found in far fewer cultures. Are proverbs similar to this one in both literal and figurative meaning to be found in just a few specific cultures of West Africa, or in many cultures over a wide area?

If we are successful in identifying a fairly specific source of a particular cultural item, just as for a linguistic item, what we have really found out is not where a particular group of people came from but where at least one member of that group came from. For broadly applicable structural features, such as some patterns of syntax and semantic organization, we can probably assume that substrate influence is likely only if we are dealing with one dominant substrate group or if the structural feature in question is found in all or most of the substrate groups in question (as is obvious from the caveat in Valdman 1978:383, and from Smith et al. 1987:79–80). The case of the Eastern Ịjọ in Berbice described in the latter work illustrates the former condition, while the above-mentioned widespread use of the same lexeme for 'buttocks' and 'base' of an arrow probably qualifies to illustrate the latter.

But for other linguistic and cultural items, it may have taken only a few individuals, perhaps even only one—and thus representation from one African language group—to establish a usage in an emerging creole (see Gilman 1986 for an opposing position). This would seem likely, for example, for activities and lexicon pertaining to a specialized craft or to priestly or shamanistic activities (e.g., names of medicinal herbs).[6] We need a model of social interaction and influence developed enough to tell us what factors cause one source group or individual to be more influential than another in a particular part of the developing culture or lexicon of a new composite group. Sheer numbers may play a role, but surely other factors, such as prestige differences among individuals and rarity of particular types of knowledge or skills, must play a part. Here current theories of cultural innovation may help us.

Let us turn now briefly to sources of information external to New World and African languages and cultures. Postma (1976), Curtin (1969, 1975), Patterson (1967), Martin (1972), and others who have studied the Atlantic slave trade have done much to narrow the field of search. But as Megenney (1986), de Granda (1978), and others have pointed out, much more remains to be done with existing slave trade records in Europe and elsewhere. (And in some cases the relevant records have been destroyed.) There is also something to be learned from slave trade documents other than archived records, such as Falconbridge (1788) or the documents amassed in works like Donnan (1965).

One further way in which we can make progress in identifying specific sources of Africanisms—or for that matter in distinguishing Africanisms from creole language items rising from other sources—is to encourage and participate in collaboration among scholars working on different parts of the total picture. A major value of a conference such as the Round Table is that it brings together just such diverse scholars: linguists who have been working on the question from the perspective of Central America, Colombia, Jamaica, Suriname, and the West African coast. In addition, and despite the fact that we linguists have our own particular contribution to make, what we are doing today needs to be extended to include scholars such as anthropologists, historians, and sociologists, both theorists and those with relevant specializations (e.g., historians of the Atlantic slave trade). The value of combining careful linguistic and anthropological fieldwork with the results of the historian's work can be seen in Price's (1975, 1976) and Voorhoeve's (1973) work on Saramaccan and other creoles of Suriname, and, perhaps, my own (Huttar 1985, 1986a) on Ndjuka; in Goodman's (1987) work on Portuguese elements in New World creoles; in Smith et al.'s (1987) work on Berbice Dutch; and in numerous contributions by de Granda to the identification of Africanisms in New World varieties of Spanish. It is encouraging to see in the identification of Africanisms this trend toward integrated use of both linguistic and extralinguistic information and paradigms of study. As long as it is recognized that the individuals and societies that have been creators and bearers of creole languages have also been creators and bearers of cultures and have lived in particular times and places, the potential contribution of such other fields to matters of interest to linguists cannot simply be dismissed by saying, "We have to do our own work."

In sum, the previous prevalence of overspecific claims about the origin of some Africanisms in New World creoles has been giving way in recent years to more caution, on the one hand, and to the use of more information so that specific claims are made on a firmer basis, on the other. It remains for us to continue to exercise due caution in our claims about specific origins and to continue the second trend in two ways. First, we must invest special effort in certain aspects of languages and cultures: discourse structure, suprasegmental phonology, semantic or cognitive organization, specialized lexicon, basic cultural values, and attitudes. Second, as mentioned in the preceding paragraph, we must inform our work as linguists with the models, knowledge, and expertise which our colleagues in other fields have to offer. We should thereby be able to serve better both our ends and theirs, as well as, I hope, in some way benefit today's creole speakers themselves.

## Notes

1. Robertson 1986; and Smith et al. 1987 provide a clear example of a source language long neglected in the origins literature turning out to be important, in this case Ịjọ for Berbice Dutch lexemes and even syntactic features.

2. His claims about morphology and especially syntax are mitigated elsewhere in his volume. A clear counterexample is given in Robertson 1986.

3. For further discussion, see Huttar 1985. On masters' ignorance of their slaves' religious practices and slaves' deliberate secrecy on the topic, see van Lier 1983:17.

4. Mühlhäusler refers to "serious gaps in our knowledge [that] include ideophones, discourse grammar, speech acts and many other areas of 'higher-level grammar' and language use" (1986:236).

5. Cf. Megenney 1986:41 on alternative hypotheses of Kikongo and Kimbundu origins for the place-name Macondo in Colombian fiction.

6. See Boretzky 1983:35 for phonological and other items which he suggests are justifiably traced to a specific African source because of their attestation in a narrow range of West African languages and in a narrow range of New World creoles.

**References**

Alleyne, Mervyn C. 1980. *Comparative Afro-American. An historical-comparative study of English-based Afro-American dialects of the New World.* Ann Arbor: Karoma.

Arends, Jacques. 1986a. Genesis and development of the equative copula in Sranan. *Substrate versus universals in creole genesis*, ed. by Pieter Muysken and Norval Smith, 103–27. Amsterdam: John Benjamins.

———. 1986b. Internal and external factors in the development of the Sranan comparative. Paper given at the Sixth Biennial Conference of the Society for Caribbean Linguistics.

Baudet, Martha M. 1981. Identifying the African grammatical base of the Caribbean creoles. *Historicity and variation in creole studies*, ed. by Arnold Highfield and Albert Valdman, 104–17. Ann Arbor: Karoma.

Berlin, Brent. 1976. The concept of rank in ethnobotanical classification: Some evidence from Aguaruna folk botany. *American Ethnopologist* 3.381–99.

Berlin, Brent, and Paul Kay. 1969. *Basic color terms: their universals and evolutions.* Berkeley and Los Angeles: University of California Press.

Bilby, K. M. 1983. How the "older heads" talk: A Jamaican Maroon spirit possession language and its relationship to the creoles of Suriname and Sierra Leone. *Nieuwe West-Indische Gids* 57.37–88.

Boretzky, Norbert. 1983a. On creole verb categories. *Amsterdam Creole Studies* 5.1–24.

———. 1983b. *Kreolsprachen, Substrate und Sprachwandel.* Wiesbaden: Otto Harrassowitz.

Broderick, S. Modupe. 1985. Time and structure in narrative: A study of internal relationships in a Krio oral narrative. *Diversity and development in English-related creoles*, ed. by Ian F. Hancock, 94–115. Ann Arbor: Karoma.

Brown, Cecil H. 1984. *Language and living things: Uniformities in folk classification and naming.* New Brunswick, N.J.: Rutgers University Press.

Carrington, Lawrence. 1987. The substance of creole studies: A reappraisal. *Pidgin and creole languages: Essays in memory of John E. Reinecke*, ed. by Glenn G. Gilbert, 77–92. Honolulu: University of Hawaii Press.

Carter, Hazel. 1987. Suprasegmentals in Guyanese: Some African comparisons.

*Pidgin and creole languages: Essays in memory of John E. Reinecke*, ed. by Glenn G. Gilbert, 213–63. Honolulu: University of Hawaii Press.

Castro, Yeda Pessoa de. 1980. *Os falares africanos na interção social do Brasil colonial*. Universidade Federal da Bahia, Publication 89.

Corne, Chris. 1987. Verb fronting in creole: Transmission or bioprogram? *Pidgin and creole languages: Essays in memory of John E. Reinecke*, ed. by Glenn G. Gilbert, 93–112. Honolulu: University of Hawaii Press.

Curtin, Philip D. 1969. *The Atlantic slave trade: A census*. Madison: University of Wisconsin Press.

———. 1975. Measuring the Atlantic slave trade. *Race and slavery in the Western Hemisphere: Quantitative studies*, ed. by Stanley L. Engerman and Eugene D. Genovese, 107–28. Princeton: Princeton University Press.

Dalby, David. 1971. Ashanti survivals in the language of the Maroons. *African Language Studies* 12.31–51.

Delafosse, Maurice. 1925. Survivances africaines chez les Nègres "bosch" de la Guyane. *Anthropologie* 35.475–94.

Donnan, Elizabeth. 1965. *Documents illustrative of the history of the slave trade to America*. New York: Octagon Books.

Falconbridge, Alexander. 1788. *An account of the slave trade on the coast of Africa*. London: J. Phillips. Facsimile edition. New York: AMS Press, 1973.

Frank, David. 1986. The structural organisation of St. Lucian Creole narrative discourse. Paper given at the Sixth Biennial Conference of the Society for Caribbean Linguistics.

Gilman, Charles. 1986. African areal characteristics: Sprachbund, not substrate? *Journal of Pidgin and Creole Languages* 1.1.33–50.

Glock, Naomi. 1986. The use of reported speech in Saramaccan discourse. *Pragmatics in non-Western perspective*, ed. by George Huttar and Kenneth Gregerson, 35–61. Dallas: Summer Institute of Linguistics and University of Texas at Arlington.

Goodman, Morris. 1987. The Portuguese element in the American creoles. *Pidgin and creole languages: Essays in memory of John E. Reinecke*, ed. by Glenn G. Gilbert, 361–405. Honolulu: University of Hawaii Press.

Granda, Germán de. 1978. Planteamientos y necesidades actuales en los estudios lingüísticos Afro-hispanoamericanos. *Estudios lingüísticos Hispanicos, Afrohispanicos y criollos*, by G. de Granda, 185–215. Madrid: Editorial Gredos.

Grimes, Joseph E., and Naomi Glock. 1970. A Saramaccan narrative pattern. *Language* 46.408–25.

Hair, P. E. H. 1970. The contribution of early linguistic material to the history of West Africa. *Language and history in Africa*, ed. by David Dalby, 50–63. New York: Africana.

Hancock, Ian. 1986. The domestic hypothesis, diffusion and componentiality: An account of Atlantic anglophone creole origins. *Substrate versus universals in creole genesis*, ed. by Pieter Muysken and Norval Smith, 71–102. Amsterdam: John Benjamins.

Hazaël-Massieux, Guy. 1985. Traces culturelles et linguistiques. *Notre librairie* 80.7–13.

Herskovits, Melville. 1941. *The myth of the Negro past*. New York: Harper and Brothers.

Holm, John. 1986. Substrate diffusion. *Substrate versus universals in creole genesis*, ed. by Pieter Muysken and Norval Smith, 259–78. Amsterdam: John Benjamins.

Huttar, George L. 1975. Sources of creole semantic structures. *Language* 51.3.684–95.

———. 1981. Some Kwa-like features of Djuka syntax. *Studies in African Linguistics* 12.3.291–323.

———. 1983. On the study of creole lexicons. *Studies in Caribbean language*, ed. by Lawrence D. Carrington, 82–89. St. Augustine, Trinidad: Society for Caribbean Linguistics.

———. 1985. Sources of Ndjuka African vocabulary. *De Nieuwe West-Indische Gids* 59.45–71.

———. 1986a. KiKongo, Saramaccan, and Ndjuka. *Language in global perspective: Papers in honor of the 50th anniversary of the Summer Institute of Linguistics 1935–1985*, ed. by Benjamin F. Elson, 563–86. Dallas: Summer Institute of Linguistics.

———. 1986b. Epenthetic *-mi* in Ndjuka: A transitive marker? Paper given at the Sixth Biennial Conference of the Society for Caribbean Linguistics.

———. 1989. The Portuguese contribution to the Ndjuka lexicon. *Estudios sobre Español de América y lingüística Afroamericana: ponencias presentadas en el 45 Congreso Internacional de Americanistas (Bogotá, Julio de 1985)*, 263–79. Bogotá: Instituto Caro y Cuervo.

Huttar, George L., and Mary L. Huttar. 1988. A humorous Paramaccan text. *Southwest Journal of Linguistics* 8.34–50.

Kay, Paul. 1971. Taxonomy and semantic contrast. *Language* 47.866–67.

Koopman, Hilda. 1986. The genesis of Haitian: Implications of a comparison of some features of the syntax of Haitian, French, and West African languages. *Substrate versus universals in creole genesis*, ed. by Pieter Muysken and Norval Smith, 231–58. Amsterdam: John Benjamins.

Lichtveld, Lou. 1931. Op zoek naar de spin. *West-Indische Gids* 12.209–30, 305–24.

Lier, R. van. 1983. *Bonuman: Een studie van zeven religieuze specialisten in Suriname*. ICA Publication no. 60. Leiden: Institute of Cultural and Social Studies, Leiden University.

Martin, Phyllis M. 1972. *The external trade of the Loango coast 1576–1870: The effects of changing commercial relations on the Vili Kingdom of Loango*. Oxford: Clarendon Press.

Megenney, William W. 1986. *El Palenquero: un lenguaje post-criollo de Colombia*. Bogotá: Instituto Caro y Cuervo.

Mintz, Sidney. 1975. History and anthropology: A brief reprise. *Race and slavery in the Western Hemisphere: Quantitative studies*, ed. by Stanley L. Engerman and Eugene D. Genovese, 477–94. Princeton: Princeton University Press.

Mühlhäusler, Peter. 1986. *Pidgin and creole linguistics*. Oxford: Basil Blackwell.

Naden, Anthony. 1986. Social context and Mampruli greetings. *Pragmatics in non-Western perspective*, ed. by George Huttar and Kenneth Gregerson, 161–99. Dallas: Summer Institute of Linguistics and University of Texas at Arlington.

Park, James F. 1980. Paragraph in Djuka deliberative discourse. *Discourse studies in Djuka and Saramaccan*, ed. by Stephen Levinsohn, 1–30. Paramaribo, Suriname: Summer Institute of Linguistics.

Patterson, Orlando. 1967. *The sociology of slavery: An analysis of the origins, development and structure of Negro slave society in Jamaica*. London: Associated University Presses.

Postma, Johannes. 1976. The Dutch slave trade: A quantitative assessment. *La traite des noirs par l'Atlantique: nouvelles approches (The Atlantic slave trade: New approaches)*, 232–51. Paris: Société Française d'Histoire d'Outre-mer.

Price, Richard. 1975. Kikongo and Saramaccan: A reappraisal. *Bijdragen Tot de Taal-, Land- en Volkenkunde* 131.461–78.

———. 1976. *The Guiana Maroons: A historical and bibliographical introduction*. Baltimore: Johns Hopkins University Press.

Robertson, Ian. 1986. Substratum influence in the grammar of Berbice Dutch. Paper given at the Sixth Biennial Conference of the Society for Caribbean Linguistics.

Singler, John Victor. 1988. The story of *o*. *Studies in Language* 12.123–44.

Smith, Norval S. H., Ian E. Robertson, and Kay Williamson. 1987. The Ịjọ element in Berbice Dutch. *Language in Society* 16.49–90.

Stassen, Leon. 1985. *Comparison and Universal Grammar*. Oxford: Basil Blackwell.

Sylvain, Suzanne. 1936. *Le créole haïtien: morphologie et syntaxe*. Wetteren, Belgium: Imprimerie De Meester.

Taylor, Douglas. 1963. The origin of West Indian creole languages: Evidence from grammatical categories. *American Anthropologist* 65.800–814.

Valdman, Albert. 1978. *Le créole: structure, statut et origine*. Paris: Editions Klincksieck.

Voorhoeve, Jan. 1973. Historical and linguistic evidence in favour of the relexification theory in the formation of creoles. *Language in Society* 2.133–45.

Welmers, William E. 1973. *African language structures*. Berkeley: University of California Press.

Wilner, John. 1986. Rhetorical questions in Sranan Tongo. Paper given at the Sixth Biennial Conference of the Society for Caribbean Linguistics.

Witkowski, Stanley R., and Cecil H. Brown. 1985. Climate, clothing, and body-part nomenclature. *Ethnology* 24.197–214.

# African Substratum: Some Cautionary Words

*Morris Goodman*

The related terms "substratum," "superstratum," and "adstratum" have been used somewhat inconsistently during the course of their history. The oldest by far is "substratum," which was introduced by the Italian linguist G. I. Ascoli in 1867. "Superstratum" was coined by the Romance scholar Walther von Wartburg in 1933, and "adstratum" (which is rarely used by creolists) one year earlier by none other than Marius Valkhoff, long before he had worked in the creole field. I have consulted twelve dictionaries of linguistic terminology (four French, four German, three English, and one Spanish) in order to compare their definitions of these terms, which are far from uniform, even though they have certain points in common. One of these common points is that each of the three terms is defined in relation to some other language for which no generally accepted designation exists, but which I will call the "reference language."

Virtually all sources agree that a substratum is a language which has in some way influenced the reference language. The only exception is Martinet (1969), who distinguishes "$\text{substratum}_1$" from "$\text{substratum}_2$." Both substrata previously existed in a particular territory, but the latter influenced the language which replaced it, whereas the former did not. The only instances of the former, most likely, are languages which had already disappeared completely from a territory before their successors arrived. Even the Amerindian languages of the United States, which had only minimal impact on those of the various colonizing peoples, have contributed a number of vocabulary items (e.g., *caucus, skunk, tomahawk, tepee*) and a few calqued expressions (e.g., *bury the hatchet*), as well as numerous place names to American (and thence to world) English.

A second characteristic attributed to a substratum by most of the sources is its ultimate replacement by the reference language in the area under consideration. Some, however, either are not explicit on this point or else seem to allow the possibility of the substratum continuing indefinitely alongside the reference language. In most creole-speaking regions, the alleged African substrata have long since disappeared, although they may survive in the very restricted role of ritual or secret languages. However, with respect to those creoles spoken on the African mainland, as in Guinea-Bissau or Sierra Leone, African languages are widely spoken alongside them and show no signs of disappearing.

Most of the sources agree further that the substratum was spoken substantially earlier than the reference language in the territory under consideration. In this respect creolists use the term rather more broadly, since the African "substrata" were introduced even later (and certainly no earlier) than the European languages in most creole-speaking regions. On the other hand, they obviously were introduced before the European-based creoles had evolved. Thus, if one considers creoles to be evolutions of their European base languages, then one cannot view the languages of African immigrants as substrata in the strict traditional sense of the term. (This issue is alluded to once more below.) Finally, a characteristic of a substratum cited occasionally by the sources (with which creolists would not quarrel) is the subordinate social or cultural status of its speakers vis-à-vis those of the reference language.

The original sense of the term "superstratum" is also somewhat different from the one some creolists now assign to it. Like a substratum it is universally defined as a language which has influenced the reference language. However, virtually all the works consulted also define it as a language introduced into an area subsequent to the reference language. In contrast, some contemporary creolists equate the term with what is also called the "base" or "lexifier" language, which necessarily must have preceded the creole in the area where the latter ultimately evolved, and which, in fact (as noted above), also generally preceded the so-called substrata in the same area.

A second frequently mentioned characteristic of a superstratum (with which all creolists would agree) is that it is the language of a militarily, politically, socially, or culturally dominant group. However, some of the sources define it more broadly as the language of any immigrant minority regardless of status. Finally, most sources define superstratum as a language ultimately supplanted by the reference language, but some allow it to persist indefinitely, and one (Pei and Gaynor 1954) even admits the possibility of a superstratum supplanting its predecessor. A classic example of a superstratum by all of the most widely accepted criteria is Norman French in Great Britain. It was the language of a conquering minority, which profoundly influenced its Anglo-Saxon predecessor yet ultimately disappeared.

The term "adstratum" (used less often than the other two) is also defined somewhat inconsistently by the various sources. Most consider it a neighbor of the reference language, interacting with it at their common borders but not necessarily either anterior or posterior to it in those areas. One source (Pei and Gaynor 1954), however, defines it as a synonym of superstratum, and another (Hartmann and Stork 1972) defines it so as to make it almost indistinguishable from "substratum."

It is noteworthy that (as far as I could determine) none of the three terms was used by any of those pioneering scholars most concerned with the genesis of pidgins and creoles: Addison Van Name, Lucien Adam, Adolpho Coelho, Hugo Schuchardt, and Dirk C. Hesseling. This is hardly surprising in the case of "superstratum" and "adstratum," since these two terms were not coined until the early 1930s, only a year or two before Hesseling's last article on creoles (1934) appeared and long after the relevant writings (and even the deaths) of the others. The reason that "substratum" was not used, however, is less clear, especially for Schuchardt and Hesseling, who both dealt extensively with the question of language contact and unquestionably knew the term. Although Jespersen discussed the notion of substratum at length in chapter 11 of *Language, its nature, development, and origin* (1922), he did not use the word at all in his extended treatment of pidgins and creoles in the following chapter. Perhaps in the case of the New World and certain other colonial areas the relevant African languages were no more indigenous than the relevant European ones and thus did not constitute a true substratum as the term was then generally understood. There may be an additional reason, however; namely, that the word had by then acquired an unsavory reputation for reasons discussed below.

To the best of my knowledge the first person to apply the term "substratum" to creole languages was the Hungarian Romance linguist Laszlo Göbl[-Galdi], in "Problemi di sostrato nel creole-francese" (1933) and another article (1934) which contains passing references to "l'influence du substrat." Though his work is not very familiar to present-day creolists, Robert Hall undoubtedly knew of it, given his familiarity with Romance linguistic scholarship, particularly that written in Italian. In fact, both titles are included in the extensive bibliography of his introductory work (1966:167). It was Hall, apparently, who introduced the term into the mainstream of contemporary creole studies in his article "African Substratum in Negro English," actually a review of Turner's *Africanisms in the Gullah dialect* (1949), which had appeared the year before. Turner, however, had not used the word. In his conclusion Hall wrote,

> The theory of linguistic substratum, at one time almost wholly discredited by the excesses of its proponents, is now being reinterpreted and, one might say, rehabilitated in the light of the more realistic picture of linguistic transfer afforded by pidgin and creolized languages (1950:54).

Why did Hall describe the substratum theory as "almost wholly discredited"? First, because features (and, in particular, changes) of attested languages were sometimes "explained" on the basis of alleged substrata about which little or nothing was known. Obviously, with such methods virtually anything could be proven. Second, some assumed that long after it had ceased to be spoken a substratum might continue to influence the reference language either through hereditary characteristics of the speakers (whether physical or psychological) or else through some sort of immaterial force. Empirically minded scholars such as Otto Jespersen, Leonard Bloomfield, and Robert A. Hall did not take such notions seriously. On the other hand, they all acknowledged the possibility that languages could influence each other during a period of bilingualism. Since no contemporary linguists would conceivably make any stronger claims than that, nor would they explain features of existing languages on the basis of extinct ones about which little or nothing is known, the discredited aspects of the substratum theory have no bearing on any current controversies.

Hall also used the term "superstratum" (though not "adstratum") in connection with pidgins and creoles, but in a more traditional sense than that now used by many creolists. He defined it (1966:97) as "the official European language which is dominant in the region where a creole [or presumably a pidgin] is spoken." Thus, French is the superstratum in Haiti, but so is Dutch in Suriname or Curaçao, and so is English in Creole French–speaking Dominica and St. Lucia. On the other hand, Hall would almost certainly not have regarded French as the superstratum in terms of its role in the formation of Haitian Creole, but only in terms of its subsequent role in Haiti once the two had become clearly distinct and separate languages. The reason for this rather subtle distinction is (I believe) that Hall regarded French genetically as the antecedent of Haitian Creole, and therefore no more its superstratum than Latin is of French. If, on the other hand, Haitian Creole were viewed as an African language with a largely French vocabulary, then French could be regarded as its superstratum in the traditional sense from the moment of contact.

Although Hall extended the meaning of the concept "substratum," it would be unjustified to lump him with those (unnamed) individuals who, according to Martinet (1969), improperly ("*abusivement*") define it as any foreign linguistic influence. Hall evidently restricted his use to the influence of an individual's native language (or, at any rate, one acquired early in life) upon any language learned significantly later, particularly if such influence is passed on to a generation of native speakers. While Hall did not say so, one might thus reserve "superstratum" for a language acquired later in life, particularly in a more formal context, such as school. If so, then "adstratum" would have to be used for those languages acquired at roughtly the same time in life (especially during childhood) and in much the same way (as in a multilingual speech community).

Of course, such usage defines these three concepts with reference to individuals rather than to entire speech communities, but they are all forms of language contact, and, as Weinreich (1953) put it, the locus of contact is the bilingual individual. What concerns pidgin and creole studies (and other branches of linguistics as well) is whether features of the speech of bilinguals can spread to other members of the speech community, and whether they can be transmitted to later generations of speakers even after the bilingual situation has come to an end. More succinctly, can language contact influence linguistic change? The most effective argument in favor of such a position is the documented existence of numerous highly specific similarities not attributable to genetic relationship yet shared by languages which are or have been in contact. These similarities are sometimes called areal features, particularly if shared by groups of contiguous languages; a group of languages sharing such features is often referred to as a linguistic area (or Sprachbund). In its earliest formulations substratum theory tried to account for such areal resemblances by positing a single common substratum (often extinct) for the entire group. Obviously, such a notion is naïve and simplistic. Certain widespread features of a Sprachbund might have originated in, and spread from, one of the languages of the group, while other features might have originated in, and spread from, a different one. With such considerations in mind, Gilman (1986) suggested that the term "Sprachbund" might be preferable to "substrate" in designating the relation between the Atlantic creoles and the languages of West Africa. However, given the way creolists have used the term "substratum" since Hall's early work, the issue is more terminological than conceptual.

While the numerous documented instances of areal features in all domains of language (phonology, morphology, syntax, semantics, and lexicon) should be conclusive evidence that language contact may indeed influence linguistic change, it would be instructive to look at some of the recent arguments advanced against such a view. I will not recapitulate those considered in Goodman (1985) except for the question of why the same alleged substratal features often recur in a wide variety of creoles. I will repeat what I said then; namely, that "some grammatical structures are much more easily transferred than others to a language in the process of being learned, specifically those which can be formed by using only syntactic arrangements of basic lexical items" (Goodman 1985:121). Weinreich (1953:41) had already made a comparable observation:

> Significantly, in the interference of two grammatical patterns it is ordinarily the one which uses relatively free and invariant morphemes in its

> paradigm—one might say the more explicit pattern—which serves as the model for imitation. This seems to be true not only in the creation of new categories . . . but also in those changes due to language contact where a new set of formants is developed to fulfill a preexisting function.

The phenomena to which Weinreich was referring are really forms of calquing, and, as Bickerton (1986a:140) observes, "Nobody disputes that there [i]s massive substratal influence in the lexicon [of creoles] through calquing as well as through direct retentions." Can one, in fact, draw a clear line between lexical and grammatical calquing, and is there any point in trying? To take a concrete example, colloquial Chicago English has expressions like *Bring it with* and *He's coming with,* obviously calqued from German *Bringe es mit* and *Er kommt mit,* even though many (if not most) who now speak this way know no German.[1] Are these expressions lexical or grammatical calques? One could easily argue either way, yet they are not different in kind from those creole expressions which seem most obviously to be African in origin, for example, 'take it go/come; big pass all,' etc.

It has also been argued that a syntactic feature of one language cannot have evolved as a result of contact with another if the feature behaves differently in some respects in the two languages. The Chicago English constructions above would differ significantly from German if the verb had been used in the infinitive, as in *Can you bring it with?* or *Should he come with?* versus, respectively, *Kannst du es mitbringen?* or *Soll er mitkommen?* in German. Yet German is obviously the source of this pattern, even though it has been adapted to the prevalent syntactic structure of English. Furthermore, a syntactic pattern calqued from another language may differ from its model as a result of subsequent historical changes. Bickerton (in Byrne 1987:xii) claims that, whereas in serial verb constructions in Saramaccan noninitial verbs may be marked for tense and negation, in their West African counterparts only the initial verb may be. Could this not simply be an African pattern adopted by Saramaccan and later modified?

Much more ingenious than the previous arguments is the one advanced by Bickerton (1986b:227–28), which builds upon the theory of an Israeli linguist named Hagit Borer claiming that syntax is invariant for all languages, and "apparent" differences are all attributable to the morphology and the lexicon. If this theory is correct, Bickerton continues (and he has no doubt that it is), and, furthermore, since in nearly all European-based creoles the morphology and lexicon are derived overwhelmingly from the base language, then whatever is not attributable in creoles to universal syntax must be attributed to that of the base, and not to that of the substratum. Even if Borer's theory is correct (an issue I will leave to others), Bickerton's corollary is a complete non sequitur. A word may be etymologically derived from one language yet acquire semantic or syntactic properties from another. For example, in Melanesian Pidgin English the words *barata* and *sista* are obviously from English *brother* and *sister,* but they refer to a sibling of respectively the same or the opposite sex, paralleling indigenous kinship terminology. Likewise, the connective *epi* in Antillean Creole is obviously from French *et puis,* but it is used to subjoin as well as conjoin noun phrases (e.g., *nom la pati epi fam la* 'the man left with the woman' and *nom la epi fam la pati* 'the man and the woman left'), a pattern found throughout most of sub-Saharan Africa and nearly all African-influenced pidgins and creoles as well.

Bickerton (*Carrier Pidgin*, April 1986) has attempted to portray his categorical rejection of syntactic substratal influence as one shared by a consensus of up-to-date opinion, stating that "most scholars in historical linguistics would say that . . . belief in substratum influence is 'misguided' and 'preposterous.' [One] should read what Lightfoot says about it in his *Diachronic Syntax*, for openers." Of course, one does not resolve academic disagreements by taking a vote, but one wonders how Bickerton arrived at his calculation that most current scholars take this position. Five introductory textbooks of historical linguistics produced within roughly the past twenty years all recognize the possibility that language contact may influence linguistic change. According to Anttila (1972:169), "The evidence as we have it today shows that syntax can be borrowed as easily as other parts of grammar." Arlotto (1972:193–95), Bynon (1977:239–56), Jeffers and Lehiste (1979, chap. 9), and Lehmann (1973:200–202) all provide examples of such borrowing, as does Comrie (1981:197–203); none of them questions its validity in principle as a possible explanation of syntactic change.

Lightfoot (1979), on the other hand, does appear to adopt a contrary position. In response to the claim that postnominal adjectives in Middle English are due to French influence, he writes (1979:206), "I resist such foreign-influence interpretations on ideological grounds; such 'explanations,' which are extremely numerous in the literature are usually unilluminating" (206). Whereas Lightfoot cites many examples of such "explanations" (especially pp. 381–83), including those of such scholars as Eric Hamp, Larry Hyman, and Robin Lakoff, he mentions no one who shares his rejection of them, nor does he ever state what his "ideological" grounds are. In fact, he makes only one systematic attempt to refute such explanations—the case of English postnominal adjectives mentioned above—and his reasoning is far from persuasive; namely, that adjectives are actually much more often prenominal than postnominal in medieval

French, and, further, that in those Middle English texts which were examined, adjectives of French origin are no more frequently postnominal than those of non-French origin. Neither argument is very strong. Rather, one should compare the placement of individual attributive adjectives in both languages on the basis of semantic equivalence as well as etymology. If there is any correlation between adjective placement in the two languages in this respect, then the case for French influence would be quite convincing. It is noteworthy that according to Lightfoot's own data (1979:207), color adjectives, though etymologically Anglo-Saxon, occur postnominally with relatively high frequency, precisely like their French counterparts.

However, Lightfoot is by no means as extreme as he tries to sound, and in fact he concedes that "to state that many of the explanations in the literature are specious as they stand is not to deny that there are genuine cases of [syntactic] borrowing" (383); as an example he cites a relative clause construction borrowed from Kannada (Dravidian) by a dialect of Konkani (Indic). Elsewhere (385), in an unguarded moment when discussing the topicalization of objects in contemporary English by placing them in sentence-initial position, he writes that "in other dialects, notably those of North Americans with a Yiddish background, the construction has already become bleached of its special effect." Evidently Lightfoot is quite ready to use contact as an explanation of syntactic change when it suits his purposes. His work can under no circumstances be said to rule it out absolutely.

In fact, no linguist of any competence whatsoever would categorically exclude the possibility of syntactic change produced by language contact. However, there still remains the extremely difficult question of deciding in specific cases whether a given feature of a given language should be explained in this way. If I may be allowed to quote myself (Goodman 1985:127),

> It can, of course, never be proved with mathematical certainty that a particular syntactic construction was introduced into a given language as a result of contact with another, since any feature so acquired could also have evolved entirely independently. Conversely, it can never be proved that any such feature was not acquired as a result of contact unless it can be demonstrated that no such prior contact took place. . . . Only by examining a large number of shared features among languages where contact is [historically] either a possible or an impossible explanation can some criteria of probability be established, however crude.

While I believe that the evidence is extremely strong that certain widespread Atlantic creole features, such as serial verbs, the comparative using *pass,* and so on, are of African origin, I do not believe that the pervasive similarities of creole languages around the world should generally be explained this way. On the contrary, African influence has, in my opinion, been greatly exaggerated by some for ideological reasons during much of the past half century. The search for universal explanations is therefore a welcome development. On the other hand, it is premature and unwarranted to assume that all (or even any) linguistic universals or tendencies, whether general or specific to creoles, are necessarily attributable to innate mental structures. Unfortunately, many creolists have failed to make this distinction.

## Note

1. It is well known that at the turn of the century German was by far the predominant immigrant language in Chicago, when at least a fourth of the city's population was foreign-born and many others were of foreign descent and spoke their parents' language.

## References

Anttila, Raimo. 1972. *An introduction to historical and comparative linguistics*. New York: Macmillan.

Arlotto, Anthony. 1972. *Introduction to historical linguistics*. Boston: Houghton Mifflin.

Bickerton, Derek. 1986a. Beyond *Roots*: Progress or regress? [Column]. *Journal of Pidgin and Creole Languages* 1.135–40.

———. 1986b. Beyond *Roots*: The five-year test. *Journal of Pidgin and Creole Languages* 1.225–32.

Bussman, Hadumod. 1983. *Lexikon der Sprachwissenschaft*. Stuttgart: Alfred Kroner Verlag.

Bynon, Theodora. 1977. *Historical linguistics*. Cambridge: Cambridge University Press.

Byrne, Francis. 1987. *Grammatical relations in a radical creole: Verb complementation in Saramaccan*. Amsterdam: John Benjamins.

Comrie, Bernard. 1981. *Language universals and linguistic typology: Syntax and morphology*. Chicago: University of Chicago Press.

Conrad, Rudi, ed. 1985. *Lexikon sprachwissenschaftlicher Termini*. Leipzig: VEB Bibliographisches Institut.

Crystal, David. 1985. *A dictionary of linguistics and phonetics*. Second edition. Oxford: Basil Blackwell.

Dubois, Jean. 1972. *Dictionnaire de linguistique*. Paris: Larousse.

Gilman, Charles. 1986. African areal characteristics: Sprachbund, not substrate? *Journal of Pidgin and Creole Languages* 1.33–50.

Göbl[-Galdi], L. 1933. Problemi di sostrato nel creole-francese. *Revue de Linguistique Romane* 9.336–45.

———. 1934. Esquisse de la structure grammaticale des patois français-créoles. *Zeitschrift für Französische Sprache und Literatur* 58.257–95.

Goodman, Morris. 1985. Review of *Roots of language*, by Derek Bickerton. *International Journal of American Linguistics* 51.109–37.

Hall, Robert A., Jr. 1950. African substratum in Negro English. *American Speech* 25.51–54.

———. 1966. *Pidgin and creole languages*. Ithaca, N.Y.: Cornell University Press.

Hartmann, R. R. K., and F. C. Stork. 1972. *Dictionary of language and linguistics*. New York: John Wiley and Sons.

Hesseling, Dirk Christiaan. 1934. Gemengde taal, mengetaal, kreools en kreolisering. *De Nieuwe Taalgids* 28.310–22.

Jeffers, Robert J., and Ilse Lehiste. 1979. *Principles and methods for historical linguistics*. Cambridge, Mass.: MIT Press.

Jespersen, Otto. 1922. *Language, its nature, development, and origin*. London: G. Allen and Unwin.

Knobloch, Johann. 1961. *Sprachwissenschaftliches Wörterbuch*. Heidelberg: C. Winter.

Lazaro Carreter, Fernando. 1953. *Diccionario de términos filológicos*. Madrid: Editorial Gredos.

Lehmann, Winfred P. 1973. *Historical linguistics: An introduction*. Second edition. New York: Holt, Rinehart and Winston.

Lewandowski, Theodor. 1976. *Linguistisches Wörterbuch*. 3 vols. Heidelberg: Quelle and Meyer.

Lightfoot, David. 1979. *Principles of diachronic syntax*. Cambridge: Cambridge University Press.

Marouzeau, J. 1951. *Lexique de terminologie linguistique*. Paris: Paul Guenther.

Martinet, André, ed. 1969. *La linguistique: guide alphabétique*. Paris: Editions Denoel.

Mounin, Georges. 1974. *Dictionnaire de la linguistique*. Paris: Presses Universitaires de France.

Pei, Mario, and Frank Gaynor. 1954. *A dictionary of linguistics*. New York: Philosophical Library.

Turner, Lorenzo Dow. 1949. *Africanisms in the Gullah dialect*. Chicago: University of Chicago Press.

Weinreich, Uriel. 1953. *Languages in contact: Findings and problems*. Publications of the Linguistic Circle of New York, no. 1.

# The Concept of Rule, Rule Borrowing, and Substrate Influence in Creole Languages

*Norbert Boretzky*

The genesis of creole languages is not directly witnessed for any creole at any time. It is therefore understandable that very different views have been taken on this issue. Some linguists seek to explain all facts from a single principle, while others try to take into account various determinants. Universalists especially are known to make monothetic claims. At best, they accept influence from base languages, but they strongly dispute the possibility of substratum influence (except phonetic). I do not wish to inquire into all the arguments put forth by the advocates of universalism; instead, I will concentrate on some of them and try to clarify whether these arguments are tenable and compatible with one another.

One of the most important arguments adduced not only by Derek Bickerton but also by several other creolists (at least until recently) has to do with the concept of "rule." Universalists maintain that influence from potential substratum languages is possible, and may be accepted, only in those cases in which a given rule in a creole is identical with one in a potential substratum (or group of substrata). In what follows I show that arguments such as this cannot be upheld, mainly because evidence from "normal" contact situations, as well as from other substratum-superstratum relations, provides convincing counterexamples.

Before pursuing this question, however, it may be helpful to note that Bickerton, who advocated the rule argument for quite some time, now seems to take a different view, dependent on a variant of the lexical learning hypothesis (LLH). According to his 1986 paper, it is not the rules or the structures of a language that are borrowed (or learned by children in first language acquisition) but rather words and morphemes. Taken literally, this seems to be a bewildering point of view; but as soon as we realize that "words" and "morphemes" must be understood as more than sequences of phonemes and that they are equipped with meaning or function as well as specific syntactic requirements, the argument sounds less strange. Further, the LLH may turn out to be not so different from the rule argument after all; Bickerton may really mean lexical entries of the transformational-grammar type with all their morphological and syntactic specifications. Roughly, this means that the abstract apparatus of rules set up earlier has been reduced and partially moved into the lexicon. As before, it is implied that the speaker must learn rules, but the rules are specific to individual words.

Applied to language interference, then, the above means that the speaker of the borrowing language is believed to take over words together with all their grammatical properties—a point of view scarcely supported by evidence. In most cases, borrowing seems to be selective. Consider the following example from a Gypsy (Romani) dialect, which borrowed from Albanian the function word *tuj,* a marker of the progressive aspect. Now, in Albanian *tuj* (or *tue*) has the following syntactic properties: it can be combined with a nonfinite form of the verb only (roughly, participle or infinitive). In a finite construction, it must be preceded by the copula 'is':

1. *ai âshtë tue qa*
   he is PROG cry (finite form)[1]
   'He is crying.'

The following Romani sentence is, however, not parallel to the Albanian:

2. *vov tuj rov- ol* (native informant)
   he PROG cry (3SG PRES)

What has been preserved from the Albanian *tuj* is the overall semantic function, but not its salient syntactic behavior.

As for creole genesis, Bickerton's thesis also has serious implications because it now becomes even more difficult than before to assume substratum influence. In the pre-LLH framework, it was enough evidence to identify a grammatical rule as identical in a creole and a substratum language. According to the LLH, one must prove that words or morphemes as phoneme sequences, and not just their meanings, have been transferred before arguing that a rule has been transferred. To support this approach, one might invoke Kinubi, the Arabic-based creole of East Africa, in which it seems that even the functions of the Arabic morphemes have been preserved to a large extent. However, we must realize that Arabic is the lexifier of Kinubi, and therefore Kinubi does behave like the Atlantic creoles vis-à-vis their potential substrata. Creolists generally agree that words and morphemes of the substrata have been transferred in exceptional cases only. This assumption entails that, despite all similarity exhibited between categories of the two groups, hardly any creole category could be descended from a similar West African category—which, of course, is in congruence with Bickerton's intention to do away with substratum influence, not by producing empirical counterevidence but by making far-reaching assumptions.

Against the above approach, problems of such importance cannot be clarified, let alone resolved, with a few remarks, as Bickerton tries to do in his 1986 paper. Rather, we must draw on other areas of language interference. From my knowledge of borrowing processes I can say with confidence that there is overwhelming counterevidence to what Bickerton contends. He does not appear to have considered the problem thoroughly enough, as evidenced by his relapsing at times into earlier positions. For example, in a discussion of verb serialization in Saramaccan, he argues (1987) that similarities between creole and corresponding West African constructions—traditionally the proof of genetic links between the two—have no standing. He claims that in a conservative creole such as Saramaccan, tense is not marked in the same way as it is in West African languages. In the latter, the tense marker can be preposed to the first verb only, whereas in Saramaccan it precedes either the first or one of the following verbs, double marking being excluded. To be sure, this is a significant difference on the syntactic level, but in order to understand the importance of this difference we must ask why in the first place the incipient creoles might have copied West African verb serializations. It was obviously not for the sake of imitating substrate syntactic patterns, but rather—as Bickerton himself assures us on various occasions—to compensate for the grave communicative deficiencies of the contact languages and to provide useful (if not absolutely necessary) new syntactic categories. If this is the case, why should we accept the dogma of total rule copying, which in this special case would include the syntactic component as well?

If I understand Bickerton correctly, he himself implicitly concedes that rules need not be copied integrally. He points out that the morphemes and function words incorporated into the creoles may lose some of the features they exhibit in the European base languages; only those required to build up new categories must be retained (Bickerton 1986:24). If base language categories are used for general patterning but not imitated in all details, why should the same procedure not be acceptable for substrate influence?

There is another incongruity in Bickerton's position. He himself emphasizes the necessity of drawing on various sources in order to construe the categories needed by a creole. Where base languages or superstrata are not accessible, or are accessible to a lesser degree, other sources have to be made available. He thus resorts to universals provided by the language bioprogram, leaving aside the substrata of a creole as possible sources. The question is why this should be so, especially when the substratum languages were present in the American colonies. There is no sense in repeating the argument that West African languages were too different to form a common substratum for the developing creoles. We must not take into account all categories occurring in West African languages, but only those present in the creoles that are comparable to West African ones. Once we pass the level of surface structures, it becomes obvious that many creole categories can be identified with West African ones, regardless of whether they are completely identical.

It is worthwhile noting again that there were no reasons for adopting any substrate words or morphemes in their integral forms, with all their morphosyntactic specifications. What was needed were morphemes with certain specific meanings as well as some abstract syntactic patterns which qualified for certain grammatical functions. A bioprogram—or whatever leads the speakers to adopt under any condition a precisely determined word order or, in the case of borrowing, to accept the borrowed rules as they are in the model language—would have to be considered a very undesirable component of the human mind, a nonfunctional monstrosity under the circumstances of creole genesis. Fortunately, speakers of the languages known to us have behaved and will continue to behave in a more sensible way than some modern linguists are able to imagine.

## The Concept of Rule and Its Relevance for Language Interference

In the previous section, various reasons were adduced for declining the need for integral rule copying, while assuming nevertheless that the concept of rule as adopted in modern linguistics (and especially in Generative Grammar) is realistic enough for the purposes of describing interference. But even this cannot be taken for granted. It is an accepted fact that the type of rule under discussion has been devised to give a synchronic description of languages. From the very beginning, generativists' interests have concentrated on the most formal level of language—syntax—and they have tended to reduce nonsyntactic phenomena to syntactic ones, insofar as this has been practicable. Semantics has been left to the lexicon and has been represented in a rather informal way. Certain phenomena, such as the traditional grammatical categories (case, person, comparative, tense, aspect, etc.) which exhibit many more properties than merely syntactic ones, have had no independent status within this linguistic theory. A concept of rule of this kind may be useful and feasible insofar as synchronic description is the main concern; however, it is inadequate for diachronic processes and language contact phenomena. I would have liked to discuss the way interference processes in all their complexity are approached in the framework of extended standard theory (EST), but unfortunately no attempts appear to have been made to handle this important problem.[2]

We know from ample experience that not only words or syntactic patterns are borrowed from one language to another, but also, and often, highly complex phenomena comprising semantic and morphosyntactic components are transferred. As far as I can see, EST does not even provide adequate descriptive devices to account for the semantic and morphosyntactic parts of a borrowed complex construction. The reason for this is clear: since syntax is treated as an autonomous system and held free of semantics, the so-called interpretive levels must be given separately. This means that the linguist has to piece together rules, or something equivalent, from different levels of language in order to describe a complex borrowing process.

One cannot help thinking that generativists deal only with isolated aspects of transferred categories simply because no complex types of rules have been worked out that would account for complex processes. However, the borrowing speakers are confronted with complex phenomena which they are more likely to interpret as units rather than isolated items. At least, it is only in rare cases that one aspect is borrowed now and another some years later, although processes of gradual adoption of model language features must not be excluded (for instance, when foreign influence is increasing).

On the whole, there are good reasons for contending that all features (component parts) which are eventually transferred are taken over concomitantly. Consider the case of the future construction in Balkanic Romani discussed as examples 8 and 10 below. How many rules are involved and in what way are they interrelated? First, an element meaning 'want, will' had to be borrowed or translated; the second solution was adopted. Second, it had to be decided whether the complementizer 'that,' which is attested in Albanian and Romanian as well as in the older stages of Greek and Bulgarian,[3] should have been copied or omitted; the second solution was adopted. Third, a decision had to be made concerning the ordering of elements (the genuine syntactic aspect). Finally, once 'want' was translated by the Romani verb *kam-*, it had to be decided whether this verb should be inflected the normal way or treated as a particle; the second, later Balkanic solution was adopted.

If all the above steps can be included within one rule, then total rule copying is achieved only if all these components are borrowed together. On the other hand, if we assume them to be separate rules, which need not be interrelated, then total rule copying would be achieved by borrowing one of the components mentioned above. As we can see, deciding whether a rule is borrowed in its totality or only in part depends somewhat on what the descriptive model allows. This is, of course, an intolerable state of affairs, which can be avoided. Once again, since we assume that borrowing is undertaken in pursuing a certain aim, it follows that the speakers should have the freedom of selecting among the components of a complex phenomenon.[4]

The problem with the concept of rule is even more complicated. Mühlhäusler (1982:412) calls attention to the fact that, perhaps because of inappropriate terminology, two concepts have often been confused: (1) rules underlying language and governing its realization, which we may call "rules of language"; (2) rules set up by the linguist in order to describe language, generally referred to as "linguistic rules." These sets of rules need not be identical. If we want to make sure that a linguistic rule is a rule of language as well, we should look for independent evidence, which is not theory dependent.

In view of the many problems that even linguists have with rules—or at least with a certain concept of rule—we might ask how normal speakers and hearers in a contact situation behave vis-à-vis a foreign language of which they have only limited command. They have access to surface structures, and they will have to interpret them without the linguist's knowledge. At most, they can make use of the vague insights they have into their own language, although these may vary from individual to individual. Moreover, this knowledge of their language may lead them to misinterpret the foreign categories. The result will be borrowing of a rather unpredictable kind. What is needed, then, is not an abstract system of universally applicable rules but rather devices which allow for the interpretation of concrete cases. The speakers' reactions depend on the concrete circumstances: degree of access, degree of competence, frequency of contacts, interest taken in the foreign language, and so on. Whatever is borrowed, it will not be the static type of rule of Generative Grammar.

## Language Interference and Substratum Influence

It might be objected that all the above observations are valid as far as "normal" interference is concerned, but they cannot be extended to substratum influence. This objection, however, would be justified only if the two situations were categorically distinct. Let us look at the typical features of both situations. In the substratum case, the native language is lost and there is a shift to the superstrate. This seems to hold for the process of creolization as well, the difference being that the shift to the new language is not perfect, obviously because of unfavorable external conditions. Apart from this difference, two languages are united here in one speaker, and the speaker transfers features from his native language into his new idiom, in either a direct or an indirect way. At this point, one of the earlier objections might be raised again. It might be argued that we should expect rules to be copied in their totality because the transfer is effected from an easily accessible mother tongue. Once again, the motives for borrowing must be taken into account in order to understand why a given model was copied only partially.

Moreover, another factor comes to bear. Since the substratum languages did not cease to be spoken in the new territories but were being used over several generations (we know this from numerous reliable reports about the linguistic behavior of the African slaves in the New World colonies), we might expect them to have undergone a process of lexical and grammatical simplification and leveling. This, of course, disallows a direct comparison between the original substratum rules and the corresponding creole rules.

What, then, are the characteristic forms (or historical stages) of "normal" interference relations? There is usually no more than a loose contact between the two languages involved, which normally leads to a limited amount of lexical borrowing. Under certain conditions the pressure from the model language may become so vigorous as to cause full bilingualism, and influence is then exerted on all levels of language. It may happen, then, that rules are totally copied (especially syntactic rules) although there seems to be no need for such total rule copying. Eventually, extreme interference may lead to two or more languages with nearly identical grammars. One such case is reported in Gumperz and Wilson (1971:155). In a small Indian town in a Marathi-speaking surrounding, the local varieties of Indo-Aryan Urdu, of Marathi, and of Dravidian Kannada converged to such a degree as to produce "a single syntactic structure" for all of them. (Much more than mere syntax was involved.)

What is most obvious about the above case is the fact that all innovations in any of the varieties go back to interference; there seems to be no case of innovation in any of the varieties that has no model in any of the other varieties. If we can prove that even in such cases rules must not be copied with all their component parts, then we have a good understanding of what is going on in creolizing languages. There is a case in point concerning gender convergence. Kannada has three genders, which are semantically determined. Marathi has three genders, too, but they are morphological, and the same holds for Urdu, which, however, has only masculine and feminine genders. Now the local variety of Marathi has adopted the Kannada rule by reorganizing its gender system on a semantic basis. The local variety of Urdu, however, did not develop a third, neuter, gender, although it made a step toward the Kannada structure: its masculine category took over the function of the neuter, now comprising both males and inanimate entities (Gumperz and Wilson 1971:155). This is clearly a case of *partial* rule convergence. From this we may conclude that total rule copying is the end of a long process rather than an instantaneous event.

Let us consider another case of complex interrelations. Turkish has an inflectional conditional formed by the suffix *-se/-sa*:

3. *siz burada kalmazsanız biz de gideceğiz*
   you here stay-COND-2PL we too go-FUT-1PL
   'If you don't stay here we will go too.'

Originally, Turkish had no complementizers, but when it came under the influence of Persian, it borrowed some elements, among them *eğer* 'if.' This *eğer* is now optionally used together with the Turkish conditional. Since in Persian there is no special conditional form of the verb, the approximation to Persian is only partial. Cases like this are quite normal.

All in all, I feel justified in drawing on various interference cases in order to corroborate my views on the impact of the potential substrate on the incipient creoles.

## Evidence from Various Contact Situations

### *Transfer of Syntactic Categories Without Transfer of the Respective Morphemes*

It is clear from language structure that pure syntactic borrowing—that is, borrowing concerning word order and similar phenomena exclusively—must be effected by merely copying syntactic patterns, because there are no special morphemes for marking word order.

4. *me vejom tire dadeha te rakerel*
   I came with your father to speak
   'I came to speak with your father.'
   *Ich kam (um) mit deinem Vater zu sprechen* (Finck 1903:44, 9).

This Sinti (= German Gypsy) sentence shows object raising in the same way German does. Since other dialects of Gypsy (or Romani, as we call it now), and especially the more conservative ones of southeastern Europe, do not exhibit this rather exotic rule, we can be sure that it has come about under the influence of German. In example 4 no words or particles have been transferred, nor have new grammatical categories been introduced in order to render the German word order. (To be sure, the new Sinti infinitive *te rakerel* cannot be understood without Slavic or German influence, but it has nothing to do with the word order problem.) This type of interference is appropriate to demonstrate that it is pointless to claim word or morpheme transfer for all cases.

For creoles, there was not much need for imitating purely syntactic patterns of West African languages because a system of grammatical categories had to be built up in the first place. Moreover, West African languages are not very homogeneous in regard to their syntactic principles.

### *Transfer of Syntactic and Semantic Categories by Way of Translation*

Bickerton seems to believe that transfer of the kind just described does not occur, because "this requires us to believe that speakers could somehow have learned the properties of morphemes without learning the morphemes themselves!" (1986:15). Now, if we look around more seriously, we will find a lot of such cases in various contact situations. For any student of language interference, Bickerton's remark will sound rather strange. However, since insights of this kind seem to be novel for creolists, I will cite evidence for such transfer from some other languages.

5. *wono hrima* (Low Sorabian; Schuster-Šewc 1974:341)
   *es donnert* (German)
   'it thunders.'
6. *wono ten cas pćić budzɨ* (Low Sorabian; Schuster-Šewc 1974:344)
   *es diese Zeit kommen wird* = *es wird die Zeit kommen* (German)
   it the time come will
   approximately: 'There will come a time . . .'
7. *wón ma kóždy swój razum* (High Sorabian)
   *es hat jeder seinen Verstand* (German)
   it has everybody his mind
   approximately: 'Everybody knows one's own mind' (High Sorabian; Schuster-Šewc 1974:342).

The two Slavic languages spoken in eastern Germany have long been under the heavy influence of German and, accordingly, have borrowed many features untypical for Slavic languages. Thus we find the German (and English) impersonal *es* 'it' with weather verbs (see 5), as well as an *es* where, apparently, preposing the subject was to be avoided (as in 6 and 7). The neuter *wono* 'it' in 6 is in full congruence with the German model, but *wón* 'he' in 7 is a masculine form that would be impossible in German. What has happened here is a partial adaptation of the German construction to Slavic patterns: *wón* masculine instead of *wono* neuter, in concordance with the masculine subject *kóždy* 'everybody'—which yields a rather bizarre construction. Although no grammatical categories of the traditional type are involved, morphemes have nevertheless been translated in order to render a semantically empty, but syntactically relevant, element. It is remarkable that two closely related languages, both exposed to the same degree of foreign influence, had the freedom to react to the superstrate in different ways.

In many other cases, markers are translated for rendering certain grammatical categories (as case, tense, aspect, etc.). An indisputable example is future tense in Romani. Romani had no specific expression for future before the Gypsies immigrated to Europe. In the course of dialect differentiation, various solutions for expressing future tense were adopted, in accordance with the languages with which Romani came into contact. Thus,

8. *ka(m) l-av/l-es/l-el etc.* (Balkanic Romani)
   want I take/you take/he takes etc.
   'I/you/he will take [it],'

which fully agrees with

9. θ*a kano/kanis/kani* (modern Greek)
   *šte pravja/praviš/pravi* (Bulgarian),

and to a lesser degree with

10. *do të marr/marrësh/marrë* (Albanian)
    want that I take/you take/he takes
    *o să fac/faci/facă* (colloquial Romanian).

Here, an original verb 'want, love' has been translated into Romani. This is semantic borrowing to the effect that a new grammatical category can be set up. Moreover, the translated verb has been reduced to a particle, again in congruence with the model languages. Finally, an original complementizer has been dropped, as was the case with modern Greek and Bulgarian. We might consider this a mere coincidence of independent developments, since verbs meaning 'will/wish/love' have been used elsewhere to convey a future meaning. But consider the following negative evidence from other Romani dialects:

11. *lava te džav/lesa te džas/lela te džal*
    I take that I go/you take that you go/he takes that he goes
    'I/you/he will go' (Russian Romani; Ventzel 1983:72).

That is, future is formed with an inflected auxiliary 'take,' for which I know only one parallel:

12. *maty- mu/maty- meš/maty- me* (Ukrainian)
    to have I take/to have you take/to have he takes
    'I/you/he will have'

from an original infinitive **jaty,* present *imu/imeš/ime,* and so on. The Roma adopted this construction when migrating from Romania to Russia and thereby passing through a Ukrainian-speaking area. The syntactic constraints do not hold, presumably because Romani lacked an infinitive, and auxiliary verbs are normally preposed to the main verb. But these differences do not count in view of an exceptional semantic congruence.

For those who are not convinced that the Romani future forms have been triggered by foreign patterns, let us have a look at the Sinti (German Romani) future tense. No special form exists. Rather, future is expressed by the unmodified present form, as is usual in colloquial German. We can interpret this state in two ways: When the Sintis' forefathers came to Central Europe, they either had no future form or they had adopted the Balkanic solution but dropped it, and they adopted the German solution in either case.

Processes like the one just described might be cited in great numbers. They entitle us to assume similar processes in creolization too, since, as I pointed out above, "normal" borrowing and substratum transfer are not totally distinct processes but together make up the greater domain of language interference. Therefore, the following typical creole phenomena (more precisely, phenomena typical of Atlantic creoles) can be derived from the West African substratum. Those who want to disprove this should make an effort to produce counterarguments of a more specific type. For reasons of space I will simply enumerate the phenomena without giving sentence examples from various creoles, since the phenomena have been discussed for a long time.

13. 'to pass' as a comparative verb (Principense, Sranan: *pasa;* French creoles: *pase;* Krio: *pas;* Saramaccan: *moro*)
14. 'to finish' as a completive marker (Portuguese creoles, Haitian, Sranan, Saramaccan: *kaba* ‹ Portuguese)
15. 'to give' as a benefactive-dative (Principense, Saramaccan: *da;* Sranan: *gi;* Haitian: *bay*)
16. 'to take' in various functions, especially associative and instrumental (Sranan: *teki;* Krio: *tek;* Saramaccan: *téi*)
17. 'to say' as a kind of complementizer (Sranan: *taki;* Krio: *se*)
18. 'to go' and 'to come' as directional verbs (Sranan, Saramaccan: *go;* Haitian: *ale;* Papiamentu: *bai;* Principense: *wɛ;* Sranan: *kon;* Saramaccan: *kó;* Haitian: *vin;* Principense: *vika*).

Since there are several different constructions with the directional verbs, I shall discuss them in detail. There are constructions with 'go/come' preceding the main verb, as in

19. *In kom shub mi doun* (Jamaican; Bailey 1966:40).
'He came (and) pushed me down.'

These are similar to English 'come to do' and 'come and do.'
There is nothing unusual about them. Other constructions with 'go/come' +

PP following the main verb might be viewed in the same way:

20. *Dem wi kyari im go a dokta* (Jamaican; Bailey 1966:36).
    'They will bring him to the doctor.'

However, there are also cases with an isolated directional verb following the main verb, and these have no equivalent in any European language, for instance:

21. *Di katn tri liin go, in liin kam (wid him).*
    'The cotton tree swayed back and forth (with him)' (Jamaican; Le Page and DeCamp 1960:175).
22. *N ap rəle doktə-a vini.*
    we are calling the doctor come
    'We are calling the doctor (here)' (Haitian; Wingerd 1977:453).

Many creoles have constructions with a double directional verb:

23. *In an Samwel gaan a riba gaan bied demself.*
    'He and Samuel went to the river to bathe' (Jamaican; Bailey 1966:132).

Taken as isolated phenomena, these constructions might be explained as independent creations or as derived from similar European constructions, although the regular use of double 'go/come' is rather unexpected. It is not by mere chance that some West African languages exhibit parallels to all the above constructions, among them Akan languages like Fante:

24. *afei egya Kweku faa no tur dεε-ɔre-kɔ-yε ha* (Welmers 1946:76)
    then father Kwaku took his rifle that he go-make hunt
    'Then father Kwaku took his gun to go hunting.'
25. *o -guanee kɔr ha mu* (native informant)
    he ran-away went bush in
    'He ran away in the bush.'
26. *o -guanee fii kurow no mu bae/kɔree* (native informant)
    he ran-away left village DET in came/went
27. *wɔ -bε -kɔ mpoano e-ko-guar*
    they will go [to the] beach to bathe
    'They will go to the beach and bathe' (Balmer and Grant 1929:134).

Note that the last type of construction is not accidental; it is, in fact, highly grammaticized. Whereas the first directional verb has full inflection, the second is closely linked to the main verb and subjected to phonological assimilation according to the rules of vowel harmony. This, of course, has not been imitated in any creole.

There seems to be another difference between the two languages: In Fante, the two directionals can stand in juxtaposition, as in

28. *me- n- ka- ba a- bɔ- hwε* (Balmer and Grant 1929:131)
    I- NEG- FUT- come AGR- come- look

'I shall not come to look.'

I was not able to find a comparable construction in any English creole. What is striking about the whole matter, however, is the overall correspondence between African languages and creoles. It would not be convincing to argue that correspondences like these came about by chance.

For Saramaccan, Bickerton (1988, and implicitly Byrne 1987) argues that the verb series formed by using the above-mentioned verbs cannot have been inherited from a West African language because in Saramaccan all verbs of a series can be tensed (viz., with *bi-*), whereas in West African languages only the first verb is capable of taking a tense marker. I have no plausible explanation for this difference, but it must be emphasized that a universal approach provides no explanation either. In my view, minor discrepancies do not invalidate transfer from the substratum.

Furthermore, a closer look at West African languages shows that Bickerton's assumptions are not quite correct. In Fante, for instance, there are verbs which cannot take tense and aspect prefixes; when they happen to come first in a verb series, the second verb will be marked for tense:

29. *me- nam tokura mu bɛ -kɔ* (Balmer and Grant 1929:116)
I walk through window will-go
'I shall go through the window.'

30. *o- fi dan no mu a-ba*
he leave house the in PERF-come
'He left the house [and] came here' (Balmer and Grant 1929:120; construction slightly changed).

31. *me- dze be-si* (Balmer and Grant 1929:116)
I take shall-fix
'I shall fix [it].'

This means that there are West African models for marking a verb other than the first verb for tense, mood, and aspect (TMA), if only in a limited number. Moreover, Akan does exhibit such a thing as TMA agreement, which is governed by rather complicated rules.

32. *ɔ-tuu mirika baa me nkyɛn* (Balmer and Grant 1929:117)
he ran came my side (with preterite inflection)
'He ran toward me.'

33. *m' a- fa sekan e- twa* (E. Hayford, personal communication)
I PERF take knife PERF/AGR cut
'I have cut with a knife.'

34. *me- ba- fa sekan e -twa* (Balmer and Grant 1929:117)
I FUT take knife AGR cut

'I shall cut with a knife.'

To be sure, tense is marked twice, unlike in Saramaccan (where it is marked only once on first, second, or third verb), and the second tense-aspect marker has a neutral shape indicating agreement only. However, the examples show that there is no simple rule.

It should be noted that languages such as Ewe also have double marking of tense, and so on. According to Westermann (1965:87), the rule of double marking is applied optionally: "The other verbs (i.e., the second, etc.) are often not conjugated, except in the future, but they are just as frequently conjugated"; for example:

35. *wó -a -gbùgbo á -va/vɛ̂*
they FUT return FUT come
'They will bring it back.'

36. *wó -tso -nɛ̂ (‹ na-e) vá-na/vá*
they take HABIT come-HABIT
'They will bring it here.'

Finally, in Akan even marking for person is not homogeneous; in certain cases the first-person singular is marked with each verb in a series:

37. *me -dze sekan me -twae* (Balmer and Grant 1929:120)
I take knife I cut (preterite)
'I cut [it] with a knife.'

All this points to the fact that the marking of verbs in West African languages cannot be captured by a simple rule. We are not in a position now to state whether there is a historical connection between Saramaccan and substrate behavior or not, and we will not be until more painstaking investigations have been carried out.

### *Evidence from Other Substrate Cases*

In the previous sections I have made the following points: (1) markers are not necessarily borrowed as such in order to constitute a new category in the borrowing language, but can be translated if they have a translatable meaning; and (2) constructions in model language and replica language need not be totally identical in order to be acknowledged as borrowings.

It could be shown that both points hold at least in situations of "normal" language contact. From the cases of normal contact discussed above, it was inferred that languages involved in creole genesis behave in the same way. Since many creolists may not accept this conclusion, I will give additional evidence from situations outside the field of creolistics in which substrata have been involved. Unfortunately, good evidence is rare because processes of this type of interference are scarcely well documented and ongoing influence on the part of the superstrate is likely to obscure substrate influence. Nevertheless, I can cite some convincing examples from Irish English and from the French spoken in Brussels.

38. *ta sé tar éis/tréis litir a scriobadh* (Irish; Henry 1957:177).
*he is after writing a letter* (Irish English)
'He has just written a letter.'

We can assume with a high degree of certainty that this perfectum proximum (*he is after writing* 'has just written') of Irish English has come about under the influence of Irish because there appear to be no traces of this construction in earlier English. From this case we learn that, first, a function has been transferred by way of translation (*tréis* = after), not by borrowing the function word; and, second, that the syntactic components of the Irish English construction have not completely been adjusted to those of Irish: word order is quite different, and the verbal noun of Irish has no real equivalent in English.

In Irish English, *it* clefting goes far beyond the restrictions it has in English. In addition to all the possibilities realized in English, in Irish English, adverbs, verbal nouns, and so on, can be clefted as well:

39. *It's badly she'd do it now* (adverb).
40. *It's flat it was* (predicate adjective).
41. *It's looking for more land a lot of them are* (verbal noun).

These constructions are not only possible in Irish, they are also used with high frequency:

42. *Ní go maith a chonaic sé iad.*
Is not well COMP saw he them
'He didn't see them well.'
43. *Is caochta atá sé.*
Is drunk COMP be he
'He is (really) drunk.'
44. *Is ag déanamh a chuid ceachtannaí ata Tadhig.*
Is at doing his portion lessons COMP-be Tim
'Tim is doing his lessons.'

Apart from frequency there are other indicators (intonation, functional variants, degree of Irish influence) that point to the Irish substratum. (For more detail, see Harris 1987, from which these samples are drawn.)

Brussels, with its unique surroundings, was Flemish until it was named the capital of the newly founded kingdom of Belgium. Following that event, it became increasingly Gallicized, partly by French-speaking newcomers and partly by the language shift of the resident Flemish population. Nowadays, the French of Brussels exhibits a great number of phenomena typical of Flemish (or Dutch in general) but not known in France. Thus, the present is often used instead of a future form in situations in which the correct meaning is clear from the context:

45\. *Tantôt vous l'avez de retour.*
'You will get it back soon' (lit.: soon you it-get 0 back),

and similarly in Flemish,

46\. *Straks krijg je dat terug.*

In this case, the substrate rule has not been brought into French by translating the function word but by using a morphologically unmarked form instead of a marked one. In the same way, the following construction, which substitutes for the "passé récent" of standard French, appears to go back to Flemish. The examples are from Baetens Beardsmore (1971):

47\. *Il est justement parti chez tante Léa* (Brussels French).
he is just gone to aunt Lea
'He has just gone to Aunt Lea's.'

48\. *Hij is juist vertrokken* (Flemish).
he is just left
'He has just left.'

49\. *Il vient de partir* (Standard French).
he come from go/leave
'He (has) just left.'

A very interesting case is the imitation of the Germanic movable preverb in the French of Brussels, which also occurs in other Romance dialects bordering Germanic languages:

50\. *bouillir au-dessus* ‹ Flemish *over-koken* 'to boil over'; *couper en bas* ‹ *af-snijden* 'to cut off'; *venir entre* ‹ *tussen-komen* 'to intervene'; *mettre près* ‹ *bij-zetten* 'add'; *savoir contre* ‹ *tegen-kunnen* 'to bear, endure' (Kramer 1981).

Similar calques have been found in the Wallonie, in French dialects spoken in the neighborhood of Alsace and Lorraine, as well as in the Rhaeto-Romanic dialects of Switzerland, but that is not evidence against substratum influence in Brussels. It simply demonstrates that the results can be identical in both varieties of interference and that loan translations at the grammatical level are very common. Again, not all components of the model have been transferred.

Creolistics is a subfield of linguistics which shares many features with other varieties of interference linguistics. It should therefore be integrated in this wider area of interference study. Conversely, results obtained in this wider field should be applied to creolistics as well. If there are universals operating during the process of creolization, similar universals should be detectable in other processes of language change. Creolization is not as extraordinary a process as some linguists believe. Although creation of novel categories does take place, it is not confined to creolization, and it occurs only to a limited degree. In all language developments we have to take into consideration the historical setting. Speakers are continuously influenced by many different factors, and nobody has ever created a language out of nothing. Linguistic models are necessary, but we should not confuse them with reality. The more ambitious a theory, the greater the danger of being seduced by its consistency and elegance, and the less the endeavor for supplying empirical evidence.

## Notes

1. The following abbreviations are used in the glosses: AGR agreement; COMP complementizer; COND conditional; DET determiner; FUT future; HABIT habitual; NEG negation; PERF perfect; PL plural; PP prepositional phrase; PRES present; PROG progressive; SG singular; TMA tense-mood-aspect; and number for person. They are all capitalized to distinguish them from the regular glosses.

2. Some efforts have been made to apply EST to the problems of code switching, but even here there is good reason for doubting the adequacy of the approach; see, for example, Muysken, di Sciullo, and Singh 1982, cited by Klavans 1985, in which far-reaching predictions about constraints on code switching are made on the basis of government-binding theory. That is, instead of asking themselves if the assumptions about government as conceived of in EST are relevant for real processes (as in code switching), the authors take it for granted that categories set up for synchronic (descriptive) purposes are adequate for everything. I propose that a test be done on the validity of such categories by first applying them to diachronic problems. It seems unlikely that, in a situation of language contact, it should be an intrinsically linguistic factor alone, and not various extralinguistic factors, that determines the cuts in switching.

3. Greek *θelo na › θe na › θa;* Bulgarian *šte da › šte*.

4. An opposing attitude reminds us of the biological orientation of historical linguistics in the mid-nineteenth century. At that time, it was held that language is a self-contained organism developing in itself and out of itself, without being subjected to external factors. This position of Schleicher et al. became outmoded as early as the turn of this century.

## References

Baetens Beardsmore, H. 1971. *Le Français régional de Bruxelles*. Brussels: Presses Universitaires.

Bailey, Beryl Loftman. 1966. *Jamaican Creole syntax*. Cambridge: Cambridge University Press.

Balmer, W. T., and F. C. F. Grant. 1929. *A grammar of the Fante-Akan language*. London: Atlantis Press.

Bickerton, Derek. 1986. *The lexical learning hypothesis and the pidgin-creole cycle*. Duisburg, Germany: Linguistic Agency, University of Duisburg.

Byrne, Francis. 1987. *Grammatical relations in a radical creole*. Amsterdam: John Benjamins.

Finck, F. M. 1903. *Lehrbuch des Dialekts der deutschen Zigeuner*. Marburg, Germany: Elwertsche Verlagsbuchhandlung.

Gumperz, J. J., and R. Wilson. 1971. Convergence and creolization: A case from the Indo-Aryan/Dravidian border. *Pidginization and creolization of languages*, ed. by D. Hymes, 151–67. Cambridge: Cambridge University Press.

Harris, J. 1987. Conservatism versus substratal transfer in Irish English. *Essener Kolloquium über Sprachwandel und seine bestimmenden Faktoren*, 1986, *Beiträge zum 3*, ed. by N. Boretzky, W. Enninger, and T. Stolz, 143–62. Bochum, Germany: Brockmeyer.

Henry, P. L. 1957. *An Anglo-Irish dialect of North-Roscommon*. Zürich: Aschmann und Scheller.

Jackendoff, Ray S. 1977. *X' syntax: A study of phrase structure (syntax)*. Linguistic Inquiry Monograph no. 2.

Klavans, J. L. 1985. The syntax of code-switching: Spanish and English. *Selected papers from the Thirteenth Linguistic Symposium on Romance Languages 1983*, ed. by L. King and C. Maley, 213–29. Amsterdam: John Benjamins.

Kramer, J. 1981. Die Übernahme der deutschen und der niederländischen Konstruktion Verb + Verbzusatz durch die Nachbarsprachen. *Sprachkontakt als Ursache von Veränderungen der Sprach-und Bewusstseinsstruktur*. Institut für Sprachwissenschaft der Universität Innsbruck. Hrsg. von W. Meid, K. Heller. Druck H. Kowatsch, Innsbruck. 129–40.

Le Page, R. B., and D. DeCamp. 1960. *Jamaican Creole*. London: Macmillan.

Mühlhäusler, P. 1982. Kritische Bemerkungen zu Sprachmischungs-Universalien. *St. Ureland (Hg.), Die Leistungen der Strataforschung und Kreolistik. Akten des 5. Symposions über Sprachkontakt in Europa, Mannheim*, 407–31. Tübingen: Niemeyer.

Muysken, P., A.-M. di Sciullo, and R. Singh. 1982. Code-mixing and government. Unpublished manuscript, University of Montreal.

Schuster-Šewc, H. 1974. Sätze mit fiktivem Subjekt vom Typ obersorbisch *wono so deščuje*/niedersorbisch *to se pada*. *Zeitschrift für Slawistik* 19.344–52.

Ventzel, T. V. 1983. *The Gypsy language*. Moscow: Nauka.

Welmers, W. E. 1946. *A descriptive grammar of Fanti*. Language Dissertation no. 39 (vol. 22, no. 3, suppl.).

Westermann, D. 1965. *A study of the Ewe language*. London: Oxford University Press.

Wingerd, J. 1977. Serial verbs in Haitian Creole. *Language and linguistic problems in Africa*, ed. by P. F. Kotey and H. Der-Housikian, 452–66. Columbia, S.C.: Hornbeam Press.

# Rules, Language Contact, Substrate, and What Not: A Reply to Boretzky

*Francis Byrne*

Norbert Boretzky's paper, at first glance, is a combination of language contact theory, a defense of the creole substrate viewpoint, and a critique of both Derek Bickerton and the rules, generalizations, and principles approach of theoretical linguistics. In effect, Boretzky argues that Bickerton's position for the viability of his universal approach vis-à-vis substratum influence is too closely associated with the formalisms and/or morphological and syntactic lexical specifications of the generative school to be effective. Boretzky claims that such abstract grammatical approaches are theoretically and methodologically inadequate to deal with contact phenomena because borrowing through contact applies selectively, not generally, as a rule-and-principles orientation warrants. Finally, Boretzky argues that since there are a number of cases in which the substrate language has had verifiable syntactic influence within some contact situations, it reasonably follows that it should likewise affect creolization. He contends that serialization is one of the more obvious instances of such transfer within Atlantic creole structure and genesis, and he supports the contention with some quite intriguing (albeit misleading) data from Akan serials.

Even though I will not argue against Boretzky's position that the substrate can syntactically influence creole languages (it seems entirely possible *given the right conditions*), I do question his arguments leading to that conclusion. Many of the points he makes are interesting and have merit. However, the arguments at times contain inaccuracies and are thereby not always entirely convincing. Below, I discuss some of the more obvious difficulties.

In Boretzky's first section, he takes Bickerton to task for modifying positions on what constitutes evidence for substrate influence on creole languages. While I do not wish, or need, to defend Bickerton, there are nevertheless some disturbing presumptions about the scientific method and the nature of rules which Boretzky uses to support his case. In regard to the latter, he critically observes that Bickerton has fluctuated from the position of total rule copying as a necessary prerequisite to prove substrate syntactic influence, to less than total rule copying, to a lexically focused theoretical approach.

I agree that the first, or total rule copying, is an extreme diagnostic for substrate influence and one which must be used with caution. Yet, to prove identity between objects under examination, certainly the more points of similarity that exist, the more empirical support there is for a conclusion of grammatical identity. If there are vague, nondistinct parallelisms, a causal relationship between elements of two or more grammars is much more tenuous and speculative and thus less convincing. If anything, I interpret Bickerton (1986b) as showing that the substratists more than likely have to rely on less empirically sound syntactic evidence to support their viewpoint because close inspections of specific patterns and elements in selected West African and creole languages show that there is not a one-to-one correspondence between them. If a linguistic link is assumed, then concrete parallel patterns are the best evidence to ensure credibility. Barring this, it seems that the next best analysis would be a systematic demonstration of partial rule transfer.

Other problems somewhat along the same lines are found with Boretzky's criticism of rule-dominated and lexically based formalisms. From the former, rules are, by their very nature, an attempt to represent and capture linguistic behavior. In this sense, they are first and foremost metaphors of perceived reality which can only be approximately accurate. As our measuring and testing devices become more sophisticated, different theories, formalisms, and analyses develop to capture the new insights. What the lexical approach represents is not some aberrant behavior but the current state of language theory. It is, in fact, a reordering of the focus of language research from a strict reliance on formalism (i.e., rules) to one based on linguistic principles. Such principles in large part emanate from individual lexical items.

In regard to differing approaches to language, Boretzky's discomfort with a lexical orientation appears to rest in his belief that it is the same as the rule-oriented analysis which Bickerton espoused in earlier work. If this were correct, it would constitute stasis at its worst, thus violating the scientific method and, in fact, Bickerton's intent. For a discipline to grow, there must be postulation, testing, and repostulation. Since syntactic theory is a relatively new discipline, the changes are necessarily rapid as fundamental tenets are proposed, debated, and modified. This can cause extreme discomfort to those who are not acquainted with current proposals. Such rapid changes also lead to erroneous interpretations of emerging hypotheses if one is not familiar with the specific details or their antecedents. This, I suspect, is the case with Boretzky, given the nature of his statements.

For one, the lexical approach as it relates to creolization is much more than learning "rules related to individual words" and taking over "words together with all their grammatical properties" (Boretzky, this volume). The intent of the theory, as I understand it, is to try to better capture the mental processes involved in the deepest form of creolization (no small objective). Since the usual lexicon in pidgins and early deep creoles is small and multifunctionality is the norm, the question here is how these items interact to form language in creolization. Evidence and language theory mandate that argument marking from the incipient creole speakers' acquired lexical items would proceed in the normal way, or like lexical items in all languages. The difference with deep creoles is that the lexical items are incorporated (i.e., reinterpreted) within a limited categorial repertoire with few configurational projections. Such "deficiencies" bring about a need for *more* governors and theta role and case markers to realize minimally adequate sentential complexity. In other words, serialization as well as other syntactic strategies of a deep creole result from the above conditions and processes, not from "learning rules . . . [and] their grammatical properties," as Boretzky states it.

Also misleading is Boretzky's interpretation of current language theory. He contends that semantics is "rather informal[ly] . . . left to the lexicon" and "traditional grammatical categories (case, person, comparative, tense, aspect, etc.) have no position of their own within this linguistic theory." To say the least, these statements are puzzling. In regard to the former, it is simply not true that semantics is informally relegated to the lexicon. Certainly the foundation of the government and binding (GB) model (Chomsky 1981, 1982, 1986) is semantically based at the sentence level on theta and binding theory, as well as logical form, which applies accepted semantic principles to test aspects of sentential strings such as well-formedness and scope. In turning to the latter, Boretzky is again mistaken in his view of the role of the "traditional grammatical categories" he mentions; all are appropriately integrated into the syntax *and/or* semantics of the various existent theoretical constructs. For example, case theory is an integral part of the GB model, as are comparatives and certainly tense and aspect,[1] among many other areas of grammar. Moreover, for a somewhat different focus from the GB model, Bresnan (1982a, 1982b) and Gazdar et al. (1985) offer diverse morphological, syntactic, and semantic orientations.

On a more positive note, Boretzky is partially correct in asserting that rules, as *previously formulated* in the syntactic literature, are inadequate to describe language diachrony, transfer, change, borrowing, and other dynamic processes. Yet even here he seems again to misunderstand scientific methodology. Rules, as a sort of measurement, are in effect hypotheses. If they are inadequate, then a scholar can try to develop a better system. Simply criticizing leads nowhere unless a more adequate alternative is substituted in its place. Scholars in the 1970s had similar if not identical misgivings, but the critical difference is that they developed an elaborate research agenda within variation theory that tried to correct the more glaring inadequacies. However, even with today's research emphasis on principles rather than strict formalism, rules developed within the generative school, and modifications they have inspired, are still the best means to illustrate linguistic patterns if one keeps in mind their metaphorical nature. There is not yet a superior alternative that could supplant the methodology.

In turning to contact phenomena, Boretzky's varied data are interesting, but the discussion suffers from the serious fallacy of argument from analogy. He seems to feel that since creoles are ultimately a result of contact, then examples of any form of contact are somehow of equal value in pushing a substratist view. If I follow his reasoning correctly, he claims that because it is possible to "transfer syntactic and semantic categories by way of translation" in a cross-section of contact situations, it naturally follows that substrate "translations" should be possible in *all* instances of creolization. The argument breaks down on this point, however, since the various outputs of contact phenomena are not equivalent. Depending on the relative influence of any of a number of demographic and linguistic variables, a wide array of results are possible, from simple lexical borrowing and code switching to varieties of a Sprachbund such as that found in the Balkans,[2] to pidginization and creolization. Nevertheless, the issue here is not the variables but the linguistic results which ensue because of their presence. While it is true that many contact codes exhibit superstrate and/or substrate influence and partial or even complete rule transfer, still to claim that because something happens in X it should occur in Y is to assume an equivalency that Boretzky has not proven and is not grammatically there.

Nor is Boretzky correct in his subtle implication that language contact, and by implication creolization, applies in a similar manner in the creation of the wide variety of contact-induced phenomena, which includes creole languages and should thereby exhibit similar properties and processes in development. The nature of his statements and his continual adducement of noncreole substrate evidence to discuss creolization lead to the conclusion that Boretzky perceives such substrate influence to apply equally in all situations. Now I know of no scholar who would venture to claim that contact phenomena result from the same type and degree of input and that evidence from one contact type proves the developmental reality of another. And just as there are different results in other language contact situations, so too have scholars such as Baker (1982), Bickerton (1984, 1986a), Byrne (1983, 1985c, 1987, 1988a, 1988c), Carden and Stewart (1988), Hancock (1986), Mufwene (1986, 1987), and Seuren (1986) concluded that different linguistic and demographic values have produced a continuum of possibilities within the creolization process itself, with the resultant languages being differentially creole from the onset. That is, the disparity in the initial formative stage leads to the observation that these languages, taken as a group, will not equally reflect optimal creole features. It would seem to be a logical extension to further state that differential creolization implies greater or lesser degrees of substrate elaboration.

The question, of course, is how these different levels of creole develop and expand during the formative period. In a pristine form of creolization in which neither the substrate nor the superstrate is sufficiently able to influence the outcome, Bickerton's view has it that a significant part of a creole's syntax develops from children's innate biologically determined grammar. Alternatively, the *extreme* form of the substrate approach, which Boretzky seems to espouse, sees a creole's syntactic expansion as emanating to a significant degree from the substrate languages present in the contact situation.[3] One of the main arguments for the latter is that serials appear in a creole whenever serialization exists in the substrate component (as was the case with the Kwa group of West African languages which were present during the development of the Atlantic creoles); conversely, creoles such as the Indian Ocean varieties do not exhibit a serial strategy when there is none in the contact languages. In defending his assumptions against problematic data and analyses in Byrne (1987), Boretzky offers the following observations: (a) no one, neither Boretzky nor universalists, has an explanation for the unusual Saramaccan serial tense patterns; and (b) Saramaccan is not unique as claimed, because Fante exhibits tense marking in serial contexts similar to Saramaccan. On both counts Boretzky is mistaken.

First, contrary to Boretzky's belief, there have been a number of explanations of Saramaccan serial tensing interspersed within serial analyses, theoretical discussions, and demonstrations of the relationship between serialization and sentential complementation.[4] The pattern to which Boretzky refers is that any given verb in a sentence containing a variety of serial types may be overtly and independently tensed with *bi*, as in the representative sentences with the instrumental role in 1b and 1c below.[5]

1. a. *dí míi téi dí páu náki dí dágu*
   the child take the stick hit the dog
   'The child hit the dog with the stick.'

   b. *dí míi bi téi dí páu náki dí dágu*
   . . . tense (TNS) . . .

The child had hit the dog with the stick.

c. *dí míi téi dí páu bi náki dí dágu*

. . . TNS . . .

'The child had hit the dog with the stick.'

One reason for the above tense patterning is that Saramaccan serial and complement clauses, with very few exceptions, are finite. With such status, not only is *bi* allowed with, for example, both *téi* 'take' and *náki* 'hit' (1b and 1c),[6] but subjects must also be present, a fact which theory and independent confirmation verify in the language (see Byrne 1985b, 1986, 1987). In at least Saramaccan, then, the evidence suggests that *each* serial verb which permits marking with *bi* is best looked at as a *finite sentential constituent*.

Another reason for the pattern is scope and spreading. As defined by Byrne (1990), scope is the interpretative range over some syntactic domain of some semantic property, and spreading is the appearance of redundant morphemes throughout a scopal domain with those formatives or constructions whose properties allow it. Now these two processes explain not only the Saramaccan serial tense patterns but such patterns in all serializing languages. That is, the reason why verbs in a serial structure *must* have the same tense interpretation is that any tense marking applies to (i.e., has scope over) the entire string. In the realm of spreading, such marking can redundantly appear in other appropriate positions.[7] As far as serialization is concerned, such positions would be finite clauses such as (almost) uniquely exist in Saramaccan, but not in many other serializing languages (hence marking only on the first verb of a serial string). Finally, the Saramaccan pattern exhibited in 1c is possible for the simple reason that the tense marker on the initial verb *téi* 'take' is not overt; because *bi* with *náki* 'hit' has only a single possible interpretation, *bi* on *téi* need not have phonological form.[8]

Boretzky's second mistaken assumption is that the Fante tense marking in example 2 below is like the Saramaccan model presented above. A close examination reveals critical differences.

2. a. *me-nam tokura mu bɛ- kɔ* (Balmer and Grant 1929:116)

I walk through window will go

'I will walk through the window.'

b. *o- fi dan no mu a- ba* (Balmer and Grant 1929:120)

he leave house the in PERF-come

'He has arrived from the house.'

To begin with, such marking with *bɛ* 'will' and perfective *a* on sentence-final verbs seems to be exclusively restricted to environments with motion verbs in matrix position. If this is correct, then I suspect, following the work of Givón

(1975) and Hyman (1975), that example 2 represents *another* areal remnant of a prior subject-object-verb (SOV) word order. Note that its limited occurrence is normal when a language has largely completed some diachronic adjustment and an SOV typology would naturally mandate verb-final marking (which should be considered identical to verb-initial marking in SVO languages, but would, of course, have different branching and a leftward tense scope domain). In comparison, Saramaccan is unambiguously SVO, with no hint of any prior SOV order, and tense appears with any verb in a number of serial types; its overt placement depends, as far as is known, solely on the discretion of the speaker.

Finally, Boretzky misses the point of *Grammatical Relations in a Radical Creole* (Byrne 1987) when he characterizes it (albeit indirectly) as being focused against the substrate position for creole serialization. To reach such a conclusion, it appears that he might have concentrated more on Bickerton's foreword to the book rather than on the book itself. In any case, the question of an African source for Saramaccan serialization is a very minor consideration; the work primarily concentrates on (a) the categorial status of certain pertinent formatives, (b) the grammatical properties of serial and complement structures, (c) the interrelationship between serialization and sentential complementation, and (d) how some Saramaccan serials have changed over time and to which categories they may eventually be reanalyzed.

One of the major conclusions from the analyses, and one which has indirect implications for the substrate view, is that serialization is, and presumably was, given the limits of the categories and structures available to the Saramaka, the only means possible to express the intricate grammatical relationships needed for sentential well-formedness and Saramaccan's status as a natural language. From this perspective, serialization was thereby a necessary and spontaneous development of particularly deep creolization. While Kwa languages could have reinforced the emerging grammatical system, they were not the main impetus in its expansion.

Given the tone and content of Boretzky's paper, he would apparently dismiss the possibility of spontaneous generation, despite the evidence, and steadfastly adhere to a causal connection for serialization between substrate and creole languages *in all instances*. Like Faraclas (1989) and Sebba (1987), his argument would again probably follow along the lines that, regardless of the results of a single analysis, whenever serialization appears in a creole, it also always exists in the substrate languages. Analyses which question or purport to disprove an extreme view of substrate serial transfer, or which at least offer a viable alternative, go against direct evidence and are thus more than likely artifacts of a transient grammatical model. This argument in its present form, however, may no longer be tenable; Bickerton (1989) argues that Seselwa, a creole of the Seychelles in the Indian Ocean, unambiguously contains serial structures[9] whose types and occurrence are comparable with any Caribbean creole. The significance of the finding to Boretzky's stance is that Seselwa had no serializing substratum from which to transfer the pattern, in a generalized form or not; its primary substrate input was from the nonserializing East African Bantu languages.

The conclusion to be drawn from the Saramaccan and Seselwa evidence is that the extreme substrate view will not work for critical elements of selected creoles. With Saramaccan, the grammatical properties of the language suggest that serialization was the only option to achieve its necessary linguistic expansion. Yet Saramaccan did have a Kwa presence, and so the claim can be made, as it has been, that serialization came from that source (despite the syntactic necessity for grammatical adequacy). Now, with evidence that serial structures may emerge in creolization without linguistic transfer, Byrne's (1987) analysis is reinforced, and the substratists will necessarily have to reevaluate their positions if Bickerton is correct. One option is for them to adopt a more moderate approach, something like that of Mufwene (1986), in which both universal (in some sense of the term) and substrate influences have a place in creole development. Similarly, they might accept, finally, the growing realization that all creolization is not the same; possibly some creoles had favorable conditions for a degree of substrate transfer,[10] while others—the deeper varieties—are best looked at as having spontaneously evolved aspects of their grammars when transfer was inadequate for linguistically acceptable expansion.

## Notes

I thank Jim Flavin, Solange Lira, Salikoko Mufwene, and Carlson Yost for making suggestions on the form or content of this paper. All errors or omissions, of course, remain my sole responsibility. The Saramaccan data cited here were collected with the assistance of grants from the National Science Foundation and the Consejo de Investigacion of the Universidad de Oriente, Venezuela, for which grateful acknowledgment is hereby made.

1. Rather than enumerate the many publications related to Boretzky's list of "traditional categories," I refer the reader to the general but comprehensive texts dealing with generative grammar currently available on the market. These include Lasnik and Uriagereka 1988; McCawley 1988; Radford 1988; and van Riemsdijk and Williams 1986, among others. In creolistics, numerous papers and books have

also been written on the subject. For example, the papers by P. Baker and Syea, Mufwene, Muysken and van der Voort, and Sankoff in Byrne and Huebner 1991 deal in part with tense, markedness, binding, and aspect, respectively.

2. Boretzky lists a few of the more important variables, and others are discussed in such works as Byrne 1983, 1985a; Lehiste 1988; and Jeffers and Lehiste 1979, chap. 9. (See these works for additional references.)

3. Substratists usually cite influence from the superstrate as also being important in creole expansion (see Muysken and Smith 1986).

4. See, for example, Byrne 1982, 1984, 1985b, 1986, 1987; Bickerton 1984; and Bickerton and Iatridou n.d.

5. The diacritics on the Saramaccan vowels in example 1 represent high tone, while lack of the same indicates low tone.

6. Actually this is not the full story. Contrary to Boretzky's contention, some Saramaccan serials additionally allow for a tense copy type pattern in which *bi* marking on the matrix verb appears to be repeated on the second:

*dí míi bi téi dí páu bi náki dí dágu*
the child TNS take the stick TNS hit the dog
'The child had hit the dog with the stick.'

7. Scope and spreading are not limited to tense marking in the world's languages but are common with many constituent types. See Byrne 1990; Carlson 1983; and Gordon 1927 for more details and examples.

8. The significance of scope and spreading is that these are integral characteristics of a particular language typology: serialization. That is, if a language adopts a serializing strategy, then at least scope, and possibly also spreading, will mandatorily be a part of the tense strategy. There is therefore nothing extraordinary about *Saramaccan serial tensing;* it is a language-specific result of particular morphological, syntactic, and semantic features. The basic operational principles involved in tense scope and variable tense marking, however, are the same in all languages allowing serialization.

9. Such a statement is, of course, contingent on one's definition of serialization. As we learn more about the phenomenon, a natural and correct consequence is to restrain the conditions with which we identify serials. This has led some scholars to take a very restricted view and allow few structure types to qualify. For example, Lefebvre 1991 argues that serials are partly a product of the lexicon. The result of her interpretation (which has considerable merit at least for Haitian Creole and Fon languages) is that many putative serials are eliminated. On the other hand, Seuren 1985, automatically eliminates any structures from contention which also function as sentential complements. The view adopted here is that of Byrne 1987:179–80: partially, serialization is a syntactic constituent configurationally dominated either by a VP or an S node. Syntactically the structures are no different from "normal" sentential complements, at least before extensive change occurs.

10. We should expect Berbice Dutch, for example, to exhibit extensive African

influence at all levels due to its early demographics. In interpreting the descriptions in Smith et al. 1987, and Robertson (this volume), where the initial contact largely involved just Ịjọ and Dutch, something very near a situation involving bilingualism probably ensued. As is usual under these conditions, the immediate linguistic result was likely similar to code switching where, in a simplification of the phenomenon, aspects of two languages combine to form a third different speech variety (such as occurs in the speech of the American Southwest where English-Spanish bilingualism is common). In any case, if conditions conducive to creolization then occurred after code switching had solidified as the descriptions suggest, many of the Ịjọ lexical items and patterns plausibly transferred to the resultant creole or creolelike speech. While Berbice Dutch is an extreme and would admit more specific African influence (i.e., Ịjọ) than other creoles with an extensive number of African substrate languages, still the point is made that the demographics of each creole is different and we could thereby expect different levels of substrate input.

## References


Baker, Mark. 1989. Object sharing and projection in serial verb constructions. *Linguistic Inquiry* 20.513–53.

Baker, Philip. 1982. *The contributions of non-Francophone immigrants to the lexicon of Mauritian Creole*. Ph.D. thesis, University of London.

Baker, Philip, and Anand Syea. 1991. On the copula in Mauritian Creole, past and present. In Byrne and Huebner, eds., 159–75.

Balmer, W. T., and F. C. F. Grant. 1929. *A grammar of the Fante-Akan language*. London: Atlantis Press.

Bickerton, Derek. 1984. The language bioprogram hypothesis. *Behavioral and Brain Sciences* 7.173–88.

———. 1986a. Beyond *Roots*: The five-year test. *Journal of Pidgin and Creole Languages* 1.225–32.

———. 1986b. Creoles and West African languages: A case of mistaken identity? In Muysken and Smith, eds., 25–40.

———. 1987. Foreword to *Grammatical relations in a radical creole: Verb complementation in Saramaccan*, by Francis Byrne, xi–xiv. Amsterdam: John Benjamins.

———. 1989. Seselwa serialization and its significance. *Journal of Pidgin and Creole Languages* 4.155–83.

Bickerton, Derek, and Sabine Iatridou. 1990. Verb serialization and empty categories. Unpublished manuscript.

Bresnan, Joan. 1982a. Control and complementation. *Linguistic Inquiry* 13.343–434.

———. 1982b. Polyadicity. *The mental representation of grammatical relations*, ed. by Joan Bresnan, 149–72. Cambridge, Mass.: MIT Press.

Byrne, Francis. 1982. *Algunos aspectos del saramacan*. Cumana, Venezuela: Universidad de Oriente.

———. 1983. Pidgin and creole languages: How, when, who, where, and why. *UDO Papers on Language* 1.23–48.

———. 1984. Instrumental in Saramaccan. *York Papers in Linguistics* 11.39–50.

———. 1985a. Language contact, creole languages, bilingualism and associated educational problems. Keynote lecture presented at the Ninth Annual Bilingual Summer Institute, University of Arizona, June 17, 1985.

———. 1985b. $pro_{prox}$ in Saramaccan. *Linguistic Inquiry* 16.313–20.

———. 1985c. The demographics of radical creolization. Lecture given at Indiana University, October 2, 1985.

———. 1986. Evidence against grammars without empty categories. *Linguistic Inquiry* 17.754–59.

———. 1987. *Grammatical relations in a radical creole: Verb complementation in Saramaccan*. Amsterdam: John Benjamins.

———. 1988a. Deixis as a noncomplementizer strategy for creole subordination marking. *Linguistics* 26.335–64.

———. 1988b. Serialization in Saramaccan. Paper presented at the Workshop on Serialization, Department of Linguistics, Southern Illinois University, April 1988.

———. 1988c. Towards a theory of theta-marking and creole depth. *Language change and contact: NWAV-XVI*, ed. by Kathleen Ferrara et al., 66–72. Texas Linguistics Forum 30. Austin: Department of Linguistics, University of Texas.

———. 1990. Tense scope and spreading in creole and West African serial verb constructions. Unpublished manuscript.

Byrne, Francis, and Thom Huebner, eds. 1991. *Development and structures of creole languages*. Amsterdam: John Benjamins.

Carden, Guy, and William Stewart. 1988. Binding theory, bioprogram and creolization: Evidence from Haitian Creole. *Journal of Pidgin and Creole Languages* 3.1–67.

Carlson, Greg N. 1983. Marking constituents. *Linguistic categories: Auxiliaries and related puzzles*. Volume 1. *Categories*, ed. by Frank Heny and Barry Richards, 69–98. Dordrecht: Reidel.

Caskey, Alexander, and Francis Byrne. 1989. Theta-marking, subjects, and finiteness in creole languages. Paper presented at the 1989 meeting of the Society for Pidgin and Creole Linguistics, Washington, D.C., December 28–29, 1989.

Chomsky, Noam. 1981. *Lectures on government and binding*. Dordrecht: Foris.

———. 1982. *Some concepts and consequences of the theory of government and binding*. Linguistic Inquiry Monograph no. 6. Cambridge, Mass.: MIT Press.

———. 1986. *Barriers*. Linguistic Inquiry Monograph no. 13. Cambridge, Mass.: MIT Press.

Faraclas, Nicholas. 1989. From old Guinea to Papua New Guinea. II: Tracing Niger-Congo influence in the development of Nigerian Pidgin. Paper presented at the Twentieth Conference on African Linguistics, University of Illinois, April 19–21.

Gazdar, Gerald, Ewan Klein, Geoffrey Pullum, and Ivan Sag. 1985. *Generalized phrase structure grammar*. Cambridge, Mass.: Harvard University Press.

Givón, Talmy. 1975. Serial verbs and syntactic change: Niger-Congo. *Word order and word order change*, ed. by Charles Li, 47–111. Austin: University of Texas Press.

Gordon, E. V. 1927. *Introduction to Old Norse*. Oxford: Oxford University Press.

Hancock, Ian. 1986. The domestic hypothesis, diffusion and componentiality: An account of Atlantic anglophone creole origins. In Muysken and Smith, eds., 71–102.

Hyman, Larry. 1975. On the change from SOV to SVO: Evidence from Niger-Congo. *Word order and word order change*, ed. by Charles Li, 114–46. Austin: University of Texas Press.

Jeffers, Robert, and Ilse Lehiste. 1979. *Principles and methods for historical linguistics*. Cambridge, Mass.: MIT Press.

Lasnik, Howard, and Juan Uriagereka. 1988. *A course in GB syntax*. Cambridge, Mass.: MIT Press.

Lefebvre, Claire. 1991. *Serial verbs: Grammatical, comparative, and cognitive approaches*, ed. by Claire Lefebvre, 37–78. Amsterdam: John Benjamins.

Lehiste, Ilse. 1988. *Lectures on language contact*. Cambridge, Mass.: MIT Press.

McCawley, James D. 1988. *The syntactic phenomena of English*. Volumes 1 and 2. Chicago: University of Chicago Press.

Mufwene, Salikoko S. 1986. The universalist and substrate hypothesis complement one another. In Muysken and Smith, eds., 129–62.

———. 1987. Pidginization/creolization: An evolutionary biology analogue. Lecture given at Northwestern University.

———. 1991. Pidgins, creoles, typology, and markedness. In Byrne and Huebner, eds., 123–43.

Mufwene, Salikoko, and Marta Dijkhoff. 1989. On the so-called infinitive in creoles. *Lingua* 77.319–52.

Muysken, Pieter, and Norval Smith. 1986. Introduction: Problems in the identification of substratum features in the creole languages. In Muysken and Smith, eds., 1–13.

———, eds. 1986. *Substrata versus universals in creole languages: Papers from the Amsterdam creole workshop*. Amsterdam: John Benjamins.

Muysken, Pieter, and Hein van der Voort. 1991. The binding theory and creolization: Evidence from 18th century Negerhollands reflexives. In Byrne and Huebner, eds., 145–58.

Radford, Andrew. 1988. *Transformational grammar: A first course*. Cambridge: Cambridge University Press.

Riemsdijk, Henk van, and Edwin Williams. 1986. *Introduction to the theory of grammar*. Cambridge, Mass.: MIT Press.

Sankoff, Gillian. 1991. Using the future to explain the past. In Byrne and Huebner, eds., 61–74.

Sebba, Mark. 1987. *The syntax of serial verbs: An investigation into serialisation in Sranan and other languages*. Amsterdam: John Benjamins.

Seuren, Pieter. 1985. Notes on the history and the syntax of Mauritian Creole. Unpublished manuscript, University of Nijmegen.

———. 1986. Predicate raising and semantic transparency in Mauritian Creole. *Essener Kolloquium über Kreolsprachen und Sprachkontakte, Beitrage zum 2*, ed. by Norbert Boretzky et al., 203–29. Bochum, Germany: Brockmeyer.

Smith, Norval, Ian Robertson, and Kay Williamson. 1987. The Ịjọ element in Berbice Dutch. *Language in Society* 16.49–90.

# Part Two

---

# *African Influence and Creole Genesis*

# The African Filter in the Genesis of Guadeloupean Creole: At the Confluence of Genetics and Typology

*Guy Hazaël-Massieux*

> And if most of the European grammatical structures in the creoles also have West African analogues this would suggest influence on the choice of those European grammatical features that do appear in the creoles (Baudet 1981).

The African phenotype is prominent among Guadeloupean speakers. In contrast with predominantly white communities such as those on Saint-Barthelemy, Les Saintes, Grands-Fonds de Sainte-Anne, and, to some extent, Désirade, most of the Guadeloupean population consists of blacks and mulattoes. However, Swadesh's (1952) lexicostatistic lists show that the basic lexicon of Guadeloupean Creole, as of other French-based creoles, is essentially French. Systematic research reveals that lexical Africanisms are limited to specific domains. The list of items is in fact comparable with those of Brazil or Puerto Rico. It is generally difficult to estimate the frequency of the items because dialectologists do not usually publish such information.

The contrast between French etymological data and those of creoles (spoken mostly by blacks) has led many creolists to assume that Africa, which seemed so discrete and almost invisible at the linguistic surface, must have provided an underlying substratum to creole. This assumption must, accordingly, account for differences between French and creole languages. Sylvain (1936)[1] summed up this substratist position adequately when she wrote that Haitian Creole is an Ewe language with a French lexicon. Her view is perpetuated today by the work of researchers, such as Lefebvre (1986), who claim that Haitian grammar is essentially African, especially Fon.

I do not deny African influence in the genesis of Guadeloupean Creole. It is actually very interesting to explore the argument Alleyne (1980) put forth in justifying the use of typological comparisons to infer genetic kinship, especially when history and anthropology suggest common origins or contacts between the compared items. But, as we are less informed about African languages and peoples than about the French ones at the time of the slave trade, I propose to begin by studying more systematically the available French data. Creolists have often attributed to the slaves all the forms which deviated from the contemporary standard French, simply because this deviance contrasted with the typically French character of the lexicon. We assume that lexical Africanisms are fairly extensive, but it seems more appropriate to examine the role of the linguistic filter of the African slaves in the makeup of the present creole than to speculate, without any precedent or model, about the deep structures which could be common to creole and African languages. Thus, it is plausible to assign the African slaves an active role in the genesis of Guadeloupean Creole. However, since the Africans must have selected from among alternative surface materials produced by French speakers under specific conditions, we must assess the shape of the original French input.

Filtering or selection concerns the pragmatic, perceptual, and interpretative levels of creolization. Pragmatic filtering allowed the selection of lexical items useful in meeting all common communicative needs of black and white inhabitants of seventeenth-century Guadeloupe; lexical Africanisms survived only in those particular domains where communication was primarily not interracial. The study of perceptual filtering establishes which elements of the phonetic form of linguistic communication were or could be perceived and retained by African slaves when they spoke with their French-speaking owners. As for interpretative filtering, we must see whether the patterns, structures, and schemes that the slaves heard were reanalyzed and reinterpreted to end in creole grammar. In doing so, we must assume three levels of reanalysis: norm, system, and linguistic type.

Coseriu (1966, 1967, 1970, 1983), who considers linguistic change as the development of a functional language, distinguishes four stages in the process: the adoption of new forms, their diffusion, a redistribution of old and new traditions, and mutation (i.e., discarding, conservation, or redeployment of items in one or more dialects).

The first contact language users in Guadeloupe are supposed to have had contacts of speech and norms; they had to communicate with and to take into account a very pregnant hierarchical authority in their working relations. Whenever they could, they overgeneralized the rules they were able to infer from the norm to which they were repeatedly exposed in the limited and stereotyped exchanges of the original *habitation* (i.e., colonial, family-size settlement). Whenever the part of the system they had inferred and overgeneralized coincided with some aspect of either their own system or their interlocutor's system, the rule was reinforced. However, if the inference proved wrong, they turned to more basic universal principles of language structure. If it is assumed that tendencies are only the diachronic expression of universals of language structure, one could think that a certain number of creole features are simply manifestations of these universals, which were shared by the types in contact. References to lost heritage then regard not only those features that were not shared by the languages in contact but also those that were incompatible with the emerging system. (I am assuming here the kinds of implicative universals proposed by Greenberg 1966, e.g., regarding constituent order.)

One could thus imagine that elements could have been retained, because from the stage of speech or norm contacts they were accepted or integrated, either by necessity (a consequence of a violent and dominating society) or because the speakers believed they recognized some patterns as corresponding to their own or interpreted them satisfactorily under the circumstances. In the latter category fall primarily lexical items, which need not have been analyzed and were adopted simply as words, or *lexies,* capable of forming sentences.

Kihm (1987a) emphasizes the frequent and uncertain character of this type of convergence. A case in point here is the interpretation of *nu* in the Port-au-Prince variety of Haitian Creole both as a first-person plural pronoun and as a second-person plural pronoun. Taylor (1977) attributes this reinterpretation to Twi or Igbo influence, which accounts for the dual value of *nu*. Actually, "normal" languages are not unidimensional; as Coseriu (1966:208) suggests, they constitute diasystems with a complex architecture.

Even in situations of limited contacts, speakers are best understood relative to their own communities; they often use expressions which might be peripheral in their own systems but whose importance may have been hypertrophied in the particular context of creole colonies. These expressions may have served as models and thus have been overgeneralized. The first consequence quite naturally would have been the creation of a unidimensional language. Bickerton (1981) characterizes Hawaiian Pidgin English as lacking anaphoric and emphatic devices as well as a regular word order. Except for the last feature, the system seems to be very close to the unidimensional language discussed here. Even though it may remain a long time in complementary distribution with other languages, it rapidly becomes relatively regular and, if not rational (as Hjelmslev 1938 says), optimized. Creole exists when the overgeneralizations tested in the exchange form paradigms accepted by speakers of different origins. They need not have the same forms; it is enough that they have a system of correspondences which ensure mutual intelligibility (more or less approximative) and thus a system which tolerates doublets; for example, the alternation of *pou/ba* observed in the French creole of Trinidad (Aub-Buscher 1976).

It is obvious that creole languages developed in situations in which slaves (or their children) could have had only a reduced *input* as a model. But Alleyne (1980) rightly disputes the thesis that the lexifier's system was deliberately reduced by its speakers, arguing that the colonists used all the resources of their language, as evidenced by fossils of inflections on some creole words. It is thus necessary to identify the language which was genuinely recognized by the slaves or their children before studying the effects of filtering or selection.

I will examine the filter effect by going from the periphery to the center; that is, by following (as much as possible) the order of understanding, if not of the learning, of French by the Amerindians and the Africans of the first colonization. The starting point must thus be the signifier, which is the object of the first reinterpretation.

On the phonetic plane, Guadeloupean Creole appears to contain a variety of popular French from the north and west Atlantic regions of France in the seventeenth century; the same may be claimed of almost all French creoles. Exceptions are only apparent and do not contradict this general statement. The presence of closed nasal vowels in Haitian seems limited to a specific domain of the vocabulary (as in the voodoo words *houngan,* and *houmfo*). The opposition is otherwise not significant, as in the variants of the indefinite article *you/youn*); in any case, this alternation seems to be the same as that in late sixteenth-century French in words such as *voisine* and *voisaine*. The sporadic attestations of /ŋ/ in Indian Ocean creoles may be accounted for in a similar manner, even when it appears in words of non-French origin. The French nouns *Garonne/Gironde* and *Coulommiers/Colombier* differ etymologically in whether the voiced plosive is pronounced by its speakers after a nasal consonant.

Overall, the list of consonants only merits attention on one or two points: the maintenance (and perhaps reinforcement) of /h/ in Normandy French, and the evolution of /r/, which was apicodental in the seventeenth century but posterior in both modern French and creole. At some time the opposition between /š/ and /s/ before /j/ was for many speakers no more relevant than the opposition between /v/ and /b/. The assumption that the basilect is more authentic when it deviates most from today's (standard) French is an old one, for, as is evident from Mongin (1984), both *boudou* and *voudou* were attested in 1682. (However, only *vlé* 'want' was then used, never **blé* or **βlé*.) It can be concluded from this that the French consonantal system did not appear to be excessively marked for Amerindian and African listeners.

As for the vocalic system, the question arises of whether only one system is at work here. In Hazaël-Massieux (1972) I assumed a variable system—the maximal realization of which would more or less coincide with one of the French varieties—with twelve distinctions. Minimally, the system has ten vowels, three of which are nasal. Accordingly, I assumed that certain features of the French system were not consistently accessible, which may account for the confusion of palatalization with lip rounding. In the minimal system the only vowels which systematically disappear are the rounded oral or nasal palatals. The most systematically absent is, of course, the rounded nasal palatal, which has been threatened for a long time in French, as much for systemic as for geolectal reasons. (The opposition between /ɛ̃/ and /œ̃/ is marked and physiologically difficult to maintain, because the wider the mouth is opened, the less it can be rounded; from the time of Middle Picard, /ɛ̃/ has been used for /œ̃/ and is the main form today in Parisian usage.)

As for the other rounded palatals, the orals, they have survived in various ways. However, if we were to refer to the peasants whom Molière (1665)[2] portrays in *Dom Juan*, the closed vowel /y/, which for a time appeared to be the realization of all the other rounded palatals, has tended to lose its roundedness since the time of popular French. One can therefore assume that the creole reinterpretation of /y/ as /i/ does not raise any particular problems. Noteworthy is the degree of aperture, which one could have thought to be marked between /ɔ/ and /o/ or between /ɛ/ and /e/. This seems to have been reinforced in the sense that the distribution of /ɔ/ in Guadeloupean Creole is wider and more stable than in current standard French.

The most significant aspects of the African filter regard syllabification. French, on the whole, allows syllables of the following types: V, CV, CCV, CCCV, VC, VCC, VCCC, VCCCC (cf. *hie* 'rammer,' *si* 'if,' *tri* 'sorting,' *strie* 'scratch,' *as* 'ace,' *halte* 'halt,' *arbre* 'tree,' *[d]extre* 'right hand'). All the syllables possible in Guadeloupean Creole are included in this list. However, even taking into account the most acrolectal variants of this creole, some syllabic patterns are always excluded. In word-initial position, consonant clusters are broken by either vocalic prosthesis or epenthesis, for example, *istilo* 'fountain pen,' *estati* 'statue,' *ispo* 'sport.' In final position, the tendency, which is also attested in popular French (now, at the relevant contact stage), is to reduce consonant clusters to single consonants. Consonant clusters are thus allowed only word medially. It may be argued, quite plausibly, that this reduction, going in the direction of being less marked, was triggered or favored by the convergence of preferred syllabic structure in popular French and in African and Amerindian languages. In any case, two special phenomena must be noted: in older

Guadeloupean Creole, there are forms such as *endé, glinsé,* and *dempi* for *aider* 'help,' *glisser* 'slide,' and *depuis* 'since.' Two explanations are conceivable. On the one hand, there are dialectal precedents in French, although it may be argued that the nasalized variants are infrequent and that the French system itself would have disfavored them. On the other hand, the realization may be attributed to African languages of the Slave Coast. It is undoubtedly in the same manner that we must account for the regressive nasalization in Guadeloupean Creole. The principal evidence for this lies in the form of the first-person singular pronoun *mwen* ‹ /mwe/ for *moi,* which coexists with its cognate *amwé* ‹ *à moi* 'help.' In contrast to the Seychelles, Martinique, and Haiti, where this phenomenon is more or less generalized, in Guadeloupe French speakers must have nasalized the vowel only sporadically.

Another significant fact is that for continuous nasal resonance of different pitches (as in *ˀõˀõ* 'no' in contrast with *hõhõ* 'yes'), tonal pitch other than intonation contour in a sentence is not typical of Guadeloupean Creole. According to Daniel Hirst (personal communication), these nasal productions could potentially be interpreted beyond all linguistic boundaries, while the lexical distinctions by the use of intonation seem to constitute a distinct mark even more incompatible with French. Note that creole accentuation, which does not imply the phenomenon of liaison (typical of French), applies to phrases rather than words.

Finally, Guadeloupean Creole has no vowel length contrast. This development may also be observed in the French lexifier itself, where length only serves to identify the syllable which has the tonic accent, that is, the last of the functional group.

The canonical form of French words is two syllables, and the erudite words which came into familiar use are drawn into this: *métro* 'underground railway,' *ciné/cinéma* 'movies,' *télé* 'television,' *radio* 'radio,' *vélo* 'bicycle,' *moto* 'motorcycle,' *cibiche* 'cigarette,' etc. Insofar as lexical words are concerned, creole seems to conform to this tendency. However, as the phonetic word retained is often the result of agglutination of the substantive and the French article, there can be various aphaereses or elisions which, while preserving the tonic syllable, delete some pretonics (and possibly the article itself). The rule actually applies to all unstressed syllables, thus in some cases it affects conjoined pronouns and auxiliary verbs when these are not stressed.

Thanks to this latter point we can now discuss the morphology of French creoles. False breaks must especially be taken into account here, since some components lose their accentual autonomy in a phrase and thus leave out cues which in isolation help identify word-boundary structures. Grammatical words (prepositions, auxiliary verbs) become especially difficult to recognize because they are unaccented. Being rather redundant in that their precise interpretation generally depends on the syntactic context of their use, they have often not been adequately identified. In spite of their high textual frequency, their semantic bleaching—compounded with the fact that they are normally used unaccented—has greatly minimized the potential to perceive their grammatical function in French. A consequence of this situation has been the reduction of lexical categories (i.e., parts of speech) in Guadeloupean Creole.

Arbitrariness and cross-systemic variation in the allocation of grammatical functions to morphemes have contributed to the failure to recognize the French grammatical morphemes. As noted by linguists such as Coseriu, there is less variation in the way experience is divided up by lexical morphemes; there must even be some universals in this area so that the most frequently shared experiences in the early contact exchanges were designated by the same words. Some of the same lexical morphemes have been extended in their use to assume grammatical functions in addition to their lexical functions. Linguists have often invoked changes in lexical categories in creole syntax (see, e.g., Stein 1984). From the inception of creoles, sentences have undoubtedly been limited to units that can be characterized as accented and lexical. This restructuring is consistent with Ludtke's (1986) observation that it is usually possible to convey grammatical meaning lexically, whereas the reverse is not true.

It is thus not surprising that in French creoles, unstressed atonic pronouns have disappeared without a trace and have been replaced by tonic forms which, having a contrastive value in addition, have taken up the grammatical function of the atonic pronouns. Likewise, French articles have either disappeared or agglutinated partially or totally to the noun; for example, *nom* ‹ *un homme* 'a man' (with deletion of the initial vowel), *lamè* ‹ *la mer* 'ocean.' They are in any case no longer functional. This departure from the French system must have been helped in part by the fact that in French, gender distinctions for the definite article were already eroded by the process of elision. In the Picard variety, the feminine form has the same phonetic realization as the French masculine. It is also noteworthy that quite early, French had recourse to a numeral for its indefinite article. All early evidence gives the form /ñõ/ written as *gnon* or *yon,* to which the accentuated form we find in today's creole *nyon* is obviously related. French has also had recourse to a deictic to reinforce the definite determiner *ce/che/he . . . la*. Being in phrase-final position, the deictic has normally been accented. Given the weakening of grammatical morphemes discussed above, only the phrase-final deictic was perceived and thus preserved in creole grammar.

In predicative phrases, the copula, like unaccented auxiliary verbs, has also disappeared. For many original creole speakers the French copula corresponded functionally to nothing in their own African languages, which explains further why, being atonic and semantically empty, it was generally not perceived. On the other hand, tense inflections on French verbs were correctly perceived, in part because they occur where word stress normally occurs and in part because they are not semantically empty. This explains why some verbs were selected in their inflected forms, for example, *vlé* < *vouloir* 'want'; *pé* < *peut* 'can, may'; *fo* < *faut* 'should, have to, must'; *fodré* < *faudrait* 'should, have to, must'; *té* < *était* 'been'; *sra* < *sera* 'will be'; *sré* < *serait* 'would be'; *alé* < *aller* 'gone.' When the same form alternated between basic denotative and grammatical usage, it was sometimes replaced by an alternative form in one of its functions. Thus, in the possession function, *avoir* 'have' has been replaced by *tenir* and *gagner,* as may be observed in the following sentence from Father Labat (1742): *Compère, toy tenir tafia?* 'Old fellow, do you have some rum?' Allomorphs of the verb *aller* have specialized so that *va* has taken up the grammatical function of future marker and *alé* has only the denotative function.

The fate of prepositions is equally interesting. The French preposition de, which in rapid speech is reduced to /d/, totally disappears from early texts. On the other hand, *à,* which is not longer but, as a vocalic item, is more audible, seems to have been more fortunate since very early on; Guadeloupean Creole has extended its usage to express possession in addition to its locative function. A careful examination, however, reveals that this creole development also has a precedent in French, in which *à* is used for both functions, though the possessive one is discouraged nowadays in standard French. This must have contributed to the selection of *à* over *de,* which is used as a possessive marker but not as a locative one. The functions of the preposition *à* were thus identified with those of similar markers in the slaves' languages: *na, la, là.* If we consider the usage of *la* in Guiana today, it is not impossible that *a* was interpreted as a variant of the locative deictic *là,* which, as noted above, is normally stressed. Prepositions which in French specify the syntactic relation of some verbs to their objects disappeared in the first formative stage simply because they were redundant in a way. In some cases, especially those involving double objects, it was assumed that a secondary predication was involved in the sentence. A second verb was then used in the predicate phrase, thus producing serial verb constructions. The only other prepositions and conjunctions that have been retained in creole are disyllabic, including those where any adverb reinforces *et* or *ou: ouben* < *ou* 'or'; *épi* < *puis* 'and, then'; *èvè* < *avec* 'with.'

As suggested above (see also Kihm 1987a, 1987b), chance similarity of form and function may contribute to the selection of a form from the lexifier. This was particularly obvious in the case of the preposition *à* with its creole variants *na/a* and of the pronominal *nu* (‹ French *nous*), which is used in Haitian Creole for both first- and second-person plural. Coincidence could even include whole phrases, such as *nan bouk* [nãbuk] ‹ *au bourg/dans le bourg* 'in town,' which may be related to Bantu clauses, as in *na mbóka* (of the same meaning) in Lingala. Recall that universals only make up for the deficiencies of the perceived input. With regard to constituent order, the position of definite and indefinite articles in Guadeloupean Creole cannot be verified by referring to universals only. Contrary to what is implied by the Greenberg (1966) method, it is striking that while the indefinite article is anteposed, as in French, the definite article is postposed instead. Though not quite French, this particular choice may not be in conflict with the Romance type. It is attested in Romanian and in Spanish (*el libro aquel*), and French itself has an occasionally postposed possessive pronoun, as in *ce livre mien* 'this book of mine.'[3] However, French does not use this order unless the postposed determiner is stress-bearing, as in the case of *mien,* which may also be used anaphorically. It could therefore be argued that the postposition of the definite article in Guadeloupean Creole was partly favored by French itself, which allows a similar construction. The fact that mostly tonic grammatical forms were selected seems to have favored the selection of a postposed definite article. Nonetheless, this hypothesis does not rule out the possibility that the structural options of some African languages, such as Ewe (Sylvain 1936), may have contributed to favoring the selection of a postposed definite article in Guadeloupean.

It seems to me that these principles of lexical pattern retention, in which perceptibility, stress, and semantic content are all significant, account adequately for other morphosyntactic features. Take, for instance, the postverbal position of the negator. It is noteworthy that Guadeloupean Creole has selected the stressed part of the French correlative negator *ne . . . pas*. Besides, this is not a creole innovation; it is an early popular French feature, evidenced by the following sentence from Jean de la Fontaine: *Fit-il pas mieux que de se plaindre?* 'Didn't he do better than complain?' The morpheme *pa,* which in French constructions with a copula or an auxiliary verb precedes the lexical predicative element, is used in exactly the same position in creole. As to why the negator precedes tense, mood, and aspect markers, it is possible that the latter were incorporated into the creole system after the former; this position of the negator may thus be attributed to rule overgeneralization.

Evidence suggests, however, that the position itself has not always been so fixed. In Ducoeurjoly (1802) the construction *té pas là* 'was not there' is attested instead of the modern sequence *pas té là*. Chaudenson (1973) has observed that the negator does not co-occur with the future marker *va*. (In Haitian Creole, which has a negative future *p[a]-ap,* the future marker itself is no longer *va* but *ap*.) The explanation for this situation may also be found in French itself, in which the form *va* requires the postposition of *pa*. For the same reason, *pa* follows the verb *vé* in all French creoles of the West Indies, as in the idiom *Ki ou vlé, ki ou vé pa* 'Whether you want or not.' The inflected forms *veux* and *voulez* require a postposed *pas*. The same explanation holds for why *pa* sometimes follows *pé* 'can/may,' as in *pé pa di ou* versus *an pa pé di ou sa* 'I cannot tell you that' versus 'I could not tell you that.'

Two other cases can be explained through filtering. It is well known that the number of certain lexical Africanisms is very limited in comparison with the demographic significance of Africans in the New World's population. Several factors may, however, account for this situation. Whenever a new instrument was introduced, a new term was adopted to distinguish it from the old one. If there was no French term for it, an African term was often adopted. The Africans brought with them to the New World knowledge, techniques, and tools which were novel to Europeans. The African words associated with these survived, especially in the domains of cooking, ethnomedicine, sorcery, religion, dance, and individual and private activities over which the masters had very little control. For instance, Josephau (1977) lists the following words: *gongonné* 'grumble'; *bigidi* 'start'; *akra* 'fritter'; *koko* 'coconut, testicles'; *zonzonné* 'irritate'; *woklo* 'mythological West African dwarf' (a prototype of rigidity); *kyololo* 'any light decoction'; *bèlè* 'drum, drum music'; *gwoka* 'drum'; *kalenda* 'old dance of African origin'; *lélé* 'stir'; *bòbò* 'whore,' etc. As the realities denoted by these words became the common knowledge of the whole of Guadeloupean society, they stopped being considered African words. Whites and blacks eating the same dishes, going to sleep with the same bedtime lullabies, and using the same bonesetters or witch doctors used the same lexical items. Some of these terms have alternates, for example, *kyou* 'ass' alternates with *bonda*. In other cases the words have remained confined to groups of black peasants; for example, *koko* 'calabash, eyeball'; *wanga* 'charm' (instead of *kenbwa*). Turiault (1874–77) distinguishes between "parler nègre" and "parler créole," which is consistent with the thesis that these terms must be of African origin.

On the pragmatic plane, we should remember that filtering could be said to be concurrent with interaction in plantation society. Indeed, in the beginning the slaves and other foreign speakers in general were exposed only to neighborhood communication of an oral type, immediately useful, hardly corrected, and unified by the "jargon" of catechism, which was itself based on the slaves' speech patterns. The French speakers were often poorly educated, as evidenced by the registers of the Catholic church. They were dialectal speakers at the height of their linguistic insecurity when they had to communicate with clerks or representatives of authority. We can assume that the model given to the slaves must have been relatively limited (utilitarian, hierarchical communication), popular (insofar as registers and stylistic levels are concerned), allusive (being oral in the appropriate contextual place), unstable (following the use of various dialectal forms), approximative (from the social and ethnic heterogeneity), and archaic (because of the important role of old settlers—*vieux-habitants*—cut off from the mother country for dozens of years).

Sticking to Coseriu's model of linguistic change presented above, I have tried to identify how selection procedures appear to have played a particularly important role in the formation of Guadeloupean and other French creoles. One could continue this research and verify how mutation, which consists of abandoning, retaining, or redistributing forms available to speakers, took place in the formation of these creoles. But this should be the subject of another research project. Nor am I going to address here the question of how these new languages rapidly became languages like any other with perhaps simply less architectural complexity; diglossia has handicapped the development of registers, stylistic levels, and lects (which I have proposed elsewhere to call, after Coseriu, "*langues fonctionnelles*"). One of the most important stages in the development of French creoles must have been the development of a class of unstressed grammatical morphemes, such as *yon*/*on* 'one/a'; *kalé* 'to be going, going'; *mwen*/*an* 'I, me'; *li*/*i* 'he, she, it'; *ba'mwen* 'for me' versus *ba mwen*/*bã* (‹ *ba ã*) 'give me.'

This study remains incomplete, especially because there is inadequate information about the structure of specific linguistic varieties that were in contact in Guadeloupe in the seventeenth and eighteenth centuries. I have nonetheless tried to show the role of filtering or selection in the formation of Guadeloupean Creole. Although the bulk of lexical material out of which this creole and others were made came from French, some principles seem to have determined which lexical items would find their way into the new languages, how they would be interpreted, and how they would be used in sentences. No useful purpose would be served in simply trying to identify common features in words between creoles and this or that African language for which we could not prove the relevant role at a relevant moment, compared with the French language.

In discussing creolization, it must be borne in mind that we are dealing with people who speak and wind up communicating with each other. It is pointless to draw up a list of universals without noting that linguistic activity itself is the first universal condition in verbal communication. The need and attempts to communicate established a realistic balance of linguistic forces between slaves and masters which made it possible to foster a new set of linguistic forms and functions. It may be helpful to liken the initial attempts by slaves to communicate with their masters and among themselves to learning to walk. A sequence of failures and more successful approximations is involved in both. While current steps fall into a paradigm with previous ones, they also differ somewhat, becoming more efficient and ready for more complex maneuvers. All of this involves some sort of experimenting. With regard to creolization, we just must bear in mind that we are dealing with communication, not communion.

## Notes

1. Sylvain's conclusion was: "En somme la principale différence du créole d'avec ces langues réside dans son système de numération. Nous sommes en présence d'un français coulé dans le moule de la syntaxe africaine ou, comme on classe généralement les langues d'après leur parenté syntaxique, d'une langue éwé à vocabulaire français" (1936:178). Curiously, no evidence is presented to support the suggestive syntactic kinship. A contemporary of Sylvain, Antoine Meillet, a historical linguist, wrote (1948) that it would be almost impossible to classify a mixed language without a word morphology, if there was such a language. After him, Haudry (1973) emphasized the difficulty in reconstructing grammatical devices, because they are replaced too quickly. How would we build again the Latin future forms if we had only Romance forms without classical attestations? Alleyne (1980) suggested an interesting answer when, as did Benveniste (1966:107), he examined the conditions under which it was possible to draw genetic conclusions from typological data.

2. Many documents, such as "Les agréables conférences de deux paysans de St-Ouen," or "La gente Poitevinerie," or the dialectal poems from Liège published by Jean Haust, reveal the frequency of all these features.

3. The following quotations support my observations: "En évitant que les loups d'aventure De mon corps tien ne feïssent leur pasture" (Marot 1968:138); "O fleuve mien!" (Du Bellay 1904:83).

## References

Alleyne, Mervyn C. 1980. *Comparative Afro-American: An historical study of English-based Afro-American dialects of the New World*. Ann Arbor: Karoma.

Aub-Buscher, Gertrud. 1976. A propos de quelques rapports prépositionnels en créole. *Actes du Treizième Congrès International de Linguistique et Philologie Romanes*, ed. by Marcel Boudreault and Frank Möhren, 1091–99, 1209–48. Laval, Quebec: Presses de l'Université de Laval.

Baudet, Martha M. 1981. Identifying the African grammatical base of the Caribbean Creoles: A typological approach. *Historicity and variations in creole studies*, ed. by Arnold Highfield and Albert Valdman, 104–17. Ann Arbor: Karoma.

Baudot, Paul Fleurus. 1923. *Oeuvres créoles de Paul Baudot*. Traduction et préface de Maurice Martin. Basse-Terre: Imprimerie du Gouvernement.

du Bellay, Joachim. 1904. *Oeuvres poétiques*, ed. by H. Chamard. Paris: Société des Textes Français Modernes.

Benveniste, Emile. 1966. "Structure" en linguistique. *Problème de linguistique générale*, ed. by Benveniste, 91–118. Paris: Gallimard, Bibliothèque des Sciences Humaines.

Bickerton, Derek. 1981. *Roots of language*. Ann Arbor: Karoma.

Céllier, Pierre. 1988. Evolution et mutation linguistique: De la copule en français aux créoles de l'océan Indien. *Etudes Créoles* 10.29–59.

Chaudenson, Robert. 1973. Pour une étude comparée des créoles et des parlers français d'outre-mer: survivance et innovation. *Revue de Linguistique Romane* 37.147–48, 342–71.

Chevillard, R. P. André. 1659. *Les desseins de son Eminence de Richelieu pour l'Amérique*. Rennes: Jean Durand.

Coseriu, Eugenio. 1966. Structures lexicales et enseignement du vocabulaire. *Actes du Premier Colloque International de linguistique appliquée*, 175–252. Nancy: Editions du Conseil de l'Europe.

———. 1967. Sistema, norma y habla. *Teoria del lenguaje y lingüística general*, ed. by E. Coseriu, 11–113. Madrid: Editorial Gredos, Biblioteca romanica hispanica.

———. 1970. Les universaux linguistiques (et les autres). Paper presented at the Eleventh International Congress of Linguists, Bologna.

———. 1983. Linguistic change does not exist. *Linguistica Nuova ed Antica* 1.51–63.

Ducoeurjoly, S. J. 1802. *Manuel des habitans de Saint-Domingue* . . . 2 vols. Paris: Lenoir.

Greenberg, Joseph. 1966. *Universals of language*. Second edition. Cambridge, Mass.: MIT Press.

Haudry, Jean. 1973. Parataxe, hypotaxe et correlation dans la phrase latine. *Bulletin de la Société Linguistique de Paris* 68.147–86.

Hazaël-Massieux, Guy. 1972. Phonologie et phonétique du créole de la Guadeloupe. Thèse de troisième cycle de l'Université de Paris III.

Hjelmslev, Louis. 1938. Relations de parenté des langues créoles. *Revue des Etudes Indo-Européennes* 2.271–86.

Josephau, Serge. 1977. Africanismes dans le créole: quelques aspects du patrimoine culturel des Antilles. Paper presented at Conférence du Centre Départemental de Documentation Pédagogique, Fort-de-France, Martinique.

Kihm, Alain. 1987a. La créolisation comme filtrage. *S'approprier une langue étrangère . . . : Actes du Seizième Colloque International "Acquisition d'une langue étrangère. perspectives et recherches,"* ed. by H. Blanc, M. Le Douaron, and D. Véronique, 290–95. Paris: Didier-Erudition, Collection le Linguiste no. 20.

———. 1987b. La matière du contact: pour un modèle lexicaliste des recontres linguistiques. Paper presented at "Contacts de langues: quels modèles?" Nice.

Labat, R. P. Jean-Baptiste. 1742. *Nouveau voyage aux Isles de l'Amérique*. Paris: J.-B. Delespine.

La Fontaine, Jean de. 1929. *Fables*. New edition by R. Radouant. Paris: Hachette. [See, e.g., "Le renard et les raisins."]

Lefebvre, Claire. 1986. Relexification in creole genesis revisited: The case of Haitian Creole. *Substrata versus universals in creole genesis*, ed. by Pieter Muysken and Norval Smith, 279–300. Amsterdam: John Benjamins.

Lüdke, Helmut. 1986. Esquisse d'une théorie du changement langagier. *La Linguistique* 22. 3–46.

Marbot, François-Achille. 1931. *Les Bambous, fables de La Fontaine, travesties en patois martiniquais par un vieux commandeur, édition revue et augmentée d'une notice littéraire et d'une traduction en français, par Louis Jaham-Desrivaux*. Paris: J. Peyronnet et Cie.

Marot, Clément. 1868. *Oeuvres complètes*, ed. by P. Jannet. Paris: E. Picard.

Meillet, Antoine. 1948. *Linguistique historique et linguistique générale*. Paris and Geneva: Champion and Slatkine.

Molière, Jean Baptiste. Poquelin dit. 1665. *Dom Juan ou le festin de pierre, comédie en 5 actes*. Paris: Collection "Classiques Larousse." [See particularly Act 2.]

Mongin, R. P. Jean. 1984. Lettres. *Bulletin de la Société d'Histoire de la Guadeloupe* 61 and 62.

Poyen-Bellisle, René de. 1894. *Les sons et les formes du créole dans les Antilles*. Baltimore: John Murphy.

Stein, Peter. 1984. *Kreolisch und Französisch*. Tübingen: Max Niemeyer Verlag, Romanistische Arbeitshefte.

Swadesh, Morris. 1952. Lexicostatistic dating of prehistoric ethnic contacts. *Proceedings of the American Philosophical Society* 96.452–63.

Sylvain, Suzanne. 1936. *Le créole haïtien: morphologie et syntaxe*. Wetteren, Belgium: Imprimerie De Meester; Port-au-Prince: chez l'auteur.

Taylor, Douglas Rae. 1977. *Languages of the West Indies*. Baltimore: Johns Hopkins University Press.

Turiault, Jean. 1874–77. Etudes sur le créole de la Martinique. *Bulletin de la Société Académique de Brest*, 2 series: 1.401–516; 3.1–111.

# Assessing the African Contribution to French-Based Creoles

*Philip Baker*

In order to begin to assess the African contribution to French-based creoles, it is first necessary to know something of the ethnolinguistic background of the people who were taken from Africa to work as slaves in plantation societies under French control. First, I summarize the available information. Words of African origin in twelve[1] French-based creoles are discussed in the following section. Eight of these are spoken in the Americas in what I will refer to as the Caribbean area: Louisiana, Haiti, Guadeloupe, Dominica, Martinique, St. Lucia, Trinidad, and Guyane Française. The remaining four are spoken in Indian Ocean territories: Reunion, Mauritius, Rodrigues, and the Seychelles. Three lists of words of African origin found in the creole languages of these territories, containing 251 items in all, are set out in appendix 1. Finally I discuss the difficulties of assessing the African contribution to the grammars of the French-based creoles. This section is followed by some concluding remarks.

## Africans in Colonial French Territories

Very little is known about the Africans taken to French territories in the Caribbean area before 1711. In Martinique and Guadeloupe, the first Africans were introduced soon after 1650. The number of slaves in Martinique had reached 14,600 by 1700, while in Guadeloupe there were 9,700 slaves by 1710 (Curtin 1969:78). The French occupation of Haiti began with Ile de la Tortue off the northern coast. The total population of 6,648 there in 1681 included 2,102 slaves, of whom 314 were children (Ministère de la France d'Outre-Mer [FOM] $G^1$ 509). By 1715 the population of Haiti included 30,653 slaves, of whom 7,826 were children (FOM $G^1$ 509), indicating that Africans had been introduced on a substantial scale in the intervening period. Small numbers of Africans were taken to Guyane Française in the second half of the seventeenth century, but they totaled only 1,400 by 1698 (Curtin 1969:78). There do not appear to have been any slaves in Louisiana before about 1718.

Although little is known of the origins of the Africans taken to these territories in the seventeenth century, the available information indicates that at least four major groups of languages were represented: West Atlantic and Manding from Senegambia, Kwa from Ghana to Nigeria, and Bantu from the Congo-Angola area. From 1711 onward, rather more is known. However, as this is discussed in some detail by Singler (in this volume), I will merely summarize the main facts as they concern the groups of languages likely to have contributed to the French-based creoles of the Caribbean area, basing my figures on table 49 from Curtin (1969:170) unless otherwise indicated. Note that these figures relate exclusively to slaves taken from Africa by the French and ignore African slaves purchased in the Caribbean area from other European nations engaged in the slave trade.[2]

Curtin (1969) distinguishes eight geographical source areas: Senegambia, Sierra Leone, Windward Coast, Gold Coast, Bight of Benin, Bight of Biafra, Angola, and Mozambique. Africans from Senegambia included speakers of both West Atlantic (notably Wolof and Fulfulde) and Manding languages (including Mandinka and Bamana, the latter better known as "Bambara"). More than a fifth of French slave exports in 1711–20 were from Senegambia, but the proportion fell thereafter and amounted to only 8.1% for the period 1711–1800 as a whole. Both West Atlantic (Temne) and Manding languages (Mende) are likely to have been represented among slaves from Sierra Leone, but this was a minor source for the French and amounted to only 0.9% for the whole period 1711–1800. Although the people living along the Windward Coast (Liberia) are overwhelmingly speakers of Kru languages, Singler (this volume) indicates that by far the greater part of the slaves embarked by the French there were speakers of Manding languages who had been brought from some considerable distance inland. Curtin (1969) indicates that the Windward Coast was the single most important source of slaves obtained by the French in the half century to 1760 but not thereafter, with the result that their proportion for the period 1711–1800 was only 16.8%. If, in order to obtain some fairly crude estimate of the proportion of speakers of particular groups of languages who were taken to the French Caribbean area, it is assumed that four out of five slaves embarked at the Windward Coast were speakers of Manding languages, and this is added to the figures for Senegambia and Sierra Leone, a combined total of 22.4% is reached for West Atlantic and Manding languages; while separate figures for these two are not calculable, it is clear that the latter would have been the better represented.

Kwa languages are dominant in both the former Gold Coast (mainly Akan languages but also Ewe) and the Bight of Benin (Ewe, Fon, etc., and the more loosely related Yoruba and Igbo). Together these areas provided 33.8% of French slave exports from 1711 to 1800, with the proportion remaining fairly constant throughout that period. Kwa languages are also spoken, though only by a minority, in the Bight of Biafra area. According to Curtin's table 49 (1969:170), this area was a source for the French only from 1781, accounting for just 1.8% of the total in the period 1711–1800. If, in order to obtain a rough indication of the proportion of speakers of Kwa languages among slaves exported by the French in the eighteenth century, it is assumed that they included one-third of those from the Bight of Biafra (i.e., 0.6%), this, added to the 33.8% from the Gold Coast and the Bight of Benin, gives a total of 34.4%.

The two remaining areas, Angola and Mozambique, are both situated in Bantu Africa. In sharp contrast to West Africa, Bantu Africa presents an almost unbroken chain of closely related speech varieties, and adjacent Bantu languages generally have 70% or more shared cognates (David Dalby, personal communication). In the period 1711–1800, the proportion of French slave exports from Angola increased steadily from 6.9% of the total in the first decade to 65.1% in the last, accounting for 35.8% for the period as a whole. For geographical reasons, Mozambique was only a minor source for the French Caribbean territories, amounting to 1.1% in all. The total for speakers of Bantu languages is thus 36.9%.

The French also obtained slaves from both West and East Africa for their Indian Ocean islands, where French-based creoles are spoken today. In order to complete the picture, I will briefly summarize the details of their peopling, drawing on figures from Chaudenson (1974) and Baker (1982a, 1982b). Though occupied from 1663, there is no mention of any African in Reunion until the census of 1704. Of the 209 foreign-born slaves whose presence was then noted, 36 were described as "caffres" (origin uncertain), 10 as being from "Guinée,"[3] 6 as being from Mozambique, and one as "More."[4] The remaining three quarters were Indians or Malagasies. (For the purposes of this paper, Malagasies, speakers of an Austronesian language, are not regarded as Africans.)[5] For the next twenty-five years most slaves arriving in Reunion were Malagasies. Meanwhile the settlement of Mauritius began in 1721 at a far more rapid pace. By the end of 1735, the 1,450 slaves in Mauritius comprised 36% from Senegambia, 33% from Madagascar, 19% from India, and 12% from the Slave Coast. In the four years to 1740 Mauritius and Reunion together received 2,429 slaves of whom 50% were from Madagascar, 29% were from Mozambique, 13% were from West Africa, and 8% were from India. Thereafter arrivals from West Africa were sporadic and ceased altogether in 1767, but a small trickle of Indian slaves continued to arrive up to 1794. The proportion of slaves arriving from Mozambique increased steadily, taking over from Madagascar as the principal source by 1765 and outnumbering Malagasy arrivals by nine to one in the period 1773–94 when by far the greatest number of slaves reached these islands. Of the other islands, Rodrigues was settled exclusively from Mauritius while the Seychelles were peopled in the early years from both Mauritius and Reunion. Following the abolition of slavery, however, substantial numbers of "rescued slaves" were "liberated" in the Seychelles. The latter were overwhelmingly Bantu and formed at least one-third of the population of the Seychelles in the latter part of the nineteenth century.

## The African Contribution to the Lexicons of French-Based Creoles

This section draws on material collected for the forthcoming *Dictionnaire étymologique des créoles*, a project based at Bamberg University under the direction of Annegret Bollée. I have incorporated fieldwork conducted by members of the project team, but more particularly I have relied on a range of published and unpublished sources, only the most important of which are listed in the References. One little-known publication which merits special mention is Josephau (1977), the main source of information for words of African origin in both Guadeloupe and Martinique.

Appendix 1 contains three lists of words of African origin found, currently or formerly, in one or more of the French-based creoles. The Bantu list has 126 items, the Kwa list has 88, and the West Atlantic and Manding list has 37. (The last two groups of languages are given in a combined list because they are spoken in an overlapping geographical area.) Note the absence of a Kru list, the Kru languages not having yet been exploited as a possible source of African words in the Caribbean creoles. The distribution of these 251 words among these creoles is set out in table 1.

A study of non-French lexical items in Indian Ocean creoles found "a broad measure of correspondence between the relative proportions of non-European immigrants of different language groups [including Malagasies, Indians, and Chinese as well as Africans] and the relative number of words adopted into Mau[ritian] from those languages" (Baker 1982b:760). This is contrasted with Reunionnais; the Malagasy contribution to its lexicon was far greater and the Bantu contribution to its lexicon far smaller than their relative contributions to the peopling of that island. A similar comparison may be attempted for the Caribbean territories for which most etymological work has been done—Haiti, Guadeloupe, and Martinique—using the language group figures given

**Table 1. Distribution of Words of African Origin among Twelve Territories**

| *Language Family* | *Bantu* | *Kwa* | *West Atlantic + Manding* | *Total* |
|---|---|---|---|---|
| Territory | | | | |
| Louisiana | 3 | — | 2 | 5 |
| Haiti | 30 (26%) | 73 (63%) | 13 (11%) | 116 |
| Guadeloupe | 23 (55%) | 11 (26%) | 8 (19%) | 42 |
| Dominica | 2 | — | 1 | 3 |
| Martinique | 20 (53%) | 12 (31%) | 6 (16%) | 38 |
| St. Lucia | 2 | 2 | 2 | 6 |
| Trinidad | 5 (31%) | 5 (31%) | 6 (38%) | 16 |
| Guyane Française | 2 | 3 | 4 | 9 |
| Caribbean area | 87 (37%) (44 etyma) | 106 (45%) (86 etyma) | 42 (18%) (23 etyma) | 235 |
| Reunion | 17 (94%) | 1 (6%) | — | 18 |
| Mauritius | 35 (73%) | 2 (4%) | 11 (23%) | 48 |
| Rodrigues | 9 (82%) | — | 2 (18%) | 11 |
| Seychelles | 63 (83%) | 3 (4%) | 10 (13%) | 76 |
| Indian Ocean | 124 (81%) (85 etyma) | 6 (4%) (3 etyma) | 23 (15%) (14 etyma) | 153 |
| Both zones | 211 (54%) | 112 (29%) | 65 (17%) | 388 |
| *Distribution of Etyma between the Two Geographical Zones* | | | | |
| Caribbean area only | 41 (28%) | 85 (57%) | 23 (15%) | 149 |
| Indian Ocean only | 82 (87%) | 2 (2%) | 10 (11%) | 94 |
| Both zones | 3 | 1 | 4 | 8 |
| Totals | 126 (50%) | 88 (35%) | 37 (15%) | 251 |

earlier and the percentages in table 1. The figures, which do not take into account slaves purchased from other European nations, were Bantu, 36.9%; Kwa, 34.4%; and West Atlantic/Manding, 22.4%. These percentages do not add up to 100 because of other language groups and a proportion of slaves of unknown origin. In order to make them strictly comparable with those in table 1 they have to be compensated pro rata, and this gives, to the nearest whole percentage point, Bantu, 39%; Kwa, 37%; and West Atlantic/Manding, 24%. Comparison of these figures with the totals for the Caribbean area in

**Table 2. Distribution of Words of African Origin among Twelve Territories, Excluding Voodoo Terms Found Only in Haitian**

| *Language Family* | *Bantu* | *Kwa* | *West Atlantic + Manding* | *Total* |
|---|---|---|---|---|
| Territory | | | | |
| Louisiana | 3 | — | 2 | 5 |
| Haiti | 22 (35%) | 28 (44%) | 13 (21%) | 63 |
| Guadeloupe | 23 (55%) | 11 (26%) | 8 (19%) | 42 |
| Dominica | 2 | — | 1 | 3 |
| Martinique | 20 (53%) | 12 (31%) | 6 (16%) | 38 |
| St. Lucia | 2 | 2 | 2 | 6 |
| Trinidad | 5 (31%) | 5 (31%) | 6 (38%) | 16 |
| Guyane Française | 2 | 3 | 4 | 9 |
| Caribbean area | 79 (43%) | 61 (34%) | 42 (23%) | 182 |
| | (36 etyma) | (41 etyma) | (23 etyma) | |
| Reunion | 17 (94%) | 1 (6%) | — | 18 |
| Mauritius | 35 (73%) | 2 (4%) | 11 (23%) | 48 |
| Rodrigues | 9 (82%) | — | 2 (18%) | 11 |
| Seychelles | 63 (83%) | 3 (4%) | 10 (13%) | 76 |
| Indian Ocean | 124 (81%) | 6 (4%) | 23 (15%) | 153 |
| | (85 etyma) | (3 etyma) | (14 etyma) | |
| Both zones | 203 (61%) | 67 (20%) | 65 (19%) | 335 |
| *Distribution of Etyma between the Two Geographical Zones* | | | | |
| Caribbean area only | 33 (34%) | 40 (42%) | 23 (24%) | 96 |
| Indian Ocean only | 82 (87%) | 2 (2%) | 10 (11%) | 94 |
| Both zones | 3 | 1 | 4 | 8 |
| Totals | 118 (59%) | 43 (22%) | 37 (19%) | 198 |

table 1 shows that Kwa is rather better represented than the population figures would suggest, while Bantu and West Atlantic are somewhat underrepresented. However, this is primarily due to the large number of terms of Kwa origin in Hai. Appendix 1 reveals that no fewer than forty-five of the seventy-three Kwa items in Hai form part of the voodoo vocabulary and are not attested in any other creole. (All of these are known only from Comhaire-Sylvain and Comhaire-Sylvain 1955). If these are excluded on the grounds that they form a specialized vocabulary known to voodoo priests rather than to the general Haitian public, eight Bantu-derived, exclusively Haitian terms belonging to the same specialized vocabulary and known only from the same source must also be excluded. The distribution of African words in these creoles is then as set out in table 2. Note that there is now an appreciably closer correspondence between the percentages representing proportions of slaves (adjusted) and lexical items according to language groups: respectively 39% and 43% for Bantu, 37% and 34% for Kwa, and 24% and 23% for West Atlantic/Manding.

The above comment is limited to Haiti, Guadeloupe, and Martinique because insufficient data are available on the other Caribbean area creoles. This is particularly regrettable so far as Louisiana and Guyane Française are concerned because both appear to have evolved initially and separately in isolation from other French-based creoles (whereas those of Dominica, St. Lucia, and Trinidad seem to be direct continuations of Martinique; see Baker 1987 and figure 1 below).

### *Words of Bantu Origin*

Most of the words in French-based creoles of the Caribbean area which can be reliably identified as being of Bantu origin are found in two languages—perhaps more properly groups of languages—of the Congo-Angola area for which adequate dictionaries exist, namely Kikongo[6] and Kimbundu.[7] The Bantu population taken as slaves to the Indian Ocean islands was drawn from an area stretching from Mozambique to Kenya, sometimes originating from points far inland (Baker 1982b:101). Dictionaries exist for more than a dozen languages of this region, and, because of the generally close relationships between neighboring Bantu languages, identical or near-identical forms are often to be found in several of these dictionaries. To save space, only one Bantu form per creole word is normally given in appendix 1, the plus sign (+) being placed after a language name to indicate that (near) identical forms occur in at least two other languages of the region. For example, Makhuwa+ *kalipa* means that forms (nearly) identical to *kalipa* are found in at least two other Bantu languages of the area.

Four of the items on the Bantu list are found in both Atlantic and Indian Ocean creoles. *Makuti* 'plaited or thatched leaves,' *sega/sika* 'kind of dance,' and perhaps *wayawaya* 'rustling of leaves' are widely distributed roots. The other item, *bangala* 'penis,' is more problematic. It is first attested in Haiti at the start of the nineteenth century (Ducoeurjoly 1802), but so far as is known is no longer current in any of the Caribbean-area creoles. It is, however, current in the French spoken throughout francophone West Africa (Racelle-Latin 1980) as well as in the creoles of Mauritius and the Seychelles. In spite of the phonetic similarity of the Kikongo form, some doubt must remain about the etymology of this word.

At least two items on the Bantu list may result from convergence with non-Bantu words.[8] *Bunda* is included among the words of Bantu origin because forms with a nasalized vowel or nasal consonant are attested more widely than those which, like the Manding forms, lack a nasal element. In the case of *senga*, D'Offay and Lionnet (1982) give no indication of the nature of this alcoholic drink. A Bantu origin seems more probable, partly because the word is found in many languages of East and southeast Africa, and partly because a Wolof word could only have reached the Seychelles via Mauritius, where no corresponding form is attested.

As was mentioned earlier, eight exclusively Haitian words relating to voodoo are of Bantu origin and are included in table 1 and excluded from table 2. Their existence is of considerable cultural interest in that they suggest that the voodoo religion, which was undoubtedly introduced into Haiti by speakers of Kwa languages from the Bight of Benin, may have attracted adherents from other ethnolinguistic groups from the eighteenth century. Note that one other Haitian word of Bantu origin associated with voodoo is also found in other creoles: *zombi*. However, this is attested in French from 1846 and might well have been introduced into Guadeloupean and Martinique creoles through French (and thus would not be a Bantu survival in the local context).

Having claimed elsewhere that Seychellois is essentially a continuation of early Mauritian (Baker 1982a, 1982b), some explanation is needed for why there are considerably more Bantu words in Seychellois than in Mauritian. There are two main reasons. First, the Seychelles received many "rescued slaves" in the second half of the nineteenth century. These were overwhelmingly speakers of Bantu languages who formed a third of the islands' population at that time and who were thus well placed to introduce African words. Second, until very recently, the Seychelles's main link with the rest of the world was via a shipping route to Mombasa (Kenya), where there exists to this day a Seychellois community bilingual in Creole and Kiswahili. Quite a number of Seychellois words of Kiswahili origin are probably to be attributed to this link.

### *Words of Kwa Origin*

The Kwa group of languages are spoken from the Ivory Coast to Nigeria. Adequate dictionaries exist for only a few members of this group, but these include all those with the largest numbers of speakers, such as Twi, Ewe, Fon, Yoruba, and Igbo. Several of these languages have both voiced and voiceless labiovelar plosives, transcribed in appendix 1 as *gb* and *kp*, respectively. Some also have retroflex consonants, noted there by a dot below the line, for example, *ḍ*.

Only *kalalu*/*lalo* 'okra' is found in creole languages of both the Caribbean area and the Indian Ocean. While no doubt from the same ultimate source as *kalalu*, it is far from certain that *lalo* owes its presence in the Indian Ocean to Kwa-speaking slaves, for two reasons. First, only one shipload of Kwa speakers is known to have reached the area (Baker 1982a:176–87). Second, the plant is almost certain to have been introduced into the Indian Ocean by the French, and thus probably bears the name in use at the place where they obtained specimens rather than the name known to a small section of the slave population in Mauritius and/or Reunion.

The detailed description of *magari* in D'Offay and Lionnet (1982)—very much abbreviated in appendix 1—does not differ in any important respect from the even more elaborate definition of Fon *gari* given in Segurola (1963). This is curious because the initial *ma-* of the Sey form looks like a Bantu class prefix, and even more so because there are no records of any Kwa speakers ever having been taken to the Seychelles. Manioc was introduced to Mauritius from the Caribbean area in the 1730s, specifically as a crop intended for consumption by slaves. As there were a few speakers of Kwa languages in Mauritius at that time, it is possible that the word and the staple were once current there, although I am not aware of any reference to either. It is thus just conceivable that both may still have been current a few decades later when the permanent settlement of the Seychelles began. The initial *ma-* of the Sey form may perhaps result from the influence of a phonetically and semantically similar Bantu word such as Nyika (a language of Kenya) *magari* 'messes of cooked grain, rice, Indian corn, etc.' (Sparshott 1887).

While forty-five of the seventy-three Haitian words of Kwa derivation relate to the voodoo cult, even when all Hai voodoo terms not attested in other creoles are excluded, as in table 2, the proportion of words of Kwa origin still exceeds that of Bantu origin in Haitian, in contrast to both Guadeloupean and Martinique creoles. Thus, for reasons which are not yet understood, speakers of Kwa languages in Hai appear to have had a greater influence on its lexicon than might be predicted from their contribution to the peopling of the territory.

### *Words of West Atlantic and Manding Origin*

This list includes words derived from languages belonging to two different groups: the rather loosely related West Atlantic groups (see, for example, the low percentages of shared cognates in Sapir 1971) and the far more closely related Manding group. Four of the words on this list are shared by French-based creoles of both the Caribbean area and the Indian Ocean. These include the ethnonyms *bãbara* and *yolof*. (The word "Bambara" was formerly applied to the Manding peoples in general and not merely, as today, to the Bamana people of Mali.) The two others are *nyamnyam,* meaning 'food' and 'eat'—which may look like an example of onomatopoeia but has these meanings and this precise form only in Wolof—and *-o,* the vocative suffix. The latter is of special interest, being found in languages of both the West Atlantic and Manding groups.

### *Other Kinds of Influence on the Creole Lexicon*

Most of the words listed in appendix 1 have become established in one or more creole languages with relatively little change in pronunciation or meaning. The etyma were found because the creole words had previously been identified as being of apparent non-French origin and because dictionaries of the relevant African languages existed and were consulted. But the African contribution to the lexicons of French-based creoles is not restricted to words which happen to look un-French. Consider the following examples from Mauritian Creole.

The Mau word for 'bed' is *lili*. Given that the agglutination of French articles on a massive scale is a feature of this creole, the "obvious" etymology is French *le lit*. However, when one discovers that the words for 'bed' or 'bedstead' in the following Bantu languages, all of which are spoken in parts of East Africa from which slaves were taken to Mauritius and in which the initial syllable, where given, is a noun class prefix, are phonetically near identical, there seems no possible doubt that the precise form of the creole word was influenced by Bantu: Taita *ulili,* Nyamwezi *wulili,* Sukuma *-liili,* Gogo *wulili,* Kaguru *ulili,* Swahili *ulili,* Bemba *bulili,* Makhuwa *olili,* Yao *cilili, mlili,* and *ulili* (three different kinds of sleeping places).

The words for 'mother' and 'father,' *papa* and *mama,* are attested in early nineteenth-century Mauritius as polite terms of address for male and female slaves, respectively. These and phonetically similar terms are found in dialectal French as terms of address for elderly people (Chaudenson 1974:795–96), so the words are "obviously" French. However, in the early nineteenth-century Mauritian texts these words are applied to comparatively young people. In several Bantu languages of southeast Africa, words meaning 'mother' and 'father' are the most polite terms of address appropriate for use when, for example, asking the way of a stranger aged from fifteen years upward. Furthermore, in one of these languages, Makhuwa, spoken by the great majority of the population in northern Mozambique and probably the first language of more Bantu slaves in Mauritius than any other, the words for 'mother' and 'father' are exactly as in creole: *mama* and *papa*. The way these words were used in nineteenth-century Mauritius clearly reflected Makhuwa usage.

Richardson (1963:13) first drew attention to several calques of Bantu forms in Mauritian creole, including the following:

> In Creole a praying mantis is called *kasbol,* literally 'break bowl,' which is the translation of the Swahili word *vunja-junga*. There is a superstition in Africa that the person on whom a praying mantis settles will break the next piece of pottery he touches.

According to the dictionary by Rechenbach (1967), it is the person who kills a mantis, rather than on whom a mantis settles, to which this superstition applies in Swahili. In Yao the word for 'mantis' is *mkakasa-ciwaga,* in which the elements are *ciwaga* 'almost any kind of pot' and *-kasa* 'shatter, break into pieces' (Sanderson 1954; note the phonetic and semantic similarity of the latter to creole *kas/e,* French *casser*).

Other calques, in addition to those noted by Richardson, probably include the standard Mauritian greetings *ki manyer* 'how are you?' (literally 'what state [are you in]?'; compare Swahili *u hali gani?* idem) and *ki nuvel,* also meaning 'how are you' (but literally 'what news?'; compare Swahili *habari gani?* idem).

It is important to appreciate that a Eurocentric linguist would not have considered any of the above examples candidates for African influence. Such examples are only likely to be spotted either by people with firsthand experience of both the relevant African language and the creole (such people are extremely rare, but Richardson happened to have been in Mauritius with the British army before working on East African languages), or by people with an intimate knowledge of a particular creole disposed to read through dictionaries of relevant African languages entry by entry. It is most unlikely that examples such as those given above are to be found only in Mauritian Creole, and it is thus to be expected that there are many more waiting to be identified in other creoles.

In general, the lists of words of African origin in appendix 1, particularly as summarized in table 2, show a fair degree of correlation between the proportion of slave immigrants associated with particular groups of languages and the proportion of creole words derived from those languages. Since that is broadly what everyone not wedded to the theory of monogenesis would expect, it is of limited interest. Many of the words in appendix 1 relate to beliefs and magic, food and drink, and music and dancing. They are features of African culture which survived slavery and the ultimate replacement of African languages by a creole language. They provide evidence, if any were needed, that speakers of particular languages once lived in particular territories, but no more than that. By contrast, calques such as the Mauritian examples given earlier seem to imply rather more, notably that they owe their presence to people who simultaneously spoke both an African language and a creole or, perhaps, people who had an African mother tongue and were acquiring a creole as a second or additional language.

A similar implication is carried by the survival of African folktales, proverbs, and riddles in creole languages. (Since the existence of African riddles in creoles of both the Caribbean area and the Indian Ocean is not widely known, three examples from Baker 1988 are given in appendix 2.) The acceptability or otherwise of this interpretation will naturally depend on one's personal view of how creole languages evolved, but note that the subtleties found in African-derived creole folktales could not possibly have been transmitted via varieties of pidgin which resembled those illustrated in chapter 1 of Bickerton (1981), not even that of his most resourceful speaker, a retired bus driver (1981:13). I will return to the possible significance of this below.

## Difficulties in Assessing the African Contribution to French-based Creoles

Suzanne Sylvain (1936) attributed many of the non-French features of Haitian morphology and syntax to several West African languages, particularly Ewe. (There was probably no adequate account of Fon available at that time.) Goodman (1964) discussed the possible influence of an even wider range of West African languages on Haitian and other French-based creoles. More recently, Lefebvre (1986) and Koopman (1986) have separately sought to derive particular features of Haitian syntax from one (Lefebvre) or more (Koopman) of the languages of West Africa. None of these authors refer to the numerically largest and linguistically most homogeneous group of immigrants, those from Bantu Africa. Even if it could be proved that Haitian Creole stabilized in the first half of the eighteenth century, as I personally think is likely, a time when immigrants from Bantu Africa formed a fairly small minority of the slave population, there would seem to be no a priori reason for assuming that they could not have influenced its evolution thereafter. In any event, they undoubtedly made a major contribution to the lexicon of Haitian and other creoles, as shown in appendix 1.

Sylvain (1936), Lefebvre (1986), and Koopman (1986) all take it for granted that Haitian Creole was an entirely separate development from Antillean French-based creoles. This seems highly questionable. Some, maybe most, of the first French settlers along the northern coast had spent some time previously in the French Antilles, and the same could well be true of their slaves. Furthermore, it is widely acknowledged that the creole spoken today in northern Haiti resembles the creoles of the Lesser Antilles far more closely than does the Port-au-Prince variety. No account of how Haitian Creole originated can simply ignore this part of its history.

Although she described Haitian as "une langue éwé à vocabulaire français" (1936:178), Sylvain did not suggest how this might have occurred. The possibility being explored by Lefebvrc is that Haitian may in part be the result of the relexification of Fon (and closely related languages) without any "pre-creole pidgin phase" (1986:283). Something of this kind may well have occurred in the case of Berbice, where one particular African language was dominant among the slave population for some years (Robertson, this volume). However, Haiti appears to have had a multilingual slave population throughout, and the proportion of immigrants whose mother tongue was a Kwa language does not seem ever to have been significantly greater than one-third. This raises the obvious question, not discussed by Lefebvre (1986), of what the majority of the slave population would have been doing linguistically while Fon speakers were busy relexifying their language. In contrast to Lefebvre, Koopman (1986) believes there was a pidgin, although she refers to this as "the contact language," and that this included some of the "common properties" of West African languages. She states that "the existence of common properties has the advantage of avoiding the search for one particular West African language that served as a basis for the syntax of Haitian" (1986:254). As there are fully a thousand languages spoken in the area from Senegal to Nigeria (Mann et al. 1987), one can appreciate the advantage to which she refers! One would have thought it would not be difficult to find a plurality of languages from that area which shared any one feature of Haitian syntax. Nevertheless, there is one feature Koopman is unable to attribute either to French or to West African languages, the "pleonastic pronoun *li*" (1986:248), that is, the use of a third-person pronoun following a third-person subject. This has been independently attributed to Bantu influence by Baker and Corne (1982:100–101) and by Mufwene (1986:144). Of course, it would be possible to amend Koopman's approach by adding the relevant Bantu languages of Angola to the list of languages examined as possible sources of Haitian features. However, even if it were possible to find at least two African languages, known to have been represented in the Haitian population at some time, for every non-French syntactic feature of Haitian Creole, it is far from sure that a coherent, convincing picture would emerge. A further hazard is that some of the features attributed to particular African languages might also be found to occur in one or more of the French-based creoles of the Indian Ocean where the languages in question were never represented.

Most substratists compare modern forms of creole languages with modern forms of African languages. In many cases they do not have much choice. However, so far as Mauritius and Haiti are concerned, quite a large number of early texts are already known. Mauritian texts from the eighteenth and nineteenth centuries reveal a number of surprises, such as the fact that the preposed marker of plurality *ban,* today one of the morphemes which occur with the greatest frequency, is not attested with this precise function before 1885. That substratists ignore early texts at their peril is suggested by the comparison of the personal pronouns of Haitian and Fon. Lefebvre (1986:292) lists only modern *mwẽ* and *u* as, respectively, the first- and second-person singular forms, but Haitian formerly had separate subject and object forms *mõ* and *mwẽ* as well as—as familiar alternatives to *u*—both *to* and *twe*. As Fon also has separate subject and object singular pronoun forms, the two systems were, to that extent, formerly more similar than Lefebvre indicates. However, while the fact that the first- and second-person plural pronouns in Fon have identical segmental representation and differ only in tone has, since Sylvain (1936), been associated with Haitian *nu* (which also functions as both first- and second-person plural pronoun), there does not appear to be any pre-1900 attestation of *nu* as the second-person plural pronoun in Haitian. Thus this seems to be a modern development not attributable to substrate influence.

Although the idea that the French-based creoles stem from a common origin no longer holds sway, there is no general consensus on the number of creoles which were separately generated. A provisional classification of these languages (Baker 1987), using three different approaches, suggested the scheme in figure 1.

Figure 1 indicates that French-based creoles were independently generated in at least five locations, numbered in chronological order according to their settlement by the French. (The vertical position of territory abbreviations also reflects the year in which the French arrived there.) "Antillean creole" refers collectively to the creoles generated simultaneously in Guadeloupe and Martinique. Speakers of these creoles subsequently settled in Dominica (Dom), St. Lucia (SLu), and, much later, Trinidad (Tri). Rodrigues (Rod) and Seychelles (Sey) were similarly settled by speakers of Isle-de-France (IdF) creole from Mauritius (Mau). The arrowheads reflect the (1) strong grammatical and lexical influence of Antillean on Guyanais some time after the independent generation

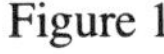

Figure 1

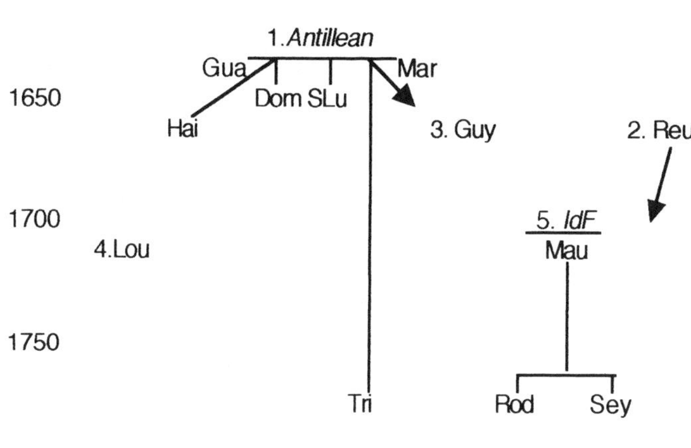


Lou Hai Gua Dom SLu Tri Mar Guy Rod Mau Sey Reu

*Dates indicate start of settlement by the French*

of the latter, and the (2) slight, purely lexical influence of Reunionnais on Isle-de-France creole. The diagonal line linking Haitian to Antillean indicates that the extent of lexical and grammatical similarity is too great for Haitian to have been an altogether separately generated creole and that it is not sufficiently great for Haitian to have been merely a continuation of Antillean. Detailed historical research on the peopling of Haiti is needed to resolve this matter.

As a result of research on the peopling and languages of the creolophone Indian Ocean territories carried out by a number of different people over the past twenty years, it is possible to draw up a scenario of how and when these creoles arose which is consistent with all the facts as they are currently known. One such account is given in Baker (1982b:806–59) and, more accessibly but in somewhat abbreviated form, in Baker and Corne (1986). This assumes that the hypothesis presented by Bickerton (1981) is basically correct in its account of how children exposed to an inadequate input language (pidgin) made an adequate creole language from that with the aid of the bioprogram. It goes on to examine the likely consequences of this in relation to three significant "events" in the demographic history of territories in which creole languages evolved: Event 1—when the number of slaves surpassed the number of members of the slave-owning class; Event 2—when the number of locally born slaves surpassed the number of slave-owning class (both foreign- and locally born); Event 3—

when the regular supply of slave immigrants came to an end. Differences in the relative timing of these events appeared to account for the fact that a creole continuum persisted in Reunion while a substantially homogeneous creole rapidly emerged in other societies with a francophone slave-owning class. This led to a hypothesis to complement that of Bickerton (1981). This complementary hypothesis (CH) makes three predictions:

1. That in all former plantation societies dependent on imported slave labor and where creole languages are spoken today, a creole-European language continuum had to exist before a substantially autonomous and significantly stable creole language could emerge;
2. That the period most favorable to the emergence of an autonomous creole is from Event 2 to Event 3;
3. That as a result of slaves arriving between Events 2 and 3 identifying a creole rather than the European language as their target,[9] there was the potential for grammatical rules to be introduced from the language or languages best represented among the slave population *during that period* (rather than, as is widely assumed though rarely explicitly claimed by substratists, during the earliest years of settlement).

Bickerton (1984) accepts predictions 1 and 2 but does not yet accept 3.

It so happens that in Mauritius throughout the period from Event 2 to Event 3 (ca. 1773–1810) the great majority of slave arrivals were from Bantu East Africa, and this was especially so between 1773 and 1794, when they accounted for nine out of ten arrivals. Among the features of Mauritian Creole which have been attributed to Bantu influence are (1) the very substantially greater proportion of nouns with an initial syllable wholly derived from a French article than in all the French-based creoles of the Caribbean area and Reunionnais (Baker 1984), (2) the "pleonastic" pronoun *li* (*i* in modern Seychellois; Baker and Corne 1986),[10] and (3) differences between the three-element tense-mood-aspect system of Bickerton's language bioprogram hypothesis (LBH) and the more elaborate Mauritian system, the first non-LBH-predicted element of which is attested from 1784 (Baker and Corne 1986).

The CH claims to provide a coherent account of the evolution of all the Indian Ocean creoles. It is consistent with all the linguistic and historical facts as they are currently known because it was specifically designed to be so.[11] While it will probably require some modification as and when additional information comes to light, the more immediate test of the validity of the CH is likely to come from applying it to the Caribbean area. While I have begun to work on this, it will be some time before the necessary information has been assembled. However, in his contribution to the 1985 Amsterdam Creole Workshop, Alleyne (1986) refers to four creoles which, in my interpretation, might seem to present problems for the CH. Two of these are Kru English (on which I have no information and thus cannot discuss) and Berbice Dutch (see Robertson, this volume). In the latter case, the European and African populations involved each belonged to a single ethnolinguistic group for some years. No new means of communication was needed for Africans to talk to Africans until other Africans of a different linguistic background arrived. Since both the LBH and the CH are concerned with societies in which the labor force included people belonging to several linguistic groups, neither hypothesis can predict anything about the Berbice situation. But all other slave plantation societies under European control had, so far as is known, a labor force in which three or more linguistic groups were represented except, possibly and briefly, in the very earliest years of their settlement. Alleyne goes on to mention territories in which one linguistic group "provided the relatively strongest substratum influence because of numerical superiority in the crucial period or marked cultural coherence leading in the case of the Akan in Jamaica to political leadership, and in the case of the Ewe-Fon in Haiti to religious leadership" (1986:303), although he does not define "the crucial period." By "numerical superiority" I assume he means that they formed the biggest linguistic group rather than that they formed the majority of the slave population, since the latter does not seem to have been the case at any time (for Haiti, see figures given above; for Jamaica, see Curtin 1969:162). This makes the second part of his sentence even more interesting because the Ewe-Fon did indeed keep their religion alive in Haiti, and their contribution to the vocabulary of Haitian is greater than that of other linguistic groups even when voodoo terminology is excluded, as indicated in table 2.

The question of why there are more Akan (Twi) words in Jamaican Creole than words from other African languages, assuming this is in fact the case,[12] is a question Le Page (1960) considered some years ago. He gave four reasons (much abbreviated here) for the strong influence of Twi speakers: (1) their (ferocious) character, (2) their greater linguistic homogeneity than other groups in the first fifty years of British rule, (3) because they established their leadership early, and (4) because they dominated the Maroons (1960:75–76). In its present form, the CH is unable to handle the possibility that one particular linguistic group may have had an influence which extended far beyond its proportion of the slave population as a whole. However, it has yet to be demonstrated conclusively that such influence exists other than in the lexicon. It is probably also worth noting that both Haiti and Jamaica are large territories when compared with any of the other creolophone islands of both the Caribbean and the

Indian Ocean. Haiti and Jamaica are also both rather mountainous, and it was possible for considerable numbers of Maroons to settle in areas outside European control where they could maintain their cultural heritage. Nothing similar was possible in the smaller islands where Maroons had to be constantly on the move to avoid being recaptured. The existence of comparatively stable Maroon settlements would undoubtedly have favored the retention of a greater number of African words and of more African cultural traditions in Haiti and Jamaica than in the smaller islands. In spite of these similarities, a major difference is the far greater degree of linguistic homogeneity found in Haiti today than in Jamaica. None of the current theories relating to creolization appears to offer an obvious explanation for why this should be so, and research is thus needed to determine whether Jamaican Creole was formerly more homogeneous than it is now. (The former would imply subsequent "decreolization," the latter that the creole failed to jell.)

Identifying African words in French-based creoles presents relatively few problems. Information already published (e.g., Curtin 1969) will in many cases suffice to indicate the range of likely source languages, and, provided adequate dictionaries exist, these can be checked for etyma. While no very firm conclusions can be drawn, in part because all these creoles also contain a number of words which are thought to be African but whose etyma have yet to be identified, it is at least clear that all linguistic groups which were reasonably well represented in the slave population of a particular territory made a broadly corresponding contribution to the non-French vocabulary of its creole. Furthermore, there is not yet any strong evidence to suggest that the timing of arrival was a significant factor. There is nothing to indicate that a linguistic group particularly well represented in the early stages of peopling a particular territory contributed a disproportionately large number of lexical items compared with another linguistic group which was equally well represented at a later stage.

Calques and cases of convergence between an African and a French word are far more difficult to identify than African words as such. This is because it is not immediately apparent that such things are of anything other than French origin. A substantial degree of familiarity with both the relevant African language and the creole is needed to spot them.

Identifying the African contribution to French-based creoles in areas other than the lexicon is a very difficult matter. The basic problem is that we do not know enough about how creole languages originated and evolved. Historical research, including searching for early creole texts as well as establishing the origins and linguistic background of the slave population, should help to clarify matters. The substratists' position would undoubtedly be strengthened if (a) it could be shown that the features of a creole they attribute to a particular African language existed in that creole at a time when there were speakers of that African language in the local slave population, and (b) the factors assumed to be responsible for the adoption into a creole of particular rules from particular African languages could be clearly specified and shown to be applicable to other creolophone societies. In the absence of such work, Bickerton's LBH will continue to command support. However, even if the LBH is basically correct, this need not necessarily limit African influence to the lexicon; with the aid of the CH and with particular reference to Mauritius, it may also help to identify the period when there was the greatest potential for substrate influence on a creole. The existence of calques and the survival of a great deal of African folklore in creole languages suggest that there must have been a period in which a proportion of the population at least was effectively bilingual in an African language and creole. There is no obvious reason why these same circumstances should not have permitted the introduction of some grammatical rules from the same African sources into creole.

Should the LBH ultimately prove incorrect, it would need to be modified or replaced by another, better hypothesis which fits all the facts. Simply proving the LBH wrong would by itself achieve nothing, leaving us with only the tried-and-found-wanting cafeteria principle.

## Appendix 1: Words of African Origin

This appendix draws on data collected between 1980 and 1985 for the forthcoming *Etymologisches Wörterbuch des Franko-kreolischen*, edited by Annegret Bollée. Full bibliographical details of the sources consulted for the overwhelming majority of African words in Indian Ocean creoles are provided in Baker (1982b). For the Caribbean area, the most important sources are Comhaire-Sylvain and Comhaire-Sylvain (1955), de St. Quentin (1872), Josephau (1977), Parsons (1943), Thomas (1869), and Turiault (1873–76). Dictionaries of African languages cited most frequently with reference to etyma of words in Caribbean creoles include Alves (1951), for Umbundu; Bazin (1965), for Bamana; Bentley (1887), for Kikongo; Christaller (1933), for Twi; Crowther (1852), for Yoruba; Delafosse (1955), for Manding; Laman (1936), for Kikongo; Missionaires (1875), for Wolof; and Segurola (1963), for Fon.

In each entry the creole word is given first, followed by a gloss and the territory or territories in which it is found. Following the semicolon, the source language name is given together with the probable etymon and a gloss of the latter. The twelve creolophone territories are abbreviated as follows: Dominica, Dom; Guadeloupe, Gua; Guyane Française, Guy; Haiti, Hai; Louisiana, Lou; Martinique, Mar; Mauritius, Mau; Reunion, Reu; Rodrigues, Rod; Seychelles, Sey; St. Lucia, SLu; and Trinidad, Tri.

*Items of Bantu Origin*

*alumãdja* "loa secondaire" Hai; Kikongo *ma-diya* "sorte de *nkisi*" (*nkisi* "fétiche, sorcellerie . . .").

*badyo* "sot" Hai, *bãdjo* "gamin des rues" Gua, Mar; Kikongo *mbadio* "nipper."

*baka* "être humain (nain) ou animal ensorcelé" Hai; Kikongo *mbaka* "a dwarf."

*bakulu* "trompeur, opportuniste" Hai; Kikongo *bakulu* "qqch qui sert à s'emparer, à faire un gain."

*bãnda* "African type of social dance" Hai; Kikongo *mbanda* "danse au son du tambour."

*baŋga* "noix de palmier" Mar; Kikongo *mbanga* "noyau des noix de palmier."

*bãgala* Hai, *baŋgala* Mau, Sey "penis"; Kikongo *bakala* id.

*bãza* "string instrument" Lou, Hai, Gua, Mar; Kimbundu *mbanza* id.

*bɛbɛ* "muet" Hai; Kikongo *bebe* "sourd-muet."

*bebeluka* "epileptic" Sey; Yao+ *-pepeluka* "stagger about."

*bekɛkɛ* "sans rien donner . . ." Hai; Kikongo *beke-beke* "qqch qui ne sert à rien . . .".

*bɛlɛ* "danse; musique populaire" Hai, Gua, Mar, Tri; Kikongo *velele* "une danse, mouvements avec les hanches . . .".

*bib* "spider" Reu, Sey; Shimaore+ *bwibwi* id.

*bilẽga* "mush made from manioc" Sey; Bemba *belengo/bilingo lutoshi* "roll between the fingers a ball of *bwali* (*bwali* "mush . . . made of meal and water").

*bobok* "tell-tale" Mau; Kiswahili *boboka* "talk indiscreetly . . .".

*bukusu* "campagnard, fruste" Gua, *pwa bukusu* "proche parents des pois d'Angole" Mar; ethnonym *Mbukusu* (southern Angola).

*bule (zẽ)* "cérémonie où l'on brise les zins d'un mort" Hai; Kikongo *bula* "frapper . . . casser."

*bunda, buda, bõda* "behind, anus" Hai, Gua, Dom, Mar, SLu; Kimbundu *mbunda* "nádegas" (+ Manding *buu-daa* "anus," Bambara *boda* id.).

*dãma* "formule incantatoire pour conjurer le mauvais sort" Mar; Kikongo *dama* "dire qqch préjudiciable, injurieux."

*daw* "kind of boat" Sey; Kiswahili+ *dau* "bateau à voile."

*dẽde* "régime de palmier à huile" Gua, Mar; Kikongo *dẽnde* "huile de palme solide à vendre."

*djon* "sorte de gris-gris" Sey; Shona+ *chaungo, jango* "charm."

*djuba* "a dance" Hai, Mar; Kikongo *nzuba* "danse de chef du pays."

*dõdosya* "zombi, revenant" Sey; Yao *ndondoča* "dead person brought back to semilife by witchcraft . . .".

*fimbo* "bâton (servant à frapper)" Sey; Kiswahili *fimbo* id.
*fula* "rite consistant à souffler des goutelettes de rhum" Hai; Kikongo *fula* "souffler, rendre par la bouche et par les narines."
*gãga, gãgã* "voodoo priest" Hai; Kikongo *nganga* "prêtre, médecin."
*gẽmbo* "roussettes, chauve-souris" Gua, Mar, Tri; Kikongo *ngembo, ngyembo* id.
*gõ(m)bo* "okra" Lou, Hai, Gua, Mar, SLu, Tri; Kimbundu *kingombo* id.
*gõgolo* Hai, *kɔkɔlɔ, koŋgoliyo* Gua, *goŋgoliõ* Mar, *gõgõ* Guy "millepede"; Kikongo *ngongolo* id.
*golegole* "frivole" Sey; Shona *gore* "an uninhibited person."
*gulu* "tortoise" Mau; Taita *nguru* id.
*humba* "sac en jute" Gua; Kimbundu *homba* "espèce de fourre-tout."
*kalamuka* "méchant" Reu; Yao+ *kalamuka* "be cunning, smart."
*kalipa* "combattant; fort" Mau, Sey; Makhuwa+ *kalipa* "fighter."
*kalkalãdye* "de façon semblable" Sey; Kikamba *ikala kalakala* "resemble," Yao *ka* "he, she, it," *-landa* "resemble."
*kamtole* "danse campagnarde populaire" Sey; Shona *kamutondore* "kind of dance (for young men and women)."
*kapileŋga* "se dit d'un homme capable" Sey; Bemba *ka* "he," *bilingana* "be active, quick, alert."
*kapkap* "frisson de fièvre" Reu; Makhuwa *kapakapa* "trembling."
*kapor* "well-built (person)" Reu, Mau, Sey; Makhuwa+ *kaporo* "slave."
*kasuku* "parrot" Sey; Kiswahili *kasuku* id.
*katiti* "bird spp." Sey; Makhuwa+ *mukatiti* "pássaro pequeno . . .".
*katutu* "petite jarre" Gua; (unspecified Angolan language) *katutu* "une cruche, un pot de terre, etc., fêlés . . .".
*katšolo* "petite pirogue" Sey; Kiswahili *nčoro* id., *ka* diminutive prefix.
*kayãbe, kayãb, kayam* "musical rattle" Reu, Mau; Nyanja *nankayambe* id.
*kayãbo* Mau, Sey, *kayãb* Reu "torn clothing"; Makhuwa *nikayampa* "rag, piece of cloth."
*kikapo* "basket" Sey; Kiswahili *kikapo* id.
*kimãga* "liquide magique" Hai; Kikongo *manga* "sortilège, charme."
*(ti-)kita* "loa pétro renommé pour sa cruauté" Hai; Kikongo *nkita* "esprit d'une personne morte de mort violente."
*kitam* "underpants" Sey; Kiswahili *kitãmbi* "narrow strip of cloth."
*kõgo* (various meanings) Hai, Gua, Mar; Kikongo *kongo*.
*koŋkway* "ugly woman" Mau; Yao+ *kongwe* "female."
*konokono* "small snails" Mau; Yao+ *likonokono* "snail."
*kurpa* "giant land snail" Reu, Mau, Sey; Makhuwa *ekhoropa* "caracol gigante."
*kuzupa* "unidentified animal in folktales" Mau, *kusupa* "lapin dans le folklore seychellois" Sey; Makhuwa *kuzupa* "hyena."
*lemba* "loa à culte familial" Hai; Kimbundu *lemba* "dieu présidant à la génération."

*likoŋgwa* "sorte de courroies pour chaise à porteur" Sey; Yao+ *likongwa* "a slave yoke."

*lompi* "vaniteux" Sey; Shona *rombi* "sitting very straight and showing importance," Bemba *lulumbi* "fame, glory."

*maboy* "fish sp." Reu; Kiswahili *maboye* "petit poisson des lagunes."

*madu(n)gu(n)* "hydrocèle" Hai; Kikongo *edungu* "scrotale hydrocèle."

*maguz* "maladif" Sey; Kiswahili *maaguzi* "medicine, remedy."

*makalapo* "musical instrument" Sey; Makhuwa *makalapo* id.

*makabe* "name of the largest surviving natural forest in Mauritius"; Gitonga *magabhi* "forests."

*makambale* Sey, *makãbale* Mau "fish sp."; Yao+ *makambale* (pl.) id.

*makatša* "kind of sweet bread roll" Reu, Mau, *mukat* id. Sey; Sukuma+ *mugaati* "bread," Yao *makača* "husks of the corncob."

*makatu* "tree sp." Sey; Kiswahili *mkatu* id.

*makluklu* "hydrocèle" Hai, Gua, Mar; Kikongo *makukluklu* "hernie scrotale."

*makõde* (place name) Mau, "fish sp." Sey; Makonde *makonde* (ethnonym, glossonym from the Mozambique-Tanzania border).

*makut(i)* "bag made of plaited leaves" Hai, Gua; "palm leaves for thatching" Sey; Kikongo *nkuta* "woven basket," Yao+ *makuti* "palm leaves for thatching."

*makwa* "black bird sp.," "fool" Reu, Mau, Sey; Makhuwa *makhuwa* "autoethnonym," "fool."

*malãga* "taro" Hai, Gua; Kikongo *ma-langa* id.

*malambo* "caleçon rudimentaire" Gua; Kikongo *mulamba* "pantalon."

*malol, maloy* "chassie" Reu, Sey; Yao *malilo-lilo* "watering of the eyes, oozing."

*malumbo* "cri d'un meneur de contredanse" Sey; Makonde *nnalombo* "mestre de dança," *ŋalombwe* "sort of signal cry."

*manimani* Mau, *mwanimwani* Sey "flashing, scintillating"; Shona *ŋaniŋani* "glittering," *manyimanyi* "iridescence."

*mapim, mapẽb* "sorghum," "popcorn" Reu; Shambala *mapemba* "maize," Yao *mapembe* "sorghum," Sena *mapim* "flour."

*mapyepye* "terreau; paille sèche" Sey; Kiswahili *mapepe* "chaff, grain, husks."

*matak* "fesses" Mau; Makhuwa+ *matako* "buttocks."

*matoŋgo* "fish sp." Sey; Kiswahili *matongo* id.

*matšapa* "worthless person" Mau; Kiswahili *mchapa* "drinker."

*mayumbe* (1) "particular group of Africans" Gua, Mar; Kiyombe *mayombe* (autoethnonym, people living in Congo, Zaire, Angola).

*mayumbe* (2) "hoe" Gua, Mar; Makonde *liyembe,* pl. *mayembe* id.

*mazãbik* "person of East African appearance" Reu, Mau, Sey; toponym *Mozambique* (cf. Kiswahili *msumbiji* id.).

(*loder*) *mazizi* "unpleasant (smell)" Mau; Kiswahili *mazizi* "cow yard, stable."

*meno* "teeth" Sey; Yao+ *meno* id.
*minimini* "lice eggs" Sey; Bemba *mini* id.
*mãgu* "fire stick" Sey; Yao *mangu* id.
*mujawa* "particular group of Africans" Mau; Makhuwa *mutcawa* "Yao."
*mukapa* "giant tortoise" Sey; Makhuwa *khapa* "turtle."
*mulãba* "bird sp." Sey; Giryama+ *mulamba* id.
*mulal* "soot" Reu, Sey; Kiswahili *mlale* id.
*mulapa* "baobab" Sey; Makhuwa *mulapa* id.
*mutya* "rustic dance" Mau, Rod; Sey; Makhuwa *mutcira* "a dance."
*niŋniŋ* "accroupi" Sey; Bondei *niŋinia* "tired of standing," Nyanja *nyanyamala* "sit on one's heels."
*pakatša, kapatša* "basket" Sey; Kiswahili *pakacha* "light basket."
*piliŋge* "argue for the sake of arguing" Mau; Tete+ *piringana* "bulhar, altercar."
*piŋgo* "small bird sp." Mau; Yao *čipingo* id.
*pum* "hernie, grosse testicule" Sey; Kiswahili+ *pumbu* id.
*pundyak* "grande quantité" Reu; Makonde *pundya* "exagerar."
*rẽmbo* "banana sp." Gua; Kikongo *nlembo* "fruit du bananier."
*sãpek* Mau, Rod; *zãbaget* Sey "favorable response to an invitation to play riddles"; Makhuwa *tcampeteke* id.
*sega* "popular local dance rhythm" Reu, Mau, Rod, Sey; *šika* "danse nègre" Hai, Gua, Mar; Nyamwezi+ *seka* "to dance"; Kikongo *xika* "play an instrument, beat a drum."
*seŋga* "boisson alcoolisée" Sey; Nyanja+ *nsenga* "beer sediment" (but Wolof *senga* "palm wine").
*simbi* "divinité des eaux" Hai; Kikongo *simbi* "esprit lutin qui hante . . . les eaux . . .".
*sirãdan* "invitation to play riddles" Mau, Rod, Sey; Makhuwa *tcirantane* id.
*sõgor* "person of African appearance" Mau, Sey; Yao *songolo* "male slave."
*sok* "hollowed out calabash" Sey; Shona+ *shokosa* "scoop out (inside of a gourd)."
*suŋgula* "monkey (in folktales)" Sey; Yao+ *sungula* "hare."
*tartar* "frame for drying fish" Sey; Makhuwa *othatha* id.
*tembo* "alcoholic drink" Sey; Bondei+ *tembo* "palm wine."
*tiŋge* "dance with hand clapping" Sey; Kiswahili *tinge* id.
*tõga* Mar; *tõgõnõ* Gua "marcher péniblement en se dandinant"; Kikongo *tonga* id.
*toto* "child" Sey; Kiswahili *mtoto* id.
*tŝakula* "light meal" Sey; Kiswahili *ča-kula* "nourriture, manger, repas."
*tun(a)* "female genitals" Mau; Makhuwa *ethuna, ethuni* id.
*tuna* "darling" Mau; Makhuwa *othuna* id.
*wãg* "Sesamum sp." Guy; Kikongo *wangila* id.
*wãga* "ensemble d'objets placés dans une demi-calebasse et déposés à un carre-

four à des fins magiques" Hai, "sorcery" Tri; Kikongo *mbwanga* "pochette à *nkisi*" (*nkisi* "fétiche, sorcellerie").

*wayawaya* "rustling (leaves, etc.)" Hai, Sey; Kiswahili *wayawaya* id.

*yāban* "particular kind of African" Reu; toponym *Inhambane* (in Mozambique).

*yaŋ* "(evil) spell" Mau; Inhambane *inyaŋgo* "medicine" (cf. *wãga*).

*zabzabina* "personne forte en gueule" Mau; Kiswahili *zabizabina* "menteur, craqueur, méchante langue . . .".

*zamba* "character in folktales" Gua, Mar; Kikonga+ *nzamba* "elephant."

*zeb* "lazy" Mau; Kiswahili *kizembe* "indolent."

*zez* "string instrument" Mau, Sey; Kiswahili+ *zeze* id.

*zombi, zõbi* "zombi" Lou, Hai, Gua, Dom, Mar, Tri; Bundu *ndjumbi* "espirito de pessoa . . . assassinada sem culpa . . .".

*Items of Kwa Origin*

*abobo* "cri poussé en se frappant la bouche avec les deux doigts . . ." Hai; Fon *awobobo, bobobo* id.

*adãmãsi* "loa" Hai; Fon ?*agãmã* "caméléon, fétiche" + -(*a*)*si* "la personne vouée à un fétiche."

*adja* "kind of (war) dance" Mar, SLu, *adjahũto* "le plus grand tambour rada" Hai; ethnonym *Adja* (Togo-Benin border area).

*agãmã* "caméléon" Hai; Fon *agãmã* id.

*agasu* "loa rada" Hai; Fon *agasu* "l'ancêtre divinisé des rois."

*agbesi, agbeto, agboe* "loa secondaire" Hai; Fon *agbe* "vodũ qui représente la mer," *agbetɔ* "la mer," etc.

*agida* "drumstick" Hai; Fon *agiḍa* id.

*aglauwedo* "loa rada" Hai; Fon *aglavũ wesu* "surnom de chien."

*ago* "pardon! excusez-moi!" Hai, Guy; Fon *agoo* "attention! gare! place!"

*agovi* "loa secondaire" Hai; Fon *agbohuĩ* "fétiche d'Abomey," *axɔvi* "prince, princesse."

*agwe* "loa de la mer" Hai; Fon *agwe* "dieu des devins."

*akãsã* "cornmeal paste" Hai; Fon *akãsã* id.

*akra* "kind of fritter" Hai, Mar; Yoruba *akara,* Fon *akla* id.

*alada, arada, rada* "African from the Slave Coast"; Gua, Mar, "group of voodoo divinities" Hai; toponym *Allada*.

*anasi* "spider" Hai; Fante *ananse* id.

*apapo* "tray used in voodoo ceremonies" Hai; Fon *akpakpo* "écuelle en bois . . .".

*asagwe* "kind of dance" Hai; Fon *asɔgwe* "percussion instrument . . .".

*asõ* "musical rattle" Hai; Fon *asã* id.

*asotɔ* (1) "kind of drum" Hai; Fon *satɔ* "gros tam-tam en bois."

*asotɔ* (2) "voodoo priest's assistant" Hai; Fon *asɔxotɔ* "player of a percussion instrument [to pacify the gods]."

*avalu* "dance of supplication" Hai; Fon *avalu* "hommage."
*avlekete* "loa secondaire" Hai; Fon *avlɛkɛtɛ* "dieu des plages."
*awoyo* "loa de mer" Hai; Fon *woyo* "la mer."
*ayida* "goddess (wife of Dambala Wedo)" Hai; Fon *ayida* "déesse de l'eau."
*ayizã* "divinité vaudouesque (maître des marchés)" Hai; Fon *aizã* "l'esprit protecteur . . . des marchés . . .".
*azagũ* "loa paysan" Hai; Fon *azagũ* "nom sous lequel on invoque quelquefois Loko."
*azenu* "magie, sortilège" Hai; Fon *azẽnu* id.
*azetɔ* "witch" Hai; Fon *azetɔ* id.
*azi* "ground nut" Hai; Ewe *azi* id.
*azili, ɛzili* "grande loa féminine" Hai; Fon *azili* "grand fétiche."
*bade* "loa du vent" Hai; Fon *gbade* "fétiche de la famille de Xɛbioso" (*xɛbioso* "fétiche de la foudre, du tonnerre").
*beke* "European" Mar, SLu, Tri; Igbo *beke* id.
*bokɔ, bɔkɔ* "voodoo priest" Hai; Ewe *bokɔ* "diviner, priest."
*da* Gua, Mar, *dada* Gua "nursemaid"; Ewe *da, dada* "elder sister, mother."
*dãbala, dãgbe* "voodoo god whose symbol is the snake" Hai; Fon *dãgbe* "serpent fétiche, python royal, divinité des Xueḍa."
*daome* "loa secondaire" Hai; Fon *dãxomɛ* "(part of) Dahomey."
*didiko* "morning snack" Gua; Twi *didi* "to eat" (+ Kikongo *diku* "aliment").
*dolo* "proverb" Guy; Fon *do lo* "dire une parabole."
*dosu* "child born after twins" Hai; Ewe *dosu* "name for a boy born after twins."
*dukunu* Hai, *dukun* Gua "sweet maize bread"; Twi *ɔ-dɔkono* "boiled maize bread."
*djɔk* "mauvais sort" Hai; Ewe *dzoka* "a charm," *dzokɔ* "laws to be observed by the owner of a charm."
*flɔ* "creux, vide" Mar; Fon *flo* "cosse, gousse vide . . .".
*gãgã* "showy" Tri; Fon *gãgã* "superbe."
*gede* "loa des cimetières" Hai; Fon *gblegɛdɛ* "fantômes."
*godo* "linge de propreté des femmes" Hai; Fon *godo* "cache-sexe."
*gogo* "behind, buttocks" Mar, Guy; Fon *gogɔ* "fesse."
*govi* "récipient rituel" Hai; Fon *govi* "petite bouteille."
*gugũ* "loa secondaire" Hai; Fon *gu* "fétiche des forgerons," *gũgũ* "féticheur masqué . . .".
*hũ* "principal tambour rada" Hai; Fon *hũ* "tambour."
*hudjenikõ* "acolyte du houngan" Hai; Gun *hũdjenikõ* "premier acolyte."
*hũfɔ* "voodoo temple" Hai; Fon *hũho* "temple," *hũfo* "danse pratiquée dans les cérémonies du culte."
*hũgã* (1) "voodoo priest" Hai; Fon *hũgã* "grand chef féticheur."
*hũgã* (2) "tambour rada" Hai; Fon *hũgã* "gros tamour en bois."
*hũsi* "female assistant of voodoo priest" Hai; Fon *hũsi* "personne vouée à un fétiche."

*hũtɔ* "tambourineur" Hai; Fon *hũtɔ* id.

*ibo* "group of voodoo divinities" Hai; *ibo, igo* "(formerly) African from the interior of the Slave Coast" Gua, Mar; ethnonym *Igbo*.

*kabakaba* "clumsily" Tri; Yoruba *kabakaba* "irregularly, roughly, unevenly."

*kãki* "kind of cake" Gua; Twi *kãŋkyew* "dɔkono" (see *dukunu* above).

*kalalu* "(soup made with) okra" Hai, Gua, Mar; *lalo* "okra" Reu, Mau, Sey; Gɛ̃ *kalalu* "broth," Pedah "sauce" (but Wolof *laalo* "liant pour le couscous"). cous").

*kata* "(rythme de) tambour" Hai; Fon *kata* "tambour et fétiche."

*kãzo* "rite où le candidat hounsi-canzo plonge ses mains dans une marmite de maïs brûlant" Hai; Fon *gãzẽ* "marmite," *kãzõ* "maladie nerveuse."

*koklo* "chicken for use in voodoo sacrifices" Hai, *kɔklɔtɛ* "sorcier, féticheur" Gua; Fon *koklo* "poule, coq."

*kuku* "hollowed out calabash" Gua, Mar, Tri; Igbo *ŋkuku* "récipient fait d'une calebasse," Twi *kuku* "pot."

*legba* "loa rada, protecteur des maisons et des routes" Hai; Fon *lɛgba* "génie protecteur d'un individu, d'une maison . . .".

*lele* "(fouet à) faire mousser" Gua, Mar; Fon *lɛlɛ do* ". . . faire tour."

*liŋlesu* "loa dangereux" Hai; Fon *lĩ* "âme," *lẽsu* "l'equivalent de vodũ."

*loko* "bois sacré . . ." Hai; Fon *loko* "(tree sp.) . . . lorsqu'il sert de support à une divinité, le Loko est considéré comme un vodũ."

*lwa* "dieu vodou" Hai; Yoruba *oluwa* "a lord, owner."

*magari* "dish made of pulped manioc" Sey; Fon *gari* "fécule de manioc . . .".

*mahi* "nom d'une danse" Hai; Fon *maxi* (ethnonym).

*nago, ãnago, nãgo* "rite et danse vodou; loa pétro" Hai; Fon *nago* "Yoruba," *nagbo* "grande féticheuse," *anago* "personne consacrée à Sakpata."

*obya* "sortilège" Tri; Twi *ɔ-bayifo* "sorcery man."

*odãsi* "personne vouée au culte de Dã" Hai; Fon *dã* "serpent," *-si* (see *adã-mãsi* above).

*ogũ* "voodoo god of war and iron" Hai; Yoruba *ŋgun* "a powerful divinity of iron and of war."

*osanye* "loa . . . qui donne la santé" Hai; Yoruba *osanyin* "dieu de la santé."

*papa-lwa* "voodoo priest" Hai; Yoruba *babalawo* "père du secret" (+ French *papa*).

*pe* "voodoo altar" Hai; Fon *kpe* "marche ou estrade . . . pour . . . y installer un fétiche."

*sato* "sorte de tambour" Hai; Fon *satɔ* "gros tam-tam en bois."

*siligbo* "loa pétro" Hai; Gun *siligbo* "dieu invoqué contre les crues de l'Ouémé."

*sobo* "loa rada" Hai; Fon *sogbo* "génie de la foudre."

*tšo* "sucre de 3[e] jet, très brun, cassonade" Mar; Fon *čočo* "huile noire extraite de l'amande de palme."

*tšotšo* "copulate" Mau, Sey; Fon *čo* "coïter."

*vodu* "ensemble de croyances, rites et danses . . ." Hai; Fon *vodũ* "déité de la religion animiste . . . toute manifestation d'une force qu'(on) ne peut definir . . .".
*wari* "a game with pebbles" Hai, Gua; (called *ware* in Ghana).
*wedo* "dénomination appliquée à plusieurs loa" Hai; Fon *Houédo* "le génie protecteur de l'ensemble des foyers d'un même père."
*zãdɔ* "rite secondaire" Hai; Fon *ãdrɔ, zãdrɔ̃drɔ̃,* "veillée nocturne avant une cérémonie religieuse."
*zẽ* "vase rituel . . ." Hai; Fon *zẽ* "pot," *wẽ zẽ* "petite poterie fétiche."
*zege* "small insect sp." Hai; Fon *zege* "scarabée an général."

*Items of Senegambian Origin*

*bãbara* (ethnic label) Gua, Mar, Mau; "sea-slug" Mau, Sey; xenonym applied to the Bamana people.
*bãbula* "drum; kind of dance" Lou, Hai, Gua, Mar, Tri; Jọola+ *bomboloŋ* "war drum made of wood."
*baka* "drum" Hai; Wolof *bakă* "battre le tamtam . . .".
*balãmbala* "*Cassia occidentalis*" Gua; Bamana *bala-mbala* id.
*baranda, baganda* "*Megalops cyprinoides* (fish sp.)" Mau; Bamana [baɣanda] "banane plantain" (related fish species are termed *banan* in both the Indian Ocean and Caribbean areas).
*bip* (expresses the sound of something falling) Hai, Gua; Wolof *bip* id.
*blokoto* Gua, *vlogodoo* Guy (sound of a horse galloping); Bamana *foro-ko-to* "bruit de galop."
*buda,* see *bunda* in the Bantu list.
*buduf* "fat, flabby person" Mau; Wolof *buduf* id.
*buki* "stupid person in folktales" Hai, SLu; Wolof *buki* "hyena."
*dẽba* "Dimba, nom traditionnel couramment porté par l'âne ou le mulet" Mar; *Demba* (a common boy's name in Senegal), Wolof *ndimbă* "cheval blanc."
*fula* "deuxième flûte de l'orchestre vaccine" Hai; Manding *fulee* "flute," Bamana *fula* "two," *fulana* "second."
*gidigidi* "tremblement persistant des membres, danse de St. Guy" Sey; Manding *gidi* "épileptique," *gidyigidyi* "secousse."
*ka* "marque tatouée sur le corps des pêcheurs . . ." Sey; Manding *ka* "coupure . . . incision . . . tatouage."
*karaŋ* "louse" Hai; Bamana+ *karanga* id., Fulfulde (Futa Toro) *karaŋgeeji* id.
*kokobe* "rendre infirme; handicapé" Hai; Manding *kokobi* "lèpre amputante."
*koŋgo* "head" Mau, Sey; Manding *kuŋo* id., Bamana *kuŋolo* id.
*lalo,* see *kalalu* in the Kwa list.
*laye* "vanner, van" Hai; Wolof *lay* "vanner."
*layu* "vannette, sorte de grand panier rond . . ." Hai; Wolof *layu* "van."

*makuklu* "imbécile" Gua; Bamana *makulu, mokokulu* id.
*mumu* "dumb person" SLu, Tri; Manding *muumunee* "dumb."
*nyamnyam* "food; to eat" Mau, Sey; *yãm* (bruit de la mastication) Hai; Wolof *nyam* "nourriture; goûter," *nyamnyam* "to eat."
*-o* (vocative suffix) Hai, Gua, Guy, Mau, Sey; Wolof *-o* id., Bamana *-o* id.
*pupu* "excrement; defecate" Hai; Wolof *puup* "aller à la selle."
*sãba* "chef de chant" Hai; *Samba* (common boy's name in Senegambia), Manding *samba* "to lead."
*seŋga,* see *seŋga* in the Bantu list.
*suku* "l'obscurité, nuit noire" Guy; Bamana *sukuru* "passer la nuit," *suko* arriver tard la nuit."
*sukunyã, sukuyã* "witch, sorcerer" Gua, Dom, Mar, Tri, Guy; Fulfulde *sukunyãdyo,* Soninke *sukunya* "sorciers mangeurs d'hommes."
*toto* "toadfish" Mau, Sey; Manding *toto* "frog," *baa-toto* "frogfish."
*tšãgomã* "crab sp." Sey; Wolof *tšagony ba, tšãgotš ba* "crab sp."
*tšak* "various states of spirituous exhilaration" Lou; Manding *čaaki* "to get drunk."
*tšolo* "disturber, trouble-maker" Mau; Bamana *čoolo* "vagabond."
*tutun* "female genitals" Mau, Sey; Bamana *tutunin* id.
*ũhũ* "yes" Tri; Bamana *ũhũ* id.
*ũũ* "no" Tri; Bamana *ũũ* id.
*was* "ostentation" Tri; Bamana *waso* id.
*welele* "rassemblement" Mar; Bamana *welele* past participle of *wele* "inviter, convoquer . . .".
*yapyap* "eat (quickly)" Mau, Sey; Wolof *yapa* "manger avidement."
*yolof* (ethnonym) Mar, Mau; Wolof *yolof* id.

## Appendix 2: Riddles

Mauritius: *Grandppâ dans lacase, so labarbe touzours dohors—Lafimée* (Baissac 1888).
Martinique: *Papa moin en didans, barbe li ca pawaîte dehors—Un clairté* (Parsons 1943).
Senegambia: "The old man is in the house, his beard is outside—Fire and smoke" (Mandinka; Gamble 1976); *[Un] homme adulte [est] ici dans [la] case, [sa] barbe [est] ici dehors—Grosse fumée* (Fulfulde; Gaden 1913).
Kwa: "Un vieillard est dans sa case, mais on voit sa barbe du dehors—Le feu" (Mina; Béart 1955); "The master is inside the hut, but his beard is outside—A fire, the smoke of which escapes through the thatch" (Yoruba; Jablow 1962).

Mauritius: *Mo gagne éne çouval, mo beau fréme li dans léquirie so laquée touzour dohors—Lafimée* (Baissac 1888).

Haiti: *M' gan ioun chouval, m' beau fermin l' lans l' équirie, quée li toujours paraître deyors—Lafimin* (Faine 1939).
Martinique: *Chuval moin, en dudans, la-cheu dehors—Lampe* (Parsons 1943).
Jamaica: *John, the mule, in the stable, his tail outside—fire in the kitchen, smoke outside* (Beckwith 1924).
Senegambia: "I tied my cow in the house, its horns are outside—smoke and fire" (Mandinka; Gamble 1976); "J'ai mis mon cheval dans la dernière de trois chambres contiguës et reliées entre elles; sa queue sorte malgré cela—La fumée" (Songhai; Ben Hamouda 1919).

Mauritius: *Mo grandmanman zamès oulé dourmi làhaut so natte, li quitte so natte li dourmi par tére—Ziraumon; Mo grandmanman li beau fére nattes tout so pitits dourmi partére—Ziraumon* (Baissac 1888).
Martinique: *Yon manman ka fè natt baille yche li, yche li toujou couché à tè—Giromon* (Turiault 1873–76).
Jamaica: "I was tying mat ever since an' I never lay down on one—Pumpkin vine" (Beckwith 1924).
Bantu: "Who is this person who weaves many mats but spends his nights on the ground—a pumpkin" (Luba; Gowlett 1975); "There is a person who is very clever at plaiting many mats, when he plaits them he does not sleep on them himself, he lies on the bare ground—Pumpkin" (Makhuwa; Harries 1942); "I have woven my many mats but I myself sleep on the ground—A pumpkin" (Nyanja; Gowlett 1975; also in Hehe, Lozi, Hoho, Mwera, etc.).

## Notes

1. The creoles of St. Barthelmy and of Grenada and the Grenadines are omitted due to lack of adequate data. (The latter may, in any case, no longer be spoken, although Parsons 1943 includes a few samples collected in about 1918.)

2. See Curtin 1969:219 for more on this. Note also that my figures are derived from Curtin's table 49 throughout, whereas Singler (this volume) draws on the same table for the period to 1750 but uses table 60 (Curtin 1969:200) for 1751 onward. Table 60 attempts to take some account of slaves purchased in the Caribbean by the French from the British and others by making adjustments to the figures in table 49 in the light of data on the slave population in a handful of plantations in Haiti in the second half of the eighteenth century. The differences between the two sets of figures do not significantly affect my discussion.

3. The precise geographical area denoted by the word "Guinée" at this time is uncertain. See Baker 1982a:204, n. 18.

4. Probably to be equated with French *maure*, the first element in the name Mauritania: Saint Louis on the River Senegal, which forms the border between Senegal and Mauritania, was among the first places the French obtained slaves.

5. Although small numbers of Malagasies are known to have been taken to the

Caribbean at different times, no one has yet identified anything of Malagasy origin in any creole of that area.

6. In addition to being a language spoken on both sides of the Congo-Zaire border, Kikongo is also an umbrella term for a large number of closely related languages, many of which have often been classified as dialects of Kikongo, which are spoken over a much wider area extending into Angola (Mann et al. 1987:150–52).

7. There are divergent views on whether the names of Bantu languages should be cited in English without the class prefix (e.g., Mbundu) or with the prefix (e.g., Kimbundu or Ki-Mbundu or kiMbundu, etc.). The practice varies from one country to another. In general, I have included the prefix whenever the name is frequently cited in this form (e.g., Kiswahili rather than Swahili) and omitted it in all other cases (e.g., Shona rather than Ic(h)ishona).

8. I am grateful to Guy Hazaël-Massieux for drawing my attention to a possible Bantu origin for *didiko* (included in appendix 1 in the Kwa list).

9. I reserve the terms "target" and "target language" for situations in which the person(s) concerned had consciously identified the desire to acquire that language. I do not believe that the first Africans who arrived in, say, Martinique or Jamaica as slaves had a conscious desire to acquire French or English as such. However, they certainly wished to communicate with people whose diverse mother tongues were not intelligible with their own. Because all slaves of all linguistic backgrounds were exposed to the language of their European "owners," words from the latter provided the starting point for intercommunication. The resulting pidginized French and pidginized English substantially solved the communication problem for foreign-born slaves. It would thus be inaccurate to represent French or English as "target languages" which slaves failed to reach. (However, for their locally born children, the acquisition of their owners' language might have seemed a desirable aim and the words "target language" could have been appropriate for them.)

10. Pleonastic *li* is comparatively rare in modern Mauritian but is well attested throughout the nineteenth century.

11. It has been suggested that the CH does not take adequate account of social factors (Alleyne 1986:302; Davis 1986:234), but such criticism relates to the very brief description of the CH in Bickerton 1984 and cannot reasonably be applied to the full account of this hypothesis in Baker 1982b:806–59.

12. So far as I am aware, no one has published figures indicating the number of Jamaican words which Cassidy and Le Page (1980) derive from Twi and other languages.

## References

Alleyne, Mervyn C. 1986. Substratum influences: Guilty until proven innocent. In Muysken and Smith, eds., 301–15.

Alves, P. Albino. 1951. *Dicionário etimológico Bundo-Português*. Lisbon: Tipografia Silvas (vol. 1); Centro Tipografia Colonial (vol. 2).

Baissac, Charles. 1888. *Le folklore de l'Ile Maurice*. Paris: Maisonneuve and Larose.

Baker, Philip. 1982a. On the origins of the first Mauritians and of the creole language of their descendants. In Baker and Corne, eds., 131–259.

———. 1982b. *The contribution of non-francophone immigrants to the lexicon of Mauritian Creole*. Ph.D. thesis, School of Oriental and African Studies, University of London. Ann Arbor: University Microfilms 8529054.

———. 1984. Agglutinated French articles in creole French: Their evolutionary significance. *Te Reo* 27.89–129.

———. 1987. Combien y a-t-il eu de genèses créoles à base lexicale française? *Etudes Créoles* 10.60–76.

———. 1988. On the origins of the Mauritian Creole riddles in Baissac 1880. *Journal of Mauritian Studies* 2.2.40–85.

Baker, Philip, and Chris Corne. 1982. *Isle de France Creole: Affinities and origins*. Ann Arbor: Karoma.

———. 1986. Universals, substrata and the Indian Ocean creoles. Muysken and Smith, eds., 163–83.

Bazin, Hyppolite. 1965. *Dictionnaire bambara-français*. Second edition. Ridgewood, N.J.: Gregg Press (first edition, Paris, 1906).

Béart, Charles. 1955. *Jeux et jouets de l'ouest africain*. Dakar: IFAN.

Beckwith, Martha Warren. 1924. *Jamaican Anansi stories*. New York: G. E. Stechert.

Ben Hamouda. 1919. Devinettes Songai. *Bulletin du Comité d'Etudes Historiques et Scientifiques de l'Afrique Occidentale Française* 2.

Bentley, William H. 1887. *Dictionary and grammar of the Kongo language*. London: Baptist Missionary Society and Trübner.

Bickerton, Derek. 1981. *Roots of language*. Ann Arbor: Karoma.

———. 1984. The language bioprogram hypothesis. *Behavioral and Brain Sciences* 7.2:173–221.

Bollée, Annegret. 1977. *Le créole français des Seychelles*. Tübingen: Max Niemeyer.

Cassidy, Frederic G., and Robert B. Le Page. 1980. *Dictionary of Jamaican English*. Cambridge: Cambridge University Press.

Chaudenson, Robert. 1974. *Le lexique du parler créole de la Réunion*. Paris: Champion.

Christaller, Johannes G. 1933. *Dictionary of the Ashante and Fante language, called Tshi (Twi)*. Basel: Basel Evangelical Missionary Society.

Comhaire-Sylvain, Suzanne, and Jean Comhaire-Sylvain. 1955. Survivances africaines dans le vocabulaire religieux d'Haïti. *Etudes Dahoméennes* 14.5–20.

Corne, Chris. 1982. A contrastive analysis of Reunion and Isle de France creole

French: Two typologically diverse languages. Baker and Corne, eds., 7–129.

Crowther, Samuel A. 1852. *A vocabulary and grammar of the Yoruba language*. London: Seeley's.

Curtin, Philip. 1969. *The Atlantic slave trade: A census*. Madison: University of Wisconsin Press.

Davis, Anthony R. 1986. Short note. *Journal of Pidgin and Creole Languages* 1.233–38.

Delafosse, M. E. F. 1955. *La langue mandingue et ses dialectes*. Paris: Geuthner.

De St.-Quentin, Alfred and Auguste. 1872. *Introduction à l'histoire de Cayenne*. Paris: J. Marchand.

D'Offay, Danielle, and Guy Lionnet. 1982. *Diksyonner kreol-franse. Dictionnaire créole seychellois-français*. Hamburg: Buske.

Ducoeurjoly, S. J. 1802. *Manuel des habitants de Saint-Domingue*. Paris: Lenoir.

Faine, Jules. 1936. *Philologie créole: études historiques et étymologiques sur la langue créole d'Haïti*. Port-au-Prince: Imprimerie de l'Etat.

———. 1939. *Le créole dans l'univers: études comparatives des parlers français-créoles*. Port-au-Prince: Imprimerie de l'Etat.

FOM. See Ministère de la France d'Outre-mer.

Gaden, Henri. 1913. *Le poular*. Paris: Ernest Leroux.

Gamble, David F. 1976. *Mandinka dilemma stories, puzzles, riddles and proverbs*. San Francisco: California State University, Department of Anthropology.

Goodman, Morris F. 1964. *A comparative study of creole French dialects*. The Hague: Mouton.

Gowlett, D. F. 1975. Common Bantu riddles. *African Studies* 34.79–145.

Harries, Lyndon. 1942. Some riddles of the Makua people. *African Studies* 1.275–91.

Jablow, Alta. 1962. *An anthology of West African folklore*. London: Thames and Hudson.

Josephau, Serge. 1977. *Africanismes dans le créole*. Fort de France, Martinique: Centre Départemental de Documentation Pédagogiques.

Koopman, Hilda. 1986. The genesis of Haitian, French, and West African languages. In Muysken and Smith, eds., 231–58.

Laman, Karl E. 1936. *Dictionnaire kikongo-français*. Brussels: Georges van Campenhout.

Lefebvre, Claire. 1986. Relexification in creole genesis revisited: The case of Haitian Creole. In Muysken and Smith, eds., 279–300.

Le Page, Robert B., ed. 1960. *Jamaican Creole*. London: Macmillan.

Mann, Michael, David Dalby, Philip Baker, Abdulaay Bari, Catherine Bozon-Verduraz, Sidia Jatta, and John Saeed. 1987. *A thesaurus of African languages: A classified and annotated inventory of the spoken languages of Africa with an appendix on their written representation*. London: Hans Zell.

Ministère de la France d'Outre-Mer. n.d. *Série G*[1]*: Recensements, Etat-civil*.

Missionnaires, Les RR PP. 1875. *Dictionnaire volof-français*. Saint-Joseph de Ngasobil: Imprimerie de la Mission.

Mufwene, Salikoko S. 1986. The universalist and substrate hypotheses complement one another. In Muysken and Smith, eds., 129–62.

Muysken, Pieter, and Norval Smith. 1986. Introduction. In Muysken and Smith, eds., 1–13.

Muysken, Pieter, and Norval Smith, eds. 1986. *Substrata versus universals in creole genesis*. Amsterdam: John Benjamins.

Parsons, Elsie Clews. 1943. *Folklore of the Antilles, French and English. Part 3*. New York: G. E. Stechert.

Racelle-Latin, Daniele (coordinator). 1980. *Inventaire des particuliarités lexicales du français en Afrique Noire*. Montreal: AUPELF and ACCT.

Rechenbach, C. W. 1967. *Swahili-English dictionary*. Washington, D.C.

Richardson, Irvine. 1963. Evolutionary factors in Mauritian Creole. *Journal of African Studies* 2.2–14.

Sanderson, G. Meredith. 1954. *A dictionary of the Yao language*. Zomba, Malawi: Government Printer.

Sapir, J. David. 1971. West Atlantic: An inventory of the languages, their class systems, and consonant alternation. *Current Trends in Linguistics 7: Linguistics in Subsaharan Africa*, 45–112.

Segurola, B. 1963. *Dictionnaire fon-français*. Ouidah: Centre Catéchétique [*sic*].

Sparshott, T. H. 1887. *A Nika-English dictionary*. London.

Sylvain, Suzanne. 1936. *Le créole haïtien: morphologie et syntaxe*. Wetteren, Belgium: Imprimerie De Meester; Port-au-Prince, Haiti: Chez l'auteur.

Thomas, J. J. 1869. *The theory and practice of creole grammar*. Port of Spain, Trinidad: The Chronicle Publishing Office.

Turiault, J. 1873–76. Etude sur le langage créole de la Martinique. *Bulletin de la Société Académique de Brest* 2.401–516, 3.1–111.

# Where Did Haitian Creole Come From? A Discussion of Hazaël-Massieux's and Baker's Papers

*Arthur K. Spears*

Recent thinking on creole genesis has focused on two explanatory matrices: universals and substratum influence. These two were the topic of Muysken and Smith (1986), the most recent major volume on the subject. However, with little reflection, it strikes one as curious that superstrate input is in so many instances discussed as though it were either an afterthought or a given, as though what needs to be explained are those properties of creoles which do *not* reflect the superstrate language. If we approach creole languages and their genesis globally, though, as indeed we must for a complete understanding, we must explain all properties of a creole language and why each is there. We are not faced with the simple task of explaining what is left in creoles after we have subtracted all that can obviously be traced to the superstrate language.

In creole genesis, various linguistic traditions interact; no one tradition will necessarily have the greatest influence. All components of that interaction need to be explained in a theory of creole genesis which, following Mufwene's (1986) statement, will have to deal with universals *and* substratum influence, and, going beyond Mufwene's principal concerns (and apparently those of most creolists), superstrate influence also. Stated differently, some putative substrate and universal features of creole languages could conceivably have been passed over during creolization in favor of a superstrate feature. One might propose that when any claimed determinants of substrate feature (or universal feature) selection do not operate, a superstrate feature is selected by default. One might, alternatively, set up universals as the default category; that is, whenever the rules, so to speak, of creole formation do not select superstrate or substrate features, for whatever reason, a universal feature results by default. This is essentially Givón's (1979) approach. The particular component of creole genesis chosen as the default category (the category the specifics of which no attempt is made to explain) is in reality a function of the theoretical perspective a particular creolist has on creole genesis, whether this perspective is explicitly stated or not.

The crucial point is that specific superstrate features should be explained. This is particularly true given that, in many cases, related creoles have incorporated different superstrate features for one and the same function. For instance, Haitian French Creole places the possessive after the noun, as in *cha mwen* 'my cat' (from the French *chat à moi*), while Guyanese French Creole places it before the noun, *mon cha* (from the French *mon chat*).[1] So, universalist and substratist theories cannot explain superstrate features in creoles by—to take one approach as an example—setting up the superstrate as the target language in second language acquisition and then claiming that the superstrate features ending up in part of the creole were just what the second language learners were able to learn. In other words, the specific superstrate features that wind up in creoles must be addressed in terms of theories and hypotheses oriented especially toward accounting for the selection and modification of superstrate features. They must explain why certain superstrate features appear in the creole while other superstrate features do not, and how those which do appear differ from the superstrate model.

## Hazaël-Massieux's Paper

Guy Hazaël-Massieux proposes to do exactly what I advocate above. His basic hypothesis, which his discussion is concerned with providing a preliminary body of evidence for, is that Guadeloupean Creole (GC) is essentially a construct of French language forms filtered and refashioned by nonnative speakers who gave birth to GC, for the most part African, but including American Indians. He uses the general model of language change developed by Eugenio Coseriu to identify principles at work in the formation of GC. We gain nothing, in Hazaël-Massieux's view, by searching out grammatical features common to creole and African languages which are absent from French. The implication of this is that a suitable general theory of linguistic change allows for the formulation of principles which explain why some French forms were incorporated but others were not, with the ensemble of incorporated forms, in line also with these principles, settling into the new grammatical configuration that is GC.

Hazaël-Massieux's hypothesis, perhaps more so than many, identifies French, not African languages, as the primary raw material for creolization, although he does recognize the role of African languages in convergence, whereby semantic and formal similarities between West African language forms and French ones favor the selection of convergent forms into the emergent creole. In addition, he recognizes actual African loans, which, in his view, result from the lack of French words to name African things which remained part of the slaves' lives; for example, items connected with cuisine, medicine, dance, and so forth. His discussion suggests, following Chaudenson (1979), that if we examine the seventeenth-century popular French that the Africans actually heard, we discover that GC is actually not so different from the actual French model, as opposed to the standard French of the time.

The primary ingredients of the hypothesis include principles relating (1) pragmatic-functional considerations, (2) sound perception, and (3) overgeneralization of grammatical rules. Pragmatic-functional considerations, to elaborate somewhat on one type, include what Le Page (1977) and others have used to explain specifics of contact language grammars: face-to-face communication, highly instrumental communication, immediate feedback, etc. According to Hazaël-Massieux, a creole exists when the overgeneralizations tested in the exchange among speakers of different origins form paradigms accepted by those speakers; it is not necessary that all speakers' systems be identical to ensure comprehension.

This may not be meant to be taken as a real definition of "creole," because it makes no reference to the existence of language norms and grammatical stability, both of which are prerequisites for creole status. The mere possibility of communication may be seen as insufficient. However, on a more liberal interpretation, it certainly does characterize the beginning point of that linguistic continuum which leads to creolization.

One fact of creole grammar which Hazaël-Massieux is able to shed some light on with his framework is future negation in Haitian Creole (HC). There are two semantically distinct futures in HC (Spears 1990:125): *va,* which comes from a conjugated form of the French verb *aller* 'to go,' and *ap,* from *après* 'after.' (There are other future constructions, but they need not detain us.) Thus, we have *pap* but not **pa va*. In HC, future negation is with *ap* only, at least putatively. Consequently, the semantic distinction between them is neutralized in negative contexts. Hazaël-Massieux proposes that creole retained only stressed items in negation, thus the first element, *ne,* of French negation is not present in creole. (Cf. a negated French sentence such as *Il ne va pas* 'He does not go/is not going.') Note that this is not a creole innovation, however, since it has long been a part of common French. He supposes, reasonably, that negation came before the introduction of preverbal tense, mood, and aspect markers; and following the French linear order, the negative element *pa* preceded the stressed verbal element. Thus, the creators of creole overgeneralized in setting up a rule that the negative element precedes the predicate. Note that the etyma of the HC preverbal markers follow the negative element in French,[2] with the exception of *va*. So, negated predicates in the emergent creole all agreed with the order of the French model, with the exception of predicates with *va*. This situation continues to the present in HC, in which only negated *ap* futures are allowed. To carry Hazaël-Massieux's line of reasoning forward, there would be pressure against *va*'s occurring negated because such a construction would go against the lexifier's system wherein *pas* normally follows the conjugated verb.

Note, however, the curious HC *pavapka* 'will not be able to' from a Port de Paix speaker (northern Haiti). I have presented the phrase undivided into morphemes because it can be analyzed as being the phonological reduction of two full forms: (1) a full form having both futures, that is, *pa va ap ka;* or (2) a form having two negative elements *pa,* that is, *pa va p(a) ka*. Both possibilities conform to the phonological rules of HC. The second morphemic analysis, however, seems the more likely since, with Hazaël-Massieux's comments, there is at least some explanation for it. (There seems to be no explanation for the first morphemic analysis.) The explanation: the two *pa*'s represent the tension between preceding and following positions for the negative element. Conceivably, *va* with the following negative element was taken from French, but pattern pressure caused *va* to appear also with the preceding *pa,* with some speakers resolving the positional conflict by placing *pa* twice, as is reflected in some present-day forms.

Though some superstrate-oriented explanations of creole grammar seem to fare well, one should nevertheless keep in mind Philip Baker's point that there are traps for "Eurocentric" linguists who might miss Africanisms based on African models which happen to be formally and semantically similar to French ones. In this regard, it would also be useful to add Baker's admonition relating to calques, for example, the Mauritian greeting *ki manyer* 'how are you?' (literally, 'what state [are you in]?'); notice the Swahili *u hali gani* and also the Swahili *habari gani* (literally 'what news?') and the Mauritian *ki nuvel*.

The real point concerning Hazaël-Massieux's discussion overall, however, is that French certainly contributed more to creole than lexicon alone, and he has provided us with a way of explaining why certain French forms have creole homologues and others do not. The approach also explains how in some cases a creole feature that does not clearly seem to be French is not necessarily African just because it corresponds to African forms. In other words, formal correspondences between creole and African languages may be not Africanisms but Gallicisms explainable on a principled basis. Hazaël-Massieux's comments can be extended to other French-lexicon creoles. If anything, his contribution serves as a break on the hasty attribution of forms to the African substratum. It also serves to place the study of creoles more within the framework of general language change, as governed by language universals and general cultural universals—to a significant extent genetically determined—which provide a restricted set of possibilities, only some of which can be actualized in a particular sociohistorical context.

This notwithstanding, an overall problem with the framework is that it does not offer much in the way of explaining subsystems of creole grammar. These subsystems raise questions such as, How do we get from the French verbal system to a creole one, and from a French determiner system to a creole alternative? Hazaël-Massieux's framework is best at explaining forms in creole, as opposed to function and meaning. So, for example, even though he provides some indications as to why certain verbal system forms ended up in creole, there is nothing to explain why a particular set of tense-mood-aspect functions and meanings are realized in creole grammar. But again, as indicated above, only if theories and hypotheses oriented toward the superstrate are combined with those dealing with universals and substrate influence will we be likely to explain fully creole genesis.

## Baker's Paper

The most important overall implication of Philip Baker's paper pertains to when creolization takes place and the role African languages play. I will pursue primarily the question of creole genesis, with special reference to Haitian Creole, drawing on Baker's and others' materials and presenting an alternative model for creolization in Haiti.

### *Haitian Creole: The Pidgin Bypass Hypothesis*

Since my concern is primarily with HC, I will take as a starting point Claire Lefebvre's discussion (this volume). Her view of the formation of HC is that it was created through interaction between French and African languages—notably Kwa languages in general, Fon in particular—without passing through a pidgin stage. She argues this must have been the case since, due to the rapid turnover in the slave population resulting from the high mortality and low birth rates slavery produced, the children who presumably might have created a creole language (using Derek Bickerton's language bioprogram) were simply not present in significant numbers. Therefore, adults must have formed HC. She hypothesizes that those adults did so through relexification and reanalysis. HC did not pass through a pidgin stage because West African morphosyntax and semantics remained basically intact while the West African lexicon was being replaced by French.

What does it mean to say there was no pidgin? Does it mean that there was never anything but French and the African languages prior to HC? If so, the question then becomes whether all relexified-reanalyzed versions of the West African languages were creoles, pidgins, or something else—maybe interlanguage—or none of the above. To avoid misunderstanding, we may have to refer to them simply as relexified-reanalyzed versions of a West African language (assuming Fon had the role Lefebvre accords it in her hypothesis). Let us refer collectively to the linguistics stages which Lefebvre hypothesizes to have led to HC as "X." It seems clear that X was neither nativized nor was its grammar stable, using "grammar" in the global sense it typically takes in studies in the generative tradition. Lefebvre, however, hypothesizes that the grammar minus lexicon was indeed mostly stable. So following that line of thought, the grammar of X was, in a sense, almost stable. Does this disqualify it from being a pidgin? It does only if we consider "pidgin" to exclude any significant continuity in grammar from substrate languages of a substrate language; but some (e.g., Bickerton and Givón 1976) have argued that such grammatical continuity can occur to some extent in a pidgin even in a plantation context. However, that grammatical continuity (in Hawaii) involved speakers from diverse substrate backgrounds and did not lead to anything that could reasonably be called a stable pidgin morphosyntax. Without arguing the point, it seems that X is outside the spirit, so to speak, of what the term "pidgin" is intended to convey. X is not an interlanguage, because, as Sarah Thomason points out (this volume), "interlanguage" assumes a desire to learn a second language and reasonable access to the second language to do so.

Nevertheless, Lefebvre's thesis raises another question. Were colonial varieties of French and Fon the only significant language varieties involved in the formation of HC? That is, could there not have been other pidgin or creole varieties, formed in different places in Haiti, which served as input into the HC of today? In a social context such as that of Haiti during the relevant period, pidgins and other creoles might well have emerged in at least some places on the island. Did they play any role in the development of HC? Baker's question (this volume) is quite relevant here: While Fon speakers were busy relexifying and reanalyzing, what were the speakers of other African languages doing?

### *The Role of Mulattoes*

We might examine the question of the social locus of creolization in Haiti from another perspective, the role of mulattoes. There was a significant number of them in the colonies from the very beginning, yet I know of no discussion in the literature on any key role that the mulatto communities may have played in the genesis of HC. It is quite possible that the mulattoes (and other nonwhite free persons) played a role comparable (though not identical) to that claimed by Hancock (1986) for the mulattoes in Lançado communities in West Africa. One plausible hypothesis would be that in mulatto groups a creole, perhaps closer to French than the HC spoken around the end of the eighteenth century, emerged and then some time later began distancing itself significantly from French during the rapid expansion of the colony in the last quarter of the eighteenth century. According to James (1963:55–56), production in Saint Domingue doubled between 1783 and 1789. During this period of expansion the demand for slaves rose quickly and the practice of seasoning slaves was dropped; the slaves were brutalized as quickly as possible into submission. One type of evidence that supports this specific form of a mulatto community–based creolization hypothesis is the attestations of eighteenth-century forms of HC closer to French than contemporary HC or that of a century or so ago. This mulatto-formed creole might have existed from the early days of the colony alongside pidgins (or some type of non–West African, non-French form of speech) spoken by the majority of the slave population. Thus, the rapid turnover in the slave population during most of the eighteenth century might have prevented a creole from forming among the majority of slaves specifically, but this did not necessarily prevent creolization everywhere.

### *The Language of Locally Born Slaves During the Eighteenth Century*

In 1789, two years before the revolution, two-thirds of the roughly half million slaves in Saint Domingue had been born in Africa. What role might they and their locally born predecessors have had in creolization? Perhaps a better-focused question would be, What language(s) did the locally born slaves speak throughout the eighteenth century? Even if we accept Lefebvre's thesis, the language situation it describes is not the only possibility. Other languages and language continua could have developed simultaneously. It seems perfectly reasonable to assume that, regardless of whatever else they may have spoken, the locally born slaves spoke a creole, especially if they tended to form a functionally and socially distinct group of slaves (e.g., house servants, craftspeople, work gang leaders, seasoners of newly arrived slaves, etc.). If they did indeed form a distinct social group, then there would have been an adequate context for them to have maintained intragroup communication (in addition, of course, to communication with other groups) laying the foundation for the formation of a creole and its intergenerational transmission.

### *A Plurilocal Hypothesis on Creolization*

To summarize, I would like to suggest that there were several possible loci of creolization. The first was what must have been a relatively socially integrated community of slaves, mulattoes, French farmers, buccaneers, and others during the second half of the seventeenth century and perhaps the very early eighteenth. This creole, if we may call it such, may actually have been more like Réunionnais in being classifiable as a variety of French, that is, a "continuation of a French linguistic tradition" (Baker and Corne 1982:121). (Note that slaves were a minority of the population.) The situation that Corne (1982:120) describes for early Réunion seems much like what the early Haitian situation must have been, in terms of broad strokes. Although the French-speaking to non-French-speaking ratios were different, there was a clear French-speaking majority in both cases. The second locus might have been the group of locally born slaves, who, though a minority, did exist throughout the history of the colony, notably in the eighteenth century. The third locus may have been the social context of the mulattry throughout the eighteenth century; their possibly streamlined French, on this hypothesis, would have developed into a creole as a distinct mulatto identity became increasingly solidified. The fourth locus might well be that in which the direct ancestor of contemporary creole was formed. This creole might have resulted from a recreolization initiated by the heavy influx of African-born slaves beginning around 1783 with the doubling in the colony's production. The halt of additional slaves coming in from Africa in the wake of the revolution would have provided the demographic stability for this creole (i.e., its various dialects)[3] to become dominant in the country.

### *Evaluating the Hypothesis*

One ostensible problem with this hypothesis is that it is not supported by Baker's discussion of African loanwords. Most are from the Kwa language family (including Ewe and Fon). Baker's figures (based on Curtin 1969) indicate that a large number of slaves coming into Haiti in the last part of the eighteenth century were Bantu language speakers. If contemporary HC were the result of a recreolization of this period (late eighteenth century), one might expect (even though this is not necessarily the case) more Bantu than Kwa loans.

Counterarguments could be presented. First, the figures for Kwa and Bantu loans, particularly after adjustment for religious items,[4] show that Bantu input is more significant than it at first seems to be, and Kwa input less. Second, the adjusted percentages for Bantu and Kwa loanwords are so close that the ratio of Kwa loans to Bantu ones provides only the weakest evidence for the claim that HC must have emerged during the early eighteenth century (see Lefebvre, this volume), possibly the late seventeenth according to one of the hypotheses entertained here, due to the numerical dominance of Kwa speakers. In fact, the claim that contemporary HC developed during the period of Kwa dominance is even less attractive given the possibility of recreolization (toward the end of the eighteenth century). Third, Baker's figures on slave arrivals and origins are based on Philip Curtin's (1969), which, as far as I can tell, ignore an important fact. The spectacular growth of Saint Domingue toward the end of the eighteenth century led to a demand for more slaves than the French themselves could import from Africa. Although the French, in the best mercantile tradition, wanted to control all of the colonists' purchases of slaves, French resources simply could not meet the demand. The British, always willing to rise to a commercial opportunity, sold slaves first imported to British islands to the colonists of Saint Domingue. By 1789 or thereabouts, 50% of slaves imported into the British islands were smuggled into Saint Domingue (Report of the Committee of Privy Council for Trade and Plantations, 1789, pt. 4, cited in James 1963:53).[5] In view of this, Curtin's (explicit) figures do not provide an accurate picture of how many slaves of each language background actually came into Saint Domingue during the late eighteenth century. Crucial is this: toward the end of the eighteenth century, there may have been significantly more Kwa language speakers coming into Saint Domingue than official French figures indicate. If this is so, then Kwa language loans in HC might reflect late eighteenth-century Kwa influence as much as earlier Kwa influence. We would then not have to consider the high percentage of Kwa-origin loans in HC as strong evidence that HC emerged early in the eighteenth century, or, more specifically, that any HC that emerged early in the eighteenth century is a direct ancestor of contemporary HC (following the plurilocal hypothesis).

The second point has to do not so much with a problem as an issue. I have hypothesized—and here I will make the hypothesis stronger for purposes of discussion—that the great influx of Africans into Haiti toward the end of the eighteenth century upset or further destabilized whatever linguistic environment had evolved. This is not to imply that that environment was in any way static. What I am implying is that if there was continuous language change due to the steady influx of slaves from Africa, that change may well have been accelerated during this period late in the century. That is to say, whatever creole or precreole was spoken by the majority of (common) slaves entered a period of Africanization. The issue is this: why would this Africanized creole, that of the majority of the black population, have become the dominant creole (assuming there were others)?

There are several possible explanations: (1) this social group (which I will refer to for convenience as "blacks") formed the majority of the population; (2) the revolution gave blacks a social power they did not have before; and (3) by this time, any prestige that may have attached to speaking any mulatto-associated dialect of creole had diminished due to the results of the revolution and the availability of French itself to serve as a distinguishing linguistic symbol. (As the mulattoes became wealthier, particularly during the second half of the century, those who could, sent their offspring to France to be educated, making French a more viable distinguishing linguistic symbol. Note that I am not implying that many did this, only that enough did.)

I might point out that the hypothesis I have sketched does agree with Baker's complementary hypothesis. What Baker's hypothesis does not deal with, which is relevant particularly for a larger island, is the possibility of different creole traditions developing and interacting with each other historically. Of course, Baker's hypothesis was developed primarily in view of events in the Indian Ocean, but it perhaps might benefit from a fuller consideration of the implications of the existence of different types of social systems for the global creolization process in a specific area.

## Notes

1. The example is from Mufwene 1986:148, 149. I have used the IPN Haitian Creole orthography to represent examples from Haitian and Guyanese.

2. For example, the HC anterior tense marker *te* comes from the French past participle of *être* 'to be': *été*. Note the French *Il n'a pas été* 'he was not/has not been.' Crucial is that in the French model, the etymon of HC *te* follows the negative element *pas*.

3. Here, one should mention an observation made by Baker (this volume) as well as others; namely, that northern HC "might originally have been a direct continuation of the Lesser Antillean creoles." This would not necessarily have had any effect on what was going on in the rest of the country, however.

4. Baker's correction of loanword figures is on the grounds that the vocabulary of voodoo is specialized, used mainly by voodoo religious leaders, and known only from the specialized study by Comhaire-Sylvain and Comhaire-Sylvain (1955). The

figures are as follows (based on Baker, after Curtin): (religious words included) Bantu, 26%; Kwa, 63%; (religious words excluded) Bantu, 35%; Kwa, 44%.

5. It seems that the percentage might more likely be 30%, *extrapolating* from Curtin's (1969) figures.

## References

Baker, Philip, and Chris Corne. 1982. *Isle de France Creole: Affinities and origins*. Ann Arbor: Karoma.

Bickerton, Derek, and Talmy Givón. 1976. Pidginization and language change: From SXV and VSX to SVX. *Papers from the Parasession on Diachronic Syntax*, ed. by Sanford Steever, Salikoko Mufwene, and Carol Walker, 9–39. Chicago: Chicago Linguistic Society.

Chaudenson, Robert. 1979. *Les créoles français*. Paris: Fernand Nathan.

Comhaire-Sylvain, Suzanne, and Jean Comhaire-Sylvain. 1955. Survivances africaines dans le vocabulaire religieux d'Haïti. *Etudes dahoméennes* 14:5–20.

Corne, Chris. 1982. A contrastive analysis of Reunion and Isle-de-France creole French: Two typologically diverse languages. In Baker and Corne, 7–129.

Curtin, Philip. 1969. *The Atlantic slave trade—A census*. Madison: University of Wisconsin Press.

Givón, Talmy. 1979. Prolegomena to any sane creology. *Readings in creole studies*, ed. by Ian F. Hancock, 3–35. Ghent: E. Story–Scientia.

Hancock, Ian. 1986. The domestic hypothesis, diffusion and componentiality. In Muysken and Smith, eds., 71–102.

Heine, Bernd. 1979. Some characteristics of African-based pidgins. *Readings in creole studies*, ed. by Ian Hancock, 89–98. Ghent: E. Story-Scientia.

James, C. R. L. 1963. *The Black Jacobins: Toussaint L'Ouverture and the San Domingo revolution*. Second edition, revised. New York: Random House.

Le Page, Robert. 1977. Processes of pidginization and creolization. *Pidgin and creole linguistics*, ed. by Albert Valdman, 222–55. Bloomington: Indiana University Press.

Mufwene, Salikoko S. 1986. The universalist and substrate hypotheses complement one another. In Muysken and Smith, eds., 129–62.

Muysken, Pieter, and Norval Smith, eds. 1986. *Substrata versus universals in creole genesis*. Amsterdam: John Benjamins.

Singler, John Victor. 1986. Lectures and handouts for the course African Languages and Caribbean Creoles. Linguistic Society of America Summer Institute, City University of New York.

———, ed. 1990. *Pidgin and creole tense-mood-aspect systems*. Amsterdam: John Benjamins.

Spears, Arthur K. 1990. Tense, mood, and aspect in the Haitian creole preverbal marker system. In Singler, ed., 119–42.

# Continuity versus Creativity in Afro-American Language and Culture

*Mervyn C. Alleyne*

The basic underlying premise of this paper is that the question of Africanisms in language is part of the larger question of Africanisms in Afro-American culture. Language is part of culture, and linguistics is (at least in some of its concerns) an anthropological science. Language is similar to other aspects of culture in that it is learned in the socialization process. It undergoes change and development in relation to social interactional processes. There are universals of language, and also of culture, pertaining to commonalities in the human experience; and there are specifics in language and culture relating to the unique experience of particular societies.

But language may be different in some senses from other aspects of culture. For example, it is the vehicle through which several other cultural behaviors and institutions are manifested. Another important difference is the link of language with modes of thought and cognitive orientations and with mental intellectual capacities. It is this latter aspect which is being emphasized now.

But it is still important to recognize the two facets of language: it is, on the one hand, a property of the mind and, on the other, a cultural institution developing through social interaction or a cultural behavior learned in the socialization process. The claim that language is already wired into the mental capacity of humans makes language different from other aspects of culture and leads to universalist mentalist interpretations of Afro-American language. No other aspect of culture is like this. Even if we may suspect that humans are already biologically wired with a capacity to generate musical forms and religious structures, no one suggests that children manifest the innate universal structures of music or religion, although there are definitely universals in music and religion in the same way that language universals exist. One might be able to construct a hypothesis that rhythm is universal and related to universal physical and motor features of humans and the universe, and that rhythm as a basic structural feature of all Afro-American music (often music is pure rhythm and no melody) is therefore not necessarily an Africanism; similarly for religion. But there has been no attempt to deal with Afro-American music and religion in this way.

My basic assumption in this paper is that language is learned, which is not to say that some aspects of a child's language behavior do not reveal a process other than, or in addition to, simple learning. But the claim here is that a child's initial deviations from adult language which may be a reflection of this innate mechanism (I do not think that all child language syntactic and semantic forms are a product of this) are not generally perpetuated into adult language. Second language learning may also be mediated by this innate mechanism, but here too my claim is that in addition to the natural cognitive processing apparatus that allows us to learn languages, there are other strategies employed in language acquisition which include behaviorist-type learning.

The assumption of this paper is therefore that environmental inputs are crucial in acculturation and cultural change as well as in language acquisition. The relevant question is how really degenerate or inaccessible or unexploitable these inputs were in the case of the emergence of Afro-American language and culture (degenerate in the case of the putative pidgin, inaccessible and unexploitable in the case of the African language and culture inputs). I shall not deal with the question of a degenerate pidgin because I know of no evidence to support the existence of a prior pidgin in Afro-American language. The notion of the inaccessibility or unexploitability of the African inputs is the foundation of a certain interpretation or hypothesis of Afro-American culture which I call the creativity hypothesis (in many ways it is the cultural analogue of the language bioprogram hypothesis). This paper contrasts the creativity hypothesis with a continuity hypothesis (which it favors), and the underlying premise is the following: to the extent that language is an aspect of culture, a theory of Afro-American language will be informed by a general theory of Afro-American culture. Stated otherwise, a theory of Afro-American language will be more powerful as it is more general in terms of accounting for Afro-American culture in general.

It may be useful to present a broader framework that might clarify what "continuity" and "creativity" are taken to mean here and what they do not mean. This framework is the long-standing debate in psychology which takes different forms and uses different terminology at different times. It has been couched in terms of nature versus nurture in human development and behavior, or, more currently, in terms of cognitive theory as against behaviorist theory. Of interest to Afro-American culture studies is that the work of A. Jensen (1969) falls within the cognitive paradigm insofar as it is based on the notion that intelligence is a biological endowment that cannot be fundamentally altered by environmental factors or that at least takes precedence over such factors. There is therefore the notion of continuity from birth or prebirth. "Continuity" here falls within the same paradigm as "creativity," with creativity referring to the idea that man is not the prisoner of inputs from his environment but is already biologically wired or programmed with certain capacities.

When applied to culture and to current studies of Afro-American culture specifically, these terms take on new meanings and we therefore have to clarify these. We first have to separate language from the rest of culture. As I stated above, language was once thought to be learned behavior; that is, children learn language through a process of stimulus and response in the guardian-child interaction; but a newer view about language, presented sometimes as absolute and categorical, claims that human beings have an innate creative capacity for language. "Creativity" here refers to the claim that the human "mentally organizes the target language structures heard and develops hypotheses about these" (Appel and Muysken 1987:87). These patterns are not a direct reflection of patterns heard in the environment. Linguistics then becomes no longer a social or anthropological science but a science of the mind, part of psychology. The most interesting direction this debate has taken is in the field of creole language genesis. And insofar as Afro-American speech of the United States, the Caribbean, and South and Central America is either creole or creole derived, this new direction has important implications for a theory of Afro-American culture. There is now a hypothesis that creole language forms are the direct product of this innate language capacity possessed by human beings but most readily accessed and manifested by children. This idea that creole languages spoken by Afro-American populations were created or generated by these universal mental processes is antithetical to the idea that they are the result of existing inputs in the environment.

In creole linguistics, therefore, there is a current debate as to whether creole languages emerged as a result of the mental creativity of speakers or whether the characteristic structure of these languages is due to continuities from the West African languages spoken by the slaves who developed these languages. In Afro-American linguistics this is what "continuity versus creativity" means.

In Afro-American culture in general, "continuity" refers to the same notion; that is, that Afro-American culture, in its most distinctive characteristics, is to be interpreted in terms of continuities from West African culture, implying also discontinuities and borrowings from the dominant culture. This has been opposed by several positions in the history of Afro-American culture studies, culminating in what may be called the "creativity" hypothesis of Afro-American culture, most closely associated with anthropologists and historians at Johns Hopkins University. I will not recount the history of these other hypotheses, which are well known and racist in their essence. Together with the current creativity hypothesis, they all reject or discount the significance of African cultural continuities in the New World.

There are three main theories about what became of African culture(s) in the New World. According to one view, Africans were stripped of their culture because of the brutalizing effects of slavery and the deliberate mixing together of slaves of different ethnolinguistic groups. Others, for example Mintz and Price (1976), agree that Africans were unable to maintain their traditional culture but believe that slaves created an original new culture in the New World. A third view is that Afro-American culture is largely an extension of African culture, though African influence is greater in some parts of the New World than in others, having become diluted in some cases and undergone changes that mask the underlying African base.

In trying to evaluate the merits of these different theories, we need to address a number of questions. For example, was the harshness of slavery an insurmountable barrier to the continuation of African culture in the New World? Were slaves deliberately and effectively mixed to prevent interaction by members of the same ethnolinguistic group, or did the ethnolinguistic distribution of slaves, especially in the crucial early period, simply reflect the geographic development of the slave trade? How culturally diverse were the Africans brought to the New World? Did the slaves quickly "orient their allegiances in New World rather than African directions" (Price 1980:194), or did they continue throughout the history of the New World to see Africa as their ancestral home?[1] Did slaves of different nations (or ethnic groups) tend at first to isolate themselves from one another and pursue their own ethnic activities (Schuler 1979:66),[2] or were new cross-ethnic bonds created—for example, bonds between "shipmates"? Another final question: Are there commonalities in the Afro-American experience, or is each Afro-American culture unique? A lot of general Afro-American studies have concentrated on commonalities without understanding how specific cases may alter the generalizations.

Common features in the Afro-American experience have attracted the attention of anthropologists and linguists alike, but each region and each segment and layer of the Afro-American population remains different and distinctive. For example, in some important ways, Jamaica is not typical of the rest of the Afro-American world. In Jamaica one African ethnic group (the Twi) provided political and cultural leadership (as did the Ewe-Fon in Haiti); throughout the post-Columbian history of Jamaica a number of Maroon communities have served as custodians of African culture (as they also have in Suriname). After the cessation of hostilities with the British, some of these Jamaican Maroon communities developed close relations with the general Afro-American population, especially in St. Thomas, Portland, St. Mary, and St. Andrew. Finally, after emancipation, small peasant communities grew up in the remote hilly areas of Jamaica, creating pockets of isolation. Though none of these features is unique to Jamaica, their combination is unique and helps to explain the distinctive course of Afro-American culture on the island.

Unlike the early racist hypotheses, the creativity hypothesis is scientifically sound and worthy of consideration. It has to be considered in the light of the effect of the ecological, social, economic, and political context of cultural history and change. Some scholars have claimed that the ecological factor has operated in an exceptional way in the Afro-American world, and they view Afro-American culture in terms of innovations or creations or reactions to this ecological context rather than as continuities or discontinuities from an African base.

Price's belief (1980:195) that the Maroons of Suriname "were faced with nothing less than the task of creating a whole new society and culture" is extreme, for it implicitly denies that they were able in some measure to reconstruct a pattern of the society and culture they had known in Africa. Maroons probably did work out new patterns of social order and cultural forms; but much depended on which groups fled to the forests first or in the largest numbers, for pioneers set a pattern to which other groups had no choice but to accommodate themselves. In Jamaica the Twi set such a pattern.

Few people now completely deny the "contributions" from West Africa to Afro-American culture. For example, Price (1980:196) speaks of "general cultural orientations" and Mintz (1970) of "those aspects of the ancestral cultures [that] they could carry in their minds." However, in the case of Jamaica, it can be demonstrated that not just "pitch, intonation and timbre" but entire functioning languages were carried to Jamaica and can still be found there even now. Not just "general cultural orientations" or "religious beliefs" but entire religions were carried to Jamaica, where they had to struggle to maintain themselves in hostile conditions. Not just "artistic or aesthetic orientations and preferences" but African musical instruments and a repertoire of songs and performances for religious and secular occasions were brought over. It is interesting to examine the different ways in which these cultural forms changed in different contexts, or, conversely, stayed intact. Price (1980:204) justifiably derides those earlier scholars who "view Suriname Maroon societies merely as a little Africa in America," for since the fifteenth century there have been no wholly intact "African" cultures even in Africa, either in the towns or in the villages.

One of the pillars of the creativity hypothesis is that there is a great variety of African cultures, and that this, together with the alleged mixing of slaves in the New World to reduce the chances of plotting and resistance by members of one ethnic group, prevented significant African cultural continuities in the New World. But again, it can be shown that this claim is disproved not only by the Jamaican case but probably also by Haiti and Cuba and Berbice; in all three places one African people dominated and assimilated others. Even where this did not happen, the basically uniform culture shared by Africans of diverse ethnic origins and transmitted to a basically uniform set of environments in the New World led to parallel changes and developments in different parts of the Afro-American world. As Abrahams and Szwed (1983:8) remarked,

> there is simply too much contrary evidence for us to accept Mintz's argument without some real qualifications. . . . Wherever Afro-Americans could interact with one another, there emerged a set of expectations, attitudes, and feelings which in great part derived from past practices. These encounters would naturally draw upon the shared experiences in Africa and the New World.

Handler and Frisbie (1972:36) concluded their study of music in Barbados with the view that "similarities in fundamental West African musical forms and expressions (and the sociocultural context in which they were found) provided a common basis for interaction among persons coming from different cultural backgrounds and a foundation upon which a shared musical tradition was established and perpetuated in New World societies." They openly oppose this opinion to the opinion of Mintz (in his foreword to Whitten and Szwed 1970:8) that

> the cultural heterogeneity of any slave group normally meant that what was shared culturally was likely to be minimal. It was not, after all, some single 'African culture' that was available for transfer nor even some generalized African cultural substratum.

However, Handler and Frisbie see no contradiction between their opposition to Mintz on this particular point and their acceptance of Mintz's broader view that ultimately Afro-American cultures "depend upon creativity and innovation far more than upon the indelibility of particular cultural contents."

The current creativity versus continuity debate has mainly addressed the culture of black people in North America. There has been much debate of late about whether "black culture" exists in the United States. This question has generally been posed within the context of slavery and the effects of slavery on the culture and psychology of enslaved Africans. Elkins (1976) sums up the different positions on slavery as "damage" and "resistance." To put it crudely, the "damage" theory holds that the powerlessness, exploitation, and brutalization of slaves resulted in their complete psychological and cultural degradation, leading in extreme cases to the creation of the personality type known as "Sambo."[3] For example, the alleged destruction of the African family under slavery, mainly through the indiscriminate sale of its members and, especially in the earliest years, the shortage of women slaves, is said to account for a number of allegedly negative personality, moral, and behavioral traits in Western Hemisphere blacks.

Supporters of the "resistance" position do not suggest that the system of slavery was permissive or benign, and they maintain that slavery was rapacious and degrading, but still they prefer to emphasize the efforts of the slaves to resist, to assert themselves, and to develop their own positive culture. They believe that this culture cannot be seen merely as a "reaction" to white oppression. Historians such as Blassingame (1972) focus on the community life of slaves. They present a picture of a life "in which family [the slave family was not destroyed either], religion and a body of lore served as mechanisms of resistance against the debilitating effects the slave system was formerly supposed to have had" (Elkins 1976:278).

This "resistance" position has become very popular among black ideologists and scholars and also among some white scholars. It has to be noted, however, that it either ignores or fails to deal satisfactorily with the apparent contradiction between the view of slavery as a brutal, oppressive, and degrading institution and the view that slaves were able to develop their own positive cultures. Second, it presents the development of this culture in too many ways as a reaction to whites and to slavery (though it sets out to do the very opposite). Third, it presents slave culture as a development of the period of slavery. It is not clear what culture the slaves had before they were slaves. Nor is it clear at what point slaves began to "develop" this culture and whether they existed in some kind of cultural void before embarking on this process of cultural development or creation.

Although many scholars still accept that New World Afro-American cultures have their roots in Africa and that continuities from the ancestral culture still persist wherever Africa-derived populations form communities in the New World, North American writings on slavery and the culture of slaves nonetheless stress the *creation* of a distinctive culture rather than the continuity of African culture(s) transplanted to the New World. Both sides in the damage versus resistance debate share the general position that slavery was the decisive factor. Either it completely destroyed or infantilized the Africans; it imposed on them white European forms of culture (which, because of the harshness of slavery, they imperfectly assimilated); or it in some way allowed them to create a distinctive culture, institutions, and organizations. In other words, the main focus is on slavery as an institution and the effects that slavery had on the lives and culture of the slaves. Even authors who take the position that slaves resisted and triumphed over the dehumanizing effects of slavery and that Africa is the mother continent for New World blacks may still fall within the orbit of the "creativity" school. Thus Levine, in a work on songs and folktales (1978), argues that slave songs constitute a distinctive cultural form, but they owe less to white influence or African origins than to the circumstances of American slave life; and he speaks of the slaves as "carving out independent cultural forms." Accordingly, he presses all the evidence and data into the same mold: for example, he represents folktales as a psychic adjustment to slavery insofar as they show how "the weak must make their way in a world of hypocrisy and superior power—by tricking not only the strong but also each other." But as Elkins (1976:282) observes, many of Brer Rabbit's tricks seem gratuitous and purposeless, and he can be downright cruel to defenseless weaker people (Brer Rabbit sacrifices his own wife and children to save himself). Elkins understandably asks whether the "adjustment" represented by these tricks can be considered positive.

A similar analysis can be applied to slave religion. Rawick (1970:151) rightly rejects the "creativity" view that religion was a release from the day-to-day world of work and a refuge in the promise of salvation, but he reaches a methodologically similar conclusion that "the religion of the oppressed usually gives them the sustenance necessary for developing a resistance to their own oppression." Simpson (1970:72) puts it more strongly:

> The shifts [*sic*] to religious cults of one kind or another comes from the nature of the slave system, the system that followed it, and the social, economic, and political treatment which those at the bottom received . . . these conditions modified character in a stressful direction and those who were most sensitive to the stress advanced new religions and secular systems to deal with their anxiety.

Slave religion may have been all of these things to some or all Africans, but it was—certainly in the case of Jamaica—first and foremost the continuity of an ancestral religion. True, there was an important link between religion and resistance; but religion was taken to the Americas from Africa and was an important basis for resistance; it was not created during the course of that resistance.

The creativity view fails to consider the possibility that preslavery cultures may have largely determined the response and adjustment of slaves to slavery. There is little doubt that animal stories featuring a spider and other animals existed in the preslavery cultures of slaves. These tales expressed a morality that Africans brought with them into slavery. But they were also part of a picaresque narrative tradition, many of whose elements are hard to square with the image of downtrodden slaves triumphing over their oppressors. On the other hand, other elements in the African moral tradition must surely have helped slaves to deal with their oppression. One reason folktales persisted during slavery was because they and their performance were an important part of African communal interaction that helped mold a new African community from diverse African elements. This is not to deny that resistance was an important factor in the emergence of Afro-American culture.

The concept of marronage, embodying political, physical, and cultural resistance, is essential for an understanding of the cultural history of the Afro-American world. A symbiotic interaction developed between culture and resistance. The will to resist required the preservation of some functional distinctiveness in culture, upon which the success of the resistance depended; and the success of the resistance in turn contributed to the preservation of an African-type base culture. The Maroon communities of Jamaica and other parts of the New World are the most striking example of this symbiosis, although from the very start resistance took other forms as well, including suicide on capture, during the Middle Passage, or on American soil; poisonings; and the development of certain personality traits (e.g., the ginal), modes of behavior, and forms of expression designed to confuse the master class. Poisoning was an art widely practiced by slaves and widely feared by the master class; it depended on preserved knowledge about herbs, roots, and barks that was part of the culture and "folklore" of Africa. Language, songs, folktales, and the Sambo and ginal personality types were imbued with ambiguities: they had one meaning for the master class and another for the slaves. Spirituals such as "Steal away to Jesus" are the best-known examples of this ambiguity,[4] but they are not the only ones; other examples can still be found throughout Afro-America (Reisman 1970a and 1970b). Finally, suicide was motivated by Africans' belief that at death their spirits would be returned to the ancestral homeland, where they would dwell in harmony with their revered ancestors. This interaction between culture and resistance was perhaps most evident in religion.

Finally, I wish to discuss an issue crucial to the acceptance of the notion of African continuities. Western writers have attached more importance than necessary to the diverse origins of Africans destined for the New World. First of all, West Africa has been widely recognized as constituting a culture area whether through historical relationships or through areal assimilation. There has been massive inter-African assimilation and acculturation throughout West Africa's history. This happened even when there was no common enemy serving as a catalyst to help bring Africans together. Enslavement in the New World enabled Africans to see beyond their differences. Cultural and ethnic unity and uniformity were not just ideological constructs promoted by the militants; they were a product of the objective conditions. Slaves began to grasp this unity almost as soon as they were captured, and they could sufficiently communicate their sense of it—whether through language, kinesics, drums,[5] or music—to organize revolts aboard the slave ships. Even if it is true (and not just a typical case of European stereotyping) that most revolts were hatched and led by Asante Africans, there was apparently no ethnic restriction on who might participate in such revolts.[6] Traveling to Jamaica on the same ship became a very important bond for Africans, who treated their shipmates as kinfolk. Patterson (1967:150) shows that for the early slaves "shipmate seems synonymous in their view with brother or sister" and

> is the dearest word and bond of affectionate sympathy amongst Africans. . . . They look upon each other's children mutually as their own. It was customary for children to call their parents' shipmates "uncle" or "aunt." So strong were the bonds between shipmates that sexual intercourse between them, in the view of one observer, was considered incestuous.

The seeds of an African community cutting across superficial boundaries between people of different ethnic origins were therefore sown as early as the crossing from Africa to the New World.

The question of community is a crucial one. The essential characteristics of a community are stability, continuity, and constant interaction, without which the slaves would have found it extremely difficult to pursue their cultural traditions. All communities are, of course, to a certain extent unstable and discontinuous: the terms are relative. With regard to Jamaica, it would be hard to argue that Maroon societies were anything but stable continuous communities. However, some scholars doubt whether the Africans who remained slaves constituted a real community and tend to see them as no more than a motley group of individuals or as tiny ethnic groups that clung together and viewed others as strangers. Mintz and Price (1976) have even argued that Africans in the New World were at first more a "crowd" than a community.

Divisions did exist among the slaves, but it is doubtful whether these were so deep as to fragment slave society into noninteracting separate and autonomous compartments. Early writers could identify different ethnic groups and different languages, but it is not clear to what extent these differences entailed ethnic rivalry or separation.[7] It is, of course, not unlikely that people of one ethnic group would stick together (for ethnic cohesion is a widespread—some would say universal—facet of human behavior and societal organization). Moreover, there are reports of exclusively Akan slave rebellions and of festivals exclusively celebrated by one ethnic group.

Beckles (n.d.) takes a different view. He speaks of "emotional unity, and a sentimental bond [that] held the plantation black communities together" (9). The form of unity cut across cultural lines but rarely withstood the full force of political praxis. Beckles cites an observer as noting in 1666 that: "They are passionate lovers one of another; and though they are born in different countries and sometimes, when at home, enemies one to another, yet when occasion required they mutually support and assist one another, as if they were all brethren." He also claims (but again without providing the evidence) that "the rebels must have developed a significant level of political consciousness in order to transcend their cultural divisive tendencies, to launch a series of collective political actions against their oppressors."

Price (commenting in Schuler 1970:143–44) says that "the majority of cases of strong ethnic organization that we know about slaves occur in the 19th rather than say the 17th century." However, he later agrees with Schuler that the "creolization" process which created "slave communities vertebrated by new Afro-American (rather than separate African ethnic) principles of organization" happened more rapidly in Suriname than in Jamaica.

Evidence from Maroon societies may shed light on the early relationships between African ethnic groups. According to Bilby (1981), contemporary Maroons still recognize four major ancestral spirits, each of which is identified with a major "tribe" or "nation" from which Maroons think they are descended.

> The only social context in which this notion of tribes comes into play is the traditional (religious) ceremony of Koromanti dance. . . . Several other tribes are cited by present-day Maroons as having contributed to early Maroon society. . . . All these individual tribes are subsumed under the one most powerful tribe, the Koromanti tribe.

There is evidence among Maroons and among Jamaicans in general of an inter-African syncretism and assimilation taking place within a broader framework of Asante (or Koromanti) dominance. Groups seem to have expressed their ethnicity in some areas but to have suppressed it in others, in favor of ethnic integration. This integration grew as creole slaves came to outnumber African-born slaves. It is interesting to observe that in England today, where different ethnic groups now experience the same subjugation, hostility, and discrimination, a similar process can be observed among West Indians from the different islands of the Caribbean. On the one hand, a distinct ethnic identity (say, Jamaican, Trinidadian, Bajan) is maintained and asserted. On the other hand, that ethnicity may be suppressed, particularly by West Indians born in England, in favor of another Caribbean ethnic identity. For instance, Jamaican language, music, and religion may be favored by Trinidadians.

So there were elements of both stability and instability, continuity and discontinuity, in slave plantation societies. There is evidence of a community of slaves interacting from the very start, and other evidence of ethnic divisions and divisions between creole and African-born slaves. There were other forms of differentiation too: by occupation (between domestics, drivers, artisans, and field slaves), by civil status (between the enslaved and the free), and by "racial" admixture (between negroes, mulattoes, quadroons, and so on). However, the discontinuities were rarely absolute. For example, even where kinship systems could not be maintained because of the absence of vital kin, basic elements of the system, such as respect for elders, could be maintained. Moreover, notions of kinship that could no longer be applied to consanguinal relations were transferred to other relations. Despite their removal from Africa and from their families, slaves continued to worship ancestral spirits in various parts of the New World.

The formation of stable integrated communities by slaves was not incompatible with dominance and leadership by one ethnic group. Scholars such as Herskovits (1941) and Bastide (1971) have always recognized that different African cultural traits preponderate in different parts of the New World. Thus, as I have said, Dahomey Fon characteristics predominate in Haiti, Yoruba in Cuba, Bantu in several parts of Latin America, and Twi-Asante in Jamaica and Barbados. Bastide (1971:8, 11) argues that predominance is not just a question of numbers, which in any case cannot be accurately established from the records. I suggested earlier that a group may have come to predominate not because it was generally in the majority but because of its importance in the early formative period of slave society. Some ethnic groups were more coherent and unified than others and could therefore maintain their traditional institutions more easily than their disorganized neighbors, who may have adopted their institutions. Gardner (1873) reports religious behavior and institutions in Jamaica that are related both in underlying principle and in detail to Akan religion; the question is whether this religion was observed by slaves regardless of ethnic origin. Another interesting question concerns the point in history at which the Akan vocabulary that predominates among Africa-derived words in the Jamaican language was adopted by other ethnic groups. The historical record provides no conclusive answer to this question, but there is no reason to doubt that there was some generalized acceptance of the norms established by the dominant group in the early period in Jamaica.[8] Gardner (1873:184) more than implies as much when he writes that "the influence of the Coromantyns seems to have modified, if not entirely obliterated, whatever was introduced by other tribes" (he is referring to religion). However, the dominant group also incorporated elements from the culture of other ethnic groups.

These are two approaches to the interpretation of Afro-American culture: one is historical and stresses continuities; the other is structural-functional and stresses creativity. I am not suggesting that the historical approach is completely satisfying, since *post hoc ergo propter hoc* is not a principle of causality. Explanation in the social sciences remains a problem that the functional approach cannot resolve. The creativity hypothesis often does not even attempt to specify the conditions of causality or the mechanisms through which the particular cultural form is produced.[9] Creativity as a psychogenetic attribute cannot be verified or substantiated outside the forms that it is alleged to generate. We therefore cannot support Rawick's claim (1970:149) that "there is no more creative and innovative culture in the New World than that of black Americans." Afro-American culture is no more and no less creative than other New World cultures. The kind of creativity demonstrated by Afro-Americans is probably a legacy of Africa. Price (1980:214) fails to see this when he contrasts the "relatively unchanging features of (Suriname) Maroon artistry which are based on a broadly African set of features" with "the celebration of artistic innovation and individual creativity which guarantees that Maroon arts are ever changing, inventing and playing with new forms and techniques," which is "American." African and Afro-American music, story telling, language, dance, and games can likewise be analyzed in terms of inventiveness within a tradition.

## Notes

1. This is what Jamaican Maroons claim. It is also borne out by slave narratives and is implicit in the high suicide rate among slaves and their belief that they would return after death to the ancestral home. Rawick (1970:162) writes of one such narrative, "Notice in the following example how the informant invokes memories of Africa, not as some distant unimaginable place, but as one that was culturally close at hand."

2. Note that this contradicts the view often stated but not quite substantiated that slaves were effectively mixed.

3. *Quashee* is Sambo's Jamaican namesake. *Quashee* connotes the following qualities: foolish, evasive, lazy, possessing a bad sense of judgment, lying, cringing, but also, contradictorily, crafty. This last quality has led some scholars to interpret the Sambo personality as a form of resistance or a means of survival and self-preservation.

4. See Fisher 1953 for evidence that the religious songs of North American slaves may have had a private meaning for slaves, different from the meaning understood by whites.

5. The use of talking drums was sufficiently prevalent and feared to provoke their prohibition.

6. Dallas (1803, 1:33) observes that "Negroes of other tribes joined the Maroons, but the Coromantee (Ashanti) language superceded the others and became in time the general one in use."

7. Long (1774:425) records that in 1769 "several new (Jonkunnu) masks appeared. The Ebos, the Pawpaws, etc., having their respective Connus." This separateness and rivalry seem to have been encouraged by the Portuguese in Brazil, who organized *batuques* (periodic displays of tribal drumming and dancing), playing one group against another in an attempt to create divisions and even animosity among slaves (Turnbull 1976:243–44). This has not been reported for Jamaica.

8. Thus, the naming of objects by Akan words was probably adopted by other groups in the early period.

9. "Universals" in studies of creole genesis are also very weak on causality, although they are often very loosely presented as if they constituted a causal agent.

## References


Abrahams, Roger, and John Szwed. 1983. *After Africa*. New Haven: Yale University Press.

Appel, René, and Pieter Muysken. 1987. *Language contact and bilingualism*. London: Arnold.

Bastide, Roger. 1971. *African civilizations in the New World*. New York: Harper and Row.

Beckles, Hilary. n.d. White power and black consciousness: Slave resistance in the English West Indies during the seventeenth century. Unpublished manuscript.

Bilby, Kenneth. 1981. The Kromanti dance of the windward Maroons. *Nieuwe West Indische Gids* 55.52–101.

Blassingame, John. 1972. *The slave community: Plantation life in the ante-bellum South*. New York: Oxford University Press.

Dallas, R. C. 1803. *The history of the Maroons*. 2 vols. London: Frank Cass.

Elkins, Stanley. 1976. *Slavery*. Chicago: University of Chicago Press.

Fisher, M. 1953. *Negro folk songs in the U.S.* Ithaca, N.Y.: Cornell University Press.

Gardner, W. J. 1873. *A history of Jamaica*. London: Frank Cass.

Handler, J., and C. Frisbie. 1972. Aspects of slave life in Barbados: Music in its cultural context. *Caribbean Studies* 11:5–40.

Herskovits, Melville. 1941. *The myth of the Negro past*. New York: Harper and Brothers.

Jensen, A. 1969. How much can we boost IQ and scholastic achievement. *Harvard Educational Review* 39.1–123.

Levine, Lawrence. 1978. *Black culture and black consciousness: Afro-American folk thought from slavery to freedom*. New York: Oxford University Press.

Long, Edward. 1774. *The history of Jamaica*. London: Lowndes.

Mintz, Sidney. 1970. Foreword to Whitten and Szwed, 1970.

Mintz, Sidney, and Richard Price. 1976. *An anthropological approach to the Afro-American past: A Caribbean perspective*. Philadelphia: Institute for Study of Human Issues.

Patterson, H. Orlando. 1967. *The sociology of slavery*. London: McGibbon and Kee.

Price, Richard. 1980. *Afro-American arts of the rain forest*. Berkeley: University of California Press.

Rawick, George. 1970. West African culture and North American slavery in North America: A study of culture change among American slaves in the ante-bellum South with focus on slave religions. *Migrations and Anthropology: Proceedings of the 1970 Annual Spring Meeting of the American Ethnological Society*, ed. by R. Spencer, 149–64. Seattle: University of Washington Press.

Reisman, Karl. 1970a. Cultural and linguistic ambiguity in a West Indian village. In Whitten and Szwed, eds., 129–44.

———. 1970b. Ethnic slave rebellions in the Caribbean and the Guianas. *Journal of Social History* 3.374–85.

Schuler, Monica. 1979. Afro-American slave culture. *Roots and Branches: Current directions in slave studies*, ed. by M. Craton, 121–37. Toronto: Pergamon Press.

Simpson, George. 1970. *Religious cults of the Caribbean: Trinidad, Jamaica and Haiti*. Institute of Caribbean Studies, Puerto Rico.

Turnbull, Colin. 1976. *Man in Africa*. New York: Doubleday.

Whitten, Norman, and John Szwed. 1970. *Afro-American anthropology*. New York: Macmillan.

# Creole Language Provenance and the African Component

*Ian Hancock*

A number of assumptions have been made regarding the role of African languages in the Atlantic Creole diaspora. Mittelsdorf (1979:99), for example, states that

> since Akan and the Bantu languages were identifiable as the main contributing languages in the Jamaican Creole lexicon, it is reasonable to assume that the search for African features in the structure and the phonology can be narrowed to those two groupings, and that any proposed Africanisms not deriving from these two are suspect.

If the identification of the provenance of African-derived morphemes in a creole were to be taken as a guide to the makeup of the creole itself, we would assume that Krio, with its overwhelming Yoruba lexical component, did not exist until after the wholesale influx of Yoruba speakers into that country after 1820, either being imported along with Nigerians who already spoke it or else coming into existence once they had settled in multilingual Freetown. Yet it is evident that an anglophone creole looking much like Krio existed on the Sierra Leone coast during the previous century—even though there is hardly a trace in modern Krio of any linguistic impact from Sherbro-Bullom, the African language spoken throughout the area in which that creole developed. In his dissertation on the origins of the Suriname creoles, Smith (1986) suggests that speakers of African languages from the Upper Guinea coast were not significantly represented in the formative situation (although this is disputable), but regarding their origin he concludes nevertheless that

> Sranan, Ndjuka, Boni, Paramaccan and Kwinti are basically derivatives of West African Pidgin English (WAPE), which in turn derives from a process of creolization via the Language Bioprogram which can be located in the region of Sierra Leone, the modern representative of which is Krio. (167–68)

There are many works dealing with the origins of the African populations in Atlantic creole societies, and these invariably use linguistic evidence as their primary focus; for example, Benjamin (1956) for Wolof in Haitian, Daeleman (1972) for the Kikongo elements in Saramaccan, Mathieu (1982) for Bantu in Palenquero, Holm and Oyedeji (1984) for Yoruba in the whole of the western hemisphere, and Smith et al. (1987) for Ịjọ in Berbice Creole Dutch, along with several other such studies. This is, of course, a quite legitimate line of pursuit, and knowing where African populations came from, and what languages they spoke, can only help us to understand the development of each individual creole. But it cannot always be assumed that the same languages provided the African component in the emergence of that creole. When Cassidy (1983:79–80) says that "Turner's linguistic evidence . . . proves beyond question that speakers of languages from as far north as Senegal, along the entire West African coast as far south as Angola, were brought to the Charleston and surrounding areas where Gullah is now spoken," this provides little information about the origins of Gullah itself, but merely helps to account for the eclectic representation of African-derived lexical items and a number of calqued forms in that language (for a discussion of the role of areal, i.e., "Balkan" features in Gullah formation, see Mufwene and Gilman 1987).

There are two opposing points of view regarding the role of African languages in the creolization process: that expounded by, for example, Alleyne (1980:138), who believes that "native [i.e., African] language transfers are more demonstrable than universal simplification errors," and, on the other hand, that of Mittelsdorf (1979:175), who believes that few features of creolization "need to be explained by reference to the linguistic background of the original population. It is only in the lexicon that the impact of the substratal African languages made itself felt to any significant extent." Mittelsdorf's anti-substratist position is shared by the universalists (see in particular Bickerton 1986), although she does not herself address this.

I have dealt with componentiality as one means of accounting not only for creole language origins but also to explain differences among those sharing a geographical and lexical base, differences which have generally been accounted for by polygenesis or varying rates of metropolitanization ("decreolization"). The African component might also be usefully addressed from this perspective.

To outline briefly what I mean by componentiality (discussed in more detail in Hancock 1986, 1987, 1988, 1992), this views each creole-forming social and linguistic matrix as an independently developed phenomenon growing out of the coming together of different proportions of its "ingredients" or components under different circumstances. Interpretations of the situation which in general support this approach include Bickerton's pidginization index and his complementary hypothesis (1984:175), the latter discussed and critiqued by Philip Baker (1982, this volume; see also Baker and Corne 1982; and Mufwene 1986 for related discussion).

These components are (a) the African languages, (b) the various dialects of metropolitan English, (c) the West African Creole component, and (d) other languages. For any specific situation, all of the following parameters must be taken into account:

1. The dates of migration and settlement
2. The proportions of speakers of different languages in each situation during the first twenty-five years, and their points of origin
3. Their social relationships
4. Their physical distribution
5. The topography of the environment vis-à-vis travel and communication
6. The rate of change over time of the population ratios
7. The changing ratio of locally born to those arriving as adults
8. Evidence of population migrations, into and out of the community

The African languages are those dealt with in the studies referred to above and potentially number in the hundreds. The various dialects of metropolitan English were regional, social, and occupational and have started to be addressed by, for example, Niles (1980), Harris (1985), Williams (1986), Rickford (1986), and Hancock (1988). "Other languages" include native American languages such as Arawak and Carib, and probably Algonkian, and others brought from the British Isles such as Irish and Scottish Gaelic, Welsh, Cornish, Jersey French, Romani, and Shelta. Little has been done on these, although Taylor (1945) began to examine Amerindian linguistic influence in the Caribbean; the role of Irish Gaelic has also received some attention.

The West African Creole component, or Guinea Coast Creole English (GCCE), according to my hypothesis, was represented by a chain of dialects spoken in Afro-European communities centered mainly on the Gambia and Sierra Leone River coasts, and later the Gold Coast and the Bight of Biafra littoral. I have dealt with its origins and dispersal along the coast elsewhere (Hancock 1980a, 1986, 1987; for a popularized account of the social situation on the Guinea Coast, see Sherry 1986, in particular chap. 17). Without repeating my claims in detail, I see the emergence of GCCE as resulting from an original ship English having been acquired as a second language by the African female partners of its speakers in the Lançado communities. This gave rise to localized varieties of a highly attenuated, though not creolized, Guinea Coast English up and down the coast. Typologically, it would have been "foreigner talk" rather than anything which had undergone creolization. On the Upper Guinea coast, this kind of English was learned as a lingua franca by the adult grumettos who worked for, but did not assimilate to, Afro-European (i.e., creole) descendants. The grumettos employed it as a second language in their interaction with the slaves awaiting shipment. What little Guinea Coast English those Africans knew nevertheless had to function for purposes of their wider communication and was retained because of that, serving as just one component in the evolution of the creole.

It is this widely dispersed creole component that accounts for the high rate of shared items in the anglophone Atlantic creoles. To illustrate: from Upper Guinea to Lower Guinea, from South America to the Central American mainland, from the Antilles to North America—throughout the whole anglophone Atlantic creole area, in fact—the second-person plural pronominal form *una* or *unu* is found. The chances of this being introduced independently in each place by speakers of specific African languages who chose that particular grammatical item to contribute and ensured its subsequent retention in the creole are logistically implausible. It must have been a part of the prediffusion creole component to begin with; no other explanation is possible. There are many such words equally widely distributed in these languages.

To return to the African component, there are, undeniably, many African items represented in the creoles. For some, such as Saramaccan, they constitute a fifth or more of the total lexicon; for others, they are restricted and, outside of their occurrence in specialized semantic domains, only account for between 2% and 4% of the everyday working vocabulary. This is true, for example, for Krio, Jamaican, Belizean, Gullah, Kittitian, Vincentian, and most others. For the Sranan-related group, it is still only about 8% (although see Huttar 1985b, for new figures for Ndjuka), while Niles (1980:148) claims that "fewer than twenty vocabulary items directly traceable to an African origin" occur in the entire Barbadian lexicon.

Mittelsdorf (1979:98) defines lexical Africanisms as (a) full morphemic retentions, (b) hybrids, (c) semantic shifts, (d) calques, and (e) word-formation devices, although the only such device she acknowledges as actually being African is iteration (see also Hancock 1980b). While she is right in maintaining that it is in the lexicon and phonology that the African component is best represented, she fails to acknowledge the semantic and grammatical material carried in that component, the source of which she attributes instead to the English dialects:

> Wherever the loss of an English feature was concerned, parallels could be found in other contact varieties of English . . . of the divergences be-

> tween Jamaican Creole and English, very few need to be explained by references to the African linguistic background of the original population. (1979:153, 175)

This is essentially the conclusion reached by Niles (1980:147) for the Barbadian situation and is an application of J. L. Dillard's "cafeteria principle," the filling of one's linguistic tray with bits and pieces from a variety of sources to account for the whole. Although the eclectic nature of the English component in the formative matrix is undeniable and accounts for the fact that Irish, Scottish, Devonian, and Kentish words can be found side by side in the same creole sentence, the approach demonstrates a certain bias to allow those varieties of English to provide the various grammatical forms, while denying the same input from the variety of African languages present in the same situation.

True to the polemic nature of creole studies, when we turn to the works of such writers as Allsopp (1975, 1983) or Baudet (1981) or Dalphinis (1985), the opposite bias is found. Baudet, for example, relying on data from four Kwa languages (Twi, Ewe, Yoruba, and Igbo), draws a series of structural parallels with them which persuade her that

> there is considerable similarity in syntactic patterns between the Caribbean creoles and West African languages, and substantial support is given to the hypothesis that creoles should be expected to exhibit those grammatical features common to all languages that provided grammatical input . . . a significant portion of the findings of this study strongly supports the case for an African substratum in the Caribbean creoles. (1981:115–16)

Unlike Allsopp and Dalphinis, Baudet is cautious in stating that universal processes, and the variety exhibited within the European languages themselves, must also be considered in the formation of the creoles. But like those who argue for a creole base originating in dialects of the metropolitan language, she does not go far enough in addressing the actual linguistic processes involved. It is not enough to rummage around in the dozens of dialects of the European languages or the hundreds of African languages to find look-alike constructions; questions such as the following must also be addressed. Why is it that only the Anglophone Atlantic creoles make use of a complementizer derived from *say* or *speak,* not found in the francophone or iberophone group? (See Frajzyngier 1984 and Mufwene 1986 for discussion of this complementizer.) What accounts for the geographically wide distribution of specific features such as nominal plurals of the type Noun Phrase + *dem,* which is extremely restricted (both geographically and by language) in Kwa and is not found at all in West

Atlantic or Bantu, but only in Manding (believed by a number of creolists not to have been significant in Atlantic creole history)? Why have English creoles selected the unmarked genitive constructions found in northern Britain, certainly, but not in any of the Irish or Scottish or southwestern or southeastern dialects which were numerically far better represented in the creole-forming situations?

Let us return to componentiality and the creolization process. In the kind of social situation which necessitated the development of a shared set of linguistic rules where one did not already exist, the locating and crystallizing of such structural and lexical features was essential. As Bickerton (1980) has hypothesized, in the absence of a target (and no single African language, or British dialect, has a structure matched by any creole), human beings must rely on an innate linguistic model, one inherent in their genetic makeup. I have argued also that where syntactic patterns happen to be shared by some, or all, of the input languages, nothing new needs to be learned, and convergence of functions will help to ensure their retention in the emerging linguistic system. The existence of such structures need not rely upon strictly universal processes. I have made such a case, examining specifically the role of the southwestern British dialects in the formative situation (Hancock, to appear). In the absence of any kind of universal lexicon, the lexical input into the creole must reflect specific sources, although, as with its structural input, this is also modified. Huttar (1973), in an important but little-known study, has shown that the semantics of creole languages are not necessarily rooted in their African or European sources. Abstract creole structure relies on syntax rather than on bound morphology to express grammatical relationships, and this lack of binding extends to lexicon as well. For example, an entry such as *happy* can be transferred into the matrix, while derivations such as *unhappy, happiness, happily,* etc., or even *being, was, were, am, are* from *be* cannot. Nor are they capable of being regenerated according to the rules of the creole component within the new system. However, no creole is pristine, consisting only of the creole component. Saramaccan, which is usually cited as the most "creole" of all creoles (Byrne 1987), appears to have a greater African component. As a result, it looks more "exotic," but this is simply the result of the same type of componential selection that gives, for example, Jamaican its more English-like character. This selection was an ongoing process, with each generation innately negotiating with the linguistic mix available for patterns to be retained or rejected in the creole. For most of the seventeenth century, and part of the eighteenth, high infant mortality rates in the Caribbean ensured that incoming Africans rather than new generations of locally born native speakers made up the biggest part of the rising population, and that the emerging model was in a state of continually being created by second-language, not first-language, speakers. With each generation, this negotiation and selection was repeated, in a kind of ongoing "rollover" process of recreolization.

While the replacement of creole by metropolitan structures and phonology is a legitimate process and can be measured and accounted for both socially and linguistically, it cannot be assumed that the presence of more English-like features in certain creoles is merely the result of their more intense decreolization. While there is no evidence that Jamaican, for instance, ever created comparatives with *pas* in a more "creolelike" way than it does now with Adjective-*er* + *than* (*biga dan mi* rather than *big pas mi*), the same creole also permits comparatives with *muoran* (*big muoran mi*). Syntactically, the latter is a creole pattern that matches the one using *pas* in other creoles. It is not that an earlier *pas* comparative decreolized in the direction of English, but rather that the English component provided the Adjective-*er* + *than* construction as an alternative while Jamaican was stabilizing. The same is probably true of the *a* + Verb versus Verb-*ing* aspectual variants (*im a ron*/*im ronin*) in the same language.

It is not in specific African language or British dialect models that we must seek the core structure of the creole component. There are African and European patterns in creole grammars, but in greater or lesser proportions, depending upon the componential makeup of each specific creole. This point is not a new one (see Mufwene 1986:193). What is "creole" about interrogative WH-adverbials is not their specific lexical forms, which are neither African nor European, but that they are nominal compounds: whether the word for 'where' is *us-say* (Krio), *o-pe* (Sranan), or *we-paat* (Jamaican), the pattern WHICH/WHAT + Noun (i.e., 'side,' 'place,' 'part') is constant. When anglophone creole grammar will not permit indirect object shift, it is adhering to an underlying creole pattern which blocks it. Benefactive 'he buy the book give the child' will permit 'he buy the book for the child' but not *'he buy the child the book' in any anglophone creole.[1]

To summarize, arguments made to date for more or less of an African input into the creoles, and those which have dwelt upon the identification of specific African languages (usually as lexical inventories) in the creole-forming situations, have failed to deal with the question in its proper context. The African and European components are external to the core process of creolization. They are significant only in that (a) they provided a discontinuous pool of linguistic material in the collective (but not shared) minds of the individuals involved, from which the creole core grammar was generated; and (b) they existed as discrete linguistic systems independently of that, which constituted components feeding into the crystallization of each specific creole language as part of an ongoing process. It is only in this second role that the identification of lexical items from specific African languages, and the location of the places of origin of their original speakers, bears relevance to creole language development.

## Note

1. I am aware that, structurally, the similarities between *big pas mi* and *big muoran mi,* and between 'he buy the book give the child' and 'he buy the book for the child' are quite different. Arguments against the first of each pair incorporating verb serialization are found in Byrne 1987 and Sebba 1987.

## References


Alleyne, Mervyn C. 1980. *Comparative Afro-American: An historical-comparative study of English-based Afro-American dialects in the New World.* Ann Arbor: Karoma.

Allsopp, Richard. 1975. The case for Afro-genesis. In Cave, ed.

———. 1983. Linguistic economies in middle-level Caribbean English attributable to African sources. Paper presented at the Second World Congress on Communication and Development in Africa and the African Diaspora, Bridgetown, Barbados.

Baker, Philip. 1982. *The contribution of non-francophone immigrants to the lexicon of Mauritian Creole.* Doctoral thesis, University of London.

Baker, Philip, and Chris Corne. 1982. *Isle de France Creole: Affinities and origins.* Ann Arbor: Karoma.

Baudet, Martha. 1981. Identifying the African grammatical base of the Caribbean creoles. In Highfield and Valdman, eds., 104–18.

Benjamin, Georges. 1956. *Survivances africaines en Amérique.* Paris: Collection Alternance.

Bickerton, Derek. 1980. *Roots of language.* Ann Arbor: Karoma.

———. 1984. The language bioprogram hypothesis. *Behavioral and Brain Sciences* 7.173–221.

———. 1986. Creoles and West African languages: A case of mistaken identity? In Muysken and Smith, eds., 25–40.

Byrne, Francis. 1987. *Grammatical relations in a radical creole.* Amsterdam: John Benjamins.

Carrington, Lawrence, ed. 1983. *Studies in Caribbean language.* St. Augustine, Trinidad: Society for Caribbean Linguistics.

Cassidy, Frederic. 1983. Sources of the African element in Gullah. In Carrington, ed., 75–81.

Cave, George, ed. 1975. *New directions in creole studies*. Papers presented at the First Conference of the Society for Caribbean Linguistics, Georgetown, Guyana. Mimeo.

Daeleman, J. 1972. Kongo elements in Saramacca Tongo. *Journal of African Languages* 11.1–44.

Dalphinis, Morgan. 1985. *Caribbean and African languages*. London: Karia Press.

Elson, Benjamin F., ed. 1985. *Language in global perspective: Papers in honor of the 50th anniversary of the Summer Institute of Linguistics, 1935–1985*. Dallas: Summer Institute of Linguistics.

Frajzyngier, Zygmunt. 1984. On the origin of *say* and *se* as complementizers in Black English and English-based creoles. *American Speech* 59.207–10.

Gilbert, Glenn, ed. 1986. *Pidgin and creole languages: Essays in memory of John E. Reinecke*. Honolulu: University of Hawaii Press.

Hancock, Ian. 1980a. Gullah and Barbadian: Origins and relationships. *American Speech* 55.17–35.

———. 1980b. Lexical expansion in creole languages. In Valdman and Highfield, eds., 63–88.

———. 1986. The domestic hypothesis, diffusion and componentiality. In Muysken and Smith, eds., 71–102.

———. 1987. A preliminary classification of the anglophone Atlantic creoles, with syntactic data from thirty-three representative dialects. In Gilbert, ed., 264–334.

———. 1988. Componentiality and the origins of Gullah. In Peacock and Sabella, eds., 13–24.

———. To appear. Componentiality and the creole matrix: The S.W. English component. In Montgomery, ed.

Harris, John. 1985. Expanding the superstrate: Habitual aspect markers in Atlantic Englishes. *Sheffield Working Papers in Language and Linguistics* 2.72–97.

Harris, John, David Little, and David Singleton, eds. 1986. *Perspectives on the English language in Ireland*. Dublin: Trinity College Centre for Language and Communication Studies.

Highfield, Arnold, and Albert Valdman, eds. 1981. *Historicity and variation in creole studies*. Ann Arbor: Karoma.

Holm, John, and A. G. Oyedeji. 1984. The Yoruba language in the New World. *Oso* 3.83–90.

Huttar, George. 1973. Sources of creole semantic structures. Paper read at the Forty-eighth Annual Meeting of the Linguistic Society of America, Chicago.

———. 1985a. Kikongo, Saramaccan and Ndjuka. In Elson, ed., 563–86.

———. 1985b. Sources of Ndjuka African vocabulary. *De Nieuwe West-Indische Gids* 59.45–71.

Mathieu, Nicolas del Castillo. 1982. *Esclavos negros en Cartagena y sus aportos lexicos*. Bogotá: Instituto Caro y Cuervo.

Mittelsdorf, Sibylle. 1979. *African retentions in Jamaican Creole: A reassessment*. Ph.D. dissertation, Northwestern University.

Montgomery, Michael, ed. To appear. *South Carolina, the Caribbean, and Africa: Linguistic and cultural perspectives*.

Mufwene, Salikoko. 1986. The universalist and substrate hypotheses complement one another. In Muysken and Smith, eds., 129–62.

Mufwene, Salikoko, and Charles Gilman. 1987. How African is Gullah, and why? *American Speech* 62.120–39.

Muysken, Pieter, and Norval Smith, eds. 1986. *Substrata versus universals in creole genesis*. Amsterdam: John Benjamins.

Niles, Norma. 1980. *Provincial English dialects and Barbadian English*. Ph.D. dissertation, University of Michigan.

Peacock, James L., and James C. Sabella, eds. 1988. *Sea and land: Cultural and biological adaptations in the southern coastal plain*. Athens: University of Georgia Press.

Rickford, John. 1986. Social contact and linguistic diffusion: Hiberno-English and New World Black English. *Language* 62.245–90.

Sebba, Mark. 1987. *The syntax of serial verbs*. Amsterdam: John Benjamins.

Sherry, Frank. 1986. *Raiders and rebels: The golden age of piracy*. New York: William Morrow.

Smith, Norval. 1986. *The genesis of the creole languages of Surinam*. Doctoral dissertation, University of Amsterdam.

Smith, Norval, Ian Robertson, and Kay Williamson. 1987. The Ịjọ element in Berbice Dutch. *Language in Society* 16.49–90.

Taylor, Douglas. 1945. Certain Carib morphological influences on creoles. *International Journal of American Linguistics* 15.140–55.

Valdman, Albert, and Arnold Highfield, eds. 1980. *Theoretical orientations in creole studies*. New York: Academic Press.

Williams, Jeff. 1986. Hiberno-English and white West Indian English: The historical link. In Harris et al., eds., 83–96.

# African Substratum: Possibility and Evidence. A Discussion of Alleyne's and Hancock's Papers

*Salikoko S. Mufwene*

Mervyn Alleyne's and Ian Hancock's papers are provocative, the first because it proposes for Jamaican Creole a substratist account that seems stronger than previous substrate hypotheses (SH), the second because it highlights how the componential hypothesis (CH) can account for the genesis of Atlantic English creoles in a curious blend of polygenesis (as far as Guinea Coast Creole English is concerned) and partial monogenesis (as far as creoles of the New World are concerned).

Strong versions of the SH (e.g., those advocated by Alleyne 1971, 1980; Koopman 1986; and Lefebvre 1986) have met with opposition from quasi-exclusive universalist positions (e.g., Bickerton 1984, 1986) and from dominant superstratist accounts (e.g., Chaudenson 1979). Both views, of course, make little room for substrate influence at the critical formative stage of the creoles lexified by Western European languages. However, Alleyne's present commitment to dominant "African continuities" (i.e., substrate influence) also seems to go against the recent appeal of the complementary hypothesis defended in this volume not only by Hancock but also by Philip Baker, which suggests a mutually enriching coexistence of the substrate and the universalist hypotheses as advocated in Baker and Corne (1986) and Mufwene (1986).[1]

Below, I discuss my target papers in turn, focusing first on Alleyne's and then on Hancock's, concomitantly placing them in broader contexts and sorting out their strengths and shortcomings, and finally concluding with general impressions on the research avenues they suggest.

## Twi Influence on Jamaican Creole

Starting from the plausible assumption that language and culture are interconnected, Alleyne makes a number of inferences, among which are the following two: (1) since black (West) African cultures share several features, the languages associated with them must also share several features, which we may for convenience characterize here as "African"; (2) since many African cultural traits have survived the brutality, oppression, and degradation of slavery, African linguistic features must likewise have survived slavery and may be identified in at least some Afro-American language varieties.

Even if these inferences should prove to be true, a problem with them is that so far the connection between language and culture has been shown not regarding the grammatical structure of language, which has been the focus of debates on creole genesis, but regarding the cataloging aspect of language (i.e., the lexicon). This is precisely where substrate influence has been the least controversial—and in fact generally minimal[2] if we ignore Turner's (1949) capitalization on proper names (as noted by Blok 1959). I know of no language and culture study which has shown correlation of culture with, for example, constituent order, internal morpheme structure in a word, or the particular morphosyntactic strategy used for expressing genericness. Unfortunately, Alleyne does not address this aspect of the second inference from his paper. This omission invites unnecessary questions on a thesis which, as I show below, could be defended plausibly on other grounds.

As Alleyne correctly observes, the thesis that Africans in the New World could not generally have used their African languages has been blown out of proportion (see Singler, this volume). For the thesis to hold, there would have had to be only one speaker of any relevant African language per plantation (and none of the slaves would have been able to speak a language other than their mother tongue). Given widespread individual multilingualism in Africa and the preferences expressed by some plantation owners for slaves from some parts of Africa, this prerequisite of the thesis which Alleyne rejects was very unlikely. It is quite plausible that some African languages were used certainly by some slaves (even if not many) on some plantations, most likely when speakers of the same African languages could be alone. The fear of conspiracy must have come from the recognition of these situations and, if I may speculate further, perhaps way after New World creoles had already taken the same shapes they now have (except for genuine cases of relexification, such as Sranan). The question really is which African languages continued to be the most used, for how long, and by what proportion of the slave population? The alleged impossibility for the African slaves to use their native, ethnic languages is simply wishful thinking about a genetic scenario whose different components remain difficult to grasp fully. We must recall that New World plantations varied significantly in size (see, e.g., Joyner 1984) and certainly also in their ethnolinguistic constituencies (even if only in terms of number of speakers of different languages rather than in the identity of the African languages represented).[3]

However, those more familiar with the typology and genetics of sub-Saharan African languages must be dismayed by Alleyne's overemphasis on common features and his neglect of lexical and structural differences among the languages brought into contact in the New World (e.g., regarding isolating vs. agglutinating morphosyntax; postnominal vs. prenominal position of tense, mood, and aspect [TMA] markers; or even contrasts in the values of TMA markers). Linguistic diversity in Africa is not a priori a strong argument against most versions of the SH (Mufwene 1990a). For instance, not all of the most commonly invoked African languages had arrived by the critical formative stage of the relevant creoles (see Mufwene's 1990a invocation of "founder principle"), a point well made in this volume by Ian Robertson with regard to Berbice Dutch. However, acknowledging the diversity affects how versions of the SH are presented. The point of this comment is that sociohistorical conditions must have varied from Jamaica to other British, French, and Dutch colonies in the New World (see, e.g., Holm 1989). They may have favored one kind of substrate influence in one polity but not another, thus making the dominant Twi influence claimed by Alleyne for Jamaican Creole (JC) conceivable.

In a different vein, I know of no study (nor does Alleyne cite one) that claims that cultural kinship (which is quite likely in the case of sub-Saharan Africa) entails linguistic kinship. While several aspects of African culture(s) have survived in the New World, due either to a common substrate core or to the kind of cultural and political dominance claimed by Alleyne, evidence for the survival of common African linguistic features is still scant. For instance, Gilman (1986) discusses only some random features which do not form a coherent structural whole. In fact, only a subset of these are part of those features which studies of creole genesis (including Alleyne 1980) have considered central. Gilman does not discuss domains such as time reference, constituent order, and complex sentence formation (particularly embedding and serialization). So we are still waiting for evidence of general or regional African linguistic continuities which form wholes and are comparable to the kinds attested in, for example, some religious practices and folk tales. (Cf. Hazaël-Massieux's position, in this volume, that most of the African linguistic influence is lexical and restricted to some cultural domains; see also Spears's reaction to the thesis.) The data presented in Lefebvre and Lumsden (1989) and Lefebvre and Massam (1988; see also Lefebvre, this volume) are a small and hopeful step for Haitian Creole, though I must observe here that French influence is far from ruled out in a few cases (see, e.g., Mufwene 1989; Hazaël-Massieux 1992). That is, convergence might be a more plausible explanation than exclusive or dominant substrate influence.

One could think of reasons why there might be cultural continuities without parallel linguistic continuities. For instance, while language was used for communication both among Africans and between Africans and non-Africans, the aspects of Afro-American culture characterized as particularly African (e.g., dance, music, folk tales, and religion) may have been confined to interaction among Africans, especially in the formative stages of the new communities. There would thus have been fewer constraints on the retention of African cultural traits than on the retention of linguistic traits, even if all the retentions were a priori based on commonality rather than other factors (cf. Mufwene 1989, 1990b, 1991). However, this argument is probably not a strong one, for as Whinnom (1971) observes, the problem of communication had to be solved primarily among the Africans themselves. So the lesser extent of cultural diversity compared with linguistic diversity may have favored a more significant retention of general or regional African cultural features, depending on the makeup of the founder population in every community. Some African linguistic features may have handicapped communication not only with non-Africans but also with some other Africans. Alternative features shared also by the lexifier may thus have been favored for communication efficiency.

Alleyne's more central and explicit thesis for dominant Twi influence on JC is, nonetheless, worthy of serious consideration, despite the above distractions. As he puts it, language, like culture, is essentially learned behavior, regardless of the role the biological blueprint may play in the learning process. The likelihood of transferring substrate features from generation to generation of creole speakers cannot be discounted a priori, even if children were involved in the crystallization of the new vernacular. Efficiency of communication normally dictates conformity with the established norm (that of the previous generation), so that, as may be observed in noncreole communities, exceptions are simply memorized instead of regularized, contrary to what some creolists (e.g., Bickerton 1984) have incorrectly assumed for creole communities.

Laying the groundwork for his position, Alleyne does well in dismissing from the outset the assumption of an antecedent pidgin for New World creoles. As characterized in the literature, the assumption makes it difficult to assume that slaves did communicate with one another on quite a variety of aspects of their lives on plantations before a significant native speaker population, with which creolization has too often been incorrectly associated, emerged in their communities. To deal with a trivial case, the kind of social interaction which led to nativization must have required a more developed linguistic system than the near-chaotic one usually attributed to pidgins (not counting expanded and stable pidgins).[4] The assumption of an expanded pidgin, as postulated by, for example, Mühlhäusler (1986) for, say, Tok Pisin and Nigerian Pidgin, would be plausible, in a last attempt to save the definition of a creole by nativization, if there were any structural or sociolinguistic features which distinguish expanded pidgins from creoles. Alleyne is right in holding firmly to the assumption that creolization does not presuppose an antecedent pidgin and claiming that the Atlantic creoles must have started as creoles. His position is supported by the assumption that the new languages must have started almost immediately to serve as primary means of communication (Mühlhäusler 1980, 1986; Valdman 1983), hence they must have become complex very quickly, even if some African languages may have continued to be used for a while by subsets of the slave populations.[5]

As Alleyne's position of creolization without prior pidginization for New World creoles becomes more plausible, so does the possibility of strong African substrate influence become more conceivable. This may be due to a variety of factors, such as commonality of substrate features where the substrate group is relatively homogeneous (the kind discussed by Ferraz 1979; Maurer 1987; Keesing 1988; and Robertson, this volume), or cultural-political dominance (the kind Alleyne focuses on in his paper), or simply the kinds of markedness factors discussed by Mufwene (1989, 1990b, 1991). The main problem remains that of presenting a sociohistorical scenario with adequate linguistic evidence that makes the thesis convincing. Alleyne claims that the Twi group was politically and culturally dominant. However, insofar as the paper discussed here is concerned, the sociohistorical evidence backing the claim remains a matter of faith.

Since, according to Alleyne, the above conception of ethnic or cultural dominance is not tantamount to numerical dominance, I can think of several scenarios which would have made the Twis dominant. For instance, the number of Twis may have been particularly significant (compared with other groups) in the original slave communities on different plantations. Their chances of transferring features of their language into the incipient vernacular and seeing these adopted by the other, smaller African groups would have been great. Assuming (based on Alleyne's position on creolization in the New World) that the initial version(s) of JC was (or were) quickly formed and stabilized (as they must have been),[6] chances are that many of the original (and putatively Twi) features would have survived as the creole was acquired by subsequent generations of slaves.[7] However, based on the way Alleyne presents his thesis, this is a speculation as good as any other. Adequate sociohistorical information may shed light on this interesting research question.

Actually, while Alleyne emphasizes that the Jamaican situation may not be typical of other settings of creolization in the New World (hence that the genetic scenarios may have varied from setting to setting), he makes no reference to the initial stages of JC. He only alludes to the Twis' leadership attributes and to their role in marronage, suggesting the impact that they must have had both culturally and linguistically on the rest of Jamaica's creole-speaking community. Neither linguistic nor cultural evidence supporting the Twis' leadership is provided. None of his claims is articulated with enough details to allow possible falsification or corroboration based on the paper alone. Thus, he simply opens an attractive avenue for future research to validate or invalidate.

It is unfortunate that the absence of linguistic evidence does not make it possible to verify whether any Twi peculiarities (as distinct from Kwa or common African peculiarities) have survived in JC. This would have allowed us to see whether the putative case of dominant Twi influence on JC is similar to that of western Bantu influence on São Tomense and Principense (Ferraz 1979) and on Palenquero (Maurer 1987), or to that of Eastern Ịjọ influence on Berbice Dutch (Smith et al. 1987; Robertson, this volume). I hope his future work will address these questions.

Finally, since Alleyne's claim that West African languages did survive and could still be found is relevant to his thesis of dominant Twi influence on JC, it would help to find out what form of Twi survived, whether or not its usage was restricted to particular domains, and how it compares with the original Twi spoken in Africa. These questions are raised especially because they would allow us to react, perhaps more adequately than we can with Warner-Lewis's (1982) data (which suggest postformative retention of Yoruba), to Chaudenson's contention (1979, 1988a) that the African languages were quickly forgotten because the slave population was generally captured young (in their teens) and would have been more inclined to learn the language that allowed them wider communication. This, of course, does not preclude the possibility of substrate influence, although it argues for an adequate acquisition of the superstrate variety to which each slave was exposed, hence it increases the possibility of superstrate influence as the primary source of creole features (see Hazaël-Massieux, this volume; Spears, this volume).

## The Componential Hypothesis

In his paper Hancock presents one of those theoretical frames within which, on the one hand, substrate and superstrate influences may be defended plausibly, and, on the other, cross-creole variation from one polity to another may be accounted for adequately by invoking differences in the sociolinguistic makeup of each setting. This regards, inter alia, the kinds of languages that came into contact with primarily the lexifier and the proportions of their respective speakers.[8] In this respect, he is doing, as he himself acknowledges, what Bickerton (1984) tried to capture with his pidginization index. Hancock does better, however, in including in his list of factors determining the shape of the resulting creole "the various dialects of [the] metropolitan [languages]." Bickerton (1984) overlooked this (see Singler 1990; Mufwene 1990b for a more explicit critique), and Arthur Spears (this volume) is quite right in commending Guy Hazaël-Massieux's paper (this volume) for bringing the superstrate "component" back into the genetic debate. As Spears correctly observes, this "component" deserves as much attention as the substrate "component" and, I am sure, also as much as the universal constraints (see Mufwene 1990a), which have caught most of the attention in the creole genesis debate of recent years, especially among anglophone creolists.

While I find Hancock's (and Bickerton's) model quite helpful, I am not so sure that Hancock's terms "components" and "ingredients" are adequate, because they do not suggest a distinction between, on the one hand, linguistic features, the actual ingredients out of which a creole is formed, and, on the other hand, factors such as "the proportion of speakers of different languages" and "the rate of change over time of the population ratios," which affect the particular selection of features which each creole makes in its own setting. In any case, the model is rewarding in several ways despite this flaw. First, it makes allowance for the determinative role that the original population plays in shaping each new contact-based vernacular. As Chaudenson (1979, 1988a, 1988b) and Baker and Corne (1986) point out, differences in the original peoplings of Réunion and Mauritius account for part of the differences in formal features of their new vernaculars. The significance of this is comparable to what population geneticists have characterized as "founder principle." This amounts to a set of features which are attested in a particular population not necessarily because the features were statistically dominant where the population originated but simply because they happened to have been dominant among the original settlers (i.e., the founder population) of the colony and therefore had a greater chance of being transmitted to the settlers' offspring.[9] Assuming the CH, it seems quite plausible to invoke the founder principle to account for some cross-basilectal differences from one creole to another; for example, the habituative expressed with an unmarked realis verb or a durative construction in Atlantic English creoles (Mufwene 1988a), or Hancock's own example about the comparative with Adjective-*er* + *than* versus Adjective + *muoran* versus Adjective + *pass*. The facts will be accounted for by invoking a higher frequency of an alternative due either to a more homogeneous proportion of

Africans in a setting or to a predilection among native speakers of the lexifier to use one of its native alternatives. (For one or another reason which determines the alternative as situationally unmarked, this was favored and selected by the new vernacular.) Only accurate historical sociolinguistic records can decide this. Since these are virtually impossible to obtain, even for committed archive researchers like Hancock, the question may remain open for quite a while, and our positions on the variation must remain speculative.

A second attractive feature of Hancock's CH lies in the fact that, in addition to the distribution of influences during the original formation of the new vernacular, it allows later influence (especially from the substrate languages) to affect the shape of any creole. In fact, it even makes room for the coexistence of competing systems within the same plantation community, the kinds of linguistic variation phenomena now accounted for by invoking decreolization too hastily. As Chaudenson (1979, 1988b) observes (see also Bickerton 1988; Baker 1990), creoles lexified by Western European languages usually started with varieties close to their lexifiers, albeit the varieties spoken by the colonists.[10] As the proportion of nonnative speakers increased, a more and more restructured variety of the lexifier now called creole emerged. This happened without necessarily displacing either the lexifier or its original first-generation, second-language approximation.

Pushed to its full capacity, Hancock's CH may be used to explain cases of postcrystallization influence on any creole, the kind that affects any language in contact with another or others. Based on my research (Mufwene 1985), the model accounts well for the fact that in Gullah, many of the African proper names inventoried by Turner (1949) have been affected by English-based phonological rules. This, I concluded, suggests that the African names were adopted after Gullah's phonological system had already been formed (with apparently a significant seventeenth- and eighteenth-century English input); thus, the African words were assimilated like foreign elements into its phonemic system. This conclusion is consistent with facts such as the following: (1) labiovelar stops, which are common in several African languages, have remained sporadic and do not have a phoneme status in Gullah, even though they have been much publicized in the literature; (2) the proportion of proper names is not matched by that of common nouns and other lexical items from African languages (Hair 1965); and (3) the ratio of Kikongo names is not matched by the Kwa-like features of Gullah grammar. Since Kikongo is Bantu and agglutinating, the third observation suggests that the ethnolinguistic makeup of the Gullah community at the time when the names were borrowed was different from the makeup of the founder population.[11]

These Gullah facts illustrate the CH's built-in mechanism for accounting for resistance to additional substrate influence when no sociolinguistic conditions disrupt established speech habits. Thus, while a higher ratio of "arriving adults" compared with "locally born" or creole slaves would increase the probability of new influence, the reverse would reduce it. In other words, there were enough model speakers of the extant creole language to ensure that its structure would change little under the influence of newcomers and for the new, noncreole slaves to learn it just like any newcomers who form a minority in any linguistic community. We must bear in mind that the newcomers did not all arrive at the same time and that the ships did not arrive as regularly as today's freighters. These facts restrict the number of cases in which recreolization (discussed below) was ever possible.

In any case, Hancock includes in his discussion of the CH the possibility of "recreolization" of the original or extant "creole." (It is not clear whether nativization is an important condition for creolization in his model, even though he speaks of the proportion of the creole population to the new-coming slaves "arriving as adults.") I personally see no justification for the putative process of recreolization either here in Hancock's paper or in Mühlhäusler's (1986), in which the notion was used earlier (see also Romaine 1988, criticized in Mufwene 1990c). Neither of these authors explains what is actually involved in "recreolization," especially whether facts similar to those that led to the original or previous creolization (viz., lack of access to the intended vernacular and development of a new one related to the original lexically but not necessarily typologically) recur.

In agreement with Alleyne's (1971) position that creoles of the New World may not have started as pidgins, I consider creolization as, roughly, the stabilization and normalization of a new, pidginlike or pidgin-based language concomitantly with its usage as a vernacular. This normally happens soon after the community born out of the contact of people from diverse ethnolinguistic backgrounds starts using the emerging language as a primary means of communication, a practice by which it develops its autonomous norms of well-formedness (Chaudenson 1988b).[12] Consequently, I interpret the putative "recreolization" as new creolization in the above sense, assuming that new conditions must have applied for the creation of a new creole.

My problem with "recreolization" as used by Hancock (and Mühlhäusler 1986 and Romaine 1988) is whether the previous creole actually became as ineffective as the lexifier during the original contact that led to its creolization, or was simply "being bent in [a new] direction" (Keesing 1988) because it was not adequately acquired by every newcomer. That is, compared with the lexifier, has the extant creole not simply been modified in contact with the new population and thus been "bent" in the direction of some postformative dominant linguistic influence (Bickerton 1984; Baker and Corne 1986; Mühlhäusler 1986; Keesing 1988)? This process is in no way different from influence on any noncreole language in a contact situation![13] Note that, according to Chaudenson (1988b) and Baker (1990), the target language at this stage of the formation of these new languages is not (the diverse dialects of) the European lexifier, as it was in the original "habitation" stage, but the speech of the current creole population, consisting of closer approximations of the lexifier. Until this question is addressed, I have the gut feeling that the term "recreolization" is used improperly here.

It is, of course, possible to see creolization (as do Alleyne 1971 and Thomason 1981) as the stabilization of a group's second-language variety. Thus "recreolization" may be charitably interpreted as the development of a second-language variety of the current creole, which is not displaced in any way and will coexist with the new variety, more or less like native varieties of American English have to date coexisted with Hispanic English. However, Hancock does not make this clear, especially since this interpretation depends primarily on his conception of "creolization."

Setting aside the issue of "recreolization," we must note that present-day creoles are normally (if not always) the result of continuous and perhaps long-term processes of restructuring motivated by various sociohistorical factors, as Hancock himself acknowledges. As Chaudenson (1988b) observes, variation in how restructuring is carried on accounts for part of the cross-regional variation in the structures of present-day creoles.

It is also possible that two kinds of developments may have taken place in the same polity, as in Réunion. According to Chaudenson (1988b), only part of the population further creolized their speech after the stage of massive influx of slaves for the plantations.[14] This could well be the case for most territories; what is missing from most claims for recreolization is lack of motivation for the creole slaves and others who lived in the *habitations* to change their speech. After all, most of them now formed a new caste between the newcomers and the plantation owners, and it was to their advantage to keep their language, which was now being approximated by the newcomers, the way it was.

Perhaps one other tacit presupposition of the "recreolization" hypothesis should be questioned here: it has been widely assumed in creolistics that the antecedents of present-day creoles were homogeneous and that current variation is due to decreolization. Claims for a diachronic process such as decreolization must be backed by diachronic, not just synchronic, evidence of variation. Inferences from synchronic variation are simply too speculative. Thus, studies like those by Brasch (1981), Rickford (1987), and Lalla and D'Costa (1989) are badly needed because they will help settle the dispute on decreolization—on a case-by-case basis.

Also worth discussing is Hancock's interesting combination of polygenesis and monogenesis in accounting for the genesis of Atlantic creoles. There is nothing bizarre in this scenario, according to which the varieties of Guinea Coast Creole English (GCCE) putatively developed independently in different forts or trade centers on the "Guinea Coast" (stretching from Gambia and Senegal to Sierra Leone), and similarities in contact situations brought about similar outcomes. On the other hand, New World Atlantic creoles may have started from those varieties of GCCE, or at least there must have been a significant input from them through slaves exposed to GCCE while waiting in the forts for their transatlantic voyage. This hypothesis should account not only for general similarities among all Atlantic English creoles but also for several features that might be considered substrate. Allowing myself to speculate, I assume that, except for those substrate features that may be attributed to a later massive influx of slaves from a particular region, correspondences could perhaps be established between aspects of, say, Gullah and the particular variety of GCCE out of which it might have developed. In the absence of a case study backing Hancock's position on the genetic relation of Atlantic English creoles to GCCE, we may conclude that the position is nothing but conjecture at this point. It is certainly worthwhile investigating while we are trying to understand creole genesis better.

Zygmunt Frajzyngier's (1984) study, which Hancock invokes somewhat differently from Bickerton's (1986) and Mufwene's (1986) invocation of the same data to play down a generalized substratist account, gives good support to Hancock's thesis that Atlantic English creoles may have started from GCCE. To be sure, cross-systemic variation, such as in the constructions *dem* + Noun ~ *di* + Noun + *dem* for nominal plural and Adjective-*a dan* Noun ~ Adjective *pas* + Noun ~ Adjective + *muoran* + Noun for the comparative, seems to pose a problem. However, Hancock's hypothesis allows for variation both in the original GCCE and among the New World varieties, especially after the massive influx of slaves subsequent to the emergence of the new languages. While variation in the substratum is a potential explanation, it is also possible that *chance*, due to variation in the superstratum, may account for part of the variation from creole to creole (Mufwene 1988a). After all, as Hancock observes, the lexifier was not homogeneously represented.

Still, the challenge remains to account in detail for cross-creole variation focusing on specific features. We may start with detailed comparisons of present-day creoles on the coast of West Africa, which may shed light on intercreole variation due particularly to differing substrate influence. There should also be more comparisons of earlier records of Atlantic creoles with the putative GCCE, as well as comparisons of present-day Atlantic creoles with their West African counterparts. An eyesore at this stage of genetic creolistics is the limited number of comprehensive independent studies of creoles, which are the prerequisite to sound comparative studies. Even after all these have been undertaken, there might still be problems if there are no corresponding studies of both the relevant African languages and nonstandard varieties of the lexifying languages, especially those of the regions from which the European settlers and indentured laborers came. Obtaining information on the seventeenth- and eighteenth-century varieties of these languages is the most frustrating part. However, it may also be an exaggeration to assume that many of these languages have undergone drastic structural changes over the last three centuries. For instance, the major change which accounts for the split of the Niger-Congo languages between the Kwa and Bantu families predates by at least several centuries the original contacts between Europeans and Africans in the fifteenth century. Chaudenson (1990) notes that changes reported in the history of Indo-European languages have generally not included features of their nonstandard varieties; many of the features reported as obsolete are still attested in today's nonstandard varieties. It seems to me that as long as there are accurate studies of both the relevant African languages and the relevant dialects of the European lexifiers in their present conditions, we might learn plenty about the genesis of Atlantic creoles in particular.

Although I have raised questions on both Alleyne's and Hancock's positions on the genesis of English Atlantic creoles, my interest in both provocative hypotheses remains strong. At face value, the two hypotheses seem at variance with each other. Charitable misinterpretation suggests, however, that Alleyne's strong position may not be exclusive of, for example, an earlier GCCE origin of JC with a subsequent strong Twi element. Nor does it suggest literally that strong Twi influence is exclusive of other influences; variation in the structure of JC might well reflect normalization in conflicting influences from different sources. In principle, Hancock's CH allows influence from one particular ethnolinguistic group to prevail when particular sociohistorical conditions are met.

Overall, it is difficult to decide on the adequacy of these hypotheses without further detailed studies to flesh them out and make them more falsifiable. At this stage of the research on substrate influence, any sociohistorically grounded hypothesis is worth considering seriously. The genesis of creoles appears to be a more complex problem than was initially assumed in the field. Insights from different approaches will certainly help us understand this general question more adequately, even if answers to the relevant subquestions do not yet seem to be forthcoming. The reality of creoles is simply not uniform from polity to polity, and I doubt that there is one single, uniform account for their respective developments. The complementarity of Hancock's and Alleyne's positions makes them both worth pursuing critically.

## Notes

1. Alleyne is not alone, as evidenced by Claire Lefebvre's paper (this volume). In fact, both his and Lefebvre's positions appear to receive general support from contributions such as John Singler's (this volume), which provide the broad sociohistorical background they need.

2. It is obvious that the vocabulary of creoles lexified by European languages is predominantly European. Even proponents of the neo-relexification hypothesis such as Lefebvre (1986, 1989; Lefebvre and Massam 1988; Lefebvre et al. 1989) operate on this assumption, for example, when they claim that French words are used according to Ewe-Fon grammar in Haitian Creole. In a different vein, Cassidy (1983) aptly observes that African words are scant in the spontaneous sample texts at the end of Turner 1949.

3. If we also consider the fact that slaves on one plantation simply did not interact with those on another every day (Joyner 1988; Baker 1990), then another relevant question is, Why are none of the New World, or more generally plantation, creoles not geographically more varied?

4. The characterization of some pidgins as stable or expanded serves no significant purpose in the opposition between pidgins and creoles, especially since for all practical purposes these pidgins have systems very similar to, and as complex as, the creoles to which they are genetically related (e.g., Nigerian Pidgin vs. Krio or Gullah). Since the so-called stable or expanded pidgins prove that nativization is not crucial to creolization, they may as well be called creoles (see Mufwene 1990a).

5. I also assume that as the slave communities identified more and more with the new vernaculars (i.e., creoles), the domains of usage of African languages must have decreased concomitantly, being restricted to some intimate family communication (where possible) and to some specific cultural activities such as religious ceremonies.

6. This assumption is concerned only with the stage of development at which a creole is identified as a different vernacular from the previous foreigner approximations of the lexifier (Chaudenson 1979, 1986, 1988b; Baker 1990).

7. The term "generation" is used here after Chaudenson (1979, 1988b) on the model of computer generations (corresponding to different periods of arrivals of slaves) rather than to refer to human age generations, as suggested by some students of creole genesis.

8. The fact that several African languages were represented on plantations of the New World does not mean there was contact between them, assuming (like Weinreich 1953) that the speaker is the locus of language contact. The relevance of this multilingualism to the selection and crystallization of African substrate features regards the competition of features it must have created for different parameters of the new systems.

9. In Mufwene 1989, 1991, statistical dominance (or higher frequency) is considered as one of the factors that may determine a feature as unmarked relative to an alternative.

10. In relation to French, Chaudenson calls the new, second-language variety "français approximatif," in contrast to the nonstandard "français populaire" spoken by most colonists and to which the slave population was normally exposed.

11. The verb "borrow," criticized as inadequate for creole genesis by Mufwene (1988b), is used here precisely to suggest that the names came in the system after the formative stage, just like European names are used in African languages without affecting these systems (Mufwene 1985).

12. Considering the case of Berbice Dutch, so far assumed to be a creole (however, cf. Mufwene 1990b), it may be irrelevant, in the proposed conception of creolization, whether a particular linguistic group was dominant at the time of stabilization/normalization and has marked the new vernacular with features of it that are not shared by other languages whose speakers subsequently became numerically dominant.

13. Romaine's use of "recreolization" is actually different from what is discussed here. It relates more to the commitment of expatriate creole speakers and their children to using a creole in a different, non-creole-speaking community than to the development of a new vernacular. The usage of the same term by all these creolists certainly does not help us develop a clear sense of what "recreolization" in its true genetic sense must be intended for.

14. Compare my comment above regarding the coexistence of a new system with a preceding one, as presumably determined in part by the nature of the social contacts. Limited social intercourse between the creole and the new groups may well have led to the normalization of the new, adstrate system.

## References

Alleyne, Mervyn C. 1971. Acculturation and the cultural matrix of creolization. In Hymes, ed., 169–86.

———. 1980. *Comparative Afro-American: An historical-comparative study of English-based Afro-American dialects of the New World*. Ann Arbor: Karoma.

Baker, Philip. 1990. Off target? [Column]. *Journal of Pidgin and Creole Languages* 5.107–20.

Baker, Philip, and Chris Corne. 1986. Universals, substrata and the Indian Ocean creoles. In Muysken and Smith, eds., 163–83.

Bickerton, Derek. 1984. The language bioprogram hypothesis. *Behavioral and Brain Sciences* 7.173–221.

———. 1986. Creoles and West African languages: A case of mistaken identity? In Muysken and Smith, eds., 25–40.

———. 1988. Creole languages and the bioprogram. *Lingustics: The Cambridge survey*. Volume 2. *Linguistic theory: Extensions and implications*, ed. by Frederick J. Newmeyer, 268–84. Cambridge: Cambridge University Press.

Blok, H. P. 1959. Annotations to Mr. Turner's "Africanisms in the Gullah dialect." *Lingua* 8.306–21.

Brasch, Walter M. 1981. *Black English and the mass media*. Lanham, N.Y.: University Press of America.

Cassidy, Frederic G. 1983. Sources of the African element in Gullah. *Studies in Caribbean language*, ed. by Lawrence D. Carrington, 75–81. St. Augustine, Trinidad: Society for Caribbean Linguistics.

Chaudenson, Robert. 1979. *Les créoles français*. Paris: Fernand Nathan.

———. 1986. And they had to speak any way . . . : Acquisition and creolization of French. *The Fergusonian impact*, ed. by Joshua A. Fishman et al., 1.69–82. Berlin: Mouton de Gruyter.

———. 1988a. Le dictionnaire du créole mauricien: où l'on reparle (à nouveau mais pour la dernière fois!) de la genèse des créoles réunionnais et mauricien. *Etudes Créoles* 11.73–127.

———. 1988b. *Créoles et enseignment du français*. Paris: L'Harmattan.

Ferraz, L. Ivens. 1979. *The creole of São Tomé*. Johannesburg: Witwatersrand University Press.

Frajzyngier, Zygmunt. 1984. On the origin of *say* and *se* as complementizers in Black English and English-based creoles. *American Speech* 59.207–10.

Gilman, Charles. 1986. African areal characteristics: Sprachbund, not substrate? *Journal of Pidgin and Creole Languages* 1.33–50.

Hair, P. E. H. 1965. Sierra Leone items in the Gullah dialect of American English. *Sierra Leone Language Review* 4.79–84.

Hazaël-Massieux, Guy. 1992. Review of *La créolisation*, ed. by Claire Lefebvre and John Lumsden. *Journal of Pidgin and Creole Languages* 7.

Holm, John. 1989. *Pidgins and creoles*. Volume 2. *Reference survey*. Cambridge: Cambridge University Press.

Hymes, Dell, ed. 1971. *Pidginization and creolization of languages*. Cambridge: Cambridge University Press.

Joyner, Charles. 1984. *Down by the riverside: A South Carolinian slave community*. Champaign-Urbana: University of Illinois Press.

Keesing, Roger M. 1988. *Melanesian Pidgin and the Oceanic substrate*. Stanford: Stanford University Press.

Koopman, Hilda. 1986. The genesis of Haitian: Implications of a comparison of some features of the syntax of Haitian, French and West African languages. In Muysken and Smith, eds., 231–58.

Lalla, Barbara, and Jean D'Costa. 1990. *Language in exile: Three hundred years of Jamaican Creole*. Tuscaloosa: University of Alabama Press.

Lefebvre, Claire. 1986. Relexification in creole genesis revisited: The case of Haitian Creole. In Muysken and Smith, eds., 279–300.

———. 1989. Instrumental *take*-serial constructions in Haitian and Fon. In Lefebvre and Lumsden, eds., 319–37.

Lefebvre, Claire, Anne-Marie Brousseau, and Sandra Filipovich. 1989. Haitian Creole morphology: French phonetic matrices in a West African mold. In Lefebvre and Lumsden, eds., 273–83.

Lefebvre, Claire, and John Lumsden, eds. 1989. *La créolisation. Revue Canadienne de Linguistique* 34.3.247–376.

Lefebvre, Claire, and Diane Massam. 1988. Haitian Creole syntax: A case for DET as head. *Journal of Pidgin and Creole Languages* 3.2.213–42.

Maurer, Philippe. 1987. La comparaison des morphèmes temporels du Papiamento et du Palenquero: Arguments contre la théoric monogénétique de la genèse des langues créoles. *Varia Creolica,* ed. by Philippe Maurer and Thomas Stolz, 27–70. Bochum, Germany: Brockmeyer.

Mufwene, Salikoko S. 1985. The linguistic significance of African proper names in Gullah. *De Nieuwe West-Indische Gids* 59.146–66.

———. 1986. The universalist and substrate hypotheses complement one another. In Muysken and Smith, eds., 129–62.

———. 1988a. English pidgins: Form and function. *World Englishes* 7.255–67.

———. 1988b. Starting on the wrong foot [Column]. *Journal of Pidgin and Creole Languages* 3.1.109–17.

———. 1989. Some explanations that strike me as incomplete [Column]. *Journal of Pidgin and Creole Languages* 4.117–28.

———. 1990a. Transfer and the substrate hypothesis in creolistics. *Studies in Second Language Acquisition* 12.1–23.

———. 1990b. Creoles and Universal Grammar. *Linguistics* 28.783–807.

———. 1990c. Review of *Pidgin and creole languages* by Suzanne Romaine. *World Englishes* 9.98–103.

———. 1991. Pidgins, creoles, typology, and markedness. *Development and structures of creole languages: Essays in honor of Derek Bickerton,* ed. by Francis Byrne and Thom Huebner, 123–43. Amsterdam: John Benjamins.

Mühlhäusler, Peter. 1980. Structural expansion and the process of creolization.

*Theoretical orientations in creole studies*, ed. by Albert Valdman and Arnold Highfield, 19–55. New York: Academic Press.

———. 1986. Bonnet blanc and blanc bonnet: Adjective-noun order, substratum and language universals. In Muysken and Smith, eds., 25–40.

Muysken, Pieter, and Norval Smith, eds. 1986. *Substrata versus universals in creole genesis*. Amsterdam: John Benjamins.

Rickford, John R. 1987. *Dimensions of a creole continuum: History, texts, and linguistic analysis of Guyanese creole*. Stanford: Stanford University Press.

Romaine, Suzanne. 1988. *Pidgin and creole languages*. London: Longman.

Singler, John V. 1990. On the use of sociohistorical criteria in the comparison of creoles. *Linguistics* 28.645–60.

Smith, Norval, Ian E. Robertson, and Kay Williamson. 1987. The Ịjọ element in Berbice Dutch. *Language in Society* 16.1.49–90.

Thomason, S. G. 1981. Review of K. C. Hill's *The genesis of language: the First Michigan Colloquium, 1979*. *Studies in Second Language Acquisition* 3.236–49.

Turner, Lorenzo Dow. 1949. *Africanisms in the Gullah dialect*. Chicago: University of Chicago Press.

Valdman, Albert. 1983. Creolization and second language acquisition. *Pidginization and creolization as language acquisition*, ed. by Roger Andersen, 212–34. Rowley, Mass.: Newbury House.

Warner-Lewis, Maureen Patricia. 1982. *The Yoruba language in Trinidad*. Doctoral thesis, University of the West Indies.

Weinreich, Uriel. 1953. *Languages in contact*. New York: Linguistic Circle of New York.

Whinnom, Keith. 1971. Linguistic hybridization and the "special case" of pidgins and creoles. In Hymes, ed., 91–115.

# Africanisms in the Grammar of Afro-American English: Weighing the Evidence

*Edgar W. Schneider*

Identifying Africanisms in Afro-American is a task which intrinsically involves weighing data and interpreting evidence in the light of conflicting theories and possibilities offered to explain the outcome of a complex historical process. Three different types of sources have been suggested to explain the linguistic constituents of pidgin and creole languages: (1) the influence of an African substratum (Alleyne 1980; Baudet 1981); (2) universal principles (Bickerton 1981, 1986); and (3) elements from the lexifier language, or the superstratum, which in most cases is European. It is debatable whether we have to assume the existence of three independent sources. Perhaps one of the first two—the substratist and universalist ones—has to be chosen as appropriate at the expense of the other (Muysken and Smith 1986). I myself am skeptical about extreme claims; I am inclined to accept Mufwene's (1986a) view that neither of these two positions is sufficient to explain all the observed phenomena and that they are not mutually exclusive (see also Mufwene and Gilman 1987). Many scholars present at the Round Table on Africanisms were much better qualified than I to judge these particular problems. I was invited primarily to provide the perspective from the third source, the superstratum influence, which, whatever its strengths may be, certainly goes beyond merely supplying lexical items.[1] Thus, in a way, my job is bound to be a rather negative one—I have to identify features which are not likely to be Africanisms rather than provide positive evidence of the kind invited by the title of this Round Table. Still, the exclusion of unlikely candidates is a valid scientific procedure and an important step toward the identification of the members appropriate to a category.

This paper is based mainly on the findings of my earlier work on the history of American Black English vernacular (BEV). Thus, my remarks primarily pertain to this variety, with which I am most familiar, but they may also be relevant for Caribbean creoles insofar as the same structures frequently occur in these. I would not find it reasonable to assume different and independent sources in such cases, because these varieties certainly constitute a continuum of Afro-American speech forms. I first single out some necessary preliminary considerations. Then I categorize linguistic forms according to the degree of English versus African or creole influence that may be assumed and discuss one example of each category in greater detail. Finally, I summarize my comprehensive assessment of the history of BEV.

## Preliminary Considerations

The first point I would like to emphasize is the importance of avoiding polemics and the need to try to exclude sociopolitical issues and motives in discussing linguistic questions. Sober minds must admit that there is reason and plausibility in each of the three competing explanations (Mufwene 1985). Contact with speakers of the superstratum variety provided much of the lexicon of creoles, and there is no reason to assume that such contact would not have affected their grammar as well; the question is just to what extent this happened. Analogously, it is equally reasonable to accept the fact that slaves transported to America must have built sentences on the model of their African native tongues, even when using newly acquired lexical material (cf. Mühlhäusler 1986:51). Finally, the idea that language develops along universal lines is too intriguing to be easily dismissed, and Derek Bickerton and others have presented some evidence in its support. Also, the process of first language acquisition, something familiar to every parent, seems to provide some corroboration. I must admit that, having just had the pleasure of seeing my little daughter going through this process, I came to feel more sympathetic to Bickerton's ideas when listening to the near pidgin she developed in transition (e.g., no copula, all verbs in the infinitive, possession expressed by sequential juxtaposition, but a regular formal distinction of completed and noncompleted verb forms, as in *geben, gebt* 'give, gave').

Second, it may be particularly fruitful to look for structures a creole shares with both of the putative parent varieties. It is natural to assume that Africans in a forced second language–learning situation would primarily have analyzed, recognized, and adopted constructions of the target variety with which they were already structurally familiar from their native-language competence. Thus, the importance of the mutual reinforcement of identical or similar structures has rightly been emphasized recently (Todd 1984: 27; Rickford 1986:269). This principle not only applies to substratum and superstratum influences but may also encompass universal tendencies. Holm (1986:261) has suggested that universals may play a role in the selection, rather than in the creation, of creole structures, and I find this a reasonable assumption.

Third, we have to keep in mind in this particular case that the superstrate was not a standard variety but a dialect, or rather a mixture of various dialects—the ones spoken by the colonists from various parts of the British Isles. The neglect of this point resulted in some confusion in the early phase of the discussion on American Black English, although it seems that the correct perspective is widely accepted nowadays (Holm 1983:19, 22; Mufwene 1985).

Fourth, at the other end of the scale, Africanness must be clearly distinguished from creoleness. Identifying the latter is comparatively easier because it consists only of pinning down structures not found in the superstratum. This is certainly an important step toward localizing Africanisms, but, as I indicated initially, Africanness and creoleness are far from being the same. Unfortunately, this distinction has also been blurred quite frequently in the debate on the genesis of BEV.

Finally, the assessment of sociohistorical conditions is, of course, crucial if we seek to support either of the positions, because the amount and kind of contact between speakers of various ethnic groups plays a major role in shaping language varieties. Bickerton is justified in demanding that the right people be shown to have been in the right place at the right time if it is claimed that one language variety influenced another. This condition applies not only to African sources but also, of course, to superstratum influence, for which little detailed evidence has been adduced. (Rickford 1986 is a noteworthy exception.) Also, this principle should not just apply to somewhat mystical overall varieties such as "West African languages" or "English dialects," but rather to more precisely defined, individual linguistic systems. Mufwene (1985) has pointed this out with respect to African influence (see also Muysken and Smith 1986) and has presented some detailed evidence along these lines, demonstrating that, perhaps surprisingly, many features of creoles appear to have been selected from languages of the Kwa group (Mufwene 1986a). As for the English sources, my own work contains some of the suggested kinds of evidence of that sort, but there are many cases in which either more precise localizations or at least quantitative assessments of the spread of some forms are required.

## Superstratum Influence: Classes of Linguistic Structures

In agreement with D'Eloia (1973), I believe that the features of Afro-American English can be classified into four different categories: (1) unequivocally English features, (2) features for which both English and African or creole models exist, (3) features which appear to be partly shaped upon English models (this source, however, is insufficient to explain the output of the process comprehensively), and (4) creole patterns which cannot be traced back to superstratum structures. For each of these four categories I will list a few examples and illustrate the problems involved by discussing one of the forms mentioned in greater detail.

Features of BEV which appear to be exclusively colonial English in origin (Schneider 1981, 1989) are the following: a number of morphological forms, such as the verbal suffix *-s* used in all grammatical persons (see Schneider 1983), most irregular verb forms, irregular noun plural forms, comparative and superlative adjectives, most pronoun forms (including *we'uns* and *you'uns;* possessive *him's,* etc.; 'absolute' *yourn, hisn,* etc.; reflexive *hisself, theirselves,* etc.; and the demonstratives *them* 'those' and *this here/them there*), *gwine* 'going,' the form *ain't* in the function of *have/be* + negation, and *a*-prefixed verbs; elements of syntax such as an invariant relativizer *what*[2] or a missing subject relative pronoun (as in *It's the devil makes folkses do bad*), the formation of indirect questions without a conjunction and with inversion (as in *He asked did he do this killin'*), multiple negation (as in *I don't know nothing*), the use of *it, they,* and zero as dummy subjects; perfective structures such as *have/had* + past participle (pp) and also a three-verb cluster *is/was/had done* + verb-pp; and the marking of the progressive aspect with the suffix *-in(g)* (while a preverbal *da/de/a,* common in Caribbean creoles, appears to be African in descent but is not found in BEV). In all of these cases, the respective forms and structures are sufficiently widespread in nonstandard English to make simple transmission a likely and reasonable assumption.

Consider, for example, the comparison of adjectives in more detail. For BEV, in addition to the standard patterns with *-er/-est* and *more/most,* redundant combinations of both are reported, as in *more cheaper* (Putnam and O'Hern 1955:22; Labov and Cohen 1973:223). In the speech of ex-slaves recorded by the Federal Writers' Project (FWP) at the time of the Great Depression[3] we also find synthetic comparative/superlatives of polysyllabic adjectives which would demand analytic constructions in the standard, such as *terriblest, honestest;* comparisons of participles, for example, *beatenest, out-fightines';* and redundant forms such as *bestes', worser*. Sound recordings made with such speakers at about the same time for the Archive of Folk Song (AFS) and stored in the Library of Congress contain only standard forms. Suffice it to note that all of these forms are widespread and frequently reported in British-English as well as American-English dialects, in studies of both earlier BEV and earlier stages of the English language (Schneider 1989:168f.). On the other hand, creoles tend to have an analytical comparative structure with postposed *pass,* which Turner (1949:214) traced back to various African models. The English type of comparative with *-er* does occur in Gullah as well (Cunningham 1970:183), and so does the marker *more,* although in the creole type of construction postponed to the adjective, as in *he big more than you* (Cunningham 1970:184). Still, the AFS tapes do contain a related example of a structure that fits into the creole pattern, namely, reduplication used for intensification (*good good,* used by Fountain Hughes; Alleyne 1980:106).

The second type of forms suggest mutual reinforcement of both English and African or creole elements; these include the deletion of the genitive *-s* of nouns, the pronoun form *you-all,* the use of pleonastic pronouns, as in *my daughter she works for . . . ,* and the formation of direct questions without inversion. Let us have a closer look at the first of these, the zero genitive. This form could have originated practically anywhere. It seems to reflect a universal tendency, which can be deduced from the observation of children's first language acquisition. It occurs in "several West African languages, such as Ibo" (Van Sertima 1976:140; Alleyne 1980:101); on the other hand, it is also widespread in English folk speech, especially in the North and the North Midlands (Wright 1905:265; Orton et al. 1978:M65, M66). Historically, this has to do with the fact that during the Middle English period the *-s* suffix spread from a class of nouns which originally had this ending to others which did not. Also, the tendency in English, in particular in American English (cf. Galinsky 1952:395), to form compounds such as *door handle* yields a formally identical construction. Pidgins and creoles typically express the relationship of possession on the basis of the African or universal model; that is, by uninflected juxtaposition, as in Gullah (Cunningham 1970:150; Van Sertima 1976:140; Rickford 1986:108), basilectal Belizean Creole (Escure 1981), and others (Alleyne 1980:101).

As for BEV, there are similar claims (e.g., Baratz 1971:39; Smitherman 1977:128), yet empirical research indicates that these are clearly exaggerated. What we really find is variable usage of the genitive marker in BEV with a great deal of inter- and intraindividual variability. For example, Walter Wolfram's Detroit study (1969:141) yielded an average deletion rate of 26.8% with lower-class blacks, with a median of 13.4%, which means that the majority of the speakers had comparatively low zero values while a few used this form exceptionally frequently. Deletion rates observed in various studies range from close to zero, as in the speech of adults and middle-class blacks, and also generally in the "absolute position" in New York City (Labov et al. 1968, 1.170), through low and medium values (Labov et al. 1968, 1.161, 169; Pope 1969: 68; Sanders 1978:58) to John Baugh's remarkable 61.1% (1983:95). Quantitatively, this is more than could reasonably be explained on the basis of the superstratum model alone, so I am inclined to attribute this to mutual reinforcement of the respective elements of various possible sources. In ex-slave speech, the respective deletion rate is 9.3% in the written sources studied (Schneider 1989:162), something confirmed by a remarkably close match of 10.3% determined on the AFS tape recordings (Schneider 1989:163). To me, this indicates that with respect to this feature in BEV and its history we have to assume not a process of change, starting out from a creole pattern of only uninflected forms and moving toward the Standard English one, but rather a comparatively stable pattern characterized by inherent variability from the outset.

The third group, forms somehow shaped upon an English source but subsequently modified in some essential way, consists of *done* as a perfective marker, *ain't* as a negator of main verb predicates—that is, as a substitute for *do/did* + negative—the tendency to use present-tense forms in past contexts as "historical present" (as well as "camouflaged forms" in general; see Brewer 1986), and, again, some pronominal patterns, such as *him, her,* and *us* as subjects (which do occur in British English but are comparatively infrequent), or *he* and *she* as possessives. Let us consider *done* in more detail. It is well known to be the regular marker of perfectiveness or completedness in the Atlantic creoles (Cunningham 1970:95; Jones 1971:83; Alleyne 1980:82), and although Joe Dillard's assumption that it is "a natural kind of relexification of Pidgin Portuguese *caba*" (1972:219) is no more than a speculative hypothesis, it is clear that this form expresses an essential creole (African or universal) category because we have related forms (such as *pinis, fek*) in French-related creoles as well. However, this is only one side of the coin. The other is that, following Traugott (1972:146) and Visser (1969:2208), *done* became the central element of a perfective three-verb cluster *have/be* + *done* + verb-pp, which gained wide currency in Middle English but was thereafter confined to the northern part of the country and also transplanted to the United States, where it has been recorded in Southern dialects in particular (Wentworth 1944:172; McDavid and McDavid 1960:17; Feagin 1979:126). Traugott (1972:193) insists on a historical connection between this diachronic and dialectal English source. Although this three-verb cluster is practically unmentioned in the context of modern BEV and has been found only incidentally in black speech (Schneider 1989:136), the evidence of the slave narratives (Rawick 1972) provides the missing link. In this source we find structures such as *had done helped, had done axed, is done growed* and also *to be done et* quite regularly and frequently but, remarkably, only in the early-settled South Atlantic states, that is, in the Carolinas and Georgia. Although these texts are, of course, not as reliable as modern tape recordings, I do not see how this remarkable result could have been achieved by any kind of editing; exactly this type of structure occurs in a number of interviews from only these three adjacent states, and this systematic distribution makes sense in the light of the historical, linguistic, and extralinguistic evidence.

What I am claiming here is that this proves a direct connection between the tense and aspect system of present-day BEV and earlier British English; however, I am not saying that this is the whole story. Apparently, the first element of this three-verb cluster, the tense marker, has been considerably weakened in white Southern English (as has been the regular marker of perfect, *have -en*) and almost completely lost in BEV. Thus, *done* has greatly gained in frequency and has acquired a widened range of structural and functional possibilities, both of which, I think, cannot be explained on the basis of the restricted currency and influence of the British source. Thus, reinforcement and modification of the role of *done* through African or creole influence appears to be very likely in this case.

The fourth class, creole constructions without any possible model in the superstratum variety, comprises the most interesting and attractive portions of the grammar of creole languages, yet it appears that this category is hardly represented at all in American BEV. The only construction that must be mentioned here is preverbal *been* as a past marker. The construction must be distinguished from a superficially similar and much more frequent one, namely, an English present perfect with *be* as part of the predicate and the preceding *have* deleted by a phonological rule. Structurally, the creole construction is followed by a verb in the infinitive or by a pp with active meaning, while the English one has either a passive pp or a verbal *-ing* form after *been*. The distinction correlates with different stress patterns: Baugh has emphasized the fact that "the stress on *been* is phonemic in black street speech" (1983:82), and he may be right in suspecting that this is a feature inherited from African tone languages. However, the problem with *been* in BEV concerns its frequency. A closer examination of the literature reveals that it has been much more frequently postulated than demonstrated, and it obviously is "relatively rare in BEV" (Fasold 1981:171; similarly even Dillard 1972:46). The only empirical attestations that I know of are by Rickford (1975) and Baugh (1983), and this conforms to what has been found in ex-slave speech: outside coastal South Carolina, this type of construction occurs hardly at all. Whether this form can be identified as an Africanism is also unclear, as it has been suggested that the tense-mood-aspect system of which it is a part is a product of the language bioprogram (Bickerton 1981:58). As Rickford (1977:207) also notes, "knowledge of African influence is completely lacking."

In conclusion, I would like to set forth the overall interpretation of my study of Earlier Black English—the speech recorded in the slave narratives—with respect to the character of this variety and, ultimately, the history of BEV. At the risk of being classified again as a representative of an allegedly narrow-minded traditionalist school, I believe the evidence at hand forces us to conclude that Earlier Black English and BEV are predominantly, though not exclusively, dialectal English in character. A vast majority of their forms and structures can be identified as, and traced back to, diachronically older elements of English dialects, some of which have died out by now in Standard English. This does not mean, however, that there was no creolization among black slaves in the United States. In the linguistic evidence we do find structures which are unquestionably creole or creole influenced in character. However, with the notable exception of southern and coastal South Carolina (an area apparently larger than the present-day spread of Gullah), these forms occur in a highly scattered fashion, are frequently restricted to the status of individual idiosyncracies, and affect only a few linguistic variables. My hypothesis is that this situation is the product of a few presumably independent creolization processes in localities with exceptionally dense black populations and on some big plantations, with a certain degree of leveling, mixing, and perhaps loss or even spreading of such forms in the postemancipation period, after the dissolution of these communities. The evidence at hand contradicts the far-reaching assumption that a supraregionally uniform "Plantation Creole," supposedly spread all over the South, ever existed. Earlier Black English is unquestionably not a creole variety, and I do not think the evidence for prior creolization is strong enough to rate it uniformly as a mesolect in the process of decreolization (although this may be just a matter of definition). Therefore, I do not believe that the simple hypothesis that present-day BEV is the descendant of a creole is correct. I am not saying that it is totally wrong, but it misses far more of the evidence than it explains, and it leaves the vast majority of relevant facts unconsidered.

Generally, I believe that, as is the case with the controversy of Africanisms versus universalisms, we should avoid extreme and biased views, for it seems that a number of conflicting influences have merged in language contact situations. Any rigid partial or monolithic theory will be inadequate for an understanding of the complex social and linguistic realities of the plantation culture. The evidence documents the existence of a considerable degree of internal structural variation. It is to be assumed that both this intraidiolectal variability and thc intcrindividual differences in the linguistic habits and abilities of black speakers have existed since the very beginning of slavery in the United States. The social frame conditions for language acquisition and usage varied considerably throughout the period of slavery, ranging between extremes from very small to big plantations, from a fairly close, even emotionally positive relationship with the white owners to a general lack of contact or even complete hostility between the races. Likewise, the linguistic varieties spoken by blacks must have covered a continuum of possibilities ranging from (presumably restricted and perhaps short-lived) creoles, on the one hand, through various intermediate stages, to a practically complete mastery of the target variety, nonstandard English, on the other. To return to my central topic: Africanisms can be expected only on one side of this continuum, and I suspect they are much more uncommon in American BEV than in Gullah or in Caribbean varieties of Afro-American English.[4]

## Notes

1. Mufwene (1986a:148) lists a few phonological but, remarkably, no grammatical items. As for phonology, Dorrill's (1986) observation that black folk speakers in the American South, as compared with their white counterparts, display both a stronger tendency to use monophthongal rather than diphthongal vowel qualities and less regional variation deserves special interest. It is probably not too speculative to hypothesize that this may be a trace of an Africanism in black speech.

2. Mufwene (1986b) suggests that this type of *what* may be analyzed as a complementizer, in which case it would have to be moved to one of the following two categories.

3. Brewer (1974) coined the label "Early Black English" for this variety, and in most of my earlier publications I have also used this name. However, Bill Stewart has convinced me that this is an inappropriate designation, for obviously speech recorded in the 1930s cannot be considered "early" in an absolute sense, by comparison with the centuries of black history in North America. Thus, I suggest a slight change of the designation and will henceforth use the term "Earlier BE"; what is important is that the speech of these ex-slaves represents a stage in the development of Black English which precedes the present one.

Dillard (this volume) challenges the reliability of the FWP ex-slave narratives as linguistic evidence (although, incidentally, more than half of the examples given in Dillard 1972 are taken from the same source, through a selection which its editor, Benjamin Botkin, explicitly admitted to have edited linguistically). Obviously, this is a crucial question. I have attempted (Schneider 1981, 1989) to single out those records which obviously do not even aim at linguistic accuracy by means of a pretest which rates the interviewers. With respect to the remaining ones, some skepticism is certainly justified: first, there is some indication that a few of the narratives were edited before being submitted to the Washington headquarters, and, second, we do not know how many of the field-workers were able to take notes in shorthand (although as professional "writers" it is unlikely that they were "often almost uneducated," as Dillard suggests), so it is possible that some stories were not recorded fully on the spot but rather written out immediately afterward from memory and notes. Thus, it is certainly true that the narratives are not absolutely reliable verbatim records, but I do believe they are sufficiently trustworthy for detailed analysis and consideration, primarily because of the internal linguistic consistency of the results and the support of comparable evidence. In a number of cases analysis of these records has yielded systematic linguistic distributions of a fairly subtle nature from different regions and by so many different field-workers and interviewees that I cannot see how this could have been achieved by any kind of bias or editing. Also, there are some fairly accurate structural correspondences with modern BEV, and there is the corroboration provided by both some closely matching data on the AFS tapes and the results of other studies of diachronic materials, for example, Harrison 1884; Jeremiah 1977; or Eliason 1956 (for details, see Schneider 1989). Thus, I admit that the speech recorded in the ex-slave narratives is neither as early nor as accurately preserved as one might want it to be, but it is the best evidence of an earlier stage of Black English that we have and are likely ever to get, and it is clearly superior to literary dialect.

4. This overall interpretation is evidently in line with the way Melville Herskovits formulated his "rainbow hypothesis": while he rated Gullah "quite African" (grade b, out of five possible degrees of Africanness), he believed the U.S. rural South and urban North to be characterized by only grade e, "trace of African customs, or absent" (see Gilbert, this volume, although he believes Herskovits to be mistaken in this respect).

## References

Alleyne, Mervyn C. 1980. *Comparative Afro-American. An historical-comparative study of English-based Afro-American dialects of the New World*. Ann Arbor: Karoma.

Baratz, Joan C. 1971. *Ain't* ain't no error. *Florida Foreign Language Reporter* 9.39–40, 54.

Baudet, Martha M. 1981. Identifying the African grammatical base of the Caribbean creoles: A typological approach. *Historicity and variation in creole studies*, ed. by Arnold Highfield and Albert Valdman, 104–17. Ann Arbor: Karoma.

Baugh, John. 1983. *Black street speech: Its history, structure and survival*. Austin: University of Texas Press.

Bickerton, Derek. 1981. *Roots of language*. Ann Arbor: Karoma.

———. 1986. Creoles and West African languages: A case of mistaken identity? *Substrata versus universals in creole genesis*, ed. by Pieter Muysken and Norval Smith, 25–40. Amsterdam: John Benjamins.

Brewer, Jeutonne P. 1974. *The verb "be" in Early Black English: A study based on the WPA ex-slave narratives*. Ph.D. dissertation, University of North Carolina at Chapel Hill. Ann Arbor: University Microfilms.

———. 1986. Camouflaged forms in Early Black English: Evidence from the WPA ex-slave narratives. Paper presented at the Sixth Biennial Conference of the Society for Caribbean Linguistics, St. Augustine, Trinidad.

Cunningham, Irma. 1970. *A syntactic analysis of Sea Island Creole ("Gullah").* Ph.D. dissertation, University of Michigan. Ann Arbor: University Microfilms.

D'Eloia, Sarah G. 1973. Issues in the analysis of nonstandard Negro English: A review of J. L. Dillard's *Black English: Its history and usage in the United States. Journal of English Linguistics* 7.87–106.

Dillard, Joe L. 1972. *Black English: Its history and usage in the United States.* New York: Random House.

Dorrill, George Townsend. 1986. *Black and white speech in the Southern United States: Evidence from the Linguistic Atlas of the Middle and South Atlantic States.* Frankfurt am Main: Verlag Peter Lang.

Eliason, Norman E. 1956. *Tarheel talk: An historical study of the English language in North Carolina to 1860.* Chapel Hill: University of North Carolina Press.

Escure, Geneviève. 1981. Decreolization in a creole continuum: Belize. *Historicity and variation in creole studies*, ed. by Arnold Highfield and Albert Valdman, 27–39. Ann Arbor: Karoma.

Fasold, Ralph W. 1981. The relation between black and white speech in the South. *American Speech* 56.163–89.

Feagin, Crawford. 1979. *Variation and change in Alabama English: A sociolinguistic study of the white community.* Washington, D.C.: Georgetown University Press.

Galinsky, Hans. 1952. *Die Sprache des Amerikaners. Eine Einführung in die Hauptunterschiede zwischen amerikanischem und britischem Englisch in der Gegenwart.* Band 2. *Wortschatz und Wortbildung—Syntax und Flexion.* Heidelberg: F. H. Kerle.

Harrison, James A. 1884. Negro English. *Anglia* 7.232–79.

Holm, John, ed. 1983. *Central American English.* Heidelberg: Groos.

———. 1986. Substrate diffusion. *Substrata versus universals in creole genesis*, ed. by Pieter Muysken and Norval Smith, 259–78. Amsterdam: John Benjamins.

Jeremiah, Milford Astor. 1977. *The linguistic relatedness of Black English and Antiguan Creole: Evidence from the eighteenth and nineteenth centuries.* Ph.D. dissertation, Brown University. Ann Arbor: University Microfilms.

Jones, Eldred. 1971. Krio: An English-based language of Sierra Leone. *The English language in West Africa*, ed. by John Spencer, 66–94. London: Longman.

Labov, William, and Paul Cohen. 1973. Some suggestions for teaching Standard English to speakers of nonstandard urban dialects. *Language, society and education: A profile of Black English*, ed. by Johanna S. DeStefano, 218–37. Worthington, Ohio: Charles A. Jones.

Labov, William, Paul Cohen, Clarence Robins, and John Lewis. 1968. *A study of the non-standard English of Negro and Puerto Rican speakers in New York City.* Cooperative Research Project no. 3288. Volume 1. *Phonological and grammati-*

*cal analysis*. Volume 2. *The use of language in the speech community*. New York: Columbia University Press.

McDavid, Raven I., and Virginia McDavid. 1960. Grammatical differences in the north central states. *American Speech* 35.5–19.

Mufwene, Salikoko S. 1985. Misinterpreting "linguistic continuity" charitably. Paper presented at the Ninth Annual Language and Culture in South Carolina Symposium, Columbia, S.C.

———. 1986a. The universalist and substrate hypotheses complement one another. *Substrata versus universals in creole genesis*, ed. by Pieter Muysken and Norval Smith, 129–62. Amsterdam: John Benjamins.

———. 1986b. Restrictive relativization in Gullah. *Journal of Pidgin and Creole Languages*. 1.1–31.

Mufwene, Salikoko S., and Charles Gilman. 1987. How African is Gullah, and why? *American Speech* 62.120–39.

Mühlhäusler, Peter. 1986. Bonnet blanc and blanc bonnet: Adjective-noun order, substratum and language universals. *Substrata versus universals in creole genesis*, ed. by Pieter Muysken and Norval Smith, 41–55. Amsterdam: John Benjamins.

Muysken, Pieter, and Norval Smith. 1986. Introduction: Problems in the identification of substratum features. *Substrata versus universals in creole genesis*, ed. by Pieter Muysken and Norval Smith, 1–13. Amsterdam: John Benjamins.

Orton, Harold, Stewart Sanderson, and John Widdowson, eds. 1978. *The linguistic atlas of England*. London: Croom Helm.

Pope, Mike. 1969. *The syntax of the speech of urban (Tallahassee) Negro and white fourth graders*. Ph.D. dissertation, Florida State University. Ann Arbor: University Microfilms.

Putnam, George N., and Edna O'Hern. 1955. The status significance of an isolated urban dialect. *Language* 31. Supplement, *Language Dissertation* no. 53.

Rawick, George P., ed. 1972. *The American slave: A composite autobiography*. 19 vols. Westport, Conn.: Greenwood.

Rickford, John R. 1975. Carrying the new wave into syntax: The case of Black English BIN. *Analyzing variation in language. Papers from the Second Colloquium on New Ways of Analyzing Variation*, ed. by Ralph W. Fasold and Roger W. Shuy, 162–83. Washington, D.C.: Georgetown University Press.

———. 1977. The question of prior creolization in Black English. *Pidgin and creole linguistics*, ed. by Albert Valdman, 190–221. Bloomington: Indiana University Press.

———. 1986. Social contact and linguistic diffusion: Hiberno-English and New World Black English. *Language* 62.245–89.

Sanders, Willease Story. 1978. *Selected grammatical features of the speech of blacks in Columbia, S.C.* Ph.D. dissertation, University of South Carolina.

Schneider, Edgar W. 1981. *Morphologische und syntaktische Variablen im amerikanischen Early Black English*. Frankfurt am Main: Verlag Peter Lang.

———. 1983. The origin of the verbal *-s* in Black English. *American Speech* 58.99–113.

———. 1989. *American Earlier Black English: Morphological and syntactic variables*. Tuscaloosa: University of Alabama Press. [Revised translation of Schneider 1981.]

Smitherman, Geneva. 1977. *Talkin and testifyin: The language of black America*. Boston: Houghton Mifflin.

Todd, Loreto. 1984. *Modern Englishes: Pidgins and creoles*. Oxford: Basil Blackwell.

Traugott, Elizabeth Closs. 1972. *A history of English syntax: A transformational approach to the history of English sentence structures*. New York: Holt, Rinehart and Winston.

Turner, Lorenzo Dow. 1949. *Africanisms in the Gullah dialect*. Chicago: University of Chicago Press.

Van Sertima, Ivan. 1976. My Gullah brother and I: Exploration into a community's language and myth through its oral tradition. *Black English: A seminar*, ed. by Deborah Sears Harrison and Tom Trabasso, 123–46. Hillsdale, N.J.: Erlbaum.

Visser, F. T. 1969. *An historical syntax of the English language*. Part 3. *Syntactical units with two verbs*. Leiden: E. J. Brill.

Wentworth, Harold. 1944. *American dialect dictionary*. New York: Thomas Y. Crowell.

Wolfram, Walter A. 1969. *A sociolinguistic description of Detroit Negro speech*. Washington, D.C.: Center for Applied Linguistics.

Wright, Joseph. 1905. *The English dialect grammar. Comprising the dialects of England, of the Shetland and Orkney Islands and of those parts of Scotland, Ireland and Wales where English is habitually spoken*. Oxford: Henry Frowde.

# The Relative Value of Ex-Slave Narratives. A Discussion of Schneider's Paper

*J. L. Dillard*

Edgar Schneider (1983, 1984, this volume) represents one of the extreme advocates for the utilization of the Work Projects Administration (WPA) ex-slave narratives (collected in the 1930s but representing slaves who reportedly had been alive at emancipation) within the conventional framework that Black English, like all other varieties of American English, represents British "folk speech" of the colonial period. He asserts (in this volume), "We have to keep in mind in this particular case that the superstrate was not a standard variety but a dialect, or rather a mixture of dialects." The very use of the term "superstrate" presupposes the theory, on the part of someone, of an African substratum in the background of Black American English (usually referred to now as the Black English vernacular). I regard this as a straw-man procedure, but that matter has been dealt with elsewhere in this volume. Schneider assumes that African substratum and British folk speech are the only choices in the formation of "Black English," and that whatever is to be explained by one of those forced choices is adequately represented by the WPA narratives. It is this issue that must be addressed here.

Since Brewer (1974), it has become fashionable to refer to the WPA narratives as representing "Early" Black English (see, for example, Bailey 1987). This is a strange periodization considering that African-derived slaves have been in what is now the United States since 1619 and presumably have had to talk to English speakers for most if not all of that time; but again the issue is one best left for other treatment. In spite of the considerable number of publications which assume that the WPA ex-slave narratives supersede all other evidence collected in the 1930s as a representation of what was spoken in the 1860s, I cannot regard that assumption as being well motivated. The ex-slave narratives were collected under known circumstances by fairly well described and recorded methods, and with some observable biases. It should be possible, then, to examine to what degree they represent the absolute truth about black speech in their own period. Surely some such examination should precede any claims about their validity for the period 1619–1865.

It seems a bit extreme even to assume, as Schneider (1981) and Bailey (1987) apparently have, that the narratives in question are representative of conditions up to seventy years earlier than the time they were written down. This rests on the tenuous assumption that ex-slaves who were alive and talking in 1865 and who were recorded in, say, 1935 had the same dialect over that seventy-year span—that the age of the informants, in spite of considerable discussion of age grading in BEV, can be ignored. Interestingly, without even considering language matters, Woodward (1974:472) saw this limitation: "The very age of the former slaves at the time they were interviewed raises several serious considerations." Of course, if emancipation were the only major social change for the population involved in slavery before World War I—and it seems very likely indeed that such a process as "decreolization" would accompany major social changes—and if it is true that the ex-slaves aged from seventy to one hundred spoke like slave children, then decreolization is pretty well ruled out. But it appears to me that the question has been begged.

Note that this seventy-two-year period (1863–1935) cuts across all three of the periods Bailey (1987) considers important and contains what he identifies as the great transitional acts (Emancipation Proclamation and the migration after World War I) that mark his major periods. This particular division into periods is based, however, on an outsider's view of what was important to the African-American population. Actually the Emancipation Proclamation produced an official and legal change that had much less influence in actuality than it did on paper; Johnson's (1934) classic study makes that point clearly. If a governmental act has to be considered a marker of a division between periods in black history, the 1954 Supreme Court decision would be more significant. For a greatly different view of periodization in Black English, see Dillard (1992:67–90). Accepting Bailey's three periods for purposes of arguments only, one can still point out a number of problems:

1. Is the immediately preemancipation slave community an adequate representation of nearly 250 years (1619–1863) in what is now the United States?
2. Are the slaves who lived until 1935 or later and agreed to be interviewed for the WPA project representative of even the immediately preemancipation slave community, particularly of the field hands?
3. Were the elicitation procedures used by the WPA field-workers comparable to those used by the Linguistic Atlas of the Gulf States (LAGS) and LAGS-associated field-workers in the 1980s?

The first question is important because claims have been made (Stewart 1967, 1968; and many others thereafter) that generally reliable records go back nearly two hundred years before emancipation. For the period up to about 1798, those records show a strikingly pidginlike language for plantation field hands in both the northern and southern parts of what is now the United States. In fact, records as late as Frederick Douglass's autobiography (1855) represent slaves newly imported from Africa speaking something quite similar to a pidgin English variety which we now know has been spoken in West Africa for at least two or three centuries. In order to deny the creolization hypothesis, one must apparently assert that all those records were faked. There must have been some kind of superimposed guidance for the recorders, who did not know each other and who recorded strikingly similar materials. Bailey's assertion (and apparently those of Schneider, Brewer, and others) seems to be that the recorders and elicitors of the ex-slave narratives were not subject to any kind of superimposed guidance.

The second question is important because Bailey (1987:33) proposes direct comparison. Since we assume that the fieldwork by Bailey and Maynor (1985), the LAGS, etc., is reliable, the question will certainly come up about the reliability of the WPA materials.

This makes the third question perhaps the crucial one. The WPA records did not simply materialize but were collected by human beings, authors with recognizable tendencies. If attestations from black author William Wells Brown's *The Colored Heroine* (1853) or from Frederick Douglass are to be dismissed because of the literary reputation of the recorder, what are we to say of the Louisiana ex-slave narratives collected and elaborately edited under the direction of the novelist Lyle Saxon? Even outside Louisiana, can we be sure that the WPA workers followed anything approximating the guidelines of dialectologists, anthropologists, or professional folklorists?

Fortunately, if we know something about Cotton Mather and his supernatural beliefs, which might cast some doubt on his quotation from "these Africans" in *The Angel of Bethesda*, we also know something about Lyle Saxon and his methods. It may also be that we can discover something of a national policy concerning the collection of ex-slave narratives which might lead us to an informed decision about reliability.

Perdue, Barden, and Phillips (1986) repeat with little more than paraphrasing Woodward's judgment (1974:472) that

> among categories of the [ex-slave] population represented by larger than their proportional numbers are urban residents, males, and former house servants, with a consequent under-representation of rural population, females, and former field hands.

The second kind of skewing is especially important because it has long been held—and not by creole origins theorists but by Frazier (1957)—that house servants and field hands had different dialects. Further, Woodward thought that the most serious sources of distortion in the Federal Writers' Project (FWP) narratives come not from the interviewees but from interviewers—their biases, procedures, and methods—and the interracial circumstances of the interview. Woodward may have been discussing primarily the events and relationships reported in the ex-slave narratives, but there is evidence of a more directly linguistic bias.

On May 1, 1937, John Lomax, then national adviser of Folklore and Folkways for the FWP, wrote to a local investigator concerning the handling of dialect. He was careful to prescribe that the narratives should be told in the language of the ex-slaves and not in that of the interviewer, but considerable responsibility was placed upon the field-workers, who seem not only to have been linguistically untrained but even questionably educated. A frequent criticism in the extensive records of the FWP is that workers were hired not because of their talents but because of their unemployed status. First director John Lomax, who was subject to severe criticism because of his lack of academic training, and others are recorded as having given frequent instructions about how the field-workers should treat dialect; for example, "Words should not be put into dialect where this did not change the pronunciation" (Mangione 1983). While this may pass for a laudable counteractive to the much-invoked eye dialect, can such workers have been qualified to make decisions of any complexity—whether a stop consonant in initial position was imploded or exploded, for example? Were these untrained and often almost uneducated field-workers able to avoid transferring syntactic structures into those of their own dialect while making longhand notes on their interviews?

It seems perfectly clear that Lomax and the others, including Lyle Saxon, assumed that there was such a thing as Negro dialect—Lomax stipulated that "the flavor of Negro speech should be preserved." Now, I happen to believe that he was right; I would also much prefer data garnered under the supervision of Lomax to that assembled by what I know from Natchitoches Parish experience to have been almost worshipers of Lyle Saxon. Still, I doubt the rigidly empirical interpretation of data which were gathered under such an extreme amount of influence from principles enunciated by Lomax.

Under these circumstances—in which dominant personalities are known to have influenced the dialect practices as well as the interview schedules of the WPA narratives—can we ignore literary texts concerning which the major objection would perhaps be that they were overinfluenced by the personal predispositions of the authors? (I am assuming, of course, that no one believes there was somewhere a Central Bias Headquarters for the Universal Distortion of the Speech of Black Characters in Literature—which would have needed to operate in English, Spanish, and Portuguese, and in a somewhat more restricted fashion in French.) The "interracial" factor as a possible distortion in the WPA narratives keeps coming up, and Perdue et al. seem committed to the idea that black interviewers would have done a better job. Under those circumstances, can we afford to overlook evidence from earlier black writers like Frederick Douglass and William Wells Brown, themselves masters of Standard English but also fully cognizant of very different dialects used by slaves who had not undergone the social changes Brown and Douglass had managed to achieve? In *My Southern Home*, Brown stipulates that most of his characters are house servants; but, then, so were a disproportionate number of those recorded in the ex-slave narratives. How about Charles Waddell Chesnutt?

Brown is perhaps the most dangerous to ignore within this tradition. An escaped slave himself, he is the subject (perhaps truly the author) of one of the many fugitive slave narratives published in perfectly standard English by the abolitionist societies. He became, obviously, a capable author and novelist, using Standard English for many of his characters, including the title character in *Clotelle, the Colored Heroine*. But he differentiates slaves from different social groups in a manner passed over by William Edward Farrison (1969) in the one lengthy study of Brown's work. Interestingly, Farrison praises every facet of Brown's writing *except* his dialect—a case of radical chic, one might say, typical of his time. Perhaps Farrison had already discovered that nearly universal conspiracy. Unfortunately, however, Farrison did not leave us his evidence of that dastardly movement. In fact, even Cleanth Brooks (1985), whose status as a critic would seem to qualify him to identify a literary conspiracy, chooses to tell us nothing of that literary trend of incredible magnitude.

The Louisiana ex-slave narratives (unpublished) in the Northwestern (Louisiana) State University (NSU) collection show at least two stages of editing of the pencil-written transcriptions of the field-workers. In some cases the "dialect" transcription—if it can be called that—is "corrected." In at least one case the material reported is changed. Lyle Saxon, who seems to have been no worse qualified than the general run of state directors of the WPA projects, put his name on *Gumbo YaYa*, which Braud (1983) judged to have been written by Robert Tallant and which she, in good company, characterized as "fakelore."

If the vast plantation literature, of which the surface is hardly scratched in the Reinccke et al. bibliography (1973), is to be discarded because many, perhaps most, of the writers were slave owners and therefore biased against the slaves, and if we are to throw William Wells Brown out with Paul Lawrence Dunbar and conscienceless participants in a racist's dialect fakery, then we may well have to throw out the WPA narratives as having been influenced by many figures in the same literary tradition. If we throw out everything which can be considered tainted by the dialect fiction tradition, we may simply wind up throwing out everything.

The sound recordings referred to by Schneider are something else. If they are truly representative of a reliable sample of even elderly ex-slave speech, they are, of course, important. I have not yet been able to listen to them. According to Bailey, who has them, the recordings themselves illustrate flawed interview techniques on the part of WPA bigwigs (personal communication). I can offer little of an objective nature on this particular matter now.

Where *other* sound recordings, representing admittedly no sampling technique whatsoever, are concerned, there are some complications. Ian Hancock (personal communication) has discovered a commercial recording by Louisiana folksinger Johnny Copeland of "I De Go Now." This "West Indian"–like *de* occurs, according to Jay Edwards (personal communication) in the area of Copeland's origin. Otherwise, *de* has admittedly not been attested—even by the most liberal interpretation of the term "attest"—outside Gullah territory. The particular kind of BEV *be* which has attracted so much attention serves some of the functions of *de* and is in some respects a kind of replacement. In its 150 years or so of use outside Gullah, including Bracketville, Texas, Gullah (Hancock 1980), *be* has acquired a "reportability" function, as in (a) *I be only eight years old,* and (b) *She be my sister,* in addition to the much-discussed *durative* function (Dillard 1985:116–19).

Of course, I am not recommending that hearsay evidence be admitted, that sound recordings be disregarded because there may have been some flaws in the eliciting technique of those who made the recordings, or that the ex-slave narratives be thrown out as evidence. In fact, those who have not had their books reviewed by C.-J. Bailey will probably not understand why I find it necessary to express this disclaimer.

Quite seriously, I suggest that the value of the ex-slave narratives may lie in a very different direction. Serious philological consideration of the records of Black English, plantation creole, Negro dialect, or whatever the stages may be called is long overdue. The WPA narratives, which are not very much unlike the plantation literature tradition—after all, the authors who participated in both had a great deal in common—have a big advantage which seems to have been overlooked. The Louisiana narratives were clearly edited for publication. Field-workers, of approximately the type described above, collected narratives in no. 2 pencil, which were edited in colored pencil and then submitted to a typist. The typescripts were apparently intended for utilization in publications, perhaps not entirely unlike *Gumbo YaYa*. I have seen an instance in which the pencil-writing interviewer, with some obvious eye dialect, writes *I noes*. The colored pencil editor has "corrected" this to *I know*. The deficiencies of the first are as obvious as those of the second. The former is as reliable as the expert on "phonetic spelling" who contributes occasionally to small-town newspapers; the latter, as a garden-variety high school English teacher, perhaps the one Martin Joos made famous as Miss Fidditch. Probably no one would seriously take a typescript made from the second WPA text as reliable linguistic data. Considering the central control from Washington, D.C., of the whole project, can we assume that no such editing was practiced upon the materials published by George Rawick and others?

No one would assume that equivalent caution is not needed in using materials collected by other methods and presented in some other fashion. The report by Frederick Douglass of what is clearly West African Pidgin English on one nineteenth-century plantation seems flawed in view of studies of that pidgin in the twentieth century:

> At the time of which I am writing [the 1820s], there were slaves who had been brought from the coast of Africa. They never used "s" in indication of the possessive case "Oo you dem long to?" means, "Whom do you belong to?" . . . "Oo dem got any peachy," means "Have you any peaches?"

The apparent inconsistency of *Oo (dem)* (apparently 'who' in the first example and 'you' in the second) and the greater likelihood of something like *(w)una* for *you dem* or *Oo dem* casts some doubt on the accuracy of the attestation. Was Douglass's memory poor or was there an editor who thought that *oo dem* looked more quaint and exotic than *peachy dem*? The writers of plantation fiction are regularly accused of such distortions. Certainly most of us would expect to find something more like *(w)una* than *oo dem* and more like *peachy dem* than *any peachy*. Or did Douglass simply get it wrong? The accuracy of his observation about the possessive (allowing for the not uncommon notion of the monolingual English speaker that *-s* is somehow inherent to possession) would seem to argue that he really heard something like what he described.

Taking into account Douglass's historical evidence can lead to possibilities even more unsettling, insofar as conventional notions of language history go. In the same paragraph, Douglass refers to "Mas' Daniel," the son of Col. Lloyd, the owner of the plantation, who "by his association with his father's slaves had measurably adopted their dialect" (1970 ed., 59). Douglass could be taken to provide the same kind of evidence as many white plantation writers: that the black varieties had a great influence on Southern white speech, at least of selected groups.

In spite of the sentimental and political incentives to the contrary, we cannot afford to be selective in our evaluation of sources. If Lyle Saxon and Robert Tallant could be wrong, so, presumably, could Frederick Douglass, William Wells Brown, and Charles W. Chesnutt. But I regard it as self-evident that the authors discussed above were more talented and proficient than the average WPA interviewer.

A philological approach might yield some results which the polemic approach has failed to produce in the last twenty-three years. Since there are at least some existing survivals of the editorial process in the Louisiana narratives, those might be a good place to start. But it would not be a good idea to approach the whole project with any such preconception as that the results should be as different as possible from the practices of the plantation novelists or that inerrancy can be established for the WPA narratives. Nor would it appear to be equitable to exempt the literary source which seems to give evidence of "metropolitan" or "rural" British dialects from the same process of examination.

We might ultimately be able to utilize the ex-slave narratives for what I think they are: representative examples of the literary tradition of black speech. Restriction of preverbal *been,* for example, to "coastal South Carolina" (Schneider, this volume) in the 1930s—or in the 1860s—would suggest an interesting hypothesis of rapid spread. By the 1960s, Loflin found it in Washington, D.C., although his analysis of the form would certainly not agree with mine; Labov (1972:53–55) reports it from Philadelphia; Fickett (1970) found it in Buffalo and reports no great migration from South Carolina; my own ears have heard it quite regularly for about seven years in Natchitoches, Louisiana. If Schneider and whatever group he represents wish to disregard the first three of those reports, then we apparently have no basis for discussion. He may feel free to explain away the last as delusion, but I still would be reluctant to drop the matter.

It would be interesting to establish the South Carolina connection, especially in view of the many indications that factors like social status of the interlocutors and notions of what is appropriate to a given communication seem to be the effective factor. Blacks in Natchitoches Parish frequently use constructions like *been* Verb*(-ed),* as in: (a) *'da been* past participle (PP), and (b) *been done* PP (in a nonpassive construction), but many of them do not use them in formal conversations, or with whites present. A student-athlete at NSU judged to be culturally very black by his professors, writing about how he prepared for a (remedial) English test, wrote that he utilized . . . *what I been know about English*. Otherwise, in thousands of themes over a fourteen-year period, no black NSU student has used that construction in writing. On the other hand, an elderly, uneducated black lady—more a friend than an informant or consultant—from whom I hear most often *I been know dat, I been had it a long time, You oughta been tol' me*, etc., produced, in a recent conversation, two consecutive sentences of the type *I 'da been done* PP (in a nonpassive construction). She acknowledges no direct non–Arkansas, Louisiana, Texas influence and would probably be entertained and amused at the notion that she speaks in a way that is somehow "South Carolinian."

## References

Bailey, Guy B. 1987. Are white and black vernaculars diverging? *American Speech* 62.32–40.

Bailey, Guy B., and Natalie Maynor. 1985. The present tense of *be* in Southern black folk speech. *American Speech* 60.195–213.

Braud, Debra. 1979. A study of *Gumbo Ya-Ya*. Northwestern (Louisiana) State University M.A. thesis.

Brewer, Jeutonne. 1974. *The verb "be" in Black English: A study based on the WPA ex-slave narratives*. Ph.D. dissertation, University of North Carolina at Chapel Hill.

Brooks, Cleanth. 1935. *The relation of the Alabama-Georgia dialect to the provincial dialects of Great Britain*. Baton Rouge: Louisiana State University Press.

———. 1985. *The language of the American South*. Athens: University of Georgia Press.

Brown, William W. 1853. *Clotel, or the colored heroine*. London.

———. [1968]. *My southern home or the South and its people, Upper Saddle River*. Ridgewood, N.J.: Gregg Press.

Dillard, J. L. 1985. *Toward a social history of American English*. Berlin: Mouton de Gruyer.

———. 1992. *A history of American English*. Essex: Longman.

Douglass, Frederick. 1855. *My bondage and my freedom*. 1970. Chicago: Johnson.

Farrison, William E. 1969. *William Wells Brown: Author and reformer*. Chicago: University of Chicago Press.

Fickett, Joan. 1970. *Aspects of morphemics, syntax, and semology of an inner-city dialect (Merican)*. Ph.D. dissertation, State University of New York at Buffalo.

Frazier, E. Franklin. 1939. *The Negro family in the United States*. Chicago: University of Chicago Press.

———. 1957. *Black bourgeoisie*. Glencoe, Ill.: Free Press.

Hancock, Ian F. 1980. Texan Gullah: The creole English of Bracketville Afro-Seminoles. *Perspectives on American English*, ed. by J. L. Dillard, 305–32. The Hague: Mouton.

Johnson, Charles. 1934. *The shadow of the plantation*. Chicago: University of Chicago Press.

Labov, William. 1972. *Language in the inner city: Studies in the Black English vernacular*. Philadelphia: University of Pennsylvania Press.

Loflin, Marvin D. 1969. On the passive in nonstandard Negro English. *Journal of English as a Second Language* 4.19–23.

Mangione, Jerre G. 1983. *The dream and the deal: The Federal Writers' Project, 1935–1943*. Philadelphia: University of Pennsylvania Press.

Perdue, Charles L., Jr., Thomas E. Barden, and Robert K. Phillips. 1986. *Weevils in the wheat: Interviews with Virginia ex-slaves*. Bloomington: Indiana University Press.

Reinecke, John, et al. 1973. *A bibliography of pidgin and creole languages*. Honolulu: University of Hawaii Press.

Schneider, Edgar. 1981. *Morphologische und syntaktische Variablen im amerikanischen Early Black English*. Frankfurt am Main: Verlag Peter Lang.

———. 1983. The origin of the verbal *-s* in Black English. *American Speech* 58.99–113.

Stewart, William A. 1967. Sociolinguistic factors in the history of American Negro dialects. *Florida Foreign Language Reporter* 5.1–7.

———. 1968. Continuity and change in American Negro dialects. *Florida Foreign Language Reporter* 6.3–14.

Woodward, C. Vann. 1974. History from slave sources: A review article. *American Historical Review* 79.470–81.

# Part Three

## *Defending and Identifying African Substrate Influence*

# African Influence upon Afro-American Language Varieties: A Consideration of Sociohistorical Factors

*John Victor Singler*

The creation of individual Atlantic creoles can be seen as a four-step process: (1) Africans were enslaved and brought together; (2) a European-lexifier speech variety arose to facilitate intergroup communication, particularly for communication between groups of Africans; (3) this language became a native language for a speech community; and (4) this language became *the* native language for a speech community.

As I have argued elsewhere (1986, 1988), the close examination of historical records makes possible a number of points about creole genesis in the Caribbean. Crucially, high mortality and low fertility were characteristic of all the colonies, but sugar colonies most of all. (The reasons why this was so are discussed below.) As a result, the period of nativization of these societies was excessively protracted. At the same time, the structure of plantation societies encouraged retention of African ethnicities and, with them, retention of African languages. The slow nativization of plantation societies argues for the slow nativization of the creoles that developed there, and the long period of creolization would have involved a long period of coexistence with African languages.[1] Thus, the historical evidence argues quite strongly for a substratal presence throughout the period of creole genesis.

This substratal presence was not manifested everywhere in the same manner and to the same degree. Consequently, it is appropriate to consider the linguistic and sociohistorical factors that constrained substratal influence. In this paper I briefly consider linguistic factors and then focus on sociohistorical ones. In particular I examine demographic and historical issues pertinent to the development of Haitian Creole.

## Linguistic Factors

In Singler 1988, I distinguished between the kind of *behavior* that creoles influenced by their substrata are most likely to display and the kind of *evidence* that creolists are most likely to accept as proof of substratal influence. That is, the best case for substratal influence is made when a particular phenomenon cannot be accounted for in any other way. However, the substratal input most likely to influence the emergent creole is that which is compatible with the superstrate, that which is linguistically unmarked, or both. Thus, two crucial linguistic factors in determining the role of the substrate in pidgin and creole genesis are the degree of congruence of the substrata with the lexifier language and the degree of linguistic markedness of the substratal input.

A third factor is the degree of substratal homogeneity. Its impact is most obvious in those cases in which homogeneity is greatest. This is illustrated in Smith, Robertson, and Williamson's (1987) study of the extensive range of Ịjọ influence upon Berbice Dutch and also in my work (1988) on the influence of Kru and Mande languages upon the extended pidgin Liberian English. There is evidence from the Liberian case that if the homogeneity of the substrate is great enough, even highly marked substratal phenomena will become part of the pidgin or creole. Homogeneity of the substrate is not a precondition for substratal influence; nonetheless, the greater the homogeneity of the substratal input, the stronger the substratal influence can be expected to be.

Finally, the particular linguistic properties of the substrate languages are themselves a factor in determining the extent of substratal influence. In ways that may be independent of linguistic markedness, some properties and parameters lend themselves to transfer more readily than do others. This can be illustrated in terms of components of the grammar. That is, if the substratal input into a pidgin or creole is properly characterized as a type of language shift, and if in the case of language shift the transference of phonology and syntax occurs first, with morphological shift occurring only later, then this bears directly on the comparative influence of African languages upon Afro-American language varieties. In particular, Kwa languages do not display extensive morphology; on the other hand, the richness of Bantu morphology is well known. In situations in which Kwa and Bantu speakers were present in significant numbers during the formative period of the pidgin or creole, Kwa influence is consistently cited as being more significant: the relative impermeability of morphology to language shift goes a long way toward explaining this.[2]

## Demographic and Historical Factors

### *On the Slow Nativization of Plantation Societies*

A good assessment of the historical context in which creole genesis occurred in the Caribbean requires an understanding of why the nativization of the region's plantation societies was so protracted. Curtin's comments in this regard are instructive:

> The slave traders responded to demand conditions, normally importing two men from Africa for each woman. Since birth rate depends on the number of women of child-bearing age, this meant an automatic reduction of 30 per cent in the potential birth rate for each group of migrants from Africa. In addition, the planters regarded female slaves as labour units, and they did little to encourage either a high birth rate or a low rate of infant mortality. When slave women found themselves in a situation without stable family life, where the demands of field work were constant, and where the rearing of children was difficult, if not actually discouraged, they simply had few children (and they knew about both abortive and contraceptive techniques). The result was a low birth rate, not merely in terms of total population, but in terms of female population. Slave populations in tropical America thus normally experienced a net natural decrease caused by very low fertility rates. (1976:319)

Kiple (1984) also examined the fertility rate of the African population of the Caribbean. Like Curtin, he notes the skewed ratio of men to women and the high incidence of miscarriage and abortion. Further, he presents reasons why the incidence of infertility was abnormally high among the African female slave population.

Coupled with the low fertility rate was a staggeringly high rate of infant mortality.[3] As part of his study, Kiple investigated and ultimately endorsed the assertion that 25% of all babies born to slaves in Jamaica died in the first two weeks, with the two most frequent causes of death being tetanus and tetany (a physiological mineral imbalance brought on by a lack of calcium or magnesium in the mother's diet). For the Caribbean in general, Kiple states that "around half of all slaves born in the West Indies did not survive infancy, while many more perished in early childhood, with tetany, infantile beriberi, and Protein Energy Malnutrition foremost among their killers" (1984:134).

At the same time, Africans tended to have a short life span once they arrived in the Caribbean. This was especially true of those who worked on sugar plantations. Sidney Mintz's study of sugar production and sugar consumption indicates that "the labor requirements [for sugar production] were horrendous" (1985:49). In their response to the extremely high turnover in their labor force, sugar growers found it cheaper to import adult slaves from Africa than to breed and rear slaves on the plantation itself.

This combination of factors yielded societies unable to reverse the natural population decrease. They were societies marked by both a disproportionately small number of children and an ongoing stream of recently arrived slaves from Africa.

### *On Determining Where in Africa Slaves Came From*

In the assessment of the demographic and historic factors attendant upon creolization, a fundamental issue is the determination of which people are the proper focus of study. To begin with, in the case of Afro-American language varieties, it is necessary to consider the degree and nature of intra-Caribbean migration. The question arises as to whether creole languages were for the most part transplanted from island to island or whether they arose anew in every colony.[4] If colony B was established by landowners and slaves from colony A, the most effective examination of substratal influence upon colony B's creole may be one that contains—or even focuses upon—the African origins of the Africans in colony A.

An additional question about demographic information and its contribution to an understanding of creole genesis is the following: In an examination of the origins of Africans brought to the New World, how long a period should be considered? That is, given the slow nativization of plantation societies and their creoles and given a substratal presence throughout—and beyond—the period of the nativization of the creole, how long a period bears upon creole genesis? Put another way, when is it appropriate to stop looking? Is the first twenty years an appropriate time span, or should it be the first fifty, or the first hundred? (Note that I do not address this as a question of how many generations. In creole societies, particularly in their earliest stages, the term "generation" has little meaning.) In his response to Bickerton (1984), Chris Corne identifies a feature in Mauritian Creole whose source is input from Indian substratal languages not present in Mauritius until after creole genesis (1984:192). Corne's example makes the point that sizable populations must be considered no matter how late their arrival.

One way of viewing this question of how long a period should be considered is to say that the first arrivals were the most important. In this view, the first people who arrived had to create what became the creole; subsequent arrivals had only to learn it. If particular groups of subsequent arrivals were particularly numerous, they might have exerted their own influence on the creole. Such late influence might be seen, however, as comparatively less likely. Or perhaps it might be considered more peripheral, ordinarily affecting only marginal or surface aspects of the grammar and not altering the fundamental principles and parameters established in the earliest period. This hypothesis that the first arrivals are the most important, while highly plausible, has yet to be substantiated. For that reason, in the present study—particularly in the discussion that follows—I treat the question as an open one and do not rule out other answers.

*Establishing the Cultural Matrix*

The relationship of first arrivals to subsequent ones must be placed within the context of what Alleyne (1971) calls the cultural matrix of creolization. Such a context includes but is not limited to demographic relationships, for example, Philip Baker's Events 1, 2, and 3 (cf. Baker 1982a, 1982b, this volume).[5] In addition to quantitative analyses, qualitative ones must be considered as well. For example, Coit (1986) argues that the *nature of contact* between superstrate and substrate speakers is a crucial variable in creole genesis. To illustrate her point she cites Corne's statement (1982:105) about Réunion that the frequency of marriages between French men and Malagasy women was the "most striking feature" of the first half century of colonization there.

Another factor that proved critical in shaping master-slave interaction was crop selection. In the first half of the seventeenth century, the principal agricultural export from the British and French colonies in the West Indies was tobacco. Sugar permanently supplanted tobacco as principal export in the second half of the century. Mintz characterizes the tobacco growers of the 1600s as generally "small-scale cultivators of limited means" (1985:52), their labor force a mixture of political prisoners, petty criminals, indentured servants, and African and Native American slaves. In contrast, "the shift to sugar production required substantial capital" (53). As Mintz notes with regard to Barbados,

> the shift from tobacco to sugar created larger estates. At the same time, the pattern enabling indentured servants to acquire land at the end of their terms disappeared. Small farms were replaced by plantations, and by the late seventeenth century and thereafter, the number of enslaved Africans rose sharply. (53)

Moreover, Mintz quotes a mid-seventeenth-century Barbadian source as saying with regard to slave owners and the acquisition of slaves, "the more they buie, the more they are able to buie" (53).

In a parallel discussion of the impact of sugar growing upon the French Caribbean, Stein states:

> With the introduction of sugar cane . . . to the French islands, colonial society and economy underwent a radical transformation. No longer were the Antilles the home of a community of prosperous farmers roughly equal

in wealth and social status; instead they became the preserve of a few great landowners who reduced their white compatriots to poverty and who imported thousands of black slaves. The introduction of sugar cane to the French West Indies was the most significant single event to occur there during the old regime [i.e., prior to the French Revolution]. (1979:6–7)

The linguistic consequences of the shift from tobacco to sugar arise from differences in the amount of contact between Africans and Europeans. On the small tobacco holdings Africans worked alongside indentured servants, but on the great sugar plantations the bulk of the large African work force would have had very limited direct contact with Europeans. Further, while an island like Martinique would have passed through a tobacco stage prior to becoming a sugar island, the rise to paramountcy of sugar came quickly after the colonization of Haiti. There was a brief period there when tobacco and, after 1669, cocoa were the major crops, but sugar soon prevailed.

## The Demography of Haiti

The case of Haiti illustrates the issues involved in interpreting the impact of sociohistorical factors upon pidgin and creole genesis.[6] In general, demographic studies of creole communities can serve only to demonstrate which linguistic sources were predominant and which, while not predominant, were present. For Haiti, the conclusions that one draws in this regard depend directly upon the time period considered to be relevant.

The French presence in Saint Domingue (Haiti) dates from sometime in the middle of the seventeenth century. Heinl and Heinl (1978) date French control from 1659. In addition to the freebooters who had resided on the Ile de la Tortue just off the northern coast of Haiti since 1630, there were by 1659 a small number of Huguenot planters present in Haiti itself. By the time of the arrival of Bertrand d'Ogeron as governor in 1665, there were approximately 400 French planters as well as the freebooters. By 1680, 4,000 slaves had been imported, according to Curtin (1969:79). Patterson (1982:481) lists the population of Saint Domingue in 1681 as consisting of 4,336 whites and 2,312 slaves.[7] Soon thereafter, Saint Domingue became France's principal sugar colony and quickly came to dominate the French Caribbean. To sustain its preeminence and to meet the growing demand in Europe for sugar, Saint Domingue continually sought more slaves. Curtin (1969:77) divides "the growth of slave population on Saint Domingue . . . into three distinct phases—rapid growth from about 1680 to 1739, slower growth (parallel to the rates prevalent on Jamaica) from

**Table 1. The Population of Saint Domingue, 1681–1789**

| *Year* | *Whites* | *Slaves* | *Free Blacks* | *Total* |
|---|---|---|---|---|
| 1681 | 4,336 | 2,312 | — | 6,648 |
| 1715 | 6,600 | 30,651 | 1,404 | 38,723 |
| 1739 | 11,540 | 117,411 | 3,588 | 132,539 |
| 1754 | 14,253 | 172,188 | 4,911 | 191,352 |
| 1775 | 32,650 | 249,098 | 7,055 | 188,803 |
| 1784 | 20,229 | 298,079 | 13,257 | 331,565 |
| 1789 | 30,831 | 434,429 | 24,848 | 490,108 |

*Sources:* For all figures except 1715, Patterson 1982:481; for 1715, Ministère de la France d'Outre-Mer, G[1] 509.

**Table 2. Estimated Slave Imports into Saint Domingue (1651–1791) by Twenty-five- and Twenty-Year Intervals**
(Saint Domingue stopped importing slaves in 1791.)

| *1651–75* | *1676–1700* | *1701–20* | *1721–40* | *1741–60* | *1761–80* | *1781–91* |
|---|---|---|---|---|---|---|
| 3,000 | 71,600 | 70,600 | 79,400 | 158,700 | 195,000 | 286,000 |

*Source:* Curtin 1969:119, 216.

1739 to 1778, then very rapid growth during the 1780's." Then, in 1791, in the aftermath of the French Revolution, rebellion in Saint Domingue brought the importation of slaves there to an end. Just how much the slave population had grown in the years between d'Ogeron's arrival as governor in 1665 and the rebellion of 1791 can be seen in tables 1, 2, and 3.[8] Taken together, these three tables provide a picture as to how many slaves were imported and at what time. Moreover, they establish that, given the high rate of mortality and the continuous increase in the number of slaves imported, the large majority of the population was African-born all the way up to 1791.

The question remains as to where in Africa the slaves of Saint Domingue came from. In the entire span of slave importation to the colony, three distinct periods emerge. The first of these extends from the founding of Saint Domingue to 1710 and thus includes the first twenty to twenty-five years after the number of slaves achieved parity with the number of owners (Baker's Event 1).

**Table 3. Estimated Slave Imports into Saint Domingue (1651–1791), Divided by Growth Period**

| *Years* | *Slaves Imported* | *Annual Average* | *Growth Rate of Slave Population* | *Era* | *Rate of Natural Decrease* |
|---|---|---|---|---|---|
| To 1680 | 4,000 | — | — | — | — |
| 1681–1738 | 204,800 | 3,530 | 7.0 | 1673–1729 | 5.4 |
| 1739–78 | 317,300 | 7,930 | 2.0 | 1739–74 | 2.6 |
| 1779–90 | 313,200 | 26,100 | 5.5 | 1776–1807 | 1.9 |
| 1791 | 25,000 | — | — | | |
| Total | 864,300 | | | | |

*Source:* Curtin 1969:79. Curtin arrives at "rate of natural decrease" on the basis of comparable figures for Jamaica.

The second period, from 1710 to 1739, covers the second half of the period of the slave population's very rapid growth. The third period is from 1740 to 1791, the year when the importation of slaves into Saint Domingue ceased.

*The Period to 1710*

The records for the first period, up to 1710, are far less extensive than those for subsequent eras. However, it is possible to get some idea of who was coming from where. In this period slaves were provided to French colonies, including Saint Domingue, by the French themselves, the English, and—most important—the Dutch. The French were slow to enter the slave trade; however, in the final quarter of the seventeenth century they did ship 50,000 slaves to various points in the New World, the largest number of slaves apparently coming from ports in the Senegambian region. The English, too, provided slaves to French colonies, the largest numbers coming from the Gold Coast, the Slave Coast, and the Windward Coast. Also, the French of Saint Domingue were in the habit of raiding Jamaica, so much so that Jamaica was sometimes referred to in Saint Domingue as "Petite Guinée."

As for the Dutch, they brought 121,500 slaves to the Western Hemisphere in the seventeenth century (Rawley 1981:94). Of these, nearly two-thirds came from the Slave Coast, that is, present-day Togo and Benin (Rawley 1981:97). Most of the rest came from Angola and the Gold Coast. If two-thirds of the slaves exported by the Dutch came from the Slave Coast, and if the ratio of slaves shipped by the Dutch to the French colonies from particular regions paralleled the overall rate, it would be fair to conclude that two-thirds of the slaves brought by the Dutch to French colonies were from the Slave Coast. In fact, the percentage coming from the Slave Coast was probably even higher than this because the bulk of the Angola slaves went to Brazil. In 1645, during Dutch control of Brazil, the governor notified the slaving company that henceforth only Bantu slaves should be sent to Brazil. Thus, the slaves imported into the French Caribbean by the Dutch in the seventeenth century would have been overwhelmingly from the Slave Coast, with a smaller group coming from the Gold Coast.

The regions in question—Senegambia, the Windward, Gold, and Slave coasts, and Angola—can be related to ethnic and linguistic groups. The Senegambian region had, in earlier periods, provided large numbers of Wolof and other speakers of West Atlantic languages. However, by the end of the seventeenth century, the largest number of Africans shipped through Senegambian ports were speakers of Northern Mande languages spoken much farther inland, particularly speakers of dialects of the Bamana (Bambara)-Malinke-Dyula cluster.[9] The Windward Coast refers to what is today Liberia and the Ivory Coast; for a number of reasons, most of the slaves from this region were from western Liberia and the regions just interior. At the end of the seventeenth century and the very beginning of the eighteenth century, these would have been speakers of Mande, especially Northwestern Mande, and—to a lesser extent—Western Kru languages. (Northwestern Mande includes Northern Mande.) Slaves brought from the Gold Coast were primarily speakers of Akan, a Western Kwa dialect cluster; and those from the Slave Coast spoke Ewe-Fon, another Western Kwa cluster. Finally, Angola refers to the coastal region from Cape Lopez south to Benguela, including the coasts of the modern-day states of Congo, Zaire, and Angola. Even though the trade routes from this section of the coast extended far inland, the slaves exported from this region would all have been speakers of closely related Bantu languages.

Taken together, the evidence pertaining to Dutch, French, and English slaving seems to indicate that in this first period, up to 1710, the largest number of Africans imported to Saint Domingue were probably Kwa, especially Ewe-Fon. There would also have been a significant number of speakers of Mande languages and smaller numbers of speakers of West Atlantic, Kru, Eastern Kwa, and Benue-Congo languages (including Bantu languages).

Still with reference to this first period, in the absence of direct information, a second way of getting at the ethnic composition of Saint Domingue is by examining evidence from another French colony, French Guiana. Although the

**Table 4. Ethnic Origins of Slaves on the Sugar Estate of Remire, French Guiana, 1690**

| | *Number* | *Percentage* |
|---|---|---|
| Senegambia | | |
| "Cap-Vert" | 3 | 4.6 |
| Fulbe | 3 | 4.6 |
| Wolof | 1 | 1.5 |
| "Bambara" | 5 | 7.7 |
| Total | 12 | 18.5 |
| Gold Coast | | |
| "Cormanti" | 3 | 4.6 |
| Bight of Benin | | |
| "Foin" | 12 | 18.5 |
| "Arada" | 7 | 10.8 |
| "Juda" | 7 | 10.8 |
| Popo | 6 | 9.2 |
| "Ayo" (Oyo Yoruba) | 1 | 1.5 |
| Total | 33 | 50.8 |
| Bight of Biafra | | |
| Calbary | 6 | 9.2 |
| Central Africa | | |
| Congo | 11 | 16.9 |
| Totals | 65 | 100.0 |

*Source:* Curtin 1969:189.

ethnic composition of Saint Domingue cannot be taken to be absolutely identical to that found in French Guiana, still, the ethnic composition of one French colony in a particular period—as revealed by the composition of a plantation in that colony—does give some insights into the ethnic composition of all French colonies at the time. The evidence is given in table 4. The first three Senegambian groups presumably make reference to speakers of West Atlantic languages, Fulbe being another name for Fula/Peulh. As for the Bight of Benin, Foin (i.e., Fon), Popo, and Arada are all names of kingdoms in the region where dialects of the Ewe-Fon dialect cluster are spoken. Juda is Ouidah, the principal fort for the Ewe-Fon region. Curtin (1969:186) suggests that Arada as a designation may mean a person sold by Arada rather than an Arada person. Even allowing for the possibility that a few of those listed as Foin, Arada, Juda, or Popo were in fact from some other ethnic group, the fact remains that nearly half of the African-born population of Remire was Ewe-Fon.[10]

### *1710–1739*

Early in the eighteenth century, the French made an effort to supply their colonies exclusively with slaves imported on French vessels. They were never wholly successful; the demand for slaves, most of all in Saint Domingue, was simply too great. Nonetheless, they did succeed in providing the greatest number of slaves.

With regard to subsequent slave importation, the figures that I use are with reference to all Africans imported by the French, not just those imported to Saint Domingue. It is true that slave owners in the Caribbean developed ethnic preferences among Africans such that "the ethnic make-up of a particular New World colony depended partly on ethnic market-preferences in that colony" (Curtin 1969:130). However, as Curtin states elsewhere (with reference specifically to the period 1748–92), "French slavers . . . delivered an approximate ethnic cross-section of their whole trade to Saint Domingue" (1976:325). The demand for slaves in Saint Domingue was so great that the planters there took whatever slaves they could get, regardless of where they were from or what the planters' preferences might have been. Moreover, Saint Domingue took the overwhelming majority of *all* Africans brought by the French to the Caribbean. Accordingly, it becomes legitimate to draw conclusions about the slaves imported to Saint Domingue based on figures for the French Caribbean as a whole.

In the second period under consideration, 1710–39, the slave population increased fourfold. The geographic distribution of French slave exports in this period is given in table 5.[11]

In this period, most Africans came from the Bight of Benin, with most of the rest coming from Angola and Senegambia. The Bight of Benin, as used by Curtin, refers to the region between the Volta and Benin rivers. "The core of this region in the eighteenth century was the somewhat narrower 'slave coast' of present-day Togo and Dahomey [now Benin]" (Curtin 1969:128), in other words, the Ewe-Fon region. (With the passage of time, more and more slaves would have come from farther inland. However, the Ewe-Fon region itself extends 150 miles inland, and most slaving in the region would not have extended that far.)

Those from Angola would have been speakers of Bantu languages. As for Senegambia, Curtin et al. (1978) say the following: "The only eighteenth-

**Table 5. French Slave Exports from Africa, 1710–39, Cumulative**

| | *1710–19* | | *1710–29* | | *1710–39* | |
|---|---|---|---|---|---|---|
| Bight of Benin | 32,840 | 62.9% | 81,040 | 62.7% | 127,580 | 57.5% |
| Senegambia | 7,110 | 13.6% | 19,970 | 15.5% | 32,300 | 14.6% |
| Bight of Biafra | 6,590 | 12.6% | 6,590 | 5.1% | 7,520 | 3.4% |
| Angola | 4,550 | 8.7% | 18,640 | 14.4% | 40,700 | 18.3% |
| Sierra Leone | 1,150 | 2.2% | 2,610 | 2.0% | 5,110 | 2.3% |
| Gold Coast | | | 390 | .3% | 8,730 | 3.9% |
| Totals | 52,240 | 100.0% | 129,240 | 100.0% | 221,940 | 100.0% |

*Source:* Richardson (1989:14); figures have been rounded.

century slave trade of real consequence was *through* Senegambia, not *from* it. The victims came from the far interior and were largely Mande" (Curtin et al. 1978:231). Specifically, they would have been Northern Mande.

Earlier, it was shown that in the first period of Saint Domingue's history, the plurality—if not the majority—of Africans were speakers of Western Kwa, particularly Ewe-Fon, with Mande speakers forming the second largest group. In the second period, the Ewe-Fon dominance continued and perhaps grew stronger still. Mande and Bantu input, though not so strong as that of Ewe-Fon, was also present.

### *1740–1791*

The figures for the third and final period are given in table 6.

In contrast to the earlier periods, the final period of slave exports was dominated not by the Bight of Benin but by Angola. The Angolan presence was most pronounced at the end of the era. Richardson estimates that in the final decade alone more than 116,000 slaves were exported from Angola by the French. In an observation that corroborates table 5, Rawley (1981:130) remarks that so great was the Angolan influx to the Caribbean that by the 1790s nearly half of Saint Domingue's African-born slave population had originated there. As for the Bight of Benin, slaves imported from there would have included significant numbers of Yoruba speakers in this period, but the largest number of slaves from the region would probably still have been Ewe-Fon. A third region, the Gold Coast, was significant early in this era, but its representation diminished over time. (Moreover, it had not been heavily represented in the previous era.)

**Table 6. French Slave Exports from Africa, 1740–89, Cumulative**

| | *1740–49* | | *1740–59* | | *1740–69* | | *1740–79* | | *1740–89* | |
|---|---|---|---|---|---|---|---|---|---|---|
| Angola | 47,970 | 37.1% | 90,890 | 40.8% | 165,580 | 47.0% | 247,560 | 49.0% | 364,020 | 49.9% |
| Bight of Benin | 40,600 | 31.4% | 71,860 | 32.3% | 96,020 | 27.2% | 139,370 | 27.6% | 194,350 | 26.7% |
| Gold Coast | 20,560 | 15.9% | 23,920 | 10.7% | 33,010 | 9.4% | 39,550 | 7.8% | 53,690 | 7.4% |
| Senegambia | 13,320 | 10.3% | 21,160 | 9.5% | 22,980 | 6.5% | 31,190 | 6.2% | 43,080 | 5.9% |
| Sierra Leone | 6,080 | 4.7% | 11,860 | 5.3% | 24,460 | 6.9% | 27,350 | 5.4% | 39,690 | 5.4% |
| Bight of Biafra | 910 | .7% | 2,960 | 1.3% | 10,620 | 3.0% | 19,900 | 3.9% | 34,260 | 4.7% |
| Totals | 129,440 | 100.0% | 222,650 | 100.0% | 352,670 | 100.0% | 504,920 | 100.0% | 729,090 | 100.0% |

*Source:* Richardson (1989:14); figures have been rounded.

Over the entire span of fifty years no region other than Angola and the Bight of Benin was responsible for so much as 7.5% of the total.

For the African population in the French Caribbean in general, the prevalence of Western Kwa, especially Ewe-Fon, persists from the late seventeenth century through the 1730s. During this same period, Mande speakers, principally Bamana-Malinke-Dyula, would also have been present but in far less significant numbers.[12] Finally, the third major group for the French Caribbean, the Bantu, were present early on but only achieved numerical dominance after 1740.

In discussing Haitian culture, Curtin states:

> In Saint Domingue, where the number of slaves imported from the Guinea Coast and Angola was roughly equal between 1748 and 1792, Dahomean culture nevertheless became dominant, since the Dahomeans formed a high proportion of the slaves in the early settlement of the colony (1976: 325). [Curtin defines the Guinea Coast as extending from Cape Mount to Cape Lopez; that is, the Windward Coast, the Gold Coast, the Bight of Benin, and the Bight of Biafra.]

"Dahomean" in this quotation can be seen as essentially (or predominantly) "Ewe-Fon." However, the transmission of culture and the transmission of language—or, more accurately, the creation of a creole culture and the creation of a creole language—are not necessarily parallel. Further, if the specific substratal input varies over time, the consequences may be different for the development of creole syntax than for the development of the creole lexicon. Earlier influences are generally hypothesized to exert greater significance in the formation of creole syntax, with subsequent substratal input less likely to exert significant influence (but cf. the Mauritian Creole example from Corne, cited above). In contrast, however, lexical items from later groups might still enter the creole with some frequency.

In the comparison of different substratal inputs in the development of a creole (where the inputs differ as to which were strongest at a particular time), the appropriate demographic and historical information must be integrated into a linguistic model that takes into account universal properties and tendencies as well as the inputs' relative congruence with the lexifier language. The frequency with which linguists from Suzanne Comhaire-Sylvain on have likened Haitian Creole to Kwa languages and the infrequency with which it has been compared with Bantu languages may be a consequence of the comparatively early arrival in Haiti of Africans who spoke Western Kwa languages and the comparatively late arrival of Bantu speakers; *or* it may be a consequence of the comparative suitability of Kwa grammar(s) as a source for creole grammar and the comparative unsuitability of morphologically rich Bantu languages as a source. The third possibility is that the two explanations converge: a late-arriving morphologically elaborated language may not have much of a chance to exert extensive influence.

The present study of the demographics of Saint Domingue does not, and cannot, by itself demonstrate the presence of substratal influence upon Haitian Creole, but it does show where best to look for the substratal input that would have wielded that influence. Beyond that, the study of the demographics of the African component of an Afro-American creole society—when it is integrated with the study of other aspects of the early stages of the society, its dynamics of race and ethnicity, of class and economic forces—leads to the identification of the social factors that shape creole genesis.

## Notes

1. While I frame my discussion of Caribbean creoles in the context of nativization, that does not mean I assume nativization to be a sine qua non for creolization in the Caribbean or anywhere else.

2. This discussion of language shift and of the status of phonology, syntax, and morphology within it draws upon a comment made by Sally Thomason at the Round Table. For a detailed discussion of language shift vis-à-vis pidginization and creolization, see Thomason and Kaufman 1988.

3. To begin with, pregnant women ordinarily had to continue working. As Kiple points out, the strenuous work they were engaged in frequently induced premature labor. Those babies that survived premature labor tended to be weaker and less able to withstand various infant diseases than were babies carried to full term.

4. A salient property of Afro-American language varieties is the depth and range of their shared linguistic features. If, as Goodman (1985:110) suggests, intra-Caribbean migration was extensive, the high degree of similarity among these varieties is more readily explained.

5. Bickerton (1984) uses Baker's work as the foundation for a quantitative pidginization index. The index is intended to assess the distance between a particular creole and its lexifier language. (In Bickerton's view, distance from the superstrate can, for certain creoles at least, be equated with proximity to the bioprogram.) Singler (1990) evaluates the index, rejecting Bickerton's formulation of it and questioning the implicit assumption that an algorithm of this type could be valid.

Elsewhere, Bickerton has introduced the possibility that I have "a time machine in the cellars of NYU" (1987:231). Documentary evidence for the analysis of sociocultural forces in the plantation societies of the Caribbean and elsewhere can be found in libraries and archives. For that reason it has not been necessary to use the machine to which Bickerton refers.

6. The work presented in this section represents an expansion of work presented informally at the 1986 NEH/NSF Creole Workshop held at the City University of New York in conjunction with the Summer Institute of the Linguistic Society of America.

7. Baker (personal communication) notes that the figure of 2,312 slaves is more correctly 2,102 slaves and, as indicated on the census document, 210 "mestis et mulastres" and "indes et indiennes."

8. The 1715 Saint Domingue census cited in table 1 and made available to me by Philip Baker has as one category the following: "Mulatres, Nègres et sauvages libres, de tous ages et sexes." (This is the source of the figure 1,404 for free blacks in 1715.) The classification reflects the fact that while those of mixed race dominated the category of *affranchis* 'free blacks,' the category was not limited to them. Any analysis of the sociocultural matrix of the genesis of Haitian Creole must look closely at the role of the *affranchis*.

The 1715 census further divides the slave population thus:

| | |
|---|---|
| Esclaves mâles Trauaillans | 12,510 |
| Esclaves femelles | 7,968 |
| Enfans | 7,826 |
| Infirmes et suragés | 2,345 |

In the count of Europeans in the census, separate categories exist for "hommes portant armes," "garçons portant armes," and "garçons au dessous de 12 ans." Similarly, there are categories for "femmes," "filles à marier," and "filles au dessous de 12 ans." For the slave population, it is not clear whether the age of twelve is the cutoff that separates "enfans" from the others. Whatever the cutoff point, it is not possible to know what percentage of those designated "enfans" were preadolescents brought from Africa and what percentage were children actually born in Saint Domingue.

9. Welmers's (1958) classification of Mande languages is the standard one. There have been subsequent adjustments, but the basic divisions have remained. Mande is divided into two branches, Northwestern and Southeastern. Northwestern Mande is further divided into Northern and Southwestern. The Bamana-Malinke-Dyula dialect cluster (also known as the "Manding" languages) is part of Northern Mande. Bamana-Malinke-Dyula is widely spoken in the Sahel and the sub-Sahelian savannah regions of the western part of West Africa. In terms of number of speakers, it dominates Northern Mande and, indeed, the Mande branch (of Niger-Congo) as a whole.

10. With reference to table 4, Bickerton (1984:176) states the following: "Curtin (1969, P. 189) cites a Cayenne plantation that in 1695 had a labor force of 65 divided among speakers of 12 languages." Bickerton introduces the table as evi-

dence of extreme linguistic diversity in plantation societies; the linguistic ties that bind "Foin," "Arada," "Juda," and Popo (ties of which Bickerton was evidently unaware) belie that claim.

11. In presenting tables drawn from Richardson (1989), I change his term "West Central Africa" to that used by Curtin, "Angola." Curtin's (1969:170) analysis of French slave exports from Africa during the period from 1711 through 1800 posits the Windward Coast as having provided almost 40% of the slave exports for the years from 1711 through 1760 (and then none thereafter). Elsewhere, Curtin et al. (1978:233) associate the intensive Windward Coast trade of the 1720s–1740s with wars and upheavals in what is today the eastern region of the Republic of Guinea. However, Jones and Johnson (1980) systematically dismantle Curtin's arguments concerning the events in eastern Guinea, the trade links between eastern Guinea and the Windward Coast, and especially the evidence for French acquisition of slaves along this coast during this period. They conclude their discussion of the period by citing Mettas (1976:32) to the effect that "Curtin's projected total of 160,800 slaves taken from the Windward Coast by French vessels between 1711 and 1760 should be reduced to 'an absolute maximum of a few thousand, doubtless a few hundred' " (1980:24–25).

Curtin's miscalculation comes largely from his use of Martin's (1931) work. Curtin equated Martin's list of ships' "places of trade" with a statement as to where these ships bought slaves. In fact, Martin frequently listed only the first place where a ship stopped in Africa. This was often a site along the Windward Coast, but as Mettas's more detailed examination of French slave ships shows, "most of the French ships which called at Cape Mount, Cape Mesurado or the River Sestos [the major stopping points on the Windward Coast] bought only wood, rice and water: they then proceeded to Whydah or beyond, where they bought their slaves" (Jones and Johnson 1980:24). Richardson's tables incorporate the corrective proposed by Mettas and Jones and Johnson.

12. Though the present emphasis is on the strong Bamana-Malinke-Dyula presence, this is not to deny the presence of speakers of Atlantic languages imported from Senegambia. As for Sierra Leone, the Africans imported from there would have been native speakers of Mande and West Atlantic languages.

## References

Alleyne, Mervyn. 1971. Acculturation and the cultural matrix of creolization. *Pidginization and creolization of languages*, ed. by Dell Hymes, 169–86. Cambridge: Cambridge University Press.

Baker, Philip. 1982a. *The contribution of non-francophone immigrants to the lexicon of Mauritian Creole*. Dissertation, University of London.

———. 1982b. On the origins of the first Mauritians and of the creole language of their descendants: A refutation of Chaudenson's "Bourbonnais" theory. *Isle de France Creole: Affinities and origins*, by Philip Baker and Chris Corne, 131–259. Ann Arbor: Karoma.

Bickerton, Derek. 1984. The language bioprogram hypothesis. *Behavioral and Brain Sciences* 7.173–221.

———. 1987. Beyond *Roots*: Knowing what's what [Column]. *Journal of Pidgin and Creole Languages* 2.229–38.

Coit, Mary V. 1986. An analysis of the historical, demographic, and social factors in Derek Bickerton's "Language Bioprogram Hypothesis." Unpublished manuscript, New York University.

Corne, Chris. 1982. A contrastive analysis of Réunion and Isle de France creole French: Two typologically diverse languages. *Isle de France Creole: Affinities and origins*, by Philip Baker and Chris Corne, 7–129. Ann Arbor: Karoma.

———. 1984. On the transmission of substratal features in creolisation. *Behavioral and Brain Sciences* 7.191–92.

Curtin, Philip D. 1969. *The Atlantic slave trade*. Madison: University of Wisconsin Press.

———. 1976. The Atlantic slave trade, 1600–1800. *History of West Africa*. Volume 1, second edition, ed. by J. F. Ade Ajayi and Michael Crowder, 302–30. London: Longman.

Curtin, Philip D., Steven Feierman, Leonard Thompson, and Jan Vansina. 1978. *African history*. Boston: Little, Brown.

Goodman, Morris. 1985. Review of *Roots of language*, by Derek Bickerton. *International Journal of American Linguistics* 51.109–37.

Heinl, Robert Debs, Jr., and Nancy Gordon Heinl. 1978. *Written in blood: The story of the Haitian people, 1492–1971*. Boston: Houghton Mifflin.

Jones, Adam, and Marion Johnson. 1980. Slaves from the Windward Coast. *Journal of African History* 21.17–34.

Kiple, Kenneth. 1984. *The Caribbean slave: A biological history*. Cambridge: Cambridge University Press.

Martin, Gaston. 1931. *Nantes au XVIIIe siècle. L'ère des négriers (1714–1774)*. Paris: Alcan.

Mettas, Jean. 1976. Pour une histoire de la traite des Noirs française: sources et problèmes. *La traite des Noirs par l'Atlantique: nouvelles approches*, ed. by Pieter Emmer, Jean Mettas, and Jean-Claude Nardin, 19–46. Paris: Paul Geuthner.

Mintz, Sidney W. 1985. *Sweetness and power: The place of sugar in modern history*. New York: Penguin.

Patterson, Orlando. 1982. *Slavery and social death*. Cambridge, Mass.: Harvard University Press.

Rawley, James A. 1981. *The transatlantic slave trade: A history*. New York: W. W. Norton.

Richardson, David. 1989. Slave exports from West and West-Central Africa, 1700–

1810: New estimates of volume and distribution. *Journal of African History* 30.1–22.

Singler, John Victor. 1986. Short note. *Journal of Pidgin and Creole Languages* 1.141–45.

———. 1988. The homogeneity of the substrate as a factor in pidgin/creole genesis. *Language* 64.27–51.

———. 1990. On the use of sociohistorical criteria in the comparison of creoles. *Linguistics* 28.645–69.

Smith, Norval S. H., Ian E. Robertson, and Kay Williamson. 1987. The Ịjọ element in Berbice Dutch. *Language in Society* 16.49–89.

Stein, Robert Louis. 1979. *The French slave trade in the eighteenth century: An Old Regime business*. Madison: University of Wisconsin Press.

Thomason, Sarah Grey, and Terrence Kaufman. 1988. *Language, contact, creolization, and genetic linguists*. Berkeley: University of California Press.

Welmers, William E. 1958. The Mande languages. *Georgetown University Monograph Series in Languages and Linguistics* 11.9–24. Washington, D.C.: Georgetown University Press.

# The Role of Relexification and Syntactic Reanalysis in Haitian Creole: Methodological Aspects of a Research Program

*Claire Lefebvre*

This paper reports on methodological aspects of a large, ongoing research program concerned with the genesis of Haitian Creole (HC). The goal of the project is to construct a theory of the genesis of HC that both explains the linguistic data and is compatible with our knowledge of the external factors that prevailed during the formation period. Although this research program is multidisciplinary, because it also involves history, it is primarily linguistic.

My working hypothesis is that relexification has played a prominent role in the genesis of HC. Accordingly, HC may ideally be defined as the result of the mapping of French phonetic strings onto West African (hereafter WA) grammatical structures. "Grammar" as used throughout this paper is defined in terms of the projections of the grammatical properties of the lexical entries. This hypothesis is akin to Sylvain's (1936) claim that HC is Ewe with French vocabulary. As a consequence of relexification, reanalysis may have taken place at all levels of the grammar within the limits imposed by the theory of parametric variation.

The hypothesis presented above is strong in comparison with more moderate positions held by, for example, Thomason (1983), Baker and Corne (1986), and Mufwene (1986), who seek to untangle the respective contributions to creole formation of substrate and superstrate languages, language universals, and several processes involved in language mixing. I believe, however, that my strong hypothesis can make a contribution to research on creole genesis. First, it logically calls for a detailed comparison of the grammar of HC both with those of the WA contributing language(s) and with French, the lexifier language; this position dictates the general methodology of the project, embedded within that of comparative linguistics in general. Second, in light of a good comparative analysis of the languages involved, the hypothesis presented here is falsifiable. Either the lexical grammatical properties of HC largely parallel those of WA contributing languages or they do not.

According to the relexification hypothesis presented above, the notion of "Africanism" in HC denotes the grammatical features of WA languages rather than lexical items retained or borrowed from these languages. It is assumed that continuity between contributing WA languages and HC lies in the grammar of these languages while discontinuity is to be found in the phonetic representation of their respective lexicons. The relexification hypothesis thus departs from several other current theories of creole genesis discussed below.

## The Hypothesized Scenario of the Genesis of Haitian Creole

An adequate scenario of the genesis of HC must answer the following questions. Which linguistic processes contributed to the formation of HC? Which languages contributed to its formation, and what were their respective contributions? When was it formed? By what age and social group and in which social context was it created? Several hypotheses, based on fragmentary data, are outlined below; they serve as guidelines for research on each of these questions.

### *What Linguistic Processes Are Involved in the Formation of Haitian Creole?*

Given our conception of relexification, we can assume that the creators of HC were presented with French phonetic strings which did not necessarily correspond to French lexical entries. Rather, a phonetic sequence was interpreted as an entity on a semantic basis and entered into the HC lexicon as a word. Examples in point are *dlo* 'water' (corresponding to the French preposition + article + noun sequence *de l'eau*) and *lari* 'street' (corresponding to article + noun sequence *la rue*). According to my hypothesis, these French phonetic matrices were mapped onto semantic units of WA languages. How this mapping was achieved and how much change took place through this process are the major questions addressed in this project.

This approach raises some questions, such as: What is the likelihood that this theory is correct? How does it differ from other approaches to creoles genesis?

The first question is related to the question of whether relexification is a process known to have played a role in language genesis. Muysken (1981) convincingly documents the emergence of Media Lengua through relexification. Media Lengua, spoken in the highlands of Ecuador, is characterized by an almost entirely Spanish lexicon and a Quechua syntax. Since it was created only sixty years ago, it is possible to reconstruct its history from readily accessible data. Media Lengua thus sets a precedent for a relexification account of the genesis of a new language, suggesting that, in principle, relexification could have played a major role in the formation of creoles. Muysken (1981:77) writes: "If it is the case that the Caribbean Creoles show numerous African survivals in their syntax and semantics, then I think we can argue that it is not interference which led to these survivals but relexification." [1] Whether relexification is the process that played a major role in the formation of HC is an empirical question that the research reported in this paper intends to address.

The thesis presented here takes issue with theories of the genesis of HC which claim, in one way or another, that HC is a variety of French. Some of these include, for instance, Faine (1937), who invokes Norman French as "the true ancestor of creole"; Hall (1950), who considers HC to be a "Romance language"; and Hyppolyte (1949), Pompilus (1955), Valdman (1978a), Wittman and Fournier (1983), and Fournier (1987), all of whom search for dialectal survivals of Middle and Classic French in HC.[2] However, the analyses of aspects of HC syntax proposed by, for example, Hilda Koopman, Claire Lefebvre, Hélène Magloire-Holly and Nanie Piou (see Lefebvre et al. 1982)[3] reveal that HC syntax shares many typological features with WA languages; these set it apart from French grammar. Systematic comparative analyses performed within the present research further reinforce this position.

The relexification hypothesis emphasizes the input of the substratum languages to HC. In this respect it accords with Alleyne's (1971, 1981) substratum theory of the genesis of creole languages, which postulates that creole languages (in particular those of the Antilles) have emerged through a gradual process of transformation of the WA languages spoken by slaves under the influence of colonial languages. His theory explains the fact that creole languages have features of both African and European languages. My hypothesis differs from Alleyne's position in two ways: first, I assume that the formation of creole languages is brought about by rather drastic, and not gradual, change; second, I assume that the special context of the emergence of creole languages has imposed constraints on the specific nature of these changes.

My hypothesis on the genesis of HC presupposes that it did not evolve from a pidgin.[4] Indeed, since the phonetic matrices of French are hypothesized to have been borrowed and mapped onto the semantics and grammar of the WA languages in Haiti at the time the creole was formed, I believe that there has never been an independent pidgin grammar distinct from those of the WA substratum languages. Rather, there was one grammar with two types of lexicons: the WA lexicons and the HC lexicon derived from French phonetic matrices. Since there appear to be well-documented cases of creoles that have evolved from a pidgin—for example, Tok Pisin (see, e.g., Sankoff 1971)—I propose that the Haitian situation was distinct from these cases.

I take issue with Bickerton's (1981, 1984) language bioprogram hypothesis, according to which creole languages, like child language, are closer to the pristine form of universal grammar than are other languages. I also dispute Seuren and Wekker's (1986) semantic transparency hypothesis, according to which the structure of creole languages reflects a universal semantic structure. In my view, HC belongs in the same language family as the WA languages which were in Haiti at the time HC was formed. This is not to say, however, that I deny the validity of the concept of universal grammar. On the contrary, I fully endorse the assumption that there exists a universal grammar and assume that the language faculty is innate, following both Chomsky (1981) and Bickerton (1981, 1984). The latter claims that the language faculty (his "bioprogram") is activated by incomplete data (a pidgin) presented to a child, a situation which leads to invention. However, I believe that the innate capacity of the human species for language consists in setting the values of the parameters which define Universal Grammar according to the data to which the language learner is exposed. Moreover, Bickerton's theory is based on the assumption that it is the children who initiate creoles. Below, I present some historical evidence that directly refutes Bickerton's theory. This evidence shows that while HC was being formed, the Haitian child population was practically nonexistent. Hence, the creators of HC had to create a new language from what they already knew, that is, their own WA languages. This point brings us naturally to the discussion of the role of second language learning in the formation of HC.

Several scholars (e.g., Valdman 1978b; Andersen 1983; Thomason 1983) have suggested that processes observed in second language acquisition have played a major role in the formation of creole. According to their approach, creoles are the result of the crystallization of a still-imperfect stage of second language acquisition. The speakers of a presumed protocreole, not having sufficient access to all the input data, create approximations, which results in a simplified system that is inherent in the second language acquisition process. The supporters of this theory have not proved that this mechanism fully explains the process of creolization. Neither have they explained why creole languages have crystallized in the form in which we know them.

On the other hand, Muysken (1981:75) claims that the development of Media Lengua through relexification cannot be associated with a particular stage in learning Spanish as a second language.[5] Measuring the influence of the second language acquisition process in the formation of HC remains an empirical question to be determined in light of comparative study of the three languages involved: HC, French, and a WA language chosen as representative of the WA substratum languages. So far, my research indicates that the speakers who created HC did not have access to the internal structure of French. A major argument in favor of this claim is seen in the fact that while the phonetic matrices of HC words are identifiable as being from French, they do not necessarily correspond to the phonetic matrices of their French etyma, as illustrated at the beginning of this section. (See Brousseau et al. 1989 for a more detailed discussion of this point.)

I bring to light the following evidence in support of the relexification hypothesis. First, I show that where the grammars of French and the WA languages differ, the grammar of HC is more like that of the relevant WA languages than that of French. Second, I suppose a high degree of similarity between the grammars of the substratum languages despite differences in their vocabularies. Third, I assume that other external conditions (e.g., multilingualism) necessary to support such a hypothesis were met at the time HC was formed. I now turn to the discussion of these points, which are embedded within the historical aspects of my scenario of the genesis of HC.

### *When Was Haitian Creole Formed?*

The following historical facts underlie my hypothesis on when HC started to take shape. At the beginning of the sixteenth century, the Spanish started to colonize the eastern section of Hispañola (today, the Dominican Republic). Slaves first arrived on this half of the island in 1503. The western half of the island (today, Haiti) was not colonized until French adventurers and buccaneers began to occupy the territory around 1668. Haitian territory remained almost uncolonized until the end of the seventeenth century, when the Dutch and the English brought in the first groups of slaves. In 1697, Spain's recognition of the western section of the island as French territory marked the beginning of the systematic colonization of Haitian territory by the French. From 1756 to 1763, the Seven Years' War interrupted the slave trade to Haiti, but it resumed in 1763. Based on these facts, drawn particularly from Cabon (192?–1940),[6] Charlevoix (1730), Curtin (1969), Daget (1975), Daget and Renault (1983), Debien (1974), Debien et al. (1961–67), Dutertre (1671), Martin (1931), Villiard d'Auberteuil (1776), Houdaille (1963, 1973), Labat (1724), Massio (1952), Mettas (1978, 1984), Moreau de Saint-Méry (1784, 1797), Nardin (1970), and Pluchon (1980), I hypothesize that HC must have been formed between the end of the seventeenth century and 1756, probably before 1740. This hypothesis is consistent with the conclusions of Singler (1986).

### *What Were the Linguistic Varieties Present at the Time Haitian Creole Was Formed?*

The identification of the period when HC was created allows us to identify the linguistic varieties that were present then. There is ample evidence to back the assumption that seventeenth- and eighteenth-century varieties of French were spoken then. As for the WA languages, the question is more complex.

According to Singler (1986, 1988), between the end of the seventeenth century and 1756, the bulk of the Haitian slaves were speakers of the Kwa languages, such as Fon and Ewe, and of the Mande languages, such as Bambara, Dyula, and Malinke. The Fon group was numerically the most important. Singler's preliminary conclusions are as follows: (1) the first slave group sent to Haiti was of the Ewe-Fon linguistic family; (2) beginning at the end of the seventeenth century and lasting until 1756, slaves out of the Fon-Ewe linguistic group were linguistically important in Haiti; and (3) after 1763, a significant number of this linguistic group continued to be sent regularly to Haiti. Hence, during the time HC is hypothesized to have been created, the Fon linguistic group was numerically important. This fact influenced the choice of Fon as the language representative of the WA languages for detailed comparative study.

My hypothesis presupposes a strong degree of homogeneity for the WA substratum languages. According to Singler (1988:56), "this assumption is certainly not without foundation." In her comparison of the properties of verbs in HC with those of WA languages, Koopman (1986:233) refers to Kru, Kwa, Mande, and Gur languages as a single entity. Her treatment is based on the fact that the languages of these language families share basic lexical properties.

### *Which Age Group Initiated Haitian Creole and in What Social Context?*

As mentioned above, I dispute Bickerton's (1984) attribution of creolization to children (see also Mufwene 1986:149–51). My hypothesis that the adult population initiated HC is based on the fact that the nativization of the Haitian population was a slow process. There was an almost total absence of reproduction among the population during the crucial period, and there was a high rate of infant mortality (see Singler 1988). Finally, I claim that HC was formed in the context of plantation working parties.

## Methodology

### *Theoretical Framework*

Among the theoretical issues raised in creole studies during the last twenty years, the following have retained the attention of most scholars: Are creoles closer to Universal Grammar than other languages? Do creoles represent the unmarked case?[7] Since creole languages are mixed languages, what part of the grammar is involved in this mixing? The first question calls for a theory of parametric variation, which allows us to identify both the points of similarity and differences within languages and the historical differences within the same language. The second question calls for a theory of markedness which provides a means of evaluating the degree of markedness of a given form or feature. Finally, the last question calls for a theory of modularity allowing for the identification of the module(s) of the grammar where massive "borrowing" can take place.

The theoretical framework developed during the last decades of linguistic research by generative grammarians offers valuable tools for studying the nature and origin of creole languages, making available a theory of Universal Grammar which allows parametric variation, a theory of markedness, and a theory of modularity. The remainder of this section explains how, in my view, the framework of generative grammar can help creolists address the above questions and how the study of creole languages offers a unique opportunity to explore and test the nature of these theoretical tools.

The genesis of HC addresses the more general questions at the heart of linguistic theory, concerned with the knowledge of language and how this knowledge develops. For generativists, the general response to these questions is based on the hypothesis that the language faculty is innate. This hypothesis has two direct consequences: first, part of language knowledge is determined by the genetic code; second, the remainder of this knowledge is language specific and must be acquired by the learner. A more specific answer to these questions of language knowledge is found in the theory of principles and parameters developed (primarily) within the framework of government and binding (Chomsky 1981, subsequent work). According to this theory, human languages differ only at the level of lexical entry (i.e., the phonological, syntactic, and semantic properties of morphemes) and along a limited number of variable parameters (e.g., the direction of theta-role and case assignment and the precise definition of grammatical principles). The test of this theory must be found in comparative studies.

Creoles are unique in many respects, and their special nature adds extra facets to a comparative study. For example, because these languages are found in multilingual contexts (substratum and superstratum languages), the study of the origins of creoles necessitates the comparison of at least three languages (or language families) that have been in close contact: the creole itself, the substratum language(s), and the superstratum language. The strict nature of the ties among these languages adds a supplementary constraint to the theory of parametric variation. Since the differences among these languages must be explained by parametric variation, the comparison should allow the determination of which phenomena are linked in a single parameter and which parameters in turn must be linked to other higher-order parameters. Consequently, the questions addressed in this project should shed new light on the format of Universal Grammar and the possibilities of variation between languages.

The relatively rapid emergence of creoles offers advantages to this framework of study. Normally, historical changes are stretched out over a much longer period, and a particular change may be hidden by other changes. In the case of creoles, however, these phenomena are presented in a concentrated form.

The relexification hypothesis is supported by recent independent studies which suggest that syntactic and semantic data are inserted into linguistic representation independent of phonological data (e.g., Jackendoff 1983; Pranka 1983; Sproat 1985). Since this separation is very marked in the formation of creoles (i.e., the phonetic matrices of HC are hypothesized to have been reinterpreted with the semantic and grammatical features of WA languages), the study of HC gives a further opportunity to explore the grammatical organization of natural languages in light of recent theoretical developments. These new theoretical developments will enable us to construct a theory of how the phonetic sequences of French were reinterpreted by the first Haitians, according to the structure of their native grammar at the levels of semantics, syntax, morphology, phonology, etc. They will also make it possible to determine what modifications in parameters had to be made to accommodate the phonetic sequences that were incompatible with the base structures of their WA languages. The documentation of these facts within this framework will result in a theory motivated by linguistic change and will permit the completion of the theory of HC genesis.

The relationship between creole languages and their source languages provides a wealth of information on the grammatical organization of natural languages. The study of the genesis of HC, and of creole languages in general, is a particular type of comparative linguistics research. I propose establishing a detailed comparison of the grammars and lexicons of HC and the languages that contributed to its formation. Comparative linguistics produced a marked turning point in the science of linguistics by allowing us to begin to identify universals of the human mind. The characteristics of creoles (their recent origins and their close association with at least two other grammars) provide linguistic theory with a unique opportunity for a very constrained comparative study.

The goals of this project, therefore, place the issues of the genesis of creole languages within the context of the larger issues that define the aims of linguistic theory, namely, knowledge of language and how this knowledge develops.

### *Language Varieties to Be Compared*

The identification of the period when HC was formed and of the language groups present during that period enables the selection of the language varieties to be compared. I consider it unnecessary to account for all the substratum languages in order to develop the theory. The systematic comparison of the grammars of HC and one substratum language is enough to demonstrate the important role of relexification and linguistic reanalysis in the genesis of the HC, particularly since the structures of the substratum languages are typologically related and there are external, historical factors which justify the particular language considered in this project.

My choice is Fon. Fon speakers were the majority during the formative period of HC, and today, influence of the Fon culture on Haitian culture (e.g., the voodoo culture) seems to be predominant (see Bastide 1967). In addition, there is a relatively high number of Fon lexical items in modern HC (Lefebvre 1986).

I should perhaps make clear that I am not attempting to trace features of HC to a specific language. Such a methodology leads to a dead end (see, e.g., the discussions in Southworth 1971:255; Goodman 1971:251). Under the assumption that the grammars of WA contributing languages are similar, I have selected one language as representative of these groups of languages and compare its grammar with that of HC within the framework of parametric variation. Since the Fon group was numerically and culturally important, it is likely that it had an important input into the grammar of HC. Hence, this choice should not be challenged because of differences observed between Fon and HC, no more than should the selection of French as the lexifier language of HC be challenged because of the differences observed between French and HC.

There is, however, a heuristic problem. Although data are available on the variety of French to which the Haitian population was exposed during the formation of HC (or at least an approximation of that variety), there is no information on the variety of Fon or the variety of HC spoken in the eighteenth century.[8] The data are just not available in the literature. Therefore, the comparison begins with twentieth-century varieties of Fon and HC, varieties potentially different from the varieties spoken in the eighteenth century. I take this fact into account in my comparative analysis and hope to lessen this problem somewhat by studying the most conservative variety of the creole, that spoken in the region of Mont-Organisé in l'Artibonite,[9] and by looking for old documents which may provide data on earlier varieties of both Fon and HC. Note that it would hardly be coincidence if the grammars of present-day HC and Fon are remarkably similar. It is very unlikely that eighteenth-century HC and Fon were completely different and just happened to drift together. Hence, I think that my thesis can be convincingly defended using only present-day varieties of Fon and HC.

### *Complete Analysis of Each of the Principal Languages*

The comparative analysis of three languages requires a preliminary analysis of each of the languages on an individual basis. It is crucial that the languages to be compared are analyzed within the same theoretical framework. The analysis of each language must cover the following areas:

Phonology
- consonantal and vocalic system
- syllabic structure
- stress patterns and tonal systems
- phonological processes at work in the language
- marked and unmarked features of each of these systems

Lexicon
- major lexical categories and the syntactic features associated with them (Are nouns, verbs, prepositions and adjectives clearly distinct?)
- minor lexical categories and the features associated with them
- categorial status of pronouns, Wh-words, etc.
- properties represented by minor categories
- referentially dependent categories; pronouns, anaphors, and reciprocals
- subcategorization properties of lexical items and the assigned thematic roles
- selectional restrictions on lexical items
- internal structure of finite semantic fields such as the pronominal system (personal, demonstrative), body parts, kinship terms, etc.
- the semantics of each lexical entry

Morphology

word-formation processes operating in the language: affixation, composition, reduplication (How are they signaled?)

position of the morphological head

elements marked by morphological features

Syntax

requirements of government and binding (categories, domains, governors/binders, etc.)

directionality of thematic role assignment

directionality of case assignment

elements that can assign case

cases assigned

interpretation of cases

syntactic properties of INFL, COMP, and DET

alpha values for movement rules (Wh-movement, NP-movement, V-movement, etc.)

types of phrasal complements and their internal structure and position in the phrase

syntactic properties of serial verbs

Analyzing each of these areas for each of the languages to be compared will allow characterization of their grammars and will provide the necessary data to undertake a comparison of various aspects of HC and of the substratum and superstratum languages.

### *Comparison of the Three Grammars*

The linguistic aspects in HC, Fon, and French to be compared are identified above. The task of comparing the three languages goes well beyond analyzing them individually and contrasting them. The data from one language must often be completed in light of those from others. A comparative analysis of the type proposed here must put forward a single analysis which will account for similar constructions in the languages studied. It must also account for differences between them, highlighting the elements that are absent in one language but present in the other.

I will illustrate this point using predicate cleft phenomena found in both HC and Fon but not in French:

1. *se* *mãže*, *žã* *ap* *mãže pẽ* (HC)
   That-is eating, John DURATIVE eat bread
   'It is EATING bread that John is doing.'

2. *nǔ* *DúDú wɛ̂,* *kɔ̀kú Dò* *è* (Fon)
something eating that-is, Koku DUR it
'It is EATING something that Koku is doing.'

The most obvious similarities between predicate cleft phenomena in both languages are the following: (a) predicate clefting involves two clauses (see Lumsden and Lefebvre 1990); (b) interpretation is on the event (not only on the verb, even if in HC the cleft position contains only the verb (Lefebvre 1989); (c) aspect is involved.

The following striking differences can, however, be observed in examples 1 and 2: (a) the cleft position contains a bare verb in HC and a full verb phrase (VP) in Fon; (b) in HC, there is a full VP in the downstairs clause, while in Fon there is a lexical trace, realized as a third-person pronoun; (c) in HC, there is no nominal morphology on the clefted predicate, while in Fon the clefted predicate bears nominal morphology (reduplication of the verb stem).

Given their striking similarities, we can hypothesize that both 1 and 2 are instantiations of predicate clefting. Hence, the analysis will have to account in a unified way for predicate cleft constructions in both languages. However, given their differences, the analysis should also account in a principled way for the particularities observed in each language. Additionally, the analysis should account for the common properties of the grammars of HC and Fon which allow predicate cleft and set them apart from French, in which there is no evidence of this syntactic strategy.[10]

The type of analysis proposed above will permit the evaluation of the degree of similarity between the grammars of HC, Fon, and French for each of the parameters of the lexicon and the grammar. It will also supply the data necessary to discuss the degree of markedness in HC (cf. n. 6).

### *Analysis of the Degree of Homogeneity in the Substratum*

The relexification hypothesis presupposes similarities between the grammars of the substratum languages despite lexical differences in their vocabularies. Therefore, a comparison of the grammars of the substratum languages is required to determine their degree of homogeneity. I plan on doing a comparison of languages from the Kwa language family and of the Mande family on phonological, morphological, lexical, and syntactic levels. The comparison of languages in these two families need not be as detailed as the comparative analysis of the three main languages. It will, however, be sufficiently documented to allow an evaluation of the degree of similarity in the grammars of the two language families pertinent to this project.

### *The Lexicons*

Since the properties of lexical entries are of primary significance for the relexification hypothesis, I will collect detailed data on the properties of the core lexicon of each of the three languages. In order to permit the manipulation and comparison of a collection of data from all three languages, I register the data in a computerized lexicon. The lexicons contain information on the internal composition of lexical items, their syntactic and semantic features, their subcategorization features, and so on. The lexicon provides not only an accessible data bank but also an important analytical tool.

### *Analysis of the Historical Data*

"A limitation on a proper understanding of the role of the substrate in creole genesis has been the lack of specific demographic and historical data about the first Africans in particular Caribbean colonies" (Singler 1988:7). The historical aspect of this project consists in the documentation of a detailed history of the Haitian people and of the external conditions that existed during the formative period of HC. This aspect requires historical research which will help determine the validity of my theory of the genesis of HC. Detailed historical information about the linguistic groups involved and the prevailing social conditions of the period are necessary.

There are two major gaps in the available data on the settlement of Haiti: (1) there is almost no information either on the period crucial to my case or on the period preceding 1756; only very incomplete information can be found in Dutertre (1671), Moreau-de-Saint-Mery (1797), Labat (1724), Charlevoix (1730–31), and Villiard d'Auberteuil (1776); (2) for some periods, the available data are often erroneous because the authors attribute ethnic and linguistic origins on the basis of the African port from which the slaves were sent to Haiti, not on the basis of their true origin (Singler 1986). In order to show to which linguistic groups the Africans who significantly contributed to the formation of HC belonged, we must look at the history of the period from the end of the seventeenth century until 1756 and reinterpret the data available in the literature, in order that each slave group can be associated with the correct language. This research program, tied as it is to the question of the settlement of Haiti, requires a careful analysis of the colonial records found in the Archives Nationales in Aix-en-Provence for the period from the end of the seventeenth century until 1756,[11] as well as the reinterpretation of the demographic data already available in the literature. The data demonstrating the low infant population at the time HC was being formed are also important for the verification of the hypothesis. Therefore, we must also examine carefully the natural rate of population growth (birth and death rates) to account for the contribution of the newly arrived slaves in the total growth of the population and the condition of the family in the slave populations.

The hypothesis that HC was formed in the context of plantation working parties requires a detailed study of the social organization of the labor on various types of plantations (e.g., sugar, coffee, and indigo) during the period before 1756. I propose to study this by compiling the archival data that will allow me to establish the following facts: (1) the distribution of the slaves according to ethnic and linguistic origins throughout the various plantations; (2) the roles and status of individuals within a plantation, and how these varied in the different types of plantation; and (3) the contribution of new arrivals in the overall growth of the population and the way the new arrivals were incorporated into plantations.

## Preliminary Findings

It is clear that the phonological shape of many HC words derives from French, not from WA languages. What must be demonstrated is that the semantic and grammatical properties of HC are not like those of French. Rather, they are similar to those of WA languages.

Preliminary findings support the general hypothesis that relexification has played an important role in the genesis of Haitian. I will discuss these in light of the constraints on relexification that have been proposed in the literature.[12]

### *Lexicon*

In both HC and Fon, the Wh-phrase contains a quantifier (*tɛ* in Fon and *ki* in HC) and a noun/pronoun, as is illustrated in table 1. Note that in some cases the Wh-particle is optional. In both languages, some Wh-phrases such as 'how many' depart from the general pattern of Wh-phrases: they are quantifiers. In HC but not in Fon, the quantifier *kumã* alternates with the Wh-phrase *ki-žã*. The difference observed between HC and Fon in the order of constituents in Wh-phrases is due to differences in the directionality parameter in the two languages. In French, Wh-phrases may take the form *Quel* + Noun, which is structurally similar to the Fon and HC data in table 1. However, French also has a full paradigm of simple Wh-words, as in the list below.

*Qui* 'Who'
*Que/Quoi* 'What'

**Table 1. Wh-Phrases in Fon and Haitian**

| *Fon* | | *HC* | | *Meaning* |
|---|---|---|---|---|
| *mɛ̌(tɛ́)* | person Wh | *ki mũn* | Wh person | 'who' |
| *é tɛ́* | that Wh | *(ki) sa* | Wh that | 'what' |
| *fí(tɛ́)* | place Wh | *(ki) kote* | Wh place | 'where' |
| | | *ki bɔ* | Wh place | 'where' |
| *kwé nũ tɛ́* | moment at Wh | *ki lɛ* | Wh hour | 'when' |
| *nɛ̀ɛ́ gbɔ̃̀* | what by | *ki žã* | Wh manner | 'how'/ |
| | | *kumã* | | 'how' |
| *nàbí* | | *kɔ̃byɛ̃* | | 'how many' |
| *àlɔ́kpà tɛ́* | kind Wh | *ki kalite* | Wh kind | 'what kind' |
| *é tɛ́ ù* | that Wh Cause | *pu ki(sa)* | for Wh that | 'why' |

| | |
|---|---|
| *Qu* | 'Where' |
| *Quand* | 'When' |
| *Comment* | 'How' |
| *Combien* | 'How much' |
| *Porquoi* | 'Why' |

Both HC and Fon are distinct from French in that they lack a paradigm of simple Wh-words. This fact is expected if relexification is a constrained phenomenon not allowing for the creation of syntactic categories that do not already exist in the language being relexified. Indeed, it has been suggested that relexification (Muysken 1981), no more than borrowing (Lefebvre 1984), does not introduce syntactic categories which do not exist in the relexifying or borrowing language. The data on Wh-phrases discussed above are in line with this constraint.[13]

From her comparison of the selectional properties of verbs in HC, French, and WA languages, Koopman (1986:242) concludes that "the picture that emerges is clear: although the phonetic shape of the HC verbs clearly comes from French, their selectional properties are rather different from those of French and strikingly similar to those observed in West African languages."

From this statement we can deduce that the phonetic matrices of the substratum WA languages were relexified by corresponding French verbs without this affecting their basic selectional properties. While in both Fon and HC we find double object constructions, as exemplified in 3, in French this construction has never been attested.

3. a. *žã ba mari yũ kado* (HC)

b. *kɔkú nɑ̃́ asíbá àkbákɑ̃́* (Fon)
X give Y (a) gift
'John/Koku gives Mary/Asiba a gift.'

Another lexical characteristic shared by both HC and Fon which sets them apart from French is serial verb constructions.

4. *žɑ̃ pɔte pul ale nɑ̃ maše* (HC)
*kɔ̀kú sɔ́ kòkló yì ∅ àxì mɛ̀* (Fon)
X take chicken go in market in
'John/Koku brings a chicken to the market.'

Although the list of serial verbs is not entirely parallel in both languages (Déchaine and Lefebvre 1986; Lefebvre 1989), this construction distinguishes them from French, which has no serial verbs. Moreover, while both HC and Fon use independent syntactic heads to encode tense, mode, and aspect, French uses a system of auxiliaries paired with verbal morphology.

Finally, French has a primitive lexical category of adjectives defined by the feature [+N +V]. In Fon and HC, adjectives share the syntactic properties of stative verbs and are thus defined by the feature complex [−N +V]. Filipovich (1987) presents a series of arguments showing that words identified as adjectives at first sight (e.g., *bèl* 'beautiful') are in fact verbs because, like verbs, they can undergo predicate cleft, they can be marked for tense, etc. These properties are exactly those of adjectives, which are also stative verbs in Fon, hence defined by the categorial features [−N +V] (Brousseau 1986). The examples below contain parallel examples for HC and Fon:

5. *li ap drol* (HC)
*é né hwé* (Fon)
he FUTURE funny
'He will be funny.'

6. *se drol, li drol* (HC)
*hwé wé, é bló* (Fon)
it-is funny he funny/does
'He is being funny.'

*Morphology*

The comparison of HC, Fon, and French morphology in Brousseau et al. (1989) supports the hypothesis that African substrate languages contributed to the HC word structure rules signaled by affixation. The fact that affixes of HC semantically parallel the Fon affixes in a systematic way, but not the French affixes—as can be seen in tables 2 and 3—also supports this view.

**Table 2. Affixes of Haitian with Respect to Affixes of French**

| | *Haitian* | *French* |
|---|---|---|
| Inversive affix | *de-* | *de-, in-, ir-* |
| base | verb | verb/adjective |
| output | verb | verb/adjective |
| Agentive affix | *-è* | *-eur* |
| base | verb | verb |
| output | noun | noun |
| Attributive affix | *-è* | *-eur, -ard, -ier, -ien* |
| base | noun | noun |
| output | noun | noun |
| Diminutive affix | *ti-* | *-et, -eau, -on* |
| base | noun | noun/adjective |
| output | noun | noun/adjective |
| Verbalizing affix | *-e* | *-e* |
| base | noun | noun |
| output | verb | verb |
| Nominalizing affix | *-ay* | *-age, -ion, -ment, -ance, -ure* |
| base | $\text{verb}_{[+\text{case}]}$ | verb |
| output | noun | noun |
| Morphological conversion | | |
| base | $\text{verb}_{[-\text{case}]}$ | |
| output | noun | |

*Source:* Brousseau et al. (1989).

The relexification hypothesis gives us a direct explanation for why there are no inflectional affixes in HC. Indeed, in Fon as in other WA languages of the Kwa and Mande families, there is no inflectional morphology. Brousseau et al. (1989) show that cases of morphological conversion in HC are adequately explained when compared with WA languages but remain unexplained when we look only at French morphology. They propose that massive incorporation of French words into Fon (and presumably other related languages) was achieved in the following way: Fon (or other WA words) would have been relexified by semantically equivalent French phonetic matrices (which did not necessarily correspond to French words, as I mentioned earlier). These phonological matrices were mapped onto (or reinterpreted according to) word structures corresponding to those familiar to the creators of HC in such a way that the

**Table 3. Affixes of Haitian with Respect to Affixes of Fon**

| | *Haitian* | *Fon* |
|---|---|---|
| Inversive affix | *de-* | *mà-* |
| base | verb | verb/adjective |
| output | verb | verb/adjective |
| Agentive affix | *-è* | *-tɔ́* |
| base | verb | verb/adjective |
| output | noun | noun |
| Attributive affix | *-è* | *-nɔ́* |
| base | noun | noun |
| output | noun | noun/adjective |
| Diminutive affix | *ti-* | *-ví* |
| base | noun | noun |
| output | noun | noun |
| Verbalizing affix | *-e* | |
| base | noun | — |
| output | verb | |
| "Action/result of" | *-ay* | copy prefixation |
| base | $\text{verb}_{[+\text{case}]}$ | verb |
| output | noun | noun (nominalization) |
| "Action/result of" | conversion | copy prefixation |
| base | $\text{verb}_{[-\text{case}]}$ | verb |
| output | noun | noun (nominalization) |
| Source/origin affixes | | *-tɔ́/-nù* |
| base | — | noun |
| output | | |

*Source:* Brousseau et al. (1989).

morphology of the lexical items contained in the HC lexicon remarkably parallels that of Fon. My analysis as reported above holds that Fon affixes have not been relexified as such, but that part of the phonetic matrices of French were reanalyzed as affixes. This proposal is in line with Muysken's (1981) claim that affixes do not relexify.

## *Syntax and Semantics*

Several aspects of the syntax of HC and Fon contrast with that of French as a result of differences in the properties of lexical entries. In this section I will concentrate on the properties of determiners in the three languages, illustrating a striking parallel between HC and Fon. (The data and analysis are basically taken from Lefebvre 1986.)

Both HC and Fon have a phrase-final determiner, as in example 7:

7. DET Pl
   *(lɔ́)* *lɛ́ɛ́* (Fon)
   *(la)* *yo* (HC)

In both languages the determiner is [+definite], as shown in examples 8 and 9:

8. *dà̃* *ɔ̃́* (Fon)
   *sɛpã* *ã* (HC)
   snake DET
   the snake [+definite]
9. *dà̃* (Fon)
   *sɛpã* (HC)
   snake (generic or [−definite])

In both languages the definite determiner shares the same semantics. It appears only in contexts in which the reference has already been mentioned in discourse, is made explicit by the situational context, or is part of the shared knowledge of the speakers.[14] Moreover, as shown in 7 above, in both languages the determiner is optional if there is a plural marker. These semantic and syntactic properties of the definite determiners in both languages set the category DET apart from that of the French determiner, which obligatorily appears prenominally (instead of postnominally) in either a definite or an indefinite form and which bears gender and number features.

Assuming that DET is a syntactic head (Lefebvre and Massam 1988), the phrase with which it occurs is its complement. It is noteworthy that in both HC and Fon, DET can take noun phrase (NP) complements, as in 8 above, and sentential complements, as in 10 and 11. In French, DET never takes a clause as its complement.

10. *súnù ɔ̃̀* *[(ḍèé)* [e] *ḍú* *dà̃* *ɔ̃́]* (Fon)
    *mun nã* *[ki* [e] *mãže sɛpã* *ã]* (HC)
    man DET COMP ate snake DET
    'The man who ate the snake.'
11. *dà̃* *ɔ̃́* *[(ḍéẽ)* *súnù ɔ́* *ḍú* [e] *ɔ́ ]* (Fon)
    *sɛpã* *ã* *[∅* *mun nã* *mãže* [e] *a]* (HC)
    snake DET COMP man DET ate DET
    'The snake that the man ate.'

Moreover, in both languages, the co-occurrence of two adjacent determiners is prohibited. In contexts in which this situation arises, one of the two determiners is not realized. (For detailed discussions of these facts, see Lefebvre 1982, 1986; Lefebvre and Massam 1988; Lumsden 1989.)

The properties of HC and Fon DET are quite distinct from those of DET in French. In the latter, DET precedes its complement, it selects only nominal phrases, and its semantic properties are different.

The similarities between the syntactic and semantic properties of DET in both HC and Fon make a strong case in favor of the relexification hypothesis in light of the following comments of Muysken on the status of function words during relexification:

> These do not *have* a meaning outside the linguistic system that they are part of, since their meanings are paradigmatically defined within that linguistic system. So when you relexify a system of function words, automatically the semantic organization of the target language comes in, and the result is at best a compromise between source and target language systems. This conclusion is relevant to the substrate debate in creole studies as a whole. If the argument is correct, we must conclude that the only African features that could have been transmitted more or less intact through relexification are those dependent on properties of content words. This means: lexically determined semantic distinctions and subcategorization features, but not syntactic properties related to function words. This consequence seems to me more or less on the right track, given the conflicting evidence for substratum so far. The strongest cases involve lexical properties of function words. (1988:15)

Assuming that Muysken is right, the syntax and semantics of DET in both HC and Fon argue strongly for relexification. Preliminary findings of the type described above support the initial hypothesis. There appears to be a systematic split in the source of information in HC lexical entries. The phonetic strings are from French, and the semantics are from Fon. These preliminary results dismiss the possibility that HC grammar is basically French. They defy the universalist hypothesis of the genesis of creoles. Finally, the relexification hypothesis and the preliminary findings that support it predict in a specific and constrained way the nature of the intersection between HC, the lexifier languages, and the substratum languages. The prediction is that the diachronic source of HC lexical entries will be systematically rather than randomly divided between the substratum and the superstratum.

## Notes

I thank John Singler and Caroline Fick for their very helpful contribution to the discussion of the historical aspects of this research program, John Lumsden for his discussion of the linguistic aspect of the project, and Salikoko Mufwene for his useful comments on an earlier version of the paper. I am also grateful to Sally Thomason and the other participants in the Round Table; their comments helped me to be more specific about some of the issues raised here. I am indebted to my students for their contribution through fruitful discussions in the course of graduate seminars related to the research reported in this paper. Finally, the scenario on the genesis of HC, which constitutes the first section of this paper, benefited from comments from the participants in the Creole Workshop organized by Gillian Sankoff as part of the LSA Summer Institute held in New York in July 1986. This research is supported by the Conseil de Recherche en Sciences Humaines du Canada, Fonds d'Aide aux Chercheurs et à la Recherche, and Fonds Institutionnel de Recherche.

1. In a more recent paper written in collaboration with Norval Smith, Muysken amends his earlier statement in allowing for relexification in language genesis only in bilingual situations: "We reject the gradual 'relexification' of believers in monogenesis (from a West African Portuguese Pidgin) or Afrogenesis, in situations of communal linguistic confrontation between, e.g. a European planter class and an African slave class. We do accept the possibility of relexification as a mechanism in forming a new language in a bilingual situation" (Muysken and Smith 1988:1).

2. See Chaudenson 1983; Valdman 1978b; and Hazaël-Massieux, this volume, among others, for a similar approach to other French-based creoles.

3. The analyses in Lefebvre et al. 1982 include base rules, determination and complementation, modal verbs, predicate clefting and verb reduplication, and relative clauses and questions.

4. The assumption that creoles have evolved from pidgins can be traced back to the 1960s. In linguistic terms, the process of creolization was characterized as the expansion or complexification of a pidgin language source, to which it added all the characteristics of natural languages (see Hymes 1971; Labov 1990; Sankoff 1971; Sankoff and Laberge 1971).

5. His claim is based on the fact that Media Lengua is very different from Quechua-Spanish interlanguage varieties (documented independently in Muysken 1979) and on the fact that it does not present the amount of variation observed in second-language learning situations.

6. The last digit of the date does not show on the manuscript.

7. Bickerton (1984) and Seuren (1983) particularly assume creole languages to represent the unmarked case. Their claim is not embedded within an explicit theory of markedness.

8. Note, however, that three hundred years in language history is a very short

time span. Moreover, as Sankoff (1980) demonstrates through her analysis of Tok Pisin, even in a situation of creole genesis, the changes observed in the language do not seem to be qualitatively more rapid than in more common situations of linguistic change.

9. Nathan Ménard of the University of Montreal, a specialist in HC dialects, has identified the region of Mont-Organisé in l'Artibonite as being both very isolated and more creole speaking. I plan to do fieldwork in this area because that is where I expect to find the most conservative creole, and therefore the variety closest to the initial phase in the formation of HC.

10. For a detailed analysis of predicate cleft phenomena along these lines, see Lumsden and Lefebvre 1990.

11. These archives contain the following pertinent documents: general correspondence between France and its colonies; the Fonds DPPC, public depository of colonial papers, in which are found the notarial minutes containing lists of goods and slaves for any property for which there had been a legal transaction; and microfilmed and nonmicrofilmed family and personal papers.

12. The Fon data reported in this section were provided by Sedjolo Agoli-Agbo from Benin. This speaker is from a rural area and is thus considered to have a more conservative dialect than the Fon speakers of the city of Kotonou. Dialectal variations within the Fon language are not taken into account here. The HC data base comes from several sources, in particular from the Haitian students who are participating in the present project: Jean-Robert Cadely, Rollande Gilles, Marie-Denyse Sterlin, and Jean-Robert Placide.

13. A theoretically plausible counterexample to this constraint is the well-known fact that HC is prepositional while Fon is postpositional. A closer look at the Fon data, however, reveals that postpositional phrases are selected by prepositions, which have mistakenly been considered verbs in the literature. These prepositions offer the right syntactic features and the right position for the French prepositions to have relexified them. The details of these facts may be found in Lefebvre 1990, 1991b.

14. See Fournier 1977 and Lefebvre 1982 for a detailed description of these facts.

## References

Alleyne, Mervyn C. 1971. Acculturation and the cultural matrix of creolization. In Hymes, ed., 169–87.

———. 1981. *Comparative Afro-American: An historical-comparative study of English-based Afro-American dialects of the New World.* Ann Arbor: Karoma.

Andersen, Roger W. 1983. *Pidginization and creolization as language acquisition.* Rowley, Mass.: Newbury House.

Baker, Philip, and Chris Corne. 1986. Universals, substrata and the Indian Ocean creoles. In Muysken and Smith, eds., 163–85.

Bastide, R. 1967. *Les Amériques noires*. Paris: Payot.

Bickerton, Derek. 1981. *Roots of language*. Ann Arbor: Karoma.

———. 1984. The language bioprogram hypothesis. *Behavioral and Brain Sciences* 7.173–221.

Brousseau, Anne-Marie. 1986. Les processus morphologiques en Fon. In Lefebvre and Kaye, eds., 281–306.

Brousseau, Anne-Marie, Sandra Filipovich, and Claire Lefebvre. 1989. Morphological processes in Haitian Creole: The question of substratum and simplification. *Journal of Pidgin and Creole Languages* 4.213–43.

Cabon, A. R. P. 192?–1940. *Histoire d'Haïti*. Volume 4. Port-au-Prince: Editions de la Petite Revue.

Charlevoix, P. F. X. 1730–31. *Histoire de l'île espagnole de Saint-Dominique*. Paris.

Chaudenson, Robert. 1983. Ou l'on parle de la genèse et des structures des créoles de l'Océan Indien. *Etudes Créoles* 6.2.157–237.

Chomsky, Noam. 1981. *Lectures on government and binding*. Dordrecht: Foris.

Curtin, Philip D. 1969. *The Atlantic slave trade: A census*. Madison: University of Wisconsin Press.

Daget, S. 1975. La traite des noirs par l'Atlantique: nouvelles approches. *Revue Française d'Histoire d'Outre-Mer* 67.

Daget, S., and F. Renault. 1983. *Les négrières en Afrique*. Paris: Karthala.

Debien, Gabriel. 1974. *Les esclaves aux Antilles françaises (17è–18è siècles)*. Basse-Terre: Société d'Histoire de la Guadeloupe.

Debien, G., et al. 1961–67. *Les origines des esclaves des Antilles*. Dakar: Institut Français d'Afrique Noire.

Déchaine, Rose-Marie, and Claire Lefebvre. 1986. The grammar of serial constructions. In Lefebvre and Kaye, eds., 471–500.

Dutertre, J. B. 1671. *Histoire générale des Antilles habitées par les Français: 1667–1671*. Volume 4. Paris.

Faine, Jules. 1937. *Philologie créole: étude historique et étymologique sur la langue créole d'Haïti*. Port-au-Prince: Imprimerie de l'Etat.

Filipovich, Sandra. 1987. Le statut des adjectifs en haitien. In Lefebvre, ed., 306–23.

Fournier, Robert. 1977. "N ap fe yu ti-koze su la" (la grammaire de la particule *la* en créole haïtien). Mémoire de Maîtrise. Université du Quebec à Montréal.

———. 1987. *Le bioprogramme et les français créoles: vérification d'une hypothèse*. Doctoral thesis, University of Sherbrooke.

Goodman, Morris. 1971. The strange case of Mbugu. In Hymes, ed., 243–55.

Hall, Robert A. 1950. The genetic relationships of Haitian Creole. *Ricerche Linguistique* 1.194–203.

Houdaille, J. 1963. Trois paroisses de Saint-Domingue au 18è siécle: étude démographique. *Population*.

———. 1973. Quelques données sur la population de Saint-Domingue au 18è siècle. *Population*.

Hymes, Dell, ed. 1971. *Pidginization and creolization of languages: Proceedings of a conference held at the University of West Indies at Mona, Jamaica, April 1968*. Cambridge: Cambridge University Press.

Hyppolite, M. P. 1949. *Les origines des variations du créole haïtien*. Port-au-Prince: Collection Haïtiana.

Jackendoff, Ray. 1983. *Semantics and cognition*. Cambridge, Mass.: MIT Press.

Koopman, Hilda. 1986. The genesis of Haitian. In Muysken and Smith, eds., 231–59.

Labat, Père Jean-Baptiste. 1724. *Nouveau voyage aux isles de l'Amérique*. Volume 2. La Haye.

Labov, William. 1990. On the adequacy of natural languages: The development of tense. *Pidgin and creole tense-mood-aspect systems*, ed. by John Victor Singler, 1–58. Amsterdam: John Benjamins.

Lefebvre, Claire. 1982. L'expansion d'une catégorie grammaticale: le déterminant *la*. In Lefebvre et al., eds., 21–64.

———. 1984. Grammaires en contact: définition et perspectives de recherche. *Revue Québécoise de Linguistique* 14.1.11–47.

———. 1986. Relexification in creole genesis revisited: The case of Haitian Creole. In Muysken and Smith, eds., 279–300.

———, ed. 1987. *Rapport de Recherche du Projet Haïti-Fon*. Université du Québec à Montréal, Groupe de Recherche sur le Créole Haïtien.

———. 1990. Establishing a syntactic category P in Fon. *Journal of West African Languages*.

———. 1991. *Take* serial constructions in Fon. *Serial verbs: Grammatical, comparative and cognitive approaches*, ed. by Claire Lefebvre, 37–79. Amsterdam: John Benjamins.

Lefebvre, Claire, and J. Kaye, eds. 1986. *Rapport de recherche du projet haïti-fon*. Université du Québec à Montréal, Groupe de Recherche sur le Créole Haïtien.

Lefebvre, Claire, Hélène Magloire-Holly, and Nanie Piou. 1982. *Syntaxe de l'haïtien*. Ann Arbor: Karoma.

Lefebvre, Claire, and Diane Massam. 1988. Haitian Creole determiner: A case for DET as a head. *Journal of Pidgin and Creole Languages* 3.213–45.

Lumsden, John. 1989. On the distribution of determiners in Haitian Creole. *Revue Québécoise de Linguistique* 18.65–95.

———. 1990. The bi-clausal structure of Haitian clefts. *Linguistics* 28.741–59.

Martin, Gaston. 1931. *Nantes au 18è siècle: l'ère des négriers (1714–1774)*. Paris: Félix Alcan.

Massio, R. 1952. Un dossier de plantation de Saint-Domingue, la caféière Ségineau, 1745–1829. *Revue d'Histoire de l'Amérique Française*.

Mettas, Jean. 1978, 1984. *Répertoire des expéditions négrières françaises au XVIIIè siècle*. Volume 2, ed. by Serge Daget. Paris: Société Française d'Histoire d'Outre-Mer.

Moreau de Saint-Mery. 1784. *Lois et constitutions des colonies françaises de l'Amérique sous le vent*. Volume 6. Paris: Chez l'auteur.

———. 1797. *Description topographique, physique, civile, politique et historique: la partie française de l'isle de Saint-Domingue*. Philadelphia. Reprint. Paris: Société d'Histoire des Colonies Françaises, 1959.

Mufwene, Salikoko. 1986. The universalist and substrate hypotheses complement one another. In Muysken and Smith, eds., 129–63.

Muysken, Pieter. 1981. Half way between Quechua and Spanish: The case for relexification. *Historicity and variation in creole studies*, ed. by A. R. Highfield and A. Valdman, 52–79. Ann Arbor: Karoma.

———. 1988. Lexical restructuring in creole genesis. Unpublished manuscript.

Muysken, Pieter, and Norval Smith, eds. 1986. *Substrata versus universals in creole genesis*. Amsterdam: John Benjamins.

Nardin, J. C. 1970. Encore des chiffres: la traite négrière française pendant la première moitiè du XVIIIè siècle. *Revue Française d'Histoire d'Outre-Mer* 209.

Pluchon, P. 1980. *La route des esclaves: négrièrs et bois d'ébène au XVIIIè siècle*. Paris: Hachette.

Pompilus, Pradel. 1955. Quelques traces du moyen-français et du français classique dans le créole haïtien. *Optique* 16.27–30.

Pranka, Paula. 1983. *Syntax and word formation*. Ph.D. dissertation, Massachusetts Institute of Technology.

Sankoff, Gillian. 1971. *The sociolinguistic situation of Tok Pisin in Papua New Guinea*. P. T. Moresby, New Guinea Research Unit.

———, ed. 1980. *The social life of language*. Philadelphia: University of Pennsylvania Press.

Sankoff, Gillian, and Suzanne Laberge. 1980. On the acquisition of native speakers by a language. In Sankoff, ed., 195–211.

Seuren, Pieter. 1983. The auxiliary system in Sranan. *Linguistic categories: Auxiliaries and related puzzles 2*, ed. by F. Heny and B. Richards, 219–51. Dordrecht: Reidel.

Seuren, Pieter, and Herman Wekker. 1986. Semantic transparency as a factor in creole genesis. In Muysken and Smith, eds., 57–71.

Singler, John. 1986. Creole genesis and historical record: The African antecedents of Haitian Creole. Unpublished manuscript.

———. 1988. The homogeneity of the substrate as a factor in pidgin/creole genesis. *Language* 64.27–51.

Southworth, Franklin C. 1971. Detecting prior creolization: An analysis of the historical origins of Marathi. In Hymes, ed., 255–75.

Sproat, Richard W. 1985. *On deriving the lexicon*. Ph.D. dissertation, Massachusetts Institute of Technology.

Sylvain, Susanne. 1936. *Le créole haïtien, morphologie et syntaxe*. Wetteren, Belgium: Imprimerie De Meester; Port-au-Prince: Chez l'auteur.

Thomason, Sarah. 1983. Chinook Jargon in areal and historical context. *Language* 59.820–70.

Valdman, Albert. 1978a. *Le créole: statut et origine*. Paris: Editions Klincksieck.

———. 1978b. Créolisation sans pidgin: le système des déterminants du nom dans les parlers franco-créoles. *Langues en contact/Languages in contact: Pidgins-creoles*, ed. by J. Meisel, 105–285. Tübingen: TBL Verlag Gunter Narr.

Villiard d'Auberteuil, M. R. 1776. *Considérations sur l'état présent de la colonie française de Saint-Domingue*. Volume 2. Paris: Grangé.

Whinnom, Keith. 1971. Linguistic hybridization and the "special case" of pidgins and creoles. In Hymes, ed., 91–115.

Wittman, Henry, and Robert Fournier. 1983. Le créole c'est du français coudon. *Revue de l'Association Québécoise de Linguistique* 3.187–202.

# On Identifying the Sources of Creole Structures. A Discussion of Singler's and Lefebvre's Papers

*Sarah G. Thomason*

The papers by John Singler and Claire Lefebvre, like most of the papers in this volume, are concerned with the elucidation of the histories of New World creole languages, and in particular with the question of whether, and how, these languages can be shown to have features of African origin. As Lefebvre points out, there is no direct attestation of Haitian Creole (HC) from the earliest period in its history; and the same is true in virtually every other case of pidgin and creole genesis. So the goal, as in any historical linguistic study, is to develop a rigorous methodology for making historical inferences about undocumented linguistic states. This problem is well known, of course. But it is less well known among pidgin and creole (PC) specialists that this very issue has been the focus of a considerable amount of research in historical linguistics over the past hundred years or so, and that, as a result, the basic methodology needed for the task is already in existence.[1]

I will begin my comments by discussing briefly the ways in which Singler and Lefebvre approach the problem of identifying the sources of creole structures. Although both authors concentrate on HC, the fundamental issues they address have general relevance beyond this particular case study. My next step will therefore be to sketch those aspects of historical linguistic methodology that are most crucial for considering the issues raised by these and other authors. Finally, I will show the specific implications of this methodology for proposals about the sources of PC structures.

Singler, like Philip Baker and a few other PC specialists, excels at careful research on the sociohistorical setting of PC genesis—research that establishes the boundaries within which purely linguistic theorizing must operate. In this paper he gives a typically lucid exposition of the factors that must be considered in any case of creole genesis and, for HC specifically, of the relevant dates and sources of slaves. His figures support Lefebvre's claim that Ewe-Fon speakers were predominant during the period when HC presumably emerged as a language (whether pidgin or creole). However, whereas Lefebvre suggests that only Fon and its closest relatives need be considered in a historical scenario for the development of HC, Singler's evidence that Mande speakers were also present in considerable numbers, and that there were smaller numbers of speakers of other languages as well, renders Lefebvre's working hypothesis dubious on demographic grounds. In studying PC genesis in a multilingual contact situation, it is surely necessary to take into account (as Singler urges) not only the lexifier language and the most prominent substrate language (if any) but also other languages whose speakers might have participated in creating the contact language. This is especially important because several independent studies have shown that in a multilingual context, a highly marked feature is likely to appear in a new pidgin or creole only if it is shared by most or all of the grammatical input languages (cf., e.g., Thomason 1983; Singler 1988). In such a case, ascribing the presence of such a feature to just one of the languages would be like ascribing a racing crew's victory to the strongest rower alone.

Singler raises one question that is rarely addressed directly in discussions of PC genesis: how long a period should be considered? He does not answer this question—no one could, given the lack of documentation of any such process—but he does refer to Corne's (1983) example of an Indian substratal feature in Mauritian Creole which must date from a period subsequent to creole genesis. He argues that such examples make it necessary to consider grammatical input even from late arrivals in a creole community and hypothesizes that the influence of late arrivals may be confined to particular grammatical subsystems. These are interesting points, but they seem to involve an implicit belief that the process of PC genesis might somehow extend beyond the emergence of the PC language. No one has presented any evidence that, once it exists as a language with its own lexical and grammatical structures, a PC language will change in a significantly different way from any other language; and there is ample evidence that a group process of language shift can lead, in any target language, to substratum-induced changes in any and all grammatical subsystems (see Thomason and Kaufman 1988, especially chaps. 5 and 9.5, for examples). The factors that determine whether such changes will occur are primarily social, not linguistic. Corne's Mauritian Creole example in fact falls into the ordinary category of shift-induced change in an existing language, so it is irrelevant to the question of how PC languages arise. The moral here is that identifying the sources of initial PC structures should be sharply distinguished, where possible, from the later historical development of a pidgin or creole language.

Since Lefebvre's paper is essentially programmatic, a critical evaluation must focus on premises and methodology rather than on research results. The primary hypothesis is, as Lefebvre emphasizes, a strong one in comparison with rival theories. The particular rival theory that I would argue for, for instance, seeks to explain PC genesis through the complex interplay of a variety of influences whose effects vary under different social conditions—lexifier language(s), other languages in the contact situation, universal structural tendencies, and universal tendencies of second-language acquisition.

I see one serious difficulty with Lefebvre's research plan if, as she indicates, the goal is to discover the sources of Haitian Creole structures. Comparing HC structures with Fon alone will not show if, and where, structural congruence exists between Fon and other relevant languages, or between Fon and structures to be expected from the operation of universal structural tendencies, L2 learning tendencies, or both. Therefore, even if the results of the HC-Fon comparison turn out to be compatible with Lefebvre's hypothesis, she would still have no evidence to support a claim that her hypothesis offers the best historical explanation for the facts. First, her approach cannot provide any systematic evidence to rule *out* other possible influencing factors.[2] Second, if rival theories account for the facts of HC equally well, and if they also account more generally for the facts of other PC languages, then the rival theories are to be preferred over Lefebvre's language-specific theory.

Lefebvre is, of course, aware of the need to motivate her historical approach by reference to wider concerns. She cites two indirect historical arguments to support her hypothesis: the evidence for relexification as the mechanism by which the Media Lengua arose (Muysken 1981) and proposals for rigid constraints on both relexification and borrowing. Neither of these arguments, in my opinion, can survive close scrutiny; the Media Lengua fails as a parallel to PC genesis, and the proposed constraints on borrowing are demonstrably invalid. I will address each of these points in turn.

Although, as Lefebvre notes, Pieter Muysken originally suggested a parallel between the emergence of the Media Lengua and PC genesis, she herself indicates in a footnote that he has changed his mind on this point (Muysken and Smith 1988:1). He is surely right the second time. The Media Lengua could only have arisen in a bilingual context, because only bilingual speakers could have had the knowledge of Spanish needed to implement a complete relexification of their native Quechua; and Muysken (1981) makes it clear that the Quechua speakers who developed the Media Lengua were fairly fluent speakers of Spanish. But no one has suggested that the slaves who developed HC or any other New World creole were at all fluent in the lexifier language.

This means that the two situations are not directly comparable. In fact, the extreme type of language mixing exemplified by the Media Lengua occurs only in situations in which most or all speakers of the borrowing language are bilingual in the source language (see Thomason and Kaufman 1988 for detailed discussion).[3]

Constraints on the transfer of structural features from one language to another have been proposed by many scholars, and Lefebvre's proposals echo some of the ones that have been especially popular. But there are well-documented cases of diffusion of all the features that she and others have cited as unborrowable. Given the right social circumstances, for instance, syntactic categories can be transferred. To give just two examples, the Indic language Shina acquired from Burushaski a peculiar infinitive construction with a discourse function (Lorimer 1937; the morphemes used in the Shina construction are native ones); and Malto, among other Dravidian languages, borrowed an entire system of numeral classifiers from Indic (Emeneau 1980:131; some of the morphemes used in the system are native ones and some are borrowed from Indic). Similarly, the claim that affixes do not relexify is refuted by evidence from a number of cases of substratum interference, for example, the transfer of a partitive case from Uralic to Russian by shifting Uralic speakers, or the transfer of illative, allative, and adessive cases from Uralic to Lithuanian by shifting Uralic speakers (Senn 1966:92). (In both instances, the morphemes used to express the new cases are Balto-Slavic morphemes; only the categories themselves were transferred, not the actual Uralic morphemes.) And finally, the view that the syntax of function words cannot be transferred from one language to another is false. Asia Minor Greek, for instance, borrowed a number of function words from Turkish, along with their syntactic properties (Thomason and Kaufman 1988:217, citing Dawkins 1916); and shifting Dravidian speakers caused the Indic particle *iti* to acquire a typically Dravidian quotative function.

In addition to her historical arguments, Lefebvre offers evidence from synchronic theory to support her hypothesis. In doing so, she implicitly assumes that historical processes of borrowing and PC genesis in bilingual or multilingual contexts will have the same linguistic properties as the abstract organization proposed by theoreticians for a single language's grammar. This unexamined assumption is extremely risky. First, one would surely expect, a priori, that extra complications might arise when elements of two or more linguistic systems are being combined. And second, the available evidence from language contact situations does not support the view that transferred lexical items in cross-language interference are merely phonetic strings that are treated as if they were totally independent of the structures into which they enter. Sometimes, to be sure, a borrowed word simply adopts the syntactic and semantic properties of a word that it replaced; but very often a borrowed word brings along its original syntax, semantics, and perhaps even its morphology—and thus potentially changes the borrowing language's structure.

For all these reasons I do not find Lefebvre's hypothesis promising as an exclusive scenario for the development of HC. Given her premises, I would expect to disagree with the theoretical conclusions she draws from her comparative study; nevertheless, the comparison itself will be valuable. In the hope of providing some guidelines that might help to evaluate the results of such studies, I will turn now to a consideration of aspects of historical linguistic methodology that are relevant for identifying the sources of initial PC structures.

I do not claim that PC genesis is just like language change. In fact, I do not think that the creation of an entirely new contact language is language *change* at all. Still, there is good reason to believe that in many ways PC genesis closely resembles a specific type of change that occurs within a single language—namely, change that results from imperfect group learning of a target language during a process of language shift. (This is what is often, though not always accurately, known as substratum interference; I will use the term "substrate interference" for convenience, but in many pidgin genesis situations, and even some creole genesis situations, its social implications are misleading.)

If I am right about this similarity, then the best theory of *either* PC genesis *or* shift-induced interference—all other things being equal—will be one which accounts for the linguistic outcomes of both processes, because that theory will be more general than a theory which accounts only for one or the other. This means that theories of PC genesis which do not take into account the partly analogous historical developments in non-PC languages start with an initial handicap. (Of course, the converse is also true.)

The first step is to invoke a uniformitarian hypothesis for evaluating historical linguistic proposals. That is, inferences about unattested linguistic states must fit with what we know about comparable situations that are either current or well documented; this is a strategy shared by all the historical sciences. In the case of the New World creoles, the evidence presented by Singler and others over the past few years points unmistakably to a long period of *pidgin* usage in many, most, or possibly all of the places where a New World creole is now spoken. The evidence is indirect but compelling: in Jamaica, Haiti, Guadeloupe, and elsewhere, Africans of the same ethnic origin were present in numbers sufficient for the African languages to be used; and they were used in the communities for some purposes for a long time after plantations were first established. Moreover, most of the language learners on these islands were adolescents or adults, not children, so the pidgin or incipient creole was presumably learned primarily as a second language, not as a first language. This means that the relevant historical situation that should be compared with the early New World PC context is second-language acquisition by groups of people—especially in language shift situations.

I should emphasize that it is important not to downplay the important *differences* between PC genesis and ordinary language shift. Probably the most striking difference between the two is the fact that in language shift a group of people are giving up their native language and adopting a target language to which they have sufficient access that they can learn both vocabulary and grammar. In pidgin genesis, by contrast, people are not giving up their native language, and they are not necessarily trying to learn a target language (TL), either; rather, they are trying to talk to each other for limited purposes, and in doing so they are creating a new contact language. In some cases, including most Atlantic creole contexts, even if there is a TL, most of the learners do not have enough access to it to learn much of its structure as well as its basic vocabulary. (Bajan may be an exception, and Réunionnais in the Indian Ocean seems to be another.) In most (but not all) cases of pidgin genesis, more than two groups of people are involved, so that more than two languages have to be considered as possible historical sources of the pidgin structures. If there are any Atlantic creole contexts in which a creole developed more or less immediately—that is, in which most people could not continue to use their native languages—then language shift is a factor; but it still is not necessarily true that there was a TL in the sense of a language that the shifting speakers were trying to learn as a whole language. I will argue below that these social differences dictate one significant methodological difference between efforts to determine the origins of initial PC structures and efforts to determine the origins of the structures of a shifted-to TL.

But in spite of the differences, I think the same basic methodological principles must govern the identification of historical sources for the linguistic features in a pidgin, or in an abrupt creole, or in a TL after a group has shifted to it. In all these cases, I believe that what is going on is a process of second-language learning: learners are making guesses about the structure of whatever they are learning, and "right" guesses are those that are accepted by the people they are talking to. In ordinary language shift, in the long run, only guesses that approximate TL structures are likely to be accepted, though the shifters' language can influence the TL significantly under certain social conditions. In such cases, most substrate interference will comprise structural features which are easy to learn; that is, they will either be universally unmarked—such as the development of fixed word-initial stress in northern Russian dialects under Uralic influence—or typologically congruent with the TL, such as the development of three new locative cases in Lithuanian under Uralic influence.

In pidgin genesis, all the participants are making guesses, and "right" guesses are those that are understood by everyone. As Le Page (1977:236) and others have observed, the learners will keep what they can of their native languages and learn what they must to communicate; so features shared by all the languages in contact will tend to turn up in the pidgin (though limitations on lexical and morphosyntactic resources will be dictated by the restricted spheres of usage). In particular, as mentioned above, the only marked features that are likely to appear in a new pidgin are those that are shared by most of the languages whose speakers are developing the pidgin. A striking example of shared marked features is the highly marked and highly stable phonemic inventory of Chinook Jargon, which includes full series of glottalized, labialized, and uvular (vs. velar) stops, as well as lateral obstruents and unusual consonant clusters.

I have outlined this scenario for pidgin (and abrupt creole) genesis to set the stage for the rest of my discussion. I do not claim it as original; it has much in common with other theories that emphasize substratum/imperfect L2 acquisition, in particular those which, like Mufwene's (e.g., 1986), combine substratum contribution with universal tendencies. For Afro-American languages, the most thorough and systematic studies of substrate influence are Alleyne (1980) and Boretzky (1983); the latter, probably because it is written in German, is too often ignored by English-speaking PC specialists. Also, in this volume, compare the partly similar views of Lawrence Carrington. I will not review the evidence for the approach here because of space limitations.

I do want to point out, though, that I disagree with many people, among them, apparently, Lefebvre, in that I do not think that *all* cases of contact-induced language change can be usefully compared with PC genesis. Cases in which native speakers of a recipient language borrow structure (as well as lexicon) from another language, unlike PC genesis and language shift, have no direct connection with imperfect language learning; rather, as emphasized above, such interference occurs only in a context of widespread bilingualism among borrowing-language speakers. The most striking effect of this social condition is that markedness considerations do not seem to play any role in the most extreme cases of this type: a glance at categories A and B of table 1, case 3 (below), shows that even highly marked structural features can be borrowed by bilinguals. So on this issue I believe that the evidence clearly refutes the *general* prediction (which has been made by Le Page 1977:232; Givón 1979:26–27; Bickerton 1981:50; and numerous other scholars) that contact-induced change leads inevitably to grammatical (especially inflectional) simplification.

Now, I will first sketch the methodological principles that apply in ordinary cases of language shift and then show how they apply in cases of PC genesis as well. If you want to argue convincingly for a case of shift-induced interference in a TL, you will need to meet four initial conditions: you must be able to identify a source language for the proposed interference feature(s); you must know what its structure was at the time of the shift; you must know what the TL structure was like before the shift as well as afterward; and you must show that the proposed interference feature(s) appeared in the TL during or right after the shift, not hundreds of years later. Although this last prerequisite is not usually a problem in cases of PC genesis, it *is* important, as I observed above, to distinguish between initial PC structures and external influence on the later development of a PC language—both lexifier language interference, especially in decreolization, and interference from new languages that come into the community, such as Indic languages in Mauritius (Corne 1983). (I will comment on some implications of this point below.) Some substratum enthusiasts used to ignore all four of the prerequisites, which explains why many historical linguists still view substratum explanations with deep suspicion.

Identifying a source language for proposed interference features in a TL means establishing that speakers of a particular language were in the right place at the right time, and that they shifted in considerable numbers to the TL. The relevance of this point for the Afro-American languages is obvious: in order to argue for contribution by African languages to the structures of any of the creoles, you first have to find out which African languages were spoken in a given place at the time of PC genesis. (I am begging the question of whether some Atlantic creoles first arose as pidgins in Africa; the same basic methodology applies in either case.) Singler's research—and now, increasingly, other people's as well—fulfills this prerequisite for the Atlantic creoles by identifying the languages spoken on particular plantations in the early years. The more general claims that have been made, for instance those based on shared features present in most or all languages of West Africa, are useful only to the extent that the generally shared features are in fact present in the languages that were spoken in a particular colony. Some of them are. But the more languages you generalize about, the fewer shared features there will be; and most shared features found everywhere in West Africa are likely to be universally unmarked and thus difficult or impossible to establish as Africanisms in Afro-American languages (as I will argue later on).

Establishing that a particular feature was present in a relevant language (group) at the time of PC genesis is not as tricky as one might predict from the fact that none of the relevant African languages is attested from such an early period. The reason is that the modern languages are readily available for study, and three hundred years is not a very long time in language history, so most structures present now were also present then. And any structures that can be reconstructed for the ancestors of some of the languages in question, such as Proto-Kwa, were almost certainly present in those languages when the PC emerged if they are currently present in relevant daughter languages.

As for the third condition, unless you want to argue that Afro-American creoles are simply changed later forms of European languages—and most PC specialists do not believe this nowadays, for good reasons—then the identification of African linguistic features in these languages cannot depend on a comparison of "before" and "after" target language structures. This means that in PC genesis the prerequisite about TL structure cannot be exactly the same as in the typical case of shift-induced interference. But the principle is still the same: in order to prove that a given Atlantic creole has African features, you have to know what the lexifier language's structure was when the language arose (either as a creole or as a pidgin). This is no trivial matter; but in spite of dialect differences and the probability of dialect diversity in most or all cases, we have a reasonably good idea of the general structural features of the relevant European languages, all of which are well attested from the period(s) of PC genesis.

So it is possible now to fulfill at least the first three of the prerequisites for identifying African contributions to initial Afro-American PC grammars, and it will become easier to fulfill all of them as detailed historical research provides more and more information about who was where when. But meeting the prerequisites for establishing African contributions does not mean that they have been established. The next step is to study the structures of all the relevant African languages in each case, and of the relevant European languages, and to identify potential sources for as many creole features as possible. (This procedure is similar to Lefebvre's research program for HC, but it is considerably broader.) This step involves a different methodology, one that is similar to methods for arguing that particular structural features arose in a TL through imperfect group learning during language shift or through borrowing by bilingual speakers into their native language.

If you are interested in finding out where a particular structure in some language came from, you need to consider two possible sources: it might have arisen from some earlier structure within the language (or its parent language) through internally motivated change, or it might have arisen as the result of language contact—that is, through interference from another language. But there is no reason to assume that these two sources are mutually exclusive; there are well-established examples of multiple causation in language change, both for strictly internal developments and for changes with both internal and external sources. In the latter case, a given structure will have arisen under the combined influence of internal drift and foreign interference, as with the phonemicization of the formerly allophonic voiced/voiceless distinction in Middle English fricatives. Multiple causation turns out to be especially important methodologically in the search for the origins of PC structures. (George Huttar, in this volume, makes a similar point.)

Sources of initial PC structures are all external, in a sense, because the linguistic development in question is a new language, not a changed later form of an old language. The possible sources are the lexifier language(s) and the other language(s) in the contact situation that gave rise to the pidgin. If more than two languages were involved, then you need to consider the possibility of a cross-language compromise among several substrate languages, or among substrate *and* lexifier languages. For all these possibilities, it is important to remember that we should not expect any feature to be identical to its source in the language(s) of origin. As Alleyne pointed out years ago (1979:200), features are often reinterpreted in the learning process; in particular, many structural features in an initial PC grammar turn out to be simpler—less marked—than the source-language features from which they arose. An example is the presence in Chinook Jargon of full pleonastic subject and possessive pronouns, a structural feature that can be traced to subject and possessive pronominal agreement affixes in the source languages.

If you believe in the bioprogram hypothesis, that is another possible source for initial PC structures. But, especially since the Afro-American languages I am focusing on apparently arose as pidgins, not abrupt creoles, I think that the role of markedness is one of selecting features from the languages in contact (often with concomitant simplification), not of creating them through innate preprogramming. Certainly markedness plays a selecting role in cases of shift-induced interference; and here again, a general theory that accounts simultaneously for what goes on with respect to universal tendencies both in language change and in PC genesis will be preferred, all other things being equal.

We can now consider a method by which the source(s) of particular features in a language in a contact situation can be established. Lefebvre is quite right when she says that her hypothesis about the sources of HC structures requires her to show that where French and West African grammars differ HC grammar resembles West African linguistic structures rather than French.[4] Of course, it is easy to establish the source of a structural feature whose form and function are traceable to a single language; but in both shift-induced interference and PC genesis, the substrate languages are more likely to contribute structure than actual morphemes. (However, African grammatical morphemes can also be found in Afro-American languages; for instance, in his paper in this volume Ian Robertson identifies several Eastern Ịjọ suffixes in Berbice Dutch.)

Table 1 illustrates three different outcomes of contact situations. In the table, "*X*-like structure" means that a feature is either identical to a structure in language *X* or is derivable from a structure of *X* by generalization and/or simplification. The features listed in the table do not exhaust the "*X*-like" structures in any of the three languages; rather, they merely exemplify the types of features that occur in the three cases. Example 1, Dravidian substrate influence on Indic languages in India, represents the typical pattern for shift-induced interference, and 2, Chinese Pidgin English, represents a pidgin analogue: neither language has substrate grammatical morphemes (category A), though both have definite substrate structural features (category B). In sharp contrast, 3—a case of heavy borrowing by bilinguals, from Turkish into Asia Minor Greek—shows many borrowed structures expressed by borrowed morphemes (category A), as well as borrowed structure alone (category B).

For all three languages, the history of the features in category B is not quite so obvious as with the category A features, since only the structures, not the actual morphemes, match structures in the substrate languages. However, all of the category B entries are features that are (a) present in, or derivable by simplification from, the substrate languages; (b) not present originally in the TL or lexifier language or borrowing language; and (c) unlikely to have arisen through a process of universally determined simplification. By far the most likely historical source, then, is one or more of the substrate languages in each instance. A creole example is the presence in Ndjuka of the double-articulated stops *k͡p* and *g͡b*, alternating—as in some relevant Kwa languages—with *kw* and *gw* (Boretzky 1983:60).

Finally, category C contains structures which match those of the substrate languages but which could also have arisen through a reasonable process of internally motivated change in a TL, or through simplification of lexifier language structures in a PC language. In a case of shift-induced interference, I think that even these features can reasonably be attributed to substrate influence, because substrate interference provides a unified explanation for their appearance in the TL. But in PC genesis we would need specific social information about the learners' access to the lexifier language before we could decide whether to propose multiple sources in shared substrate/lexifier–language structures or contribution from substrate grammars alone. And if we lack such information—as we will in most cases—then the determination of the historical sources of features present in, or derivable from, both substrate and lexifier

**Table 1. Varying Results of Language Contact**

1. Shift-induced interference from Indic in Dravidian (Emeneau 1980)
   A. Innovated Dravidian-like structures with Dravidian morphemes:

      None

   B. Innovated Dravidian-like structures without Dravidian morphemes:

      Retroflex consonants
      Syntax of particle *api* (cf. Drav. **-um*)
      Second causative construction
      NEG conjugation (in some modern Indic languages)
      Inclusive/exclusive 'we' (in some modern Indic languages)

   C. Innovated Dravidian-like structures also plausible as internally motivated change:

      Syntax of quotative particle *iti*
      Agglutinative no. + case suffix sequences
      System of echo-word formation
      Absolutive constructions unlike other Indo-European absolutives
      Rigid SOV word order

2. Chinese Pidgin English (Cantonese substrate) (Shi 1986)
   A. Cantonese-like structures with Cantonese morphemes:

      None

   B. Cantonese-like structures without Cantonese morphemes:

      English *v* → /b/ (but /f/, which Cant. has, remains)
      Lack of oral C / ___ # (but Nasal remains / ___ #)
      Lack of plural personal pronouns (cf. Cant. *ngaw* 'I' vs. *ngaw-day* 'we, us')
      Obligatory use of numeral classifier *piece*
      Copula with predicate noun but not with predicate adjective
      Yes/no Q construction with Verb-no-Verb
      Predicate-initial NEG
      Deletion in discourse of topic-connected NP from comment sentence

   C. Cantonese-like structures that are also like (simplified) English:

      Lack of $\theta$, ð
      Lack of *r*
      Few consonant clusters
      Lack of inflectional morphology
      Adverbial derivational suffixes
      SVO word order

**Table 1. Continued**

3. Borrowing (by bilingual Greek speakers) from Turkish into some Asia Minor Greek dialects (Dawkins 1916)
   - A. Innovated Turkish structures with Turkish morphemes:
     - Third-person possessive suffix (occasional)
     - Turkish agglutinative verb inflection (occasional)
     - Superlative formation with particle *an*
     - Derivational suffixes (added to Greek verbs)
   - B. Innovated Turkish-like structures without Turkish morphemes:
     - Vowel harmony with new V phonemes /ö ü ï/
     - [q] allophone of /k/ in back-vowel environments
     - Morphophonemic rule /k/ $\rightarrow$ *ğ* / ____ + *i*
     - Agglutinative noun and verb inflection (with Greek suffixes)
     - Several Turkish word order patterns
     - Loss of definite article except in accusative case (where Turkish marks definiteness)
   - C. Innovated Turkish-like structures also plausible as internally motivated changes:
     - Devoicing of word-final obstruents
     - Loss of $\theta$, ð
     - Loss of most adjective-noun agreement inflection
     - Loss of grammatical gender

languages will remain permanently beyond our reach. So, for instance, the presence of nasalized vowels in Haitian Creole cannot be assumed to be an exclusive French contribution, because the relevant African languages also have phonemically nasalized vowels. Similarly, SVO word order cannot be claimed as an exclusive African contribution, since French is also an SVO language. In other words, we can be sure about the sources for some initial Afro-American creole structures, but not about the sources of all of them.

I have not said much about the problem of identifying changes in PC languages after the period of origin. The pidgins I know most about have not changed appreciably except in lexicon, but probably all Afro-American languages have undergone significant structural change during their histories. Some of this change surely resulted in structural expansion as pidgins acquired new spheres of usage and became creolized; but all of it was change in an existing language, not PC genesis. The search for sources of innovations in a fully crystallized PC language is subject to the same methodological constraints as in any other kind of language change: both external and internal causes must be considered, and the total picture for external causation resembles examples 1 and 3, *not* example 2. In cases like that of Indian immigration to Mauritius, the relevant example is 1; cases of decreolization are much more likely to resemble example 3. Moreover, as Lawrence Carrington points out (in this volume), an Atlantic creole feature of African origin could have entered the PC either when it first emerged as a language or later on, through interference—provided, of course, that the relevant African language(s) was/were spoken in the community both at the beginning and later. Finally, it is important to keep in mind the fact that changes that simplify a language's structure, at least locally, frequently arise *both* through internal drift *and* through external causation, especially in shift situations. So individual simplificatory changes cannot, in themselves, be used as evidence of present or former pidginization or creolization.

I will close with a warning: neither the basic issue of PC origins nor the question of change in a fully crystallized PC language will be solved by any one simple explanatory statement that applies equally to all the languages. Just as PC genesis is similar to shift-induced language change in some respects and different from it in other respects, so the histories of individual PC languages are similar in some ways and different in others. Both social and linguistic factors varied at the time the PCs arose, and all these variations surely influenced the linguistic outcome of PC genesis.

## Notes

1. I will therefore argue against Lefebvre's view (as expressed orally in February 1988 at the conference from which this volume arose) that if creoles arose through a sharp break in transmission, we need a new methodology to study creole genesis, because traditional historical linguistic methodology is irrelevant. I believe that the issue of an appropriate methodology is an empirical one, and my point is that there is, in fact, ample evidence that the methodological constraints on studies of ordinary language change must also be applied in studying pidgin and creole genesis.

2. Lefebvre's paper does have a paragraph describing a plan to compare Kwa languages with Mande languages, but she argues that this comparison "should not be as detailed as the comparative analysis of the three main languages." And she does not, according to her description, plan to investigate the possible influence of other languages or of universal tendencies of any kind.

3. This means that Lefebvre's invoking of Muysken's (1981) discussion in her dismissal of second-language learning as an important factor in PC genesis is un-

justified. Given that the Quechua speakers in question were bilingual in Spanish, of course imperfect learning played no role in the development of the Media Lengua; but imperfect L2 acquisition must at least be considered seriously in the case of the Atlantic creoles, because full bilingualism in the lexifier language was presumably conspicuously absent among the majority of slaves.

4. However, I don't believe she takes the approach far enough. She does not, for instance, consider the various weightings that must be given to different kinds of features, especially features that vary along a marked-unmarked continuum; and she apparently assumes that the phonological structures of HC were *not* affected by African structures. Separating out the phonology (or any other highly structured grammatical subsystem) is bound to reduce the value of a comparative study, because crucial evidence is liable to be ignored.

## References

Alleyne, Mervyn C. 1979. On the genesis of languages. *The genesis of language*, ed. by Kenneth C. Hill, 89–107. Ann Arbor: Karoma.

———. 1980. *Comparative Afro-American: An historical-comparative study of English-based Afro-American dialects of the New World*. Ann Arbor: Karoma.

Bickerton, Derek. 1981. *Roots of language*. Ann Arbor: Karoma.

Boretzky, Norbert. 1983. *Kreolsprachen, Substrate und Sprachwandel*. Wiesbaden: Otto Harrassowitz.

Corne, Chris. 1983. Substratal reflections: The completive aspect and the distributive numerals in Isle de France Creole. *Te Reo* 26.65–80.

Dawkins, R. M. W. 1916. *Modern Greek in Asia Minor*. Cambridge: Cambridge University Press.

Emeneau, Murray B. 1980. India and linguistic areas. *Language and linguistic area*, ed. by Anwar Dil, 126–65. Stanford: Stanford University Press. Reprinted from *India and historical grammar*. Annamalai University Department of Linguistics Publication no. 5 (1965), 25–75.

Givón, Talmy. 1979. Prolegomena to any sane creology. *Readings in creole studies*, ed. by Ian F. Hancock, 3–35. Ghent: E. Story-Scientia.

Le Page, Robert B. 1977. Processes of pidginization and creolization. *Pidgin and creole linguistics*, ed. by Albert Valdman, 222–55. Bloomington: Indiana University Press.

Lorimer, D. L. R. 1937. Burushaski and its alien neighbors: Problems in linguistic contagion. *Transactions of the Philological Society* 1937.63–98.

Mufwene, Salikoko S. 1986. The universalist and substrate hypotheses complement one another. *Substrata versus universals in creole genesis*, ed. by Pieter Muysken and Norval Smith, 129–63. Amsterdam: John Benjamins.

Muysken, Pieter. 1981. Halfway between Quechua and Spanish: The case for relexification. *Historicity and variation in creole studies*, ed. by Arnold Highfield and Albert Valdman, 52–78. Ann Arbor: Karoma.

Muysken, Pieter, and Norval Smith. 1988. Question words and reflexives in the creole languages. Unpublished manuscript.

Senn, Alfred. 1966. *Handbuch der litauischen Sprache*. Heidelberg: Carl Winter.

Shi, Dingxu. 1986. *Chinese Pidgin English: Its origin and linguistic features*. M.A. thesis, University of Pittsburgh.

Singler, John Victor. 1988. The homogeneity of the substrate as a factor in pidgin/creole genesis. *Language* 64.27–51.

Thomason, Sarah Grey. 1983. Chinook Jargon in areal and historical context. *Language* 59.820–70.

Thomason, Sarah G., and Terrence Kaufman. 1988. *Language contact, creolization, and genetic linguistics*. Berkeley: University of California Press.

# The Ịjọ Element in Berbice Dutch and the Pidginization/Creolization Process

*Ian Robertson*

The debate on the formation of creole languages of the Caribbean in particular, and of the wider world in general, has now polarized around the substratum and the universalist positions. Supporters of the universalist position argue that the claim for African substratum influence is more sociohistorical than linguistic, and that, in at least one case (that of Hawaii), it is not even sociohistorically valid. Since similar linguistic features may be found in creoles which do not have the same substratum influence, the presence of those features in any one creole could not be accounted for by substratum influence (Bickerton 1974, 1984).

Bickerton has proposed the language bioprogram hypothesis (LBH) to explain creole language genesis.

> The LBH claims that the innovative aspects of a creole grammar are inventions on the part of the first generations of children who have pidgin as their linguistic input, rather than features transmitted from pre-existing languages. The LBH claims, further, that such inventions show a degree of similarity, across wide variations in linguistic background, that is too great to be attributed to chance. Finally, the LBH claims that the most cogent explanation of this similarity is that it derives from the structure of a species specific program for language, genetically coded and expressed, in ways still largely mysterious, in the structures and modes of operation of the human brain. (1984:173)

The LBH makes children the agents of expansion in the creolization process. It argues that similar or common creole grammatical features can more plausibly be seen as the direct result of children making use of innate language-learning mechanisms to "expand" and render more complex the grammar of the pidgin language to which they were exposed, and which they must now use as both their primary means of communication and their native language. According to Bickerton, when linguistic facts in support of substratum theory have been uncovered, they have been far too few to make a convincing case.

In addition, such facts may be outweighed by the myriad others which cannot be readily traced to any substratum language(s). Thus far, Bickerton's dissatisfaction with the lack of linguistic support for the substratum theories appears justified.

In contrast to universalist arguments, substratum theories, whatever the specifics of their formulation (e.g., Whinnom 1965; Alleyne 1971; Allsopp 1976), focus on the role of the substrate language(s) in the creolization process. In the case of the Caribbean, the substrates must obviously be West African. The fact that some features common to Caribbean creoles may also be found in creoles which do not have a West African substrate is not considered to constitute any embarrassment to this explanation because it is viewed as perfectly normal for languages to derive identical grammatical features, categories, and processes from different sources without the mediation of any innate characteristics.

The most recent of the substratum arguments is perhaps Alleyne's (1980), which documents common features across a wide range of Caribbean creoles and indicates the extent to which many of these may be considered retentions and metamorphoses of various West African languages. His position is that

> Africans of varying linguistic and geographical origins (but confined to West Africa) underwent language change arising primarily out of new communicative needs within their own number, and secondarily, out of communicative needs with Europeans (in this case, English, themselves of various dialects and geographical origins within the United Kingdom). It is axiomatic of all such change arising out of language contact that there will be transmission or continuities from the native language of the people undergoing linguistic change. . . . Of course in many instances these transmissions and continuities are eventually discarded, and the newly adopted language may show absolutely no trace of the former native language. (1980:138)

The absence of further evidence has left these two contending sets of theories in a position of virtual stalemate. One major impediment has been the inability to identify the specific substratum source(s). Berbice Dutch (BD) is a Caribbean creole uniquely placed to offer further evidence on this debate.

In earlier works (Robertson 1979, 1983), I provided an analysis of the grammar of BD, a creole still spoken by fewer than one hundred speakers on the Berbice River in Guyana. Smith et al. (1987) indicate quite clearly that the seminal African substratum input into BD came from Eastern Ịjọ (EI), with the Kalabari dialect perhaps the major contributor, though there is evidence for significant contributions from other EI dialects.

Alleyne (1980:143) notes that "since the earliest contacts could well have been the most linguistically important, it may be useful to examine them more closely." This paper attempts, therefore, to examine more closely the influences of Eastern Ịjọ on the grammar of Berbice Dutch. The survey is limited to those few features which the current availability of documents on EI and the level of sophistication of linguistic analysis allow.

## Historical Background

### *Berbice*

Bickerton (1981:45) argues that

> one would think that the first task in constructing any substratum theory would be to show that the necessary groups were in the necessary places at the necessary times.

There is no specific historical information available on the ethnic distribution of slaves on Berbice plantations during the first sixty years after the colony's establishment. There is, however, a very sound argument for assuming that the necessary group, Eastern Ịjọs, was in the necessary places at the necessary time.

In 1627, Abraham Van Pere, a director of the Zeeland Chamber of the Dutch West India Company, was granted permission to sail to the South American coast and establish a colony. According to Netscher (1888), Van Pere's application was addressed both by the Zeeland Chamber itself and by the Assembly (Committee) of Nineteen. Both bodies approved the request, but the proposals of the Committee were more generous because they included the granting of Van Pere's request that he be allowed to take along six Negroes.

Accordingly, Van Pere set out on September 24, 1627, to found what later became known as the Berbice colony. Apparently, the party of sixty-six was made up of twenty households of three people each and six Negroes. These Negroes would have been the first Africans in the new colony coming, ironically, from Holland. From the very outset, therefore, there was an African presence in the Berbice colony.

The slow growth of the Berbice colony is well documented. According to Netscher (1888), the initial focus was on trade in annatto, letter wood, and tobacco. Forty-four years after the initial settlement Adrian van Berkel, who was employed by the original patroon of Berbice as secretary and purchaser and who lived in Berbice between 1670 and 1689, documented the existence of a mere five plantations on the Berbice colony, all of them company owned, and a trading post on the Canje. In between those two dates, one of the few reliable population estimates for Berbice points out that in the mid-1630s the population was forty whites and twenty-five Africans.[1]

Van Berkel named only three of the plantations, but, unless the other two were among those destroyed by an Amerindian uprising which was reported to have destroyed several plantations in 1687, the other two may have been Oosterfant and New Vlissingen, the only other estates existing in 1712. There is no evidence on the location of the latter.

Van Berkel provides no specific information on the number of slaves on the plantations in his time, 1671–74. A reasonable estimate may be arrived at, however. According to Netscher (1888), there were, in 1720, six sugar and two cacao plantations, one large fort, one small fortress, four outposts, one church, and one smithy. The last three of these would not have had any significant number of slaves. The total number of slaves at this time was 895. If the slaves were evenly distributed across the remaining nine locations, the average holding would have been about 90.[2]

Given five plantations, and given that these plantations required a large number of slaves, it seems reasonable to assume a slave population of between 400 and 500 in Van Berkel's time. Van Berkel himself testifies to the relatively large numbers of slaves: "We had to take stock and muster the slaves to learn how many of them had died and how many had been born. Here on the first estate I had business to occupy me three or four hours" (1948:14–15).

One important feature of the Berbice plantations, the company plantations in particular, is the chronic short supply of slaves and the heavy reliance on creole slaves as a consequence. This was part of the policy from the very outset, and as late as 1764, the largest single group of slaves tried for participating in a massive revolt in the previous year was creole. The number of Europeans in Berbice must have stabilized around fifty, for, as late as 1735, Galbo-Elephantus (1735) comments: "The colony *begins* to be quickly peopled, Captain E——having brought over twenty two passengers; so that there are already more than *sixty* planters here" (my emphasis).

## *Dutch–Eastern Ịjọ Contact*

Although history is silent on Berbice between 1627 and 1667, there is much information on the parallel period on the West African coast. According to Northrop (1978), the Ịjọs have inhabited the Eastern Niger Delta for centuries. Their presence there, according to Hair (1967), antedates the arrival of the Europeans by several centuries. Prior to the arrival of the Europeans, the Ịjọs engaged in fishing and the production of salt, both of which they traded with the inland farming communities. Northrop argues that it was with the fishing group that European contact was established and maintained over a significant period. There was much intergroup warfare, and Ịjọs are known to have kept other Ịjọs as domestic slaves in precolonial times.

According to Ryder (1965:195), "the Dutch supplanted the Portuguese as Chief European traders on the coast of Guinea by the end of the second decade." The period of greatest Dutch activity in West Africa, from about 1635 to 1655, would represent the time during which the early Berbice slaves would have arrived in the colony. Contemporary sources establish that the main slave trade was with the Caravalies (i.e., Kalabari Ịjọs), with the majority of the shipments made from the Bight of Biafra.

According to Hair (1967:235–36),

> Sandoval (1627), a priest working with African slaves in the Caribbean, distinguished between "Caravalies naturales e puros" and "Caravalies particulares," without unfortunately making it clear who the former were: the latter traded with the native-Calabars (at New Calabar?) but did not speak the native Calabar language.

Dapper (1668) noted considerable trade in slaves by the Dutch at Bonny and New Calabar in the early seventeenth century. Hair (1967:234) cites Pacheco Perreira (1500) as indicating that the "Bonny River" (part of the Niger Delta) became an important center for Dutch trade in the 1640s.

At the critical time, therefore, the Dutch were trading in slaves, mainly with the Kalabari, and were transporting these slaves to the Caribbean. It is not unreasonable, therefore, to assume that the vast majority of slaves in Berbice at that time were of Eastern Ịjọ origin and that prominent among these were Kalabari.

The unusual case of one group of West Africans selling their own group into slavery is perhaps explained by the subgroupings noted by Sandoval. Hair (1967:252) cites Robert Horton on this:

> Oral traditions and corroborative material evidence (captured sacred tusks) suggest that between 1500 and 1600, the town of Bile was at least as prominent as New Calabar and Bonny in the slave trade, and that Bile got its slaves by sacking neighbouring Delta villages, rather than by trade with the hinterland.

Smith et al. (1987) have clearly established that the BD lexicon is more fundamentally influenced by Kalabari than by any other Ịjọ dialect, a position in perfect accord with historical facts pertaining to Dutch trading with the Ịjọs in the seventeenth century. Furthermore, given the Dutch contact with the Ịjọ territory and the seminal nature of the Eastern Ịjọ dialects in the formation of Berbice Dutch, it seems reasonable to accept that Ịjọ slaves must have predominated on the early Berbice plantations.

The above seems to argue that the development of BD must have taken place on the early plantations before the Ịjọ numerical dominance was lost. In this context the large number of Ịjọ survivals is better accounted for since they would have been very well established before the inputs from other languages became available.[3]

## Berbice Dutch and Creolization

Among the creole languages of the Caribbean area, BD is uniquely placed to allow for the critical examination of several assumptions. Since it is the only creole language for which the principal substrate influence can be clearly identified, there is much scope for the examination of the roles of the input languages in the processes of creolization. It may allow for identification of some of the actual processes of creolization and may shed considerable light on whether the creolization process could have been exclusive to children nativizing a pidgin.

Other assumptions may also be scrutinized in light of the specific evidence available from BD. The assumption of heterogeneity of ethnic input at the substrate level of creolization may be challenged, as well as the assumption that this nascent language was necessary for communication across slave groups of different ethnic origins. This paper is concerned with identifying the influences of EI on the grammar of BD and with the implications these may be seen to have for the pidginization and creolization processes.

According to Alleyne (1980:138), "the order of total discarding of former native language elements is (1) vocabulary, (2) morphology, (3) syntax, and (4) phonology." Given the high percentage of EI lexical survivals noted by Smith et al. (1987), it seems reasonable to expect that the influence of EI on BD grammar would be significant if Alleyne's order is at all valid.

On the level of the morphology, Robertson (1979:1983) draws attention to the use of several suffixes in BD, a feature unique among the creoles of the Caribbean area. Smith et al. (1987) note that at least two of these suffixes are of EI origin. To these may be added several others identified by Kouwenberg (1987). The remainder of this paper examines these suffixes and several other areas in which EI dialects have influenced the grammar of Berbice Dutch. Undoubtedly, other areas of possible influence need to be examined, but this survey focuses on exemplification of some types of evidence which BD may be seen to provide.

*Suffixes*

Robertson (1979) identifies *-te* as one of two markers with past time reference (the other being the preposed particle *wa*). The form *-te* is more correctly labeled perfect (PERF) if the emphasis is on current relevance or on predications which may not yet have been concluded. The form may often be translated into English as a simple past:

1. *oori laakii-te*
   he laugh PERF
   'He laughed.'
2. *eenshii bugrav -t(e) o hiirii*
   we bury PERF her here
   'We buried her here.'
3. *a fal -te*
   he/she/it fall PERF
   'He (she, it) fell.'

However, there are several instances in which the use of *-te* does not clearly indicate that the action or state is complete. The issue is essentially one of focus.

4. *eke pash-te eeni fa sins eeni kal kal tokaapuu*
   I care (*te*) them from since they small small children
   a. 'I have taken care of them since they were very young children.'
   b. 'I took care of them since (during the time that) they were very young children.'

In example 4, the act of taking care of the children has lasted for a number of years. It clearly started in the past, but there is no clear indication that the process is complete. In fact, for some of the people referred to it is still continuing. If, in fact, the process were complete, the sentence could be given the alternative translation 4b.

5. *oorii gruii-te wiirunii*
   she grow (*te*) Wiruni
   'She has grown up on the Wiruni.'
6. *a koro -te*
   it fall (*te*)
   'It has fallen.'

The suffix *-te* may be added to certain state verbs, for example, *niin-te* 'know'; *furstan-te* 'understand'; *biun-te* 'think, believe'; *blente-te* 'to have become blind'; *pote-te* 'to have become old.'

The use of the perfect with apparent stative predicators may be explained in a number of ways. Alleyne (1986) suggests that the categorization of predicators on the state/nonstate parameter may not be identical in English and creole, and consequently any predication which enters into a combination unacceptable in the language of the gloss may simply be reflecting this difference in categorization. Jaganauth (1987) assumes what may be considered a more acceptable position; that is, that the stative/dynamic distinction, as noted by Givón (1979), represents extreme ends on what may be considered a continuum of stability and that some states are, as a consequence, more compatible with perfect than others. This position seems more satisfactory because it does not deny the obvious stative qualities of the equivalent of 'know,' 'see,' 'blind,' 'old,' etc.

Both *blente-te* and *pote-te* possess parallel adjectival forms, *blente* and *pote*. The use of the suffix *-te* with these forms seems to signal a state that has been entered into. Efebo (1967:12) points out that in Nembe "adjective verbs" take the same endings as other verbs. In such cases *-te* is used to signal a state that has been entered into:

7. *Or ebi -te* (Nembe)
   it good has-become
   'It has become good.'
8. *Togu bei duba-te* (Nembe)
   boy the big has-become
   'The boy has become big.'

The suffix *-te* in BD thus appears to be a direct transfer from EI, retaining its "perfect" meaning as well as the ability to be used with stative predicators.

A second suffix, *-a,* is used to signal iterative and durative (DUR) aspects in BD.

9. *eke stuudii-a da wat een doz mii-a juu*
   I study (DUR) is what they does do (DUR) you
   'I am wondering what it does to one.'
10. *eke muu-a kiirikii*
    I go DUR church
    a. 'I am going to church.'
    b. 'I go to church.'

There are no specific time values inherent in the use of this suffix.

Kouwenberg (1987) observes that the form is really a shortened form of *-are,* the present continuous suffix in the Kalabari, Okrika, and Ibani dialects. Thus the suffix *-a* represents a borrowing with expansion in meaning and reduction in form. The full form is exceedingly rare in BD. Its presence is important, however, since there would otherwise have been no clue to the source of this suffix. The continued use of this form is one good index of the wide range of factors that may have come into play in the creolization process and may hint at one very important reason for the failure to isolate specific substratum influences. The full form *-are* would have been reduced over time to *-a* by a set of relatively low-level phonetic changes. If this process of reduction had been complete, the substratum influence would have been obscured by a low-level phonetic process, a "plausible process" of the kind Bickerton (1984:183) rejects on the basis of lack of specificity.

There is in BD some evidence that the Guyanese Creole English (GCE) preposed durative particle *a* is used simultaneously with the suffix *-a:*

11. *ju kiikii dat dii jerma a set-a dii tshroon eenshi fa*
you see that the lady DUR sit DUR the throne us of
'You see that the lady (Queen) sits on the throne.'

12. *ene a kor -a*
rain DUR fall DUR.
'It is raining.'

The double marking of the durative seems to be the beginning of a process of transition in which the GCE preposed particle *a* is used alongside the BD suffix. This process of double marking is quite normal in such transition situations (cf. Bickerton's 1975 discussion of *doz* and *juuz tu*). If this transition from BD *-a* to GCE *a* had ever been completed, it would have been impossible to speak of any substratum influence here. Evidence of this kind seems to caution that the lack of specific evidence of substratum influence may be a function of a number of factors. This lack should not be used as proof that such evidence never existed.

Robertson (1979, 1983) points to the fact that one means of signaling plurality in BD is by the use of the suffix *-apuu*. The use of this suffix is extended to include also the plural personal pronouns *eenshia* 'we,' *eeniiapu* 'they,' and *jenda* 'you.' As Kouwenberg (1987) points out, it is likewise extended to adjectives functioning as nominals:

13. a. *kali -apu*
'small ones'
b. guu-je
'big one.'

In all EI dialects, *-apu* is used with items which have the feature [+HUMAN]. It functions both as a nominalizer and as a pluralizer. However, the class distinction of EI nouns is not carried over into BD. Consequently, the use of *-apuu* is generalized to all plural nouns and plural nominalizers.

Robertson (1979:53) draws attention to the suffixing of *-je* to personal pronouns, suggesting a number of Dutch sources for the suffix. Kouwenberg (1987) notes this suffix is also of Kalabari origin and used, according to Jenwari (1977), as the nominalizing suffix on singular nonhuman forms.

This use of nominalizers is unusual among creoles of the Caribbean area. It is important to note that the use of neither of these nominalizers—for example, in *kali-apu* 'small ones' and *guu-je* 'big one'—is obligatory in BD. What is of even greater significance is the fact that BD requires neither the feature specifications [+HUMAN] for pluralization nor [−HUMAN] and SINGULAR for nominalization. The factors governing these selections are not obvious, but their identification and further investigation are likely to add to the understanding of the factors influencing creolization.

### *Negation*

The principal negator in BD is *kaane:*

15. *eke niimii diida kaane*<br>
    I know that not<br>
    'I do not know that.'

It may be derived by fusion of the negative suffix in EI (e.g., *-gha* in Nembe, *-ke* or *-ka* in Okrika) and the Standard Dutch (SD) *nee* 'no.' This latter is reflected in the BD negator *neene* 'no.' By far the most frequent manifestation of *kaane* is *-ka*.

Three features of this negator are relevant to this paper. First, it is the only obligatory negator in BD. Several other negators may be used along with it, but none of these ever occurs without it except when the influence of GCE stress on *ka* is taken into account (Robertson 1983, 1984).

Second, *ka* occurs in sentence-final position:

16. *eke niimii ka*<br>
    I know not<br>
    'I do not know.'
17. *Juu na wa kiikii da wii ka*<br>
    you did not see is who not<br>
    'You did not see who it was.'

The only exception made to this sentence-final rule occurs when following the rule would lead to a misinterpretation:

18. *eke nii ka ash o jenda*<br>
    I know not if he there<br>
    'I do not know if he is there.'

If, as is normal, the negator is placed at the end of the sentence, the following results:

19. *eke nii ash o jenda ka*
I know if he there not
'I know if he is not there.'

This is clearly a different message. It is one of the few known instances where the *ka* negator is not in final position.

Third, *ka* may also be used to negate indefinite quantifiers:

20. *een gutu ka*
one thing not
'Nothing.'

21. *ek a mii-a een gutu ka met dii ene*
I did do one thing not with the rain
'I did nothing because of the rain.'

22. *en kene ka*
one person not
'Nobody.'

In EI, the negator is suffixed to the verb. Since EI has an SOV word order, the negator frequently occurs in sentence-final position. There is one exception in Nembe where the negator precedes the perfect or future suffixes:

23. *Ain bo -gha-te* (Nembe)
it come not has
'It has not come.'

24. *O bo -gha-nyuu* (Nembe)
he come not will
'He will not come.'

It is important to note that while this negator is a suffix in EI dialects, it is best treated as an enclitic in BD. The full form does appear independently as one potential response to alternative questions. The reduced forms occur, however, as cliticized. The principal negator in BD may therefore be considered to result from the convergence of two forms: one EI, one SD. Its distribution is clearly influenced by that of the EI negator. Given the fact that the EI negator is a suffix, it is possible to speculate on the influence this might have on the encliticization of the reduced forms of *kane*.

### *Third-Person Pronouns*

EI third-person singular pronoun forms vary according to case, gender, and emphasis. Efebo notes that in Nembe "there are two forms of the subject pronoun, long and short. The long pronouns are used for emphasis or to make plain which person is referred to" (1967:1). The selection of the form is determined by the case and gender of the antecedent and by whether it is human.[4] The short Nembe subject forms of the third-person pronoun are *o* 'he,' *a* 'she,' and *ain* 'it.' The long forms are *ori* 'he,' *are* 'she,' and *ain* 'it.'

In BD, the third-person singular pronouns are *a, o,* and *ori,* derived from EI short forms *a* and *o* and from the long form *ori,* respectively. BD has no gender distinctions, as the following examples show:

25. *a bii a sukuu fii mu-ka*
he say he want to go not
'He said that he did not want to go.'

26. *oorii pan -t eke bii . . .*
he tell (PERF) me say . . .
'He told me that . . .'

27. *een fragi-t o hus . . .*
they ask (PERF) him how . . .
'They asked him how . . .'

28. *a bii a sukuu fi mu-ka*
she say she want to go not
'She said that she did not want to go.'

In object position, both forms are often replaced by the unstressed schwa. By contrast with these two, there is no case restriction on *oorii*. It occurs in subject, object, and genitive positions. It may also be used to form the reflexive, as in *oorii-selfu*. The other third-person singular pronouns are never used to form the reflexive or the genitive.

The EI distinction of stress or emphasis is evident in a few cases in BD. In the following discourse (examples 29 and 30) the speaker feels the need to distinguish between two females who could both have been the antecedent of *oorii*.

29. *een naam adii, een naam luusii*
one name Audie, one name Lucy
'One named Audie, one named Lucy.'

30. *oorii jende toto maikonii*
she (the former) LOCATIVE at Mahaicony
'She is at Mahaicony.'

In the following case, three male participants are involved. The incidence of *oorii* is not accidental, particularly where the third party is introduced. At this point *oorii* is stressed. Significantly, the speaker then resorts to *a* in the final part of the utterance, since there is no possibility of further confusion.

31. *so toto dii dispensa laate*
so when the dispenser arrived
'So when the dispenser arrived,'

*oorii loosh -te dii stitsh*
he loose PAST the stitches
'he opened the stitches'

*an twa bande di bwa an pii-te di*
and put bandages the hand and give PAST the
'and put bandages on the hand and gave the'

*kene tablit*
person (man) tablets
'man tablets'

*an diida waatii heelp-te dii kene*
and that what help PAST the person(man)
'and that was what helped the person'

*an dii kene pan -t oorii*
and the man tell (past) him
'and the man told him.'

*so oorii nou buu -te dida shii tiibii*
so he now take PAST in that his head
'So he, having taken that in'

*anga bii dii dispensa*
LOC say the dispenser
'says the dispenser'

*moi -ka so a suukuu fi mu -ka*
good not so he want to go not
'is not any good, therefore he does not want to go.'

The BD third-person plural pronoun is identical with the proto-Ịjọ form *eni*.

*Postpositions*

Although BD has an SVO word order, postpositions are used in several locative and temporal constructions (Robertson 1979).

32. *een doz twa o kundg been*
they usually throw it (your) anus in
'They usually throw it in the anus.'

33. *eke mu koop brot shap anga*
    I go buy bread shop LOC
    'I will buy bread in the shop.'
34. *eke habu ande bokap eke warii ondro*
    I have some fowls my house under
    'I have some chickens under my house.'

This use of postpositions, as noted by Smith et al. (1987), is a direct transfer from EI, in which the order of elements is SOV:

35. *bele-bi- o nama tuua*
    pot the in meat put
    'Put the meat in the pot'
36. *wari- bi- o*
    house the in
    'in the house'

In the EI dialects of Kalabari, Bile, and Okrika, *anga* means 'side.' In BD, the form is used in locative phrases when no specific locative postposition (directional or spot) is used.

37. *hiirii anga*
    here LOC
    'Here.'
38. *a jende eke warii anga*
    it there my house in
    'It's somewhere in my house.'

### *Demonstrative*

One final area of Ịjọ influence of great significance needs to be mentioned. In the Nembe dialect, the demonstrative is formed by postposing the definite article to the noun. BD uses the same strategy for signaling the proximal demonstrative:

34. Nembe: *mi wari mi*
    BD: *di wari di*
    the house the
    'This house.'

### *Discussion*

Mühlhäusler appears to support Bickerton's (1984:184) argument against the usefulness of seeking one-to-one correspondences between substratum and creole languages when he claims that "as regards the determination of substratum influence nothing is more misleading than a simple static comparison between languages" (1986:123).

Mühlhäusler and Bickerton are both correct in this. But the analysis of the contribution of substrate languages must start with concrete evidence of some substrate input. The simple one-to-one correspondences allow for identification of specific input, but the case cannot be closed on such obvious evidence. The larger issues of identifying what has actually happened to these inputs, which grammatical subsystems tend to be affected and which not, and what conclusions may reasonably be drawn from these sets of information are of much greater import.

These are the investigations most likely to allay Bickerton's suspicions about unspecified "plausible processes of change" (1984:184) which may have obscured the substratum input. Thus far, creolists have been asked to take too much of the substrate case on faith. BD provides considerable evidence that substrate languages were not simply innocent bystanders in the creolization process.

BD is the only Caribbean creole language for which the substrate input can be isolated with reasonable specificity. This fact may, in the first instance, encourage creolists to challenge the view that the substrate input was of necessity heterogeneous. Linguistic heterogeneity at the substrate level, and the consequent need for a stable communication medium, has always been assumed to be the prime motivation force behind the emergence of the pidgin antecedent of the creole. The case of heterogeneity has always been based on the socio-historical assumption that slaves in any colony were mixed. Little cognizance was given to the possibility of dominance from any single linguistic group. There is at least some preliminary support for this possibility. Smith (1987) suggests Kikongo dominance in Sranan, and the case for Twi has been mooted for Jamaica (Cassidy 1961).

That slave populations were mixed is an incontrovertible fact, but no linguist has rigorously applied the requirement that such mixing must have taken place at the right time and in the right places if it was to be a relevant factor. Even where these criteria are met, it still seems necessary to establish whether linguistic dominance could have been established in spite of mixing. Bases for such dominance could often extend beyond the simple numcrical. In religious activity, for instance, the dominant priest could well have imposed the language of his group even though that group may have been a minority one in the colony.

The linguistic evidence of substratum influence provided here is quite protracted and may best be summarized as follows: (a) the retention of suffixes in BD, (b) the use of third-person pronominal forms, (c) the retention of the negator *ka,* (d) the use of the same strategy to indicate definiteness and the proximal demonstrative, and (e) the use of postpositions.

The substratum influence here cuts across a range of grammatical subsystems sufficient to reject the argument that these substrate languages did not have a seminal input into the creolization process. However, they do not provide easy or automatic answers to a range of questions the substratist must address.

A significant one is: What factors determine the systems on which substratum influence would be readily manifested? In the case of the BD pronouns, for instance, only the third-person singular and plural are selected from the substrate. The first and second are selected from the superstrate. This contrasts significantly with the Jamaican Creole case, in which only the second-person plural form is selected from a substrate.

As regards the "plausible processes" of change, BD suffixes seem to suggest that these should not be dismissed as easily as Bickerton (1984) attempts to do. It may be argued, for instance, that had the reduction of *aare* to *a* been completed, the evidence of substratum influence would have been reduced to mere conjecture. Further, there is some evidence of the intrusion of the GCE proposed particle *a* in place of the suffix. Such a change, if completed, would have completely removed any evidence of substrate influence on the initial creolization process.

Prior to the discovery and exploration of the Ịjọ connection, Robertson (1983) noted that inflectional suffixes in BD were significant in that they must have survived the pidginization process. This argument is made more convincing now by the fact that all these suffixes are clearly of EI origin.

Le Page (1967:86) believes that "since the inflectional categories of two languages in a contact situation rarely coincide, inflection is the commonest tragedy in a contact situation." It seems pointless to argue, based on the assumption that pidginization is correlated with simplification and creolization with reacquisition of complexity, that these suffixes were lost during the pidginization stage and reinserted in the creolization process. If this were the case, one would still have to account for the fact that the choice has been made from the substrate and that suffixes rather than separate particles are used, a practice not in keeping with those of other Caribbean creoles.

Another issue is the use of postpositions. Contrary to the obvious unlikelihood that an SVO language would retain postpositions, BD has done so. Such postpositions are relatively few, being restricted to temporals and locatives, but they represent a challenge to the view expressed by Bickerton (1981:50):

> Languages, even creoles, are systems, systems have structure and things that are incompatible with that structure cannot be borrowed. *SVO lan-*

> *guages cannot borrow a set of postpositions, to take an extreme and obvious case*. (my emphasis)

BD does precisely that.

Given the high level of EI lexical retentions in BD, one could, in fact, expect more grammatical retentions than have so far been noted. Such a high level of transfer is perfectly compatible with the position advanced by Mühlhäusler (1986:115) that when relatively homogeneous substrate groups are involved, "transfer would seem to be perfectly viable as universal solutions become necessary in mainly heterogeneous communities." As far as the slave population was concerned, Berbice was a relatively homogeneous slave society at the time of creolization.

Mühlhäusler's observation brings into focus the question of the roles of input languages in the creolization process. Clearly, the nativization process in BD drew heavily on EI. Bickerton (1984:175) argues that

> Bruner and Feldman (1982) are right in pointing out that input from a variety of fully developed human languages was also potentially available. *However, . . . there is no evidence that children, in acquiring a pidgin natively, are able to use the latter kind of input, and much evidence that they cannot, or perhaps do not need to*. (my emphasis)

It seems distinctly possible that the analysis of creolization which makes children totally responsible for expansion must also be reconsidered. The position is based on a particular interpretation of nativization which is perhaps more narrow than that proposed by Hall (1966:xiii):

> Creolization is simply one manifestation of a broader process, which, for want of a better term, we can call "nativization." A language is nativized when it is taken over by a group of speakers who have previously used some other language so that the new language becomes the native language of the group.

This view of nativization does not exclude a priori adults, who, by force of circumstances, may need to adopt a new mode of communication. At the same time it does not, and perhaps it cannot, deny the role of children in the nativization process. The BD evidence suggests that it is necessary to reconsider the role of adults in the creolization process. Clearly in this case they were not idle spectators, even though the use of creole slaves in Berbice was quite early and widespread.

Another assumption BD obviously challenges is the following position: "Although there are here and there some sweeping similarities which tease you and provoke you to go on with the search, you never find any language which has quite the same kinds of structures as the creole language does" (Bickerton 1979:3).

The strongest support BD provides for the universalist position lies in the details of the actual transfers. Clearly the retention of two aspect markers, durative/iterative and perfect, from a complex system must be explained, as must the generalization of the use of plural [+HUMAN] marker and the retention of nominalizers. Perhaps the universalist preoccupation with predication systems, tense, mood, and aspect marking in particular, has left too little time for the universal factors underlying development in other systems. Gender distinctions, for instance, are not manifested early in children's acquisition of pronominal forms—a fact which may well provide an explanation for the tendency not to have such distinctions in creole languages, though South-Central Niger-Congo languages as a general rule do not have sex-based gender distinctions. Even in Ịjọ the use of such distinctions varies from dialect to dialect (Williamson 1971:283–84). Perhaps Mühlhäusler's (1986) observation that borrowed constructions must fit into the grammar of the developing creole would account for the ease with which gender distinctions, which are not uniformly applied anyway, are lost in the creolization process.

BD is the only Caribbean creole for which an African source language has been identified. Analysis of its subsystems points to significant retentions, transfers, reductions, and expansions in several areas of the grammar. These are much more numerous and significant than the glib universalist position has led us to believe. Though as yet they cannot be said to make a satisfactory case for a purely substratum theory of the processes of creolization and pidginization, these features raise a number of new challenges while offering an opportunity to determine the roles of universals and substrate influences in the creolization process.

## Notes

1. This information was provided by Mrs. A. Benjamin, a researcher in Berbice history, who refers to a document found in the Portuguese archives.

2. There is no clear indication of the time at which sugar was introduced into Berbice, but this must have taken place before 1660 because the crop is known to have been established in the Essequibo colony in the 1650s.

3. An earlier version of this paper (February 1988) presented considerable historical evidence and argument against the position taken by Smith et al. (1987) on

the origin of BD. It is now clear that there could have been no general Guyana Dutch Creole of which Skepi Dutch is a mere remnant.

4. Williamson (1971:283) observes that gender systems in Ịjọ may be more, or less, elaborate depending on whether the written variety is included.

## References

Alleyne, M. C. 1971. Acculturation and the cultural matrix of Caribbean creoles. *Pidginization and creolization of languages*, ed. by Dell Hymes, 169–86. Cambridge: Cambridge University Press.

———. 1980. *Comparative Afro-American: An historical-comparative study of English-based Afro-American dialects of the New World*. Ann Arbor: Karoma.

———. 1986. Perfect and passive. Paper presented at Sixth Biennial Conference of the Society for Caribbean Linguistics, University of the West Indies, St. Augustine, Trinidad.

Allsopp, S. R. R. 1976. The case for Afrogenesis. Paper presented at the Inaugural Conference of the Society for Caribbean Linguistics, Georgetown, University of Guyana.

Baudet, Martha. 1981. Identifying the African grammatical base of the Caribbean creoles: A typological approach. *Historicity and variation in creole studies*, ed. by Albert Valdman and Arnold Highfield, 104–18. Ann Arbor: Karoma.

Bickerton, Derek. 1974. Creolization, linguistic universals, natural semantax and the brain. *University of Hawaii Working Papers in Linguistics* 6.124–41.

———. 1976. Creole tense aspect systems and universal grammar. Paper presented at the Inaugural Conference of the Society for Caribbean Linguistics, Georgetown, University of Guyana.

———. 1981. *Roots of language*. Ann Arbor: Karoma.

———. 1984. The language bioprogram hypothesis. *Behavioral and Brain Sciences* 7.173–221.

Cassidy, Frederic G. 1961. *Jamaica talk*. London: Macmillan.

Dapper, O. 1668. *Naukeurige beschrijuinge der Afrikaensche gewesten*. Amsterdam.

Dunstan, Elizabeth. 1969. *Twelve Nigerian languages*. New York: African Studies.

Efebo, L. Awotua. 1967. *Nembe made easy*. University of Ibadan, Institute of African Studies, Occasional Paper 6.

Elephantus, Galbo. 1735. *A voyage to the new colony of Berbice in 1735*. Trans. by L. Christian W. B. Jamieson, 1877. Crab Island: Van de Kock and Son.

Gilman, Charles. 1986. African areal characteristics: Sprachbund, not substrate? *Journal of Pidgin and Creole Languages* 1.33–50.

Hair, P. E. H. 1969. An ethnolinguistic inventory of the Lower Guinea Coast before 1700. Part 2. *African Language Review* 8.225–56.

Hall, Robert A., Jr. 1966. *Pidgin and creole languages*. Ithaca, N.Y.: Cornell University Press.

Jaganauth, Dhanaiswari. 1987. *Predicate structures in Guyanese Creole*. M.A. thesis, University of the West Indies, Mona, Jamaica.

Jenewari, C. E. W. 1977. *Studies in Kalabari syntax*. Ph.D. dissertation, University of Ibadan.

———. 1983. Defaka: Ịjọ's closest linguistic relative. *Current approaches to African linguistics*. Volume 1, ed. by Ivan R. Dijhoff, 85–111. Dordrecht: Foris.

Kouwenberg, Silvia. 1987. Eastern Ịjọ–derived words in Berbice Dutch. Unpublished manuscript.

Le Page, R. B. 1967. Review of *Pidgin and creole languages*, by R. A. Hall. *Journal of African Languages* 6.83–86.

Mühlhäusler, Peter. 1986. *Pidgin and creole linguistics*. Oxford: Basil Blackwell.

Muysken, Pieter. 1981. Creole tense/mood/aspect systems: The unmarked case? *Generative studies on creole languages*, ed. by Pieter Muysken, 181–99. Dordrecht: Foris.

Netscher, P. M. 1888. *History of the colonies of Essequibo, Demerara and Berbice*. Gravenhage: Martinus Nijhoff. Reprint. Georgetown: *Daily Chronicle*, 1929.

Northrup, David. 1978. *Trade without rulers: Pre-colonial economic development in southeastern Nigeria*. Oxford: Clarendon Press.

Robertson, Ian E. 1979. *Berbice Dutch: A description*. Ph.D. dissertation, University of the West Indies, St. Augustine, Trinidad.

———. 1983. The significance of Berbice Dutch suffixes. *Studies in Caribbean language*, ed. by Lawrence Carrington, 211–16. St. Augustine, Trinidad: Society for Caribbean Linguistics.

———. 1984. Characteristics of a post-creole transition. Paper presented at Fifth Biennial Conference of the Society for Caribbean Linguistics, Mona, Jamaica.

Robertson, Ian E., and Silvia Kouwenberg. 1987. Marking of tense mood aspect in Berbice Dutch. Paper presented at Fourth Essen Colloquium on Creole Languages and Language Contact.

Ryder, A. F. C. 1965. Dutch trade on the Nigerian coast during the seventeenth century. *Journal of the Historical Society of Nigeria* 3.195–210.

Smith, Norval. 1987. *The genesis of the creole languages of Suriname*. Doctoral dissertation, University of Amsterdam.

Smith, Norval, Ian Robertson, and Kay Williamson. 1987. The Ịjọ element in Berbice Dutch. *Language in Society* 16.49–90.

Van Berkel, A. 1948. *Travels in South America between the Berbice and Essequibo rivers and in Suriname: 1670–1689*. The Guiana Edition. Trans. by W. E. Roth. Georgetown: *Daily Chronicle*, 1948.

Whinnom, Keith. 1965. The origins of the European-based pidgins and creoles. *Orbis* 14.509–27.

Williamson, Kay. 1971. The Benue-Congo languages and Ịjọ. *Current trends in*

*linguistics*. Volume 3, ed. by Thomas Sebeok, 245–306. The Hague: Mouton.
———. 1975. The syntax of verbs of motion in Ịjọ. *Journal of African Languages* 2.150–54.
Wolff, Hans. 1959. Niger Delta languages. I: Classification. *Anthropological Linguistics* 1.32–53.

# Phonological Features Common to Some West African and Atlantic Creole Languages

*John Holm*

African influence on the phonology of the Atlantic creoles has been assumed at least since Van Name (1869–70:124). Schuchardt (1882:895) asserted that many of the phonological similarities among the Atlantic creoles of different lexical bases could be attributed to their common African substratum, which he demonstrated by comparing specific phonological features of Mbundu, São Tomé Creole Portuguese (CP), Papiamentu Creole Spanish, and Sranan Creole English. Although this century has brought a number of broad comparative studies of Atlantic creoles and West African languages, most have focused on syntax rather than phonology, with the notable exception of Boretzky (1983).

This paper deals with the importance of substrate influence on the phonology of the Atlantic creoles. It starts from the position that these creoles' phonology—like their lexicon, semantics, and syntax—is likely to reflect the influence of not only their substrate but also their superstrate and sometimes their adstrate languages, as well as creole-internal innovations, universals of adult second language acquisition, and the convergence of all or some of these factors. Having discussed the other sources of influence elsewhere (Holm 1988:105 ff.), I will focus here on the substrate. However, the mechanism of such influence on creole phonology requires some reference to universals, not in the sense of innate linguistic structures (Bickerton 1981) but rather the universals of adult second language acquisition that play a role in pidginization. Valdman (1983), building on the work of Schumann (1978) and others, makes a strong case for the parallels between pidginization and second language learning, claiming that both processes involve cognitive and linguistic universals. The crucial difference is that in the case of pidginization there is a restriction of information about the target language that is determined by the social situation (i.e., trade, slavery, etc.). In creolization, the pidgin-speaking community's restricted version of the target language is nativized, perpetuating many first language (or substrate) features that are already in the pidgin. Thus later monolingual creole speakers have features of African languages in their speech although they themselves have no knowledge of their forebears' native languages.

The actual mechanism for the retention of substrate features is no more mysterious than the mechanism for the transfer of first language features to a second language. These are the same processes, the only difference being that the latter occurs at the level of the individual while the former occurs at the level of the entire speech community. The kinds of phonological changes that can result from language contact were outlined some time ago by Weinreich (1953). Transfer results from a speaker identifying a phoneme in the second language with one in his first language and then subjecting it to the latter's phonetic rules. This can result in underdifferentiation (the merger of two sounds that are distinct in the second language but not in the first), overdifferentiation (the imposition of phonemic distinctions from the first language on allophones of a single phoneme in the second), or outright substitution (using a phoneme from the first language for a similar but distinct phoneme in the second). There can be similar transfer in intonation and syllabic structure.

Since there is evidence that creoles acquire their features from a number of different sources (superstrate, substrate, and adstrate languages; creole-internal innovations; universals of second language acquisition; and combinations of all or some of these), the question often arises as to which of these is the source of a particular feature. The only workable methodology is to gather the relevant data from each possible source; if similar features can be found in only one of these, that would appear to be the source of the creole feature in the absence of any alternative explanation. If similar features can be found in more than one potential source, then one must try to evenhandedly weigh the relative likelihood of each source (or the convergence of sources) having provided the creole feature in question. Of course, some fundamental difficulties impede each step. Our knowledge of the actual source dialects at the time of contact is seriously restricted in the case of the European superstrates and nearly nonexistent in the case of the African substrate languages, although we can infer a good deal from later varieties of related dialects. Information on a particular feature's distribution is needed not only in investigating possible substrate sources but also in weighing the possible influence of language universals. We can only hope that future research will be informed by better knowledge of the ethnolinguistic origins of the early speakers of Afro-American language varieties as well as by more detailed and accurate studies of the relevant African languages. However, we also need more focused comparative studies of language universals with a broader data base (e.g., Stassen 1985), including universal patterns in phonology. In the meantime, a great deal can still be accomplished with our limited current resources, particularly if we can come to see our primary objective as the advancement of creole studies as a whole, rather than the advancement of a particular theoretical position within creole studies.

One phonological feature common to some Atlantic creoles and West African languages is the coarticulated stops. The case for this feature having resulted from substrate influence is quite straightforward: these phonemes are not found in the European superstrates and they are relatively rare among the world's languages, so their presence in the creoles could hardly be attributed to the influence of language universals. However, a number of West African languages have both voiced and voiceless labial-velar coarticulated stops. Each contrasts with the corresponding labial or velar stop (e.g., Yoruba *gbọ́* 'to hear' versus *bọ́* 'to nourish' versus *gọ* 'to embarrass') and acts as a single consonant in the CV syllabic pattern. They are found in the eastern West Atlantic languages as well as in Mande, Kru, Gur, and Kwa languages, and some northern Bantu languages.

Saramaccan has both /gb/ and /kp/, often in words of African origin for flora and fauna; for example, *gbono-gbono* 'moss' and *kpasí* 'vulture' (Alleyne 1980:50 refers to them as implosives). Donicie and Voorhoeve (1963:v) note that Saramaccan /gb/ and /kp/ have the allophones [gw] and [kw], respectively; indeed, /kp/ has replaced /kw/ in some words of European origin such as *kpéi* 'slobber' (cf. Dutch *kwijlen*). According to Boretzky (1983:62), /gb/ and /kp/ in some dialects of Ewe correspond to /gw/ and /kw/ in other dialects of the same language. Saramaccan /gb/ and /kp/ often correspond to Sranan /gw/ and /kw/, respectively, as in *dagbe* versus *dagwe* 'type of snake' and *kpiñi* versus *kwinsi* 'squeeze' (cf. dialect *squinch*). Ndjuka also generally has /gw/ and /kw/ like Sranan, but while Sranan lacks the coarticulated stops, some Ndjuka speakers use variants of certain words with them, such as *gwé* or *gbé* 'leave' (cf. *go away*), *kwo-kwo* or *kpo-kpo* 'type of fish soup' (George Huttar, personal communication). Alleyne speculates that such pairs resulted from allophones in the earliest Surinamese creole(s), as well as in some of the African languages which were the mother tongues of some pidgin speakers. Boretzky's data on Ewe dialects seem to support this hypothesis. Alleyne further surmises that the [kw] allophone came to predominate and eventually replace [kp] in those varieties that remained in contact with Dutch, which lacks the coarticulated stop.

Bickerton claims that Saramaccan "preserves the coarticulated and prenasalized stops characteristic of many West African languages but of no other creoles" (1981:122). Besides their presence in Ndjuka, noted above, coarticulated stops are found in a number of other Atlantic creoles. The creole Portuguese of Príncipe has /gb/, which Günther (1973:41, 45) describes as a labial-velar plosive and treats as an integral part of the creole's phonological system. However, Ferraz (1975:155) treats it as an implosive which "is not a productive unit in the incorporation of borrowings, and is only found in archaic borrowings from African languages"; for example, *igbegbé* 'snail,' *igbɛ́* 'testicles.' Both /gb/ and /kp/ are part of the phonological systems of Krio (Fyle and Jones 1980:xix), Liberian (Singler 1981:25), and Nigerian Pidgin English (Mafeni 1965). Boretzky (1983:60) suggests that these may represent more recent (i.e., nineteenth-century) borrowings from neighboring African languages; indeed, most words with these phonemes do occur in loanwords, such as Liberian *gbasa jamba* 'cassava leaf' from Vai and *kpiti* 'fists' from Klao (Kru). Turner (1949:241) mentions the occasional use of coarticulated stops in Gullah, but Mufwene (1985:158) suggests that they "intruded only at a later stage into the original Gullah phonological system, that they did this essentially only with the African 'loan words' they occur in, and that they are not part of its core phonological inventory."

However, the origin of certain palatals in the Atlantic creoles is much more complicated. The case for African substrate languages having been the sole source of such palatalization is less convincing than in the above case of the coarticulated stops. While the evidence I give below suggests that substrate languages played a significant role in the development of some kinds of palatalization in the creoles, we can by no means exclude the influence of language universals or the influence of superstrate features that are now archaic or regional.

Palatalization, the raising of the tongue toward the hard palate, often occurs as a secondary feature of articulation, as in the initial sound of the standard British pronunciation of *dew* as opposed to *do*. Such palatalization affects several sounds in a number of the Atlantic creoles. Since the symbols used to indicate palatalization are not always consistent, table 1 is provided to make clear the notation used in the discussion below. In many languages there tends to be palatalization of obstruents immediately preceding front vowels, especially the high ones. For example, the Latin phoneme /k/ developed the allophone [tš] before the higher front vowels /i/ and /e/; in Italian /tš/ is now a phoneme, with contrasting pairs such as *ciarpa* /tšarpa/ 'scarf' versus *carpa* 'carp.' Similarly, Latin /g/ developed the allophone [dž] before higher front vowels but remained a velar elsewhere; in modern Italian there is a phonemic contrast between the two in *giusto* /džusto/ 'just' and *gusto* 'taste.'

Palatalization is also a feature of many African languages. For example, in a southern variety of Kongo the alveolar phonemes /t/, /s/, and /z/ all palatalize before the high front vowel /i/ to their respective alveopalatal allophones [tš],

**Table 1. Symbols Used to Indicate Palatalization**

| | | *Alveolar* | *Alveo-palatal* | *Palatalized Alveolar* | *Palatal* | *Velar* |
|---|---|---|---|---|---|---|
| Plosive | − voiced | t | tš | ty | ky (c) | k |
| | + voiced | d | dž | dy | gy (j) | g |
| Fricative | − voiced | s | š | sy | — | — |
| | + voiced | z | ž | zy | — | — |

[š], [ž]; for example /tobola/ 'to bore a hole' is phonetically [tobola], but /tina/ 'to cut' is phonetically [tšina] (Ferraz 1979:51). It should be noted that the alveopalatal affricate /tš/ can result from the palatalization of either the alveolar /t/ (as in Kongo) or the velar /k/ (as in Italian), just as its voiced counterpart /dž/ can result from the palatalization of either alveolar /d/ or velar /g/.

There can also be correspondence between palatals and palatalized alveolars; for example, /ky/ in some Twi dialects corresponds to /ty/ in other dialects of the same language, and a similar correspondence exists between their voiced counterparts /gy/ and /dy/ (Westermann and Bryan 1952:90). In general, African languages with palatal consonants fall into two broad categories; in the first, palatal and the corresponding nonpalatal sounds are allophones of the same phoneme (like late Latin [k] and [tš]); in the second, they constitute separate phonemes (like Italian /k/ and /tš/).

In Portuguese, as in Italian, alveopalatals are distinct phonemes that contrast with their nonpalatal counterparts, for example *chapa* 'metal plate' (/šapɐ/, earlier /tšapɐ/) versus *tapa* 'slap.' However, the creole Portuguese of São Tomé has developed a system in which its alveopalatals are in complementary distribution with their nonpalatal counterparts, apparently under the influence of substrate languages like southern Kongo discussed above. According to Ferraz (1979:41), São Tomé CP alveopalatals [tš], [dž], [š], and [ž] occur only before high front /i/, /ĩ/, and the semivowel /y/, while the corresponding nonpalatals [t], [d], [s], and [z] occur elsewhere. In words of Portuguese origin, nonpalatal alveolars have been palatalized before the high front vowels, as in *kẽci* /kẽtši/ 'hot' (‹ *quente*), *daji* /dadži/ 'age' (‹ *idade*), *dɔši* 'sweet' (‹ *doce*), *kwaži* 'almost' (‹ *quase*), while Portuguese alveopalatals in this position have remained alveopalatals. Elsewhere, however, Portuguese alveopalatals have been depalatalized, as in São Tomé CP *bisu* 'animal' (‹ *bicho*), *zɛmɛ* 'moan' (‹ *gemer*), while nonpalatal alveolars have remained the same. There are rela-

**Table 2. Palatalization in Caribbean Creole French**

| | Affricates | Palatalized Alveolars | Palatalized Velars | Depalatalized Velars |
|---|---|---|---|---|
| *tiens bien* 'hold on well' | tšɛ̃be | | kyɛ̃be | kɛ̃be |
| *coeur* 'heart' | tše | tyɔ | kyɛ | kɛ |
| *diable* 'devil' | džab | dyab | gyab | |
| *gueule* 'snout' | džɔl | | gyɔl | |

*Source:* Stein 1984:24–25.

tively few exceptions to these rules, although some are attested in words recently borrowed from Portuguese, such as *dozi* 'twelve' (‹ *doze*) replacing the older São Tomé *dɛš ku dosu* (literally, 'ten and two'). The parallels between the patterning of alveopalatals and nonpalatal alveolars in São Tomé CP and southern Kongo are striking, particularly in comparison with the patterning of these sounds in Portuguese. It seems clear that substrate languages like southern Kongo imposed this part of their phonological system on São Tomé CP.

In Papiamentu, some Spanish consonants followed by a palatal glide have been reinterpreted as alveopalatals, for example, *džente* 'tooth' (‹ *diente*) and *šete* 'seven' (*siete*). There has also been palatalization before /i/, as in *kušina* 'kitchen' (‹ *cocina*) and *duši* 'sweet' (‹ *dulce*).

In Negerhollands Creole Dutch, /s/ and /š/ appear to have merged into a single phoneme tending to have the allophone [š] before /i/ and [s] elsewhere, for example, [ši] or [si] 'his' (‹ Dutch *zijn*) but [pus] 'push' (‹ English *push*; Stolz 1986:72). Moreover, [t] varies with [ty] and [tš] before /i/, as in *biti* or *bitji* (i.e., [bityi]) and *bitši*, all 'a little bit' (‹ Dutch *beetje*; Bradford 1986:86).

Caribbean varieties of creole French tend to palatalize French /t/ and /d/ before the glide /y/, and /k/ and /g/ before any front vowel (all of which are high or mid in French, whether rounded or not). This can be seen in Goodman (1964) and in the examples in table 2, given in the notation discussed above. The forms are from the creoles of the Lesser Antilles, French Guyana, and Haiti; some are variants within the same dialect.

This pattern is partially parallel to Twi dialect variation between /ky/ and /ty/, on the one hand, and /gy/ and /dy/, on the other, as discussed above. In this context it is interesting that Lesser Antillean Creole French alveopalatals can be followed by /w/, as in *tšwizin* or *twizin* 'kitchen' (‹ *cuisine* /kɥizin/), and *zedžwi* or *zedwi* 'needle' (‹ *les aiguilles* /lɛz egɥiy/; Valdman 1978:53).

Although /w/ is back and nonpalatal, its lip rounding preserves a feature of the French high front rounded semivowel /ɥ/ and may correspond to similar labialization of certain monophonemic segments in Twi dialects represented as /kw/ (or /tw/) and /gw/ (or /dw/). Before /i/ these palatalize to [tšw] and [džw], respectively, whence the pronunciation of the language's name [tšwi] (Boretzky 1983:64; Westermann and Bryan 1952:90).

While New World varieties of Creole French have /s/ and /š/ as two distinct phonemes that generally correspond to their French counterparts, there is occasionally some variation, as in Haitian [šošɛ] or [sosyɛ] 'witch' (< *sorcière*). Early texts of Louisiana Creole French show alternation not only between /s/ and /š/ (e.g., *çassé* 'to hunt' from French *chasser* versus *chien* 'dog' from the same French word) but also between /z/ and /ž/ (e.g., *manzé* 'to eat' from French *manger*; Hall 1992). The Isle-de-France varieties of creole French in the Indian Ocean ordinarily have no alveopalatals, for example, Mauritian *sɛz* 'chair' (< French *chaise*) and *lazã* 'money' (< French *l'argent*; Valdman 1978:53). Stein (1984:24) notes that /š/ and /ž/ are not found in the Malagasy language of Madagascar, generally considered an important substrate language of the Isle-de-France creoles but not the New World varieties.

Certainly palatalization, like other aspects of the phonology of the creoles based on French and other languages, has been attributed to many influences besides substrate languages. In a comparative study of the phonology of French dialects, Canadian French, and the French-based creoles, Hull (1968, 1979) points to the importance of maritime French in the spread of a number of features. Canadian French has palatalized forms like /tšur/ 'heart' (< *coeur*) and *quienbin* 'catch, hold' (< CF *kyɛ̃be* idem). Hull notes that "palatalized /k/ and /g/ are found throughout northern France, and were virtually standard in the 17th century, so obviously would have occurred in MarF" (1968:258).

Alleyne (1980:56 ff.) deals with palatalization in a number of English creoles, representing the feature as /j/ instead of /y/. He traces the palatal plosives in the Surinamese creoles to two sources. First, /k/ and /g/ developed palatal allophones before front vowels, for example, Saramaccan *kína* or *tjína* 'food taboo' and *géi* or *djéi* 'to resemble' (De Groot 1981). Second, the alveopalatals /tš/ and /dž/ in English and Portuguese were reinterpreted as palatalized alveolars, as in *djombo* 'jump' (< English *jump*) and *tjuba* 'rain' (< Port. *chuva* idem). Since these also occurred before back (i.e., nonpalatalizing) vowels, a phonemic split took place because the palatalization alveolars now contrasted with velar stops, for example, Saramaccan *tjubí* 'hide' versus *kúbi* 'a kind of fish.' Later influence from English and Dutch established velar [k] before front vowels, particularly in Sranan, leading to variants such as *kina* or *tjina* 'leprosy.' It also led to forms such as *waki* 'watch' (via *watji*) and *wégi* 'wedge' (via *wédji*).

The Surinamese creoles generally have /s/ where English has /š/ (e.g., Sranan *sípi* 'ship,' *físi* 'fish'), but Ndjuka has the allophone [š] before /i/ and the glide /y/ (e.g., [šípi] 'ship,' [šyɛŋ] 'shame') and even /wi/ (e.g., [šwíti] 'pleasant' ‹ English *sweet*; George Huttar, personal communication), suggesting a connection to the palatalization of labialized consonants found in Twi and Caribbean Creole French, as discussed above.

In Gullah, Turner (1949:24) notes that "[c]—The voiceless palatal plosive . . . usually occurs . . . in positions where *ch* would be used [in General American English] . . . [and] before front vowels, including [a], as a subsidiary member of the [k]-phoneme. In this position it is sometimes slightly affricated." Its voiced counterpart [dž] is similarly used for English /dž/, especially among older speakers, as an allophone for /g/ in words like *jadn* 'garden' (Turner 1949:24). In Gullah, palatal [šy] or [š] can also replace /s/ before front vowels, as in [šyiəm] or [šʌm] 'see them,' much like allophones of /s/ in Ewe, Ibo, and other West African languages (Turner 1949:26, 247).

Alleyne (1980:58) points out that while decreolizing shift from palatalized stops to English alveopalatal affricates is virtually complete in Jamaican Creole English and other varieties in the Caribbean proper, there are lexical remnants of an earlier variation between velars and alveopalatals, for example, Jamaican *kitibu* or *tšitšibu* 'firefly' and *gaagl* or *džaagl* 'gargle.' As Cassidy and Le Page (1980:238) note, the intermediate form for the last was probably /gyaagl/. The palatals /ky/ and /gy/ occur in a number of Jamaican words (e.g., /kyaad/ 'card,' /gyaadn/ 'garden') in which they would not be expected because they do not have a high front vowel. Cassidy and Le Page (1980:lviii) note that in seventeenth-century British usage [k] and [g] occurred before back vowels like /ɔ:/ (preserved in Jamaican Creole English /kaad/ 'cord' and /gaadn/ 'Gordon'), while the palatals [ky] and [gy] occurred "before low-front [a] and [a:]." Note that while [a] is a low back vowel in American usage, it is indeed low front in Internation Phonetic Alphabet terms.

According to Harris (1987), Middle English /a/ had varying reflexes in early Modern English, including low front [æ] and mid front [ɛ], which led to the palatalization of adjacent velars. Despite the later backing of the vowel itself, Harris sees the preservation of this palatalization in an on-glide after the velar (e.g., *kyat* 'cat,' *gyas* 'gas') and an off-glide before it (e.g., *bayg* 'bag'). The latter is lexically selective in the Caribbean (e.g., *hayg* 'hag,' *blayk* 'black'; Warantz 1983:84) but regular in Ireland. Although Irish Gaelic has palatalized velars, this in itself "cannot explain the fact that the distribution of palatalization [e.g., in contact English in Ireland and the Caribbean] faithfully mirrors historical contrasts in the superstrate" (Harris 1992), leading to the conclusion that the relevant palatalization of historical velars took place in England itself and "was well represented in the speech of English colonists in both Ireland and the New World. If the West African and Irish Gaelic substrata did make any contribution to the establishment of the feature in the emergent contact vernaculars, this is likely to have been at best reinforcing or 'preservative' " (Harris 1987).

Certain Surinamese Creole English words also seem likely to have been based on such archaic or regional British forms as *kyabbage* 'cabbage' (cf. Saramaccan *tjábisi* idem). Jamaican has the word *john-crow* /džánkra/ 'buzzard,' which Cassidy and Le Page (1980:250) derive from *carrion crow* via a shift of the initial sound from /ky/ to /ty/ to /dy/ to /dž/. Part of this process may have occurred in Suriname (cf. Sranan *djankro* and Ndjuka and Saramaccan *djankoo* idem), after which the form with the palatalized alveolar spread to Jamaica and elsewhere via diffusion.

In the case of palatalization, evidence for substrate influence on the Atlantic creoles must be considered in conjunction with the converging influence of language universals and influence from superstrate features that are now archaic or regional. The case for the last is clear in both the French and English creoles; the Portuguese creoles of the Gulf of Guinea preserve the palatals in the superstrate's phonemic inventory, but they have reorganized the possible occurrence of these sounds according to the rules of allophony in their substrate languages. The latter phenomenon represents fairly straightforward evidence of substrate influence on creole phonology, as does the preservation of coarticulated stops in the creoles, which can be attributed to no other possible source. Bickerton's suggestion that substrate influence can occur on the level of phonology and lexicon but not on the level of syntax must be rejected as both illogical and implausible.

Constraints on length preclude a closer examination of other phonological features common to many of the Atlantic creoles that suggest the retention of features in substrate African languages. These include the inventory of both vowels and consonants in basilectal varieties, and particularly syllabic structure rules. Further evidence of this can be found in certain aspects of the creoles' nasal vowels, remnants of vowel harmony, prenasalized stops, and phonemic tone, as well as the alternation of certain apical and labial consonants (Holm 1988:105–43).

*Acknowledgments*

I thank the following colleagues for their helpful comments on an earlier draft of the material on which the present paper is based: Norbert Boretzky, Hans den Besten, Luiz Ivens Ferraz, Morris Goodman, John Harris, George Huttar, R. B. Le Page, Philippe Maurer, Salikoko Mufwene, John Singler, and Sarah Grey Thomason. Of course, I alone am responsible for any shortcomings.

**References**

Alleyne, Mervyn. 1980. *Comparative Afro-American: An historical-comparative study of English-based Afro-American dialects of the New World*. Ann Arbor: Karoma.

Bickerton, Derek. 1981. *Roots of language*. Ann Arbor: Karoma.

Boretzky, Norbert. 1983. *Kreolsprachen, substrate und sprachwandel*. Wiesbaden: Harrassowitz.

Bradford, William. 1986. Virgin Islands Dutch Creole: A morphological description. *Amsterdam Creole Studies* 9.73–99.

Cassidy, F. G., and R. B. Le Page. 1980. *Dictionary of Jamaican English*. Cambridge: Cambridge University Press.

De Groot, A. 1981. *Woordregister Saramakaans-Nederlands*. Paramaribo.

Donicie, Antoon, and Jan Voorhoeve. 1963. *De Saramakaanse Woordenschat*. Amsterdam: Bureau voor Taalonderzoek in Suriname van de Universiteit van Amsterdam.

Ferraz, Luiz Ivens. 1975. African influences on Principense Creole. *Miscelânea Luso-Africana: Colectânea de estudos coligidos*, ed. by M. Valkhoff et al., 153–64. Lisbon: Junta de Investigações Científicas do Ultramar.

———. 1979. *The creole of São Tomé*. Johannesburg: Witwatersrand University Press.

Fyle, C. N., and E. D. Jones. 1980. *A Krio-English dictionary*. Oxford: Oxford University Press/Sierra Leone University Press.

Goodman, Morris. 1964. *A comparative study of creole French dialects*. The Hague: Mouton.

Günther, Wilfried. 1973. *Das portugiesische kreolisch der Ilha do Príncipe*. Marburg: Marburger Studien zur Afrika- und Asienkunde.

Hall, Gwendolyn. 1992. *Africans in colonial Louisiana: The development of Afro-Creole culture in the eighteenth century*. Baton Rouge: Louisiana State University Press.

Harris, John. 1987. On doing comparative reconstruction with genetically unrelated languages. *Papers from the Seventh International Conference on Historical Lin-*

*guistics*, ed. by A. G. Ramat, O. Carruba, and G. Bernini, 267–82. Amsterdam: John Benjamins.

Holm, John. 1988. *Pidgins and creoles*. Cambridge: Cambridge University Press.

Hull, Alexander. 1968. The origins of New World French phonology. *Word* 24.255–69.

———. 1979. On the origin and chronology of the French-based creoles. *Readings in creole studies*, ed. by Ian Hancock et al., 201–15. Ghent: E. Story-Scientia.

Mafeni, Bernard. 1965. *Some aspects of the phonetics and phonology of Nigerian Pidgin*. M. Litt. thesis, Edinburgh University.

Mufwene, Salikoko. 1985. The linguistic significance of African proper names in Gullah. *De Nieuwe West-Indische Gids* 59.149–66.

Schuchardt, Hugo. 1882. Kreolische Studien I. Ueber das Negerportugiesische von S. Thomé (Westafrika). *Sitzungsberichte der kaiserlichen Akademie der Wissenschaften zu Wien* 101.889–917.

Schumann, John. 1978. *The pidginization process: A model for second language acquisition*. Rowley, Mass.: Newbury House.

Singler, John. 1981. *An introduction to Liberian English*. East Lansing: Michigan State University African Studies Center.

Stassen, L. 1985. *Comparison and universal grammar*. Oxford: Basil Blackwell.

Stein, Peter. 1984. *Kreolisch und Französisch*. Tübingen: Max Niemeyer.

Stolz, Thomas. 1986. *Gibt es das kreolische Sprachwandelmodell? Vergleichende Grammatik des Negerholländischen*. Frankfurt am Main: Verlag Peter Lang.

Turner, Lorenzo. 1949. *Africanisms in the Gullah dialect*. Chicago: University of Chicago Press.

Valdman, Albert. 1978. *Le créole: structure, statut et origine*. Paris: Klincksieck.

———. 1983. Creolization and second language acquisition. *Pidginization and creolization as language acquisition*, ed. by Roger Andersen, 212–34. Rowley, Mass.: Newbury House.

Van Name, Addison. 1869–70. Contributions to creole grammar. *Transactions of the American Philological Association* 1.123–67.

Warantz, Elissa. 1983. The Bay Islands English of Honduras. *Central American English*, ed. by John Holm, 71–94. Heidelberg: Groos.

Weinreich, Uriel. 1953. *Languages in contact: Findings and problems*. The Hague: Mouton.

Westermann, Diedrich, and M. Bryan. 1952. *Handbook of African Languages*. Volume 2. *Languages of West Africa*. Oxford: Oxford University Press.

# Vowel Length in Afro-American: Development or Retention?

*Hazel Carter*

This paper concerns a problem raised by Alleyne (1980) in connection with the vowel system of Afro-American as a whole, and Jamaican, Guyanese, and Gullah in particular; namely, vowel length. Very few Afro-American languages have vowel length; hence, where it occurs, it needs explanation, in terms either of development within the languages themselves or of retention from English or African languages. Having examined a wide spectrum of comparative evidence, Alleyne concludes:

> It seems that the earliest forms of Afro-American dialects made no distinction between long and short vowels. Long vowels in Saramaccan and Ndjuka . . . are a later development as a result of the coalescence of two vowels after the application of a vowel epenthesis rule and an intervocalic liquid deletion rule. . . . *English syllabic nuclei, which at the time of initial contact between Englishmen and Africans were differentiated by length were interpreted as nuclei of neutral length.* It is not clear whether tense/lax distinctions existed in the English of the time. If they did, they were apparently not transferred into Afro-American; so that pairs, like English *fit, feet* . . . became undifferentiated. (1980:39; my emphasis)

After observing that modern Jamaican and Guyanese forms "reflect the earlier absence of quantity as a basis of phonemic distinction," he continues (41):

> *phonemic length began to be introduced into Jamaican and Guyanese as a result of English influence*. . . . Quantity was introduced into the systems of Jamaican and Guyanese, but the associated quality distinction (high/lower high; tense/lax) is less well established . . . the difference that exists between 'fit' and 'feet' or 'pull' and 'pool' is exclusively one of length at one pole of the Jamaican continuum [i.e., the basilect].

In sum, then, Alleyne's hypothesis is that the earliest form(s) of Afro-American had no phonemic vowel length distinction and that in varieties such as Jamaican, vowel length was introduced through the influence of English.

The principal focus of this paper is Jamaican Creole English, hereinafter referred to simply as "Jamaican." I first want to comment on two premises of Alleyne's hypothesis, namely, that in the early stages of Afro-American there was no vowel length distinction, and that Jamaican thus developed it at a later stage. There is very good evidence for the former in the vowel systems of Krio and Pidgin (i.e., West African Pidgin English), which have neither phonemic nor phonetic vowel length,[1] and I have elsewhere (Carter 1987b) given support to the view that the ancestor of Krio and Pidgin was probably the ancestor of at least some transatlantic creoles. Given this, the second point to some extent follows; however, as Alleyne himself stresses (1980:33), he does not postulate *one* common ancestor, and he lists four possible interpretations of the data, of which he prefers the following: "the common source is . . . a common substrate structure . . . a common set of structural features" which "left traces, to varying degrees," in different parts of the Afro-American language area. My viewpoint differs somewhat from Alleyne's in that I prefer not to minimize the *variation in the substrate,* and particularly the fact that African languages, even those closely related, sometimes have considerable differences in their phonological systems. I suggest that this variation persisted, in the form of competing systems or subsystems, in the phonology of the first Afro-Americans, and that its effects can be discerned even today. In the case of Jamaica, this situation has been repeated or reinforced by later, nineteenth-century input from speakers of African languages.

Second, I find it rather difficult to accept Alleyne's explanation of Jamaican vowel length as due to the influence of English, and after reviewing the evidence, I will propose a different conclusion. In order to do this, it will be helpful to explain what I understand by vowel length, examine the nature of "vowel length" in Jamaican, and compare this both with what is known of the English system of the relevant period and with certain phonological features of the African languages relevant to the case, especially in regard to assimilation of adoptives (these points will not necessarily be dealt with in this order). In an interesting reversal of this process, we have the history of African words coming into Jamica in the nineteenth century.

## Reflexes of English Vowels in Jamaican

Modern United Kingdom Standard English (hereinafter referred to as UKSE)[2] now has no phonemic length distinctions; earlier forms of English, such as Middle English (ME) of the eleventh to fifteenth centuries, had such distinctions, but during the Great Vowel Shift they were replaced by distinctions of quality. In particular, four of the long vowels of ME were diphthongized, /iː/

→ /ay/, /u:/ → /aw/, /ɔ:/ → /əw/, and /a:/ → /ey/.[3] Other long vowels were raised, for example, /e:/ → /i/ and /o:/ → /u/, and distinguished again by quality from the (formerly) short vowels /e/ → /ɛ/ and /o/ → /ɒ/. Alleyne's hypothesis requires that English should have still maintained the length distinctions at the time when Jamaican, Guyanese, and Gullah began to acquire or develop them. Jamaica was settled from the early seventeenth century, so at least some quantity distinctions should have survived into this period, and perhaps even longer. We do not really know when phonemic length finally vanished from English; however, according to Alleyne, "it would seem from our Afro-American comparative work that there may have been no qualitative distinction, but only length distinction, for mid front vowels of 16th–17th century English" (1980:43). That is, vowel length is considered to have persisted in at least part of the English vowel system during the formative period of Jamaican.

There are certain problems in the concept of vowel length which will be taken up later; meanwhile, according to the *Dictionary of Jamaican English*, by Cassidy and Le Page (1981; hereafter *DJE*), there are three long vowels in Jamaican: /ii/, /aa/, and /uu/. I have replaced the phonetic brackets used by the *DJE* with phoneme slashes in appropriate cases, and for UKSE I am using the transcription by Ladefoged (1975), replacing *DJE* [a:] with /a/, [ɔ:] with /ɔ/, and [ɒ:] with /ɒ/, since I hold to the view that modern UKSE has no phonemic vowel length.

Jamaican /ii/ corresponds to UKSE /i/, derived from several ME sources, including /e:/ and /ɛ:/ and the diphthong /ei/, for example, /bliid/ 'bleed' and /bliit/ 'bleat,' to which I would add /disiivin/ 'deceiving.' Thus it seems clear that the raising of /e:/ to /i/ had occurred. The *DJE* reports some variation in /i/ and /ii/ usage, such as [aslip ~ asliip] 'asleep,' said to reflect similar variations in English of the seventeenth century.[4] The examples given are all of stressed final syllables. The [ii] is, however, also the result of a development /ui/ → [wii] within Jamaican: /du + it/ → [dwiit] 'do it,' which is tentatively attributed to the influence of Akan initial /dw/; the vowel length, however, is not explained.

The /ii/ does *not* correspond to the output of ME /i:/; it is quite clear from forms such as /hays/ 'ice' and /tayl/ 'tile' that the diphthongization of /i:/ → /ay/ had already taken place.

Jamaican /aa/ corresponds to two vowels in modern UKSE: (1) /a/ ← ME /a/, lengthened (still in the ME period) before certain consonants, hence /paas/ 'pass,' /yaad/ 'yard,' /haaf/ 'half,' /faada/ 'father'; and (2) /ɔ/ ← ME /au/ (or /aw/), hence /braad/ 'broad,' /aak/ or /haak/ 'hawk,' /yaak/ 'York,' /laan/ 'lawn,' /aal/ 'all.' (Diphthongal pronunciations are said to have survived in English until late in the seventeenth century.) Some cases, according to the

*DJE*, represent a seventeenth-century lengthened variant of ME short /o/ or /a/, as in /klaat/ 'cloth' and /daag/ 'dog.' The *DJE* also notes variation between /a/ and /aa/ in, for example, /daag ~ dag/ 'dog'; several, though not all, of these are of final stressed syllables. A similar example is [káakrwóč] 'cockroach,' in which [aa] corresponds to /ɒ/ of UKSE ← (unlengthened) ME /o/; compare [kákakrwó] 'the cock is crowing,' in which the same UKSE vowel is represented by Jamaican [a].

The Jamaican /aa/ does *not* correspond otherwise to the descendant of ME /a:/, which in UKSE is /ey/ and in Jamaican is /ye/, as in /fyes/ 'face.' The *DJE* attributes this to Northern and Scots dialect usage, but in any case, the Jamaican form suggests either a date of entry after the diphthongization(s) in English or an independent, though parallel, development of a rising diphthong as a means of differentiation from English /æ/ → Jamaican /e/. To me this further suggests that length distinction was unlikely to have remained in English, and that what Jamaicans heard was a qualitative distinction.

The Jamaican /uu/ corresponds to the UKSE /u/, for which the *DJE* gives examples /ontruut/ 'untruth' and /ruudnis/ 'rudeness (sex)'; compare also /kúuldringk/ 'cool drink' and, from personal data, /brúumwíd/ 'broomweed.' UKSE /u/ is derived from, among others, ME /o:/, /ou/, and /eu/.

The /uu/ does *not* correspond to the output of ME /u:/, which in UKSE is /aw/; in Jamaican the reflex of this is /ow/, as in /hows/ 'house.' The *DJE* says that

> ME [u:] began to be diphthongized in most English dialects (but not in Scots) in the fifteenth century to [ʊu] and the first element was progressively lowered giving [əʊ] or [ʌ̈ʊ] in the sixteenth and seventeenth centuries. Jamaican [oʊ] is thus close to the seventeenth-century Southern or later Northern English usage. (liv)

Again, one has to assume either a participation in the English development or a similar parallel one. Either way, there is no necessity to postulate a still-existing length distinction in English. According to the *DJE*, "There is a certain amount of alternation between JC /uu/ and /u/, particularly in final position," but no examples are given.

Several points arise from this brief survey.

Firstly, it seems quite clear that *the development of the qualitative differences that were to replace phonemic length as distinctive features was well on its way in the sixteenth and seventeenth centuries*. Jamaican is therefore at least as likely to represent perceived differences of quality as of length, and in some cases clearly does so. I am willing to concede that both types of distinction may have existed concurrently for a time, such that the output of ME /e:/ was long as well as high, namely [i:]; and there is no doubt that many speakers of English still have an entrenched belief in a length distinction, for example, that the "ee" of *seen* is a long vowel and that the "i" of *sin* is a short one.[5] (Additionally, there are certain vowels, such as [ʌ], derived from the former short vowels, which are not found in stressed final position and hence are felt to be somehow different from those which may be found in this position; the difference is often thought to be one of length.) The fact is that we really do not know when the process was completed; all we know is that *phonemic* length was certainly on its way out during the relevant period.

Secondly, the /ui/ → [wii] development in Jamaican has not happened in English; it is an internal Jamaican change and, as I will show, is entirely typical of African language phonology.

Thirdly, the variation between "long" and "short" vowels in a number of words suggests either multiple (dialectal) origins, as suggested by the *DJE*,[6] or instability in the system, possibly from the coexistence of competing subsystems.[7]

## Long and Double Vowels: "Length" in African Languages

Vowel length is a vexed question, and the definition of "long vowel" causes considerable difficulty. I take the usual starting point, that a *long vowel* (or diphthong) should function as the nucleus of a single syllable, while if there are two syllabic nuclei, it is a case of *juxtaposed* or *double vowels*. This, of course, throws the burden back onto the definition of "syllable."

For a tone language, the definition "tone bearing unit" may be used. This still raises problems when the tonal system is a complex one in which rising and falling tones are distinguished, but for languages with a clear High, Low, or Mid surface tone distinction, the definition serves very well. In such cases, vowel "length" can often be analyzed as juxtaposed vowels, each serving as the nucleus of a separate syllable, as in Angolan Kongo, a two-tone language. Here it can be demonstrated that, in surface realizations, all four theoretical possibilities exist: HL, LL, LH, and HH:[8]

| | | |
|---|---|---|
| HL: | *-sáalá* | 'remain' |
| LL: | *kasaala* | 'that he may remain' |
| LH: | *Nzaámbi* | 'God' |
| HH: | *(osìnga) ssáál' (ee?)* | '(are you going) to stay behind(?)' |

At least four types of vowel system (in respect of length) are represented among African languages.

*True phonemic long vowels, contrasting with short vowels*. For true phonemic vowel length we may take a language such as Arabic, in which a long vowel is the nucleus of one syllable and contrasts with a short vowel, as in *dira:satun* 'studying' versus *madrasatun* 'school.' It is not possible to give a precise definition for "syllable" in Arabic, only to rely on a first language speaker's assessment of how many syllables there are in a word. It should be noted that the placement of vowel length is not predictable from any phonological feature, such as position in the word, though it is, of course, predictable in many cases from patterns of derivation.

*Phonetic but not phonemic length*. Frequently vowel length in a language of this kind is *positionally conditioned,* as in Swahili and many other Bantu languages, in which the penultimate syllable of a prepausal word is lengthened, usually with compensating reduction of the final vowel (often whispered or even deleted): *asante sa:na* 'thank you very much,' *kari:bu* 'come in (singular),' *karibu:ni* 'come in (plural).'

*Double vowels; no phonemic length distinction*. Twi (Twii) is one of the many West African languages with this system: *áa* relative marker, 'which, who' (cf. *a* 'when'), *naa* marker of past continuous (cf. *na* 'mother'), *ntáabóo* 'planks,' *kyé ǹ séé* 'dish.'

*No phonemic or phonetic length; no double vowels*. My firsthand knowledge of West African languages of the relevant area does not include any of this type; one possible candidate is Margi, a language of northern Nigeria.[9] Very important for the purposes of this study, however, is that both West African Pidgin English (WAPE) and Sierra Leone Krio exhibit this kind of vowel system: WAPE *àkpara, kwara* 'harlot' ‹ Efik *akparaa*[10]; WAPE *nkandá*, K *kandá* 'skin, hide' (cf. Kongo *nkkaanda*); WAPE, K *watá* 'water' ‹ English.

Among the modern descendants of the African languages spoken by the first Afro-Americans, the great majority are tonal; many have CV syllabic systems and are syllable timed; most important, the majority have double rather than phonemically long vowels. It is reasonable to suppose these shared characteristics are a common heritage and also characterized the African languages of the sixteenth and seventeenth centuries.[11] Present-day Mende, Twi, Ewe, and Yoruba, for example, are all languages of this kind.

This is not to say that double and phonetically long vowels cannot coexist in a language—they often do. In Shona,[12] [téér:ra] 'listen!' consists of four syllables, of which the third is long. Each [é] is the nucleus of a separate syllable, and so is [é:]; however, [é:] is not phonemically distinct from [é] but derives its length from its position within the word, as penultimate syllable. *Stylistic lengthening* is also found; again in Shona, a *final* vowel may be lengthened for stylistic reasons, as in shouting over a distance, in greetings, and in other kinds of formal speech or chanting, such as praise poetry. Double vowels and vowel length are very fragile creatures, as will become abundantly clear by the end of this paper. In Bantu languages, for instance, a surface double vowel can often be interpreted as the reflex of a proto-Bantu *VV; but the double protovowel has shifted to a single vowel over a large area in Guthrie's zones B, L, M, F, E, G, and P—that is, a central belt running from the west and curving upward to the northeast (see Guthrie 1967:68, topogram 3). Conversely, modern languages often show double or long vowels which are reflexes of proto-Bantu *V. A very common source of this is a phonological rule *V → V:/__NC; that is, V is lengthened when it occurs before NC. This has taken place in Angolan Kongo, a language very relevant to the Afro-American situation; however, lengthening in this case has given rise to surface vowel doubling *phonetically* indistinguishable from the double vowels derived from a double protovowel or underlying *VV. The derivation from *VNC can, however, be detected in some cases by the following argument.

Verbs in Angolan Kongo belong to one of two tone classes, distinguished by having high tone on the first stem syllable (TCI) or the second (TCII). (The H in TCI is a "moving" tone, which shifts one syllable to the left in certain conditions.) When verbs of TCI acquire a third stem syllable, they also acquire a second H: *-sála* 'work' (contrast *-natá* 'carry'), *-sádilá* 'work for; use' (contrast *-natína* 'carry for'), *-nóka* 'rain,' and *-nókená* 'rain on.' Some verbs with [VV] show this third H (*-sáalá* 'remain,' *-yéelá* 'be ill'), suggesting analysis as /CVCVCa/ stem, C2 =0. Verbs with [VVNC], however, do not show a second H until the stem builds up to *four* surface syllables: *-váanga* 'make, do,' *-váangamá* 'get made, get done'; *-súumba* 'buy,' *-súumbilá* 'buy for'; which suggests analysis of the unextended stem as /CVNCa/. The tone assignment is apparently made before the "lengthening" rule comes into operation. The analysis is supported by Guthrie's comparative series (CS) for these items: **-cád-* 'work' and **-nók-* 'rain,' but **-çíád-* 'remain,' **-béėd-* 'be ill,' and **-páng-* 'make,' **-cúmb-* 'buy.'

This exercise illustrates some of the problems raised by vowel length in African languages: at the underlying or systematic phonemic level Kongo has no long vowels, and on the surface it has only double vowels; in between, however, hence in a very abstract sense, it can be said to have vowel length.

Even within synchronic systems, vowel doubling and vowel length are subject to fluctuation. Double vowels derived from both the "long" and underlying double vowels of Kongo are subject to reduction in certain morphophonological conditions, of which I cite one combination: the first of the double vowels must be in the first stem syllable, and the stem must, by addition of postposed morphemes, be increased so that three syllables follow the affected vowels, as in the following, in which the extra syllables are provided by radical extension: *-váanga* 'make, do,' *-váangamá* 'get done/made,' *-vángakaná* 'be feasible'; *-dyaáta* 'tread, walk,' *-dyaátisa* 'drive (a car),' *nn-dyatísilu* 'way of running (an organization).' In the next case they are due to compounding (which may be considered a subset of the same rule): *Ndzaámbi* 'God,' *Ndzambi-ámphuungu* 'the High God (lit. God of the highest point).' The reduction does not apply to elements occurring later in the stem, as in *bévvaangaangá* 'they make,' *dívvangakanaangá* 'it is feasible.' There are other exclusions, however. Whether these should be regarded as blocking conditions for the P-rule rather than additional P-rules resulting in contraction, the fact remains that vowel length is very variable, even within one relatively homogeneous system. This point will become important when we examine Jamaican vocabulary derived from Angolan Kongo.

What I have said concerning variability within a system applies even more so when one considers the dialects of a language. Certain Kongo dialects do not operate the long vowel *V → VV/__NC rule and hence cannot be said to have long vowels at any level. Some Shona speakers lengthen the penultimate much more than others, and in some dialects certain particles, such as the question indicator *heré?,* show none, or show it on the final.

## Reanalysis of Jamaican Vowel Length

In approaching vowel length in Jamaican, despite difficulties of interpretation of surface pitch phenomena, I work from the hypothesis that it is a tone language and that pitch changes can therefore be correlated with syllabicity. Alleyne (1980:70–72) notes Lawton's (1963) correlation of "stressed long vowel" with falling pitch, as in *máatá* 'mortar' and *bíitá* 'beater.' [13] Here, obviously, I concur rather with the analyses of DeCamp (1961) and Bailey (1966) in interpreting this as a double vowel with HL tone pattern, each vowel being the nucleus of a separate syllable.

If this is accepted, *Jamaican has no long vowels, but rather double vowels,* each functioning as the nucleus of a separate syllable. Thus /máatá/, /bíitá/, and /káakrwóč/ all have three syllables. (My own very limited acquaintance with Jamaican leads me to believe that phonetic vowel length *does* occur but is a stylistic device for emphasis.) Jamaican, then, shares two features with many

African languages but not with English: it is tonal, and it has double rather than long vowels.

There is perhaps another shared phonological feature. In many African languages there operates a principle of *maintenance of syllable count,* such that if a sound shift results in deletion or contraction of a segment functioning as a syllabic nucleus, it is compensated for by doubling of an adjacent segment, thus providing a substitute nucleus. One typical example is that of Zambian Tonga, in which nominal prefixes with vowels /u/ and /i/ regularly show such a change: /mu+ofu/ → [mooh$^w$u] 'blind person,' /mú+embo/ → [mwéembo] 'trumpet,' /mí+embo/ → [myéembo] 'trumpets.' It seems to me that the Jamaican sound change /ui/ → [wii] is precisely comparable and not matched by anything in English, which has not the requisite syllabic structure to need "compensation" of this kind.[14]

I suggest that these are not chance similarities, mere accidental typological resemblances, but *survivals of a phonological system in which there was, indeed, no phonemic vowel length, but some of whose speakers had first languages with double vowels and a very strong syllabic identity, plus—and possibly because of—a systematic exploitation of pitch differences in terms of tone*.

It is not yet clear whether Jamaican should be classed as syllable timed, though to my ear it is certainly more so than UKSE. Stress seems to play a part in the suprasegmental system, but not as a basis for stress timing. One thing does seem fairly clear, however: syllabification tends to be on the African pattern of CV, open syllables unless the consonant is word-final. Thus in /káakrwóč/ the syllables are /káa+krwóč/ rather than the English /kók + rəuč/. English, by contrast, is stress timed and intonational, permitting CVC syllables, and no longer has any phonemic length distinctions. However, as already noted, English still has *phonetic* length, which is relevant in the context of contact between speakers of different language types in that *perception* is involved, not merely—and perhaps not even principally—the underlying system.

## Phonetic Length in Modern English

Phonetic vowel length in UKSE is governed by a set of phonological variables, summarized as follows.

*Stress.* Stressed syllables tend to have greater length: in *pity* [pɪtɪ], the first, stressed, vowel is longer than the final, unstressed, vowel, though both are of the same quality.

*Number of syllables in foot.* English is a stress-timed language in which the unit is a foot, consisting of a stressed syllable in initial position plus any unstressed syllables up to the next stressed syllable (which begins another foot). Feet are of roughly equal length, so that the greater the number of syllables which have to be accommodated within the foot, the less length they will have: *'come* in *'Do* ¦ *'come* ¦ *'too* will be longer than in *'Don't* ¦ *'come to the* ¦ *'door,* since in the first case, *come* occupies a whole foot, while in the second, two more unstressed syllables are squeezed into the foot.

*Closed or open syllable.* Open syllables have longer vowels or diphthongs, thus *fee, car, for, moo, fur, my, coy, cow,* and *new,* when uttered in isolation, have longer vowels and diphthongs than *feet, cart, fort, mood, furl, mite, coin, frowst,* and *cute.* (Vowels derived from the historically short vowels do not occur in stressed open syllables; for example, the vowels of *fit, fat, got, put, but,* and *bet.*)

*Voicing of following consonant.* Vowels and diphthongs before a voiced consonant are longer than those before a voiceless consonant: compare *feed/feet, card/cart, form/fort, mood/moot, furl/first, mile/mike, frown/frowst, cube/cute, fin/fit, fad/fat, hog/hock, pull/push, buzz/bus, beg/bet.* (When a nasal is followed by a consonant, this rather than the nasal is the determining factor; cf. *bend/bent.*)

## Adoptives from English in African Languages: Assimilation or Innovation?

I have demonstrated (Carter 1987a) that modern African languages with double vowels assimilate certain English vowels to their own systems as *double vowels;* the determining factors are that the vowel in question must be stressed, and it must also occur regularly (especially in citation context) as sole occupant of the metrical foot. Moreover, the so-called short vowels /ɪ/, /æ/, etc., are treated thus, not merely the long vowels /i/, /u/, etc. Thus, final stressed syllables, including monosyllabics, which occupy a whole foot in citation forms are assimilated as double vowels in languages like Twi and Yoruba, while stressed vowels which do not occupy a whole foot, such as the first of a di- or trisyllabic, are assimilated as short vowels. The following Yoruba examples illustrate this: *fíimu* 'film,' *páanu* 'pan, corrugated iron,' *búréeki* 'brake,' but *lɛ́ta* 'letter,' *ópuna* 'opener.'

Languages with penultimate lengthening tend rather to assimilate stressed vowels as one vowel, whatever the context; most, of course, add epenthetic vowels to closed final syllables, so that the vowel is now penultimate and meets the condition for positional lengthening, as in Shona *ródhi* [ró:di] 'road,' *róri* [ró:ri] 'lorry'; compare *rótari* [róta:ri] 'lottery.'

In none of these cases has English influence been suggested. Yoruba, Twi, and others have not changed their phonological systems under pressure from English; they have introduced no new feature (apart from accepting some previously uncommon tone patterns). Double vowels, penultimate lengthening, or both already existed in these languages before English adoptives came on the scene; what the speakers have done is to assimilate perceived length to the already existing system.

Likewise, if the double vowel interpretation of length in Jamaican is accepted, this opens the way for an explanation in terms of *assimilation of some feature of English to an African system,* rather than influence in the sense of introduction of a feature directly from English. As I have already suggested, the existence of the phonemic length feature in English of the period is at the very least open to doubt; and even if it should be proved beyond doubt, I suggest that *Jamaican did not take over the feature of length, but adapted it as a double vowel*. It is noticeable that the examples of variation in the *DJE* nearly all concern final stressed syllables: [aslip ~ asliip] 'asleep,' [dag ~ daag] 'dog,' [juju ~ juu] 'dew.'

## Jamaican Kumina Language

During the mid-nineteenth century there was an influx of indentured laborers from Africa, principally from Sierra Leone and Angola (see particularly Schuler 1980 for documentation). The Angolan group left strong traces in the Kumina religious sect, including the use of many items of vocabulary derived from Kongo and, less so, Kimbundu. As already shown, Angolan Kongo has double vowels, and though there is much variation, the distribution is according to clear phonological rules.

Among the descendants of these Kongo speakers the situation can only be called chaotic. Words with double vowels in modern Kongo have been contracted in Kumina; occasionally there is the reverse, but more often than not there is no stability and the variation is not regular. Even in the speech of one person, one will find variations such as *bízi*/*bíizi* 'meat, flesh; (body)' ‹ Kongo *mmbízi;* nowhere in Kongo does this have a double vowel. Table 1 gives a list of words of which the etyma are reasonably certain, showing the modern Kongo form. Pitch or tone for the Kumina forms varies greatly, and I have not marked it. It may, however, be stated that the pitch patterns do not regularly correspond to the tone patterns of the present-day Kongo item, nor do the long or double vowels always exhibit the customary Jamaican fall; for example, *booló* by the side of *bóólo* 'bread, cake' (the second closer to Kongo).[15]

**Table 1. Kumina Forms and Meanings with Their Kongo Etyma**

| *Kumina Form* | *Kongo Form* | *Kumina Meaning* | *Kongo Meaning* |
|---|---|---|---|
| Kumina V ‹ Kongo VV | | | |
| *gandu* | *ngaándu* | alligator | crocodile |
| *gwandul* | *waándu* | red peas | peabean |
| *maza* | *maáza* | water | water |
| *mazi* | *maázi* | oil | oil |
| *mwana* | *mwaána* | child | child |
| *ngonde, ngombi* | *ngoónde* | moon | moon |
| *panga (mi)* | *umphaáni* | give me | give me |
| *sembele (mbele)* | *sseéngele* | machete | axe |
| *yeto* | *yeéto* | the whole nation | we, us |
| Variable | | | |
| 1. Reflex of Kongo VV: | | | |
| *(m)be(e)le* | *mmbeéle* | knife, machete | knife |
| *bilo(o)ngo* | *nlloóngo** | obeah | medicine |
| *(m)bo(o)lo* | *mmboólo* | bread | bread; cake |
| *bo(o)ngo, liboongo* | *mmbóongo* | money | goods, money |
| *(n)du(u)mba* | *nnduúmba* | girl | girl |
| *fwi(i)di* | *fwíidi* | dead | s/he is dead |
| *go(o)mbe, ko(o)mbo, ko(o)nve, -i, kinkhombo* | *nkhóombo*<br>*ngoombé* | cow; goat | goat<br>cow |
| *ji(i)mbu* | *ndzíimbu* | money | money |
| *(n)ke(e)nto, kent* | *nkkéentó* | woman | woman |
| *ki(i)nzu* | *kiinzú* | bowl, pipe; pots; black | pot (sing.) |
| *ku(u)nga* | *nkkuúnga* | talk/sing; play drum | song |
| *kukwela, -e, kukweele* | *kukyéele* | morning; before day | it has dawned |
| *kwe(e)nda, kwe(e)nga* | *kweénda* | go; come | to go |
| *la(a)mba* | *-láamba* | cook | cook |
| *le(e)ka* | *-léeká* | lie down; sleep | lie down; sleep |
| *ma(a)lu, -o* | *maalú* | feet | feet |

**Table 1. Continued**

| *Kumina Form* | *Kongo Form* | *Kumina Meaning* | *Kongo Meaning* |
|---|---|---|---|
| *ma(a)mbu* | *maambú* | talk; sing | words; affairs |
| *me(e)so* | *meéso* | eye/s | eyes |
| *mu(u)ngwa* | *muúngwa* | salt | salt |
| *pa(a)ngya* | *mpháangi* | friend | elder sibling/ cousin |
| *po(o)ngo, puungu, puungu* | *mphúungu* | thunder | highest point |
| *ya(a)ya* | *yaáya* | old lady, mother; man | mother; maternal relative |
| 2. Reflex of Kongo V: | | | |
| *(m)bi(i)zi* | *mmbízi* | meat; body | animal; meat |
| *(n)gu(u)lu, -a* | *ngulú* | hog (pig) | pig |
| *mala(a)vu, -a* | *malavú* | rum | palm wine |
| *si(i)ka (guma), sekia (goma)* | *-síka* | play (drum) | strike drum; shoot |
| 3. Occurring with both VV and V in Kongo: | | | |
| *(n)gang' awoka* | *ngaánga* | | doctor |
| | *ngang' áwwuka* | God | doctor of healing |
| *gang' ankisi* | *ngang' ánkkisi* | obeah man | fetish doctor |
| *yakala* | *yakála* | | man |
| *male(e)mbe* | *malé(e)mbe* | greetings | gently; greetings |
| | *malémbe-malembe* | | gently |
| *(ki)(n)Za(a)mbi* | *ndzaámbi* | God | God |
| *(ampungu)* | *ndzambi-ámphuungu* | God; thunder | God of the highest point (the High God) |
| *VV in both languages* | | | |
| *(m)but' amuuntu* | *mmbút' amuúntu* | big man | elder |
| *mwiiv(i)* | *mwiívi* | thief | thief |

**Table 1. Continued**

| *Kumina Form* | *Kongo Form* | *Kumina Meaning* | *Kongo Meaning* |
|---|---|---|---|
| *nduungu* | *nnduúngu* | pepper | pepper |
| *niini* | *nwíini* | to drink | he has drunk |
| *nzwaandi* | *ndzó-aándi* | my yard | my house |
| *swiike* | *-swéeka* | run | hide |
| *taata* | *taáta* | father | father |
| *voonda* | *-vóonda* | get a blow | kill, injure |
| *wiilaanga* | *-wíilaangá* | listen, hear | be hearing |
| *wiiza* | *wiiza!* | going away | come! |
| *yaandi* | *yaándi* | man; home; far | s/he |
| | *kwaándi* | | his home |
| | *kwanndá* | | far away |

*The Kumina form is probably taken from a northern dialect; Angolan Kongo does not have the *bi*- prefix.

The most striking aspect of this list is the great variability of the Kumina forms. Indeed, there is probably more variation than is listed here, since for some of the forms I have only one attestation. Secondly, the greatest variability is found for forms which have VV in Kongo, and of these, a very high proportion (16:21) are long vowels, that is, the result of the NC rule. Thirdly, while there are cases of "contraction" of Kongo VV → Kumina V, there are no cases of Kongo V → Kumina VV without a variant Kumina V form. Apart from those instances of regular variation within Kongo itself (group 3), only four of the total of forty-nine items have V in Kongo; all others are from Kongo VV. All cases of Kumina VV/V variation are penultimate, though this may be accidental.

The interpretation of these data is not easy, but at the very least they suggest two competing vocalic subsystems. In one, there is a tendency for all vowels to be short, as postulated by Alleyne for early Afro-American (that is, there is no length distinction); in the other, there is a double (or possibly even long) vowel, distinguished from the single or short vowel. If both subsystems were still present on the island when the Kongo speakers arrived, and had already led to variations of the [dag ~ daag] kind, it is hardly surprising that confusion resulted as to their own system while they were gradually trying to assimilate to their surroundings. There would have been the tendency to contract, hence *gandu, maza, mwana,* [16] and *kombo, mambu, meso;* the original Kongo system would have been maintained by some, reinforced by the double vowels of Jamaican, hence *koombo, maalu, meeso,* and *nduungu, taata, voonda*. As confusion became rife, the short-long variation would extend to reflexes of Kongo V, hence *mbiizi, malaavu, siika* side by side with "correct" *mbizi, malavu, sika*.

The variability in the Jamaican system as a whole may, I suggest, have a similar explanation. If one group of speakers had learned (proto-)Pidgin, they would accommodate all English vowels as single within their system; the same would apply to speakers of languages with phonetic but nonphonemic vowel length. However, those with a vowel system with neither phonemic nor phonetic length but with double vowels, like those of Twi, Yoruba, and Kongo, would perceive some English vowels as double and others as single, and assimilate them accordingly. This seems to me the most plausible explanation for variations such as /i/ ~ /ii/, /a/ ~ /aa/, and /u/ ~ /uu/.

It may be that English length distinctions had persisted and are reflected in the double vowels; but whether this be the case or not, my contention is that these double vowels *did not develop through English influence* on the Afro-American system. They were already there in the subsystem of certain speakers, and what we have today is the result of accommodation of English vowels to this (sub)system, not a feature introduced into the system as a result of contact with English.

## Postscript

The foregoing argument does not explain the constraints on the occurrence of long or double vowels in Jamaican, in particular the limitation of the double vowels to /ii/, /uu/, and /aa/, an apparent correlation of doubling with extreme height and lowness. In a comment at the Round Table, Lawrence Carrington suggested there might be some phonetic characteristic of the mid vowels which functioned to block doubling, or, conversely, some feature of the extreme vowels which promoted the process. The only possibility which occurs to me is that extreme vowels may be expected to require more effort, so it is reasonable to suppose that they require a longer articulation time.[17] In Akan, mid vowels do not occur as phonemic nasal vowels, though underlyingly oral mid vowels may be nasalized by adjacency to a nasal consonant. That is, mid vowels certainly form a distinct subset in these languages.

This raises the more general question of the relative stability of certain vowels within a system. I am not aware of any explanation of this kind which accounts for the Great Vowel Shift, or even its predecessors or successors within the Indo-European field, but I welcome comments from scholars working in this area.

## Notes

I express my appreciation to John Rickford for his profound and careful discussion of this paper at the Round Table and for pointing out errors in the manuscript of this version.

1. This applies to forms of African as well as English origin; for example, *akpara/kwara* 'harlot,' derived from Efik *akparaa*. There may be stylistic lengthening, however.

2. John Rickford has justifiably taken me to task for using the abbreviation BE for British English, rightly pointing out that it is currently employed to mean Black English. I accept the reproof and here replace it with UKSE (United Kingdom Standard English), specifically RP (received pronunciation).

3. This is, of course, an oversimplification. Bynon 1977:82 shows the long vowels resulting from the (first stage of) the Great Vowel Shift as /i:/, /e:/, /ɛ:/, /o:/, and /u:/, with all the Old English long vowels "replaced" except /a:/ and /ɔ:/. Diphthongization of what had been OE /a:/ and /ɔ:/ came later.

4. According to the *DJE*:

> The Jamaican situation [in respect of /i/ ~ /ii/ variation] would appear to reflect two facts: first, educated English usage in the sixteenth to seventeenth centuries varied a good deal in respect to vowels derived from ME /ī/, ME /ĭ/ and ME /ē/ . . . ; secondly, [i] and [ɪ] appear to be allophones of the same phoneme in both Twi and Ewe. Thus JC /kril ~ kriil/ *creel* /brim/ *bream* /siniki/ *sneaky* /hib ~ heb/ *heave* /aslip ~ asliip/ *asleep* certainly reflect the loss of "quantity" as a basis of phonemic distinction, but . . . vowel-quality rather than quantity is in any case the primary basis of phonemic distinction in RP also, and Jamaican variations are paralleled by seventeenth-century variations in England (*DJE*, xlv).

See note 7 for the modern situation.

5. Further, as pointed out by several conference participants, regional dialects of English almost certainly maintained length distinctions into the seventeenth century.

6. "Jamaica may itself turn out to be an important source of information about seventeenth to eighteenth century regional English usage" (*DJE*, xliii).

7. Beverly Hall-Alleyne (personal communication) says that the variation no longer persists; in her examples the double vowel variant has prevailed, e.g., /daag/, /sliip/. The *DJE* was first published in 1967 and was largely based on fieldwork

by Cassidy in 1952; the variation recorded then, therefore, probably reflects older speech forms.

8. Despite the exclusion of *HH in the underlying tonal pattern of any individual item, HH freely occurs on the surface as the result of elision and transfer. I have not given details of the way in which surface pitch data have been analyzed in terms of tone in Kongo; readers are asked either to take the analysis on trust or apply to me for elucidation.

9. According to Hoffmann (1963:21), "Generally speaking, vowels in Margi seem to be of a medium length, neither extremely short nor extremely long. As no minimal pairs with an opposition short vowel:long vowel were found, the rare examples, where a long vowel had been marked, have been disregarded, and no attempt has been made to indicate vowel length."

10. Dennis Winston (personal communication), correction of the form *akpara* given in Carter 1987a.

11. This is not to minimize the point made by Charles Gilman at the Round Table that African languages have almost certainly changed over the intervening centuries; but the modern languages are virtually the only available evidence.

12. As so often, I quote from a language well known to me, where I am sure of my facts, rather than a more relevant language in which I am less confident.

13. Alleyne follows Lawton 1963 in showing final low pitch for these items; I interpret the phonetic data differently and assign *high* tone to the final syllable.

14. When English had long vowels, disappearance of a consonant could lead to compensation by lengthening, as in 'drown' ‹ ME [dru:n] ‹ OE druncnian.

15. This indeed suggests a possible analysis in terms of true vowel length. I have not pursued this possibility here.

16. A form *móna* 'child,' probably from Kimbundu, exists also.

17. This in turn would provide conditions favoring diphthongization. However, evidence from the Great Vowel Shift does not entirely support this, because although the extreme vowels were (eventually) all diphthongized, the high vowels were replaced by shift of the mid vowels. See also note 7.

## References

Alleyne, Mervyn. 1980. *Comparative Afro-American: An historical-comparative study of English-based Afro-American dialects of the New World*. Ann Arbor: Karoma.

Bailey, Beryl Loftman. 1966. *Jamaican Creole syntax: A transformational approach*. Cambridge: Cambridge University Press.

Bynon, Theodora. 1977. *Historical linguistics*. Cambridge: Cambridge University Press.

Carter, Hazel. 1987a. Suprasegmentals in Guyanese: Some African comparisons.

*Pidgin and creole languages: Essays in memory of John Reinecke*, ed. by Glenn G. Gilbert, 213–63. Honolulu: University of Hawaii Press.

———. 1987b. Three creole pitch systems. Paper presented at the African Linguistics Conference, Montreal.

Cassidy, Frederic G., and Robert B. Le Page. 1981. *Dictionary of Jamaican English*. Second edition. Cambridge: Cambridge University Press.

De Camp, David. 1961. Social and geographical factors in Jamaican dialects. *Creole language studies*. Volume 2, ed. by Robert B. Le Page and David De Camp, 61–84. London: Macmillan.

Guthrie, M. 1967–71. *Comparative Bantu*. Farnborough: Gregg Press.

Hoffmann, Carl. 1963. *A grammar of the Margi language*. London: Oxford University Press.

Ladefoged, Peter. 1975. *A course in phonetics*. New York: Harcourt Brace Jovanovich.

Lawton, David. 1963. *Suprasegmental phenomena in Jamaican Creole*. Ph.D. dissertation, Michigan State University.

Schuler, M. 1980. *Alas, Alas Kongo: A social history of indentured African immigration into Jamaica, 1841–1865*. Baltimore: Johns Hopkins University Press.

# Phonological Features in Afro-American Pidgins and Creoles and Their Diachronic Significance. Comments on the Papers by Holm and Carter

*John R. Rickford*

It is a pleasure to comment on these papers by John Holm and Hazel Carter because they are both well written and well researched, and because the study of pidgin-creole phonology is an important but neglected topic. As Holm noted in the conference version of his paper, recent argumentation against Africanisms in Afro-American varieties has been syntax based, and the phonological similarities of these varieties have not been considered significant for theories of their genesis and development. This critique, of course, does not apply to Alleyne (1980) or Boretzky (1983), but the neglect of phonology in creolistics is very real, and it goes beyond the substratist-universalist controversy. For instance, none of the fourteen articles in Muysken and Smith (1986) deals with phonology; and only one of the twenty-one articles in the first six issues of the *Journal of Pidgin and Creole Languages* deals with phonology. Even in this volume, phonology-based papers are clearly in the minority.

It is important to counteract this underrepresentation because generalizations based on data from only one domain are invariably contradicted or challenged by data from other domains. For instance, Bickerton's (1975:18) claim that variable rules would be inappropriate for the Guyanese situation because of the extensiveness of invariant patterning there is more valid for morphosyntax than phonology (Rickford 1979), a function of the sociolinguistic generalization that phonological features tend to show gradient social stratification, while grammatical features tend to show sharp stratification with more pronounced differences between groups (Wolfram 1969:121).[1] A second example is Labov's (1972:322) classic characterization of sociolinguistic variables as "alternative ways of saying the same thing," which turned out to work well for phonology but not for morphosyntax (Lavandera 1978). A third example involves the issue of Africanisms, the focus of this conference. While the source of many pidgin and creole syntactic features may be a matter of controversy, no one could fail to concede after reading Alleyne (1980), Boretzky (1983), and Kihm (1986) that some of the distinctive phonological features of Afro-American pidgins and creoles represent the influence of their African substrates.

But it is not enough to introduce phonological features simply as a foil to syntactic ones. Having agreed that it is important to consider all domains, we still have a great deal of hard thinking and research to do about the ways in which syntax, morphology, phonology, and the lexicon line up in terms of susceptibility to diffusion and in terms of their significance for our theories of creole genesis and development.

Let me quickly sketch some of the issues which occur to me. First, Holm noted in an earlier version of the paper in this volume that "borrowing is generally considered to occur most readily on the level of the lexicon and least readily on the level of syntax, with phonological borrowing occupying an intermediate position." But Weinreich (1953:67) noted at least three different nineteenth-century and early twentieth-century opinions about the relative susceptibility of the various domains to borrowing or interference. Although everyone agreed that words were lent and borrowed most readily, Whitney (1881) felt that suffixes and inflections came after words, with sounds last; Dauzat (1938) felt that sounds and syntax came after words, with morphology last; and Pritzwald (1938) suggested that phonology came after lexicon, with morphology and syntax last. Weinreich essentially disagreed with all of them, noting that before meaningful comparisons were possible, we would need to devise means of formulating the degree of integratedness of a system and measuring the affected portion of each domain. I think he meant by this that while it is relatively easy to point to instances of borrowing with respect to individual features, it is harder to come up with reliable measures of the overall degree of influence in an entire domain and to compare relative influence across domains meaningfully.[2]

Second, one difference between phonology and syntax—and it is one that challenges Holm's general theme that both dimensions must be given equal weight in untangling issues of creole genesis—is that because of the myriad combinations into which even a small inventory of phonemes can enter, it is difficult to argue that a language lacks "sufficient" phonological distinctions. No one ever says of Hawaiian or Ndjuka, for instance, that if they had more than five or seven vowels, they would be able to differentiate more words or concepts. In syntax or semantics, however, it is conceivable (although admittedly controversial) that a language might be underequipped for the range of uses which native speakers require, and it is, of course, this limitation which Bickerton (1981) postulates as a condition for his hypothetical bioprogram to "kick in" as a pidgin is nativized. Neither Bickerton nor anyone else has argued for the operation of a corresponding phonological bioprogram, however, and it is partly in the absence of any such argument that local substratal effects in phonology seem less controversial. Of course, other considerations involving universals do apply to phonological features, as Holm notes.

A third issue is that creoles appear to differ from pidgins in their greater phonological flexibility or capacity for morphophonemic variation, especially insofar as the reduction of tense-aspect and other grammatical morphemes is concerned (Labov 1990; Mühlhäusler 1986:206). This is one area in which work on Afro-American varieties with an eye to the potential effects of substratal, superstratal, and universal influences is very much needed. Bendix's (1983) paper on sandhi phenomena in Papiamentu, African, and other creole languages is one of the only recent works dealing with this subject. I should note that detailed study of such phonological variability will require recorded, naturalistic, connected speech data, and not simply the citation forms readily available in published works. It will also require better recording equipment and more careful attention to the recording process.[3] The extra effort and expense are likely to be worth it. For instance, Caribbean creoles share with American vernacular Black English a systematic but apparently unique rule by which initial voiced stops in tense-aspect auxiliaries can be variably deleted (*da* ~ *a, go* ~ *o, dõ* ~ *õ,* and so on; see Rickford 1980). This is an obvious candidate for substratal African influence, a possibility increased by the fact that Nigerian Pidgin English displays similar variability (Nicholas Faraclas, personal communication).

Phonological variability in African and Afro-American varieties is in fact a recurrent theme in the papers by Holm and Carter. It seems clear that we need to study such variation more carefully and directly than we have in the past, and that creolistics as a field needs to use more sophisticated means of analyzing and accounting for variation. This is an issue to which I will return in discussing these papers individually, especially Carter's.

## Holm's Paper

### *Mechanism for the Retention of Substrate Features*

Holm's general approach is commendable in two respects: his openness to other influences besides substratal transfer and his reference to the transfer model of Weinreich (1953), whose taxonomies and insights are too often ignored by students of language contact. With respect to other influences, however, one wonders why universals are artificially restricted to universals of adult second language acquisition when the relevance of first language and other universals has been so forcefully argued in recent years (see, for instance, Bickerton 1983, a rebuttal of Valdman 1983, which Holm cites approvingly; as well as papers by Mufwene and others in Smith and Muysken 1986).

Weinreich's transfer model is also more complex than Holm suggests, in at least two respects. First, in addition to the processes of overdifferentiation, underdifferentiation, and phone-substitution which Holm mentions, Weinreich (1953:18–19) mentions a fourth possibility: reinterpretation of distinctions, which is more difficult to identify because its effects are almost invisible on the surface. Second, and more important, Weinreich insists that structural correspondences between two languages only help to establish what is *possible* in terms of interference or transfer between them; what *actually* happens in particular cases is also determined by nonstructural factors relating to individual language users (e.g., which other languages they know) and to the social statuses of their communities (e.g., size and relative prestige). Thomason and Kaufman (1988:35) agree: "It is the sociolinguistic history of the speakers, and not the structure of their language, that is the primary determinant of the linguistic outcome of language contact."

Holm is not alone in minimizing or ignoring the nonstructural factors; even a prominent sociolinguist such as Trudgill (1986), while overtly tipping his hat to Weinreich, overwhelmingly favors structural over nonstructural factors as explanations for the effects of interdialect contact. But I think Weinreich's more genuinely sociolinguistic approach was right; we need such an approach to explain why some of the phonological adaptations we find in pidgins, creoles, and other cases of second language acquisition do not match what we might predict from the straightforward operation of substrate effects. For instance, Mühlhäusler (1986:141) shows that there are some "surprising" differences between the shapes of English loanwords in Tok Pisin's principal substratum language, Tolai, and their cognates in early Tok Pisin: English 'biscuit' comes out *bisket* in early Tok Pisin, but *patiket* in Tolai, and English 'strong' comes out *strong* or *sitirong* in early Tok Pisin, but *torong* in Tolai. Similarly, some of the adaptations English loanwords undergo in West African languages ('step' realized as *sitɛ̃mbu* in Yoruba; Carter 1988:239) are not found in the English-based Caribbean creoles for which such languages were substrates. In both cases, the explanations for the differences undoubtedly involve both structural *and* nonstructural factors, including the fact that the source language speakers have borrowed a few words into their essentially unchanged native systems, but the pidgin and creole speakers have participated in a different sociolinguistic process involving mutual linguistic accommodation and language shift (Thomason and Kaufman 1988).

*Coarticulated Stops*

With respect to the coarticulated stops /kp/ and /gb/, the case for their being derived from African substrates is clear in view of the factors cited by Holm: their presence in a number of relevant West African languages,[4] their absence in relevant European languages, and their rarity or markedness worldwide. Holm does a good job of marshaling evidence from Alleyne (1980:50), Boretzky (1983:60), and other sources to show that coarticulated stops occur not only in Saramaccan (contra Bickerton 1981:122) but in other creoles, including Ndjuka, Príncipe Creole Portuguese, Krio, Liberian, Nigerian Pidgin English, and Gullah. At the same time, the fact that these coarticulated stops are relatively rare and have a limited functional load, being mainly restricted to African-derived words, reduces their significance.

Although the "Africanness" of these coarticulated stops may be "straightforward," there are some open questions about their development and distribution in Afro-American varieties which Holm does not mention. One is the fact, noted by Alleyne, that /gb/ is more common than /kp/ in non-African-derived Saramaccan words; that is, we have more examples like *gboto* 'boat' than *kpiñi* 'squeeze out.' Why should this be? Alleyne speculates that "there may have been some interlingual identification between African [gb] and European [b], arising perhaps from the absence of [b] in some of the African languages or dialects used in the contact situation" (1980:50). This may well be, if relevant West African languages without [b] exist, but another explanation may simply be that [gb] is commoner than [kp] among West African languages. Southern Bambara and Maninka, for instance, both have /gb/ but not /kp/ (Welmers 1973:48).

A second, related issue is that in Saramaccan these coarticulated stops did not simply replace European-derived /p/ and /b/, but also (perhaps more commonly) /kw/ and /gw/, indicating that the interlingual identification between West African and European consonant systems was not as straightforward as we might otherwise have imagined.

Finally, there is the synchronic variation in several of the African and Afro-American languages between [kp] and [kw], and [gb] and [gw], to which Alleyne, Boretzky, and Holm all refer. This may relate to the phonetic fact, noted by Welmers (1973:47), that the coarticulated stops are often heard as involving a *w* off-glide because the bilabial release is slower or weaker than the velar. And this in turn may account for the interlingual identification between the coarticulated and labialized stops referred to above.

One open issue Holm does mention is the question of whether the words with coarticulated stops in Gullah and in Krio, Liberian, and Nigerian Pidgin English, which are primarily if not exclusively African derived, represent recent (nineteenth-century) borrowings. This seems very likely in the case of the West African varieties, but less so in the case of Gullah. I agree with Mufwene (1985:157–58) that coarticulated stops are marginal in Gullah, and I share his fascination with the issue of why they were preserved in some but not other words. But Saramaccan, in which the possibility of recent borrowings is slimmer if not nonexistent, poses similar problems, clearly the result of irregular retention from an earlier stage. I do not see why a similar explanation could not apply to Gullah, and I am not convinced by existing arguments or evidence that the Gullah features represent more recent borrowings. Why should nineteenth-century Gullah speakers have been better disposed to adopt such a distinctively non-English feature than their seventeenth- or eighteenth-century counterparts, whose exposure to English would have been more limited and whose familiarity with African languages greater? In any case, it is an intriguing issue.

### *Palatalization*

With respect to palatalization, one cannot help but be impressed by the wealth of evidence Holm introduces, from a variety of languages both past and present, and by his readiness to admit superstratal and other influences. And yet, with the exception of one or two cases—such as the distribution of alveopalatal [tš], [dž], [š], and [ž] in São Tomé Creole, which suggests stronger influence from Southern Kongo than from standard Portuguese—one is almost embarrassed by the richness of possible influences. With substrates, superstrates, and universals all likely to yield the same result in so many cases, influence from any one source is especially difficult to prove.

In future work on this variable it may be useful to consult Bhat's (1978) comparative study of palatalization, as much for its summary data on over one hundred instances of palatalization in a wide variety of languages as for its recommendation that the three constituent processes of palatalization (tongue fronting, tongue raising, and spirantization) be distinguished. As Bhat notes (51–54), tongue raising tends to affect apicals, and the height rather than frontness of the following vowel is important; tongue fronting, by contrast, tends to affect velars, and the frontness of the following vowel is more important than its height. These generalizations help us to anticipate the solution to the mystery of why Jamaican has /ky/ and /gy/ in words like /kyaad/ 'card' when, according to Holm, "they would not be expected because they do not have a high front vowel." Since velar palatalization is an instance of tongue fronting, we expect the frontness (rather than height) of the vowel to be crucial, and, of course, Holm's sources show this to have been the diachronic conditioning in this case. In a similar vein, while it does not appear to affect the substantial point (originally Alleyne's), it is technically incorrect to describe the back vowels which follow /tj/ and /dj/ in Surinamese *tjuba* and *djombo* as "nonpalatalizing," because the crucial conditioning in the case of tongue-raising palatals like these is vowel height, not frontness.

An important source of evidence in several of the cases of palatalization Holm discusses is the existence of synchronic variability in the creoles, as attested in lexical doublets such as Lesser Antillean *tšwizin* ~ *twizin* 'kitchen' and triplets such as Negerhollands *biti* ~ *bitji* ~ *bitši* 'a little bit.' Based on my experience in transcribing spoken texts (Rickford 1987), I suspect that morphophonemic variability of this type is even commoner in connected speech than is usually reported and that it was so even in the past, at least since creolization took place.

A related point about palatalization—and it applies to other features, too—is that despite its ubiquity, written records of creole speech from earlier times are often limited, like modern written representation, in giving absolutely no orthographic indication of its existence (using *cat* instead of *cyat* or *kyat*). The moral, of course, is to be cautious in the use of such written records. But it may also be helpful to study the synchronic relations between Afro-American speech and its representations in popular literature and the media to get some idea of how much we can depend on such representations in reconstructing the past. In popular representations of vernacular Black English, for instance, consonant cluster simplification is often indicated, but not the neutralization, before nasals, of [ɪ] and [ɛ].

Holm's concluding section is, like most of his paper, evenhandedly and judiciously argued. The following statement, however, comes as a bit of a surprise, since the focus of the paper up to this point has been on substrate influence on phonology: "Bickerton's implication that substrate influence can occur on the level of phonology and lexicon but not on the level of syntax must be rejected as both illogical and implausible." What is lacking is any explicit theoretical justification for the expectation that substrate influence in any one domain should imply or guarantee similar influence in other domains. Holm may have had in mind a principle of the type which Thomason and Kaufman (1988:60) adopt on the basis of their research:

> If a language has undergone structural interference in one subsystem, then it will have undergone structural interference in other subsystems

> as well, from the same source. Not necessarily in all subsystems . . . lexical interference may be negligible in cases of interference through shift; and considerable structural interference may occur without including externally-motivated changes in the inflectional morphology. But we have found *no* cases of completely isolated structural interference in *just one* linguistic subsystem.

However, the authors do go on to note that in borrowing, "limited phonological restructuring can occur without concomitant syntactic restructuring" (60), citing the case of Nguni dialects of Bantu, which have borrowed clicks from Khoisan (and which retain them primarily in Khoisan loanwords) but show no syntactic interference from Khoisan.[5] Given the similarity between this Nguni case and what some have suggested about coarticulated stops in Afro-American creoles—namely, that they are largely restricted to African words and *may* represent recent borrowings—we should probably be cautious about invoking Thomason and Kaufman's principle as justification for Holm's more general conclusion.

## Carter's Paper

Carter's paper is more difficult to discuss than Holm's because it covers more subtopics. Carter focuses on areas in which the phonetic facts and appropriate phonological analyses are more open to question (vowel length, quality, and tone), includes more new data ("new" to creolistics, at least), and raises the issue of variability more acutely. Moreover, Alleyne's (1980:35–43) discussion of Afro-American vowels, the springboard for Carter's paper, is silently present throughout the paper. I found it necessary to read and reread Alleyne's discussion to understand Carter's more fully, and in what follows I will probably appear to be commenting on his argumentation and evidence as much as hers, but hopefully not unduly so.

### *Alleyne's Hypothesis*

The starting point for Carter's paper is a hypothesis elaborated in Alleyne (1980:38–43), which she summarizes as follows: "The earliest form(s) of Afro-American had no phonemic vowel length distinction, and that in varieties such as Jamaican, vowel length was introduced through the influence of English." At the risk of going over some of the ground Carter covers, I wish to consider Alleyne's proposals in a little more detail.

Alleyne (1980:38, 76) characterizes the earliest Afro-American phonological system as a four-tiered one:

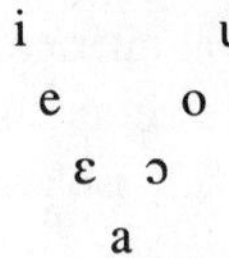

The lax mid vowels [ɛ] and [ɔ] are described as having a low functional load and occurring mainly in African words (39–41), so the system is essentially three-tiered (i/u, e/o, a). In addition to lacking a productive tense/lax distinction for the mid series, the system also lacks any vowel length or tenseness/closeness distinction for the high vowels, any means of distinguishing between 'beat' [i] and 'bit' [ɪ], or between 'fool' [u] and 'full' [ʊ].

What is Alleyne's evidence for this claim? Not early written records or texts (none are cited), but the fact that modern varieties such as Saramaccan and Ndjuka, generally the most conservative and least Anglicized varieties of Afro-American, appear to have a similar system. For instance, both 'big' and 'see' have the same vowel (*bígi, sí*) in these varieties, as do 'root' and 'pull' (*lútu, púu*).[6] Although these varieties do have some long vowels ("double" by Carter's analysis), these are seen as "a later development as a result of the coalescence of two vowels after the application of a vowel epenthesis rule and an intervocalic liquid deletion rule. Thus 'self' → *selefi* → *seépi*" (1980:39).

Modern Jamaican, Guyanese, and Krio vowel systems are more complex than this, but Alleyne sees their additional distinctions, once again, as representing postgenesis developments, in these cases the result of the continuing influence of English. The primary evidence for this claim is the synchronic variability between forms like [kril] and [kriil] 'creel' in Jamaican and [beg] and [bɛg] in Krio, which he sees as "residues of the earlier lack of phonemic distinction" (42).

### *Carter's Hypothesis*

While agreeing that Krio and West African Pidgin English (WAPE) provide some support for the absence of vowel length in early Afro-American, Carter suggests that vowel length variability was present in Afro-American from early on, and that this in turn was a function of variable or competing West African subsystems rather than English influence. English, she argues, is unlikely to have been the source of phonemic vowel length in Jamaican and similar varieties because the Great Vowel Shift, which transformed distinctions of length into distinction of quality, was essentially over at the time these varieties were being formed (seventeenth century on). Furthermore, Jamaican's putative long vowels are better analyzed as double vowels with HL tone pattern (*íi, áa, úu*). This makes them less likely to have come from English, which has neither double vowels nor distinctive tone, than from African languages, many of which do have such features.

Much of Carter's paper is devoted to a survey of African languages. This is very interesting, but it is easy to get mired in detail. One essential point is, however, that most of the relevant African languages have double rather than phonemically long vowels; thus their speakers assimilate perceived length in English loanwords (in stressed syllables which occupy a whole foot, for instance) with double vowels, as in Yoruba *fíimu* 'film.' Another key point is that vowel doubling and vowel length are highly variable in African languages—from one language, dialect, and style to another, as well as in diachronic changes and synchronic morphophonemic variation within a single language. Such variability is evident today in Jamaican Kumina ([kinzu ~ kiinzu] ‹ Kongo [kiinzú] 'pot'), and it suggests to Carter the existence of two competing subsystems among the mid-nineteenth-century Angolan and Sierra Leonean immigrants from whom Kumina is derived: one in which only short vowels are allowed, and one in which double or long vowels are also permitted. She suggests that the variation in Jamaican English itself (e.g., /asliip ~ aslip/) might have originated in the same way, through the clash between African subsystems which permitted phonemic double or long vowels and those which did not.

In the remaining sections of this discussion I will comment on various aspects of the alternative hypotheses, beginning with narrower issues about the length and quality of English, West African, and Afro-American vowels and concluding with larger issues relating to their variability.

### *Length of English Vowels during the Formation of Afro-American*

Carter, I think, proves her case that "the development of the qualitative differences which were to replace phonemic length as distinctive . . . [in English] was well on its way in the sixteenth and seventeenth centuries." This is clear from her demonstration that Jamaican /ii/, /aa/, and /uu/ do not correspond to Middle English (ME) long /i:/, /a:/, and /u:/, respectively, but to the outputs of ME /e:/, /a/, and /o:/ (and to other specified vowels), raised and otherwise modified by the Great Vowel Shift.

Equally justified is her conclusion that "Jamaican is therefore at least as likely to represent perceived differences of quality as of length, and in some cases clearly does so." To this I would add, however, that those vowel quality differences are even more ubiquitous than she suggests, and that they occur in Guyanese and Gullah as well, despite the tendency of Alleyne (1980:35, 41–43) and others to represent and discuss these vowel systems as if length but not quality were the only phonetically discernible and phonemically significant feature. For Gullah, this is clearly not the case, since Turner (1949:15–20) distinguishes between [i] and [ɪ], [e] and [ɛ] in terms of relative retraction and closeness or height.[7] In Guyanese, comparable differences of vowel tenseness or height also exist (see Allsopp 1958:6; Rickford 1979:191–93, 1987:8–9). Even Devonish (1989:75), who opts for the following normalized representation of GC vowel phonemes, recognizes that in the high and mid pairs the vowels are distinguished by relative tenseness or peripherality as well as by length.[8]

ii i u uu
ee e o oo
aa a

Jamaican also seems to have a comparable combination of length and quality; Cassidy and Le Page (1980:xxxix) describe /ii/, at least, as "long, high, *tense*," in contrast with /i/ "short, high, *lax*" (emphasis added). It is all too easy, given the prevalence with which Cassidy's phonemic orthography is used for Caribbean creole English vowel systems, to forget that /ii/ versus /i/ often represents a difference of vowel quality as well as length.

Having agreed on these two counts with Carter, however, I wish to disagree with her argument that "Alleyne's hypothesis *requires* that English should have still maintained the length distinctions at the time when Jamaican, Guyanese, and Gullah began to acquire or develop them." I think what is fundamentally at issue—in the difference between the Surinamese and non-Surinamese varieties, and in the inferences we can draw from this and other evidence about the development of Afro-American—is the *number* of vowel distinctions involved and their *variability* rather than just their *nature*. Jamaican, Guyanese, and Gullah clearly share distinctions between /ii/ and /i/ (and comparable pairs) with English, but not Saramaccan and Ndjuka (reportedly). Whether these distinctions are interpreted primarily in terms of quality or length, the more decreolized varieties could have acquired them after their initial formation, through their longer and more intimate association with English. The phonetic issues are not without interest and significance, but deciding them one way or another does not materially affect the larger issues.[9]

### *Jamaican (and Guyanese) Vowels: Double or Long?*

A similar argument applies to Carter's analysis of Jamaican as possessing double vowels (with two syllabic nuclei) rather than long vowels (with a single, long syllabic nucleus). It is a refreshing and attractive analysis, especially in view of the neat way it links up with historical facts (e.g., relevant African languages have a similar system) and accounts for some of the synchronic features (e.g., Jamaican /dwiit/ derived from /du it/ to maintain syllable count). But there are reasons to be cautious about it. In Guyanese, at least, /maatá/ and /biitá/ both have, to the ears of this native speaker and others I have consulted, two syllables, not three, the initial syllable consisting of a single long vowel, or as Devonish (1989:89) analyzes it, a single complex nucleus with two moras. It would be good to have acoustic or native speaker support for the double vowel analysis in Jamaican and to know how extensively it applies in the lexicon. Is /dwiit/ 'do it' really two syllables? Does this analysis apply also to /iin/ as a variant of /in/ 'in'? Moreover, as Devonish (personal communication) has asked, how come Jamaican attests only the HL tone pattern in these adjacent double vowels (/máata/) while the full spectrum of possibilities (HL, LL, LH, HH) is reflected in words with nonadjacent vowels?[10] Contrast Saramaccan, in which adjacent double vowels and alternative tone patterns are better established, as in *dɔ́ɔ* 'door,' *gɔɔ́* 'grow,' and *dóón* 'drum' (Alleyne 1980:41). Finally, the Jamaican pattern of assimilating English adoptives does not really match that of languages like Yoruba with true double vowels. Yoruba *fíimu* 'film' exemplifies the Yoruba tendency to assimilate English stressed vowels which occupy a whole foot as double, but the comparable Jamaican item does not have a double vowel (*flɪm, fɪm*); contrariwise, Yoruba *lɛta* 'letter' represents the Yoruba tendency to assimilate English stressed vowels which do not occupy a whole foot as short, but Jamaican *bíita* 'beater,' which has a double or long initial vowel rather than a short one, could not have been derived according to the same principle.

Again, these are interesting phonetic and phonological issues in their own right. But whether we analyze Jamaican as possessing long or double vowels, or both (as Shona does), we can ask why it makes such distinctions where Saramaccan and Ndjuka do not. (Recall that Surinamese double vowels derive from elided liquids and do not match the putative Jamaican double vowels in distribution.) Was Afro-American originally invariant and lacking in length and quality distinctions for the high and mid vowels, as Alleyne claims?

### *Variability and Other Issues*

Interestingly enough, Carter's position on early Afro-American vowel length is more prototypically Alleyne-like than Alleyne's, insofar as it stresses African rather than English origins and variable/complex rather than invariant/simplified initial systems. Throughout Alleyne's 1971 paper (and in many parts of Alleyne 1980), the thesis is advanced that differences in native West African systems and differences in opportunities and motivation for acculturation to English meant that early Afro-American must have been variable from its very inception. Consider, for instance, the following passage:

> In neither lexicon, phonology nor syntax was the Proto-Afro-American dialect stable, uniform or durable. . . . It is likely that in any Afro-American community there would have been, from the very beginning, considerable intra- and interidiolectal variation. . . . Fluctuation in the phonological systems of Afro-Americans during the formative period was also due to differences in the native phonological systems of Africans . . . fluctuations on the morphophonemic level may also have existed as a result of dialect differences within the English of the contact situation. (Alleyne, 1980:75–76)

Carter certainly reveals enough variability within and across the native vowel systems of relevant African languages to make it likely that early Afro-American was not invariantly lacking in length and quality distinctions and that some of the variation in modern Jamaican, as in modern Kumina, might reflect competing West African systems.

Having essentially agreed with Carter (and with prototypical Alleyne) on this, however, I must confess that a number of issues remain unresolved. I will mention only two.

First, why do Surinamese varieties lack distinctions of vowel length, doubling, or tenseness while Jamaican, Guyanese, and Gullah do not? Carter does not address this issue, but to follow through on her line of argumentation, we might suppose that the relevant substratal systems for Suriname did not permit phonemic vowel length or doubling, while at least some of those for other parts of the Caribbean did. It is unlikely that such a neat, demographically based vowel system differentiation can be established (for instance, we know from Hancock 1969:17 that "at least one-third of the slaves imported into Surinam were from Angola," and from Carter's paper that Angolan Kongo includes double vowels), but in order to pursue the question we need a list of the relevant contact languages for each territory and information on their vowel systems, especially with respect to length and doubling.

Alleyne's argument that the Surinamese varieties differ from the others because of their more limited exposure to English is a simpler one, although it is still a puzzle why the former should lack distinctive vowel length and quality despite possible reinforcing substratal influences (see n. 9). One solution, although not the type Alleyne would favor, I think, is to recognize a tendency for pidgins and early contact varieties to lose vowel length and other phonological distinctions found in both their lexifier and substratum languages (Heine 1975:3; Mühlhäusler 1986:148) and to suggest that the Surinamese and West African varieties are frozen at a "pidginizing" stage of this type. But since the Surinamese creoles are as complex as other Caribbean varieties, sometimes more so in many other features, this "solution" raises new problems and puzzles of its own.

Second, I think it will be necessary to recognize more intrasystemic morphophonemic variation in Jamaican, Guyanese, and Gullah (perhaps also in Saramaccan, Ndjuka, and Sranan) than either Carter or Alleyne seems prepared to accept, and to analyze it more directly, using more sophisticated means. Both authors seem to regard morphophonemic variation between tense and lax or long/double and short vowels as exceptional, but I suspect that a closer analysis of connected speech will reveal it to be more widespread (see Cassidy 1961:42–43, and Carter's own description of Kumina), and that quantitative or implicational approaches will better reveal its nature and conditioning (De Camp 1971:358–62; Rickford 1979, chap. 7). For instance, according to Alleyne (1980:41), "some words whose cognates in English may have had the shorter (lax) vowel acquired [in Jamaican and Guyanese] long vowels: [i:n] 'in,' [wi:k] 'wick,' [i:f] 'if.' " One is likely to infer from this that only the long or tense vowel variants persist. But I know from my native Guyanese experience that the short/lax vowel variant is actually more common. The following entry for /iin/ in Cassidy and Le Page (1980:234) suggests as much for Jamaican: "A common dial pronunc of *in* (though the usual pronunc at all levels is /in/ [ɪn])." Diachronically, Carter still seems to envisage the formation of Jamaican as due to competition between two or more different but invariant West African systems. However, her discussion of the modern reflexes of those systems reveals more inherent, intrasystemic variability. Her fascinating Kumina data display considerable inherent variability, although the terms "confusion" and "chaotic" imply a view of it as exceptional and unprincipled which is probably unjustified. I would like to see more creolists wade into the analysis of such inherent variability directly and with more sophisticated analytical tools. The process should be informative and insightful in both synchronic and diachronic terms.

## Notes

1. For instance, with only a few exceptions (such as the use of /a:/ instead of /ɔ:/ in words like 'God'), speakers at all levels of the Guyanese continuum share non-English or creole pronunciations such as /tʌŋ/ for 'town' (compare British/ American SE /taʊn/) or /fèerí/ for 'fairy' (with high tone or prominence on the second syllable instead of the first; see Devonish 1989:92). But they are more sharply stratified in terms of their everyday use of morphosyntactic creole features such as the use of anterior *bin* or focus/cleft-marking *a* (*a tiif ii tiif di buk*).

2. Relevant to this issue too is Thomason and Kaufman's (1988:37–40) observation that the relative susceptibility of a domain in one language to influence from another depends on whether borrowing or language shift is involved, the former favoring the lexicon, the latter favoring phonology and syntax. Creole genesis is a subtype of language shift.

3. Uher or Nagra reel-to-reel tape-recorders, capable of high-fidelity recording speeds of 3¾ or 7½ rps, are ideal. Even the best cassette recorders are limited insofar as they have fixed (slow) speeds. Researchers need to be prepared to spend as much, or more, on their recording equipment as they do on their computers, recognizing that the former critically limits the quality of the data to be analyzed.

4. By "relevant" African and European languages, I mean here and throughout this paper those languages likely to have been involved in the formation of Afro-American varieties, such as Twi, Yoruba, and Mende, on the one hand, and English, French, and Dutch, on the other.

5. Sarah Thomason, in fact, reiterated this point and this example in the discussion period following Holm's paper. She also observed that prestige constraints impinge more powerfully on syntax than phonology, with the result that nonstandard African-derived features are less likely to persist in syntax than in phonology.

6. The system also includes at least one diphthong (/ai/) and a nasality distinction.

7. Turner's discussion is couched in phonetic terms, but it is evident throughout that the distinctions are intended to be phonemic. For instance, after discussing Gullah [i] and [ɪ], Turner observes that "in Fante, [i] and [ɪ] likewise belong to separate phonemes" (1949:19). Furthermore, the texts at the end of the book exemplify relevant phonemic contrasts, for instance between [bɪt] 'bit' and [bit] 'beat' (262).

8. Devonish notes (1989:75), as Cassidy and Le Page (1980:xlv) and Alleyne (1980:41) also do, that differences of tenseness, height, and length "coincide in GC

as they do in many languages." His argument for accepting length as phonemically criterial in GC is the fact that the pair [a:] and [a] differ only in length. Note too that it is an idealized basilect, omitting [ʌ] (compare Rickford 1987:9).

9. Of course, since many of the relevant West African languages have a tense/lax or close/open distinction for the high vowels [i/ɪ, u/ʊ), the mid vowels [e/ɛ, o/ɔ], or both (Welmers 1973:20–21; Bendor-Samuel 1989:23, 56, 128, 414), it is difficult to understand why the Surinamese and West African English-based pidgins and creoles do not make a similar distinction. Alleyne (1980:43) seems to be aware of the potential problem here but turns it on its head. According to him, "although African certainly has [ɛ], Afro-American uses [e] in English cognates such as 'bed.' " He uses this observation as evidence that English vowels at the time of early Anglo-African contact were distinguished by length instead of quality. Since Carter effectively repudiates the latter claim, the puzzle still remains, suggesting that substratal influence cannot tell the whole story.

10. Although I have not yet seen it, Hubert Devonish (personal communication) informed me that Wittle (1989) has analyzed Jamaican as having long (one-syllable) vowels rather than double vowels (with two equally prominent syllabic nuclei).

## References

Alleyne, Mervyn C. 1971. Acculturation and the cultural matrix of creolization. *Pidginization and creolization of languages*, ed. by Dell Hymes, 169–86. Cambridge: Cambridge University Press.

———. 1980. *Comparative Afro-American: An historical-comparative study of English-based Afro-American dialects of the New World*. Ann Arbor: Karoma.

Allsopp, Richard. 1958. *Pronominal forms in the dialect of English used in Georgetown (British Guiana) and its environs by persons engaged in non-clerical occupations*. Volume 2. M.A. thesis, London University.

Bendix, Edward. 1983. Sandhi phenomena in Papiamentu, African and other creole languages. *Studies in Caribbean languages*, ed. by Lawrence D. Carrington in collaboration with Dennis Craig and Ramon Todd Dandare, 112–23. St. Augustine, Trinidad: Society for Caribbean Linguistics.

Bendor-Samuel, John, ed. 1989. *The Niger-Congo languages*. Lanham, Md.: University Press of America.

Bhat, D. N. S. 1978. A general study of palatalization. *Universals of human language*. Volume 2. *Phonology*, ed. by Joseph H. Greenberg, assisted by Charles A. Ferguson and Edith A. Moravcsik, 47–92. Stanford: Stanford University Press.

Bickerton, Derek. 1975. *Dynamics of a creole system*. Cambridge: Cambridge University Press.

———. 1981. *Roots of language*. Ann Arbor: Karoma.

———. 1983. Comments on Valdman's "Creolization and second language acquisition." *Pidginization and creolization as language acquisition*, ed. by Rodger Andersen, 235–40. Rowley, Mass.: Newbury House.

Boretzky, Norbert. 1983. *Kreolsprachen, Substrate und Sprachwandel*. Weisbaden: Harrassowitz.

Carter, Hazel. 1988. Suprasegmentals in Guyanese: Some African comparisons. *Pidgin and creole languages: Essays in memory of John E. Reinecke*, ed. by Glenn G. Gilbert, 213–63. Honolulu: University of Hawaii Press.

Cassidy, Frederic G. 1961. *Jamaica talk: Three hundred years of the English language in Jamaica*. Basingstoke and London: Macmillan.

Cassidy, Frederic G. and Robert B. Le Page. 1980. *Dictionary of Jamaican English*. Second edition. Cambridge: Cambridge University Press.

Dauzat, Albert. 1938 [1927]. *Les patois*. Paris: Delagrave.

De Camp, David. 1971. Toward a generative analysis of a post-creole continuum. *Pidginization and creolization of languages*, ed. by Dell Hymes, 349–70. Cambridge: Cambridge University Press.

Devonish, Hubert. 1989. *Talking in tones: A study of tone in Afro-European creole languages*. London: Karia Press.

Hancock, Ian F. 1969. A provisional comparison of the English-derived Atlantic creoles. *African Language Review* 8.7–72.

Heine, Bernd. 1975. Some generalizations on African-based pidgins. Paper presented at the International Conference on Pidgins and Creoles, Honolulu, Hawaii.

Kihm, Alain, 1986. Nasality in Kriol: The marked case? *Journal of Pidgin and Creole Languages* 1.81–107.

Labov, William. 1972. *Sociolinguistic patterns*. Philadelphia: University of Pennsylvania Press.

———. 1990. On the adequacy of natural languages. 1: The development of tense. *Pidgin and creole tense-mood-aspect systems*, ed. by John Singler, 1–58. Amsterdam: John Benjamins.

Lavandera, Beatriz. 1978. Where does the sociolinguistic variable stop? *Language in Society* 7.171–82.

Mufwene, Salikoko S. 1985. The linguistic significance of African proper names in Gullah. *Nieuwe West-Indische Gids* 59.149–66.

Mühlhäusler, Peter. 1986. *Pidgin and creole linguistics*. Oxford: Basil Blackwell.

Muysken, Pieter, and Norval Smith, eds. 1986. *Substrata versus universals in creole genesis*. Amsterdam: John Benjamins.

Pritzwald, Kurt Stegmann von. 1938. Sprachwissenschaftliche Minderheitenforschung: Ein Arbeitsplan und eine Statistik. *Wörter und Sachen*, n.s., 1.52–72.

Rickford, John R. 1979. *Variation in a creole continuum: Quantitative and implicational approaches*. Ph.D. dissertation, University of Pennsylvania.

———. 1980. How does DOZ disappear? *Issues in English creoles: Papers from the 1975 Hawaii Conference*, ed. by Richard R. Day, 77–96. Heidelberg: Julius Groos Verlag.

———. 1987. *Dimensions of a creole continuum: History, texts and linguistic analysis of Guyanese Creole*. Stanford: Stanford University Press.

Thomason, Sarah Grey, and Terrence Kaufman. 1988. *Language contact, creolization and genetic linguistics*. Berkeley: University of California Press.

Trudgill, Peter. 1986. *Dialects in contact*. Oxford: Basil Blackwell.

Turner, Lorenzo Dow. 1949. *Africanisms in the Gullah dialect*. Chicago: University of Chicago Press.

Valdman, Albert. 1983. Creolization and second language acquisition. *Pidginization and creolization as language acquisition*, ed. by Roger Andersen, 212–34. Rowley, Mass.: Newbury House.

Weinreich, Uriel. 1953. *Languages in contact: Findings and problems*. New York: Linguistic Circle of New York.

Welmers, William E. 1973. *African language structures*. Berkeley: University of California Press.

Whitney, William Dwight. 1881. On mixture in language. *Transactions of the American Philological Association* 12.1–26.

Wittle, Desiree. 1989. *A reanalysis of Jamaican syllable structure*. Undergraduate final paper, Caribbean Studies, University of the West Indies, Mona, Jamaica.

Wolfram, Walt. 1969. *A sociolinguistic description of Detroit Negro speech*. Washington, D.C.: Center for Applied Linguistics.

# An Africanist Approach to the Linguistic Study of Black English: Getting to the Roots of the Tense-Aspect-Modality and Copula Systems in Afro-American

*Charles DeBose and Nicholas Faraclas*

## Africanisms, Creole Genesis, and Black English

As creolists, much of our concern about Africanisms in Afro-American has been shaped and determined by the debate concerning creole genesis. This debate has been characterized by sharp contention between proponents of various genetic theories (monogenesis vs. polygenesis, substrate influence vs. language universals, etc.). By concluding that neither an exclusively substratist nor an exclusively universalist position accounts adequately for the structures found in Afro-American, the University of Amsterdam Workshop in 1985 set a proper tone for the discussion of Africanisms in Afro-American at this Round Table. In our contribution we wish to stress that the processes of pidginization, creolization, and decreolization involve the complex and creative interaction of many factors, including (but not restricted to) substrate and universal elements, and that no monocausal explanation is sufficient at any stage. Furthermore, the product of this interaction is an independent, coherent system in its own right rather than a hodgepodge of borrowed features and lexical items. No variety of Afro-American illustrates these points more effectively than does Black English (BE).

### *The Black English Challenge to the Study of Africanisms*

Because BE bears more surface similarity to Standard English (SE) and less surface similarity to African languages than do most other Afro-American language systems, the BE data force us to confront head-on the complex nature of the task of research on Africanisms. The first challenge posed by the BE data relates to the definition of the term "Africanism" itself. If "Africanism" were to be defined solely in terms of surface features and lexical items, we would be forced to conclude that few Africanisms exist in BE. In our opinion, this definition is unnecessarily restrictive and tends to trivialize whatever influence substrate language patterns may have had on Afro-American.

If, however, the definition is broadened to include systems (i.e., holistic, meaningful patterns that underlie surface phenomena), striking resemblances between African languages and such highly decreolized varieties as BE become apparent. Moreover, it is only when these resemblances are understood in terms of the African language patterns that motivated them that a comprehensive account is possible of the surface realizations of similar patterns in BE.

The second challenge posed by the BE data involves the possibility of identifying a particular African language as the substrate for a particular variety of Afro-American. While investigators of a less decreolized variety of Afro-American might be tempted to isolate a single African language or a small group of African languages as the substrate for that language, such a task would be impossible in the case of BE. We contend that the search for a single substrate language is as futile as the search for a single cause for creole genesis. The search for a single substrate language ignores the sociolinguistic realities of West African society and of Afro-American diaspora communities.

The very rich multilingual and multicultural tradition that typifies West African coastal societies and the potent pidginization and creolization dynamics that this tradition has set into motion undoubtedly predate the arrival of the Portuguese in the fifteenth century. While West Africa is one of the most diverse regions of the world in terms of the number and genetic affiliation of its languages, constant and intimate interethnic contact over thousands of years has forged a profound typological unity among the languages of the area. In this study, therefore, we define "substrate" as the systems, structures, and features that characterize the hundreds of languages spoken along the West African coast as an area and typological unit (see Gilman 1986).

The third challenge posed by the BE data regards the integrity of Afro-American languages as separate linguistic systems. The higher prestige of the lexifier languages and the fact that researchers are highly literate in those languages make it extremely difficult for creolists to maintain the unbiased attitude required for the linguistic study of Afro-American. Because of its high degree of surface similarity to English, BE has suffered inordinately from an Anglocentric approach to its analysis (see Turner 1949 for a discussion of how similar biases affected the study of Gullah). Up to the present, no comprehensive account of the verbal system of BE has been proposed. This is due less to any lack of intelligence on the part of those who have studied BE in the past than to their commitment to the derivation of BE forms from English forms without any consideration of the substrate systems. Once the substrate systems are considered, however, a comprehensive, highly regular, and elegantly simple BE verbal system emerges that accounts not only for the data that were successfully dealt with in former analyses but also for the numerous data that forced past researchers to revert to ad hoc rules, makeshift subsystems, and lists of exceptions.

### *An Africanist Approach to the Study of Black English*

In this paper we outline an Africanist approach to the study of BE which proposes developmental scenarios that relate BE systems to corresponding systems in West African languages. The model of BE upon which our scenarios are based builds on previous efforts to validate the existence of a basilectal BE system in connection with claims of either a creole ancestry for BE, continuing influence of an African substratum, or both (Stewart 1966, 1968; Dillard 1972; DeBose 1976a, 1976b, 1977, 1983a, 1983b, 1988).

Mufwene (1983) provides a highly coherent defense of the creolist hypothesis based on similarities between the verb system of basilectal BE and the Caribbean Anglophone creoles (CACs). Our research corroborates and expands upon Mufwene's analysis of the basilectal BE verb system. Although he limits his argument to the defense of creolist hypotheses for BE genesis and refrains from addressing the question of an African substratum, the common systemic features that Mufwene postulates for basilectal BE and the CACs are also widespread among the languages of West Africa in areas from which many of the ancestors of BE speakers were taken as slaves.

### *Data Samples*

To date we have collected approximately one hour of spontaneous speech from each of ten BE speakers. This constitutes the BE speech data base for the present study. The empirical substance of the data gathered thus far does not differ radically from that of data previously reported in the literature. Our greater success in achieving a coherent overall analysis is due more to our access to native speaker intuitions, on the one hand, and to our familiarity with West African language structures, on the other, than to any new revelations in the data.

Generalizations concerning the substrate are based on a sample consisting of all of the languages of southern Nigeria for which detailed grammatical descriptions exist (see Appendix). The languages in the sample are among the most widely spoken languages in the region, and taken together they include the mother tongues of at least 60% of the population of southern Nigeria and at least 30% of the coastal population of West Africa. Genetically, the languages in the sample represent almost every major division of the two branches and four subbranches of Niger-Congo found in southern Nigeria (Faraclas 1987, 1988). An ideal substrate sample would, of course, include all of the major linguistic groupings found along the entire West African coast, but such a data base does not as yet exist. The southern Nigerian sample represents the most comprehensive effort to date in this direction and is therefore used in this study.

For the sake of clarity and simplicity, all substrate examples used in this work are taken from Nigerian Pidgin (NP). We wish, however, to emphasize the fact that the features listed in this work are so widespread in southern Nigeria that almost any one of the languages in the sample could have provided an equally comprehensive and satisfactory set of parallel forms. No arbitrary "cafeteria style" inventory of examples is necessary to illustrate the considerable morpho-syntactic correspondence between NP and the languages of southern Nigeria, whether considered individually or as an areal-typological unit.

### *Analysis of the Black English Verbal System*

Even at this preliminary stage, the main contours of the BE verbal system are clear. Using a very eclectic version of the grammatical construction model for grammatical analysis (Fillmore 1987; Fillmore et al. 1983–84) we have identified a few constructions that account systematically for nearly 100% of the relations observed in our data. According to Fillmore (1987:3), what distinguishes construction grammar most from other grammatical models is

> (1) that it aims at describing the grammar of a language in terms of a collection of *grammatical constructions* each of which represents a *pairing of a syntactic pattern with a meaning structure* and (2) that it gives serious attention to the structure of *complex* grammatical patterns instead of limiting its attention to the most simple and universal structures. (emphasis in original)

In the next section we describe the constructions that make up the BE verbal system, paying particular attention to the tense-aspect-modality and copula subsystems. In the following section the matrix of motivating factors that underlies each of the major components of the BE tense-aspect-modality and copula subsystems is discussed. As elaborated thus far, Grammatical Construction Theory seeks to explain the existence of a particular construction A in a particular language by citing a constellation of similar or parallel constructions (B, C, D, etc.) in the same language which can be said to *motivate* it (i.e., constructions B, C, and D together motivate construction A). Generally, we will follow this procedure in our descriptions of BE verbal constructions, but, given the fact that BE falls along a linguistic continuum that includes a West African or Caribbean substrate and an English superstrate, we group together constructions found along the entire continuum in our matrices of motivating constructions. As such, these matrices provide a rigorous yet supple framework for the formulation of plausible historical scenarios for the development of the BE verbal system.

## The Subject + Predicate Construction in Black English

The main contours of the BE tense-aspect-modality and copula systems are highlighted in this section as we focus upon certain properties of BE predicates which we have found to be reliable predictors of their syntactic behavior and semantic interpretation. In the following discussion, the terms "subject" and "predicate" are used for syntactic elements of BE sentences unless we explicitly state otherwise.

The subject + predicate construction consists of a subject directly followed by either a nonverbal predicate (examples 1a–1c), a derived verbal predicate (examples 1d and 1e), or a verbal predicate (examples 2a–2d). The derived verbal predicates are those in which the main verb is delimited in some way, such as by the suffix *-in* or the preverbal marker *done*.

1. a. *We tired.* 'We are tired.'
   b. *He a teacher.* 'He is a teacher.'
   c. *They at home.* 'They are at home.'
   d. *She walkin home.* 'She UNFOLDING STATE walk home.'
   e. *I done walk home.* 'I RESULTATIVE STATE walk home.'

Verb forms similar to the English infinitive, simple present, simple past, and past participle frequently occur in BE, but such variation does not play a primary role in the tense-aspect-modality interpretation of BE sentences. Sentence 2a, which has a nonstative verb, derives a completive aspect interpretation from the lexical stativity parameter (LSP, described below) regardless of the surface form of the verb. Sentence 2b, however, which has a stative verb, derives a noncompletive (perfective) aspect interpretation from the LSP. When a verb variant similar to the English infinitive is selected (examples 2c and 2d) many BE informants assign to such sentences a noncompletive (habitual) aspect interpretation in contrast to the completive aspect interpretation specified for 2a or the noncompletive (perfective) aspect interpretation specified for 2b.

2. a. *I go/went/gone/home.* 'I COMPLETIVE (PAST) go home.'
   b. *I been at home.* 'I NONCOMPLETIVE (PERFECT) at home.'
   c. *I go(z) home.* 'I NONCOMPLETIVE (HABITUAL) go home.'
   d. *I be(z) at home.* 'I NONCOMPLETIVE (HABITUAL) at home.'

The classification of 2c as noncompletive/habitual aspect, notwithstanding its similarity to the English simple present tense, is motivated by its syntactic and semantic parallelism with sentences like 2d, in which *be* occurs with the suffix *-z* instead of the English simple present form *is*. Furthermore, the suffix *-z* occurs in BE with all persons.

The noncompletive/habitual predicates of 2c and 2d are realizations of one of two major subconstructions (defined below) of the BE subject + predicate construction. The sentences in examples 1a–1e, and 2a and 2b all derive their aspect and tense interpretations from the LSP. The noncompletive/habitual predicates of 2c and 2d are considered to have zero stativity, however, in that they are not subject to the LSP.

The two major subconstructions of the subject + predicate construction are characterized by several important constraints on their syntactic patterning, including: (1) the selection of negative markers and (2) the use of irrealis proverbs and other preverbal irrealis markers (defined below).

### *Negative Markers and Other Proverbs*

Much of the evidence in support of our analysis of BE predicates lies in the patterns of co-occurrence observed between different types of predicates and different subsets of a class of markers, referred to here as "proverbs." Proverbs occur optionally in the syntactic position immediately preceding the predicate and following other optional markers (specified below) which may occur between the subject and predicate. The proverb class includes the negative proverbs *ain't* and *don't*; proverbs proper such as *is, do, was/wudn't, has/hadn't,* and *did/didn't*; and irrealis proverbs such as *will/won't* and *can/can't*. The proverb class of markers may precede the subject in interrogative sentences, as below:

3. a. *Ain't they at home?*
   b. *Is you been at home?*
   c. *Can you go home?*
   d. *Do you be at home?*

### Ain't *versus* Don't *Negation*

BE sentences such as those in examples 1 and 2 are negated with either *ain't* or *don't,* depending on the type of predicate. Habitual aspect verb predicates generally take *don't* negation, whereas other predicates may not be negated by *don't,* as illustrated below:

4. a. *I don't go home.*
   b. *I don't be at home.*
   c. **We don't tired.*
   d. **I don't went home.*

Predicates which do not take *don't* negation are negated by *ain't,* as below:

5. a. *He ain't a teacher.* 'He is not a teacher.'
   b. *I ain't went home.* 'I didn't/haven't go(ne) home.'

BE predicates, whether negated by *ain't* or *don't,* as well as those which directly follow the subject, are interpreted as realis modality unless they are marked otherwise, that is, contextually, by following an irrealis proverb or by containing an irrealis predicate marker (defined below).

### *Irrealis Modality Proverbs and Predicates*

Irrealis modality may be expressed in BE by placing a predicate directly after an irrealis proverb, as in 6a, or an irrealis predicate marker, as in 6b–6d.

6. a. *He will be a teacher.* 'He will be a teacher.'
   b. *She gon be a teacher.* 'She is going to be a teacher.'
   c. *Im 'on be at home.* 'I'm going to be at home.'
   d. *We finta go home.* 'We are about to go home.'

Unlike irrealis proverbs, irrealis predicate markers may not optionally precede the subject in an interrogative construction and may follow a negative or tense-marking proverb. Only irrealis/habitual verb predicates (defined below) may directly follow an irrealis proverb or irrealis predicate marker. However, as examples 6a–6c show, certain nonverbal predicates may follow an irrealis proverb + *be,* or an irrealis predicate marker + *be.*

### *The Irrealis/Habitual Verb Construction and the Unmarked Predicate Construction*

The syntactic properties of BE predicates examined thus far strongly support the existence of an irrealis/habitual verb subconstruction of the BE subject + predicate construction. As it turns out, when the semantic properties of BE predicates are considered, there is ample evidence in support of another major subconstruction which accounts for all BE predicates except those classified as irrealis/habitual predicates. We shall refer to all such predicates as instances of the unmarked predicate construction. They are unmarked in the sense that in the absence of special markers or contextual cues, such predicates derive their tense and aspect interpretation from the LSP.

### *The Unmarked Predicate Construction and the Lexical Stativity Parameter*

Mufwene (1983) observes that the assignment of tense and aspect values to BE sentences appears to conform to a LSP used by linguists to describe the verbal systems of Caribbean English creoles. Mufwene's version of the LSP is equivalent to the factitive tense-aspect familiar to West Africanists (Welmers 1973). While our work corroborates Mufwene's attribution of a significant role to the LSP in BE, we expand Mufwene's basic model, which recognizes two degrees of stativity in finite BE predicates—[+stative] and [−stative]—to include a third [+/−stative] category. Such an adjustment makes it possible to account for certain BE predicates which behave at times as [+stative] and at other times as [−stative]. The general principle of the LSP is as follows: If there are no contextual cues to the contrary, a stative predicate is normally interpreted as nonpast in tense and noncompletive in aspect, while a nonstative predicate is normally interpreted to be in the past tense and in the completive aspect.

We follow Mufwene in characterizing unmarked nonstative verbal predicates as [−stative] and the predicates delimited with either *-in* or *done-* as [+stative]. The LSP accounts adequately for the examples in the previous section. For instance, 2a is assigned a [+past] and [+completive] interpretation, whereas sentences (1a–1e) are assigned a [−past, −completive] interpretation.

A problem arises, however, in the interpretation of unmarked predicates that contain a stative verb. As will be shown below, unmarked BE stative verb predicates behave syntactically like [−stative] predicates in most (but not all) cases. Semantically, however, there are a number of instances in which the tense and aspect interpretation of unmarked predicates containing stative verbs such as *know* or *think* is ambiguous, as in 7a, or parallels that of [+stative] nonverbal predicates, as in 7b.

7. a. *I aint know about it.* 'I don't/didn't, know about it.'
   b. *I think he walk home.* 'I NONCOMPLETIVE PRESENT think that he COMPLETIVE PAST walk home.'

The proposed [+/−stative] value becomes helpful here. Using this modified version of the LSP, the syntactic patterns displayed by unmarked predicates may be accounted for by a comprehensive yet simple set of constraints on the unmarked predicate subconstruction. To fully account for those constraints we must first consider certain properties of BE subject nouns and pronouns, not discussed up to this point, which serve as key criteria for the subclassification of predicates.

*Special Pronouns and z-Suffixed Pronouns and Nouns*

Because our analysis permits the occurrence of all types of BE predicates directly after subjects, we can automatically account for 1a–1e, in which nonverbal and derived verbal predicates occur without a copula proverb. There is no need to invoke contraction and deletion processes, as previous analyses conducted from an Anglocentric perspective have done, to account for the absence of surface forms of *is* and *are* where such forms are expected to occur in English. In order to account fully for the occurrence in BE data of forms which resemble English contractions, our analysis recognizes special variants *I'm, it's, that's,* and *what's* of the pronouns *I, it, that,* and *what* which happen to resemble the English contractions of the same forms. Our analysis of them as single morphemes is supported by the fact that they tend to occur in complementary distribution with their simple pronoun equivalents. Only simple variants of *I, it, that,* and *what,* for example, occur with irrealis/habitual verbs and unmarked nonstative verbal predicates, hence the ungrammaticality of 8a and 8b:

8. a. **I'm be at home.* 'I HABITUAL at home.'
   b. **It's rain all night.* 'It COMPLETIVE PAST rain all night.'

On the other hand, simple variants of *I, it, that,* and *what* tend to be unacceptable when followed directly by a nonverbal predicate, as in the following examples:

9. a. **What happenin?* 'What is happening?'
   b. **That a book.* 'That is a book.'
   c. **It cold.* 'It is cold.'
   d. **I at home.* 'I am at home.'

The special pronoun analysis is also supported by the acceptability of the simple subject pronouns *you, he, she, we,* and so on, in the same environments where special forms of *I, it, that,* and *what* occur:

10. a. *I'm at home.* 'I am at home.'
    b. *He at home.* 'He is at home.'
    c. *They at home.* 'They are at home.'
    d. *It's cold.* 'It is cold.'

e. *We cold.* 'We are cold.'
f. *What's cookin?* 'Greetings!'
g. *She cookin.* 'She is cooking.'

Our analysis accounts for other properties of BE subjects which resemble English contractions by means of a special -*z* suffix that may be added to any simple subject pronoun or noun, as below:

11. a. *I-z at home.*
b. *We-z cold.*
c. *Her mother-z a teacher.*

The behavior of BE special pronouns and *z*-suffixed nouns and pronouns supports our modified version of the LSP to the extent that nonstative verb predicates always select simple subject pronouns, whereas other unmarked predicates, depending on their value for the feature [stative], may select certain special or suffixed pronouns as well.

*Syntactic Constraints on the Unmarked Predicate Construction*

In the preceding discussion we identified three syntactic properties of unmarked BE predicates which reliably predict their value for the feature [stative]. One is the selection of the proverbs *is* and *was/wudn't* as opposed to the proverbs *had/hadn't* or *did/didn't;* a second is the selection of simple versus special *z*-suffixed pronouns; and a third is occurrence in serial irrealis/habitual verb constructions following *be* versus nonoccurrence after *be*.

Derived Verb + *in* and irrealis predicates marked by *(g)on* or *finta* take the proverbs *is* and *was/wudn't,* whereas nonstative verb predicates always select the proverbs *had/hadn't* or *did/didn't*. Stative verbal predicates, resultative state *done* + Verb, and perfect *been* predicates behave like derived Verb + *in* and irrealis predicates in selecting the *is* proverb, but tend not to select *was/wudn't*:

12. a. *Is you done ate breakfast?* 'Have you eaten breakfast?'
b. *Is you been at home?* 'Have you been at home?'
c. *They had done went home.* 'They had gone home.'
d. *She had been at home.* 'She had been at home.'

Stative verbs usually behave like nonstative verbs in selecting the proverbs *had/hadn't* or *did/didn't*:

13. a. *Had you thought about it?* 'Did/had you think/thought about it?'
b. *I didn't know that.* 'I didn't know that.'

The proverb *is* has marginal acceptability, however, with some stative verbs:

14. *Is you thought about it?* 'Did/have you think/thought about it?'

Stative verbs also usually behave like nonstative verbs in only selecting simple subject pronouns, but *z*-suffixed pronouns are marginally acceptable with stative verbs, as illustrated by the unacceptability of 15a compared with the acceptability of 15b:

15. a. **I-z think about it.* 'I think about it.'
    b. *I-z thought about it.* 'I (have) thought about it.'

Nonverbal, derived verbal, and *been* predicates and irrealis modality markers freely accept *z*-suffixed pronouns and the special pronouns *it's, that's,* and *what's*. The special pronoun *I'm* is usually selected with nonverbal predicates, irrealis predicates, and Verb + *in* predicates. *I'm* is rarely selected with *done* + Verb and *been* predicates, however, except in conservative lects such as Samaná English (DeBose 1983a, 1988).

Unmarked predicates which select the proverbs *was/wudn't* as well as *is,* and the special pronoun *I'm,* also occur in serial constructions with the irrealis/habitual verb *be*. Such predicates conform to all the above-mentioned correlates of [+ stative] predicates and may be said to have a higher degree of stativity than *done* + Verb predicates which occur in irrealis/habitual constructions following *be,* as in example 16, but rarely select the pronoun *I'm* or the proverb *was/wasn't*.

16. *She be done walk home.* 'She HABITUAL-RESULTATIVE STATE walk home.'

Derived verbal *done* predicates appear to be more stative than perfect *been* predicates, which never follow *be,* and rarely select the pronoun *I'm*. Perfect *been* and other stative verbs share with nonstative verbs selection of the proverbs *had/hadn't* and/or *did/didn't* and nonoccurrence in serial constructions with *be;* but they are more stative than nonstative verbs in terms of their occasional co-occurrence with *z*-suffixed pronouns and the proverb *is*.

### *Realis Modality and Neutral Modality Markers*

To complete our description of the general contours of the BE subject + predicate construction, we must account briefly for two syntactic classes which occur optionally between the subject and predicate or proverb and predicate. One of these classes we label "realis modality adverbs," and in it we include the "remote perfect adverb" *been* and what Spears (1982) calls the "semi-auxiliary" *come*. This class occupies the position directly after the subject. The other class, "neutral modality markers," occupies the position between adverbs and proverbs. The two most common neutral modality markers are *must(a)* and *might(a)*. When one of these markers co-occurs with a proverb, the two produce the so-called double modal constructions observable in sentences 17:

17. a. *We might will go home.* 'It might be the case that we will go home.'
    b. *She must ain't at home.* 'It must be the case that she is not at home.'

The adverb *beén* (pronounced with heavy stress) adds to the propositional content of the sentence the delimitation 'long since':

18. a. *I beén at home!* 'I have long since been at home.'
    b. *We beén go there!* 'It has long since been the case that we go there.'

*Beén* can co-occur with a neutral modality marker as in 19a or a neutral modality marker and a proverb as in 19b:

19. a. *We beén might go there!* 'It has long since been the case that we might go there.'
    b. *We beén might can go there!* 'It has long since been the case that we might be able to go there.'

The adverb *come* adds to the propositional content of a sentence an element of the speaker's indignation. Syntactically *come* is restricted to the environment directly preceding a Verb + *in* predicate. It never occurs in the negative mode.

20. *She come blabbin her mouth.* 'SPEAKER is indignant about the fact that she was talking indiscreetly.'

Having completed our account of how BE functions as a linguistic system synchronically, we can now turn our attention to how the BE verbal system has developed diachronically. In the next section we show how superstrate, substrate, and universal factors could have provided the raw materials, the structural matrices, the functional models, and the inspirational sparks from which the BE speaking community has creatively forged a living language.

## Scenarios for the Development of the Black English Verbal System

In this section, the tense-aspect-modality and copula systems of BE and its superstrate and substrate languages are compared in order to formulate plausible scenarios for the development of the BE verbal system. The semantic and syntactic structures cited here as representative of the substrate are those shared by the languages of southern Nigeria. Specific forms are taken from Nigerian Pidgin. It should be noted, however, that the structures which typify the languages of southern Nigeria are almost identical to those which characterize the great majority of Afro-American language varieties, and that the forms used in Nigerian Pidgin are strikingly similar to those used in the English-lexifier creoles of the Caribbean.

Figure 1. The semantics of tense, aspect, and modality in the languages of southern Nigeria:

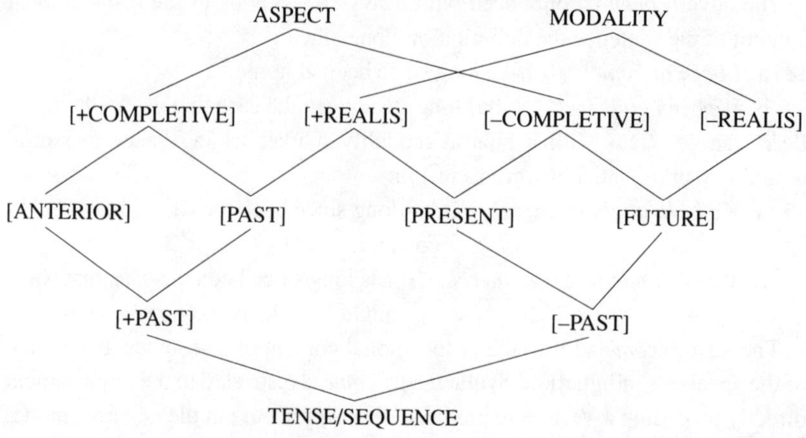


*Tense-Aspect-Modality Systems*

A schematic diagram of the web of relations that hold between the semantic components of the tense-aspect-modality systems found in the languages of southern Nigeria would look something like figure 1.

In the languages of southern Nigeria, aspect and modality distinctions are primary and tense distinctions are secondary. Most tense distinctions are not regularly signaled morphosyntactically. The tense interpretation of a predicate normally depends either on how it is marked for aspect and/or modality or on other contextual cues.

The aspectual subsystem has a completive pole and a noncompletive pole, while the modality subsystem has a realis pole and an irrealis pole. The lines that link the poles on the web diagram are default paths, showing how the subsystems interrelate. If a predicate is assigned a given polar value *a,* it will normally be interpreted to have the other polar values linked to polar value *a* by a line on the diagram. For example, a predicate marked [+completive] will normally be interpreted as referring to an event in the past, and it is usually not necessary to use any special morphosyntactic markers to signal its value for tense. Likewise, [−realis] predicates are normally interpreted to be in the future tense:

21. *A dón* *sík.*
I COMPLETIVE sick
'I got/have become sick.'

Figure 2. The semantax of tense, aspect, and modality in the languages of southern Nigeria. (LSP = Lexical Stativity Parameter; SM = Special Marker)

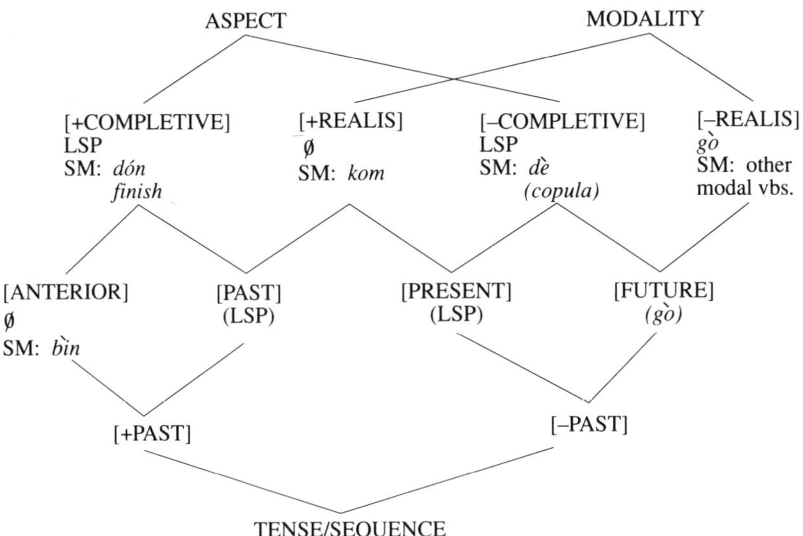


Combinations of markers or special markers must be used when two or more nonlinked polarities are involved:

22. *A gò dòn sík.*
I IRREALIS COMPLETIVE sick
'I will get/will have become sick.'

The morphosyntactic machinery normally used in southern Nigerian languages to signal the semantic relations outlined in figure 1 are shown in figure 2.

Realis predicates are not usually marked as such, while irrealis predicates are consistently signaled by modality markers or modal verbs. Since all predicates are assumed to be [+realis] unless marked otherwise, a very strong argument can be made for the primacy of modality distinctions in the languages of southern Nigeria. In most of these languages, the general irrealis marker is the most commonly used of all tense-aspect-modality markers (Faraclas 1987, 1988). Special realis modality markers, in almost every case a reflex of the verb meaning 'come,' are available as well in most southern Nigerian languages.

If there are no contextual cues to the contrary, the LSP assigns the values [+completive], [+past] to [−stative] predicates, and [−completive], [−past] to [+stative] predicates:

23. *A ting sé ím gó Légos.*

I think that she go Lagos.

'I think ([+stative] [−completive], [−past]) that she went ([−stative] [+completive], [+past]) to Lagos.'

Besides the LSP, southern Nigerian languages have the means to signal aspectual distinctions more explicitly by using a reflex of the locative copula as a special noncompletive marker (*dè* in NP) and a reflex of a verb meaning 'finish' or 'be done' (*finish* or *don* in NP) as a special completive marker:

24. *A gó Légos.* but *A dè gó Légos.*
I go Lagos. I NONCOMPLETIVE go Lagos.
'I went to Lagos.' 'I am going/always go to Lagos.'

As mentioned above, in most of the languages of southern Nigeria tense distinctions are normally inferred from aspectual or modality values. Adverbials of time such as 'yesterday,' 'today,' or 'tomorrow' are often used in ambiguous cases. An [anterior] sequentiality marker (*bin* in NP) is usually available as well:

25. *A gó bìn dón sík.*
I IRREALIS ANTERIOR COMPLETIVE sick
'I will have gotten sick.'

The English tense-aspect-modality system can be diagrammed somewhat similarly to that of the languages of southern Nigeria, but with some key differences, as shown in figure 3.

In contrast to the previous diagrams, the lines that link the various values for each component of the English tense-aspect-modality system represented in figure 3 do *not* represent default interpretation paths. Since each component (except [+realis]) is regularly marked and such default interpretation principles as the LSP do not play a central role in the English system, these lines show how the morphosyntactic behavior and semantic interpretation of each component are embedded in the system.

Tense is of primary importance in the English system, with the simple past (*-ed*) forms of verbs signaling [+past] tense and the simple present forms marking [−past] tense. Either the head or the proverb of all predicates must be overtly marked for one of these values. No special nonderived anterior sequence marker exists.

While [+realis] predicates are normally not overtly marked as such, [−realis] predicates are usually signaled by the use of a modal verb followed by the infinitive form of the predicate head or proverb (the infinitive without a preceding modal verb is used in the marginal irrealis subjunctive). The simple present forms and the infinitive forms for most verbs are in the majority of cases indistinguishable from one another at the surface.

Figure 3. The semantax of tense, aspect, and modality in English

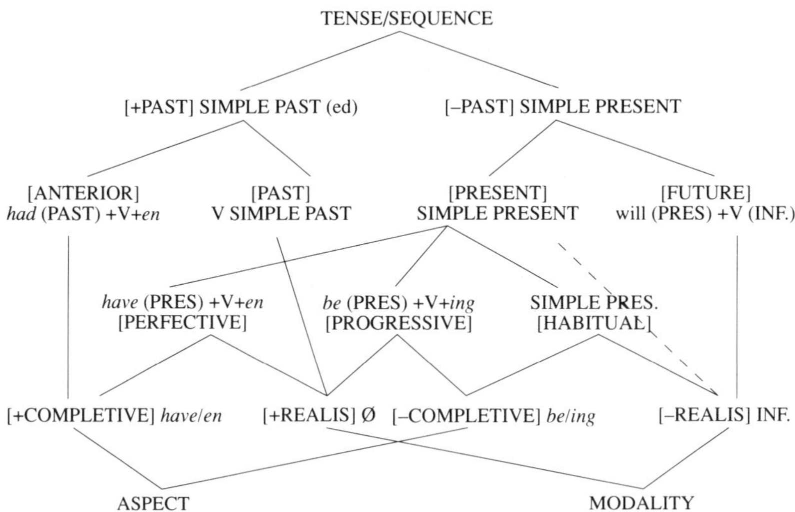


Aspect is less crucial in defining the English system than are tense and modality, in that it need not be overtly marked. The discontinuous morpheme *be* (Verb)-*ing* is used to signal [−completive] aspect, while *have* Verb-*en* is used to mark [+completive] aspect. Since all predicates must be marked for tense in English, [+completive] and [−completive] aspects are never marked as such at the surface. Instead, mixed tense-aspect categories such as present perfect and past progressive are expressed in surface realizations. Furthermore, aspectual interpretations are frequently derived from the context of sentences in the simple past or present tense, for example, the frequent habitual aspect interpretation of the simple present.

The web of tense-aspect-modality relations in BE is shown in figure 4.

Modality plays a major role in defining the basic constructions (UP vs. I/HP) and the default interpretation paths (LSP) that characterize the BE tense-aspect-modality system. BE predicates in the unmarked construction are [+realis], and those in the other basic construction may be interpreted as irrealis modality or habitual aspect. Special [+realis] markers such as *come* are also used in certain pragmatic contexts (Spears 1982).

All BE predicates are assigned a value for the aspectual feature [completive]. In unmarked predicates the value for [completive] is determined by the LSP, as outlined above. All irrealis/habitual predicates are [−completive]. Special markers are available to signal that the aspectual value associated with

Figure 4. The semantax of the BE tense-aspect-modality system. (LSP = Lexical Stativity Parameter; SM = Special Marker, UP = Unmarked Predicate; I/HP = Irrealis/Habitual Predicate)

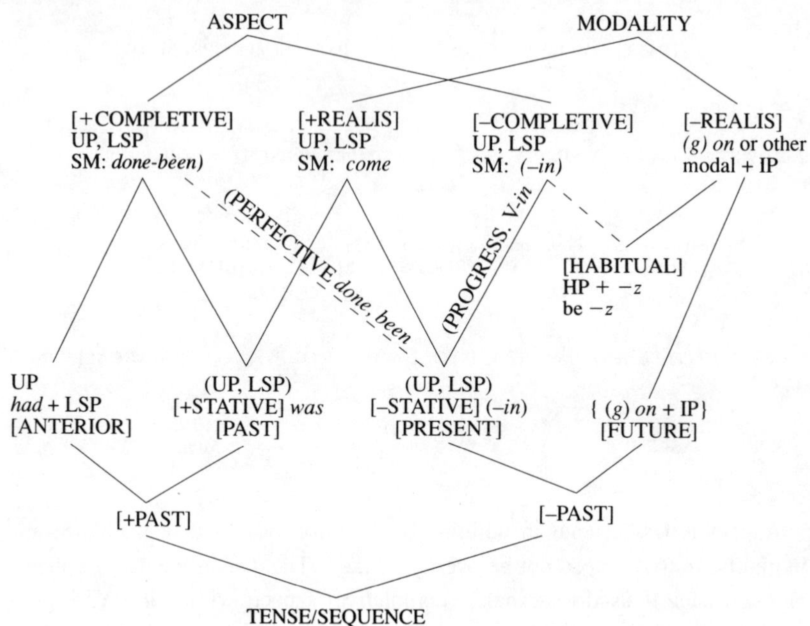


a given predicate is contrary to that which would have been assigned to it by the LSP. The unfolding state *-in* suffix is used to stativize [−stative] predicates, making them eligible for the assignment of a [−completive] value for aspect by the LSP. The proverb *do(n't)* and the verb suffix *-z* are used to override the [+completive] value assigned to [−stative] predicates by the LSP and replace it with a [+habitual] aspectual interpretation (DeBose and Faraclas 1988).

Tense values for most BE predicates are derived from aspectual values determined by the LSP in the case of the present and past, or from modality values associated with the use of the irrealis predicates in the case of the future. Special markers are available to signal that the tense value associated with a given predicate is contrary to that which would have been assigned to it by the lexical stativity parameter. The proverb *was* is used to mark past tense with [+stative] predicates, and the *-in* suffix is used to mark the present form of [−stative] predicates. Selection of the preverbal marker *done,* which is [+stative], overrides the default past-tense interpretation assigned to nonstative predicates by the LSP, without changing their [+completive] aspectual interpretation (De-

Bose and Faraclas 1988). Anterior sequence is signaled by the form *had,* which must be followed by a [−stative] (or [+/−stative]) predicate.

Forms corresponding to the English simple past versus simple present are used to make tenselike distinctions in some lects of BE, but these patterns are highly variable and account for very restricted subsets of BE predicates; they cannot be said to define the general functioning of the BE system in any way.

Mixed tense and aspect meanings are associated with some BE forms. The suffix *-in* consistently conveys a progressive meaning which combines present tense with noncompletive aspect. The unmarked copula verb *bèen* and the prefix *done-* often convey a perfective meaning which combines past tense and noncompletive aspect.

### *Copula Systems*

In the languages of southern Nigeria, copulas are used (1) as proverbs to link predicative noun phrases, locatives, and, marginally, "adjectives" (which are usually stative verbs and may be used without a copula) to the subject; and (2) as noncompletive aspect markers. There are usually several different copular forms which serve different proverbal functions:

26. a. *Hàlíma nà tícha.*<br>
NAME IDENTITY COPULA teacher<br>
'Halima *is* a teacher.'

b. *Hàlíma dé Légos.*<br>
NAME LOCATIVE COPULA lagos<br>
'Halima *is* in Lagos.'

c. *Hàlíma dé bíg.* OR: *Halima big.*<br>
NAME LOCATIVE COPULA big (adj.) NAME big (verb)<br>
'Halima *is* big.'

d. *Hàlíma dé wàka.*<br>
NAME NONCOMPLETIVE walk<br>
'Halima *is* walking.'

e. *A nó bì tícha.*<br>
I NEGATIVE IDENTITY COPULA teacher<br>
'I *am* not a teacher.'

In English the copula has similar proverbal and noncompletive marker functions, as shown in the glosses to example 26. Generally, only the verb *be* is used in all of these cases, and it is marked for person, number, and tense as are all finite English verbs. Since every English sentence must be marked for tense, the copula must always be present in all of these environments, and the copulaless version of example 26c, is impossible. Because tense is obligatorily marked, a purely noncompletive aspectual category is impossible at the surface, so the present-tense form of *be* could perhaps be said to signal the mixed tense-aspect category progressive when it is used as an aspectual marker.

In BE several different copular forms alternate with zero in both the proverbal and noncompletive marker functions listed above. The forms *be* (irrealis/habitual) and *bèen* (unmarked) are syntactically verbs, but semantically they mark noncompletive (habitual versus perfect) aspect. The form *is* is optionally used as a nonpast proverb, and the form *was* is obligatorily used as a proverb for the past tense. Like all proverbal forms in BE, *is* and *was* have special negative forms and are subject to presubject inversion in yes-no questions. Following general BE patterns, *is* and *was* are not inflected for person or number.

Although some observers have implied that the BE copula occurs in the same environments as does the copula in English, a more precise statement of the distribution of the BE copula would have to take into account the use of some forms of the BE copula before *done-* and *been* or the use of *ain't* before all unmarked predicates. The optional absence of the copular proverb (*is*) before stative predicates in the present tense is accounted for by the fact that the LSP automatically assigns noncompletive aspect and nonpast tense to such predicates, and therefore no proverb is needed for the specific purpose of tense marking.

### *Motivations for the Black English Tense-Aspect-Modality and Copula Systems*

*Modality.* The use of modality markers and modal predicates to distinguish irrealis from realis modality in BE is a pattern found both in the superstrate and the substrate, as well as in languages universally. The existence of a reflex of the verb meaning 'go' as an irrealis future marker is common to BE and the substrate languages and is similar in form (but not in meaning) to the *be going to* construction in English. The distinction between an imminent and remote future or between an unsure and sure future (*finta* vs. *(g)on* in BE) is found in BE, English, and the substrates. BE shares with the substrates the marking of realis modality by means of a reflex of the verb meaning 'come,' although its specialized use as a marker of indignation seems to be an innovation in BE. The tendency for the verbs meaning 'go' and 'come' to become tense-aspect-modality markers is a widely recognized language universal.

*Predicate constructions.* The use of two separate constructions to distinguish unmarked from irrealis/habitual predicates in BE situates the BE system at an intermediate point between the substrate system (in which one predicate construction prevails throughout) and the superstrate system (in which five constructions—simple present, simple past, present participle, past participle, and infinitive—are used). In form, the BE irrealis/habitual verb construction could be seen as the fusion of elements from the English simple present (for example, the *-z* suffix, *do* proverb, and *don't* negation) and infinitive constructions (with, for example, ∅ tense, no person or number marking). The relative unimportance of tense and the use of a reflex of the copula to mark noncompletive aspect in BE irrealis/habitual predicates could be motivated by similar features found in substrate languages as well. It should be noted, however, that while a reflex of the copula is used to mark noncompletive aspect as such in the substrates, in BE *be* marks a more particular form of [−completive] aspect, namely, the habitual aspect. The habitual *-z* suffix, which can be said to be motivated by the English third-person simple present *-s* inflection, is analogously extended to all person and number environments.

*Copula environments and the lexical stativity parameter.* As noted above, copular proverbs and the copula-derived habitual marker are not obligatory in BE in environments where aspect and tense interpretations would be predicted by the LSP. Since both BE substrate and BE superstrate languages commonly employ copular proverbs (before nominal, adjectival, and locative predicates), on the one hand, and copula-derived noncompletive markers, on the other, the existence of these structures in BE may be said to be motivated from both directions. It is likely, moreover, that these environments for copula proverb use and the development of copula-derived aspectual markers correspond to universal language patterns, which may be cited as a motivating force as well.

The occurrence of nominal, adjectival, locative, and derived stative predicates directly after a subject with no intervening copular proverb or copula-derived aspect marker in BE has no superstrate motivation. In the BE substrate languages, most items that convey adjectival meanings in English are actually stative verbs and are most commonly used directly after a subject marker with no intervening copular proverb, although a copular proverb may often be optionally inserted here (just as in BE; see example 26c above). We may conclude, therefore, that the copulaless structures found in BE are motivated by the subject + stative verb/adjective construction in the BE substrate, which BE has innovatively extended to nominal, locative, and derived stative predicate environments.

This use of nominal, locative, adjectival, and derived predicates as stative predicates immediately after a subject has important implications for the operation of the LSP in BE. In most of the BE substrate languages all predicates contain either a [+stative] or a [−stative] verb, with predicates containing a [+stative] verb being [+stative] and those with a [−stative] verb being [−stative]. In BE, the LSP accommodates itself to a system containing many nonverbal and derived predicates by assigning the value [+stative] to them. Note that nonverbal and derived [+stative] predicates far outnumber the [+stative] verb predicates and English-influenced forms such as the special pronouns, and suffixed pronouns co-occur more regularly with nonverbal or derived predicates than with [+stative] verbs (mirroring their usage in English). Thus, a new class of [+/−stative] predicates, consisting of predicates containing [+stative] verbs and whose semantic interpretation and syntactic behavior lie midway between that of [−stative] and [+stative] predicates has emerged.

Although the composition of the [+stative] and [−stative] categories to which the LSP applies in BE can be said to be motivated to a fairly high degree by superstrate categories, the actual operation of the LSP in assigning tense and aspect values is almost identical to that of the LSP in the substrate languages. In short, the LSP can be seen as a substrate-motivated semantic filter through which new forms (from whatever source) are integrated into the BE verbal system.

*Tense and aspect*. In English, tense is of primary importance and aspect is of secondary importance, but the opposite is true in BE and its substrates. The development of mixed tense and aspect categories such as progressive and perfect in BE seems to be bringing the BE system gradually closer to the English system.

The split of [−completive] aspect into progressive tense or aspect, on the one hand, and habitual aspect, on the other, also mirrors the English tense-aspect-modality web more than it does that of the substrates. Just as the copular noncompletive marker from the substrates seems to have become specialized as the habitual marker in BE, so does the superstrate present participle suffix *-ing* seem to have been adopted as a marker for the BE progressive (in the form of the stativizing suffix *-in*).

BE stressed adverbial *béen* 'long since' and unstressed unmarked predicate *bèen* (which often takes on a perfective marking function) may be considered to be motivated by both the past-participle form of the verb *be* in English and the substrate anterior marker *bìn* in NP. The BE anterior proverb *had* is similar in form and syntactic behavior to the superstrate anterior proverb, but it resembles substrate forms in that it is sensitive to the LSP. The resultative state stativizing marker *done-* in BE could be said to be motivated by the past-participle form of the verb *do* in English and the completive aspect marker in the BE substrates (*dón* in NP). As does *bèen, done-* often takes on a perfect marking function in BE, but its primary function is to derive [+stative] predicates from verbs, allowing them to occur with forms normally used only with [+stative] predicates, such as copular proverbs. The use of *done-* after a copular proverb, in fact, is one of the main arguments for classifying it as a prefix, although the actual morphosyntactic status of *done-* must be investigated further.

The analysis of motivations for the BE tense-aspect-modality and copula systems, in terms of general contours as well as the specific features discussed above, clearly establishes that substrate patterns play a major and crucial role. Although the importance of input from superstrate and universal sources cannot be denied, our assessment of their role would be hopelessly distorted and practically meaningless if we did not take substrate factors into consideration. To ignore the role of the West African substratum in the motivation of the BE system would be analogous to trying to motivate modern English from French without acknowledging the Germanic roots of the English language.

Our success in getting to the African roots of BE owes a great deal to the areal-typological definition of substrate employed in our analysis and our access to a representative data base of languages of the West African area, as well as to our willingness to approach the study of BE without the Anglocentric biases that have clouded much of the previous work on BE. A key element that marks our approach as distinct from most previous analyses of BE is our focus upon systems rather than isolated features. While this analysis does not deal with the entire BE system, we feel confident that we have identified a core system that cannot be ignored in any satisfactory account of BE.

## APPENDIX: Source Grammars

Bamgbose, Ayo. 1966. *A grammar of Yoruba*. West African Language Monographs 5. Cambridge: Cambridge University Press.

Barnwell, Katherine G. L. 1969. *A grammatical description of Mbembe—A Cross River language*. Ph.D. dissertation, University College, London.

Clark, David J. 1969. *A grammatical study of Ekpeye*. Ph.D. dissertation, University of London School of Oriental and African Studies.

Emmenanjo, E. Nnolue. 1978. *Elements of modern Igbo grammar*. Ibadan: Ibadan University Press.

———. 1985. *Auxiliaries in Igbo syntax: A comparative study*. Bloomington: Indiana University Linguistics Club.

Faraclas, Nicholas. 1984. *A grammar of Obolo*. Bloomington: Indiana University Linguistics Club.

Jenewari, Charles J. 1977. *Kalabari syntax*. Ph.D. dissertation, University of Ibadan.

Kaufman, Elaine M. 1969. *Ibibio grammar*. Ph.D. dissertation, University of California, Berkeley.

Kuperus, Julie. 1978. *Esquisse du système verbal de l'oro du Nigéria*. Thèse de maîtrise, University of Paris.

Meier, Paul, Inge Meier, and John Bendor-Samuel. 1975. *A grammar of Izi*. Norman: Summer Institute of Linguistics and University of Oklahoma Press.

Stanford, Ronald. 1967. *The Bekwarra language of Nigeria: A grammatical description*. Ph.D. dissertation, University of London School of Oriental and African Studies.

Thomas, Elaine. 1978. *A grammatical description of the Engenni language*. Arlington: Summer Institute of Linguistics and University of Texas Press.

Williamson, Kay. 1965. *A grammar of the Kolokuma dialect of Ịjọ*. West African Language Monographs 2. Cambridge: Cambridge University Press.

**References**

DeBose, Charles E. 1976a. *Be*-insertion: A zero-copula analysis of Black English deep structure. Paper presented at the Fifth Pacific Coast Regional Meeting of the American Dialect Society.

———. 1976b. The Black English basilect and the notion of fossilization. Paper presented at the CATESOL Mini-Conference, California State University, Fresno, 6 November.

———. 1977. The status of native speaker intuitions in a polylectal grammar. *Proceedings of the Third Annual Meeting of the Berkeley Linguistics Society*, 465–74. Berkeley Linguistics Society.

———. 1983a. Samaná English: A dialect that time forgot. *Proceedings of the Ninth Annual Meeting of the Berkeley Linguistics Society*, 47–53. Berkeley Linguistics Society.

———. 1983b. A reanalysis of the Black English verb system as decreolization. Paper presented at the Conference on African Linguistics, Madison, Wisconsin.

———. 1988. *be* in Samaná English. *Occasional Paper* no. 21. St. Augustine, Trinidad: Society for Caribbean Linguistics.

DeBose, Charles E., and N. Faraclas. 1988. The role of the feature stative in Black English predicates. Paper presented at Winter meeting of the Linguistic Society of America, New Orleans.

Dillard, J. L. 1972. *Black English: Its history and usage in the United States*. New York: Random House.

Faraclas, Nicholas. 1987. Creolization and tense-aspect-modality system of Nigerian Pidgin. *Journal of African Languages and Linguistics* 9.45–59.

———. 1988. Nigerian Pidgin and the languages of southern Nigeria. *Journal of Pidgin and Creole Languages* 3.177–97.

Fillmore, Charles. 1987. *On grammatical constructions*. Reader, Linguistics 120A, University of California, Berkeley.

Fillmore, Charles, George Lakoff, and Paul Kay. 1983–84. Lecture notes, Linguistics 290. University of California, Berkeley.

Gilman, Charles. 1986. African areal characteristics: Sprachbund, not substrate? *Journal of Pidgin and Creole Languages* 1.33–50.

Mufwene, Salikoko S. 1983. *Some observations on the verb in Black English vernacular*. Austin: African and Afro-American Studies Research Center, University of Texas.

Spears, Arthur. 1982. The Black English semi-auxiliary *come*. *Language* 58.850–72.

Stewart, William A. 1966. Social dialect. *Research Planning Conference on Language Development in Disadvantaged Children*. New York: Yeshiva University.

———. 1968. Continuity and change in American Negro dialects. *Florida Foreign Language Reporter* 6.

Turner, Lorenzo Dow. 1949. *Africanisms in the Gullah dialect*. Chicago: University of Chicago Press.

Welmers, William E. 1973. *African language structures*. Berkeley: University of California Press.

# Black Identity, Homeostasis, and Survival: African and Metropolitan Speech Varieties in the New World

*Charles Gilman*

This paper treats a larger aspect of Africanism than the formal survival of grammar and lexicon in Afro-American languages. The data on substantive Africanisms are vast and rich, and many of the contributions to this book add to this richness. Rather than further enlarge these data, I will discuss the kind of ideological and social mechanisms that have prevented African characteristics from being swamped by the European lexifiers, so that the languages continue to be distinct after many centuries of pressure toward unification with the official varieties which coexist with them in every country where they thrive.

The problem is similar to one in thermodynamics. Every system tends toward a state of entropy in which all areas are uniform. If we find a continued area of distinctness—an island of warmth in a cool environment, or of coolness in the midst of heat—we know there must be mechanisms which maintain the separation (blankets, heaters, insulation keeping the place warm, or fans and air conditioners keeping it cool). Likewise, there must be heterostatic mechanisms maintaining the Afro-American varieties distinct in an atmosphere where so many forces—schools, job requirements, social status, radio, and television—press for their assimilation or eradication. My research task has been to sift through the studies of scholars who have considered other aspects of Afro-American culture and gather together passing observations which will allow us to understand the nature and reasons for this heterostasis, for the continued resistance of Afro-American languages to the pressures for conformity to an official standard.

I need two terms: "homeostasis" and "heterostasis." I use "homeostasis" to describe both the external pressure for assimilation and the internal mechanism that identifies a particular language variety as marked by its particular forms and structures. Heterostasis is its opposite, forming the resistance to homogenization and maintaining the boundary between speech forms that continue to coexist as separate entities. Consider a speaker who has the choice of using a more creolelike or a more metropolitanlike form. It is only through the agency of such individuals that material can pass from the metropolitan variety to the creole, or in the other direction.

If the choices of such individuals are consistently made in a single direction in a speech community, either the creole or the metropolitan variety will disappear. When both the creole and the metropolitan variety continue to persist either as identifiably distinct forms or as distinct points in a continuum, there must be forces within each group of speakers which maintain the varieties. Labov (1966:84) called these opposing forces "pressures from above" and "pressures from below." Rickford (1980:177) characterized them as pressures encouraging movement in the direction of the acrolect or standard language, and pressures favoring the basilect or creole language. Rickford (1985) has discussed the ethnic division between blacks and whites in the Sea Islands as a sociolinguistic boundary keeping their speech distinct. Ethnic division is only one of many factors which operate as heterogenetic forces maintaining the New World African-related languages distinct from their metropolitan lexifiers.

Continuity and boundary have been the chief themes of the study of divergence, convergence, and replacement of speech norms, whether these are conceived as separate languages or as varieties of a single language. The early conflict in historical linguistics between the family tree model and the wave model viewed these processes as antithetical, but observation shows that both must be present in any real bivarietal language situation. This results from the permeability of language, as opposed to the complete genetic isolation of biological species from one another, and from the status of language varieties as recognizable social entities or norms existing apart from the usage of individual speakers (see Whinnom 1971, and Mufwene 1987 for other discussions of biological versus linguistic distinctness). Pohl (1978:87) showed how the border between France and Belgium acts as a "barrier or filter" between north and south.

Trudgill (1983) developed a complex formula involving interaction, population, distance, preexisting linguistic similarity, influence, time lag, prestige, and covert prestige to explain the direction of diffusion in a dialect area. It appears that the forces maintaining the distinctness of creoles from the metropolitan forms are the same social constructs which maintain languages or their varieties distinct in noncreole situations. In the context of African-derived societies of the New World, an African-related social identity is seen as the theme maintaining the distinctness of African-related varieties—pidgins, creoles, and African languages—from the metropolitan languages of the colonized areas.

The original view of comparative linguistics emphasized geographical isolation as a heterogenetic force in dialect split and language formation (Bloomfield 1933:321–45). The clearest examples in creole studies are African-related varieties which, as a result of migration or political changes, are separated from their original chief metropolitan lexifiers, such as Saramaccan and Ndjuka in Suriname, Samana (DeBose 1983), French creoles in Trinidad and other former French colonies in the English-dominated Caribbean area (Le Page and Tabouret-Keller 1985:52), and Papiamentu. Another example is a geographical barrier which separates the creole-speaking and metropolitan-speaking areas. This occurred widely in the early Maroon communities (Price 1976, 1979; Le Page and Tabouret-Keller 1985:71). Black and mixed-race privateers in the Leeward Islands between 1780 and 1830 (McGlynn 1987) were another example of a geographically separated community. Angolar is an example of a Maroon creole in the Old World (Ferraz 1983:121). Haiti is the nearest approximation in the Western Hemisphere to a geographical area entirely dominated by the African-related variety.

A second heterogenetic factor familiar from the recent history of Europe has been the complex of factors that make up nationality: religion, geographical origin, and ethnic identity. All of these continue to be important in promoting the continued existence of African-related varieties alongside their metropolitan lexifiers in the African diaspora of the New World. Pitts (1985:302) concluded that ritualized effect should be added to region, history, and socioeconomic differences as major factors in linguistic variation.

The effects of religion are most striking in the cases of the syncretic religions such as voodoo, Candomble, and so on (Simpson 1978). Although the maintenance of extensive competence in Yoruba by some priests and diviners as in Brazil and Cuba is unusual, many adherents to these religions have a large African-derived vocabulary for gods and paraphernalia which distinguishes the religious register of their language from the metropolitan variety and marks it as specially identified with the African traditions preserved in the religions. Brandão's (1986) recognition of religious identity as a symbolic strategy in Brazil shows the connection between these rituals and their social significance.

A less striking case is the preservation of a more extremely divergent creole for liturgical use in spirit religions in Jamaica and the use of creole in voodoo. The early Obeah men in Jamaica were generally natives of Africa (Edwards 1794, reprinted in Sennett 1985:20). Although such well-organized cults did not survive in the United States except where they were reintroduced from Latin America and the Caribbean, African supernatural practices remained alongside Christianity in the form of magical practices. Many slave plantations had a respected and feared hoodoo man or magician, and these were often African-born and spoke African languages (Sernett 1975:100). Christian missionaries to the slaves were warned not to preach in Black English, but this advice was not always followed, as evidenced by the evangelical material reprinted by Sernett which shows clear Black English characteristics (1975:67, 69).

There was some sporadic direct African influence on black American Christianity into the twentieth century, as in the case of the African Universal church, founded by Laura Adorkor Kofey (Newman 1987:139). Members of this church studied Xhosa-Zulu and prayed in a language called "Banta." Today, black preachers in the United States use the alternation of Black English with more standard English as a consistent rhetorical device, beginning the sermon with standard forms and gradually building up to a climax using more Black English forms. Pitts (1985) claims that black sermons use more vernacular forms than normal speech, but prayers use less.

A third type of religious heterogeneticism is the neologism of the Rastafarians (Pollard 1983, 1986; Sutcliffe and Wong 1986, chap. 3), which differentiates them from others by the use of language, thus increasing their linguistic distance from the metropolitan variety. They are able to speak to each other "in words and gestures opaque to outsiders" (Barrett 1974:193). This illustrates what should be better understood with regard to all African-related varieties: their continued distinctness relies not only on the preservation of older creolisms but also on the continued innovation in directions distinct from the metropolitan varieties, recreolization as a heterogenetic factor alongside decreolization as a homeogenetic one.

The ethnic identity of Afro-American populations is composed of physical, cultural, and economic factors. Integrationist political ideology and ethnocentric values have perhaps prevented many researchers from fully appreciating ethnic identity as a source of pride and solidarity, assuming that the low social and economic status assigned to African populations would drive them to strive to assimilate to metropolitan norms. A good example is Andersen's (1983:5) generalization that "increased social mobility causes the speakers of the creole to restructure their language by incorporating into their speech features from the prestige language." The assumption in this statement—that prestige is always unidirectional and that creoles always evolve in this direction—must be balanced by a recognition of the heterogenetic forces that act in the contrary direction. Joos (1971:187) suggested lack of solidarity between European and colonized peoples as a factor in pidgin formation, and the incipient solidarity among the colonized as tending to convert pidgin into creole. The phenotypic characters of Africanness and the continued hostility and persecution by Euro-Americans have made decreolizing aspirations unrealistic in most situations, and the pride in African derivation can be well documented in African populations at all stages of their history.

The assumption that it is always the metropolitan varieties which have prestige simply because their speakers have economic and political power flies in the face of the evidence for continued promotion of Africanicity as a positive value, first in the Maroon communities and slave rebellions, then in the black economic projects of Marcus Garvey and even Booker T. Washington, and finally in the present Black Power and nationalist movements (Sutcliffe and Wong 1986, chap. 6). Dalphinis (1985:92) states that the new status of Caribbean languages "indexes a common culture which becomes more and more important." Jamaican Creole forms are a strong affirmation of black identity among urban black youths in England (Montgomery 1986:86). Bolinger (1980:46) identifies Black English as a secret language that promotes solidarity and intracommunication while excluding outsiders. Milroy (1980:194) points out that "a highly focused set of vernacular norms is able to symbolize solidarity and loyalty to a set of values of a non-institutional kind." Barbag-Stoll (1983:47) similarly describes how Nigerian students living in Britain use pidgin as an act of identity to establish the feeling of unity with other Nigerians.

In considering the effect of ethnicity on heterogenetic factors impeding complete decreolization or replacement of the pidgin, it is important to distinguish between those creole languages which are regarded as a marker of ethnicity and those which are not. For example, although Yiddish is identified with Jews, one can be a Jew without any knowledge of Yiddish, while speaking French is a defining characteristic, for example, for French Canadians or Frenchmen. Among the New World creoles, Saramaccan, Ndjuka, and perhaps Gullah are languages of ethnic identification in this sense, while speaking or not speaking Jamaican Creole is not a necessary defining character either of Jamaican nationality or of creole ethnicity in Jamaica. Isolation from the area of metropolitan lexifier political domination can produce such identity—as among the creoles of Spanish-speaking areas, for whom creole English becomes an ethnic marker. Krio in Sierra Leone and Portuguese Creole in the islands off West Africa (Washabaugh and Greenfield 1983:116) are languages of ethnic identity for their speakers. In a totally different geographical area, Sankoff (1980:24) discusses how Tok Pisin is used as a language of solidarity among its speakers.

Consideration of the above points shows that the barriers and heterogenetic forces maintaining the separate identity of African-related language varieties are not uniform throughout the New World but are different in different countries, and among different groups in the same country.

Geographic isolation from the lexifier operates to maintain English-lexified languages of Suriname, Papiamentu in Curaçao, and Mosquito Coast English in Spanish-speaking Central America, but not Jamaican Creole or Haitian Creole, or Black English in the United States. Religion maintains separate varieties among almost all black communities, but the effect is much more remarkable in the syncretic religions which use a large African vocabulary, prayers and songs in African languages, etc., than in revivalist churches identified with similar Euro-American churches. Practitioners of new nationalist religions like the Rastafarians or the Black Muslims constitute a third group, emphasizing innovation rather than retention of archaic African speech characteristics.

The identification of African-related speech varieties with black race or ethnicity is much stronger in places like Haiti and Jamaica, where there is no large segment of the black community using the metropolitan variety, than in the United States or Brazil, where it is usual for many ethnic blacks to have speech patterns unmarked for this identity (for Brazil, see Bortoni-Ricardo 1985:10).

There is a pervasive assumption in sociolinguistics that the African-related varieties are to be assigned a negative value. The terms "acrolect" and "basilect" are one example; the most basilectal forms are those furthest from the local norms of white speech. The designations H and L are another example; H is clearly a mnemonic for "high" and L for "low." Dalphinis (1985:92) shows how such terms mirror the prejudice against creole languages. A third example is the common usage of "standard" to refer to the metropolitan variety of the lexifier, as though there were no nonstandard metropolitan forms, or any standardized creoles. Likewise, the designation of pidgins and creoles as resulting from "inadequate" inputs (Andersen 1983:11) labels them with a stigma of nonsufficiency. The use of the expression "covert prestige" (Labov 1966:108; Trudgill 1983:155) for what I am designating as heterogenetic force assumes the point of view of the speaker of the metropolitan variety, for whom the prestige of his own norms is overt and that of others is therefore covert. Siegel (1987), who uses the terms "integrative" and "segregative" orientation for the attitudes associated with homeogenetic and heterogenetic forces, regards maintenance of nonmetropolitan varieties as inadequate learning of a target language.

It may be pointed out that even black scholars who have mastered the language of academe must thereby lose the prestige orientation understood by heterogenetic speakers. The different prestige of the same language varieties in different domains is discussed in Britto (1986:148). This domain split is shown by the Grenadian school teachers described in Le Page and Tabouret-Keller (1985:185) who refuse to acknowledge that they speak Patois but laugh at Patois jokes.

The most extreme case of this assumption of the prestige of the metropolitan variety is the common statement of the "life cycle" theory, according to which decreolization is the final stage of the cycle; this ignores the enormous literature which expresses the view that stabilized pidgins or creoles may underlie many of the standard languages of the world. Woolford has described several distinct theoretically possible paths along which a pidgin may develop (Woolford and Washabaugh 1983:2). Decreolization is one outcome, standardization of the creole as a separate language is a second, and heterostasis, with the continued existence of both the creole and the lexifier as elements of a bilingual, diglossic, or continuum speech community, is a third.

It must be clear by this time that continued heterostasis requires that both the metropolitan variety and the creole have positive values, even though these may be expressed along different scales, and even though, as Marta Dijkhoff points out in her comments (in this volume), this positive value is balanced by negative features as well. Brown and Levinson (1987:110) describe switching into the code associated with in-group and domestic values as a way of encoding positive politeness. I will discuss several situations in which African identity and African-related speech clearly have positive value, and the negative implications of the conventional designations "basilect," "L," "covert prestige," and the like are therefore inappropriate.

Maroon communities and slave revolts are excellent early examples of the establishment of speech communities in which approximation of metropolitan speech varieties would definitely not confer high prestige. Dalphinis (1985:26) suggests that Maroon societies in St. Lucia were important in the development of "Patwa." It is notable that it is often among the descendants of Maroon communities that existing African-related speech varieties are most clearly different from the metropolitan.

A second example is the prestige universally accorded to Africans as sorcerers or leaders of syncretic religions. The prestige of these Africans derived from their superior knowledge of the authentic sources of the knowledge represented by their practices. Brazilian practitioners of Yoruba religion still go to Nigeria to study, thereby confirming the high prestige of Africans as opposed to Euro-Americans in this domain.

A third area in which black varieties of speech enjoy high prestige is that of contemporary black nationalist political movements. The many instances of well-educated black political leaders giving speeches in black-marked varieties—for example, Stokely Carmichael's political speeches, or Patwa in St. Lucia (Dalphinis 1985:94)—are clear evidence for the high prestige of black speech in these areas.

A fourth important area is the use of African-related forms in poetry, song, theater, and other art forms, in which the artist affirms the positive value of the African-related heritage by choosing the speech forms most characteristic of it. Trudgill (1983:147) shows how white British pop singers imitate the pronunciations of black Americans in their songs. Sutcliffe and Wong (1986, chap. 4) discuss the use of the Jamaican "Afro-Lingua" in reggae "Deejaying," and Angrosino (1987) has described the choice of the "Nation Language" of poor blacks by poets writing works to be read accompanied by instrumental "dubs" of reggae songs.

I have not yet discussed the role of social class in the heterostasis of the metropolitan-African dichotomy. Milroy (1980:202) cites Levinson (1978) as pointing out that dense multiplex networks associated with an ethic of solidarity and reciprocity are universal in low-status communities. Barbag-Stoll (1983:44) quotes Rens (1953) as stating that a common lingua franca in Suriname helped slaves to identify themselves as a group different from their masters. The frequent association of African-related speech forms with poverty and low socioeconomic status in the New World reflects the history of Africans. They were first brought as slaves or indentured workers, and then their descendants were kept in low positions through segregation and discrimination.

The development of continua with large mesolects, as in Jamaica, reflects a situation of considerable social mobility in which individuals moving up and down the social scale develop speech forms with elements of both the metropolitan and the African-related varieties. As Le Page and Tabouret-Keller (1985:73) put it, "linguistically the coloured middle class has bridged the gulf between Creole-speaking workers and expatriates." The retention of sharp linguistic barriers between creole and metropolitan forms, as in Haiti (Winford 1985:349–50), reflects a similarly sharp social class distinction between a small ruling elite which uses the metropolitan variety and a continually impoverished mass which uses creole (Simpson 1978:62). Similarly, the existence of two discrete repertoires among blacks in London (Sebba, cited by Le Page and Tabouret-Keller 1985:157) reflects a sharp distinction between the old native British majority and the group which continues to identify with its recent Caribbean origin. Barbag-Stoll (1983:117) cites a Nigerian play in which Pidgin is a mark of working-class identity.

The continuum model is oversimplified, however, in that it fails to take account of lateral stratification among the lower classes. In the early days of slavery in the Catholic countries of Brazil, Haiti, and Cuba, slaves were permitted to form ethnic associations through which African languages, dances, and religious beliefs could be perpetuated (Simpson 1978:57). Edwards (1983:306) shows how rural people in Guyana choose an identity represented by creole, and Kernan, Sodergren, and French (1977:43) similarly describe rural Belizean Creole as sharing a certain inherent prestige with English as against urban creole. In Liberia, on the other hand, the urban mesolect has higher prestige than the rural varieties (Singler 1987:137). Different lower-class groups such as Asians, or poor whites in the United States, use forms different from those used by the descendants of Africans, and different religious groups use different varieties of creole.

This lateral stratification applies to ethnic distinctions among the black groups themselves, as in the distinction between West Indians and black Americans in New York (Basch 1987), between Gullah and Black English vernacular (BEV) in the South, or between Garifuna (black Caribs) and Creoles in Belize. The latter distinction goes back to slavery days when Maroons were designated by a different name than Caribs because they weren't members of a clan (Wright 1987). Rather than a continuum with the metropolitan variety at the top and a single basilectal variety at the other pole, the model in these cases should be a truncated triangle with different basilectal varieties, both African-related and metropolitan, at the bottom and less stigmatized metropolitan varieties and local standards at the top.

The continuum model also may create a false impression that the creoles or African-related varieties are necessarily always at the bottom of the scale. Different historical conditions, as well as different relations among lower-class groups, produce different configurations. In triglossic situations such as West Africa or New Guinea (Abdulaziz-Mkilifi 1972; T'Sou 1983), the creolized variety occupies a relatively high social position, marking an urbanized or Westernized population able to command more money and power than the rural population, which speaks the traditional ethnic languages. If the pidgin or creole in such situations is lexified from an indigenous rather than a European language, as is the case with Kikongo ya Leta (Kituba), Police Motu, etc., the direction of historical change is not decreolization toward the lexifier but rather continued innovation away from the lexifier, symbolizing the relatively high status of the urban, modern pidgin or creole, as opposed to the rural, low-status lexifier.

Some simplified statements of the life cycle theory may produce the false impression that decreolization or replacement is the necessary fate of all creoles. This overemphasizes the homeogenetic force pulling toward the metropolitan variety and ignores the heterogenetic factors outlined here. The creole may become a new standard and cease decreolizing, remaining distinct from the lexifier and following its own independent development. Alternatively, the social stratification of which the metropolitan-creole dichotomy is one of the signs may be stabilized, resulting in a continued evolution of the two varieties in parallel, as Standard and nonstandard English have done for the last three centuries in Britain and the United States.

Although I have treated heterogenetic forces separately for convenience in discussion, it is clear that in fact they overlap, and that they must coexist in order to be strong enough to balance the homeogenetic pull toward uniformity with the metropolitan languages which are official almost everywhere in the New World. Dalphinis (1985:31) tells us that Patwa was the language of revolt, African perpetuation, and African religions in St. Lucia. Slave religion, African-related or Christian, was an important factor in slave revolts in Jamaica, Haiti, the Virgin Islands, Cuba, and North America, the most famous U.S. examples being the Gullah Jack and Nat Turner revolts (Suttles 1971:98). The African-related church of Laura Adorkor Kofey was closely related to the economic movement of Marcus Garvey (Newman 1987), and Rastafarianism also grew out of Garveyism. Rastafarianism combines the factors of low social status, pride in blackness, identity with Africa, religion, and geographical identification with the West Indies to provide a strong heterogenetic complex producing increased divergence from the metropolitan variety. Pulis (1987) has described Dread labor-exchange networks as a positive alternative to the money economy. The Sea Islands combine geographical distinctness, religion (Jones-Jackson 1985), and social class factors to maintain the separation of their speech both from local white English and from other varieties of BEV. Saramaccan combines geographical separation, political distinctness, rurality, and religion, as well as ethnic identification.

The retention of many creole features in certain areas may be explained by the existence of numerous heterogenetic forces. These forces have developed most strongly among Maroon societies like the Saramaccans and successful black-dominated revolutionary societies like Haiti, where political domination has allowed other heterogenetic factors like religion to act most definitively. In Brazil and the United States, on the other hand, the homeogenetic pull of continued political domination by a large, powerful group of metropolitan speakers has rendered less effective the heterogenetic forces, which, however, continue to operate.

Milroy (1980:195), one of the first to affirm the strength of heterogenetic forces without stigmatizing them as covert or inadequate, reports that no unitary model has been found to account for the two opposing ideologies of status and solidarity in an integrated way. Hopefully the present study will contribute to the development of such a model.

Although the heterogenetic forces described in this paper are the same as those associated with dialect split and linguistic nationalism in other areas of the world, they are unified among the societies discussed by the twin factors of African origin and black physical identity. All the distinctly Afro-American religions, which provide such a strong force for the maintenance of Afro-American speech varieties separate from the metropolitan variety, are either directly derived from religions of Africa or show strong similarities with areal features of African religious beliefs and practices. With a few exceptions, such as white creole speakers in Louisiana or Asians in the Caribbean and the Guianas (Le Page and Tabouret-Keller 1985:62; Rickford 1985:112), almost all the creoles of the New World are spoken by populations with African biological ancestry. Their political movements are clothed in a rhetoric of blackness which leads to an identification of heterogenetic forces in the maintenance of their speech as the expression of a black, African identity asserting itself against the dominance and the homeogenetic force of metropolitan speech, equally identified as white in the social context of the New World. Thus Gumperz and Cook-Gumperz (1981:441) show that the pronunciation "thang" (thing) in Los Angeles marks blackness. Smitherman (1980:163) states that blacks need to have a code undecipherable by whites. Baugh (1983:3–4) suggests that black speech in the United States is preserved by a combination of isolation and active resistance. And Barrett (1974:8) says, "As a positive symbol for the Black man, Blackness suggests an 'anti-racist' racism; a self-definition based on African referents." Blackness serves the function identified by MacDonell (1986:110) of discourse which finds its meanings by reference to an ideological position and serves as a weapon in struggle.

While there is (as linguists and anthropologists constantly try to remind the public at large) no necessary connection between race and language, several colleagues have reminded me that creoles may become the center of identification for non-African groups. In her response to this paper, Marta Dijkhoff mentions the Jews and Dutch with regard to Papiamentu, and Guy Hazaël-Massieux mentions white Creoles in parts of the French-speaking Caribbean, to which I may add the rural Asians in Guyana. Despite these exceptions, history has generally maintained the unity of black physical identity and African cultural tradition, with the results presented above. Even in the exceptional cases in which Afro-American language becomes the vehicle for cultural struggle by a non-African population, each such situation has evolved from an earlier one in which the language variety was used in common between people of African origin and the present speakers.

The continued coexistence of metropolitan and African-related speech forms in the New World has been described as resulting from the homeostasis of two forces. On the one hand are homeogenetic forces pulling toward decreolization or replacement by the metropolitan varieties. On the other hand are the heterogenetic forces resulting in the maintenance or increase of the distinctness of the African-identified forms. This model provides a corrective to the excesses of both the conflict models of society, according to which one group must eventually dominate the other completely and replace all its institutions, and functionalist theories which assume a harmonious division of society into cooperative, mutually supportive groups. As long as the opposing forces remain in balance, the two speech forms will continue to exist as distinct varieties in the speech community, changing in independent ways rather than assimilating toward one another. The life cycle model, with decreolization as its foreordained outcome, is only one pathway through the network of alternatives. Which path is taken will depend on the choices and the exertions of the black descendants of Africans who speak these languages.

## References

Abdulaziz-Mkilifi, M. H. 1972. Triglossia and Swahili-English bilingualism in Tanzania. *Language in Society* 1.197–213.

Andersen, Roger W. 1983. *Pidginization and creolization as language acquisition*. Rowley, Mass.: Newbury House.

Angrosino, Michael V. 1987. The poetics of class consciousness: Dub poetry and West Indian identity. Paper presented at the Eighty-sixth Annual Meeting of the American Anthropological Association, Chicago.

Barbag-Stoll, Anna. 1983. *Social and linguistic history of Nigerian Pidgin English*. Tübingen: Stauffenberg Verlag.

Barrett, Leonard E. 1974. Soul-force: African heritage in Afro-American religion. Garden City, N.Y.: Anchor.

Basch, Linda. 1987. Ethnicity, class, and migration: Changing dimensions of West Indian identity in New York. Paper presented at the Eighty-sixth Annual Meeting of the American Anthropological Association, Chicago.

Baugh, John. 1983. *Black street speech*. Austin: University of Texas Press.

Bloomfield, Leonard. 1933. *Language*. New York: Holt, Rinehart and Winston.

Bolinger, Dwight. 1980. *Language, the loaded weapon*. London: Longman.

Bortoni-Ricardo, Stella Maris. 1985. *The urbanization of rural dialect speakers: A sociolinguistic study in Brazil*. Cambridge: Cambridge University Press.

Brandão, Carlos Rodrigues. 1986. Religious identity as a symbolic strategy: Brazilian dimensions. *Social Science Information (Informations sur les Sciences Sociales)* 25.229–57.

Britto, F. 1986. *Diglossia*. Washington, D.C.: Georgetown University Press.

Brockriede, Wayne, and Robert L. Scott. 1972. Stokely Carmichael: Two speeches on black power. *Language, communication and rhetoric in black America*, ed. by Arthur L. Smith, 176–94. New York: Harper and Row.

Brown, Penelope, and Stephen C. Levinson. 1987. *Politeness: Some universals in language usage*. Cambridge: Cambridge University Press.

Dalphinis, Morgan. 1985. *Caribbean and African languages: Social history, language, literature and education*. London: Karia Press.

DeBose, Charles E. 1983. Samana English: A dialect that time forgot. *Proceedings of the Ninth Annual Meeting of the Berkeley Linguistic Society*, ed. by Amy Dahlstrom et al., 47–53. Berkeley: Berkeley Linguistic Society.

Edwards, Walter A. 1983. Code selection and shifting in Guyana. *Language in Society* 12.295–311.

Ferraz, Luiz Ivens. 1983. The origin and development of four creoles in the Gulf of Guinea. In Woolford and Washabaugh, eds., 120–25.

Gilman, Charles. 1987. Stolen paradigms: Stammbaum to black box. *Papers in the history of linguistics. Studies in the History of the Language Sciences* 38, ed. by Hans Aarsleff, Louis G. Kelly, and Hans-Josef Niederehe, 3–11. Amsterdam: John Benjamins.

Gumperz, John, and Jenny Cook-Gumperz. 1981. Ethnic differences in communicative style. *Language in the U.S.A.*, ed. by Charles A. Ferguson and Shirley Brice Heath, 430–45. Cambridge: Cambridge University Press.

Jones-Jackson, Patricia. 1985. Religious patterns in the Sea Islands and the Caribbean. Paper presented at the Ninth Annual Language and Culture Symposium, University of South Carolina, Columbia.

Joos, Martin. 1971. Hypotheses as to the origin and modification of pidgins. *Pidginization and creolization of languages*, ed. by Dell Hymes, 187. Cambridge: Cambridge University Press.

Kernan, Keith T., John Sodergren, and Robert French. 1977. Speech and social prestige in the Belizian speech community. *Sociocultural dimensions of language change*, ed. by Ben G. Blount and Mary Sanches, 35–50. New York: Academic Press.

Labov, William. 1966. Hypercorrection by the lower middle class as a factor in linguistic change. *Sociolinguistics, Janua Linguarum*, Series Major 20, ed. by William Bright, 84–113. The Hague: Mouton.

Le Page, Robert B., and Andrée Tabouret-Keller. 1985. *Acts of identity: Creole-based approaches to language and ethnicity*. Cambridge: Cambridge University Press.

Levinson, Stephen C. 1978. Sociolinguistic universals. Mimeo.

MacDonell, Diane. 1986. *Theories of discourse: An introduction*. London: Basil Blackwell.

McGlynn, Frank. 1987. Manumission: The gift of freedom? Paper presented at the Eighty-sixth Annual Meeting of the American Anthropological Association, Chicago.

Milroy, Lesley. 1980. *Language and social networks*. Oxford: Basil Blackwell.

Montgomery, Martin. 1986. *An introduction to language and society*. London: Methuen.

Mufwene, Salikoko S. 1987. Pidginization and creolization: An evolutionary biology analogue. Lecture at Northwestern University, 5 May.

Newman, Richard. 1987. *Black power and black religion*. West Cornwall, Conn.: Locust Hill Press.

Pitts, Walter. 1985. Linguistic variation as a function of ritual structure in the Afro-Baptist church. *Proceedings of the Eleventh Annual Meeting of the American Anthropological Society*, ed. by Mary Niepakiy et al., 294–304. Berkeley: Berkeley Linguistic Society.

Pohl, Jacques. 1978. Communication field and linguistic field: The influence of the border (France and Belgium) on the French. *International Journal of the Sociology of Language* 15.85–90.

Pollard, Velma. 1983. The social history of Dread Talk. *Studies in Caribbean language*, ed. by Lawrence D. Carrington, Dennis Craig, and Ramon Todd Dandare, 46–62. St. Augustine, Trinidad: Society for Caribbean Linguistics.

———. 1986. Innovation in Jamaican Creole: The speech of Rastafari. *Focus on the Caribbean. Varieties of English Around the World* 8, ed. by Manfred Görlach and John A. Holm, 157–66. Amsterdam: John Benjamins.

Price, Richard. 1976. *The Guiana Maroons: A historical and bibliographical introduction*. Baltimore: Johns Hopkins University Press.

———. 1979. *Maroon societies*. Baltimore: Johns Hopkins University Press.

Pulis, John W. 1987. The valley of Jehosaphat: Historical consciousness and cosmology among Rastafarians in Jamaica. Paper presented at the Eighty-sixth Annual Meeting of the American Anthropological Association, Chicago.

Rens, Lucian Leo Edward. 1953. *The historical and social background of Suriname Negro English*. Amsterdam: North Holland.

Rickford, John R. 1980. Analyzing variation in creole languages. *Theoretical orientations in creole studies*, ed. by Albert Valdman and Arnold Highfield, 165–84. New York: Academic Press.

———. 1985. Ethnicity as a sociolinguistic boundary. *American Speech* 60.99–125.

Sankoff, Gillian. 1980. *The social life of language*. Philadelphia: University of Pennsylvania Press.

Sernett, Milton C. 1975. *Black religion and American evangelism*. Metuchen, N.J.: Scarecrow Press.

———, ed. 1985. *Afro-American religious history: A documentous witness*. Durham, N.C.: Duke University Press.

Siegel, Jeff. 1987. *Language contact in a plantation environment: A sociolinguistic history of Fiji*. Cambridge: Cambridge University Press.

Simpson, George Eaton. 1978. *Black religions in the New World*. New York: Columbia University Press.

Singler, John Victor. 1987. The city, the mesolect, and innovation. *Journal of Pidgin and Creole Languages* 2.119–47.

Smitherman, Geneva. 1980. White English in blackface. *The state of the language*, ed. by Leonard Michaels and Christopher Ricks, 158–79. Berkeley: University of California Press.

Sutcliffe, David, and Ansel Wong. 1986. *The language of the black experience*. Oxford: Basil Blackwell.

Suttles, William C. 1971. African religious survivals as factors in American slave revolts. *Journal of Negro History* 56.97–104.

Trudgill, Peter. 1983. *On dialect: Social and geographical perspectives*. New York: New York University Press.

T'Sou, B. K. 1983. Triglossie et réalignement sociolinguistique. *Contrastes* 6.101–13.

Washabaugh, William, and Sidney M. Greenfield. 1983. The development of Atlantic creole languages. In Woolford and Washabaugh, eds., 106–19.

Whinnom, Keith. 1971. Linguistic hybridization and the "special case" of pidgins and creoles. *Pidginization and creolization of languages*, ed. by Dell Hymes, 91–115. Cambridge: Cambridge University Press.

Winford, Donald. 1985. The concept "diglossia" in Caribbean creole situations. *Language in Society* 14.345–56.

Woolford, Ellen, and William Washabaugh, eds. 1983. *The social context of creolization*. Ann Arbor: Karoma.

Wright, Pam. 1987. The Ethnic Mirror: Words as the history of Carib ethnicity. Paper presented at the Eighty-sixth Annual Meeting of the American Anthropological Association, Chicago.

# Language as a Struggle for Survival. A Discussion of Gilman's Paper

*Marta B. Dijkhoff*

In language variation, two opposing forces have been identified by different names in the literature: pressures from above or below (Labov 1966) and integrative or segregative forces (Siegel 1987). Creolization and decreolization are the linguistic results of these two forces, while covert and overt prestiges are sociological features associated with them. These forces are also the basis of a distinction between two polar varieties in the so-called postcreole continuum, namely, acrolect and basilect, corresponding respectively to the distinctions high versus low and standard versus nonstandard.

In his paper Gilman introduces two new terms for the same forces: "homeostasis," corresponding to pressures from the official, standard language to assimilate the low, nonstandard variety; and "heterostasis," corresponding to the opposite, resistant force that strives to maintain the difference. To justify these new terms Gilman claims that they correct the excesses of current conflict models of society, in which complete dominance and replacement are the final outcome. This is predicted by, for example, the life cycle theory of creoles and functionalist theories about society, which assume a harmonious division into cooperative mutually supportive groups.

It is not clear, however, when and how Gilman's two opposing forces operate, for his examples cover a wide range of languages and language varieties in different settings and periods of time. The forces affect not only speech varieties like Black English, Gullah, and Jamaican Creole, which coexist with the standard and official varieties of their lexifiers, but also creole languages like Saramaccan, Ndjuka, and Papiamentu, which coexist with a standard official language (Dutch in this case) that has contributed relatively little to their structures or lexicons.

The two opposing forces affect all sorts of language varieties, regardless of whether they are markers of ethnicity, are metropolitan, are associated with prestige, are opposed to traditional ethnic languages, or are urban and opposed to rural varieties in noncreole speech situations. Gilman covers quite a variety of situations, including Maroon communities and slave revolts, the prestige of African sorcerers and leaders of syncretic religions, art and literature, African-related forms in songs, and black nationalist political movements (e.g., Garveyism and Rastafarianism as positive heterostatic forces at different times).

Heterostasis and homeostasis therefore seem to be never-ending laws of nature which, as social mechanisms, affect not only creole languages but language in general. According to Gilman, heterostatic "forces maintaining the distinctness of creoles from the metropolitan forms are the same social constructs which maintain languages or their varieties distinct in noncreole situations."

However, should we be as cautious as Gilman in his likening of heterostasis in creoles to that in noncreole languages? Is there any reason for assuming creole language varieties to be an exception to general principles? Why can we not think of, perhaps, the Romance languages as the result of the interaction of the same pressures that now affect creoles relative to their lexifiers? Unfortunately Gilman does not elaborate on this question. We thus miss the advantage of alternative or additional insights that new terms like his tend to suggest, especially in the field of creolistics, in which concepts like "language continuum," "creolization," and "decreolization" seem to have been defined solely by the distribution of speech forms and by the geneses of the languages, which almost always mention slavery and oppression.

The purpose of Gilman's paper is to identify various heterostatic forces which prevent the assimilation or replacement of one norm by another. However, his heterostatic forces seem to have a negative origin, like "lack of solidarity between European and colonized peoples, . . . the phenotypic characters of Africanness, and . . . persecution by Euro-Americans." They do not seem to occur on their own; they are mostly a reaction to the opposite homeostatic forces. It seems like the fate of the besieged who has no chance to win but one way or another keeps fighting or dies.

Furthermore, heterostatic forces manifest themselves at the periphery of society, where no real power can be derived. While cultural and ethnic identity, solidarity, intracommunication, and exclusion of outsiders are undoubtedly positive values, they are also limitations on domains of influence. Gilman sees the outcome of all this as depending on "the choices and the exertions of black descendants of Africans who speak creole languages" (varieties are not mentioned this time). This conclusion seems rather simplistic, for there are other forces (psychological, political, economical, and social) involved in the whole process. The development of a language might not depend solely on its native or original speakers. For example, Papiamentu, sadly enough, became more widely accepted by descendants of its original speakers, the blacks, only after it had become the language of communication between two different white groups: the Jews and the Dutch.

Proponents of the life cycle theory of creoles have assumed three possible outcomes: decreolization, standardization of the creole as a separate language, or continued existence of both the creole and the lexifier as elements of a bilingual, diglossic speech community. However, there are not many examples in which standardization is the final outcome. Even when it is, the new language is still kept outside the power structure of society and is not used in, for example, law and education. Besides, the fact that a creole language becomes standardized does not preclude coexistence of the creole and its lexifier. Standardization might in fact mean systematic and constant borrowing by the creole language from the lexifier. This is a situation typical of Papiamentu, which keeps borrowing from Spanish and, to a lesser extent, from Dutch in order to expand its vocabulary when necessary.

We can conclude, therefore, that the two opposing forces go on being active. Standardization surely does not eliminate the struggle of the opposing forces, and the besieged have to continue fighting or die.

## References

Labov, William. 1966. Hypercorrection by the lower middle class as a factor in linguistic change. *Sociolinguistics, Janua Linguarum*, Series Maior 20, ed. by William Bright, 84–113. The Hague: Mouton.

Siegel, Jeff. 1987. *Language contact in a plantation environment: A sociolinguistic history of Fiji*. Cambridge: Cambridge University Press.

# Substantive Africanisms at the End of the African Linguistic Diaspora

*Selase W. Williams*

The term "Africanism" is generally used to refer to elements of material culture, behavioral patterns, traditions, or ceremonies that are found outside Africa but can be traced to indigenous African cultural origins. While Africanisms have been readily acknowledged among people of African descent in the West Indies and in South American countries like Brazil, few of the characteristic cultural patterns found among people of African descent who live in North America have been accorded the status of Africanisms. This exclusion reflects the pervasive Eurocentric devaluation of the cultural phenomena that exist in African-American society. In fact, Nathan Glazer and Daniel Patrick Moynihan (1963) set the tone for other American students of culture when they asserted that "the Negro is an American and nothing more. He has no culture to value or protect."

Despite centuries of enslavement of the most brutal kind, African Americans have retained a great deal of that which is African in their music, their physical gestures and coordination, their religious beliefs and practices, and their modes and systems of communication. Some of these phenomena are difficult to define and describe because of the cultural transformations they have undergone as a consequence of the disruptive forces of enslavement and persistent cultural oppression. In addition, the tools used to describe European culture are frequently inadequate to accurately describe indigenous and creolized African cultures. Yet these modified forms contrast with European cultural forms in the American context and are readily observable.

Lomax (1970) was able to describe the homogeneity in African and Afro-American musical style only by comparing "both white and black" musical data from Africa, western Europe, and the New World. More recently, Hall (1990) has demonstrated African religious retentions in Florida. The most obvious of the African cultural forms in the United States are the hip, shoulder, and head movements in African-American popular dances. Clearly not European and strikingly similar to various traditional African dance movements,

African-American dance forms are New World expressions of African culture for which it is difficult to find appropriate English descriptors.

I argue below that many of the characteristic features of African-American speech may, in fact, be Africanisms that have not been recognized as such because the most visible component of the language—its vocabulary—is largely of English origin. Thus, those features of African-American speech that do not follow some accepted pattern of English are almost automatically thought to be distortions of English.

However, to qualify as a *substantive Africanism,* a unique African-American speech feature must be demonstrated to be systematically related to a phonological, syntactic, or semantic pattern found in one or more indigenous African languages, the speakers of which have a direct historical connection with the African Americans using the feature(s) in question. In the following pages I demonstrate the effectiveness of tracing certain phonological characteristics of African-American language to African sources by using comparative African linguistic data and sociohistorical facts surrounding the enslavement of African peoples in the Old South. The comparative linguistic data inform us of the compatibility of the African-American linguistic forms with a selected group of African languages, while the sociohistorical facts indicate the historical connection(s) between certain African ethnolinguistic groups and African peoples enslaved in the various parts of the antebellum South.

My research was based on the hypothesis that linguistic variation found in African-American speech communities does not necessarily signal change in progress, but may in fact constitute reflexes of different African source languages. In other words, the African languages spoken by significant numbers of enslaved Africans served as filters through which they received the language of their new social context. To test this hypothesis, the variant pronunciations of the word-final consonant in English words such as *with* by African Americans during the early 1900s are examined here.

The English word *with,* which contains a word-final voiceless interdental fricative [θ] in Standard American English, is characteristically realized in African-American speech as [wɪt], [wɪd], or [wɪf]. Although one or more of these realizations appear in the transcriptions of researchers who have studied African-American language, there has been little serious discussion of the variant pronunciations. Exceptions to this generalization are discussed in Dorrill (1975) and Butters and Nix (1986), about which more is stated below. Students of "Black English" would probably conclude that these three pronunciations are accounted for as either free variation, a consequence of the postcreole continuum, or general American regional dialect influences. However, an unexplored fourth possibility is that these variants are due to the phonological patterns of different African languages originally spoken by the Africans enslaved in different regions of the Old South, making the variant pronunciations substantive Africanisms.

Given the nature of this reconstructive research and the kind of data and evidence available for analysis, the results reported here are necessarily tentative. Throughout the paper, two fundamental assumptions are maintained. First, in a culture contact situation in which one cultural group is enslaved by another cultural group, the enslaved group will be forced to incorporate some of the enslaver's language into its communication system. Second, the enslaved group will preserve the syntactic, phonological, and semantic substance of its original language(s) within the resulting communication system.

These basic assumptions underlie the substratum school of thought on creolization, represented in the writings of, for example, Turner (1949), Stewart (1968), Dillard (1972), and Alleyne (1980). On the other hand, I do not subscribe to the position that neither linguistic universals nor superstrate language features influence the language forms that result from culture contact situations. In fact, Mufwene (1986) convincingly argues that the universalist and the substrate hypotheses complement one another. However, I do maintain that ethnocentricity and prior linguistic conditioning are the principal forces operant in language contact situations.

Prompted by the results of my research on Sierra Leone Krio (Williams 1971, 1976, 1977), one might hypothesize that the numerically dominant African language group would have the greatest influence on the resultant language system in a creolizing context. Those works point out that the Yoruba, who provided the substantive syntactic, phonological, and semantic structures onto which English was grafted during the creolization process, constituted the largest ethnolinguistic group in that community. However, in the pages below I demonstrate that the principle of *ethnolinguistic compatibility* plays an equally important role in determining the final shape of a creolized language. Thus, in reconstructing the linguistic history of a creolized language, it is necessary to know not only the relative size of the various linguistic groups involved but also the degree of compatibility that exists between the suspected substratal system(s), the superstratal system(s), and the resulting creolized system.

## Impediments to the Study of Africanisms in the United States

Before the research on variant pronunciations of word-final [θ] in African-American speech is presented, it might be useful to outline some of the numerous factors that have stifled the study of Africanisms in the U.S. context. One can legitimately ask why North America has not been considered fertile ground for research on Africanisms. It is a widely known fact that African peoples were brought to these shores in bondage in large numbers, that they played a fundamental role in the building of America, and that their presence and contributions span a period of more than 350 years. Nonetheless, the debate over the existence of African cultural elements in North America continues.

Even Melville Herskovits (1941), the most widely recognized scholar of African retentions and continuities (see next section), focused his attention on the West Indies and South America rather than on North America. An outstanding exception, among early scholars in this area, is Lorenzo D. Turner (1949), whose work on the Gullah language elevated the debate from one based on speculation to one based on demonstration. While some recent publications should be credited with identifying substantive Africanisms in North America (e.g., Thompson 1969; Vass 1979; Asante and Asante 1985; Stuckey 1987; Holloway 1990), the majority of those who write on African Americans do not attribute their unique or prominent characteristics to African cultural sources.

A cultural explanation for the differences witnessed between European Americans and African Americans should be a logical one. However, persistent stereotypes and misperceptions of African Americans prevent the majority of American scholars from seeing an undistorted reality. This distorted picture of reality is further reinforced by European intellectual traditions based on normative research and social Darwinism. Normative research reduces all non-European cultural phenomena to inferior status, while social Darwinian theories prove those inferior cultural forms to be genetically generated. Terms like "minority" lead to the misperception that African peoples never existed in large enough numbers, in relation to the European-American population, to be culturally influential. Works such as Wood (1974), which reveal that the African population in some states reached more than 50% during the slavery period, seem to have made no difference.

Another factor that contributes to these misperceptions is the common knowledge of the brutal and oppressive nature of slavery. The conscious efforts of the planters to completely eradicate African culture are well documented. In fact, most African material culture and other overt manifestations of African cultures *were* effectively destroyed. What is not understood is that there is more to culture than material objects. A great deal of what constitutes culture resides at the subconscious level, what might be called cultural programming (e.g., values, patterned behaviors, preferences, and modes of expression). Linguistic competence falls into this category.

Dalby (1972) provides us with another reason for the misperception that few

Africanisms exist in North America. It is his contention that many words and phrases of African origin have made their way into general American English. For most users of the language, these terms have lost their historical identity and are simply viewed as *Americanisms*. One such word identified by Dalby is "jazz," which he has traced back to the Wolof language of Senegambia. Similarly, jazz, as a particular type of music, has become accepted simply as "American" music.

There is also a prevalent belief that African Americans were quickly assimilated into European culture and never went through the creolization process witnessed in other parts of the African diaspora. While the language and culture of the Sea Islands present clear evidence of the nature and extent of Africanisms that existed in the American context of an earlier day, there are those who argue that Gullah is not typical of African-American culture. For instance, Davis (1971:91), in assessing the language of African Americans, states, "The question, however, is not whether Gullah is creole, but, rather, whether all the dialects spoken by American Blacks are so."

Much of the research conducted on African-American language during the 1960s, as an outgrowth of the Chomskyan revolution, was directed toward determining whether its deep structure was the same as, or different from, that of Standard American English. If the deep structures were different, then African-American language had its own integrity, but if their deep structures were not different, then any differences were trivial and this nonstandard dialect could not possibly be African.

Research on variable rules in the African-American speech community typically demonstrated a close correlation between nonstandard speech forms and low socioeconomic status and/or low educational attainment. This suggested that the speech of most African Americans differed from that of most European Americans not because of different cultural and linguistic histories but because of their relative positions on the socioeconomic ladder. Such analyses diverted attention away from research that would test the hypothesis put forth in this paper.

Should one conclude from this discussion that the various theoretical frameworks and methodologies designed by European and European-American scholars are inappropriate for the study of African-American language? Not categorically. However, it does suggest that Eurocentric research on African-American culture will shed little or no light on the true nature of this cultural phenomenon. Research conducted from a Eurocentric frame of reference will interpret the characteristic features of African-American speech as little more than "bad English." An Afrocentric frame of reference forces a different set of questions, the answers to which may be sought using any variety of approaches. The research presented in this paper is Afrocentric in that it turns to Africa, first and foremost, in trying to explain cultural phenomena found in the African-American community.

## Methodological Considerations

Africanisms can be placed into two different categories: *retentions* and *continuities*. An African retention is a cultural element that is identical, or nearly identical, with an element in the African source culture, in both form and function. On the other hand, an African continuity is a modified version of an African cultural element or a foreign element that has been modified to conform to an African cultural pattern. Continuities are, by definition, more difficult to study. This is especially true in the case of African continuities in North America because accurate records of the history of African cultural forms were not kept with any degree of consistency. Furthermore, North America is at the end of the African diaspora in the New World.

I selected the variant pronunciations of the word-final voiceless interdental fricative in English by African Americans for three reasons: (1) little attention has been paid to this phenomenon in the literature on African-American language; (2) since the research involves a form of linguistic reconstruction, I felt that phonological evidence would be more accessible than syntactic or semantic evidence in older documents; (3) none of the presumed African source languages were found to have [θ] in their sound inventories, making any phonetic interpretation of that sound by African Americans a prime candidate for an African continuity.

The variant pronunciations of word-final [θ] can probably be found in every major urban center in the United States. Yet, to attempt to trace the African origins of these variants by studying urban language patterns would not be very revealing. The urban centers are too far, both geographically and temporally, from the original language contact sites. Ideally, one would like to have data from distributional studies of the sound patterns of rural African Americans in all of the states of the Old South (i.e., Virginia, North Carolina, and Georgia) from different time periods since the enslaved Africans first started arriving. However, no such systematic body of data or anything close to it exists. In the absence of such data, the most reliable early data available were sought.

The linguistic data on African Americans used here came from four major sources. *Studies in areal linguistics* (Kurath 1972) provided sketchy but linguistically reliable data taken from the linguistic atlas project for the region in question. Turner's *Africanisms in the Gullah Dialect* (1949) provides both linguistic descriptions and transcriptions of speech that I consider characteristic of the South Carolina and Georgia coasts. Data from central Georgia come from the Uncle Remus stories of Joel Chandler Harris (1892). The authenticity of Harris's renditions of central Georgia speech is validated by Sumner Ives in *The phonology of the Uncle Remus stories* (1954).

Comparative linguistic data on the African languages which were presumed to be involved in the language contact situation in question were compiled on a checklist of African consonantal features (see figure 1, below). Ten languages were selected as representative of the various ethnolinguistic groups which, according to historians, were imported to America in the largest numbers: Bobangi, Ewe, Fanti, Igbo, Kongo, Mandingo, Mende, Ngola, Wolof, and Yoruba. The checklist attempts to characterize these languages with respect to the presence or absence of word-final consonants, interdental fricatives, and labial fricatives. The information for the checklist was gathered from a variety of dictionaries, grammars, and word lists with publication dates ranging from 1870 to 1970. Because the sources differ considerably regarding the amount of linguistic detail provided, the symbols that appear on the checklist should be viewed as rough phonetic representations. The checklist will be discussed in more detail later.

The most comprchensive work on the provenience of the various ethnolinguistic groups imported into slavery in the United States is *The Transatlantic Slave Trade: A Census*, by Philip D. Curtin (1969). Although this was my primary source for information on the ethnic distribution of enslaved Africans, some insights were gained from other sources.

## Ethnolinguistic Distribution of Enslaved Africans in the United States

Curtin reminds us that the eighteenth century was the most important period of the slave trade in terms of the direct importation of Africans into the United States. The Atlantic slave trade was abolished by law in 1808. Even though the fact that Africans continued to be imported into the United States well after 1808 is well known, a review of the previous century gives a wide-angle snapshot of those involved in the trade.

During this period, South Carolinians had a strong preference for Africans from the Senegambia region (principally Bambara and Malinke), with a secondary preference for peoples from the Gold Coast (presumably Ewe, Fanti, and Twi). In addition, they were prejudiced against Africans of short stature and especially disliked those from the Bight of Biafra (i.e., Ibos). Virginians, on the other hand, appear not to have indicated ethnic preferences for African bondsmen. Curtin (1969:156) makes the following observation about the neighboring states of North Carolina and Georgia:

> The South Carolina slave market supplied many of the slaves for North Carolina and Georgia, and small samples of Georgia slave imports from Africa after 1766 show a heavy but non-quantifiable bias toward Senegambia, Sierra Leone . . . thus approximating the South Carolina pattern.

Despite the expressed preferences for bondsmen from particular ethnolinguistic groups, a statistical analysis of their distribution suggests that actual purchases may have been determined more by availability or the presumed skills of individuals than by preference of the slave owners for physical or personality types. In addition, the numbers reveal quite clearly that the ethnolinguistic makeup of enslaved Africans varied from state to state.

Figures on Virginia for the period 1710–69 as presented by Curtin (1969: 157) are as follows: Bight of Biafra, 37.7%; Gold Coast, 16.0%; Angola, 15.7%; and Senegambia, 14.9%. Compare the figures for South Carolina for the period 1690–1807 (Curtin 1969:157): Angola, 39.6%; Senegambia, 19.5%; Windward Coast, 16.3%; and Gold Coast, 13.3%.

In addition to the enslaved populations emanating directly from Africa, Curtin suggests that at least 4% of those entering by way of South Carolina and about 14% of those entering via the Chesapeake were reexports, mainly from the West Indies. Since a large share of those enslaved in the West Indies originated from the Gold Coast and the Bight of Biafra, these reexports to Virginia would have increased the Gold Coast and Bight of Biafra numbers.

In all probability a variety of African languages were spoken by significant numbers of African bondsmen in North America. Using that set of languages, figure 1, a preliminary checklist of African consonantal features, was constructed.

A number of important insights are gained even from a cursory review of the checklist. For instance, none of the languages has either of the interdental fricatives [θ] or [ð] in its sound inventory. This is very significant because we would expect speakers of a language not possessing these sounds to replace them with a sound from their respective inventories. The fact that African Americans characteristically replace these sounds with another consonant seems to follow logically. The factors which influence the choice of the replacement sound will be discussed in the next section.

Notice also that word-final consonant clusters are virtually nonexistent in

**Figure 1. Comparative African Consonantal Features**

| | *I* | *II* | *III* | *IV* | *V* | *VI* | *VII* | *VIII* | *IX* | *X* | *XI* | *XII* | *XIII* |
|---|---|---|---|---|---|---|---|---|---|---|---|---|---|
| | θ/ð | *CC#*[1] | *C#* *[−nasal]* | ŋ | ŋ# | *n#* | *m#* | *r#* | *r* | *f* | *∅* | *v* | β |
| Mandingo | − | − | − | + | + | − | − | − | + | + | − | − | − |
| Mende | − | − | − | + | + | (+)[2] | ? | − | − | + | − | + | − |
| Fanti | − | − | − | (+)[3] | − | + | + | (+) | + | + | − | − | − |
| Ewe | − | − | − | + | + | + | + | − | + | + | + | + | + |
| Yoruba[4] | − | − | − | + | + | + | ? | − | + | + | − | − | − |
| Igbo | − | − | − | + | − | − | + | + | + | + | + | + | + |
| Bobangi | − | − | − | + | − | − | − | − | − | − | − | − | − |
| Kongo | − | − | − | + | − | − | − | − | − | + | − | + | − |
| Ngola | − | − | − | + | − | − | − | − | + | + | − | + | − |
| Wolof | − | (+) | + | + | + | + | + | + | + | + | − | + | − |

[1]CC stands for a sequence of two consonants; #, for word boundary.
[2]Usually becomes a nasalized vowel.
[3]Welmers reports that it only occurs before (K).
[4]Intervocalic [r] is reduced to [∅] in many common words in normal speech.

the languages considered here. The one exception is Wolof, yet even this language has very restricted occurrences of this feature, which correlates with the regular sound pattern of African-American speech, in which a word-final consonant sequence is characteristically reduced to a single consonant (e.g., [slɛpt] › [slɛp]).

The third feature, word-final nonnasal consonant, is likewise lacking in all of the languages reviewed except Wolof. It is the absence of this feature that reinforces or promotes the morpheme structure condition alluded to above. What is demonstrated is an uncompromising preference in these African languages for a CVCV morpheme structure. Note that although many of the languages represented on the checklist do allow word-final nasal consonants, most of the Congo-Angolan languages do not even allow that. In fact, in a few of the languages in which a word-final nasal consonant is present phonemically, it is realized phonetically as nasalization on the preceding vowel.

The appearance of word-final [r] in only three of the languages on the checklist again points to the likely relationship between the sound systems of these African languages and the sound system of African American. The deletion of postvocalic [r] is the feature in African-American speech that results in the pronunciation [pričə] for *preacher* and [pok] for *pork*. So prominent a part of African-American speech is this feature that many white musical groups which try to duplicate a "soulful sound" accentuate it.

Clearly there are systematic correspondences between African American and the selected African languages. The fact that the lexical items used by African Americans are not the same items used by historically related African peoples does not negate their substantive linguistic ties. A more refined listing of consonantal, vocalic, and suprasegmental characteristics would probably be even more revealing.

## Variant Pronunciations of [θ] in the Linguistic Reconstruction of the Old South

The variant pronunciations of [θ] noted in the literature on African-American speech are [d], [t], and [f]. According to Kurath (1972), virtually all of the "Negroes" from Delmarva Peninsula, the Virginia Tidewater, and the northeastern corner of North Carolina pronounce 'with' as [wɪf]. A review of the Gullah language of coastal South Carolina and Georgia demonstrates that both word-initial and word-final [θ] are pronounced as [t], as in [tiŋ] 'thing' and [fet] 'faith.' On the other hand, Joel Chandler Harris, in his renditions of African-American speech in central Georgia, wrote *with* as "wid," suggesting the pronunciation [wɪd].

Thus, at the first level of analysis, I concluded that the distribution of the variants in question was the following: [f], Virginia and North Carolina; [t], South Carolina and Coastal Georgia; [d], Central Georgia.

However, a clearer picture of this phonological phenomenon emerges when a larger sample from both central Georgia and the Gullah area is considered. Ives's (1954) study of Harris's renditions of African-American speech in central Georgia reveals that the [d] pronunciation found in words like *with* corresponds to [ð], the voiced interdental fricative, whether it occurs in word-initial, word-medial, or word-final position. Examples included in his study are the following: *them* › "dem" [dɛm], *this* › "dis" [dɪs], *neither* › "needer" [nidə], *with* › "wid" [wɪd].

The majority of Harris's renditions of words containing word-final *-th,* however, reflect an [f] pronunciation. Words like *mouth, both,* and *breath* are offered as examples of this phenomenon. Similarly, although Turner's transcriptions of Gullah speech show [t] where one would expect the voiceless interdental fricative [θ], *with* is transcribed as [wɪd], suggesting that the final sound in *with* was different from the final sound in a word like *faith* for the general regional dialect.

The above data suggest the following distribution pattern:

| | | | |
|---|---|---|---|
| Central Georgia | word-final [θ] | › | [f] |
| | word-final [ð] | › | [d] |
| Coastal Georgia/South Carolina | word-final [θ] | › | [t] |
| | word-final [ð] | › | [d] |
| Virginia/North Carolina | word-final [θ] | › | [f] |
| | word-final [ð] | › | [d?] |

This regular pattern clearly indicates that the variant forms are not in free variation. The origins of these pronunciations of English "th" sounds have yet to be determined. Let us turn back to the figures concerning the provenience of various African groups in the Old South.

In the coastal areas of Georgia and South Carolina, 39.6% of the enslaved Africans were from Angola. Bobangi, Kongo, and Ngola on the consonantal checklist represent this ethnolinguistic area. While Bobangi is not spoken within the modern political borders of Angola, but rather in Zaire (formerly the Belgian Congo), it is assumed that enslaved Africans reportedly taken from Angola may have originated from neighboring areas such as Zaire. Notice that although both Kongo and Ngola have [f] in their sound inventories, neither of the three languages allows any word-final consonants. Consistent with the data, it is highly unlikely that the speakers of these languages, either individually or collectively, would have chosen [f] as a replacement for [θ]. None of the languages is very favorably disposed toward labial fricatives, especially not in word-final position. Since [t] and [d] are among the most universally unmarked consonants, these are natural choices for the Angolan languages.

Independent support for this hypothesis comes from Sierra Leone Krio, a creolized language known to have been largely shaped by speakers of Yoruba. Native speakers of Krio, like those of Gullah, have adopted the [t] pronunciation of [θ] in both word-initial and word-final positions (e.g., [θɪŋk] › [tɪŋk] 'think' and [tiθ] › [tit] 'teeth'). A glance at the checklist reveals that Yoruba and the Angolan languages have very similar distributions for their consonants. In addition, the number of Yoruba personal names in Gullah recorded by Turner suggests that a significant number of Yoruba speakers may also have been enslaved in coastal Georgia and South Carolina and would have used the same pronunciation strategies there as in Sierra Leone.

In Virginia and northeastern North Carolina, the largest segment of the enslaved population (37.7%) was Ibo-speaking people from the Bight of Biafra. The second largest group was from the Gold Coast (16.0%), some of whom were surely speakers of Ewe, while an almost equally large group was from Senegambia (14.9%), some of whom were surely Wolof speakers. Two of these languages, Ibo and Ewe, have both voiced and voiceless pairs of bilabial and labiodental fricatives, while Wolof allows the labiodental fricative in word-final position, as reflected in the name of the language itself. The [f] pronunciation of word-final [θ] found to be characteristic of African-American speech in Virginia and northeastern North Carolina is completely compatible with the sound systems of Ewe, Ibo, and Wolof. Again, it appears that the choice is a linguistically "natural" one.

Finally, the area of central Georgia, according to Curtin, should have had roughly the same ethnolinguistic makeup as South Carolina. If this were the case, we would expect to find [t] pronunciation in that area, whereas we actually find [f]. How can this be explained?

Remember that in this area there was a discrepancy between the strong preference for Africans from Senegambia (19.5%) and the Gold Coast (13.3%), on the one hand, and the actual statistics that indicate that almost 40% of the enslaved Africans in Georgia came from Angola. It may well be the case that slave owners from the central part of the state held the strong preference for Senegambians and those from the Gold Coast, leading to an ethnolinguistic composition quite different from that on the Georgia coast. This would have made the ethnic composition of central Georgia similar to that of Virginia.

Littlefield's (1981) research provides us with one possible reason for one ethnolinguistic group to be selected for slave labor in a given geographical area while other groups were preferred in a different area. The various African ethnic groups were known for their skill and experience in certain occupations. While the Angolans, the Kongos, and the Mendes may have been highly valued for their rice-farming skills, the Wolofs of Senegambia and the Ewes of the Gold Coast may have been better suited for industries located in central Georgia, which was certainly not a primary rice-producing area.

The discussion in this section demonstrates that the selection and distribution of enslaved Africans by British colonists in North America had linguistic consequences for today's African Americans and, to a greater or lesser degree, for the European Americans in those areas. Information on the sources of enslaved Africans in various areas of the South can assist us in determining the ethnolinguistic group(s) most directly responsible for the linguistic systems that exist in those areas. However, a number of factors make it highly unlikely that any single linguistic feature found in an African-American community could be traced back to a single African source language. What we are likely to find is that features common to a number of African linguistic groups will manifest themselves in the language of African Americans in areas where members of those particular linguistic groups were enslaved. For instance, the [f] pronunciation of word-final [θ] in English appears in some areas because the ethnolinguistic groups enslaved in those areas have a wider distribution for labial fricatives and allow word-final consonants. The [f] pronunciation is not found in some areas because in the presumed source languages labial-dental fricatives occur only in restricted environments. Both of these cases demonstrate the principle of ethnolinguistic compatibility. Research on clusters of features in conservative pockets of the Old South is expected to be even more revealing.

## The British Dialect Hypothesis

A number of scholars, including Brooks (1935), Howren (1971), and Mufwene (1985), have suggested that many, if not all, of the linguistic features thought to be African-American language features have their origins in British dialects of the seventeenth and eighteenth centuries. For instance, Mufwene (1985:157) states that

> even though second language acquisition is generally less perfect than the speech of native speakers, it can be assumed that, in a number of respects, the speech of the slaves in the beginnings of the South Carolina colony was similar to, and based on, that of the British colonist.

While Mufwene's conception of the genesis of the creolized languages of the Atlantic allows for a kind of re-Africanization of those languages, his hypothesis constitutes a serious challenge to theories of Afrogenesis, regardless of their particulars. Although the underlying assumption (i.e., that African linguistic structures were eradicated upon contact with the European) is incorrect, the British dialect hypothesis is not without foundation. Constance Davies (1934) indicates that in eighteenth-century English, [f] and [v] occurred interchangeably with [θ] and [ð], yielding pronunciations which she represents as "heyff" for *hithe*, "Merdifes" for *Meredith's*, and "livef" for *liveth*. Further support comes from Martyn Wakelin (1972:98), who states:

> The simplication of [θ] to [f] is a well-attested and widely spread phenomenon. Although generally associated with Cockney and London pronunciation (as in [sa:fɛnd] 'Southend'), it is in fact characteristic not only of the Home Counties as a whole but of areas further afield. It can, for example, be heard in Leeds.

The literature on British dialects, then, clearly supports the proposition that at least some of the British colonists were pronouncing word-final [θ] as [f]. However, such evidence alone does not support the contention that this was the only form to which the enslaved African population was exposed.

There are numerous questions to be answered by proponents of the British dialect hypothesis:

1. Was [f] in free variation with [θ] in word-final position for those who came from the relevant dialect regions of England?
2. What was the settlement pattern in the United States for those British colonists who spoke the [θ] › [f] dialects?
3. If the [θ] › [f] British dialects were so prevalent at the time of the founding of the original colonies, why was that feature not preserved in New England and spread to other regions of the United States?
4. How does one account for the variant pronunciations of word-final [θ] in African-American speech?

Within the Afrocentric framework outlined in this paper, the varied pronunciation of word-final [θ] is accounted for as a consequence of differential African source languages. The presence of British colonists who spoke the [θ] › [f] dialect would simply have provided further reinforcement for the [f] pronunciation among those Africans who had already selected that variant on independent grounds (i.e., linguistic interference). The absence of [θ] › [f] in New England and in the rest of the United States could be explained by the fact that there were few Africans in the linguistic community to fuel the incipient [θ] › [f] change.

Finally, researchers such as Greibesland (1970), Dorrill (1975), and Butters and Nix (1986) have argued that the differences between black and white speech in the South in general are not very great, and are in fact quantitative, not qualitative. The implication here is that both African-American and European-American language origins in the South are the same—the origins, of course, being European dialects of the seventeenth and eighteenth centuries. Countering such claims are scholars like Dillard (1972), who argue that African-American language has always been the creative and innovative force, while European-American language has been the imitative force in black-white contact. This can be witnessed in various cultural arenas other than language. Why should we expect it to be any different in the linguistic arena? Those who point out the minor differences in the speech of African Americans and European Americans in the South today should be reminded that integration, especially in the area of education, has been operating for more than twenty years and may be having a leveling effect on black-white language differences.

The research reported above is surely not the final word, largely because of the nature of the data on which it depends. To fully test the hypothesis formulated in this paper, fieldwork is required in the conservative rural areas of the South. Accurate, fully consistent linguistic data on African-American and European families which have long been native to their respective communities are essential, although this type of information may be increasingly more difficult to find. In addition, further information on the internal slave trade is needed to determine with greater precision the ethnolinguistic groups enslaved in various areas of the South. Finally, further support for the position defended in this paper may be adduced, applying similar methodology, from cultural traditions other than language; for example, folktales, basket making, herbalism, and religious traditions. Even this preliminary research, however, should convince the reader of the enormous opportunities that exist for meaningful research on, and the reconstruction of, African-American culture.

## References

Alleyne, Mervyn C. 1980. *Comparative Afro-American: An historical-comparative study of English-based Afro-American dialects of the New World*. Ann Arbor: Karoma.

Ansre, Gilbert. 1961. *The tonal structure of Ewe*. M.A. thesis, Hartford Seminary Foundation. Hartford, Conn.

Asante, Molefi, and Kariamu Asante, eds. 1985. *African culture: The rhythms of unity*. Westport, Conn.: Greenwood Press.

Brooks, Cleanth. 1935. *The relation of the Alabama-Georgia dialect to the provincial dialects of Great Britain*. Baton Rouge: Louisiana State University Press.

Butters, Ronald, and Ruth Nix. 1986. The English of blacks in Wilmington, North Carolina. *Language variety in the South*, ed. by Michael Montgomery and Guy Bailey, 254–63. University: University of Alabama Press.

Crosby, K. H. 1944. Introduction to *The study of Mende with phonetic introduction to Mende*, by Ida C. Ward. Cambridge: W. Heffer and Sons.

Curtin, Philip D. 1969. *The Atlantic slave trade: A census*. Madison: University of Wisconsin Press.

Dalby, David. 1972. The African element in American English. *Rappin' and stylin' out*, ed. by Thomas Kochman, 170–86. Champaign-Urbana: University of Illinois Press.

Davies, Constance. 1934. *English pronunciation: From the 15th to the 18th century*. London: J. M. Dent and Sons.

Davis, Lawrence M. 1971. Dialect research: Mythology and reality. *Black-white speech relationships*, ed. by Walter Wolfram and Nona E. Clarke. Washington, D.C.: Center for Applied Linguistics.

Dillard, J. L. 1972. *Black English: Its history and usage in the United States*. New York: Random House.

Dorrill, George T. 1975. *A comparison of Negro and white speech in central South Carolina*. Ph.D. dissertation, University of South Carolina, Columbia.

Gamble, D. P. 1958. *Elementary Wolof grammar*. London: Research Department, Colonial Office.

Glazer, Nathan, and Daniel Patrick Moynihan. 1963. *Beyond the melting pot*. Cambridge, Mass.: MIT Press.

Gregersen, Edgar. 1977. *Language in Africa: An introductory survey*. New York: Gordon and Breach.

Greibesland, Solveig C. 1970. *A comparison of uncultivated black and white speech in the upper South*. Ph.D. dissertation, University of Chicago.

Hall, Robert L. 1990. African religious retentions in Florida. *Africanisms in American culture*, ed. by Joseph E. Holloway, 98–118. Bloomington: Indiana University Press.

Harris, Joel Chandler. 1892. *Uncle Remus and his friends*. New York.

Herskovits, Melville. 1941. *The myth of the Negro past*. New York: Harper and Brothers. Reprint. Boston: Beacon Press, 1958.

Holloway, Joseph E. 1990. *Africanisms in Afro-American culture*. Bloomington: Indiana University Press.

Howren, Robert. 1971. The speech of Ocracoke, North Carolina. *A various language*, ed. by Juanita Williamson and Virginia Burke. New York: Holt, Rinehart and Winston.

Ives, Sumner. 1954. *The phonology of the Uncle Remus stories*. Publications of the American Dialect Society, no. 22. Gainesville: University Press of Florida.

Kurath, Hans. 1972. *Studies in areal linguistics*. Bloomington: Indiana University Press.

Littlefield, Daniel. 1981. *Rice and slaves: Ethnicity and slave trade in colonial South Carolina*. Baton Rouge: Louisiana State University Press.

Loman, Bengt. 1967. *Conversations in the Negro American dialect*. Washington, D.C.: Center for Applied Linguistics.

Lomax, Alan. 1970. The homogeneity of African–Afro-American musical style. *Afro-American anthropology*, ed. by Norman E. Whitten, Jr., and John F. Szwed, 181–201. New York: Free Press.

MacBriar, Rev. R. Maxwell. 1870. *A grammar of the Mandingo language*. London: Printed for the Wesleyan-Methodist Missionary Society.

Mufwene, Salikoko. 1985. The linguistic significance of African proper names in Gullah. *Nieuwe West-Indische Gids* 59.146–66.

———. 1986. The universalist and substratum hypotheses complement one another. *Substrata versus universals in creole genesis*, ed. by Pieter Muysken and Norval Smith, 129–62. Amsterdam: John Benjamins.

Stewart, William. 1968. Continuity and change in American Negro dialect. *Florida Foreign Language Reporter* 6.3–4, 14–16, 18.

Stuckey, Sterling. 1987. *Slave culture: Nationalist theory and the foundations of black America*. New York: Oxford University Press.

Thompson, Robert F. 1969. African influence on the art of the United States. *Black studies in the university*, ed. by Armstead Robinson, 122–70. New Haven: Yale University Press.

Turner, Lorenzo D. 1949. *Africanisms in the Gullah dialect*. Chicago: University of Chicago Press.

Vass, Winifred. 1979. *The Bantu speaking heritage of the United States*. Los Angeles: Center for Afro-American Studies, UCLA.

Wakelin, Martyn F. 1972. *English dialects: An introduction*. London: The Athlone Press of the University of London.

Ward, Ida C. 1941. *Ibo dialects and the development of a common language*. Cambridge: W. Heffer and Sons.

Welmers, William E. 1946. *A descriptive grammar of Fanti*. Ph.D. dissertation, University of Pennsylvania.

Whitehead, John. 1899. *Grammar and dictionary of Bobangi language*. London: Gregg International Publishers. Reprint 1967.

Williams, Wayne R. 1971. Serial verb constructions in Krio. *Studies in African Linguistics*, supplement 2.

———. 1976. *Linguistic change in the syntax and semantics of Sierra Leone Krio*. Ph.D. dissertation, Indiana University.

———. 1977. The so-called relativized and cleft predicates in Krio: One step closer to an understanding of creolization. *Language and linguistic problems in Africa*, ed. by Paul Kotey and Haig Der-Houssikian, 467–78. Columbia, S.C.: Hornbeam Press.

Wood, Peter H. 1974. *Black majority: Negroes in colonial South Carolina from 1670 to the Stono rebellion*. New York: W. W. Norton.

# The Africanness of Counterlanguage among Afro-Americans

*Marcyliena Morgan*

Since Herskovits's *Myth of the Negro Past* (1941) there has been considerable discussion of the role of Africanisms in the development of the language, culture, and social reality of Afro-Americans in the United States. In linguistics this discussion has focused on whether the language of Afro-Americans largely results from African languages, archaic forms of English, or universal rules of language change. This paper departs from this tradition in two respects. First, I present evidence that in the United States there were two separate levels of language development: one having to do with well-known, yet diverse and often conflicting, processes of language change such as language shift, maintenance, choice, death, etc.; the other the result of a conscious attempt on the part of U.S. slaves and their descendants to represent an alternative reality through a communication system based on ambiguity, irony, and satire. Second, I argue that this other aspect of language development resulted largely from substratal influences.[1]

Before going into the social and historical background to this bilevel view of language development, I should clarify what I mean by two "levels." Clearly we are not in the presence of two entirely separate Black English languages, with separate syntax, phonology, and vocabularies. Rather, this second level, referred to here as "counterlanguage," has to do with the development of a speech economy in which the "ways of speaking" inherited from Africa have been reshaped by the historical experience of Afro-Americans in America.

## U.S. Slavery and Total Institutions

E. Goffman (1961:xiii) defines "total institution" as "a place of residence and work where a large number of like-situated individuals cut off from the wider society for an appreciable period of time, together lead an enclosed, formally administered round of life." He includes in his characterization of institutions the following: those established to care for persons felt to be both incapable and harmless or incapable but unintended threats to the community, and those established to pursue some worklike and instrumental task.

The above description of total institution aptly captures the unique character of American slavery in that it accounts both for the treatment of slaves during slavery, including the paternalistic and humanitarian justifications of slavery that were prevalent,[2] and for denial of civil rights to ex-slaves after abolition.

Because the reality of a total institution is defined by those outside it, an underlife (Goffman 1961) or antisociety (Halliday 1978) develops which is counter to the reality of the total institution. A communication system emerges to support this underlife. Halliday (1978) refers to this system as antilanguage and defines it as the means of realization of a subjective reality which does not merely express this reality but actively creates and maintains it. The language is secret because the reality is secret and values are defined by what they are not. This system is referred to as counterlanguage here in order to highlight its function as an alternative reality and to focus on its special conception of information and knowledge.

The notion that U.S. slaves communicated contradictory meanings among themselves while in the presence of those who did not recognize that the slave reality was being contradicted may at first appear a complicated example of language development. However, this is not true for two reasons. First, as a total institution, U.S. slavery required that slaves exhibit childlike behavior in the presence of whites. This behavior, which supported the paternalistic and humanitarian rationalizations of U.S. slavery, was reinforced through a communication style imposed on slaves which interpreted any expression of ideas, direct eye contact, or questions as potentially aggressive acts. Second, in response to this repressive and regimented communication environment, slaves developed a system of intragroup communication based on the use of ambiguity and irony in African songs and public announcements. Thus, in the case of Afro-Americans in the United States, indirect speech was an aspect of the counterlanguage because it was a shared norm among the slaves while white plantation owners and overseers had little knowledge of it.

## Indirect Speech in African Contexts

By examining documents dating from the eighteenth century and conducting field research on the African continent, folklorists and anthropologists have constructed detailed examples of the function and use of indirectness in African societies. In his exploration of the widespread use of satiric songs in West African societies Piersen found that "subtlety and wry indirection are the requirements of African verbal wit, and the demonstration of verbal skill more than circumspection demanded a satire by allusion" (1971:22).

In African societies expressions of praise, shame, and ridicule were announced to the entire village through satirical songs. Rattray (1923) described the Apo ceremonies of the Ashanti through which satire was institutionalized and ridicule of authority was sanctioned. In Dahomey, Herskovits witnessed a monthly social dance known as *avogan* in which residents satirized those of neighboring sections: "Crowds come to see the display and watch the dancing . . . to listen to the songs and laugh at the ridicule to which are held those who have offended members of the quarter giving the dance" (1966:138–39).

While names are ordinarily omitted during these songs, everyone present is aware of the identity of the target of the ridicule. Herskovits provides an example of a Dahomean woman who masked her ridicule of her co-wife, a princess, by referring to her as a "man of rank."

> To you I bring news
> With you I leave word
> That a man of rank who kills and then steals is here.
> (138–39)

Atkins (1970) found that in Sierra Leone, satiric songs were used to parody domestic and neighborly disputes as well as to convince villagers to adhere to proper social order. Perhaps the favorite vehicle for African satire was work songs (Piersen 1977:17). While exposing the weaknesses, strengths, and vices of chiefs and leaders, work songs also had a wider application. The target of their satire was often a misdeed or injustice inflicted by a powerful authority. For example, Merriam (1959) reports that the work song of Bashi women on a coffee and quinine plantation in the Belgian Congo (Zaire) became progressively critical of the plantation owner, who was withholding rations. The song included a threat to take their labor elsewhere if rations were not restored.

While indirect communication is found in songs throughout Africa, it is also part of the speech economy of the entire community. In Hausa, Hunter writes, "the appropriate way to attack someone verbally is with well chosen metaphorical or figurative language, with proverbs, puns, cloaked disapproval" (1982:392). Indirect speech is also ritualized in such practices as *bo akutia* among the Ashanti. Levine (1977:8) describes this practice as one in which a person brings a friend to the home of a chief or some other official who has offended him but of whom he is afraid. In the presence of the offender, the aggrieved individual pretends to have an altercation with his friend, whom he verbally assails and abuses freely. Once he has expressed or demonstrated his feelings in the presence of the person against whom they are really intended, the brief ritual ends with no overt acknowledgment by any of the parties involved of what has actually taken place.

In modern Akan society a person is judged as honorable, intelligent, etc., by his ability to manipulate language (Saah 1984). This level of judgment is so important that an Akan chief does not risk his status by speaking directly to villagers. Rather, he is spoken to and speaks through a spokesman who is valued for his ability to use proverbs and figures of speech; that is, for his ability to be indirect. Kofi Saah reports one case in which a chief was dethroned because villagers believed he lacked the verbal wit necessary to complain about lack of services and manipulate the government into agreeing to provide those services. In his discussion of the use of proverbs, metaphors, and euphemisms in Akan languages, Saah reports:

> Subjects like death, menstruation, defecation, and so on are regarded by the Akans and other people as things not to be spoken about in plain language . . . though these things have their own names in the language, euphemisms are used as a strategy to skirt the taboo word. (1984:369)

Saah further illustrates his observation with a report on Ghanaian television's description of the funeral of Nana Akyin VI, chief of Ekumba. Under Akan influence, thc announcer could not say that the chief died or was buried, so she reported (in English) that the chief "went to his village," a literal translation from Akan.

Irvine (1974:176) reports the function of indirectness in greetings in Senegal. In Wolof, who greets first (rather than the form or content of the greeting) indicates both the status and the responsibility of the interlocutors. The lower-status person speaks first and can ask favors of the higher-status person but not vice versa. When it is not clear whose status is higher, interlocutors often jockey for the low-status position because lower status implies that the higher-status person is obligated to contribute to the support of the lower-status person. Irvine (1982) also examines the communication of affect in Wolof. In this language one cannot understand a communicative event by simply interpreting the content of what is said. In fact, what is said is often not what is meant. Irvine refers to this as the sincerity problem because the observer cannot be sure that person X "really" experiences the affective state attributed to him or her.

The above discussion illustrates the use of indirect forms of communication in many aspects of life throughout Africa. These indirect forms were also used by slaves in the Caribbean and the United States. Though the historical experience of plantation slavery is shared by those of African descent in both regions, the development of indirection as a speech norm differed because the nature of plantation and postbellum society also differed (as suggested by n.2). While indirectness in the Caribbean retains many of its African characteristics, it has become a communication norm throughout society. In the United States, however, indirection has been expanded to a "way of speaking" with intragroup "norms of interpretation" (Hymes 1972) which signal both the social reality of the antisociety as well as solidarity among African descendants. Comparisons of indirectness in the United States and the Caribbean further illustrate that counterlanguage is particular to the Afro-American community in the United States.

## Indirect Speech in African America

The satiric songs that were common to Africa also appeared in the New World. Phillippo (1843) found that in Jamaica, the slave songs "had usually a ludicrous reference to the white people, and were generally suggested by some recent occurrence." Caines (1804) on the British island of St. Christopher wrote: "the Negroe dress every occurrence in rhyme, and give it a metre, rude indeed." Piersen (1977:25) provides a satiric song sung by slave women in 1807 to welcome Europeans arriving at the dock in Port Royal.

> New-come buckra,
> He get sick.
> He take fever.
> He be die.
> He be die.
> New-come buckra, he get sick . . .

In 1724 Father Jean Baptiste Labat wrote that slave songs in Haiti were "satirical to excess . . . few people apply themselves with greater success to knowing the defects of people, and above all of the whites, to mock among themselves" (Piersen 1977). As in Africa, slave work songs were often used for satirical purposes. Levine offers this example from Abram Harris:

> My old Missis promised me
> Dat when she died, she gwine set me free.
> But she lived so long en got so po
> Dat she lef me diggin wid er garden ho. (1977:138–39)

In the United States, the focus of songs, though similar to those of Africa and the Caribbean, walked a very narrow line; the stinging satire at the heart of the songs described above functioned in secrecy and went largely unnoticed. The surprise of whites when they happened to observe clear cases of satire is revealed in Piersen's (1977) report of an occurrence in Charleston in 1772: a South Carolinian was scandalized when he secretly beheld a Saturday night country dance of slaves. According to Wood (1974:342), "The entertainment was opened by men copying (or taking off) the manners of their masters, and the women those of their mistresses, and relating some highly curious anecdotes, to the inexpressible diversion of that company."

In order to hide their message, the satire of the work songs, while present, often favored other slaves as targets rather than the overseer or plantation owner. Thus a song from the 1840s sung by the leading oarsman Big-Mouth Joe criticized fellow slaves as lazy, worthless, etc.[3]

> One time upon dis ribber,
> Long time ago—
> Mass Ralph 'e had a nigger,
> Long time ago—
> De nigger had no merit,
> Long time ago—
> And now dere is in dis boat, ah,
> A nigger dat I see
> Wha' ia a good for nuthing shoat, ah, . . . (Hubbell
> 1954:244–45)

As Levine points out, that is not to say that songs never directly criticized whites and even slavery. Because in the United States the satire was counter-language, it was not always possible to know when a song was satirical. For example, the following song recorded by Harriet Brent Jacobs (1973:449) in the nineteenth century ridicules stingy whites by asking God to bless them with money.

> Poor Massa, so dey say;
> Down in de heel, so dey say;
> Got no money, so dey say;
> Not one shillin, so dey say;
> God A'mighty bress you, so dey say.

Punishment for satire did not end with emancipation. For over a hundred years after the end of slavery there were no black men and women—only boys and girls—and they behaved and spoke accordingly under the threat of death.[4] In 1870, a freedman reported to David Macrae: "I was once whipped because I said to missis, 'My mother sent me.' We were not allowed to call our mammies 'mother.' It made it come too near the way of the white folks" (Levine 1977:139).

The system of counterlanguage which developed during slavery included warnings as well as praise and satire.[5] During the postbellum era, counterlanguage relied on ambiguity and functioned as satire about blacks or whites in the presence of whites and as satire or praise in the presence of blacks.[6]

While the above examples illustrate that indirect communication functioned in the Caribbean and the United States much as it did in Africa, it was also shaped by the particular slave experiences of both populations. For example, in recent descriptions of the communication styles of Antigua (Reisman 1970, 1974) and Barbados (Fisher 1976), indirection appears in songs and public announcements, but it is also apparent in discourse in the form of passing remarks or "dropping remarks." An example of this speech event is described by Fisher (1976:231): "A woman chose to wear an overly bright shade of lipstick to a party. She overheard a woman say, 'Oh, I thought your mouth was burst' to a man whose lips were perfectly in order."

The "dropped remark" described above is strikingly similar to the Ashanti *bo akutia* ceremony discussed earlier. According to Fisher (1976:231), in order for a dropped remark to occur and be recognized as such, a suitable context must be created by the speaker, who "lays in wait" until the remark can be embedded in casual conversation or unmarked speech: "the more awkward the fit between the dropped remark and the casual, non-incendiary message to the sham receiver, the more potent the effect." The speaker must make certain the target is in hearing range before the remark is dropped. Yet, the targeted overhearer cannot acknowledge that the message has been received because that would be admitting guilt. Rather, dropped speech events can only be understood in terms of a "shift" in bystanders and receivers.

The use of dropped remarks or "noise," while part of the speech events of these communities, is viewed by its members as "unruly, disruptive, stubborn, disorderly" (Reisman 1974:123) and "rude and unmannerly" (Fisher 1976:235). In Caribbean societies, these speech events are part of the communication norm, and the subjective assessment of these events is based on societal indicators of class and status. In the United States, however, these events are part of the counterlanguage and therefore are valued precisely because of the ambiguity inherent in the interaction.

## Africanisms in Indirect Speech in the United States

In an effort to determine the extent to which indirect communication operates among Afro-Americans in the United States today, sixty black women and fifty-six white women between the ages of seventeen and seventy-five were asked to determine in the following narrative, "Regina's Other Story,"[7] whether the target of the response to Doretha's remark was Doretha or the general audience.

> *Regina's Other Story*
>
> I was talking to some close women friends of mine and another close friend of mine that they hadn't met, Doretha, joined us. Well, Doretha and I have been friends for years, but my other friends don't know her as well as I do. Anyway, we were all sitting around talking about how our lives have changed and Doretha said, "One thing I like about my life is that I don't have to have any babies if I don't want to. I think any woman who has more than two kids is crazy and needs her head examined." Now, no one said anything, but two of my friends have four kids apiece and one of them was pregnant with her third child. Well, a little later on, after we had been drinking and laughing a little bit, I was talking to one of the girls and Doretha was sitting nearby. So my girlfriend says very loudly so that everyone could hear, "I'm sorry that I have so many kids. I guess women like me just don't have any sense and should just forget it and have our tubes tied!" I was so embarrassed that I didn't say anything.

Note that the loud response of thc girlfriend was an accusation or attack on the character of the intended target, though it may have also been true of the others in the audience. Both black and white women were asked questions to determine whether they detected ambiguity in who was being addressed. The women's responses reveal two different perspectives on indirect reference. While both groups agreed that there was ambiguity, only the white women sought to determine a motivation for it. On the other hand, the black women ignored all statements which provided background or explanation for the indirectness. In fact, as table 1 illustrates, when asked if they thought Doretha knew whether the women had more than two children, nearly twice as many blacks (64.28%) as whites (36%) believed that she was aware of that fact.

Moreover, when asked why Regina was embarrassed, only slightly more than 5% of the white women thought it was because Regina thought the girlfriend was attacking her while 5 times as many blacks (25%) considered that a possibility (table 2).

The response of the two groups of women to "Regina's Other Story" presents a clear example of the existence of counterlanguage. The black women's response to the first question: "Do you think Doretha knew that some of the other women had more than two children?" only recognizes that the indirect reference occurred—whether what was said was an insult was immaterial. For

**Table 1. "Regina's Other Story," Question 1: Do you think Doretha knew that some of the other women had more than two children?**

| | White | | Black | |
|---|---|---|---|---|
| | *No.* | *%* | *No.* | *%* |
| Yes | 7 | 12.5 | 15 | 25 |
| No | 36 | 64.3 | 21 | 35 |
| Maybe | 13 | 23.2 | 24 | 40 |

**Table 2. "Regina's Other Story," Question 2: Why was Regina embarrassed?**

| | White | | Black | |
|---|---|---|---|---|
| | *No.* | *%* | *No.* | *%* |
| Because of what her girlfriend said. | 17 | 30.4 | 18 | 30 |
| Because of what Doretha said. | 36 | 64.3 | 27 | 45 |
| Because she thought her girlfriend was talking to her. | 3 | 5.3 | 15 | 25 |

whites, the evaluation of the event was based on Doretha's intention—whether she "meant" to insult the women. Yet in the counterlanguage, as well as in the African examples discussed earlier, intention of the speaker is not considered; rather it is the context in which the speech event occurs, the framing of the event, and how targets, hearers, and overhearers interpret what is said that determines what is meant. Thus the black women in the study could choose between two realities or communication norms while the whites had access to only one.

The above discussion examines the extent to which indirect discourse in African languages is related to indirectness in the Caribbean and Afro-American speech behavior in the United States. I have proposed that indirect speech in the United States was the source of a counterlanguage which still exists today among Afro-Americans in the United States. Although indirect discourse in the

Afro-American community in the United States is similar to that in the Caribbean, I have proposed that the major difference between the two has to do with its previous and continued function in the United States as counterlanguage.

In closing, I recently came across an interesting example of the use of indirectness and its apparent acceptability among educated blacks. Three black literary scholars and critics discussed black literary criticism in the journal *New Literary History* (1987). In the very heated and energetic attack on the discussant (Joyce Joyce), one of the commentators criticized her for hosting such an intense and culturally sensitive debate in a white publication. Joyce's response to their analysis of both her ideas and motives included a criticism of the nature of the rebuttals from the two commentators:

> He [one of the commentators] has, however, as we can deduce from his language, no hesitation in attempting to make me appear mindless and backwards in the eyes of white society. . . . Both [of the commentators] broke the important code of the signifying tradition: they failed to attack by subversion—to speak in such a way that the master does not grasp their meaning. (1987:383)

Although an indirect written attack by the commentators probably could not have helped Joyce "save face," the fact that she suggests that using a form of indirectness would have been the "black thing to do," and that nonblacks would not have understood that another level of communication was being used, is one indication of the continued importance of counterlanguage and its function and acceptability within the Afro-American speech community in the United States.

## Notes

I am grateful to Gillian Sankoff, Barbara Hoejke, Salikoko Mufwene, DeLores Weaver, and Thomas Morton for their valuable comments on this paper.

1. This level is actually what Afro-Americans call "using a different code." Unlike linguists, Afro-Americans use "code" to represent a style shift which may occur in the presence of whites. The shift may be one of accent to "sound" white, a change to vernacular speech to fit some whites' perceptions of black speech, or a shift to counterlanguage (explained below) to communicate intragroup in the presence of whites. The psychological aspect of this type of shifting is what Du Bois (1961), in his discussion of the black community, characterized as "double consciousness," the simultaneous juggling of two opposing realities. The point is not whether what is said, especially in the presence of nonblacks, is ambiguous;

the context is by definition ambiguous. The question is when and whether black participants communicate to each other through the counterlanguage.

2. One unresolved issue in the history of American slavery is U.S. slaves' overall lack of widespread resistance to slavery as compared with slaves in the Caribbean. This issue is important because it has generated arguments that the "nature" of U.S. slavery was humane compared with slavery in the Caribbean (Elkins 1959). Since the paternalistic argument of U.S. slavery viewed slaves as inferior beings who had to be guarded against themselves and who had to be cared for in every aspect of life, it is likely that paternalism in U.S. slavery was one factor which shaped the nature of the resistance to slavery. Yet it is unwise to suggest that the type of resistance to slavery is an indication of how slaves felt about their bondage. Bryce-LaPorte (1971) argues that unlike slavery in the Caribbean, where there was no paternalistic rationale for slavery and where widespread rebellion occurred, resistance in the United States tended to be individual and isolated; it was marked by recalcitrant behavior or resistance to the system itself.

3. While this does not depart from the African satirical songs described earlier, the point is that the satire was carefully directed.

4. This "tell them what they want to hear" approach to intergroup communication continues to be a part of the communication norm of the speech community (Smitherman 1977). In 1863, Lucy Chase wrote: "The habit of the Negro is to say whatever he thinks his interrogator wishes him to say" (Levine 1977:467). McDavid and McDavid (1951:26) further confirmed the extent of this attitude when they found that blacks more than whites were willing "to accept as authentic the responses suggested by the field worker, no matter how deliberately far-fetched some of these suggestions might be."

5. Genovese (1972), Smitherman (1977), Levine (1977), and others provide work songs used to warn other slaves of danger or give information about escapes to freedom. In fact, Smitherman (1977:48), who attributes her analysis to Du Bois (1961), writes:

> They [slaves] moaned "steal away to Jesus" to mean stealing away FROM the plantation and TO freedom. . . . They sang triumphantly "this train is bound for Glory," but the train they were talking about was the "freedom train" that ran on the Underground Railroad.

6. Kochman (1981) provides extensive discussion on various aspects of indirectness. Of course, as Mitchell-Kernan's (1972) description of the phenomenon reveals, "signifying" or "the dozens" was an outcome of counterlanguage. I do not discuss signifying here because it may serve multiple functions in the black speech community (e.g., age grading) and therefore requires an analysis much broader than I attempt here.

7. This narrative was actually part of a larger study (Morgan 1989) in which informants heard three narratives and were asked a series of questions about their interpretation of the events.

## References

Atkins, John. 1970. *Voyage to Guinea, Brazil, and the West Indies*. 1735. London: Frank Cass.

Bryce-LaPorte, Roy Simon. 1971. The slave plantation: Background to present conditions of urban blacks. *Race, change and urban society*, ed. by Peter Orleans and William Russell Ellis, Jr., 257–84. Beverly Hills: Sage.

Caines, Clement. 1804. *The history of the General Council and General Assembly of the Leeward Islands*. St. Christopher: R. Cable.

Du Bois, William E. B. 1961. *Souls of black folk*. 1903. New York: Fawcett Edition.

Elkins, Stanley. 1959. *Slavery—A problem in American institutional and intellectual life*. Chicago: University of Chicago Press.

Fisher, Lawrence. 1976. Dropping remarks and the Barbadian audience. *American Ethnologist* 3.227–42.

Genovese, Eugene D. 1972. *Roll, Jordan, roll: The world the slaves made*. New York: Vintage Books.

Goffman, E. 1961. *Asylums*. Garden City, N.Y.: Doubleday.

Halliday, M. A. K. 1978. *Language as social semiotic—The social interpretation of language and meaning*. Baltimore: University Park Press.

Herskovits, Melville J. 1941. *The myth of the Negro past*. New York: Harper and Brothers.

———. 1966. *The New World Negro*. Bloomington: Minerva Press.

Hubbell, Jay. 1954. Negro boatmen's songs. *Southern Folklore Quarterly* 18.244–45.

Hunter, Linda. 1982. Silence is also language: Hausa attitudes about speech and language. *Anthropological Linguistics* 24.389–95.

Hymes, Dell. 1972. Models of the interaction of language and social life. *Directions in sociolinguistics: The ethnography of communication*, ed. by John J. Gumperz and Dell Hymes, 35–71. New York: Holt, Rinehart and Winston.

Irvine, Judith. 1974. Strategies of status manipulation in Wolof greeting. *Explorations in the ethnography of speaking*, ed. by Richard Bauman and Joel Sherzer, 167–91. Cambridge: Cambridge University Press.

———. 1982. Language and affect: Some cross-cultural issues. *Georgetown University Roundtable on Language and Linguistics*, ed. by Heidi Byrnes, 31–47. Washington, D.C.: Georgetown University Press.

Jacobs, Harriet Brent (Linda Brent). 1973. *Incidents in the life of a slave girl*. 1861. New York: AMS Press.

Joyce, Joyce A. 1987. Reply—'Who the cap fit': Unconsciousness and unconscionableness in the criticism of Houston A. Baker, Jr., and Henry Louis Gates, Jr. *New Literary History* 18.371–84.

Kochman, Thomas. 1981. *Black and white styles in conflict*. Chicago: University of Chicago Press.

Levine, Lawrence. 1977. *Black culture and black consciousness*. Oxford: Oxford University Press.

McDavid, Raven, and Virginia McDavid. 1951. The relationship of the speech of American Negroes to the speech of whites. *American Speech* 26.3–17.

Merriam, Alan. 1959. African music. *Continuity and change in African culture*, ed. by William Bosnan and Melville Herskovits. Chicago: Phoenix Books.

Mitchell-Kernan, Claudia. 1972. Signifying, loud-talking—and marking. *Rappin' and stylin' out: Communication in urban black America*, ed. by Thomas Kochman. Champaign-Urbana: University of Illinois Press.

Morgan, Marcyliena. 1989. *From Down South to Up South: The language behavior of three generations of black women residing in Chicago*. Ph.D. dissertation, University of Pennsylvania.

Phillippo, James. 1843. *Jamaica: Its past and present state*. Philadelphia: James M. Campbell.

Piersen, William. 1977. Puttin' down ole massa: African satire in the New World. *African folklore in the New World*, ed. by D. J. Crowley. Austin: University of Texas Press.

Rattray, R. S. 1923. *Ashanti*. Oxford: Clarendon Press.

Reisman, Karl. 1970. Cultural and linguistic ambiguity in a West Indian village. *Afro-American anthropology: Contemporary perspectives*, ed. by Norman E. Whitten, Jr., and John Szwed, 129–44. New York: Free Press.

———. 1974. Contrapuntal conversations in an Antiguan village. *Explorations in the ethnography of speaking*, ed. by Richard Bauman and Joel Sherzer, 110–24. Cambridge: Cambridge University Press.

Saah, Kofi K. 1984. Language use and attitudes in Ghana. *Anthropological Linguistics* 28.367–77.

Smitherman, Geneva. 1977. *Talking and testifying: The language of black America*. Boston: Houghton Mifflin.

Wood, Peter. 1974. Black majority. *South Carolina Gazette*. September 17, 1772. New York: Alfred A. Knopf.

# Part Four

## *Some Historiographical Notes*

# Africanisms in the American South

*Michael Montgomery*

In 1904, Thomas L. Broun of Charleston, West Virginia, published a three-page essay in the *Publication of the Southern Historical Association* on the etymology of the verb *tote*. Relying largely on four current dictionaries, Broun, an amateur linguist, argued against the possible African derivation of the word that had been suggested by two of the dictionaries (*Webster's* and *The Century*), but he took two very different tacks in doing so. He began in a scholarly manner, pointing out proposed etyma for *tote* from Latin (*tollo* 'to carry away') and Old English (*totian* 'to lift up, to raise'). Then, as if to clinch the case, he concluded his piece with an ipso facto argument that "very few words, if any, have been introduced into the English language through Southern negroes, certainly no verb, and *tote* is a verb" (1904:296). Although no one knows what specifically inspired or provoked Broun to make this contribution to an etymological discussion, two points are clear.

First, Broun's piece was not isolated; it was part of a general discussion and came on the heels of at least eight other statements on *tote* that appeared in several journals (*American Notes and Queries*, *Modern Language Notes*, and *The Nation*) over the previous decade, and it thus was a contribution to a longer-standing etymological debate. Second, the supposition that *tote* is an Africanism went back much further; the word was recognized as a Southernism at least as early as 1781 by Rev. John Witherspoon of Philadelphia in a series of papers called "The Druid" in the *Pennsylvania Journal* (Mathews 1931:25). Noah Webster in his 1828 edition of *An American Dictionary of the English Language* came as close as anyone in his day to labeling the word an Africanism, calling it "a word used in slaveholding countries; said to have been introduced by the blacks."

Thomas Broun's argument for the non-Africanness of *tote* was clearly the typical one, at least in the printed debate of that time. All the writers who preceded him, some of them anonymous, denied either the Africanness or the southernness of the term in an apparent attempt to discredit the view (unstated in the debate) that the word originated among blacks or Southern whites. Rather than taking such denials only at face value, we should ask just what they imply and what picture they provide. To this writer they imply at least two things: (1) that the question of African influence on American English was open to debate, and (2) that there must have been some adherents to the Africanist point of view in the nineteenth-century South to inspire such a denial. Just as forms labeled nonstandard and stigmatized in seventeenth- and eighteenth-century grammar books tell us something about the colloquial language of the day, denials and labels such as those by Broun indicate discussion of and credibility given to the influence of African patterns on Southern English.

The point I make here is that there were etymological discussions by both lexicographers and amateur philologists over the Africanness of *tote* and a number of other terms like *goober* and *buckra,* particularly in the South, and that these discussions reach back into the nineteenth, and occasionally the eighteenth, century. The record of these discussions is often difficult to find, but tucked away here and there in the literature are comments, observations, and letters to editors speculating about, or denying, the possible African etymology of specific words. A number of these are listed in the References.

This paper has three objectives. The first is to create a perspective and to characterize the understanding of the possibility of Africanisms in American English, particularly in the South, prior to the publication of Melville Herskovits's *Myth of the Negro Past*, the watershed work in the field, and to put this understanding into the context of American dialect study of the period. The pieces of this puzzle are diverse and often hard to piece together, so the picture drawn here is a sketchy one, in most ways more suggestive than conclusive.

The second objective is to outline research potentials on Africanisms in the Southern United States and suggest ways that their range and intensity can be investigated. We now know a fair amount about Africanisms and other substratal elements in Sea Island Creole, or Gullah, along the South Atlantic Coast, at least enough to begin making comparisons with other creoles, as a result of the expert work of Cassidy (1983, 1986), Hancock (1969, 1987), Stewart (1968), Mufwene and Gilman (1987), and others, but as yet the same cannot be done for linguistic forms or features—lexical, grammatical, phonological, or otherwise—in the interior South. Further research is necessary.

Third, this paper begins one direction of further research by showing how materials from the Linguistic Atlas of the Gulf States project constitute an important source of data on language patterns in the interior American South and how they offer the prospect of comparative data on some African-derived forms; in short, how they enable us to begin to answer the questions raised in the previous paragraph.

My perspective on Africanisms in the American South is based on material collected for the *Annotated Bibliography of Southern American English* (McMillan and Montgomery 1989). Most of the items that deal with the issue of Africanisms, such as the one by Thomas Broun, are little more than instances of philological puzzle solving, but several are longer and will be given some attention here. In general, the bibliographical record reveals that in the nineteenth and early twentieth centuries material on black American speech was being collected and there was considerable curiosity about its possible Africanness. In addition, the pidginization of Southern black speech was mentioned at least half a century earlier than Herskovits's work, which appeared in the second quarter of the twentieth century.

## Are There Africanisms in Southern American English?

The most familiar material discussing the extent of Africanisms in American English is the early commentary on Gullah, especially as presented in Lorenzo Dow Turner's introduction to *Africanisms in the Gullah Dialect* (1949). Turner reviews the literature to assess the degree to which writers before him considered the possibility of Africanisms. Among several others, he cites the following passage from the foreword to Ambrose Gonzales's collection of stories, *The Black Border*:[1]

> These Gullahs seized upon the peasant English used by some of the early settlers and by the white servants of the wealthier colonists, [and] wrapped their clumsy tongues about it as well as they could, and, enriched with certain expressive African words, . . . the words are, of course, not African, for the African brought over or retained only a few words. (1922:10, 17)

Also quoted is Reed Smith of the University of South Carolina, who stated that

> what the Gullahs seem to have done was to take a sizeable part of the English vocabulary as spoken on the coast by the white inhabitants from about 1700 on . . . and reproduce it changed in tonality, pronunciation, cadence, and grammar to suit their native phonetic tendencies, . . . the result has been called by one writer "the worst English in the world." (1926:22)

There is little disputing Turner's assessment that nearly all writers on the subject traced "practically all of the peculiarities of Gullah to early English" (1949:10), and it doesn't take deep reading to relinquish doubts about the Anglocentrism of early folklore and dialect studies on the Sea Islands and elsewhere in the South. However, this is hardly the entire story.

While scholars normally sought older British analogues for cultural phenomena, both black and white, to most Southerners the Africanness of black culture was impossible to deny, especially in the domains of music, dance, and religion. Innumerable comments were made in the colonial and antebellum periods indicating this, as by Thomas Jefferson in his *Notes on the State of Virginia* (1954:140–41). Although the Africanness of black speech was seldom noted per se, authors occasionally cited forms that posed difficulty for derivation from English, forms that we know today are Africanisms. William Francis Allen, in the introduction to his *Slave Songs in the United States*, mentions *buckra,* the proper names *Cuffy, Quash,* and *Cudjo,* the verb *churray* 'to spill,' and the pronoun *oona* (1867:xxv) in Gullah. He also observes that the language contact situation on the Sea Islands produced a variety of speech, "a patois" (xxv) with "no distinctions of gender, case, number, tense, or voice" (xxx). Other nineteenth-century compilers and commentators, particularly Harrison (1884) and Brinton (1887), also cite forms of African heritage, the latter identifying supposed numerals from a speaker of the Amerindian language Nanticoke as being from Mandingo.

Despite the scattered printed observations, private discussion and interest about the level of African input were most likely far greater. For striking evidence of this there is no better figure to examine than John Bennett (1865–1956). A newspaperman and free-lance writer from Ohio, Bennett moved to Charleston in the late nineteenth century for health reasons. He integrated himself into Charleston society and became intensely interested in the local culture. In two essays he wrote on Gullah (1908, 1909), more substantial than anything written before his time, he catalogs and glosses numerous Gullah words and phrases and comments briefly on Gullah's formative elements: "Though its intonation may thus be African, its vocabulary is English; . . . the number of African words, phrases, and idioms retained is, comparatively, small" (1908:337–38). Yet it is clear from his private notebooks[2] and from his correspondence (Anderson n.d.) that he had a long-term and very keen interest in tracing local words back to African languages. Piecing together bits of information from travelers' accounts such as Winwood Reade's *The African Sketch Book* (1872) and Georg Schweinfurth's *The Heart of Africa* (1874) and from early books on African languages such as Robert Needham Cust's *Modern Languages of Africa* (1884), Bennett was able to either puzzle out or confirm the African sources of *yam, voodoo, banjo, duppy, buckra, mumbo-jumbo, okra, pinder, goober, coonjine, cootah,* and many other words. He also assiduously recorded numerous rhymes and songs that had un-English words and tried to trace them to the few specific African languages about which anything had been written.

Bennett neither published his private research on African etymologies nor revealed an inkling of this interest in his two essays on Gullah. Why? Although he may have considered his findings too tentative or thought his work too amateurish, another explanation appears far more likely: the subject was too explosive. If words such as *yam* and *pinder* and many others came from Africa, this most likely implied a greater African contribution to white culture of Low Country South Carolina than could have been discussed in print. Bennett states on page 16 of his notes on Gullah:

> On close observation and research in the Coast Country of South Carolina there appear certain other remnant traces of considerable interest, some apparently unknown to lexicographers, for the great part unnoted by observers, and for the rest unattended by local students, as part of *a great question already forced upon them in too many ways to be welcome*. (emphasis mine).

The point here is that the psychology revealed by this point of view would have greatly restrained public discussion of Africanisms, but researchers were already working in private in the direction of more accurate recognition of the African element in Southern American English.

Above I surveyed a sample of the linguistic commentary. Work of the same type was far more common among folklorists, a host of whom began collecting black folklore in the late nineteenth century, much of it of linguistic interest. The American Folk-lore Society was founded in 1888 to collect "Relics of Old English Folk-Lore (ballads, tales, superstitions, dialect, etc.) and Lore of Negroes in the Southern States of the Union" (*Journal of American Folklore* 1:3). The American Dialect Society was founded the next year with similar antiquarian goals. However strange it may seem to later generations of scholars, this antiquarianism inspired folklorists to venture not only up into the remote hills of Kentucky and North Carolina but also into the unknown territory of black society to collect folklore—not ballads but songs, rhymes, chants, stories, folktales, and other verbal lore. Black communities were commonly assumed to be repositories of holdovers from previous centuries. In the early years of the *Journal of American Folklore*, in fact, more material was published on black folklore than any other American group, including those arch-archaizers, the Southern mountaineers.

Thus, many of these early collectors saw themselves as involved in an urgent salvage operation. What we would call their Anglocentrism—their preoccupation with finding English, Irish, and Scottish carryovers among pockets of American society—was the motivation, as well as a measure of romantic inspiration, which initially sent them into the field. Rather than seeing the Anglocentric view as nothing more than blinders for folklorists and linguists, we should understand it in a dispassionate light as a perfectly logical intellectual point of view in the late nineteenth and early twentieth centuries—and a reflection of its time. Three points can help us understand this.

## Reasons for Anglocentrism

First, there was scant knowledge of African languages before the 1930s. In his report to the American Council of Learned Societies in 1941, Turner lamented the serious handicaps faced by linguists because of "the lack of ethnological studies of the different tribes on the West [African] Coast" and the "lack of adequate grammars and dictionaries of the West African languages" (1941:72). These handicaps explain why Turner spent most of the 1930s doing his own spade work on West African languages. It would not have been easy for Reed Smith in 1926, and it was extremely difficult for our Thomas Broun or anyone else in 1900, to make a strong case for the African origin of any word. This makes the efforts of John Bennett even more impressive. African etymologies were at best only suppositions. When offered in dictionaries, they were phrased in passive sentences (for example, *tote* was "said to be an African word introduced by Southern negroes" by *The Century*). Thanks largely to Turner, Herskovits, and other researchers, scholars experienced a quantum jump in the knowledge of African languages in the 1930s. But if African languages were in no sense points of reference for earlier writers on black speech in the United States, what was?

One thing that the point of reference certainly was not was the white speech of the day. Little descriptive work had been done by 1930, and the linguistic notion of the primacy of speech patterns over writing gained significant acceptance only later. It was literary English, in particular the education of scholars—both black and white—in the English classics that gave them their points of reference in comparing language patterns. Shakespeare, Spenser, Chaucer, and other Renaissance authors were standard reading for generations of students in the English-speaking world, at least in the higher grades. Gullah was described as "Elizabethan" or "Jacobean" for the same reason that so many commentators called black usages "Elizabethan" or "Chaucerian" and for the very same reason that other commentators labeled southern Appalachian speech in the same way: these writers knew their classics, especially sixteenth-century literature. Literary forms from Renaissance English, notably from Shakespeare, were the only "data" most writers were familiar enough with to use for comparisons. Thus, the terms "Shakespearean" and "Elizabethan" in popular usage have meant little more than "old-fashioned."

This explains, at least in part, why even an august scholar like George Philip Krapp of Johns Hopkins University emphasized the English connections of black speech. Krapp, a scholar of international repute in the history of the English language, knew every stage of the language so thoroughly that he could hardly fail to find a plausible English source for any form he heard in black speech. His statements that "many of the characteristics of Negro English which are assumed to be the peculiar property of the Negroes are merely archaic survivals of good old English" (1924:190) and "it is reasonably safe to say that not a single detail of Negro pronunciation or of Negro syntax can be proved to have any other than an English origin" (191) can thus be put into perspective. This tendency to view dialect forms as Elizabethan carryovers explains why essays have appeared for years with titles like "Uncle Remus Spake the Queen's English" (Polk 1953), and why Reed Smith, a preeminent scholar of English balladry in the 1920s, suspected English-dialect analogues for everything in Gullah. Anglocentrism was thus not just a default position reflecting the lack of knowledge of African languages; many early writers were intimately familiar with elements of the English superstrate (as we would term it today) as represented by belles lettres and popular literature.

A third important point is that there was a rather primitive understanding of language contact situations, although there certainly are intimations of the notion of pidginization before Herskovits and some discussion of the interactional processes involved in the black-white contact crucible in the South as well. Recall that William Francis Allen referred to black speech as a "patois," the common term for a rural dialect in that day, especially one influenced by language contact. Giles Jackson and G. Webster Davis wrote in *The Industrial History of the Negro Race in the United States* that "the Negro uses in many instances a kind of pigeon [*sic*] English or dialect. The whites heard this jargon on southern plantations and copied it, and thus the language of the whites and blacks on southern plantations had a strange similarity" (1908:112). In the same essay quoted earlier, Krapp (1924:134) describes the pidginization of black speech in a scenario he saw as consistent with his Anglocentrism:

> From the very beginning the white overlords addressed themselves in English to their black vassals. It is not difficult to imagine the kind of English this would be. It would be a very much simplified English—the kind of English some people employ when they talk to babies. It would probably have no tenses of the verb, no distinctions of case in nouns or

> pronouns, no marks of singular or plural. . . . Its vocabulary would be reduced to the lowest elements. In short, it would be a language of very much the same kind as those which have developed elsewhere under similar circumstances. It would have resemblances to the Beach-la-Mar of the Western Pacific, the Pidgin English of China, and the Chinook Jargon of Western America.

The similarity of black American speech to anglophone Caribbean creoles was pointed out by at least two sources independent of and roughly contemporaneous with Herskovits. Damon (1934:134), in referring to eighteenth-century black songs, says that "the dialect, which sounds like a cockney, Frenchified English, sprinkled with such words as *buckra, banjo, massa, pickaninny,* was probably fairly close to West Indian speech." Also, Stoney and Shelby (1930:ix–x) in an essay prefacing their collection of Gullah tales, say that "the branches of the family tree of Gullah are American, the trunk is West Indian and the roots English and African." We may thus conclude that a number of earlier observations laid the groundwork for the connections that Herskovits and Turner were soon to establish. While not minimizing the fundamental and pioneering contributions of these two scholars, my discussion provides a somewhat fuller view of the field, complementing that presented by Glenn Gilbert elsewhere in this volume.

## Research Possibilities

The published record surveyed above is only one part of the material available to explore the extent of Africanisms in Southern American English. As I mentioned, folklorists collected a wealth of verbal lore from blacks in the nineteenth and early twentieth centuries, largely in the form of songs, rhymes, chants, hymns, proverbs, and other such supposedly conservative genres. Much of this lies untapped in journals and unmined in archives around the country; five such cases are noted here.

Some of the richest material is that collected at Hampton Institute in Virginia for the *Southern Workman*, a journal published between 1872 and 1939. Two examples of probable Africanisms among a multitude that could be cited are *tingany* 'flour' and *harberdidie* 'turkey buzzard' (*Southern Workman* 1895, 24.78). *Strange Ways and Sweet Dreams*, Donald J. Waters's 1983 anthology of brief items on folklore and ethnology, provides a representative sample of material from the Hampton Institute archive.

Another little-used source is the lifetime of material on black folklore collected by Newbell Niles Puckett located in the library at Case Western Reserve University in Cleveland and elsewhere. Only a fraction of this was published in Puckett's magnum opus, *Folk Beliefs of the Southern Negro* (1926). Intensely interested in the issue of Africanisms in his day and ahead of everyone else but Herskovits, Puckett discusses a number of unusual terms, including several found in Louisiana voodoo songs such as *macaya, ouarasi, mawa,* and *ouanga,* that suggest his material should be mined for further data.

A third potential source of Africanisms is material on Louisiana French Creole going back to that collected by Alcee Fortier in the 1880s and 1890s. Reinecke et al. (1975:278–91) list 180 items dealing with this creole, including many substantial collections of folklore in the form of theses and dissertations at Louisiana State University. Little of this has been sifted for Africanisms.

Fourth, the many records compiled by the Work Projects Administration, particularly those archived in state and university libraries throughout the South, need to be mined for linguistic and other types of Africanisms. The republished *Drums and Shadows* volume (1986), drawing on material collected by the Savannah unit of the WPA, contains a number of Africanisms, such as *mosojo* 'pot' and *diffy* 'fire,' that are not noted elsewhere.

A fifth source of material on Africanisms in Southern English will now be dealt with in more detail—data from the Linguistic Atlas of the Gulf States.

## Africanisms in the Deep South

In his well-known book on the history and usage of Black English, J. L. Dillard spends eight pages (1972:115–23) addressing a central question pertinent to this paper's discussion: How much of it is African? Citing the lexical borrowings identified by Mitford Mathews in *Some Sources of Southernisms* and Raven McDavid in his review of Turner's *Africanisms in the Gullah Dialect*, Dillard suggests other possible lexical and grammatical forms borrowed or relexified from African languages into American English. Dillard vigorously opposes the view that the Africanness of Gullah is, at least historically, unique among mainland varieties of speech: "There is hardly any reason to assume," he says, "that any of the Africanisms listed by Turner were limited to the Gullah area in the eighteenth and nineteenth centuries" (1972:117). Not only must Africanisms have been widespread among blacks elsewhere in the South, he hypothesizes, but they must have made considerable inroads into the white population as well. Confirming these hypotheses is crucial to Dillard's basic case because it would lend validity to the argument that American black speech as a whole had a Gullah-like progenitor. Moreover, documenting the spread of Africanisms in American black speech, and in white speech as well, appears to be a key to understanding the influence of black, creole, and African influences on white society. The existence and distribution of Africanisms across the South are empirical questions, but how can they be investigated?

Until quite recently, it has been unclear how to produce evidence that would enable us to explore Dillard's hypotheses. As presented in his book, they are contentions based on a review of the literature and scattered observations by himself and other linguists, including some of the early commentators mentioned here. To explore these views, a large body of linguistic data, ideally from across the social and ethnic spectrum in the South, is required. Such a corpus of data does, in fact, exist and is in the process of being edited. These data are the basic materials of the Linguistic Atlas of the Gulf States (LAGS), which consists of several components: field records (i.e., the tape recordings), protocols (the worksheets for the questionnaire), idiolect synopses (the one-page summary of forms for each informant), the concordance of approximately three million items keyed by line numbers to the protocols, and other ancillary materials, including the handbook, all published by University Microfilms and the University of Georgia Press.

## Linguistic Atlas of the Gulf States

For those unfamiliar with the LAGS project, a brief summary is in order. Directed by Lee Pederson of Emory University from the beginning, LAGS is a broad-based study of regional and social dialects based on interviews with more than nine hundred primary informants recorded from 1968 to 1983 in eight Southern states: Tennessee, Arkansas, Louisiana, Mississippi, Florida, Alabama, Arkansas, and Texas (as far west as the Balcones Escarpment). LAGS is the largest, most inclusive research project on Southern speech yet conducted; it provides basic texts for studying the region's speech and a description of the sociohistorical and sociolinguistic contexts necessary for their interpretation. Ultimately, the project seeks to achieve four additional interrelated goals: an inventory of the dominant and recessive patterns of usage in the Gulf states; a global description of regional and social varieties of Southern speech; an abstract of regional phonology, grammar, and lexicon; and an identification of areas of linguistic complexity which require further study (Pederson 1977:28; Bailey 1989).

From its inception LAGS has been an extension of the direct method of dialect geography initiated by Jules Gilliéron in France and refined by Hans Kurath in the United States. This method involves the following: selection of a network of communities, including focal, relic, and transitional communities, on the basis of the history of the region; conversational interviews with natives of these communities conducted with a questionnaire of selected items; and recording of the responses in finely graded phonetics. The informants are of three types: folk informants with a grade school education or less (40%); common informants with a high school education (35%); and cultivated informants with a college education (25%). Blacks make up 22% of the sample, which also includes informants whose native language is Spanish, French, or German. Although faithful to the methods and the questionnaire of other regional linguistic atlas projects, LAGS has been innovative in several ways. For example, every interview was taped, totaling nearly 5,500 hours of recording for the project as a whole. In addition, most interviews elicited at least 1 hour of free conversation, and approximately 160 informants in urban areas were given a supplementary set of questions about city life.

Most earlier work on Africanisms focused on lexical forms, and the same is true for LAGS. Words are much easier to document, map, and in many ways interpret than grammatical and phonological forms. Questions on the LAGS worksheets were not designed specifically to elicit Africanisms, but a number of them are cataloged in the LAGS concordance (Pederson et al. 1986) because they arose during the course of interviews. The lexical files are the most completely edited so far (Pederson et al. 1990), but in the immediate future it will be possible to examine the phonological and grammatical data for Africanisms as well. Since all LAGS interviews were tape-recorded, eventually this material will be available for intonational study as well.

Below I examine the patterning of three Africanisms: *pinders, goobers,* and the loan translation *hoppergrass*. LAGS lexical data are being edited to reveal social, generational, and ethnic patterns as well as geographical ones, thanks to a set of microcomputer analysis programs. The LAGS Codemap program, used to create figures 1, 2, and 3, presents a tabular breakdown by race (W = white, B = black), class (L = lower, M = middle, U = upper), and generation (according to age ranges 13–30, 31–60, and 61–99) for the speakers in each of eighteen subgroups who provide a given form, out of the total number in that group who were interviewed. It also codes the forms for each subgroup according to letters and numerals and presents a map plotting these letters and numerals across the eight-state LAGS territory.[3]

From the codemap for *pinders* (from Kongo *mpinda;* see figure 1) we can see that it was known by a slightly lower number of whites (73/717, or 10.2%) than blacks (29/193, or 15%). The term is clearly recessive, with more than three quarters of the speakers (78/102) who knew it being over sixty years of age,

Figure 1. Codemap for *Pinders*

Code 1: Race/Class/Age

| | | | |
|---|---|---|---|
| 1 = W/L/13-30 | 0/5 | A = B/L/13-30 | 1/13 |
| 2 = W/M/13-30 | 1/67 | B = B/M/13-30 | 0/13 |
| 3 = W/U/13-30 | 0/10 | C = B/U/13-30 | 0/0 |
| 4 = W/L/31-60 | 4/25 | D = B/L/31-60 | 3/19 |
| 5 = W/M/31-60 | 0/117 | E = B/M/31-60 | 4/25 |
| 6 = W/U/31-60 | 1/33 | F = B/U/31-60 | 0/5 |
| 7 = W/L/61-99 | 21/149 | G = B/L/61-99 | 18/84 |
| 8 = W/M/61-99 | 43/257 | H = B/M/61-99 | 3/35 |
| 9 = W/U/61-99 | 3/54 | J = B/U/61-99 | 0/3 |
| Totals | 73/717 | Totals | 29/193 |

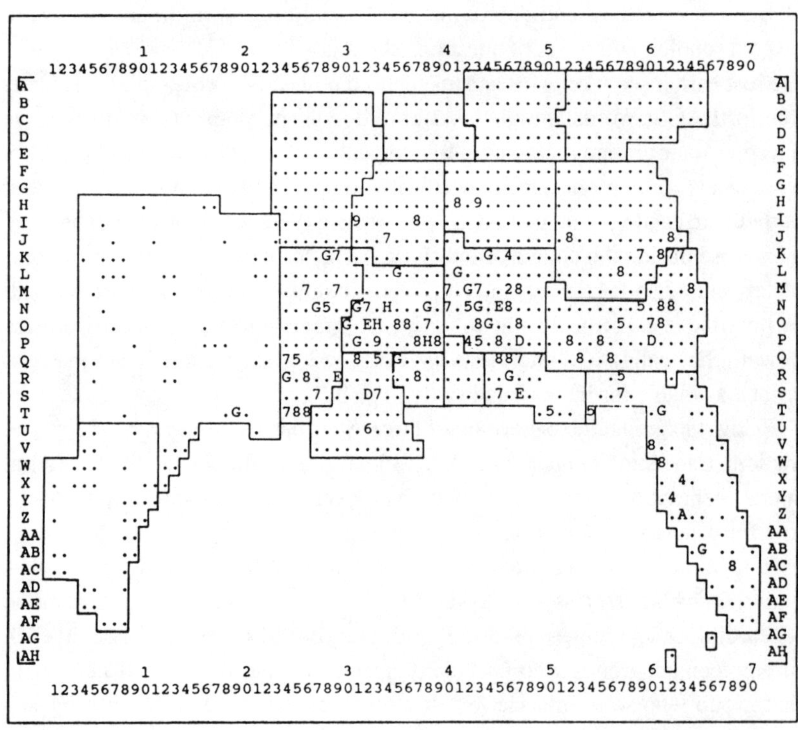

and only 2 speakers of the 108 under thirty years old knowing the term. The geographical spread is quite clearly confined to the Black Belt, most intensively in Alabama and Georgia, with no appearance of the word in the upper South (Tennessee, north Georgia, etc.) and only one in Texas.

On the other hand, the pattern for *goobers* (akin to Kongo *nguba;* shown in figure 2) shows that the term has moved into the mainstream vocabulary in the South. It is not much less widespread among younger whites (34/82, or 41.5%) than among older whites (218/460, or 47.4%) and in fact is known by more whites overall (333/717, or 46.4%) than blacks (72/197, or 36.6%). The term has diffused throughout the South, including into the mountain areas of Tennessee and north Georgia, although its occurrence is more intense in the lower South, especially in Alabama and Mississippi.

A type of form less widely recognized in Southern English for its probable Africanness is the loan translation. To determine the African elements in American English, Dalby (1972:174) notes that "we need also to look for so-called calques or loan translations, in which African phrases and expressions were translated literally into English by speakers of West African languages and then retained in black speech with their original African meanings." Among the examples he cites are *bad-eye, bad-mouth, big-eye,* and *day-clean*. Two others most likely showing African influence are *hoppergrass* and *peckerwood* (Lee Pederson, personal communication) in that they follow a verb + noun pattern more typical of West African languages than English, which employs the noun + verb compounding sequence (as in *woodpecker* and *grasshopper*) much more often.

As figure 3 shows, the distribution of *hoppergrass* gives further evidence that the form may well be an Africanism, because it is far more prevalent among black speakers (82/197, or 41.6%) than among whites (63/717, or 8.8%) in the LAGS territory. While only 30.1% (8/26) of younger blacks knew the term, nearly half of the middle-aged ones (24/49, or 49%) and 41% (50/122) of the older blacks knew it.

This brief look at three forms having African influence shows how conclusions can be drawn about the prevalence of individual forms across racial, social, and generational lines in the LAGS territory. In addition, LAGS codemaps reveal aspects of the geographical spread of forms that will help researchers reconstruct earlier stages of the region's speech patterns. These maps thus show the spread of Africanisms both through the population and through the region. Beyond this, they provide one way to answer the larger question of the influence of blacks on white speech, and vice versa, as well as one kind of

Figure 2. Codemap for *Goobers*

Code 1: Race/Class/Age

| | | | |
|---|---|---|---|
| 1 = W/L/13-30 | 3/5 | A = B/L/13-30 | 2/13 |
| 2 = W/M/13-30 | 26/67 | B = B/M/13-30 | 4/13 |
| 3 = W/U/13-30 | 5/10 | C = B/U/13-30 | 0/0 |
| 4 = W/L/31-60 | 5/25 | D = B/L/31-60 | 8/19 |
| 5 = W/M/31-60 | 59/117 | E = B/M/31-60 | 11/25 |
| 6 = W/U/31-60 | 17/33 | F = B/U/31-60 | 2/5 |
| 7 = W/L/61-99 | 64/149 | G = B/L/61-99 | 30/84 |
| 8 = W/M/61-99 | 126/257 | H = B/M/61-99 | 14/35 |
| 9 = W/U/61-99 | 28/54 | J = B/U/61-99 | 1/3 |
| Totals | 333/717 | Totals | 72/197 |

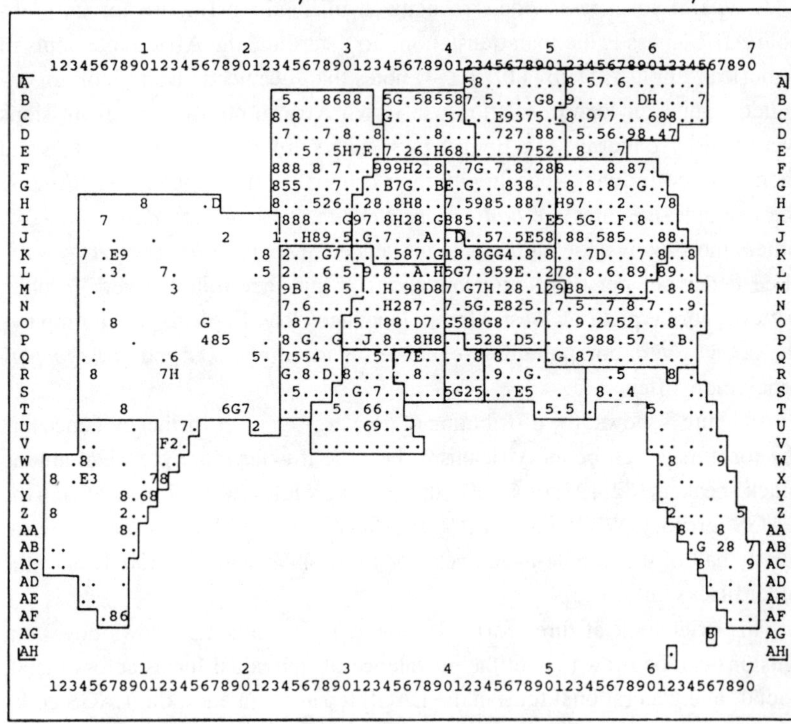

Figure 3. Codemap for *Hoppergrass*

Code 1: Race/Class/Age

| | | | |
|---|---|---|---|
| 1 = W/L/13-30 | 1/5 | A = B/L/13-30 | 5/13 |
| 2 = W/M/13-30 | 3/67 | B = B/M/13-30 | 3/13 |
| 3 = W/U/13-30 | 0/10 | C = B/U/13-30 | 0/0 |
| 4 = W/L/31-60 | 2/25 | D = B/L/31-60 | 12/19 |
| 5 = W/M/31-60 | 11/117 | E = B/M/31-60 | 9/25 |
| 6 = W/U/31-60 | 3/33 | F = B/U/31-60 | 3/5 |
| 7 = W/L/61-99 | 13/149 | G = B/L/61-99 | 38/84 |
| 8 = W/M/61-99 | 23/257 | H = B/M/61-99 | 10/35 |
| 9 = W/U/61-99 | 7/54 | J = B/U/61-99 | 2/3 |
| Totals | 63/717 | Totals | 82/197 |

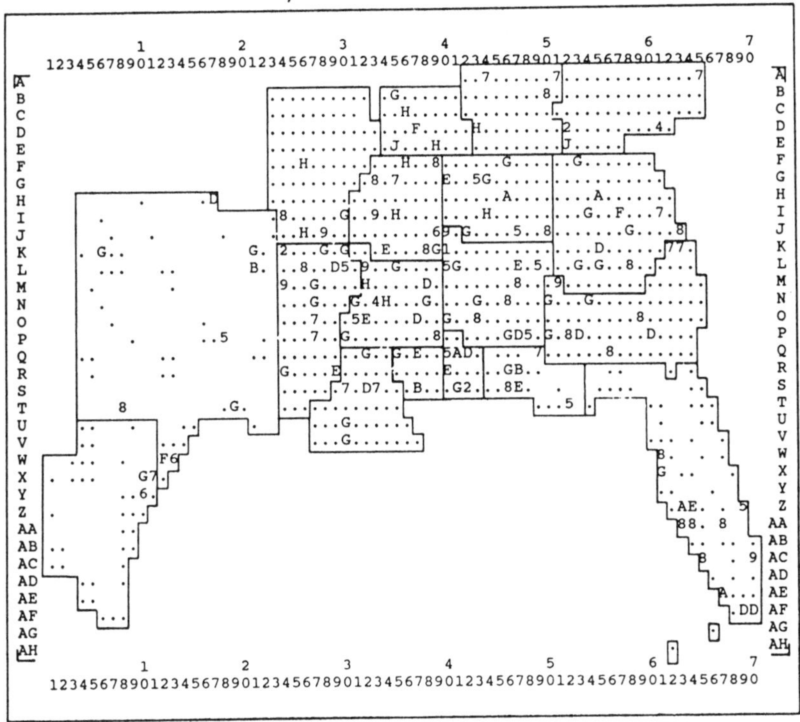

index, in terms of different percentages of occurrence, for supposing that some forms such as *hoppergrass* exhibit African influence.

Many more Africanisms are tucked away in the LAGS concordance that would be profitable to examine in the way done here, including *cush, cush-cush, gumbo, hoodoo, juke,* and *voodoo*. They occur with a lower frequency than researchers would like, but in many cases the concordance indicates the syntactic context and a scribal note about the usage of the term as well. The information is enough to give us a baseline while the archives collected by folklorists and other scholars are investigated and fresh studies are undertaken.

This paper has had the historiographic goal of deepening our understanding of the extent to which early scholars and commentators appreciated the African contributions to Southern American English. It has had the bibliographic goal of identifying lesser-known items, particularly untapped archives and resources for filling in the picture of these African elements, and has shown how data from the Linguistic Atlas of the Gulf States project are helping to do this. Many contours and details of this picture remain to be sketched in, but the outlines are now clearer.

## Notes

1. The twelve-page foreword has Gonzales's name at the end, and although Turner and nearly everyone else have assumed that Gonzales wrote it, this view has been pointedly opposed by William Stewart, the most prominent scholar of Gonzales's work. Stewart (personal communication) argues that the sentiments expressed in the excerpt quoted here are uncharacteristic of Gonzales and that the latter's health was too fragile at the time for him to have written the essay.

2. Bennett's material on Gullah, located in file 21-176-1 of the John Bennett Collection at the Historical Society of South Carolina in Charleston, consists of forty 8½-by-14-inch pages onto which he pasted personal notes, excerpts from books, and a wide variety of other items. Thanks go to Steve Hoffius of the Historical Society staff in helping the author find and copy this material.

3. Many thanks to Lee Pederson of Emory University, director of the Linguistic Atlas of the Gulf States, for making both the data and the Codemap program available.

**References**

A., C. H. 1891. "Tote." *American Notes and Queries* 6.190.

Allen, William Francis. 1929. *Slave songs of the United States*. 1867. New York: Peter Smith.

Anderson, Mary L. n.d. Letters of two friends: The Yates Snowden–John Bennett correspondence. Unpublished manuscript.

Anonymous. 1888. On the field and work of a journal of American folklore. *Journal of American Folklore* 1.3–7.

B., W. G. 1894. "Tote." *Nation* 58.121.

Bailey, Guy. 1989. Linguistic atlas of the Gulf states. *Encyclopedia of Southern culture*, ed. by William Ferris and Charles Wilson, 788. Chapel Hill: University of North Carolina Press.

Baskerville, W. M. 1891. The etymology of English "tote." *Modern Language Notes* 6.180–81.

Bennett, John. 1908–9. Gullah: A Negro patois. *South Atlantic Quarterly* 7.332–47, 8.39–52.

Brinton, D. G. 1887. On certain supposed Nanticoke words, shown to be of African origin. *American Antiquarian and Oriental Journal* 9.350–54.

Broun, Thomas L. 1904. The word "tote." *Publication of the Southern Historical Association* 8.294–96.

Bruce, J. Douglas. 1893. "Tote." *Modern Language Notes* 8.251.

Bruce, Philip A. 1894. "Tote." *Nation* 58.121.

Cassidy, Frederic G. 1983. Sources of the African element in Gullah. *Studies in Caribbean language*, ed. by Lawrence D. Carrington et al., 75–81. St. Augustine, Trinidad: Society for Caribbean Linguistics.

———. 1986. Some similarities between Gullah and Caribbean creoles. *Language variety in the South: Perspectives in black and white*, ed. by Michael Montgomery and Guy Bailey, 30–37. University: University of Alabama Press.

Cust, Robert Needham. 1883. *A sketch of the modern languages of Africa*. London: Trübner.

Dalby, David L. 1972. The African element in American English. *Rappin' and stylin' out: Communication in urban black America*, ed. by Thomas Kochman, 170–86. Champaign-Urbana: University of Illinois Press.

Damon, S. Foster. 1934. The Negro in early American songsters. *Papers of the Bibliographical Society of America* 28.132–63.

Dillard, J. L. 1972. *Black English: Its history and usage in the United States*. New York: Random House.

G., B. W. 1894. "Tote." *Nation* 58.121.

Gonzales, Ambrose. 1922. *The black border: Gullah stories of the Carolina coast*. Columbia, S.C.: The State Press.

Hancock, Ian F. 1969. The English-derived Atlantic creoles: A provisional comparison. *African Language Review* 8.7–72.

———. 1987. A preliminary classification of the anglophone Atlantic creoles, with syntactic data from thirty-three representative districts. *Pidgin and creole languages: Essays in memory of John F. Reinecke*, ed. by Glenn G. Gilbert, 264–333. Honolulu: University of Hawaii Press.

Harrison, James A. 1884. Negro English. *Anglia* 7.232–79.

Herskovits, Melville J. 1935. What has Africa given America? *New Republic* 84.91–93.

———. 1941. *The myth of the Negro past*. Boston: Beacon Press.

Jackson, Giles B., and D. Webster Davis. 1908. *The industrial history of the Negro race of the United States*. Richmond, Va.: Virginia Press. Reprint. Freeport, N.Y.: Books for Libraries Press, 1971.

Jefferson, Thomas. 1954. *Notes on the state of Virginia*. Ed. by William Peden. Chapel Hill: University of North Carolina Press.

Krapp, George Philip. 1924. The English of the Negro. *American Mercury* 2.190–95.

McDavid, Raven I., Jr. 1950. Review of *Africanisms in the Gullah dialect*, by Lorenzo D. Turner. *Language* 26.223–33.

McMillan, James B., and Michael Montgomery, eds. 1989. *Annotated bibliography of Southern American English*. Tuscaloosa: University of Alabama Press.

Mathews, Mitford McLeod. 1931. Rev. John Witherspoon (1722–94). *The beginnings of American English: Essays and comments*, 13–30. Chicago: University of Chicago Press.

———. 1948. Africanisms in the plantation vocabulary. *Some sources of Southernisms*, 86–129. University: University of Alabama Press.

Mufwene, Salikoko, and Charles Gilman. 1987. How African is Gullah, and why? *American Speech* 62.120–39.

Pederson, Lee. 1977. Toward a description of Southern speech. *Papers in language variation: SAMLA-ADS collection*, ed. by David L. Shores and Carole P. Hines, 25–31. University: University of Alabama Press.

Pederson, Lee, Susan Leas McDaniel, Carol Adams, and Michael Montgomery, eds. 1990. *Regional matrix for the linguistic atlas of the Gulf states*. Volume 4 of *Linguistic atlas of the Gulf states*. Athens: University of Georgia Press.

Pederson, Lee, Susan Leas McDaniel, and Marvin H. Bassett, eds. 1986. *The linguistic atlas of the Gulf states: A concordance of basic materials*. Ann Arbor: University Microfilms.

Polk, William T. 1953. Uncle Remus spake queen's English. *Southern accent: From Uncle Remus to Oak Ridge*, 57–71. New York: Morrow.

Puckett, Newbell Niles. 1926. *Folk beliefs of the southern Negro*. Chapel Hill: University of North Carolina Press.

Reade, Winwood. 1873. *The African sketch book*. 2 vols. London: Smith, Elder.

Reinecke, J. E., S. M. Tsuzaki, D. DeCamp, I. F. Hancock, and R. E. Wood, eds. 1975. *A bibliography of pidgin and creole languages*. Honolulu: University of Hawaii Press.

Schweinfurth, Georg. 1874. *The heart of Africa: Three years of travels and adventures in the unexplored regions of central Africa from 1868 to 1871*. 3 vols. London: Sampson.

Smith, Reed. 1926. *Gullah*. Columbia: University of South Carolina Bulletin no. 190. Reprinted in 1965. Eric Document 034 191.

Stewart, William A. 1968. Continuity and change in American Negro dialects. *Florida Foreign Language Reporter* 6.2.3–4, 14–16, 18.

Stoney, Samuel Gaillard, and Gertrude Mathews Shelby. 1930. The family tree of Gullah folk speech and folk tales. *Black genesis: A chronicle*, ix–xxv. New York: Macmillan.

Tillman, Nathaniel. 1942. A possible etymology of "tote." *American Speech* 17.128–29. [West African origin suggested.]

Turner, Lorenzo Dow. 1941. Linguistic research and African survivals. *The interdisciplinary aspects of Negro studies*, ed. by Melville J. Herskovits. American Council of Learned Societies Bulletin 32.68–89.

———. 1949. *Africanisms in the Gullah dialect*. Chicago: University of Chicago Press. Reprinted, with introduction by David De Camp. New York: Arno Press, 1969.

Twining, Mary A. 1977. *An examination of African retentions in the folk culture of the South Carolina and Georgia Sea Islands*. 2 vols. Bloomington: Indiana University Press.

W., G. B. 1894. "Tote." *Nation* 58.121.

Waters, Donald J., ed. 1983. *Strange ways and sweet dreams: Afro-American folklore from the Hampton Institute*. Boston: G. K. Hall.

Webster, Noah. 1828. *An American dictionary of the English language*. New York: Converse.

Woodson, Carter G. 1936. *The African background outlined, or handbook for the study of the Negro*. Washington, D.C.: Association for the Study of Negro Life and History.

Work Projects Administration. 1940. *Drums and shadows*. Reprinted, with an introduction by Charles Joyner. Athens: University of Georgia Press, 1986.

# Historical Development of the Creole Origin Hypothesis of Black English: The Pivotal Role of Melville J. Herskovits

*Glenn G. Gilbert*

The evidence was all around them, but few saw it, and no one really knew what to make of it: thus can we describe pre-Herskovitsian thinking about the provenience and survival of African languages and cultures in the New World. Melville Herskovits proposed that the acculturation of Africans in the New World left considerable opportunities for the direct and indirect survival of African cultural traits, including language; that acculturation to African values affected Europeans as well; that the hybrid Afro-European cultures of the New World are not inferior copies of a European model but are valuable cultural creations worthy of study in their own right; and that the degree of intensity of the African component decreases as one moves north in an arc beginning in Suriname and ending in the Northern states of the United States—what one could call the rainbow hypothesis.

This paper begins with a section which places Herskovits's work in historical perspective. It then focuses on the development of his thought in the late 1920s and early 1930s, the time when his thinking was radically redirected from its traditional, assimilationist cast toward the creole origin hypothesis. Elsie Clews Parsons and Hugo Schuchardt's contributions to the hypothesis and their influence on Herskovits are briefly discussed. The paper ends with a brief look at the rainbow hypothesis—the componential analysis of the intensity of cultural survivals—especially with regard to Herskovits's exaggeration of the linguistic differences between the Sea Islands and the mainland Southern United States, and finds this exaggeration to support William Stewart's notion of a compromise worked out by Herskovits and the assimilationist sociologist E. Franklin Frazier.

## Herskovits in Historical Perspective

Herskovits's work of fifty years ago represents a turning point. Studies going back to the 1860s had provided steadily increasing insights into the origin and development of black dialect in the United States and its relation to the dialects of English spoken by whites of English-speaking descent, European ethnics, Amerindians, Hispanics, and others, at the same time and in the same geographic locations. His predecessors, William Francis Allen (1867), Addison Van Name (1869–70), James A. Harrison (1884), and Hugo Schuchardt (1893, 1914), built up a tradition very different from that of the "dialectologists." His mentors, teachers, and scientific and financial backers, Elsie Clews Parsons and Franz Boas, were much more influential as contemporaries than were George P. Krapp (1924, 1925) and H. L. Mencken (1919), for instance. Clearly, too, the original contributions of his wife, Frances (Shapiro) Herskovits (e.g., 1966; and M. Herskovits and Herskovits 1934, 1936), have been underrated and deserve to be reassessed. Herskovits represented a rallying point for contemporaries such as Lorenzo Dow Turner (1949), Claude M. Wise (1933), Wise's student T. Earl Pardoe (1937), and John Reinecke. He encouraged Turner's studies of Gullah in much the same way that Boas and Parsons had promoted his own fieldwork in Suriname. (In hindsight, Turner appears as a kind of bridge, ultimately reuniting the dialectologists and the creolists.) It is also interesting to note that Reinecke, an unknown but promising scholar from Hawaii, was provided with the means (whether Herskovits was directly involved is not known) to finish his studies at Yale, where much of the input to his monumental dissertation (1937) was provided by the very library that Van Name had built up over many years.

The best-known living representatives of the Herskovitsian tradition are without doubt William Stewart (e.g., 1966–67, 1969, 1974) and J. L. Dillard (e.g., 1968, 1972). Unfortunately, Stewart has published very little since 1974, and Dillard, although a prolific writer, seems to have withdrawn from active dialogue with his critics. Throughout the 1970s and 1980s a younger generation of less confrontational dialectologists, sociolinguists, and variation theorists has explored new avenues of reconciliation of the dialectologist and creolist positions. Ralph Fasold (1972), for example, provided very reasoned arguments in favor of a more moderate creolist position, and William Labov's change of heart (recognizing the deep-seated differences between black dialect and other dialects, based on their disparate histories) at the time of the Black English trial in 1979 in Ann Arbor was nothing short of sensational (Labov 1982). On the other hand, creolists such as Robert B. Le Page (Le Page and Tabouret-Keller

1985; Le Page 1987), Ian Hancock (e.g., 1986, 1987), Salikoko Mufwene (e.g., 1987), and Geneviève Escure (e.g., 1988a, 1988b; Escure and Gilbert 1988) have recently begun to question the belief that most African slaves in the New World originally spoke nothing but creole basilect and have been decreolizing toward the metropolitan standard ever since. For them, the covert prestige of nonstandard forms, expressed through "acts of identity," may well neutralize any perceived advantage of the standard. The assumption of a steady decrease in the linguistic distance between Black English and other dialects in the United States, which most people had previously assumed as desirable and inevitable, began to be questioned in the early 1980s, primarily due to the work of Labov and his students in the mid-Atlantic East (e.g., Ash and Myhill 1986; Labov and Harris 1986; Myhill and Harris 1986; see also Gilbert 1988), and Guy Bailey and his students in the central Gulf South (e.g., Bailey and Maynor 1987; Bailey 1987). It is becoming increasingly evident that black dialect is here to stay and that it will attract the attention of linguists and other social scientists well into the next century, and beyond.

## Melville Herskovits

The closest thing to a biography of Herskovits is George Eaton Simpson's (1973) evaluation of his work in the Leaders of Modern Anthropology series. Beyond this, there is his obituary (Merriam 1964) and a complete list of his publications in the *American Anthropologist* (Moneypenny and Thorne 1964). His papers, manuscripts, and wide-ranging correspondence (communications from his correspondents and carbon copies of his own typewritten letters to them) have been preserved in the Herskovits Room of the Africana collection at the Northwestern University library (Evanston, Illinois). Fortunately, all of the material has been expertly cataloged and is easy for researchers to work with.

Herskovits was born in 1895 and died in 1963. His B.A. in history from the University of Chicago was awarded in 1920; his M.A. (1921) and Ph.D. in anthropology (1923) were from Columbia. It was in New York that he was profoundly influenced by Alexander A. Goldenweiser of the New School for Social Research and by Franz Boas at Columbia. Throughout his life, the dual themes of history and anthropology were inextricably intertwined in his thinking.

In 1924 he married Frances S. Shapiro in New York. She exerted a continuing influence on him throughout their long marriage, and she coauthored a number of books on the Caribbean and Africa with him, starting with *Rebel Destiny, among the Bush Negroes of Dutch Guiana* (1934) and *Suriname Folklore* (1936). Because she figures so prominently in his early work in Suriname, which began in the summer of 1928, a separate study of Frances Herskovits as a creolist and anthropologist in her own right would doubtless yield further insights.

Although Herskovits's dissertation was on the East African cattle complex, he spent most of the 1920s studying the physical anthropology of blacks in the United States, working first in Harlem and later at Howard University in Washington, D.C. Because Howard in those years attracted some of the best black academics of the post–World War I period, it was perhaps no accident that he came into contact there with the black sociologist E. Franklin Frazier, who was later to become the chief spokesman of the conservative forces seeking to turn back the creole paradigm (Simpson 1973; Stewart 1974).

In 1927 he began his long academic career at Northwestern University, and it was there that "he saw a new light," to use the mystical (and entirely accurate) phraseology of William Stewart. Until 1928 he was not prepared to admit that African cultural traits (including any kind of African language substratum) played an essential part, or perhaps any part whatsoever, in black life in the United States. His studies of blacks' physical anthropology pointed to a massive amount of admixture with whites and Indians, much greater than the U.S. Census was willing to admit (coupled with a surprisingly small amount of variability of physical type), so that he was ultimately able to affirm the existence of a novel people of a new physical type, the American black.

In "Acculturation and the American Negro" Herskovits describes how his preoccupation with physical anthropology led to a new interest in acculturation:

> It was not long before the opportunity to watch at the same time this phenomenon of the manner in which these American negroes had become essentially a part of the general American culture impressed itself upon me. . . . [Further study] has brought new instances of the extent to which the acculturation has taken place. (1927a:216–17)

In his first book, *The American Negro: A study in racial crossing* (1928), which deals largely with physical anthropology, he admits that there must have been stages of acculturation, but that by the early twentieth century almost all traces of it had been obliterated. Here he pleads agnosticism: "The stages of acculturation through which they passed after their arrival in this country have never been adequately described, nor, so far as one can see, are they likely to be" (1928:xiii). Upper Manhattan, which never ceased to fascinate him, was a case in point: "Harlem, the greatest center they have created, is to all intents and purposes an American community peopled by individuals who have an additional amount of pigmentation in their skins" (57).

I find no record of Herskovits traveling in the Southern states during those years. His knowledge of U.S. black culture appeared to be confined mainly to New York and Washington; he spared no pains to emphasize its European character and to minimize possible African survivals. For him, equality for blacks (actual or potential) could only mean blacks outdoing the Europeans, on their own terms at their own game.

Nevertheless, he continued his lively interest in Africa and the Caribbean, and it is in the book reviews from 1926 to 1928 that we begin to see the first stirrings of a change of heart. For example, in a review of Newbell Nile Puckett's *Folk beliefs of the southern Negro*, written in the summer or fall of 1926, he criticizes Puckett's knowledge of Africa (which was a problem with most writers of the time) and his dim view of African cultures. In a more moderate vein, he continues: "Yet some of his suggestions, such as the derivation of voodoo from the vodu of the Ewe, or goober (peanut) from guba, an African word for the ground-nut, are interesting" (1927b:310). But then, pulling back from a direction he did not care to (or feared to?) follow, he is quick to note: "He clearly recognises the paucity of African survivals to be noted in this country, which is important" (310). Puckett spent many pages trying to trace deep-seated African survivals in American black religion—charms, emotionalism, frenzy—but Herskovits was unconvinced: "it is difficult to see that much of a case for African elements in American Negro religion can be established" (311). Nevertheless, Herskovits felt somewhat uneasy in the light of Puckett's observations and called for "much more research" into both African and U.S. black culture.

His anthropological apprenticeship under Boas becomes evident in his review of W. B. Seabrook's *Lo, the poor Haitian*, written in fall 1928 or early winter 1928–29, in which he criticizes the author for not looking beneath the surface of the cultural phenomena he is observing: "his results show a lamentable willingness to accept surface values" (1929:198). Herskovits's new concern for the superficial versus the deep-seated cultural behavior nested behind it hints at changes in his thinking. But it hardly prepares us for the vastly different viewpoint expressed in his review of Martha Beckwith's *A study of Jamaican folk-life*, written hardly a year later, after his second summer in Suriname:

> Although certain phases of the life of the New World Negroes, especially their folk-lore and religious practices, have been subjected to intensive study, the general outlines of their cultural behavior have rarely received any attention at all. Such beginnings in this direction as have been made have been submerged in the general assumption that practically all aboriginal African traits of culture have been stamped out by the repressions of

> slavery. So widespread is this assumption that today it is taken for granted by almost all students of the Negro, and it furnishes the basis for the subsidiary hypothesis that we must look to Europe of the late seventeenth century, rather than to Africa, for the sources from which the present-day behavior of the New World Negroes derives—to Elizabethan England, for example, when the Negroes of the United States and English-speaking colonies of the Caribbean Sea are being considered.
>
> To what extent is this assumption justified? The answer to this question can only be vouchsafed us after long research, but I am convinced that the prevailing concept will be strongly modified as further investigation is carried out. The value of Miss Beckwith's book lies in the fact that in giving us an ethnological account of the life of the Jamaican Negroes, it sets us upon a path of reexamination of this hypothesis that should lead to a new concept of the number of Africanisms which the New World Negroes have preserved. (1930a:332)

The change in Herskovits's thinking from his former position of thorough eradication of all African cultural traits, through assimilation to the culture of the Europeans, to the view that he was to hold for the rest of his life—the persistence of large numbers of overt and covert ("hidden") African survivals, including language, scattered rainbowlike and intensifying in a southerly direction—is directly linked with his two summers of fieldwork among Sranan and Saramaccan speakers in Suriname in 1928 and 1929. Years later, Frances Herskovits related that

> his field experience in Suriname in 1928 and 1929 had a profound influence on his thinking, and though he was scarcely conscious of this at the time, the findings in both the Bush and the city of Paramaribo began shaping his concepts on acculturation.
>
> My husband began outlining the opening paper of this volume ["The Negro in the New World," 1930b] on board a cargo boat that was taking us from Trinidad to the United States in the late summer of 1929, after our second field trip to Suriname. It was a leisurely voyage, and he welcomed the opportunity to visit several islands in the Caribbean where the Dutch freighter that had taken us down to Paramaribo did not stop. Here in Barbados, Antigua, St. Lucia, St. Kitts, and Dominica, he played the African game *wari* (which he had learned in Suriname) with the men on the docks, and talked to them about his stay among the Bush Negroes and his enjoyment of the drumming at the *winti* dances in the city of Paramaribo. He was already well on his way into his ethnohistorical researches. (1966:viii)

The "profound influence on his thinking" described by Frances Herskovits soon appeared in his writing. In a review of Samuel Stoney and Gertrude Shelby's *Black Genesis*, written only a few months after his return from the second field trip to Suriname, he criticizes the authors because they emphasize "early English" elements in the English-related Caribbean creoles while ignoring widespread and glaring African survivals:

> The lack of grammar attributed to Negro English simply means that there is a lack of English grammar—something far different, for grammar is structure, and Negro English, whether spoken in Dutch Guiana, the West Indies, or America, has as rigid rules as any language. . . . The amount of early English in West Indian and Guiana speech is not as large as the authors seem to think, and Cruickshank's work, which is one of the few identifiable ones mentioned, stresses, as a matter of fact, the Africanisms in the speech rather than the old-English elements. And it is surprising, in view of the fact that, according to Mr. Du Bose Heyward's preface, one of the authors is acquainted with the Guianas, that recognition of the identities of Gulla with the "taki-taki" of Dutch Guiana identities, grammatical structure and phonetic usage, which I found in the text in great numbers, is not indicated. (M. Herskovits 1930c:314)

Melville and Frances Herskovits traveled together in the summer of 1928 (their first field trip to Suriname) with a physician, Dr. Morton C. Kahn, who had been to the colony three times in the early 1920s for studies of tropical medicine and public health, and whose prior experience and contacts were invaluable to them. (Herskovits related, for example, how they owed their good health on this and many other tropical field trips in the Caribbean and in West Africa "in very great measure to his Spartan training in tropical hygiene" [Herskovits and Herskovits 1936:viii].)

It is interesting to compare Herskovits's distinction between "lack of grammar" and "lack of English grammar," quoted above, with Kahn's remarks (which were more typical of the time) on "talkee-talkee" syntax, contained in his 1931 book about the Bush Negroes (Ndjukas) of Suriname:

> The individual words are strung together with very loose grammatical construction, varying with the idiosyncracies of the speaker. The nouns and verbs have no regular order; instead they are twisted around for convenience and emphasis. The implied meaning is usually not difficult to grasp. (Kahn 1931:163–64)

What induced Herskovits to abandon his studies of blacks in Harlem and college students in Washington, D.C., and set out for the northern coast of

South America, of all places the one least likely to support his assimilationist hypothesis? It was perhaps his own nagging doubts about his former views, of which we gain some hint from his book reviews of those years, coupled with the encouragement and support of colleagues and mentors—above all, Elsie Clews Parsons and Franz Boas. In the words of Melville and Frances Herskovits:

> Our first field trip was made under the auspices of the Columbia University Council for Research in the Social Sciences; our second under those of Northwestern University; and both were made possible by the generous support of Dr. Elsie Clews Parsons. It is a privilege to express here our deep appreciation to Dr. Parsons, not alone for this support, but for the initial indication of Suriname as a fruitful area for research into African survivals in the New World, and for the many suggestions concerning the handling of the data which she has given us. To Professor Franz Boas we are indebted for much that we can name—the endorsement of the Suriname project, its direct sponsorship, and counsel on method—and for much more that does not lend itself to enumeration, above all, the inspiration of his work. (1936:vii)

## Elsie Clews Parsons and Herskovits

Accordingly, our discipline owes much to the intervention of Elsie Clews Parsons (1875–1941). Parsons not only directed the Herskovitses' attention to Suriname, but she underwrote many of the expenses incurred by their research there. (The bulk of her papers have been preserved but remain unanalyzed. Her correspondence over many years with Melville Herskovits is cataloged among his papers.) A prolific researcher in her own right, the author of twenty-seven volumes of folklore and ethnographic studies, from a wealthy family and of independent means, she not only put the idea in their heads that Suriname was the place to go, *she financed their trip*. She had traveled repeatedly to the Caribbean in the years after World War I to study the folklore of the islands, and she was surely not unaware of the effect that a visit to the Dutch colony would have on this unusual pair of researchers. For our science, the result was like putting a match to gunpowder.

Her collections of folklore from the Sea Islands, the Bahamas, the Antilles, the Cape Verde Islands, and other areas adjoining the Middle and South Atlantic basins contain many footnotes comparing similarities among the various folk traditions, but her introductions and analyses are tantalizingly short. Nevertheless, there are indications that she intended, eventually, to write considerably more about Creole English and Creole French in the Caribbean. In the foreword (an unnumbered page) to the posthumous publication of her *Folk-lore of the Antilles, French and English* (vol. 3, 1943), the editor, Gladys A. Reichardt, observes:

> The third volume . . . stops where . . . its author regrettably and suddenly stopped her work on Dec. 19, 1941 [Parsons suffered a fatal heart attack in New York, shortly after returning from yet another trip to South America]. She had planned . . . to include the following: Verse, Folk Beliefs, Linguistic Notes and Glossary of Dialectic Terms in French and English, and Provenience and Distribution. These we must do without since they are matters too complicated for a foreign hand.

One wonders what, if any, of this material might still be preserved among her papers. For the present, we must do with short observations such as the following:

> During my final editing of the tales I happened to be engaged in collecting Portuguese-Negro tales from Cape Verde Islanders in Massachusetts and Rhode Island. Resemblances between the Bahama and the Cape Verde Islands tales, not only in patterns but in minor details, I found startling. Whatever may have been the provenience of the tales in Africa, Portuguese or other, I have no doubt that by far the greater number of the Bahama tales were learned there—learned, not in America, but in Africa. (*Folk-tales of Andros Island, Bahamas*, 1918:xii)

> A number of the dialectical forms of the Bahamas and the Sea Islands appear in the English spoken in Sierra Leone [based on the report of Cronise and Ward 1903]: um (them), too (very), fo' (to). (And eighteen further items; *Folk-lore of the Sea Islands, South Carolina*, 1923:xvii, fn. 5)

> There are several dialectical expressions common to the Bahama-Islanders and the Sea-Islanders. There is, too, the same confusion of gender and of number, based, I surmise, upon indifference in Africa to these linguistic distinctions. The persistence of the indifference in Negro dialects, in English, French, and Portuguese, is an interesting fact in the psychology of language. (1923:xx)

> As for the peculiar intonation of certain Sea-Islanders—an intonation which somewhat recalls that of a Frenchman speaking English—I have made no attempt to indicate it. Nor have I learned as yet what must be the historical reason of it. (1923:xxi)

It was clear to her that more African traits have survived in the Caribbean than in the United States (including the Sea Islands). For example, in assessing survivals of African music, sung during the telling of certain tales, she notes: "In the Bahamas and West Indies, song is still a part of narrative. In the Southern States it is passing or has passed out" (1923:xix). The idea of a greater or lesser number of African survivals linked with the passing of time since the settlement of the New World and the individual demographic histories of the colonies stretching from Suriname to British North America was probably not original with her. (Schuchardt, for example, hints at it in a number of places in both his published and unpublished work.) Yet it surely was a key consideration in steering Herskovits to Suriname, not only to Paramaribo and the adjacent coastal strip but to the Saramaccans in the interior as well.

## Schuchardt and Herskovits

Schuchardt's "Creole Study 10: On the Negro English of West Africa," dating from approximately 1893, emphasizes the African substratum in the English-related New World creoles and views Gullah as a link language intermediate between the Caribbean creoles and the Black English of the interior South. According to Gilbert (1985:33):

> He proposes to distinguish the Black dialect of the Sea Islands of South Carolina and Georgia, "which is still a genuine creole (North Am. NE), from those varieties which have moved nearer to English, more or less (North Am. NE)," although he is "well aware of the fact that we can hardly think of drawing a neat boundary between them." In these passages, Schuchardt [is saying] that the Sea Islands dialect (or Gullah) is still a creole and that there is a continuum of decreolization affecting all of Black English to varying degrees.

This astonishing piece of work, which anticipated Parsons by twenty years and Herskovits by thirty-five, unfortunately did not appear in print until almost a century later in English translation (Gilbert 1985) and in the original German (Viereck 1987). In Schuchardt's 1914 monograph on Saramaccan, a summing up of his views and final statement of his lifelong preoccupation with the "mixed languages" that arose from the European colonial expansion,

> similar ideas are expressed, although the wording is not so clear cut. He does not explicitly call Gullah "still a genuine creole," as he does in "Creole Study X." In my introduction to the 1980 translation of [this

> monograph], I tried to sum up his sometimes rather rambling exposition by stating: ". . . Schuchardt anticipates in essence the hypotheses of Melville Herskovits, Lorenzo Dow Turner, William Stewart, and others, with regard to the creole origin of Black English in the United States, the historical role of Gullah and the Afro-Caribbean creoles, the decreolization process, and the post-creole continuum." Being familiar with his writing and general theoretical position, it was quite clear that the creole-origin theory of Black English in the United States was so self-evident for him that he did not even bother to state it explicitly. (Gilbert 1985:33)

Herskovits, who could read German and Dutch, among other languages, was familiar with Schuchardt's 1914 work (alone of Schuchardt's published work on creoles) but cited it only in connection with the knotty problem of where the Portuguese component of Saramaccan came from (Herskovits 1931). Predictably, Herskovits thought it was brought by the ancestors of the Saramaccans directly from West Africa, where it represented a remnant of the Portuguese substratum underlying the pidgins and creoles spoken there. Schuchardt, faute de mieux, subscribed to the "traditional" view that Portuguese was introduced by Sephardic Jewish planters who had come from Brazil with their slaves. It is conceivable that other parts of Schuchardt's monograph had an indirect effect on Herskovits's thinking regarding *English* in the Caribbean and the southeastern United States, but no direct influence can be demonstrated, so far as I can determine. Thus, Herskovits in effect "rediscovered" the creolist hypothesis (paradigm) of the origin and development of Gullah, and Black English in the Southeast generally, in the United States.

## Scales of Intensity of Survival of African Traits

It is important to realize that Herskovits treated language as an integral part of cultural behavior generally, and that the notion of "acculturation" applies to every aspect of culture across the board. Another key principle is that faint, hard-to-detect traces of the products of acculturation can be better detected by comparing the same elements in historically related societies where the "substratum" is much more salient. As early as 1930, in "The Negro in the New World: The Statement of a Problem," Herskovits set up a "scale" of African survivals "north of Brazil," oriented from a greater to a lesser number of survivals along a generally south-north axis: (1) Maroons in Suriname; (2) coastal dwellers in Suriname; (3) Haiti; (4) Santo Domingo; (5) islands of the British, Dutch, and Danish West Indies; (6) Sea Islands of the United

States and savannahs of southern Georgia; (7) blacks in the Southern United States; and (8) completely acculturated blacks in the (Northern) United States (1930b:149–50).

The scale presented in table 1 illustrates how this principle, which can be called the rainbow effect, persisted in his thinking, although now given in considerably more detail. The scale provides for twenty-one geographic locations (with Brazil included) and lists ten cultural categories (including language), rated for five degrees of retention. In the language column, note the "quite African" (b) rating for the Sea Islands (identified by Herskovits as Gullah Islands), as opposed to "trace of African customs, or absent" (e) for the U.S. rural South and urban North, a gap all the more striking because "only the greatest degree of intensity is indicated for each group." The Sea Islands turns out to be rated two steps above the Virgin Islands and Trinidad (Toco), and one step above Guyana, Suriname (Paramaribo), Haiti (peasant and urban), and Jamaica (Maroons and general). In its low level of retention, the non-Gullah part of the United States shares company with the black Caribs of Honduras and urban Trinidad (Port of Spain).

Although the Sea Islands and the U.S. rural South and urban North also differ in three of the remaining nine cultural categories (technology, economic organization, and folklore), the gap for language between the Sea Islands and the rest of the United States seems unjustifiably large. Herskovits exaggerated retention on the Sea Islands and minimized it elsewhere. This looks like good evidence for what William Stewart (1974:3–6) calls "the Herskovits-Frazier compromise," with regard to African language substrate influence, whereby Herskovits freely admitted intensive survivals on the Sea Islands, but denied their existence on the mainland (outside the narrow coastal strip facing the islands), thus apparently acceding to Frazier's "assimilationist" view, at least for those cultural traits having to do with language. (Incidentally, Stewart's 1974 article, "Acculturative Processes and the Language of the American Negro," is an absolutely outstanding piece of work, with good arguments and numerous sources to support his position.)

Beyond his possible desire to compromise with Frazier, Herskovits may have been influenced by Lorenzo Dow Turner, with whom he carried on a frequent correspondence from the late 1930s until his death. (Turner, who portrays African retentions in Gullah as being very extensive, published very little prior to his 1949 book, *Africanisms in the Gullah Dialect*. His influence was thus relatively slight until the late 1940s.)

For other types of cultural survivals, Herskovits admitted of no such disparity between the Sea Islands and the mainland: the gap applies mainly to

**Table 1. Scale of Intensity of New World Africanisms**
(Only the greatest degree of retention is indicated for each group.)

| | *Technology* | *Economic* | *Social Organization* | *Nonkinship Institutions* | *Religion* | *Magic* | *Art* | *Folklore* | *Music* | *Language* |
|---|---|---|---|---|---|---|---|---|---|---|
| Guiana (bush) | b | b | a | a | a | a | b | a | a | b |
| Guiana (Paramaribo) | c | c | b | c | a | a | e | a | a | c |
| Haiti (peasant) | c | b | b | c | a | a | d | a | a | c |
| Haiti (urban) | e | d | c | c | b | b | e | a | a | c |
| Brazil (Bahia-Recife) | d | d | b | d | a | a | b | a | a | a |
| Brazil (Porto Alegre) | e | e | c | d | a | a | e | a | a | c |
| Brazil (Maranhão, rural) | c | c | b | e | c | b | e | b | b | d |
| Brazil (Maranhão, urban) | e | d | c | e | a | b | e | d | a | b |
| Cuba | e | d | c | b | a | a | b | b | a | a |
| Jamaica (Maroons) | c | c | b | b | b | a | e | a | a | c |
| Jamaica (Morant Bay) | e | c | b | b | a | a | e | a | a | a |
| Jamaica (general) | e | c | d | d | b | b | e | a | b | c |
| Honduras (black Caribs)[1] | c | c | b | b | b | a | e | b | c | e |
| Trinidad (Port of Spain) | e | d | c | b | a | a | e | b | a | e |
| Trinidad (Toco) | e | d | c | c | c | b | e | b | b | d |
| Mexico (Guerrero) | d | e | b | b | c | b | e | b | ? | e |
| Columbia (Choco) | d | d | c | c | c | b | e | b | a | e |
| Virgin Islands | e | d | c | d | e | b | e | b | b | d |
| U.S. (Gullah Islands) | c | c | c | d | c | b | e | a | b | b |
| U.S. (rural South) | d | e | c | d | c | b | e | b | b | e |
| U.S. (urban North) | e | e | c | d | c | b | e | d | b | e |

a: very African; b: quite African; c: somewhat African; d: a little African; e: trace of African; ?: no report.

The derivations of the listings are as follows:

Guiana, Brazil (Bahia and southern Brazil), Trinidad, and Haiti: field research, and various published works bearing on the Negro peoples of these countries.

**Table 1. Continued**

Brazil (north-urban and rural): unpublished reports of fieldwork by Octavio Eduard in Maranhão.

Jamaica: firsthand contact with the Maroons and other Jamaican Negroes, though without opportunity for detailed field research; and for the general population, the volume *Black Roadways in Jamaica*, by Martha Beckwith.

Cuba: various works by F. Ortiz, particularly his *Los Negroes Brujos*, and R. Lachetãneré's *Manuel de Santeria*.

Virgin Islands: the monograph by A. A. Campbell entitled "St. Thomas Negroes—A Study of Personality and Culture" (*Psychological Monographs* 55.5 [1943]), and unpublished field materials of J. C. Trevor.

Gullah Islands: fieldwork by W. R. Bascom, some results of which have been reported in a paper entitled "Acculturation among the Gullah Negroes" (*American Anthropologist* 43 [1941]:43–50).

United States: many works, from which materials of African derivation have been abstracted and summarized in my own work, *The Myth of the Negro Past*.

[1]Carib Indian influences are strong in this culture.

*Source:* Simpson 1973:152–53, from Herskovits 1945.

language. In this he was shown to be mistaken by Stewart in a series of articles from the 1960s, and by Stewart's associate and protégé, J. L. Dillard, in his widely read book *Black English* (1972). At best, Herskovits's position was not always clear (cf. Stewart 1974:5–6, 38, fn. 8).

In the late 1920s and the 1930s a spirit of change was "in the air," which eventually led to a radical reassessment of the black contribution to the hybrid Afro-European cultures of the New World. Although Herskovits was at the center of this movement, other scholars played an important role as well: for example, the language sociologist John E. Reinecke, the Louisiana phoneticians Claude M. Wise and T. Earl Pardoe, and the eminent black American linguist, dialectologist, and Africanist Lorenzo Dow Turner. A more detailed study would have to take their contributions and mutual interactions into account.

This new way of viewing the hybridization of cultures could be interpreted as a full-fledged paradigm shift in the social sciences, in the Kuhnian sense, and it undoubtedly could be profitably treated from that point of view. The reason that Herskovits's name figures so prominently in this regard, and that he succeeded where Schuchardt and Parsons had failed, is that Herskovits embraced the hypothesis early in his career, promoted it at every opportunity, stayed with it consistently for the rest of his life, was an excellent social science popularizer in a variety of general magazines and newspapers, occupied a prestigious academic position at a major university in the urban Northern United States, was generally recognized as *the* authority on Africanisms in the New World, bolstered his arguments about language with a whole range of other cultural values, and, most important, he was right.

## References


Allen, William Francis. 1867. *Slave songs of the United States*. New York: Peter Smith.

Ash, Sharon, and John Myhill. 1986. Linguistic correlates of interethnic contact. In Sankoff, ed., 33–44.

Bailey, Guy. 1987. Are black and white vernaculars diverging? Papers from a NWAVE panel discussion. *American Speech* 62.32–40.

Bailey, Guy, and Natalie Maynor. 1987. Decreolization? *Language in Society* 16.449–73.

Cronise, Florence M., and Henry W. Ward. 1903. *Cunnie Rabbit, Mr. Spider and the other beef*. London: Swan Sonnenschein.

Dillard, J. L. 1968. Non-standard Negro dialects—convergence or divergence? *Florida Foreign Language Reporter* 6.2.9–12.

———. 1972. *Black English: Its history and usage in the United States*. New York: Random House.

Escure, Geneviève. 1988. Topic structures as language universals. *Journal of Pidgin and Creole Languages* 3.159–76.

———. 1988b. Creole acrolects as innovations. Unpublished manuscript.

Escure, Geneviève, and Glenn G. Gilbert. 1988. Acrolectal speech in Roatan. Paper presented at the seventh biennial meeting of the Society for Caribbean Linguistics, Nassau, College of the Bahamas, 24–27 August.

Fasold, Ralph W. 1972. Decreolization and autonomous language change. *Florida Foreign Language Reporter* 10.1–2.9–12, 51.

Frazier, E. Franklin. 1957. *The Negro in the United States*. Rev. ed. 1949. N.p.: Macmillan.

———. 1965. *Black bourgeoisie*. First paperback ed. 1957. New York: Free Press.

———. 1974. *The Negro church in America*. 1963. New York: Schocken Books.

Gilbert, Glenn G., ed. and trans. 1980. *Pidgin and creole languages: Selected essays of Hugo Schuchardt*. Cambridge: Cambridge University Press. [Contains an English translation of the introductory section of Schuchardt 1914.]

———. 1985. Hugo Schuchardt and the Atlantic creoles: A newly discovered manuscript "On the Negro English of West Africa." *American Speech* 60.31–63.

———, ed. 1987. *Pidgin and creole languages: Essays in memory of John E. Reinecke*. Honolulu: University of Hawaii Press.

———. 1989. Review of *Diversity and diachrony*, by D. Sankoff. *Language* 64.810–13.

Hancock, Ian. 1986. The domestic hypothesis, diffusion and componentiality: An account of Atlantic anglophone creole origins. In Muysken and Smith, eds., 71–102.

———. 1987. A preliminary classification of the Anglophone Atlantic creoles, with syntactic data from thirty-three representative dialects. In Gilbert, ed., 1987, 264–333.

Harrison, James A. 1884. Negro English. *Anglia* 7.232–79.

Herskovits, Frances S., ed. 1966. *The New World Negro: Selected papers in Afroamerican studies by Melville J. Herskovits*. Bloomington: Indiana University Press.

Herskovits, Melville J. 1927a. Acculturation and the American Negro. *Southwestern Political and Social Science Quarterly* 8.211–24.

———. 1927b. Review of *Folk beliefs of the Southern Negro*, by Newbell Nile Puckett. *Journal of American Folk-lore* 40.310–12.

———. 1928. *The American Negro: A study in racial crossing*. New York: Alfred A. Knopf.

———. 1929. Lo, the poor Haitian. Review of *The magic island*, by William Buehler Seabrook. *Nation*, February 13, 198–200.

———. 1930a. Review of *Black roadways: A study of Jamaican folklife*, by Martha Warren Beckwith. *Journal of American Folk-lore* 43.332–39.

———. 1930b. The Negro in the New World: The statement of a problem. *American Anthropologist* 32.145–55.

———. 1930c. Review of *Black genesis*, by Samuel G. Stoney and Gertrude M. Shelby. *Annals of the American Academy of Political and Social Science* (Philadelphia), July 1930, 313–14.

———. 1931. On the provenience of the Portuguese in Saramacca Tongo. *West-Indische Gids* 12.545–57.

———. 1945. Problem, method and theory in Afroamerican studies. *Afroamerica* 1.5–24.

Herskovits, Melville, and Frances S. Herskovits. 1934. *Rebel destiny: Among the Bush Negroes of Dutch Guiana*. New York: Whittlesey House.

———. 1936. *Suriname folk-lore*. New York: Columbia University Press.

Kahn, Morton C. 1931. *Djuka: The Bush Negroes of Dutch Guiana*. New York: Viking Press.

Krapp, George Philip. 1924. The English of the American Negro. *American Mercury* 2.190–95.

———. 1925. *The English language in America*. 2 vols. New York: Century.

Labov, William. 1982. Objectivity and commitment in linguistic science: The case of the Black English trial in Ann Arbor. *Language in Society* 11.165–201.

Labov, William, and Wendell A. Harris. 1986. De facto segregation of black and white vernaculars. In Sankoff, ed., 1–24.

Le Page, Robert B. 1987. The need for a multidimensional model. In Gilbert, ed., 1987, 113–29.

Le Page, Robert B., and Andrée Tabouret-Keller. 1985. *Acts of identity*. Cambridge: Cambridge University Press.

Mencken, H. L. 1919. *The American language*. New York: Albert A. Knopf.

Merriam, Alan P. 1964. Melville Jean Herskovits 1895–1963. *American Anthropologist* 66.83–91.

Moneypenny, Anne, and Barrie Thorne. 1964. Bibliography of Melville J. Herskovits. *American Anthropologist* 66.91–109.

Montgomery, Michael B., and Guy Bailey, eds. 1986. *Language variety in the South*. University: University of Alabama Press.

Mufwene, Salikoko. 1987. Review of *Language variety in the South*, by M. B. Montgomery and G. Bailey. *Journal of Pidgin and Creole Languages* 2.93–110.

Muysken, Pieter, and Norval Smith, eds. 1986. *Substrata versus universals in creole genesis*. Amsterdam: John Benjamins.

Myhill, John, and Wendell A. Harris. 1986. The use of the verbal *-s* inflection in BEV. In Sankoff, ed., 25–31.

Pardoe, T. Earl. 1937. *An historical and phonetic study of the Negro dialect*. Ph.D. dissertation, Louisiana State University, Baton Rouge. [See the comments on this work in Reinecke et al. 1975:513–14.]

Parsons, Elsie Clews. 1918. *Folk-tales of Andros Island, Bahamas*. New York: George Stechert.

———. 1923. *Folk-lore of the Sea Islands, South Carolina*. Cambridge, Mass., and New York: American Folk-lore Society.

———. 1943. *Folk-lore of the Antilles, French and English*. Volume 3. New York: American Folk-lore Society.

Reinecke, John E. 1937. *Marginal languages: A sociological survey of the creole languages and trade jargons*. Ph.D. dissertation, Yale University, New Haven.

Reinecke, John E., Stanley M. Tsuzaki, David De Camp, Ian F. Hancock, and Richard Wood. 1975. *A bibliography of pidgin and creole languages*. Honolulu: University of Hawaii Press.

Sankoff, David, ed. 1986. *Diversity and diachrony*. Amsterdam: John Benjamins.

Schuchardt, Hugo. ca. 1893. Kreolische Studien X: Über das Negerenglische in Westafrika. Manuscript. [English translation in Gilbert 1985; German text printed in Viereck 1987.]

———. 1914. *Die Sprache der Saramakkaneger in Surinam*. Amsterdam: Johannes Muller. [The long, interesting introduction by Schuchardt to Schumann's Saramaccan dictionary, which Schuchardt presents here for the first time in print, is available in English translation in Gilbert 1980.]

Simpson, George Eaton. 1973. *Melville J. Herskovits*. New York: Columbia University Press.

Stewart, William A. 1966–67. Nonstandard speech patterns. *Baltimore Bulletin of Education* 43.2–4.52–65.

———. 1969. Urban Negro speech: Sociolinguistic factors affecting English teaching. *Florida Foreign Language Reporter* 7.1.50–53, 166.

———. 1974. Acculturative processes and the language of the American Negro. *Language in its social setting*, ed. by William W. Gage, 1–46. Washington, D.C.: Anthropological Society of Washington.

Turner, Lorenzo Dow. 1949. *Africanisms in the Gullah dialect*. Chicago: University of Chicago Press.

Van Name, Addison. 1869–70. Contributions to creole grammar. *Transactions of the American Philological Association* 1.123–67.

Viereck, Wolfgang, ed. 1987. Hugo Schuchardt. Kreolische Studien X: Über das Negerenglische in Westafrika. *Anglia* 105.1–27. [The first printed version of the original German text.]

Wise, Claude M. 1933. Negro dialect. *Quarterly Journal of Speech* 19.523–28.

# Postscript

*Salikoko S. Mufwene*

One need not be a substratist to realize the significance of the present collection of papers toward understanding some of the mechanisms of creole genesis, especially how African languages have contributed differentially to the structures of Afro-American language varieties (AALV). Among many things, this book highlights the complexity of the subject matter of Africanisms interpreted as contributions of African languages to systems of AALVs. While it answers a few questions, it also spells out many theoretical and empirical issues that scholars will have to address in order for further progress to be made on the topic.

It would be illusive for me to pretend to realize what all the questions are and then synthesize them in a few pages without any distortion or personal bias. I would, in fact, avoid writing this concluding chapter if it were not for a request of the participants in the 1988 Round Table that I write a postscript with questions for future research that follow from the debates at the meeting and these proceedings. Having myself participated in much of the literature on creole genesis (mostly trying to reconcile substratists, superstratists, and universalists), I hope my bias will be moderate enough to make this exercise worthwhile. I cannot deny the fact that the few questions formulated below reflect my own interest in the ongoing debate.

A convenient question to start with is, What kind of contact situation leads to creolization? As is obvious from both this anthology and the literature on substrate influence in AALVs, the least disputable evidence of African influence is attested in Berbice Dutch (BD). The source for several BD features that are both unusual among AALVs and atypical of Dutch is Ịjọ, a language in sharp typological contrast with its Kwa neighbors. For instance, BD has the same form and position for the markers of nominal plural, tense-aspect, negation, and postpositions as Ịjọ. Also, unlike in most other AALVs, Ịjọ has contributed up to 30% of the vocabulary of BD (Smith et al. 1987). Such high lexical influence makes claims of strong Ịjọ influence hard to dispute, despite the role of a filtering system that may be associated with, though not fully located in, Universal Grammar (Mufwene 1990a).

To be sure, BD developed in sociohistorical conditions which so far appear to be untypical of those traditionally associated with pidginization and creolization. In particular, it seems to have started essentially out of the contacts of the Ịjọ with Dutch slavers at the mouth of the Kalabari River in West Africa, thus involving only two languages rather than a multitude. This atypical situation (at least based on what is commonly assumed of pidginization and creolization) prompts some questions: Is it justified to assume that BD is a creole?[1] If it is, then should we stick to the assumption that creolization is conditioned in part by extensive societal multilingualism? Again, if BD is a creole, is its situation really atypical or have we simply missed certain things about the genesis of other AALVs and creoles? For instance, could it simply be that, as suggested by Robert Chaudenson (especially 1979, 1986, 1988), the materials selected by a creole derive primarily from the varieties spoken in the original contacts between the superstrate and the substrate groups? That is, is any subsequent restructuring that leads to pidginization or creolization[2] constrained in part by the shape of what actually serves as the target (which need not be identical with the native variety of the lexifier) and by the proportion of the population that prompts the restructuring?

Disregarding the case of lexical contributions, are the formal typological conditions that affected the development of BD so different from those that affected the development of other AALVs? Witness, for instance, the circumstances that led to Bantu influence, which is likewise indisputable, in the structures of São Tomense (Ferraz 1979) and Palenquero (Maurer 1987), regarding, for example, the sentence-final position of the negation marker in both AALVs. In both cases Bantus formed the most important ethnolinguistic group from the beginning of the colony. In these cases, as in that of BD, is it not the same kind of condition as (the majority of) the substrate group forming a typologically homogeneous group (Thomason 1983; Mufwene 1986; Thomason and Kaufman 1988)?

I do not wish to suggest that typological kinship of the substrate languages or kinship between them and the lexifier answers all the questions about selection of features by the relevant creole. As must be obvious by now, the lexifier or the dominant substrate group may itself have presented several options from which choices had to be made thanks to a variety of factors (see, e.g., Mufwene 1991a). However, it seems to me that if progress is to be made in genetic creolistics, the question of which particular sociohistorical and language contact conditions are conducive to creolization must be addressed explicitly. The papers published in this volume lay the groundwork for questioning the definitions of pidgin and creole proposed by Hall (1966), which were justified by knowledge that is partly outdated today.

In a somewhat different vein, Norbert Boretzky makes quite a provocative point in claiming that "all innovations in any of the varieties go back to interference; there seems to be no case of innovation in any of the varieties that has no model in any of the other varieties" (this volume). This contention (shared by Mufwene 1990b) is consistent with observations by Thomason (1983) and Hagège (1985) that most creole features attributed to the putative language bioprogram are actually shared by many of the languages in contact. On the other hand, it raises the following questions for future research: What is the role of Universal Grammar in creole genesis? What principles have constrained and/or regulated how creoles select their formal features from the alternatives that their selections competed with?

As alternatives to Bickerton's language bioprogram (1981, 1984, 1988, 1989) qua Universal Grammar, studies such as Seuren and Wekker (1986), which focuses on semantic transparency, and Mufwene (1989, 1991), which assumes a context-based model of markedness, address the above question, but they are far from answering all the relevant questions. For instance, where either the lexifier and/or any of the languages in contact avail alternative morphosyntactic strategies that are equally viable for the emerging creole, how are the factors that determine the selection of features to be ranked relative to each other? Can these factors be weighted regardless of the factor of time? Were all the factors that may appear to be relevant now equally significant at the time the features were being selected? Were all the features that are now attested in creoles selected at more or less the same time? If not, under what conditions can reversals in the selection of features possibly occur? Are the above considerations consistent with the fact that several morphosyntactic alternatives may have always coexisted in a creole for more or less the same function, for example, the usage of both *a* + Verb and *de* + Verb durative constructions in Jamaican Creole?

To date, there is no single genetic study of any AALV that is based on a holistic examination of its grammatical system compared with the substrate and/or superstrate systems. Without returning to the structuralist maxim of "La langue est un système où tout se tient," originally intended for the now less convincing assumption that all parts of a grammatical system are coterminous (Mufwene 1992), the curiosity concerning how some positions would stand such a test is hard to repress. Such an approach might shed a lot of light on the selection processes that determine the features of individual creoles. For one thing, it will certainly shift part of the attention now monopolized by morphosyntactic characteristics (dealing with form only) to semantics. This will be informative because it may reveal which particular meaning components are more central than others. Also, the suggested holistic approach leads to the ineluctable question of whether the genetic influences that determine the selection of the morphosyntax are necessarily coextensive with those that determine the selection of the semantics. Even studies such as those by Claire Lefebvre and her associates at the University of Montreal do not lead us to such considerations yet, although their research agenda has certainly taken the proposed holistic orientation.

There are also several questions of detail that deserve attention. One such has been raised by Frajzyngier (1984) regarding the complementizer *sɛ* in English AALVs. If it is really due to substrate influence, why is there no such complementizer in French AALVs like Haitian Creole (HC)? Under what particular conditions can substrate influence produce in a creole structural features for which there is no conceivable model (albeit reinterpreted in some cases) in the lexifier? What are the peculiarities of those conditions that in the case of Oceanic English pidgins produced structural features such as the transitive marker for which there is no obvious model in the lexifier?

If *sɛ* in English AALVs is truly due to substrate influence, the above question may be reformulated as follows: If the sociohistorical conditions of the genesis of HC are as hypothesized by John Victor Singler and by Claire Lefebvre (this volume), suggesting, in fact, influence similar to that of Oceanic languages on Pacific English pidgins, why was the French verb *dire* 'say' not reinterpreted as a complementizer? Answering this question and the like in future research may shed significant light on some issues regarding the genesis of pidgins and creoles.

Elliptical possessive constructions such as those listed below in Gullah also raise interesting questions.

1. *dæ də ǰi:n buk; dɪsya də mi o:n*

   'That is Jean's book; this is my own.'

Since Jamaican Creole has constructions such as in example 2, it may be assumed to differ from Gullah not so much in the ellipsis strategy as in the morphosyntactic strategy for marking possession.

2. *da a fi ǰin buk; disya a fi mi*

However, on account of the way HC marks possession (in postposing the possessor noun phrase (NP), it may not be justified to assume that it behaves like Gullah regarding elliptical possessive constructions.

3. *sa a sɛ liv žã, sa a sɛ pa mwɛ̃*
this DEICTIC be book John part me
'That is John's book; this is mine.'[3]

The HC strategy is reminiscent of nonstandard French, as in example 4, from which it differs partly in not having an elliptical counterpart. Note the presence of *pa* 'part, share' in 3.

4. *Celui-là est le livre à Jean; celui-ci est à moi.*
that-one be the book to John this-one be to me
'That (one) is John's book; this (one) is mine.'

Both Gullah and Jamaican Creole prepose the possessor NP, just as they do their other determiners and on the same pattern as English. The question suggested by, for example, Guy Hazaël-Massieux's paper is: What, aside from the relative homogeneity of the substrate languages (as might be assumed of some features of Pacific English pidgins or creoles), constrains the influence of the lexifier on the structural features of a creole?

While it is obvious that both the lexifier and (some of) the substrate languages constrain the features selected by creoles, the question arises of how to reinterpret the role of Universal Grammar in these contact-based restructuring processes. For instance, in comparing features of HC with those of Mauritian Creole (e.g., their possessive constructions, in which the pronoun is preposed in Mauritian but postposed in HC), what accounts for the different selections made by the two creoles? Also, the following question arises: Are the constraints that regulate the selection of features from the lexifier the same as those that regulate the selection of features from the substrate languages? To what extent do these principles cohere with the sociohistorical, ethnolinguistic constraints suggested in Singler's and Philip Baker's papers and in several others before them?

Hancock (1980, 1986, this volume) suggests that Guinea Coast Creole English may have played an important role in the formation of AALVs. Could other non-European-based African contact varieties have played a similar role? This general question has not been addressed in the literature. Was bilingualism in precolonial Africa so significant that it precluded almost everywhere the development of pidginlike contact varieties, as suggested by Hulstaert (1989) regarding the development of Lingala?[4] Generally, how do the pidginization and creolization of European languages differ from those of African languages such as have resulted in Sango, Kituba, and Lingala? Since the same terms are used for these historical processes, what are their common characteristics?

In a different vein, serial verb constructions (SVC) have been adduced as star evidence by both substratists (e.g., Alleyne 1980) and universalists (e.g.,

Bickerton 1981, 1984; Byrne 1987) to defend their respective positions on the genesis of creoles. In light of recent studies (see, e.g., Joseph and Zwicky 1991), it appears that the traditional association of this syntactic phenomenon with isolating languages was mistaken. Claims of the nonexistence of SVCs in the European lexifiers of AALVs is invalidated, even if only partially, by Pullum (1990), who shows that SVCs or similar constructions occur in English. These are generally headed by the verbs *go* and *come,* subject to some formal constraints. The ensuing question is whether SVCs support any particular genetic hypothesis in a manner that is different from the selection of other features in pidginization and creolization and apparently also in other cases of contact-induced linguistic restructuring.

Questions of all kinds may be raised; certainly there are many more now than when Turner (1949) and Alleyne (1980) were published. I hope that future research will definitely go beyond these milestones and this book and that it will address not only the questions formulated above but also numerous relevant ones that I have overlooked.

## Notes

1. This question, also discussed in Mufwene 1990a, was raised in one of the debates by John Holm. See also Holm 1988, 1989.

2. As in Mufwene 1990b, I am assuming that where creoles have developed from antecedent pidgins they differ from the latter basically in that they are used as vernaculars while pidgins are not. Other structural differences between them are assumed to follow from this difference. Creolists who distinguish between creoles formed by children and those formed by adults suggest ipso facto that nativization, with which creolization has long been associated, is not a necessary factor or agent.

3. I am grateful to Michel Degraff for this example.

4. Like Samarin (1982, 1990), Hulstaert attributes the formation of Lingala to colonial rule and characterizes its genesis as due to the participation of non-Bantu interpreters in the colonial conquest.

## References

Alleyne, Mervyn C. 1980. *Comparative Afro-American: An historical-comparative study of English-based Afro-American dialects of the New World.* Ann Arbor: Karoma.

Bickerton, Derek. 1981. *Roots of language.* Ann Arbor: Karoma.

———. 1984. The language bioprogram hypothesis. *Behavioral and Brain Sciences* 7.173–221.

———. 1988. Creole languages and the bioprogram. *Linguistics: The Cambridge survey*. Volume 2. *Linguistic theory: Extensions and implications*, ed. by Frederick J. Newmeyer, 268–84. Cambridge: Cambridge University Press.

———. 1989. The lexical learning hypothesis and the pidgin-creole cycle. *Wheels within wheels: Papers of the Duisburg symposium on pidgin and creole languages*, ed. by Martin Pütz and René Dirven, 11–31. Frankfurt am Main: Verlag Peter Lang.

Byrne, Francis X. 1987. *Grammatical relations in a radical creole: Verb complementation in Saramaccan*. Amsterdam: John Benjamins.

Chaudenson, Robert. 1979. *Les créoles français*. Paris: Fernand Nathan.

———. 1986. And they had to speak any way . . . : Acquisition and creolization of French. *The Fergusonian impact*, ed. by Joshua A. Fishman et al., 1.69–82. Berlin: Mouton de Gruyter.

———. 1988. *Créoles et enseignment du français*. Paris: L'Harmattan.

Ferraz, L. Ivens. 1979. *The creole of São Tomé*. Johannesburg: Witwatersrand University Press.

Frajzyngier, Zygmunt. 1984. On the origin of *say* and *se* as complementizers in Black English and English-based creoles. *American Speech* 59.207–10.

Hagège, Claude. 1985. *L'homme de paroles*. Paris: Librairie Arthème Fayard.

Hall, Robert A., Jr. 1966. *Pidgin and creole languages*. Ithaca, N.Y.: Cornell University Press.

Hancock, Ian F. 1980. Gullah and Barbadian: Origins and relationships. *American Speech* 55.17–35.

———. 1986. The domestic hypothesis, diffusion and componentiality: An account of Atlantic anglophone creole origins. *Universals versus substrata in creole genesis*, ed. by Pieter Muysken and Norval Smith, 71–102. Amsterdam: John Benjamins.

Holm, John. 1988. *Pidgins and creoles*. Volume 1. *Theory and structure*. Cambridge: Cambridge University Press.

———. 1989. *Pidgins and creoles*. Volume 2. *Reference survey*. Cambridge: Cambridge University Press.

Hulstaert, Gustaaf. 1989. L'origine du Lingala. *Afrikanistische Arbeits-Papiere*. Institut für Afrikanistik, University of Cologne.

Joseph, D. Brian, and Arnold M. Zwicky, eds. 1990. *When verbs collide: Papers from the 1990 Ohio State mini-conference on serial verbs*. Department of Linguistics, Ohio State University.

Maurer, Philippe. 1987. La comparaison des morphèmes temporels du papiamento et du palenquero: Arguments contre la théorie monogénétique de la genèse des langues créoles. *Varia Creolica*, ed. by Philippe Maurer and Thomas Stolz, 27–70. Bochum, Germany: Brockmeyer.

Mufwene, Salikoko S. 1986. The universalist and substrate hypotheses complement one another. *Substrata versus universals in creole genesis*, ed. by Pieter Muysken and Norval Smith, 129–62. Amsterdam: John Benjamins.

———. 1989. Some explanations that strike me as incomplete [Column]. *Journal of Pidgin and Creole Languages* 4.117–28.

———. 1990a. Creoles and Universal Grammar. *Issues in creole linguistics*, ed. by Salikoko Mufwene and Pieter Seuren. *Linguistics* 28.783–807.

———. 1990b. Transfer and the substrate hypothesis in creolistics. *Studies in Second Language Acquisition* 12.1–23.

———. 1991. Pidgins, creoles, typology, and markedness. *Development and structures of creole languages: Essays in honor of Derek Bickerton*, ed. by Francis Byrne and Thom Huebner, 123–43. Amsterdam: John Benjamins.

———. 1992. Why grammars are monolithic. *The joy of grammar: A festschrift in honor of James D. McCawley*, ed. by Diane Brentari, Gary Larson, and Lynn MacLeod, 225–50. Amsterdam: John Benjamins.

Pullum, Geoffrey K. 1990. Constraints on intransitive quasi-serial verb constructions in modern colloquial English. *When verbs collide: Papers from the 1990 Ohio State mini-conference on serial verbs*. Working Papers in Linguistics 39, ed. by Brian D. Joseph and Arnold M. Zwicky, 218–39.

Samarin, William J. 1982. Colonization and pidginization on the Ubangi River. *Journal of African Languages and Linguistics* 4.1–42.

———. 1990. The origins of Kituba and Lingala. *Journal of African Languages and Linguistics* 12.47–77.

Seuren, Pieter, and Herman Wekker. 1986. Semantic transparency as a factor in creole genesis. *Substrata versus universals in creole genesis*, ed. by Pieter Muysken and Norval Smith, 57–70. Amsterdam: John Benjamins.

Smith, Norval, Ian E. Robertson, and Kay Williamson. 1987. The Ịjọ element in Berbice Dutch. *Language in Society* 16.1.49–90.

Thomason, Sarah G. 1983. Chinook Jargon in areal and historical context. *Language* 59.820–70.

Thomason, Sarah G., and Terrence Kaufman. 1988. *Language contact, creolization, and genetic linguistics*. Berkeley: University of California Press.

Turner, Lorenzo Dow. 1949. *Africanisms in the Gullah dialect*. Chicago: University of Chicago Press.

# Contributors

**Mervyn C. Alleyne** is a professor of linguistics at the University of the West Indies, Mona Campus, in Kingston, Jamaica. He is one of the foremost defenders of the African substrate hypothesis on the genesis of creoles of the New World. This is most elaborately defended in his seminal *Comparative Afro-American* (1980), which his *Roots of Jamaican Culture* (1988) places in the broader context of culture contact. He is a former review editor of the *Journal of Pidgin and Creole Languages* and is vice-president of the Association pour la Promotion des Etudes Créoles.

**Philip Baker** is a former journalist turned linguist after a long stay in Mauritius. He is a coauthor of *Isle de France Creole* (1982) and of the *Dictionary of Mauritian Creole* (1987). In 1990 and 1991 he was the columnist of the *Journal of Pidgin and Creole Languages* and is one of the authors of the complementary hypothesis on creole genesis, allowing for combined influence of the language bioprogram and substrate languages in the structures of creoles.

**Norbert Boretzky** is a professor of linguistics at the University of Bochum. His *Kreolsprachen, Substrate und Sprachwandel* (1983) is one of the most documented defenses ever written for African substrate contributions to Atlantic creoles.

**Francis Byrne** is an associate professor of linguistics at Shawnee State University at Portsmouth, Ohio, and president of the Society for Pidgin and Creole Linguistics. At the time of the Round Table on Africanisms, he was one of the strongest defenders of the language bioprogram hypothesis, attributing to the language bioprogram grammatical features of Saramaccan that distinguish it from English and Portuguese. This position is expressed in *Grammatical Relations in a Radical Creoles* (1987). He is a coeditor of *Development and Structures of Creole Languages* (1991) and *Atlantic Meets Pacific* (1993).

**Lawrence D. Carrington** is a professor of linguistics at the University of the West Indies, St. Augustine, Trinidad. He is the author of *St. Lucian Creole* (1984) and the editor of, in 1983, the often-cited *Studies in Caribbean Language* and, more recently, the *Dictionary of St. Lucian Creole* (compiled by Jones Mondesir, 1992). He is the columnist for the *Journal of Pidgin and Creole Languages* (1992 and 1993).

**Hazel Carter** is a professor of African linguistics at the University of Wisconsin, Madison. She is one of the rare researchers on Atlantic creoles who are also accomplished Africanists. Moreover, she works on one of the least studied aspects of creoles: their prosodic features. Among her numerous papers on the subject matter is "Suprasegmentals in Guyanese: Some African Comparisons" (in *Pidgin and Creole Languages,* edited by Glenn Gilbert, 1987).

**Charles DeBose** teaches in the Department of English, California State University, Hayward. He is the first to have used Samaná English, spoken by descendants of African Americans who migrated to the Dominican Republic in the nineteenth century, to determine whether or not African American vernacular English has decreolized. See "Samaná English: A Dialect That Time Forgot" (in *Proceedings of the Ninth Meeting of the Berkeley Linguistics Society*).

**Marta B. Dijkhoff** is a researcher at the Instituto Lingwistiko Antiano in Willemstad, Curaçao. Originally impressed by the language bioprogram hypothesis, she is now leaning toward the complementary alternative. Her work on structural features of Papiamentu questions some details of conventional analyses; for instance, "On the So-called 'Infinitive' in Atlantic Creoles" (coauthored with Salikoko Mufwene, *Lingua* 77:319–52, 1989) and "Complex Nominals and Composite Nouns in Papiamentu" (in *Varia Creolica,* edited by Philippe Maurer and Thomas Stolz, 1987).

**J. L. Dillard** is a professor of English emeritus at Shawnee State University. He is one of the sharpest critics of the English dialect account of the origin of African American vernacular English features. He assumes that this language variety started as a Gullah-like variety, which has decreolized under the influence of white middle-class English. These positions may be found in, for example, *Black English* (1972) and *A Social History of American English* (1984). The latest of his numerous books on the subject matter is *A History of American English* (1992).

**Nicholas Faraclas** is an assistant professor of linguistics at the University of Papua New Guinea. He is also an Africanist, having done field work and published on Kwa languages of Nigeria. Among his publications are "Creolization and the Tense-Aspect-Modality System of Nigerian Pidgin" (*Journal of African Languages and Linguistics* 9:45–59, 1987) and "Nigerian Pidgin and the Languages of Southern Nigeria" (*Journal of Pidgin and Creole Languages* 3:177–97). He subscribes to the substrate hypothesis, which, according to him, accounts likewise for several features of Tok Pisin, which he has also studied.

**Glenn G. Gilbert** is a professor of linguistics at Southern Illinois University, Carbondale, and the editor of the *Journal of Pidgin and Creole Languages*. A significant component of his work has been historiographical, as evidenced by his *Pidgin and Creole Languages: Selected Essays by Hugo Schuchardt* (1980) and *Pidgin and Creole Languages: Essays in Honor of John Reinecke* (1987).

**Charles Gilman** is a freelance linguist with wide-ranging field research experience, having worked particularly on Cameroon Pidgin English and on Zairean Swahili. He has also studied African linguistics, knowledge that underlies his often-cited "African Areal Characteristics: Sprachbund, Not Substrate?" (*Journal of Pidgin and Creole Languages* 1:33–50, 1986). He is among the first to have used the "feature selection" metaphor in studies of creole genesis.

**Morris Goodman** is a professor of linguistics at Northwestern University. He is to date one of the most insightful critics of the language bioprogram hypothesis, as evidenced by his review article on Derek Bickerton's *Roots of Language* in the *International Journal of American Linguistics* 51:109–37 (1985). His *Comparative Study of French Creole Dialects* (1964) remains an important reference, along with his more recent papers assessing the importance of the Portuguese element in Papiamentu and Saramaccan.

**Ian Hancock** is a professor of linguistics at the University of Texas at Austin. He has worked on Sierra Leone Krio and Texas Gullah and is one of the originators of the complementary hypothesis. His work has been informative on the history of English settlements on the West African coast and the development there in the sixteenth and seventeenth centuries of Guinea Coast Creole English, which putatively contributed to the development of English creoles in the New World, as expressed in, for example, "Gullah and Barbadian: Origins and Relationships" (*American Speech* 55:17–35, 1980). His current work on Romani is also from the point of view of language contact.

**Guy Hazaël-Massieux** is Maître de Conférence at the Université de Provence. He is probably one of the best bridges between the extreme dialectologist, substratist, and universalist hypotheses on the genesis of French creoles. According to him, the grammatical features of these creoles are generally retentions from the colonial nonstandard varieties of their lexifier, although African languages may have helped select them. See, for example, "En quoi peut-on dire que les créoles à lexique roman sont des langues néo-romanes?" (in *Hommage à Madame le Professeur Maryse Jeuland,* 1983) and "Les plus anciens textes des créoles français de la Caraïbe" (in *19è Congrès de Linguistique et Philologie Romanes,* 1986).

**John Holm** is a professor of linguistics at Hunter College and the Graduate Center of the City University of New York. He has worked on Miskito Coast Creole English and is one of the strongest defendants of the substrate hypothesis. His two-volume *Pidgins and Creoles* (1988, 1989) is already widely cited. The second of them, *Reference Survey,* is the most elaborate compendium on pidgins and creoles worldwide ever compiled. He has also coauthored and coedited several other books, including *Dictionary of Bahamian English* (1982) and *Atlantic Meets Pacific* (1993).

**George Huttar** is a professor of linguistics at the Summer Institute of Linguistics, Dallas. He has worked primarily on Ndjuka, a Portuguese-based creole of Suriname, and has published some of the most informative articles on the nature of African substrate influence and its compatibility with the language bioprogram hypothesis. Among his work on the subject matter is "Sources of Ndjuka African vocabulary" (*Nieuwe West-Indische Gids* 59:45–71, 1985).

**Claire Lefebvre** is a professor of linguistics at the Université du Québec à Montréal. She is the author of the new relexification hypothesis that attributes to West

African Kwa languages, especially the Ewe-Fon cluster, the primary responsibility for Haitian Creole's grammatical features. She is, however, now open to French influence. She has coauthored or edited several works, including *Syntaxe de l'haïtien* (1982) and *Les langues créoles et la théorie linguistique* (*Canadian Journal of Linguistics* 34, no. 3, 1989). She is the editor of *Travaux de Recherche sur le Créole Haïtien*.

**Michael Montgomery** is a professor of linguistics at the University of South Carolina at Columbia. His research of the past decade and a half has focused on grammatical peculiarities of nonstandard varieties of Southern English. He has coedited *Language Varieties in the South: Perspectives in Black and White* (1986) and compiled, with James McMillan, the *Annotated Bibliography of Southern American English* (1989). He is now one of the editors of the *SECOL Review*.

**Marcyliena Morgan** is an assistant professor of linguistic anthropology at the University of California, Los Angeles. She is one of the editors of *Pragmatics* and edited *The Social Significance of Creole Language Situations* (in press). She works on the ethnography of African American vernacular English, focusing on gender and on the language of rap music.

**Salikoko S. Mufwene** is a professor of linguistics at the University of Chicago. One of the authors of the complementary hypothesis, he is now working on a population genetics analog of feature selection in creole genesis. These views are expressed in, for example, "Transfer and Substrate Hypothesis in Creolistics" (*Studies in Second Language Acquisition* 12:1–23, 1990), "Pidgins, Creoles, Typology, and Markedness" (in *Development and Structures of Creole Languages*, edited by Francis Byrne and T. Huebner, 1991), "Africanisms in Gullah: A Re-examination of the Issues" (in *Old English and New,* edited by Joan Hall et al., 1992). He coedited *Issues in Creole Linguistics* (*Linguistics* 28, no. 4, 1990) and wrote the column for the *Journal of Pidgin and Creole Languages* (1988 and 1989). He is now its associate editor.

**John R. Rickford** is a professor of linguistics at Stanford University and a former editor of the *Carrier Pidgin*. He is the leading variationist in using quantitative analysis to shed light on decreolization, the process that makes a creole less and less different from its lexifier. His *Dimensions of a Creole Continuum* (1987) illustrates both the general orientation and high quality of his work. He has edited several works and published prolifically on African American English. Among the most recent are "Grammatical Variation and Divergence in Vernacular Black English" (in *Internal and External Factors in Syntactic Change,* edited by M. Gerritsen and Dieter Stein, 1992).

**Ian Robertson** is a senior lecturer at the University of the West Indies, St. Augustine, Trinidad. It is thanks to him that creolists have now become very interested in Berbice Dutch (Guyana), the only Atlantic creole in which African linguistic influence (attributed primarily to Eastern Ịjọ, Nigeria) is not controversial. He is a coauthor of "The Ịjọ Element in Berbice Dutch" (*Language in Society* 16:49–90, 1987).

**Edgar W. Schneider** is a professor of English linguistics at the University of Regensburg and the most articulate and prolific defender of the dialectologist position on the origin of African American vernacular English. See, for example, *American Earlier Black English* (1989), in which he also defends the position that this variety has not decreolized. Among his recent publications is "The Cline of Creoleness in English-Oriented Creoles and Semi-creoles of the Caribbean" (*English World-Wide* 11:79–119, 1990).

**John Victor Singler** is an associate professor of linguistics at New York University and the associate editor of the Creole Language Library. He works on Liberian Settler English and its connection with African American vernacular English. His sociohistorical research of the past few years, especially on Caribbean French creoles, has been seminal in helping many of us realize the conditions under which African substrate languages may have determined structural features of creoles of the New World. His "Homogeneity of the Substrate in Pidgin/Creole Genesis" (*Language* 64:27–51, 1988) explains why the substrate is not excluded by the language bioprogram. He edited *Pidgin and Creole Tense-Mood-Aspect Systems* (1990).

**Arthur K. Spears** is an associate professor of linguistics at the City University of New York. To some, he is known for his work on African American English, particularly for "camouflaged" features in its system, a case demonstrated by him in "The Black English Semi-auxiliary *Come*" (*Language* 58:850–72, 1982). He has also worked on Haitian Creole, as illustrated by "Tense, Mood, and Aspect in the Haitian Creole Preverbal Marker System" (in *Pidgin and Creole Tense-Mood-Aspect Systems,* edited by John Singler, 1990).

**Sarah G. Thomason** is a professor of linguistics at the University of Pittsburgh and the editor of *Language*. She is a coauthor of the often-cited *Language Contact, Creolization, and Genetic Linguistics* (1988). Among her many papers are "Chinook Jargon in Aareal and Historical Context" (*Language* 59:820–70, 1983), in which she shows how features of the Jargon may be traced to languages in the contact situation, and "On Interpreting 'The Indian interpreter' " (*Language and Society* 9:167–93, 1980).

**Selase W. Williams** is the director of the Pan African Studies Department at the California State University, Northridge. He is among the first students of Atlantic creoles in the generative grammar era, having written his Ph.D. dissertation on Krio. He is also one of the first in this generation of scholars to support the

African substrate hypothesis. His work, mostly unpublished, is from the perspective of Afrocentrism. His published work includes "The So-called Relativized and Cleft Predicates in Krio: One Step Closer to an Understanding of Creolization" (in *Language and Linguistic Problems in Africa*, edited by P. F. A. Kotey and H. Der-Houssikian, 1977).

# Author Index

# Language Index

# Subject Index